Stephen Széchenyi
and the Awakening of Hungarian
Nationalism, 1791–1841

Stephen Széchenyi

and the Awakening of Hungarian Nationalism, 1791–1841

BY GEORGE BARANY

PRINCETON, NEW JERSEY
PRINCETON UNIVERSITY PRESS
1968

Publication of this book has been aided by the Whitney Darrow Publication Reserve Fund of Princeton University Press, by the Faculty Research Fund of the University of Denver, and by the Graduate School of International Studies at the University of Denver.

Printed in the United States of America
by The Maple Press Company, York, Pennsylvania

To

S. HARRISON THOMSON
Teacher, Scholar, Friend

Preface

Professor George Barany has written a big and important book about the "father" of Hungarian nationalism, Count Stephen Széchenyi.

Westerners know too little about Széchenyi, a great Hungarian and a great man. Barany makes a contribution to their knowledge and, it is likely, to Hungary's and the world's knowledge of Széchenyi as well. Barany does more. He makes a contribution to our knowledge of nationalism. His book is based on sustained, thorough, and exhaustive research in the archives and libraries of France, Austria, England, the United States, the Vatican, and Sweden, and on materials from Hungary. He has uncovered new sources and on the basis of these he reaches different if not always new conclusions of major importance for understanding the history of central Europe.

This is not all. In lucid English (his second and adopted language) he skillfully handles the evidence in the voluminous materials in several languages on his subjects, Széchenyi and nationalism, and as he does so he presents a new information on European diplomacy in and about the Habsburg Empire as well as on the flow and interchange of ideas in Europe and even America.

Though Barany deeply admires his hero, Széchenyi, he not only analytically describes his successes and strengths but critically examines his failures and weaknesses, even his hypocrisies. Thus he is able to arrive at a rare balance of judgment on controversial issues.

As Professor Barany says, Széchenyi, a rich aristocrat and one-time soldier, considered himself above all a Magyar, gave his loyalty to the Habsburg dynasty, and preferred order to revolution. Yet he was also an internationalist, opposed oppression of other nationalities in Hungary, admired England—its government and its economic institutions—and pushed Hungary into the mainstream of European development with his innovative ideas in bridge, road and railway building, in horse racing and breeding, and in the establishment of the Hungarian casino (club).

Torn between the old tenacious Hungarian world of aristocracy and feudal privilege and the nascent world of liberalism and industrialism, Count Széchenyi suffered great tensions. He found partial release in his manifold activities. But in his public as well as private life he went from one crisis to another, often contemplated taking his own life, and finally, indeed, did so.

Generally a believer in progress, he was at times profoundly pessimistic. Most often he arrived at an equivocal middle-of-the-road position, only to be bitterly criticized by the reactionary Metternich and opposed by more liberal Hungarians such as Kossuth. He became a "monument" of the Hungarian nation but never its political leader.

Professor Barany was educated in Hungary and the United States. His education in Hungary (Szeged) was not quite completed in 1944 when he, a Jew, was sentenced by the Nazis to hard labor on the Russian front. After three years in a Russian prison camp, he returned to Hungary in 1947 to complete his education and find employment. In the late fall of 1956 he arrived in the United States (Camp Kilmer, New Jersey) with "two handbags." At this point the writer of this Preface, then Executive Secretary of the American Historical Association, was able to suggest that he study with Professor S. Harrison Thomson at the University of Colorado. At Colorado he obtained his Ph.D. in 1960 with a fine dissertation on Széchenyi, which, much amplified, has become this book. At the University of Denver since 1960, he has established a remarkable reputation as a teacher and producing scholar.

When Professor Barany asked me if I would write the Preface to this book, I at first thought I should decline for I knew so little of Hungarian history. But I agreed because I was a friend, a fellow historian, and fellow student of nationalism, and because I knew that I would learn much from his book about nationalism, Széchenyi, and Hungary.

I have learned much.

Barany shows, for example, with irrefutable evidence, that nationalism has aristocratic as well as bourgeois origins and that an aristocrat could be deeply committed to and involved in the economic changes leading to modernity. He reveals, too, the torture and anguish of a dreamer who tried to act during times of great stress, and thus teaches us (cold comfort though this be) that men before us have lived in times of anxiety and have, however tragic the human condition, continued to dream.

BOYD C. SHAFER

Acknowledgment

My first word of appreciation goes to the man to whom this study is dedicated. It was upon the suggestion of S. Harrison Thomson, Professor Emeritus of the University of Colorado, Boulder, that I decided, some 10 years ago, to write my doctoral dissertation on Széchenyi and the Age of Reform in Hungary. Besides his guidance and professional help, I greatly benefited from the criticism of Professor Willard A. Fletcher of the University of Texas, Austin, who was the second reader of my thesis, and of my sister-in-law, Florence Wallach Freed, who read the first draft. Their remarks, as well as those made by Boyd C. Shafer, James Wallace Professor of History at Macalester College, St. Paul, Minnesota, and Bickford C. O'Brien, Professor of Russian history at the University of California, Davis, both of whom were members of my examination committee for the doctorate, gave valuable help when I resolved to continue my research on Széchenyi and his times after the completion of my doctoral work.

In this second phase of my endeavors, the friendship and encouragement given by Hans Kohn, Professor Emeritus of the City College of New York, has been an invaluable source of inspiration. Indeed, his and S. Harrison Thomson's examples have shown me *how enriching and awe-inspiring the study and teaching of history can be in old and new worlds, if cultivated with moral fortitude, incessant effort and humility.* Professor Kohn read Chapters I–V before I submitted the manuscript to the publisher. My colleague in the Department of History at the University of Denver, Professor Theodore R. Crane, obliged with Chapters VII–X. And Chapter VI was scrutinized by another friend, Thomas R. Mark, Professor of English Literature at Colorado State University in Fort Collins. The advice thus received, supplemented by the benevolent comments of Professors István Deák, from Columbia University, and Peter F. Sugar, from the University of Washington, Seattle, the two readers for Princeton University Press, were most helpful in eliminating many shortcomings of the manuscript. For the remaining ones, and the views expressed in the book, I alone am responsible.

ACKNOWLEDGMENT

It would be difficult to itemize all the assistance given to me by archivists and librarians. I am indebted to Dr. Richard Blaas, Director of the *Haus-, Hof- und Staatsarchiv* in Vienna and to practically every coworker on his staff, especially Deputy Director Dr. Anna Coreth, *Amtsrat* Anton Nemeth, and *Archivsekretär* Robert Stropp. My thanks are due to the staff of the British Public Record Office in London, where I occasionally had to impose with special requests on Miss Daphne H. Gifford, Principal Assistant Keeper in the Repository and Technical Services Section, and Mr. L. G. Seed, Head of the Photographic Section; to the French *Archives Diplomatiques du Ministère des Affaires Etrangères* in Paris when I had the guidance of *Conservateur* Mlle Françoise Demanche; to the Swedish *Kungl. Krigsarkivet* in Stockholm, where I was the beneficiary of the efficient aid of Director Dr. Bertil Broomé and his secretary, Mrs. Åsa Schreck; and to the *Archivio Segreto Vaticano* in Vatican City, where Professor Sergio Damiani helped me overcome the problems of a language barrier.

Facsimiles and transcripts of Crown-copyright records in the Public Record Office appear by permission of the Controller of H. M. Stationery Office. Similarly, I am obliged to the above-mentioned Austrian, French, Swedish, and Vatican archives for permission to publish documents related to Széchenyi's activities and Hungary's history in the 19th century. The list would be incomplete, however, if I did not recognize the help received, on various occasions, in the manuscript divisions of the British Museum, the Library of Congress, and the different branches of the National Archives in Washington, D.C.

Of the librarians on whom I had to impose repeatedly, I should like to mention Dr. Friedrich Rennhofer, Leader of the *Katalog Abteilung,* and Mr. Johann Zach, Leader of the *Zentral Katalog,* both from the *Österreichische Nationalbibliothek; Bibliotheksoberrevident* Clemens Hösslinger, from the *Staatsarchiv,* Vienna; Miss Marta Papp, Chief Librarian of the Historical Institute of the Hungarian Academy of Sciences, Budapest; and Dr. Francis S. Wagner in the Library of Congress. In one instance, Miss Susan Parsons, from the Reference Department of the library of the Boston Athenaeum, was especially generous with her help. Closer home, I am indebted to the staffs of the libraries of the University of Colorado and the University of Denver.

For authorization to use parts of my articles, which appeared previously in scholarly publications, I am grateful to Professors S. Harrison Thomson, editor of the *Journal of Central European Affairs,* R. John Rath, editor of the *Austrian History Yearbook,* Louise E. Luke, editor of the *Slavic Review,* and Ralph A. Loomis, editor of the *Papers of* the Michigan Academy of Science, Arts, and Letters. For permission to use illustrations pertinent to Széchenyi's life, I wish to thank the Historical Institute and its deputy director, Professor György Ránki, the Hungarian Historical Association and its Secretary General, Professor Iván T. Berend, and the Hungarian Academy of Sciences. For the reproductions, after which the two maps in the book were drawn, I am in the debt of Dr. Rudolf Kinauer, director of the map collection of the *Nationalbibliothek*, Vienna, and of Professor Endre Arató, Budapest. The maps in our study were prepared by Mr. Dennis D. Siglinger, from the Department of Geography at the University of Denver. Miss Joyce A. Little helped me with the index.

I should like to record my gratitude for the grants of the Joint Committee on Slavic Studies of the American Council of Learned Societies and the Social Science Research Council (1963 and 1966); the Graduate School of International Studies and the Social Science Foundation of the University of Denver; the Austrian Ministry of Education; the Faculty Research Fund of the Graduate School and the College of Arts and Sciences of the University of Denver. The generous financial support of these institutions enabled me to do research, to travel, to buy microfilms, to have some free time for writing, and to publish my book.

Among those who have encouraged me at the University of Denver over the years, I wish to express my sincere thanks to Vice-Chancellor of Academic Affairs Wilbur C. Miller, Deans Josef Korbel and Edward A. Lindell, Chairman Allen D. Breck and every member of the Department of History: although I cannot list them all by name, I want them to know how highly I value their readiness to help whenever I needed their advice.

I am deeply obliged to Professor Boyd C. Shafer, former executive secretary of the American Historical Association and managing editor of the *American Historical Review* and now chairman of the Department of History at Macalester College, for having graciously consented to write a preface to my study and for having given so much of his time to read it in proof. May I also gratefully acknowledge the assistance received from Princeton University Press, especially from Associate Director and Editor R. Miriam Brokaw, and my editor, Roy A. Grisham.

My last "thank you" goes to Suzy, my wife, who has shared my tribulations for many years. This book is also hers—as is my love.

GEORGE BARANY

Denver, Colorado
July 15, 1968

Contents

Abbreviations

Archival and Manuscript Materials

AUSTRIAN:

HHStA	Haus,- Hof- und Staatsarchiv, Vienna
CAa	*Kabinettsarchiv, Staatskonferenzakten*
CAs	*Kabinettsarchiv, Separatkonferenzakten*
MKA	*Minister Kolowrat Akten*
StKI	*Staatskanzlei, Interiora, Intercepte*

BRITISH:

PRO	Public Record Office (London)
F.O./7	*Foreign Office, Austria*
BrM	British Museum (London)
AP	*Aberdeen Papers*

FRENCH:

AMAE	Archives du Ministère des Affaires Etrangères, Paris
CPAu	*Correspondance politique, Autriche*
MDAu	*Mémoires et documents. Fonds français et fonds divers, Autriche*

SWEDISH:

KKa	Kungl. Krigsarkivet, Stockholm
KTNh	*Kriget i Tyskland, 1813–1814, Nordarméns högkvarter.* Handlinger från diverse personer (The War in Germany, 1813–1814. Headquarters of the Northern Army. Papers from Various Persons)

UNITED STATES

NA	National Archives, Washington, D.C.

VATICAN:

ASV   Archivio Segreto Vaticano
  SSE   *Segreteria di Stato, Esteri*

Major Collections of Széchenyi's Works, Letters, and Papers.

SzIM   *Gróf Széchenyi István Munkái.* Összegyüjti és kiadja a
                Magyar T. Akadémia (The Works of Count
                Stephen Széchenyi. Collected by the Hungarian
                Academy of Sciences), 9 vols. (Budapest: Athe-
                naeum, 1884–96)

Levelek   *Gróf Széchenyi István levelei* (Letters of Count Stephen
                Széchenyi), ed. Béla Majláth, 3 vols. (Budapest:
                Athenaeum, 1889–91) Vols. III, IV and VI of
                SzIM.

Szülőihez   *Gróf Széchenyi István levelei szülőihez* (Letters of Count
                Stephen Széchenyi to His Parents), ed. Antal Zichy
                (Budapest: Athenaeum, 1896). Vol. IX of *SzIM*

Beszédei   *Gróf Széchenyi István beszédei* (Speeches of Count
                Stephen Széchenyi), ed. Antal Zichy (Budapest:
                Athenaeum, 1887). Vol. II of *SzIM*

Cikkei   *Gróf Széchenyi István hirlapi czikkei* (Newspaper Articles
                of Count Stephen Széchenyi), ed. Antal Zichy,
                2 vols. (Budapest: Athenaeum, 1893–94). Vols.
                VII and VIII of *SzIM*

SzIM²   *Gróf Széchenyi István Munkái.* II. Sorozat. A Magy.
                Tud. Akadémia megbizásából sajtó alá rendezi
                Szily Kálmán (The Works of Count Stephen
                Széchenyi. 2d Series. Published on behalf of the
                Hungarian Academy of Sciences by Kálmán
                Szily), 2 vols. (Budapest: Magyar Tudományos
                Akadémia, 1904–1905)

SzIÖM   *Gróf Széchenyi István Összes Munkái.* Kiadja a Magyar
                Történelmi Társulat (The Complete Works of
                Count Stephen Széchenyi. Published by the
                Hungarian Historical Association), 12 vols. (Buda-
                pest: Magyar Történelmi Társulat, 1921–39)

Naplók   *Gr. Széchenyi István naplói* (The Diaries of Count
                Stephen Széchenyi), ed. Gyula Viszota, 6 vols.
                (Budapest: Magyar Történelmi Társulat, 1925–
                39). Vols. X–XV of *SzIÖM*

Széchenyi és Kossuth   Gr. *Széchenyi István irói és hirlapirói vitája Kossuth Lajossal* (Count Stephen Széchenyi's Literary and Journalistic Debate with Louis Kossuth), ed. Gyula Viszota, 2 pts. (Budapest: Magyar Történelmi Társulat, 1927–30). Vol. VI of *SzIÖM*

Döblingi hagyaték   Gr. *Széchenyi István döblingi irodalmi hagyatéka* (Count Stephen Széchenyi's Posthumous Papers of Döbling), ed. Árpád Károlyi and Vilmos Tolnai, 3 vols. (Budapest: Magyar Történelmi Társulat, 1921–25). Vols. VII–IX of *SzIÖM*

A kelet népe   *A kelet népe* (The People of the Orient), ed. Zoltán Ferenczi (Budapest: Magyar Történelmi Társulat, 1925). Vol. V of *SzIÖM*

Hitel   *Hitel. A taglalat és a hitellel foglalkozó kisebb iratok* (Credit. The Analysis and the Minor Works Dealing with Credit), ed. Ifj. Béla Iványi-Grünwald (Budapest: Magyar Történelmi Társulat, 1930), Vol. II of *SzIÖM*

Pol. isk.   *Gróf Széchenyi István politikai iskolája, saját müveiből összeállitva* (Count Stephen Széchenyi's Political School, Compiled from His Works), ed. János Török, 3 vols. (Pest: Heckenast, 1864)

Adatok   *Adatok gróf Széchenyi István és kora történetéhez, 1808–1860* (Data Concerning the History of Count Stephen Széchenyi and His Times, 1808–1860), ed. László Bártfai Szabó, 2 vols. (Budapest: Au. edn.,1943)

Other Major Source Publications and Collections of Documents

Fontes   *Magyarország Ujabbkori Történetének Forrásai—Fontes Historiae Hungaricae Aevi Recentioris*

FontesAu   *Fontes Rerum Austriacarum—Österreichische Geschichtsquellen*

KLÖM   *Kossuth Lajos Összes Munkái* (The Complete Works of Louis Kossuth), 11 vols. (Budapest: Magyar Történelmi Társulat, 1948–66)

APF   *Archives parlementaires de 1787 à 1860. Recueil complet des débats législatifs et politiques des chambres françaises*, imprimé par ordre du sénat et de la chambre des députés, sous la direction de M. J. Mavidal . . . et de E. Laurent, *Première Série* (1787–1799)

AÖG   *Archiv für österreichische Geschichte*

BFSP	British and Foreign State Papers
FKgÖ	Forschungen zur Kirchengeschichte Österreichs
MÖIG	Mitteilungen des österreichischen Instituts für Geschichtsforschung
QSGO	Quellen und Studien zur Geschichte Osteuropas
VKNGO	Veröffentlichungen der Kommission für neuere Geschichte Österreichs

Serials and Periodicals

AH	Acta Historica
AHR	American Historical Review
AHY	Austrian History Yearbook
ASz	Agrártörténeti Szemle
BS	Balkan Studies
BSz	Budapesti Szemle
D	Der Donauraum
EEQ	East European Quarterly
ÉTTK	Értekezések a Társadalmi Tudományok Köréből
H	Historica
HQ	The Hungarian Quarterly
HZ	Historische Zeitschrift
ITK	Irodalomtörténeti Közlemények
JCEA	Journal of Central European Affairs
JMH	Journal of Modern History
NHQ	The New Hungarian Quarterly
ÖOH	Österreichische Osthefte
PMA	Papers of the Michigan Academy of Science, Arts, and Letters
RDM	Revue des Deux Mondes
RER	Revue des Etudes Roumaines
RH	Revue Historique
RHMC	Revue d'Histoire Moderne et Contemporaine
RHo	Revue de Hongrie
SEA	South-Eastern Affairs
SEER	The Slavonic and East European Review
SH	Studia Historica
SR	The Slavic Review
SOA	Südosteuropäische Arbeiten
SOF	Südost-Forschungen
Sz	Századok
TSz	Történelmi Szemle
VAO	Veröffentlichungen der Arbeitsgemeinschaft Ost
WHS	Wiener Historische Studien

Stephen Széchenyi
and the Awakening of Hungarian
Nationalism, 1791–1841

. . . ein guter Mensch, in seinem dunklen Drange,
ist sich des rechten Weges wohl bewusst.

GOETHE, Faust, Part I
Prolog im Himmel

I declared Count Stephen Széchenyi last November (as he him-
self mentioned) the greatest of all Hungarians at the crowded
assembly of Pest County, and the multitude resounded with un-
ceasing acclamations; and I also repeated this word in the Pesti
Hirlap. *This word belongs to the* Credo *of my soul. . . . . I*
would blush in shame before myself if I should forget even for a
moment about the respect that every Hungarian owes to the
immortal merits of Count Stephen Széchenyi, and no one feels
this more deeply than I, who have called him and sincerely call
him now, at this moment, too, with these lips which have never
been and never will be contaminated by cowardly flattering and
deceiving politics, the greatest Magyar.

LOUIS KOSSUTH, June 26, 1841
Pesti Hirlap

CHAPTER I

Captatio Benevolentiae

For over a hundred years Louis Kossuth, leader of the Hungarian Revolution of 1848–49, has been thought of in the United States as the embodiment of Hungary's best traditions. In popular imagination, political oratory, and American history textbooks, the name of Kossuth is a symbol of his nation's desire for progress and its struggle for independence. From the days of the "Kossuth excitement" in the early 1850s to the exhibition of Kossuth documents in the Library of Congress at the end of 1958 and to the Kossuth stamps in the "Champions of Liberty" series, this century-old Kossuth tradition has been a very special historico-psychological manifestation of the United States' interest in Central Europe, particularly Hungary: its ideological foundations were expressed in classic terms by the two resolutions in behalf of Hungarian freedom supported by Abraham Lincoln in September 1849 and January 1852.[1] During the same period of time, however, no comprehensive study has been published in the United States or, for that matter, elsewhere outside Hungary, about Count Stephen Széchenyi,[2] Kossuth's forerunner and later political opponent. Yet the latter repeatedly called Széchenyi "the Greatest among the Magyars."[3]

[1] Roy P. Basler, *The Collected Works of Abraham Lincoln*, 8 vols. and index (New Brunswick, N.J.: Rutgers University Press, 1953–55), II, 62, 115f., 118.

[2] One reason for this may be that "Széchenyi's main works have not been translated from the Magyar." Robert A. Kann, *The Multinational Empire*, 2 vols. (New York: Columbia University Press, 1950), I, 381. There may, however, have been an interest in Széchenyi in the Anglo-Saxon world in the second part of the 19th century, as shown by the four articles published anonymously under the title, "The Great Magyar," in Charles Dickens' journal *All the Year Round* in 1870 (New Series, III, 450–56, 476–80, 498–504, 522–28). This series of articles was based on Saint-René Taillandier's study of Széchenyi published in the *Revue des deux mondes* in 1867 (Aug. 1, Oct. 15, 1867, pp. 628–61 and 864–903, respectively).

[3] In a speech in which he expressed his thanks to the estates of Pest county shortly after his release from prison in June 1840, Kossuth referred to Széchenyi as "the man whose equal I do not know in my nation's annals." Gyula Viszota, ed., *Gróf Széchenyi István írói és hírlapírói vitája Kossuth Lajossal* (Count Stephen Széchenyi's Literary and

3

Why is it that a nation assigned the epithet "greatest" to a man who seemed to have failed as a practical politician? For there can be no doubt that in the years preceding the revolution of 1848, Hungarian public opinion and the nation at large chose the way of Kossuth. This meant that somewhere between the official course of the imperial government and the ferment of Hungarian political life, Széchenyi's ideas got lost and the "greatest Hungarian" failed as a practical politician. Or is there any more important test of statesmanship and greatness than success in politics? Was Kossuth's apotheosis of Széchenyi sincere, or was it just one of his skillful political maneuvers to raise his potential opponent above all human standards and thus declare him to *quantité négligeable* for all practical purposes, as an able literary historian suggested?[4] But even if Kossuth really meant what he said, he might have been wrong: did Hungarian public opinion ever reverse his judgment concerning Széchenyi? Or was Széchenyi, as Julius Szekfű thought,[5] "a unique phenomenon," "a miracle never to be repeated" in Hungarian history, who had a message for posterity which his own contemporaries, in a mysterious way, were blind enough to overlook? In the latter case, were there any "objective" historical factors which prevented his fellow countrymen from "understanding" him and which influenced the leaders of Austria to ignore his suggestions, or was his personality too enigmatic and unstable for political leadership?[6]

To be sure, one key to the solution of the Széchenyi "mystery" must

---

Journalistic Debate with Louis Kossuth), cited hereafter as *Széchenyi és Kossuth*, 2 vols. (Budapest: Magyar Történelmi Társulat, 1927), I, 788f. This work is Vol. VI of *Gróf Széchenyi István Összes Munkái* (The Complete Works of Count Stephen Széchenyi), cited hereafter as *SzIÖM*, published in *Magyarország Ujabbkori Történetének Forrásai—Fontes Historiae Hungaricae Aevi Recentioris,* cited hereafter as *Fontes*.

At another county meeting of Pest in November 1840, Kossuth called Széchenyi "the Greatest among the Magyars," and repeated this epithet in a lead article of *Pesti Hirlap* in June 1841. Gyula Viszota, ed., *Gróf Széchenyi István naplói* (The Diaries of Count Stephen Széchenyi), cited hereafter as *Naplók*, 6 vols. (Budapest: Magyar Történelmi Társulat, 1925–39), V, 422 (Vol. XIV of *SzIÖM* in *Fontes*); Zoltán Ferenczi, ed., *A kelet népe* (The People of the Orient) (Budapest: Magyar Törénelmi Társulat, 1925), pp. 62, 360, 421. (Vol. V of *SzIÖM* in *Fontes*). See also Kossuth's letter to Ladislas Teleki, May 8, 1860, in László Bártfai Szabó, ed., *Adatok gróf Széchenyi István és kora történetéhez, 1808–1860* (Data Concerning the History of Count Stephen Széchenyi and His Times, 1808–1860), cited hereafter as *Adatok*, 2 vols. (Budapest: [author's edition], 1943), II, 881.

[4] Antal Szerb, *Magyar Irodalomtörténet* (Hungarian Literary History) (Budapest: Révai, 1947), pp. 280, 286, first edn: Kolozsvár-Cluj, 1934.

[5] Gyula Szekfű, *A mai Széchenyi* (Present-day Széchenyi) (Budapest: Magyar Kulturális Egyesületek Szövetsége, 1935), pp. 24f.

[6] For the former opinion see Elemér Mályusz, "A reformkor nemzedéke" (Generation of the Reform Era), in *Századok*, LVII (1923), 32–60. For the latter opinion see Louis Eisenmann, *Le compromis austro-hongrois de 1867* (Paris: Société Nouvelle de Librairie et d'édition, 1904), pp. 652f.

be found in his personality, although this approach raises new difficulties. As a captain of hussars, previously unknown in his country's public life, he became the founder of the Academy of Sciences at the age of 34. As a member of one of the leading Hungarian magnate families, intermarried with the Austrian, Bohemian, Croatian, and Italian nobilities, he started a radical reform movement in the homeland he hardly knew as a youth. He was one of the great landowners in Hungary, yet he raised his voice in the interest of the serfs and advocated the gradual elimination of all privileges. A citizen of the world, he had spent most of his life abroad before he was 30 and kept his private diaries in German, sometimes in Italian, French, and English, only occasionally inserting a few Hungarian words; nevertheless, he was the first to utter a speech in the Magyar tongue in the upper chamber of the Hungarian Diet, and his writings marked the beginning of modern political prose in Magyar. A man with strong sensual impulses, a dandy of the Congress of Vienna, he turned out to be one of the most ethical thinkers of his nation. An ardent patriot, he preferred in his romantic and somewhat mystical national feeling Magyars to Germans, Romanians, or Slavs, but he was the first among his countrymen to raise his voice in opposition to any discrimination against other peoples at a time when Magyar chauvinism seemed to have overpowered all minds. As a Christian humanist, he preached and practiced tolerance toward Protestants, Jews, and Muslims as well; but he could become rigid and intolerant wherever he saw dishonesty, dirt, and ignorance in his beloved fatherland, or whenever he found himself failing in his duties toward God or his fellow men.

He was an adherent of the Habsburg dynasty and of the Austrian Empire, realizing the interdependence of Hungary's regeneration and the strengthening of the Monarchy; but he wrote hundreds of pages of the most violent and sarcastic criticism of Francis Joseph and Austrian neo-absolutism in the 1850s. An impatient agitator advocating the modernization of Hungarian society and the emancipation of all underprivileged classes, he attacked vigorously what he believed to be false glorification of the Hungarian past so cherished by the nobility; yet, while scourging the "national" vices and ridiculing the feudal practices and outmoded customs, he strived to prepare a firm ground for the country's future by preserving the organic continuity of the nation's constitutional life and by "ennobling" the moral forces of its traditional ruling classes. He was a champion of liberty and progress, giving these concepts a special moral aspect by demanding both from the nation and from the individual a high degree of sobermindedness and discipline; always more admired and respected than loved, he despised demagoguery, mistrusted popular enthusiasm, and remained in the strict sense of the word an "aristocrat" at the bottom of his heart until the very end of his life. His views were enlightened and liberal concerning most important religious, social, and economic questions of the day; also, he advocated the "golden mean" and was in favor of moderation in all walks of life. Still, he did not hesitate a moment to sacrifice his remaining popularity by attacking Kossuth with crusading zeal and bitterness when, in his opinion, the latter's policy threatened the country with deadly danger. By his economic reforms, he laid the foundations of modern Hungary; he was the first Hungarian statesman to realize the primary significance of economic matters in modern societies; yet, he rejected any kind of materialistic philosophy, had the courage to dream for his people, and always kept his eyes directed toward the lofty ideals of Eternal Truth, Justice, Equity, and Virtue—ideals which in his opinion could be reached by nations and individuals alike only through Christian perfectionism.

In his political affairs, however, Széchenyi advocated realistic goals and practical methods, and warned against passions and emotions; yet in his agitation for reform, he used poetic words to catch the fancy of his countrymen; his whole "system" and philosophy of life was highly idealistic. A pioneer of Western ideas in Hungary and an admirer of the achievements of the Anglo-Saxon world, he endeavored to discover and understand the secret of the Hungarian nation's peculiar vitality. Regarded by many as a "cold calculator," he became the "martyr of the heart," for he was driven insane by his excited imagination which compelled him to foresee political trends and consequences which no one else but he could recognize in time. Having first died a spiritual death, he later recovered and again began to work for his fatherland, only to commit the most controversial act of his life: a devout Catholic, who throughout his mature life went to confession and received Holy Communion, he was finally forced into suicide by the Austrian police in a fit of utter despair.

Even from these few dramatic highlights of Széchenyi's career, one must conclude that there were extraordinary circumstances and conflicts dominating his inner as well as public life. The human drama symbolized by Széchenyi's fate had a considerable impact on the thinking of those who knew him. An interesting example of this is a letter written to Disraeli by "Professor Metternich"[7] during his exile at Brighton, England. The 75-year-old ex-chancellor chose the example of Széchenyi as an object lesson to illustrate and justify his own political philosophy to

[7] Epithet used by Disraeli in a letter to Mrs. Disraeli, Jan. 7, 1849, in William Flavelle Monypenny and George Earle Buckle, *The Life of Benjamin Disraeli*, 6 vols. (New York: Macmillan, 1916–20), III, 130.

Disraeli who was about to take over the leadership of the English conservatives. The letter, dated October 2, 1848—that is, at a time when the reaction to the revolutionary events of Spring 1848 had already gained momentum all over the continent—put a strong emphasis on the principle of order and the importance of military strength, only to continue with a characterization of Széchenyi as follows:

. . . Il me reste de vous faire part d'un fait charactéristique. Vous connaissez peut-être personnellement le Comte Etienne Szécheny [sic]—il a été souvent en Angleterre—ou, si tel n'est pas le cas, son nom vous sera présent, parce qu'il paraît dans les feuilles du jour. Le Comte S. est l'un des fauteurs les plus marquant des changements que dans son organisation intérieure a éprouvé la Hongrie dans le cours des dernières 25 années. Idéologue et à la fois homme d'action; patriote chaud mais exalté; ambitieux dans la double direction due bien général et de sa personnalité, c'est lui qui a introduit dans son pays les produits de la vapeur; les courses de chevaux; les clubs, appelés en Hongrie casinos, et l'idée de la nationalité Hongroise, servie par la diffusion de la langue Magyar que le bas peuple parlait *seul* jusqu'à l'année 1825. Toutes les affaires se sont jusqu'en 1830 traitées *en latin*. . . .

Le Comte S. arrivé au point où la raison s'est montrée à nu devant lui, c'est elle qui lui a fait défaut. La tête lui a tourné et il se trouve aujourd'hui dans une maison de santé près de Vienne. La faculté ne renonce pas à l'espoir de le guérir et je partage cet espoir, vu la circonstance suivante. Il a des moments lucides et dans ces moments il rentre dans les faits historiques. "Le P. de M. m'a toujours averti du mal que je faisais. Il m'a dit: Ne touchez pas aux fondements de l'édifice sans quoi il croulera en entier. Je n'ai point su profiter de cet avertissement; j'ai tué mon pays!" Alors il rentre en fureur.

Bien des amitiés, mon cher Disraeli. Ma lettre renferme de l'étoffe pour l'orateur au Parlement et pour romancier. Vous ne m'en voudrez pas.[8]

In his answer of October 12, 1848, Disraeli replied to his "dear master," "You were quite right in saying that there was stuff in it both for the statesman and the poet, for the principles indicated may guide a troubled Cabinet, and the fate of Szécheny [sic], whom I knew only by reputation, is dramatic and fulfils the laws of poetic justice."[9] Be

[8] *Ibid.*, pp. 189f. Cf. Richard Metternich-Winneburg, ed. *Aus Metternichs nachgelassenen Papieren.* Geordnet und zusammengestellt von Alfons v. Klinkowström, 8 vols. (Vienna: Braumüller, 1880–84), VIII, Docs. No. 1,701 and 1,734, pp. 34, 185.

[9] Széchenyi's life presented a challenge not only to politicians, writers, and historians, as suggested by Metternich and Disraeli, but also to medical and psychiatric research. Lombroso, for example, tried to support his ideas that "genius was a special morbid

this as it may, the expressions used by the two conservative "philosophical statesmen" concerning Széchenyi clearly point out one of the basic questions of all Széchenyi research: how is it possible that Széchenyi, considered a loyal supporter of the Habsburg dynasty, a staunch defender of the Austrian Empire's unity against Kossuth, was also thought of as the initiator of the "subversive activities" resulting in the revolutionary explosion of 1848 in central Europe?[10]

Naturally, Metternich's "I told you so" attitude requires critical examination, and an attempt to this effect will be made in this book. At this point one may only refer to Franktiše Palacký who, according to the French historian Saint-René Taillandier, suggested immediately after the Austro-Hungarian Compromise of 1867 and on the eve of his departure for the Slavic Congress in Moscow that Széchenyi was "A great figure . . . the only Magyar who is respected by other races. If the Austrian government were inspired by his principles and if all the Magyars resembled him, we would not be forced to accept the invitation of the Russians."[11]

The prominent Czech historian-statesman's comment further broadens the issues raised by Metternich and Disraeli. The question is not only why and how the well-to-do scion of a leading aristocratic family decided to embrace the cause of his previously despised fatherland's "regeneration," to use Széchenyi's own term, but also *whether* reform, sincerely accepted and intelligently applied in time, could be a substitute for either strong-fisted absolutism or revolution? One could even ask whether there is such a historical moment *at all* in a politically and socio-economically underdeveloped area, especially since central Europe was and largely continued to be such an area before and after 1848? Approached from this angle, the "Széchenyi question" ceases to be an exclusively Hungarian problem although Hungarians have been inclined to interpret,

---

condition" and that there was a "resemblance between genius and insanity" among others also by citing the example of Széchenyi. Cesare Lombroso, *The Man of Genius* (New York: Scribner's, 1896), pp. 87–90.

[10] As a supplementary footnote to the opinion of leading contemporary statesmen of the Austrian Empire, it is rather interesting to cite the opinion of the revolutionary Viennese daily *Die Constitution* about Széchenyi—in the spring of 1848. In a series of articles aimed at the popularization of revolutionary Hungary among the "dear Austrian brethren" (*liebe Brüder Österreicher*), the author, M. Töltényi, presents Széchenyi as father and prime mover of the Hungarian opposition to the "hated Metternich" ("Ungarn." *Die Constitution*, No. 16, Apr. 8, 1848, pp. 211f.) and calls Kossuth the "disciple" of Széchenyi despite the fact that he was aware of the Széchenyi-Kossuth controversy since the publication of *A kelet népe* in 1841 ("Ungarn." *Die Constitution*, No. 17, Apr. 10, 1948, p. 244), where Széchenyi himself sharply rejected all such generalizations.

[11] Saint-René Taillandier, "Hommes d'Etat de la Hongrie. Le comte Stéphan Széchenyi," *Revue des deux mondes*, Aug. 1, 1867, 2d Period, LXX, 653f.

until very recently, the flow of their modern history in the light of the Széchenyi-Kossuth controversy.

Indeed, the personal and psychological side of Széchenyi's life, in addition to his public career, has traditionally been a significant field for research; to it have been devoted the efforts of several generations of Hungarian historians, writers, and psychologists. From the publication of the first Széchenyi monograph in 1832[12] to the recent appearance of a not-quite-complete bibliographical survey of about 350 pages,[13] summarizing the main trends of Széchenyi historiography for 1851–1918, there has been an almost continually growing Széchenyi literature which would now fill a small library. From this awe-inspiring 135-year-old historiographical tradition I have attempted to learn what I consider to be most important for the understanding of Széchenyi's life and times. I have also tried to avail myself of the golden opportunity so few Hungarian historians have had, namely, to find out what Széchenyi and Hungary meant to the world beyond the empire of the Habsburgs. It is out of these intertwined endeavors that the present book was born.

[12] József Balásfalvai Orosz, ed., *Gróf Széchenyi István mint író* (Count Stephen Széchenyi as a Writer) (Pozsony: K. Snischer, 1832).

[13] Zoltán Varga, *A Széchenyi-ábrázolás fő irányai a magyar történetirásban (1851–1918)* (The Main Trends of Széchenyi Interpretation in Hungarian Historiography, 1851–1918) (Budapest: Akadémiai kiadó, 1963).

CHAPTER II

In the Footsteps of the Forefathers

Si Deus pro nobis quis contra nos?—If God is with us who is against us?[1]—The device of the Széchenyis' coat-of-arms was born in the fighting spirit of the anti-Turkish campaigns and in the intolerant atmosphere of 16th-century religious wars. The ancestor of the family was Michael Széchenyi who fought bravely in the Habsburg armies against the Turks in the mid-16th century.[2] Bártfai Szabó in his three-volume family history[3] tried to trace the Széchenyi line back to the noble Zách family of 14th-century Anjou Hungary. This theory, however, seems to be only a myth.[4]

The first Széchenyi whose name looms large in Hungarian history was a former student of the University of Vienna and a protégé of Peter Cardinal Pázmány who reconquered Hungary for Catholicism in the first half of the 17th century. It was this George Széchenyi whom

---

[1] Iván Nagy, *Magyarország családai czimerekkel és nemzedékrendi táblákkal* (The Families of Hungary, Their Coats of Arms and Genealogical Tables), 12 vols. (Pest: Ráth M., 1857–65), x, 517–25; and Constant von Wurzbach, *Biographisches Lexikon des Kaiserthums Oesterreich*, 60 vols. (Vienna: Universitäts-Buchdruckerei, 1856–91), xli, 224–89.

[2] Miksa Falk, *Gróf Széchenyi István és kora* (Count Stephen Széchenyi and His Time) (Pest: Emich G., 1868), p. 2, quotes a passage of Nicholas Istvánffy's Hungarian history (*Historia Regni Hungarici*, xxii) also referred to in the diploma issued by Emperor Leopold I, which awarded a member of the family the title of a count.

[3] László Bártfai Szabó, *A Sárvár-felsővidéki gróf Széchényi család története* (History of the Count Széchényi de Sárvár-Felsővidék family), 3 vols. (Budapest: 1911–26). This is the most comprehensive monograph on the Széchenyi family to date. (Cited hereafter as *Széchényi család.*)

[4] For a careful evaluation of the documents relevant to the Széchenyi family's origin, see Nagy, *Magyarország családai*, pp. 517ff.; Vilmos Fraknói, *Gróf Széchenyi Ferencz, 1754–1820* (Count Francis Széchenyi, 1754–1820) (Budapest: Magyar Történelmi Társulat, 1903), pp. 6ff.; and István Friedreich, *Gróf Széchenyi István élete* (The Life of Count Stephen Széchenyi), 2 vols. Budapest: Szt. István Társulat, 1914–15), i, 3.

Ferdinand II, Holy Roman Emperor and King of Hungary, elevated along with his mother and his brother Lawrence to the nobility.

The Széchenyis adamantly supported the cause of the Habsburgs in Hungary.[5] Pázmány's disciple became in 1685 the successor of the great cardinal as Archbishop of Esztergom and Primate of Hungary at the age of 92. Though lacking the political tact and elasticity of Pázmány, he was still a remarkable person. According to his political concepts, the Habsburg dynasty was the defender of the faith against the Turks as well as against Protestant heretics, in whose persecution he excelled. Loyalty to the Habsburgs and an uncompromising attitude toward Protestantism were the safeguards of Hungary's survival in the view of this high prelate of low birth who once summarized the purpose of his actions in these terms: "What tyranny and evil heresy destroyed I shall restore for the sake of God and fatherland."[6]

In his crusading support of the counterreformation, George Széchenyi defied "bad" and "frigid" Catholics; he cynically went along with the most repulsive and absolutistic measures of Leopold I, which were destined to suppress any possible resistance in Hungary. Yet he protested resolutely to his monarch when the latter's actions seemed to infringe upon rights incorporated in the Hungarian constitution.[7] As Bishop of Győr (Raab), he financed the construction of many beautiful baroque buildings for ecclesiastic and educational purposes. He made rich contributions to different institutions and endowments, spending also large sums to promote the military efforts of the imperial forces. He gave another fortune to relatives, thus making him the founder of the family's wealth. Ruthless in his business transactions, tyrannical in his personal and family relations, George Széchenyi reached the patriarchal age of 103—leaving the memory of his tremendous activity to a long line of Széchenyi descendants. Among them, one—Stephen—was particularly intrigued by the vitality of his ancestor during the deplorable years he spent in a mental institution near Vienna at Döbling.[8]

[5] "In the year 1620 we had left Szécsény, Nógrád county, and moved with my father Márton Széchenyi to Gyöngyös, Heves county . . . . Then Gabriel Bethlen's host burnt our house in Szécsény." This excerpt from the family chronicle of Lawrence Széchenyi, cited by Fraknói, *Széchenyi Ferencz*, p. 8, suggests that the parents of George and Lawrence sided with Ferdinand II.

[6] Deed of foundation of the Academy of Buda, 1687, cited by Fraknói, *ibid.*, p. 25.

[7] His dramatic appeal to Emperor Leopold I is in a letter dated Apr. 12, 1671. "Ad Imperatorem Leopoldum," in Jac. Ferdin. de Miller, ed., *Epistolae archiepiscoporum Georgii Strigoniensis et Pauli Colocensis e comitibus Szécsényi*, 2 pts. (Pest: Trattner, 1807), Pt. 1, 22ff. The work was in Stephen Széchenyi's library. Cf. László Bártfai Szabó, *Gróf Széchenyi István könyvtára* (Count Stephen Széchenyi's Library) (Budapest: Magyar Nemzeti Muzeum, 1923), p. 63.

[8] Andreas Angyal, *Barock in Ungarn* (Budapest: Danubia, n.d.), p. 71; Fraknói. *Széchenyi Ferencz*, pp. 16, 24ff.; B. Szabó, *Széchényi család*, I, 123–201. For Stephen

A nephew, Paul, differed greatly in personality from George Széchenyi. Inclined to the contemplative life, he entered the Order of St. Paul at the age of 20 to become a teacher and scholar; in 1673 he became prior of a monastery. It was his uncle's influence and drive which started the modest young monk on his ambitious ecclesiastic career ending in the archiepiscopal see of Kalocsa. As the second highest dignitary of the Hungarian Roman Catholic Church, Paul Széchenyi distinguished himself not by proselyting Protestants to the Catholic faith but by his religious tolerance and tactfulness. Several times he was asked to mediate between Leopold I and the Hungarian national party led by Prince Francis II Rákóczi who, in a letter which explained to Paul Széchenyi the causes of his fight against the Habsburgs, signed himself as "your son most ready to serve you."[9]

Paul Széchenyi never hesitated to defend his nation's rights and interest at the court of Leopold. He asked moderation from the party of opposition, too, revealing, as he himself wrote to Rákóczi on more than one occasion, even at the obvious risk of infuriating the court, his "innate Hungarian soul."[10] In his endeavors to mediate between Vienna and Rákóczi, the archbishop was helped by the diplomatic representatives of the Protestant powers, England and the Low Countries. The latter, who would have liked to separate Rákóczi from Louis XIV, doubted the sincerity of both the court party and the Hungarian insurgents but trusted the integrity of Paul Széchenyi.

The mediation failed: the archbishop himself became the stumbling block of the Viennese court and of Rákóczi's followers as well, the forces of both parties devastating his estates. Frustrated and disillusioned, Paul Széchenyi withdrew from public life, trusting the restoration of Hungary's peace henceforth rather to heaven than to mortals, for, as he put it,

---

Széchenyi's attitude see his letters of May 24 and June 12, 1858 to A. Tasner, in Béla Majláth, ed., *Gróf Széchenyi István levelei* (Letters of Count Stephen Széchenyi), 3 vols. (Budapest: Athenaeum, 1889–91), III, 684, 695. This set, hereafter cited as *Levelek*, constitutes Vols. III, IV, and VI of *Gróf Széchenyi István Munkái* (Count Stephen Széchenyi's Works), 9 vols. (Budapest: 1884–96), published by the Hungarian Academy of Sciences and referred to henceforth as *SzIM*.

[9] *"Filius servire paratissimus,"* Feb. 5, 1704, in Miller, ed., *Epistolae*, Pt. I, 75ff. Cf. Fraknói, *Széchenyi Ferencz*, p. 34, n. 3.

[10] Jan. 28, 1704, in Miller, ed., *Epistolae*, Pt. I, 71–74. Cf. Fraknói, *Széchenyi Ferencz*, p. 32, n. 1. See also C. Höfler, "Abhandlungen zur Geschichte Österreichs unter den Kaisern Leopold I, Josef I, Karl VI.—I. Zum ungarischen Ausgleich im Jahre 1705. Nach den Aktenstücken der diplomatischen Correspondenz des Grafen Wenzel Gallas, Kais. Gesandten in London." *Archiv für österreichische Geschichte*, XLIII (Wien: 1870), Pt. III, pp. 199–282, esp. 205f.; Emile Horn, *François Rákóczi II, Prince de Transylvanie* (Paris: D. Perrin, 1906), pp. 169–97, 231–44, 250–65, 306ff.; and Freiherr von Hengelmüller, *Franz Rákóczi und sein Kampf für Ungarns Freiheit, 1703–1711*, I (Stuttgart-Berlin: Deutsche Verlagsanstalt, 1913), pp. 108ff., 120–26, 136, 140–56, 160ff., 169–74, 185f., 199–206.

"During the time of the fateful revolution I spared not trouble or pains to restore the ardently desired peace for the fatherland; but, to the immeasurable sorrow of the good, all means have been exhausted in vain. . . ."[11] Exactly 140 later these bitter words written in a report to the pope on March 11, 1708 could have been signed as well by another Széchenyi—called the "Greatest Magyar."

The patriotic archbishop was survived by his younger brother George (II), a brave soldier who was given the title of Count in 1967 both for his deeds in the Turkish wars and, as the royal diploma stated, for the merits of the two Széchenyi archbishops.

Compared to the first two generations of notable Széchenyis, the succeeding half-century failed to produce any outstanding personalities in the family. To be sure, the family's loyalty to the Habsburgs was never in question. Many Széchenyis held important positions in the court, the administration, and the army. There were several chamberlains among them; and when the throne of Maria Theresa was in danger, there were three Széchenyis in active service to offer *vitam et sanguinem* for the Queen of Hungary. By the end of the eighteenth century, however, there was but one representative of the male line of the family—Count Francis who was to become the father of Stephen, the reformer.[12]

In his book *A kelet népe* (People of the Orient), Stephen Széchenyi paid his respects to his father in the following terms:

> Oh how often as a young boy, did I see my poor father grief-stricken. . . . At that time, I was unable to understand his grief. How great it must have been! Later I learned and now I know that he had been bemoaning the low condition of our nation. . . .
>
> Ever since my father who excelled in so many civic virtues, went to his grave without hope as a "Magyar," I never ceased to compare other nations' signs of existence to the thread of life of the Magyar to find out whether or not there was any hope for his resurrection. This has been the most profound duty of my life.[13]

[11] Miller, ed., *Epistolae*, Pt. II, 282f.; Fraknói, *Széchenyi Ferencz*, pp. 38ff. See also Gyula Lánczy, "Széchenyi Pál érsek s a nemzeti politika" (Archbishop Paul Széchenyi and National Policy), pp. 1–39, in *Magyar történeti jellemrajzok* (Character Sketches from Hungary's History) (Budapest: Athenaeum, 1882).

[12] Fraknói, *Széchenyi Ferencz*, pp. 40–67; Friedreich, *Széchenvi élete*, I, 7f. The exclamation "our life and blood for our monarch" refers to the famous scene in September 1741, when Maria Theresa, tears in her eyes and the infant Joseph, the future emperor, on her arm, asked the Hungarian diet for help against her enemies in the Austrian War of Succession. Cf. C. M. Knatchbull-Hugessen, *The Political Evolution of the Humgarian Nation*, 2 vols. (London: The National Review Office, 1908), I, 197–200.

[13] Zoltán Ferenczi, ed., *A kelet népe* (Budapest: Magyar Történelmi Társulat, 1925), Vol. v of *Gróf Széchenyi István Összes Munkái* (Complete Works of Count Stephen Széchenyi, cited hereafter as *SzIÖM*, published in *Fontes Historiae Hungaricae Aevi Recentioris*

One wonders to what extent various interpretations of Francis Széchenyi's life have been romantically idealized because of filial piety and his son's importance in Hungarian history. Far from being a victim of a conflict of loyalties to king and nation as Paul Széchenyi had been,[14] Francis Széchenyi also lacked the vigor and energy of the primate ancestor, although he did not hesitate either to suppress his complaining serfs or to act highhandedly against other noblemen who opposed him.[15] He was accused of opportunism; and a certain lack of moral firmness was exemplified by his change of heart from a youthful atheism to the religious mania of his last years.[16]

Still, it is going too far to stress only the negative aspects of Francis Széchenyi's character. His educational background until the age of 18 was "Hungarian" and provincial compared with that of most sons of leading magnate families.[17] Subsequently, however, the two years spent in the enlightened and cosmopolitan atmosphere of the *Theresianum* in Vienna (Martini and Sonnenfels were among his professors), his travels in western Europe, England, and later Italy, his long association with the Viennese illuminati, Austrian and Hungarian freemasons, his connections with and generous support of almost all significant representatives of his country's cultural life and, in the early 1800s, his intimacy with the Redemptorist saint, Clement Hofbauer, Friedrich and Dorothea Schlegel and the Austrian-Catholic romantic circle raised him far above the intellectual level of most of his contemporaries.[18]

(cited henceforth as *Fontes*), pp. 215f. A translation of this passage in Frederick Riedl, *A History of Hungarian Literature* (New York: Appleton, 1906), p. 153, is not based on the complete text of the Hungarian original.) All translations of Széchenyi, unless indicated otherwise, were rendered by the present writer. Though the "first" in English, these translations are meager efforts to convey the original pathos and flavor of Széchenyi's unique style, impossible to imitate even in Hungarian.

[14] Friedreich, *Széchenyi élete*, I, 9–14.

[15] Fraknói, *Széchenyi Ferencz*, pp. 171–76, 263–70; Ferenc Eckhart, *A bécsi udvar gazdaságpolitikája Magyarországon 1780–1815* (The Economic Policy of the Court of Vienna in Hungary, 1780–1815) (Budapest: Akadémiai kiadó, 1958), p. 254.

[16] Gyula Viszota, ed., *Gr. Széchenyi István naplói* (Count Stephen Széchenyi's Diaries), 6 vols. (Budapest: Magyar Történelmi Társulat, 1925–39), II, 85 (Nov. 21, 1820). This work, constituting Vols. x–xv of *SzIÖM* in the *Fontes* edition will be referred to hereafter as *Naplók*.

[17] Viktor Padányi, *Széchenyi kulturája* (Széchenyi's Cultural Background), Tom. I, Fasc. I, Sectio Geographico-Historica, *Acta Universitatis Szegediensis* (Szeged: 1943), pp. 12f. For the education of the Hungarian artistocracy see Gyula Kornis, *A magyar művelődés eszményei, 1777–1848* (Hungarian Cultural Ideals, 1777–1848), 2 vols. (Budapest: Magyar Kir. Egyetemi Nyomda, 1927), I, 491–510.

[18] For the relationship of Francis Széchenyi and the Hofbauer circle, see Antal Fekete, *Gróf Széchenyi István vallásossága* (Count Stephen Széchenyi's Religious Outlook), No. 16 of *Palaestra Calasanctiana* (Budapest: 1936), pp. 34–41; esp. 58–65. However, there is no proof of Clement Hofbauer's direct influence on Stephen Széchenyi. (pp. 109f)

Francis Széchenyi adjusted himself carefully throughout his public and private life to the prevailing atmosphere of the Viennese court and to the latest shift of imperial politics. He was "enlightened" during the reign of Joseph II, vigorously supporting the emperor's policies. His sympathies turned toward the Hungarian national cause in the 1790s when the cause became fashionable under Leopold II who himself seemed to have favored this extrovert "Magyarism" manifest in clothing and speech as an outlet of more dangerous dissatisfaction. Finally, he became more and more conservative and even an archreactionary in the last 25 years of his life, thus closely following the "development" of his third sovereign, Francis II.[19] But such an interpretation does not do justice to the complex character of Francis Széchenyi. It presents his most consistent political attitude, his loyalty to the throne—so remarkably in the line of *the* Széchenyi tradition—as mere political opportunism. It also excludes the possibility that the two extremes of Francis Széchenyi's life, his activity as an enlightened reformer and his conversion to religious bigotry, may have been sincere and psychologically understandable, that is, "consistent."[20] Moreover, it ignores other important characteristics of his which, in some form or another, were present in all phases of his life—his tolerant attitude toward Protestantism (which at that time was almost identical with Hungarian nationalism[21]) and his magnanimous support of cultural and charitable institutions in both the Austrian and Hungarian parts of the empire.[22]

It is well known that members of the national opposition disliked the idea that Francis Széchenyi accepted important offices under Joseph II at a time when some patriots declined imperial appointment. But Joseph II was far from being isolated with his reform plans in Hungary. In fact, his efforts were supported by many Hungarians whose loyalty to their nation could hardly be questioned. In a letter answering one of those who reprimanded him for his support of the emperor, Francis Széchenyi pointed out: that the Hungarian constitution had to be changed; that this transformation had to be initiated from above with the help of imperial authority; that in Hungary there were 40 thousand noble legislators and five million slaves; and that the former would

[19] Padányi, *Széchenyi kulturája*, pp. 20ff.

[20] Even Padányi admits that Francis Széchenyi's constant loyalty to a Supreme Authority contains certain ethical values, yet he considers him completely "denationalized" and lacking any patriotic feelings. This standpoint is exaggerated, as shown by Fraknói, *Széchenyi Ferencz*, p. 98 and n. 1.

[21] Henry Marczali, *Hungary in the Eighteenth Century* (Cambridge: Cambridge University Press, 1910), p. 223.

[22] Fraknói, *Széchenyi Ferencz*, pp. 112, 120–29, 140–47, 193–248, 360; Wurzbach, *Biographisches Lexikon*, XLI, 248ff.

never resign their privileges, nor voluntarily admit the principle of equality of noblemen and peasants.[23]

This letter was written in 1785. One year later he resigned his position as royal commissioner, giving his illness as an excuse. Széchenyi *was* sick, but in addition he may have realized that the emperor's radical reforms could not possibly be put into practice against the determined opposition of Hungarian public opinion. Thus his resignation was a sign of his independent thinking as well as his weakness of character; independent thinking did not let him ignore Hungarian national feeling, but weakness of character prevented him from speaking up against his monarch, as the great Széchenyis—both past and the one yet to come— would undoubtedly have done.

After his temporary retirement from politics Francis Széchenyi went on his "long journey" to the West, stopping in Prague, Berlin, Göttingen, Spaa, Liège, Dunkirk, and Calais. He spent the greater part of his trip in England. He carefully studied English industry and agricultural conditions, drew sketches of buildings and machines, and visited sessions of Parliament. He intended to write a book on contemporary England, and although the plan never materialized fragments of his work are extant in the family archives.[24]

Francis Széchenyi's experience abroad and deep interest in economic affairs may have helped him in improving the financial situation of the Széchenyi estates. Upon receiving the family estate from his mother in 1775, like many a Hungarian magnate, he had to take over heavy debts; within a quarter of a century he managed to cut his debts in half, and in the last 20 years of his life he considerably increased the family fortune.[25] He instilled his sympathy toward England and interest in financial matters in his son, Stephen, who also inherited his father's oversensitive nervous system. Before turning, however, to this problem, let us briefly examine Stephen Széchenyi's maternal background.

With papal dispensation, Francis Széchenyi married Julia Festetich, the young widow of his elder brother.[26] *L'adorable* and *l'incomparable* Julie, the *eingefleischter Engel*—as she was called in the letters of her admirers—aroused his interest even during the lifetime of his brother, Joseph. In one of his letters to Francis, Joseph alluded to this attraction: "you trespassed the line, when promising to inform me of everything, yet you had a greater regard for my wife than for your own brother." No wonder that Francis had to overcome the reluctance of both his

---

[23] Fraknói, *Széchenyi Ferencz*, pp. 92–112. The letter was written to Count Forgách by Széchenyi's secretary, Hajnóczy, undoubtedly with the approval of the former.

[24] *Ibid.*, pp. 107–114.

[25] *Ibid.*, pp. 85f., 319–29.

[26] *Ibid.*, p. 89. It cost him 10,000 Italian thalers.

own mother and his father-in-law to be before he could lead his beloved bride to the altar in August 1777.[27]

The Festetich family was just as distinguished as and even wealthier than the Széchenyis. Julia spent her youth in Vienna but received a strongly Hungarian education.[28] She was the sister of Count George Festetich, patron of Hungarian literature and founder of the *Georgicon* in Keszthely on the banks of Lake Balaton (the *Plattensee*). Established on the estate of George Festetich, the *Georgicon* was the first agricultural institute of the Monarchy. Its curriculum reflected some of the pioneering ideas of a Slovak-Hungarian Lutheran minister, Samuel Tessedik, whose writings and shortlived vocational school for peasant youngsters (1779) anticipated the Swiss educator Johann Heinrich Pestalozzi. In half a century, 1797 to 1848, nearly 1,500 students, mostly natives of Hungary, attended the scientific agricultural courses given at the *Georgicon*.[29] From 1817 to 1819, the year of his death, George Festetich organized yearly cultural festivals, called *Helicon* of Keszthely. By inviting prominent writers and scholars to participate in the symposiums, the aging count wished to pay his respects to the literati at a time when, in the words of the poet Berzsenyi the great men of the country regarded the Magyar vernacular as the idiom of gypsies and treated writers as one treats jesters. One may add that the Festetichs, like the Széchenyis, were traditionally pro-Habsburg. Still, George Festetich, as a lieutenant colonel in 1790, was a supporter of the "Party of Liberty" negotiating with the Prussians and was first in rank among the four authors of the Graeven Hussar regiment's petition "to the honorable estates of the sublime fatherland," demanding Hungarian officers and Hungarian language for the Hungarian army corps.[30] Hence it is safe to assume that Francis Széche-

[27] *Ibid.*, pp. 87–90.

[28] Padányi, *Széchenyi kulturája*, pp. 31–35. In Padányi's opinion the firmness of Julia Festetich's character far outweighs that of Francis Széchenyi. There is no biography of Stephen Széchenyi's mother.

[29] Jerome Blum, *Noble Landowners and Agriculture in Austria, 1815–1848, Series LXV, No. 2 of the Johns Hopkins University Studies in Historical and Political Science* (Baltimore, 1948), pp. 127f.; Moritz v. Kármán, *Ungarisches Bildungswesen* (Budapest: Kön. Ung. Universitätsdruckerei, 1915), pp. 106f.; Ludwig v. Gogolák, *Beiträge zur Geschichte des slowakischen Volkes* (Munich: Oldenbourg, 1963), p. 151. For a contemporary French visitor's remarks, F. S. Beudant, *Travels in Hungary, in 1818*, pp. 122f. in Richard Phillips and Co., *New Voyages and Travels; consisting of Originals and Translations*, IX (London: 1923).

[30] Kálmán Benda, ed., *A magyar jakobinus mozgalom iratai* (Documents of the Hungarian Jacobin Movement), 3 vols. (Budapest: Akadémiai kiadó, 1952–57), I, 207–58. Published in *Fontes*; Dezső Kereszturi, "Festetits György és a magyar irodalom" (George Festetits and Hungarian Literature), *Irodalomtörténeti Közlemények*, LXII (1963), 557–62; Robert Gragger, *Preussen, Weimar und die ungarische Königskrone*, #6 of *Ungarische Bibliothek* (Berlin-Leipzig: W. de Gruyter, 1923), pp. 75, 85 and 142, n. 181. For a contemporary account of the first *Helicon* festival, see Daniel Berzsenyi's letter in *Történeti Lapok*, I (July 26, 1874), 272.

nyi's marriage to Julia Festetich, disapproved by his mother and disliked by her father but looked upon favorably by her brother, George, strengthened his ties with the national party of Hungarian patriots.

After losing their firstborn infant, George, the couple had two sons, Louis and Paul, and two daughters, Frances and Sophie, when the youngest of the family, Stephen, was born on September 21, 1791.

It was a strange year, that year of Grace 1791. As a sign of man's ever-present desire to conquer space, the Hungarian paper *Hadi és Más Nevezetes Történetek* (Military and Other Notable Events) printed a sketch of Blanchard's balloon and of "the Viennese crowd in the wood of the Prater waiting on May 29, 1791, for the takeoff of the ball which, however, failed to materialize this time." The same paper, published in Vienna twice a week by radical intellectuals, informed its readers about the revolutionary changes in France. In August and September it discussed the Declaration of the Rights of Man and Citizen and, within a fortnight after the event, presented the sensational news of the approval of the new French constitution by Louis XVI.[31] This was September 13, about a week before the birth of Stephen Széchenyi. On the next day the king, who had in June tried to escape from France, confirmed the constitution by oath. The National Assembly accepted La Fayette's motion for a general amnesty, and on September 15 it was decided that a solemn *Te Deum* be held on Sunday, September 20, since the Revolution had come to its happy end.[32] Emperor Leopold II was greatly relieved by his brother-in-law's decision, thus causing his sister Marie-Antoinette to exclaim, *"Quel malheur, que l'empereur nous a trahis."*[33]

Actually, her imperial brother had many problems of his own. Using the "Jacobin" May Constitution, which in the words of R. R. Palmer "ignited a center of conflagration in Eastern Europe secondary only to the French Revolution,"[34] Prussia and Russia were preparing for Poland's second partition, which meant rivalry and trouble among the

[31] Zoltán Trócsányi, "Uj életformák" (New Ways of Life) in Vol. v (*Az uj Magyarország*—New Hungary, ed. Gyula Miskolczy) of *Magyar Művelődéstörténet* (Hungarian Cultural History), ed. Sándor Domanovszky et al. (Budapest: n.d. [1939]), pp. 244f.; György Bónis, *Hajnóczy József* (Joseph Hajnóczy) (Budapest: Akadémiai kiadó, 1954), pp. 112–18.

[32] *Archives parlementaires de 1787 à 1860. Recueil complet des débats législatifs et politiques des chambres françaises*, imprimé par ordre du sénat et de la chambre des députés, sous la direction de M. J. Mavidal . . . et de E. Laurent, *Première Série* (1787–99), xxx (Paris: 1888), 620f., 635, 646.

[33] "What a misfortune that the emperor has betrayed us." Quoted in Georges Lefèbvre, *La Révolution Française*, Vol. xiii of *Peuples et Civilisations*, ed. Louis Halphen and Philippe Sagnac, new ed. (Paris: 1951), p. 223.

[34] R. R. Palmer, *The Age of the Democratic Revolution*, 2 vols. (Princeton, N.J.: Princeton University Press, 1959–65), i, 443ff., ii, 139ff.

three conservative monarchies in eastern Europe. In addition, ever since the last years of Joseph II's reign, there had been a revolutionary fermentation in the Habsburg Empire itself. In Hungary, many noblemen, in particular the Protestants, looked toward Hohenzollern Prussia, some of them even going so far as to offer the Hungarian crown to the Prussian king. Others, due perhaps to their connections with English freemasons, may have thought of importing a ruler from England whose constitution, so they theorized, was similar to that of Hungary. Indeed, it is possible that further research might detect an impact of American constitutional ideas on the thinking of educated Hungarians.[35] Oddly enough, while the latter were trying to broaden their political horizon by establishing new links with the West, Johann Gottfried Herder in 1791 prophesied the disappearance of the Magyar from the community of nations, a prediction which was to haunt the generation of Stephen Széchenyi.[36]

Yet the Hungarians were rather active about the same time. They had to compromise with Leopold II after he had come to terms with the Prussians in July, 1790, but national feeling still ran high in the Diet of 1790–91 and the different commissions of the Diet kept on pressing for reforms.[37] The Hungarians repudiated the authoritarian trends of Josephinism, but their endeavors nevertheless were its spiritual children and reflected the ideas of the French Revolution. As soon as French events took a sharp turn to the left, however, the enthusiasm of the Hungarian estates decreased. With their memories of the violent peasant outbursts of the eighties in Hungary and Transylvania still fresh, they were also mindful of the radical pamphlets circulating among their serfs. Some of them were written with the encouragement of Leopold II who intended to continue his older brother's work of enlightened reform

[35] In addition to Gragger's study cited in n. 30 above, see Marczali, *Hungary in the Eighteenth Century*, pp. 222f.; Denis Silagi, *Ungarn und der geheime Mitarbeiterkreis Kaiser Leopold II*, #57 of *Südosteuropäische Arbeiten* (Munich: Oldenbourg, 1961), pp. 22–36 and *id., Jakobiner in der Habsburger-Monarchie*, Vol. VI of *Wiener Historische Studien* (Vienna-Munich: Herold, 1962), pp. 55–64, 86–100; Éva H. Balázs, *Berzeviczy Gergely, a reformpolitikus, 1763–1795* (Gregory Berzeviczy, the Reformer, 1763–1795) (Budapest: Akadémiai kiadó, 1967), pp. 9f., 151–55, 163f. and n. 42, 180.

[36] Johann Gottfried Herder, *Ideen zur Philosophie der Geschichte der Menschheit*, Pt. IV, Book XVI, Ch. 2, pp. 66off. in *Herders Werke*, ed. Eugen Kühnsmann (Vol. 77 of the series *Deutsche National-Literatur*, Historisch-kritische Ausgabe), ed. Joseph Kürschner (Stuttgart: n.d.). Herder's subsequent, more optimistic remarks regarding the development of the Magyar language and literature went unheeded in Hungary. Cf. Tibor Joó, *A Magyar nemzeteszme* (The Magyar National Idea) (Budapest: Franklin, n.d. [1939]), p. 106.

[37] For the reform movement of the 1790s, see Elemér Mályusz, "A reformkor nemzedéke" (Generation of the Age of Reforms), *Századok*, LVI (1923), 17–75. For the policies of Leopold II vis-á-vis Hungary and their international ramifications, cf. Adam Wandruszka, *Leopold II*, 2 vols. (Vienna-Munich: Herold, 1964–65), II, 49–90, 312–20, 330–34.

in subtler (and sometimes less subtle) ways. So it turned out that when the so-called Martinovics conspiracy was detected and cruelly quashed by the court in 1794–95, all potential political opposition in Hungary was frightened into silence.

The movement of the Hungarian Jacobins was directed by abbot Ignatius Martinovics, a highly educated but utterly ambitious man who under Joseph II held the chair of experimental physics at the German University of Lemberg (Lvov). Martinovics was a follower of French revolutionary ideas and had at first enthusiastically supported the reforms of Joseph II; then, during the reign of Leopold II, he became one of the agents of the court and sent regular reports about the activities of the Viennese illuminati. He did not give up completely his own ideas of reform. Turned down by Leopold's successor, Francis, after his father's death, and spurred on by a strange combination of wounded vanity, resentment against court reaction, and perhaps a sincere desire for social progress, Martinovics set out to organize two societies: one of them, the Association of Reformers, destined for the lesser nobility, the other, the Association of Liberty and Equality, for the radical intelligentsia. The noble reformers were kept in ignorance of the existence of their more radical counterparts. The Association, however, was to use members of the first group as its tools only to eliminate them after the successful first phase of the planned insurrection. Through the two organizations, the ringleaders tried to channel and rally the sympathy of intellectuals toward the French Revolution and the dissatisfaction of certain segments of the nobility with the reactionary policies of Vienna. Thus the Martinovics movement endeavored to exploit the radicals' longing for social reform as well as the national party's constitutional opposition to the court.

The Hungarian Jacobins, however, were entirely unknown to the lower classes and had no public support. They had no time to put their plans into practice, for after a few weeks of watching, in July 1794, the police suppressed their embryonic organization. Seven death sentences and dozens for long imprisonment were meted out in a series of trials held in the spring of 1795. The severity of the punishment came as a shock to the educated and to the sympathizers with liberal reform. Among the arrested there were many noblemen from "good families"; one of those executed was even a count. French republican ideas were popular among the instructors and students of the University of Pest and at the Calvinist College of Sárospatak; most leaders of Hungarian literary life, like John Batsányi, Francis Verseghy, Ladislas Szentjóbi-Szabó, and Francis Kazinczy were involved in the movement and were imprisoned for many years. A heavy cloud of suspicion hung over the heads of those who reputedly held enlightened views: the reading of a declaration issued by the Martinovics circle or the participation in translating a French revolutionary poem or pamphlet would have been sufficient cause for detention.[38]

Francis Széchenyi's former secretary and intimate protégé, Joseph Hajnóczy, was one of those sentenced to death. According to the traditional interpretation, the liquidation of the Martinovics conspiracy was the great turning point in Francis Széchenyi's life. Although he was not even asked to testify at the trial, as a contemporary remarked, "he himself must have felt that he used to be a freemason in his earlier years."[39] He was not involved in the conspiracy himself, but it was a close call, for Vienna suspected powerful supporters behind the Martinovics group.[40]

In addition to his past as a freemason, Francis Széchenyi took an active part in the works of the 1790–91 Diet, cautiously supporting the goals of the "national" party and the ideas of religious freedom and general taxation. In 1792, however, he resigned his seat in the urbarial commission, established by the Diet for the improvement of the peasant's lot, and advised the king to dissolve all the Dietal committees in charge of reform proposals. In Fraknói's opinion, the committees were not liberal enough for Széchenyi;[41] more probably Széchenyi, who was warned by primate Joseph Batthyány that his name was in the "Black Book" at court,[42] was anxious to "compensate" for his former "sins" and get back into royal favor.

The question of royal favor in the case of Francis Széchenyi is an important one. Fraknói overemphasized the importance of Francis Széchenyi's "diplomatic mission" to the emperor's brother-in-law, King Ferdinand IV of Naples in early 1793; also, in his opinion, Stephen Széchenyi was born in the imperial palace of the Viennese *Augarten*,

[38] In addition to the works by Benda, Silagi, and Palmer already cited, see also Peter F. Sugar, "The Influence of the Enlightenment and the French Revolution in Eighteenth Century Hungary," *Journal of Central European Affairs*, xvii (1958), 331–55; Ernst Wangermann, *From Joseph II to the Jacobin Trials* (Oxford: Oxford University Press, 1959). For a recent comprehensive survey of the pertinent literature see Kálmán Benda, "A jozefinizmus és jakobinusság kérdései a Habsburg Monarchiában" (Problems of Josephinism and Jacobinism in the Habsburg Monarchy), *Történelmi Szemle* viii (1965), 388–421.

[39] Fraknói, *Széchenyi Ferencz*, pp. 168–71. For Francis Széchenyi's intimate relationship with Hajnóczy see Benda, ed. *Magyar jakobinusok*, i, 42–50, ii, 102, 364f.; B. Szabó, *Széchényi család*, ii, 323–33, 375f.; and Bónis, *Hajnóczy*, pp. 24–45, 51f., 54, 57f., 63, 86, 97, 108, 110, 138, 163–67 and n. 94.

[40] Elemér Mályusz, ed., *Sándor Lipót főherceg nádor iratai, 1790–1795* (Papers of Archduke Alexander Leopold, 1790–95) (Budapest: Magyar Történelmi Társulat, 1926), p. 853. Doc. 182 (Apr. 20, 1795), report to Francis II, published in *Fontes*.

[41] Fraknói, *Széchenyi Ferencz*, pp. 164f.

[42] B. Szabó, *Széchényi család*, ii, 356.

which allegedly had been put at the disposal of the expectant mother as a royal gesture.[43] In fact, Stephen was born in a room on the second floor of the beautiful baroque building in the *Herrengasse,* rented since 1788 by the Széchenyi family and known even today as the Wilczek Palais.[44]

As for Francis Széchenyi's problem of loyalty, it may be said that still in the lifetime of Joseph II, Széchenyi had been denounced as one of those trying to establish contact with Prussia in behalf of the Hungarian malcontents. On that occasion, he was also identified as one whose wife was a member of the Festetich family.[45] Only a few months later instructions sent by Leopold II to his son, the recently elected Archduke-Palatine Alexander Leopold, described Francis Széchenyi and his secretary Hajnóczy as two "very dangerous" persons, both belonging to the "red American lodge and in correspondence with the court of Berlin." In this list of "dangerous persons and party chiefs who showed themselves as opponents of the court at the present Diet," Francis Széchenyi's name followed the names of four members of the Festetich family, one of whom was George, his brother-in-law. On August 17, 1791, about a month before Stephen Széchenyi was born, another message to the arch-duke-palatine repeated the warning that the Festetichs and Széchenyis must not be trusted.[46]

---

[43] Fraknói, *Széchenyi Ferencz,* pp. 144f., 148–63. Wurzbach follows Fraknói concerning the place of Stephen Széchenyi's birth. *Biographisches Lexikon,* XLI, 251.

[44] The original 16th-century structure, a historical monument under the protection of the city of Vienna, was rebuilt in the first half of the 18th century, when it became the property of *Landmarschall* Charles Ignatius Lembruch. According to a plaque placed on the facade of the building by the Austrian Association for Literature, two famous writers, Franz Grillparzer (1812–13) and Joseph von Eichendorff (1810–12) have lived in the palace, which was purchased by the Count Wilczek family in 1825. In 1941, on the occasion of the 150th anniversary of Széchenyi's birth, the Hungarian government intended to place a commemorative plaque on the building an intention which was declared an accomplished fact by Géza Hegyaljai-Kiss in his article "Auf den Spuren des 'Grössten Ungarn' in Wien," *Ungarn,* II, 621. However, I was unable to find any Széchenyi marker in the summer of 1964. According to Count Hans Gregor Wilczek, who had heard of the intention of the Hungarian authorities during the "Széchenyi Year" at the time, and to whom I am indebted for this information, the plan failed to materialize for some reason, perhaps because of the war. In 1966 "Hungarians living abroad" placed a plaque of red marble on the building commemorating Count Stephen Széchenyi.

[45] Gragger, *Preussen, Weimar und die ungarische Königskrone,* pp. 33–36, 92 and n. 52.

[46] Docs. 45 and 50, in Mályusz, ed., *Sándor Lipót iratai,* pp. 443 and 455, respectively. The documents were part of Leopold II's "Black Book," the title of which was *Die Calculation der Menschen.* Concerning the *loge rouge américaine,* see Docs. 15 and 4 in Vols. I and II of Benda, ed., *Magyar jakobinusok,* pp. 578–99 and 36f., respectively. According to Martinovics, the Franco-American Union's aim was, among others, to promote the ideas of the French and American constitutions and its members were obliged "to defend with all [their] strength, in writing, orally and also with sword in hand the present condition of France and America against all despots." Doc. 37/a., *ibid.,* I, 581 and 584.

With his connections in Vienna and in the surroundings of the pala-tine, Széchenyi could not possibly have been unaware of the suspicion of the court. The danger of his situation was more than a product of his own imagination—it was very real.[47] In early 1791 he asked Franz Gotthardi, the leader of Leopold II's secret service in Hungary, to put in a good word for him in Vienna.[48] Széchenyi's awareness of being a suspect may have been confirmed by Leopold's son and successor who warned him to abstain from Hungarian politics.[49] As the years went by fear and anxiety appear to have caused a certain split in his personal-ity. Hence his zeal in supporting Francis II's regime and his violent attacks in an easy on "the spirit of the age" (*Vom Zeitgeist*) upon the ideals of the Enlightenment. In his last work the aging Széchenyi took a strong stand against the principles of natural law, equality of classes, freedom of press, and constitutionalism. Advocating the restora-tion of the monastic orders in the Monarchy and the readmission of the Jesuits, restored by the pope in 1814, he proposed that philosophy, history, public law, and some of the sciences be taught by priests and that books be strictly censored. Condemning what he regarded as the defiance of authority on every level, he suggested that Catholicism be strengthened as the religion of the state. Without intending to hurt the Protestants, he thought that some of their privileges, such as the election of ecclesiastic officers and educational autonomy, ought to be extended to the Roman Catholic Church.

These ideas, of course, represented a break with the Josephinian tradi-tions so deeply entrenched in the Austrian system of government by the end of the 18th century. Financing numerous enterprises such as Bible translations, periodicals, and other activities propagating the Catho-lic faith in the fight against religious indifferentism, Francis Széchenyi became even before writing *Vom Zeitgeist,* which never appeared in print, a most prominent figure of the Catholic revival, second only to his close friend St. Clement Maria Hofbauer. Between 1815 and 1820 his house in Vienna was the center of the movement of Catholic regeneration and the dozen or so persons belonging to the inner circle around him replaced, to a large extent, the Schlegel circle of which Széchenyi himself was a member in earlier years. Indeed, his palace was, along with that of the nuncio's, an important outpost in the struggle against Gallicanist trends in the German lands and a means of communication with the Holy See in Rome.[50]

---

[47] Cf. Benda, ed., *Magyar jakobinusok,* III, 780.

[48] Silagi, *Ungarn und der geheime Mitarbeiterkreis,* p. 42.

[49] Georg Széchenyi, *Graf Stephan Széchenyi* (Cologne-Detroit-Vienna: Amerikanisch-ungarischer Vlg., 1961), pp. 6f.

[50] A Hungarian translation of Francis Széchenyi's *Vom Zeitgeist* was published by Antal Zichy in *Budapesti Szemle,* XVII (1886), 1–17. For Francis Széchenyi's role in the

Thus the former enlightened reformer turned into a religious zealot in his last years, spending the greater part of the day in prayers on his knees. It was to this period of his father's life that Stephen Széchenyi referred, in November 1819, as to a period of alienation in the parental house since the saintly asceticism of clergymen surrounding his parents, especially if they were young, seemed to be strange to him.[51] This disturbing feeling was intensified by a friend of his father's who once remarked that he had seen Francis Széchenyi as an atheist, an ardent patriot, a zealous royalist, and as a praying friar (*Betbruder*), drifting always with the current.[52] As noticed by the novelist Sigismund Kemény, the "Hungarian Balzac," such a contrast in the respected father's attitude could not but have a very strong psychological impact on an impressionable young man, especially if he had the inquisitive mind of a keen observer like Stephen Széchenyi.[53]

Beyond the personal element and psychological gap which separated Stephen Széchenyi's generation of 1848 from that of his father's, which reached maturity before the French revolutionary wars, there were other

---

Catholic revival of the early 19th century see John Hofer, *St. Clement Maria Hofbauer*, tr. from the 3d German edn. (New York-Cincinnati: F. Pustet, 1926), pp. 369ff., 374–379, 383 n., 387, 390, 396, 422, 457f., 462, 517, 522–25; Fritz Valjavec, *Der Josephinismus* (Munich-Vienna: Vlg. Rohrer, 1944), pp. 41, 46 n.3, 75 n.1, 99 n.1; id., *Geschichte der deutschen Kulturbeziehungen zu Südosteuropa*, 4 vols. (Munich: Oldenbourg, 1953–65), IV, 32f.; Georg Brandhuber, "J. M. Sailers Rechtfertigung," *Historisches Jahrbuch*, LII (1932), 75f.; Eduard Winter, "Differenzierungen in der katholischen Restauration in Österreich," id., pp. 445f.; id., *Die geistige Entwicklung Anton Gunthers und Seiner Schule* (Paderborn: Vlg. Schöningh, 1931), pp. 36, 57–63, 90, 129; id., *Der Josefinismus*, 2d. edn. (Berlin: Rütten und Loening, 1962), p. 223; Katalin Gillemot, *Gróf Széchenyi Ferenc és bécsi köre* (Count Francis Széchenyi and His Viennese Circle) (Budapest: 1933), pp. 21–73. For important documents relevant to the Josephinian tradition in the Habsburg lands see Ferdinand Maas, ed., *Der Josephinismus*, 5 vols. (Vienna-Munich: Vlg. Herold, 1951–61), constituting Vols. 71–75 of *Fontes rerum Austriacarum*, 2 Abtg., *Diplomataria et Acta*. For some of the specific aspects of Gallicanism and Josephinism in Hungary, cf. the neo-conservative and nationalistic interpretation by Antal Meszlényi, *A jozefinizmus kora Magyarországon* (The Age of Josephinism in Hungary) (Budapest: Stephaneum, 1934). See also Paul P. Bernard, "The Origins of Josephinism: Two Studies," *The Colorado College Studies*, No. 7 (Feb. 1964).

[51] Nov. 5, 1819, Viszota, ed., *Naplók*, I, 705.

[52] Nov. 21, 1820, *ibid.*, II, 85. See also the unfavorable judgment of another contemporary, published by Imre Lukinich, ed., "Hunkár Antal emlékiratai" (Antony Hunkár's Memoirs), *Hadtörténelmi Közlemények*, 1926, pp. 104f. Kazinczy, too, questioned Francis Széchenyi's patriotic motives; his derogatory remarks are cited by Gillemot, *Széchenyi Ferenc és bécsi köre*, pp. 10f.

[53] Zsigmond Kemény, "Széchenyi István" (Stephen Széchenyi) in Antal Csengery, ed., *Magyar szónokok és státusférfiak* (Hungarian Orators and Statesmen) (Pest: 1851), 371f. In his last article on Széchenyi, Béla Iványi-Grünwald, one of the leading Széchenyi scholars in this century, went so far as to suggest that Stephen Széchenyi's recurrent guilt complex should be interpreted in terms of his ambivalent relationship with his father. Béla Iványi-Grünwald, "Széchenyi amulettje" (Széchenyi's Amulet), *Uj Látóhatár*, March-April 1960, pp. 111–16.

important factors that affected the fabric of Hungarian society and the outlook of its ruling nobility in the 18th century. At least one of these needs to be mentioned at this point, namely the change in the components and aims of nationalism in Hungary. It was in the latter half of the 18th century that the remainders of a sense of Christian mission— rooted in the medieval Hungarian kingdom and strengthened by more than 150 years of warfare against the Turks, anti-Habsburg traditions, and Protestant dissent, as well as the feudal nobility's class-conscious constitutionalism—began to change from a Hungarian "estates" nationalism into a modern, Magyar national consciousness. In the initial phase of this process Hungarian feudal nationalism was still primarily a political-legal, i.e., a premodern and *a*-national, phenomenon, in spite of its predominantly Magyar character[54] and Protestant—especially Calvinist—outlook. But by the mid-19th century, Magyar nationalism had been influenced by the Enlightenment, liberalism, and a cultural revival stimulated chiefly by German romanticism.[55] Since, however, Magyar nationalism continued to be imbued with the traditional political-legal aspects of retarded Hungarian socio-economic conditions, the ties between its "feudal" and "modern" phases remained manifold and strong. This "symbiosis," which not only characterized the views of the "historical" classes but also influenced the outlook of the rest of the populace, was one of the peculiarities of Magyar nationalism until very recently.[56]

[54] Although the overwhelming majority of the Hungarian nobility was Magyar, the line between Magyar and non-Magyar was not sharply drawn. The powerful Hunyadi family in the 15th century was of Romanian origin, the Zrinyis in the 16th were Croats, and half of Kossuth's kinship was Slovak. Royal favor and intermarriage, economic and political advantages, the medieval Hungarian constitution's indifference toward nationality, and the permanent immigration of privileged foreigners into the country made for natural assimilation or "Magyarization." On the other hand, Hungarian historians strongly emphasize the existence of a reverse trend of "de-Magyarization" since Mohács (1526), a process strengthened by the alien dynasty, repeated foreign invasions, the repopulation of the country with non-Magyars, and the increasing impoverishment and social destitution of large segments of the nobility. According to the calculation of Elek Fényes, *Magyarország statistikája* (The Statistics of Hungary), 3 vols. (Pest: Trattner-Károlyi, 1842), 1, 64, 118, out of Hungary's population of 11,187,288 in 1840 (without Transylvania), 544,372 persons belonged to the nobility. The latter figure included "about 58,000 Slavs, 21,666 Germans and Rumanians, thus leaving 464,705 Magyar-speaking nobles."

[55] For the general background see Georges Weill, *L'eveil des nationalités et le mouvement liberal*, Vol. xv of *Peuples et Civilisations*, ed. Louis Halphen and Philippe Sagnac (Paris: F. Alcan, 1930), and more recently, Félix Ponteil's study under the same title in the same series. For the special role played by the Hungarian Calvinist (Reformed) Church in the maintenance of Magyardom, cf. Marczali, *Hungary in the Eighteenth Century*, pp. 288–300.

[56] For the Magyar pride of Hungarian peasants and "sandal" nobility, see the remarks of a French writer who visited Hungary in 1846. Hippolyte Desprez, "La Hongrie et le movement magyare," *Revue des deux mondes*, Dec. 15, 1847, pp. 1,071f.

To be sure, after the defeat of the Rákóczi uprising the landed nobility made its peace with the dynasty by accepting at the Diet of 1722–23 the Pragmatic Sanction. This fundamental law, the interpretation of which was contested both during the period preceding the revolution of 1848 and the negotiation which led to the Compromise of 1867, transformed the Hungarian elective kingdom into a hereditary monarchy and recognized the "indivisible and inseparable" links that tied Hungary to the rest of the Habsburg domains. The trend toward centralizing absolutism, confirmed under Maria Theresa and Joseph II, curbed the political independence of the Hungarian nobility without, however, breaking their local autonomy in the counties or their influence on domestic affairs in the diet. It is for this reason that the nobility in both Hungary and Croatia were not only a privileged class but remained "the ruling nation itself" before 1848.[57]

This ruling nobility frustrated many progressive reforms in Hungary during the 18th century. The refusal to give up their tax exemption was tied to a tariff system which hurt Hungary's economic development and at the same time strengthened the trend toward economic separatism. This ultimately helped Kossuth in his agitation for a politically motivated Industrial Protective Union, which was but a manifestation of modern economic nationalism on Hungarian soil.[58]

Joseph II's policy has rightly been criticized by Hungarian historians who do not always recall that centralization also meant the elimination or transfer of administrative units previously under Vienna's direct supervision to the Hungarian central authorities. Such action reinforced Hungarian claims to all territories reconquered from Turkey, which formerly belonged to the Crown of St. Stephen. It is true that the trend was largely reversed under Leopold II; nevertheless, it was during Joseph II's reign that the first successful steps were taken to reincorporate Transylvania into Hungary.[59] Leopold II's return to the "divide and rule"

[57] G. E. Rothenberg, *The Austrian Military Border in Croatia, 1522–1747*, (Urbana, Ill.: University of Illinois Press, 1960), p. 84. For an English translation of the Hungarian *Pragmatic Sanction* see Geoffrey Drage, *Austria-Hungary* (London: J. Murray, 1909), pp. 751ff.

[58] For details and bibliography see Julius Miskolczy, *Ungarn in der Habsburger-Monarchie* (Vienna-Munich: Vlg. Herold, 1959), pp. 20–33, 63ff., 71–79. For Kossuth see Domokos Kosáry, *Kossuth és a Védegylet. A magyar nacionalizmus történetéhez* (Kossuth and the Protective Union. [Contribution] to the History of Magyar Nationalism) (Budapest: Athenaeum, 1942). For the problems involved cf. R. W. Seton-Watson, "Metternich and Internal Austrian Policy—II," *The Slavonic and East European Review*, XVIII (1939), 137ff.

[59] Friedrich Walter, "Die Wiener Südostpolitik im Spiegel der Geschichte der zentralen Verwaltung," in Friedrich Walter and Harold Steinacker, eds., *Die Nationalitätenfrage im alten Ungarn und die Südostpolitik Wiens* (Munich: Oldenbourg, 1959), pp. 20ff.

policies of Joseph's predecessors[60] and the continuation of this policy by Francis I, who wanted to keep all peoples in a state of mutual distrust,[61] and by Metternich, who intended to balance the aspirations of different nationalities against each other, contributed in large measure to the rise of both Magyar and non-Magyar nationalisms by generating an atmosphere of suspicion that brought disastrous consequences to all parties involved, including the administration.

The widespread discontent bordering on rebellion in several areas of the Habsburg monarchy just before Joseph II's death gave the Hungarian estates an opportunity to put pressure on the dynasty to confirm their ancient liberties. Law X, which was enacted by the Diet of 1790-91, stressed that Hungary was an independent and free kingdom with a constitution of its own and was to be governed in accordance with its own laws and customs and not according to the norms applied to other provinces. Act XII, passed by the same Diet, declared that the legislative authority was vested both in the crown and the estates.[62] The latter, incidentally, based some of their arguments in favor of the new legislation on the Social Contract and other political theories of the Enlightenment.[63] As Szekfű has said, the Hungarian nobility, representing only five percent of the population, began to justify their old privileges by resorting to modern political terminology in the name of the entire people, the overwhelming majority of whom were peasants whose fate the same nobility refused to improve for 50 more years. Thus the various laws passed during the last decade of the eighteenth century assisted

[60] *Ibid.*, pp. 9-19, 23-27. As justification for the reversal of the "administrative dualism" begun under Joseph II (and resumed in the Compromise of 1867), Prince Kaunitz suggested, in 1791: "Je sichtbarer und bedenklicher die absicht ist, die man heget, aus Hungarn, Siebenbürgen und der illyrischen nation eine vim unitam zu machen, desto räthlicher und nothwendiger wird das principium divide et impera . . . ." Cited *ibid.*, p. 23, also *ibid.*, *Die österreichische Zentralverwaltung*, I, 2d half, Pt. 1, No. 35 of *Veröffentlichungen der Kommission für neuere Geschichte Österreichs* (Vienna: A. Holzhausens Nachf., 1950), p. 82; for the incipient "administrative dualism" ("Verwaltungsdualismus") in the Empire, see *ibid.*, pp. 16-23, 65. For the reversal of Joseph II's policy see also Ernst Wangermann, *From Joseph II to the Jacobin Trials*, p. 87.

[61] Francis is reported to have described his peoples to the French ambassador in these words: "Chacun garde son voisin. Ils ne se comprennent pas, ils se détestent. De leur antipathies naît l'ordre, et de leur haine réciproque la paix générale." Quoted, after L. Leger, *Histoire de l'Autriche-Hongrie* (Paris: 1897), p. 454, by Paul Henry, "Le problème des nationalités," in *L'Europe du XIXᵉ et du XXᵉ siècle*, ed. M. Beloff, P. Renouvin, F. Schnabel, and F. Valsecchi (Milan: Marzorati, 1959), pp. 175f.

[62] Henrik Marczali, ed., *A magyar történet kutfőinek kézikönyve—Enchiridion fontium historiae Hungarorum* (Budapest: Athenaeum, 1901), pp. 765f. For an enumeration of the laws enacted by the Diet of 1790-91 and for an English summary of the more important ones, see Robert Townson, *Travels in Hungary, with a Short Account of Vienna in the Year 1793* (London: G. G. and J. Robinson, 1797), pp. 156-80.

[63] Bálint Hóman and Gyula Szekfű, *Magyar Történet* (Hungarian History), 2d edn., 5 vols. (Budapest: Kir. Magy. Egyetemi Ny., 1935-36), V, 56f., 73f.

the estates in confirming their traditional position,[64] even though the prevalence of more radical trends during the French Revolution and the discovery of the Martinovics plot (which was partially a reaction against the reestablishment of estates' supremacy)[65] served Vienna well in keeping the revived Hungarian feudal nationalism under control. Still, Acts X and XII of 1791 proved to be points of departure for increasingly broadening demands aimed at achieving independent Hungarian statehood within the Habsburg domains, especially during the second quarter of the nineteenth century. A first rate constitutional lawyer like Kossuth was able to reinterpret Act X in such a way that it implied that Hungary was to be granted a parliamentary form of government with a responsible ministry and to have a voice in directing the foreign policy of the empire.[66]

Or, to put it differently, the nobility played the role of the "third estate" in an area where a Western-type bourgeoisie either was entirely absent or was lacking in social prestige and too weak numerically and economically to give leadership to the movement to modernize national life. Admittedly, the most progressive elements of the nobility attempted to strengthen the middle classes, and these contributed to the Westernization of Hungarian society and political life. Still, the dominant role of the nobility, unchallenged before 1848 and voluntarily accepted after 1867, left a lasting imprint on the development of the Magyar intelligentsia and the evolution of modern nationalism in Hungary.[67]

It was the nobility which, as a reaction against the "Germanization" of Joseph II, took up the fight in 1790 and thereafter, first for equal rights, then for the supremacy of the Magyar idiom.[68] Similarly, the

[64] It has rightly been pointed out that "Magyar nationalism was not the monopoly of the magnates and gentry," and that the wave of national enthusiasm that swept Hungary during the last years of Joseph II's life went well beyond the closed ranks of the privileged classes. Soon, however, the political initiative passed again into the hands of the estates and the "Fourth Estate relapsed into a disillusioned inactivity." Wangermann, *From Joseph II*, pp. 3f., 34f., 52–57. For the reform movement of the 1790s see Elemér Mályusz, "A reformkor nemzedéke," esp. pp. 19–28, 36–39.

[65] For the rejection of the traditional concept of the Magyar "political nation" by Martinovics, see Endre Arató, *A nemzetiségi kérdés története Magyarországon—1790–1848* (History of the Nationality Question in Hungary—1790–1848), 2 vols. (Budapest: Akadémiai kiadó, 1960), I, 63–67.

[66] See the instructions given by Pest county to its deputies to the Diet of 1847, in István Barta, ed., *Kossuth Lajos az utolsó rendi országgyülésen, 1847–48* (Louis Kossuth at the Last Feudal Diet of 1847–48), Vol. XI of *Kossuth Lajos Összes Munkái* (Kossuth's Complete Works), in *Fontes* (Budapest: Adadémiai kiadó, 1951), esp. pp. 171–74. Also Kossuth's speech in the Diet, Nov. 22, 1947, *ibid.*, pp. 315–21, 325–28.

[67] Hugh Seton Watson, "'Intelligentsia' und Nationalismus in Osteuropa, 1848–1918," *Historische Zeitschrift*, CXCV (1962), 335f, 339f.

[68] The pertinent documentation is available in Gyula Szekfű, ed., *Iratok a magyar államnyelv kérdésének történetéhez* (Documents Concerning the History of the Magyar Idiom as a State Language) (Budapest: Magyar Történelmi Társulat, 1926), in *Fontes*.

pioneers of the 18th-century Magyar literary and cultural revival were mainly members of Maria Theresa's noble guard. This literary movement was inspired by the French and German Enlightenment and also drew heavily on classical, chiefly Latin, examples. Its promoters were "Westernizers" who set out to create a literature for the Hungarians with the intention of elevating their culture to the level of the rest of Europe. The enlightened idea of progress was colored by cultural nationalism from the outset, as was the case with other underdeveloped societies in eastern Central Europe and elsewhere. To take roots, civilization had to be spread in the vernacular, and to spread civilization became the duty of every good patriot.

The aim of the more conservative "Magyar" school was similar. The most popular author of the school, Andrew Dugonics, was politically motivated. Out of resentment against the policy of Germanization he published his novel *Etelka,* the first bestseller in the Magyar tongue, in 1788. The plot concerned Árpád's conquest of Hungary. Himself of Slavic extraction and cosmopolitan only in the unscrupulous use of foreign literary sources, Dugonics revealed his xenophobia by contrasting the virtues of the "truly" Magyar leading characters in the book with the unscrupulousness of a number of evil and intriguing advisors, all of whom were Slavs, that is, foreigners. Another work, describing the journey of a village notary to Buda (*Egy falusi nótáriusnak budai utazása*), was published by Joseph Gvadányi in 1790. It was a violent satire on Joseph II's regime and reflected its author's shock over the fact that the ancient Magyar capital was full of foreigners. Strongly critical of the cosmopolitan culture of the Hungarian aristocracy, Gvadányi's epic poem typified the self-centered conservative outlook of the lesser nobility, whose horizon was confined to the narrow limits of Hungary.

Thus during the incipient phase of modern Magyar nationalism, political, linguistic and cultural issues were closely interrelated.[69] Moreover, the appearance of modern Magyar national consciousness coincided

---

For a critique of Szekfű's collection see Arató, *A nemszetiségi kérdés*, 1, 310f. For the violent dissatisfaction with Austrian rule that appears to have permeated the different segments of Hungarian society, and the "national hatred against the Germans," see the account of an Englishman who spent five months in Hungary in 1793: "Everything German was despised, and this people were liable to be insulted if not protected by the Hungarian dress; for the patriots were more than usual attached to their manners and dress; and the *moustaches*, which, with the polished part of society, were grown out of use, were again introduced." Townson, *Travels in Hungary*, pp. 96f., 138–41, 149–53.

[69] For literary trends of the last 18th and early 19th centuries, see G. F. Cushing, "The Birth of National Literature in Hungary," *The Slavonic and East European Review* XXXVIII (1960), 459–75.

with the awakening of the non-Magyar peoples in Hungary, frequently spurred on by the same trends—Josephinian reform, Enlightenment, and Romanticism—which were instrumental in stirring up their Magyar counterparts.[70] Yet if there were some common denominators among the catalysts that prepared the gradual transformation of politically insignificant and vague patriotic feelings into linguistically and ethnically oriented national pride among Magyars, Slovaks, Romanians, Croats, and Serbs (however different these groups might have been in sociological, religious, and historical background or relationship with the dynasty and state), other factors, deriving from the differences just mentioned, contributed to the same general direction of the new nationalisms developing in east Central Europe—all seemed to lead toward increased identification with the kinsfolk speaking the same or a closely related language.

Naturally, there were important variations of the theme among "historical" nations, such as Magyars or Croats, whose traditional ruling noble classes were recognized as constituting the *natio,* and peasant peoples, whose new elites were mainly clergymen, educators, literati, or merchants. But the growing historicism among all these groups, manifest in the revival or creation of myths about the lost national grandeur of one's own people that had to be restored in order to accomplish a more civilized and dignified human existence for the benefit of the entire nation, made the leitmotif itself unmistakable. If the estates of the Catholic Croats were willing to support the Hungarian Diet against Joseph II's centralist reforms, agreeing even to the dissolution of the special military frontier districts for reasons of their own, they nonetheless resented the attempts to establish a national army under Hungarian officers with Magyar as a language of command, and protested against the substitution of Magyar for Latin as the official language of the state. At the same time, the Croats' Southern Slav brethren, the Serbs, always sensitive to the fate of their Orthodox coreligionists in the declining Ottoman Empire and to the changes affecting Danubian and Balkan trade, demanded, under the leadership of their clergy and commercial bourgeoisie a large degree of territorial autonomy, which the Hungarians opposed. Whereas the Serbs were able to refer to their old privileges received from the dynasty, the leaders of the Uniate and Orthodox Romanians, who were the majority of the population of Transylvania, requested the same privileged status which the three constitutionally

---

[70] Gogolák, *Beiträge,* p. 196 *passim;* Keith Hitchins, "Samuel Clain and the Rumanian Enlightenment in Transylvania," *Slavic Review,* XXIII (1964), 660–75; John C. Campbell, "The Influence of Western Political Thought in the Rumanian Principalities, 1921–1848: the Generation of 1848," *Journal of Central European Affairs,* IV (1944), 262–73; Stephen Fischer-Galati, "The Origins of Modern Rumanian Nationalism," *Jahrbücher für Geschichte Osteuropas, Neue Folge,* XII (1964), 48–54.

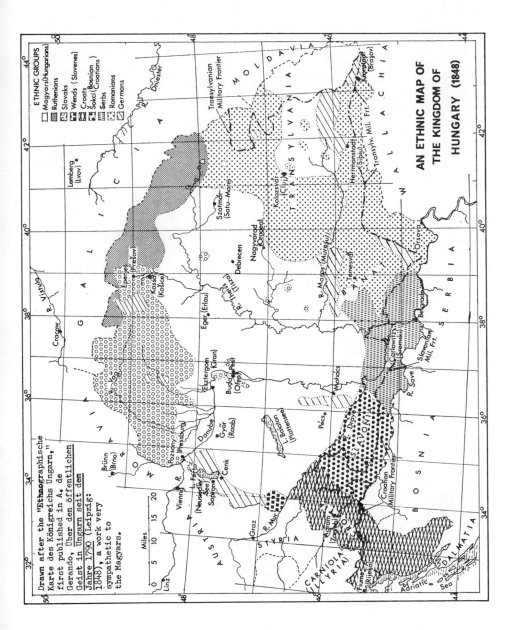

Drawn after the "Ethnographische
Karte des Königreichs Ungarn,"
first published in A. de
Gerando, über den öffentlichen
Geist in Ungarn seit dem
Jahre 1790 (Leipzig:
1848), a work very
sympathetic to
the Magyars.

ETHNIC GROUPS

☐ Magyars(Hungarians)
▨ Ruthenians
▤ Slovaks
⊤ Wends (Slovenes)
▦ Croats
▩ Bosnian
▦ Sokci Croatians
▦ Serbs
▨ Romanians
▨ Germans

AN ETHNIC MAP OF
THE KINGDOM OF
HUNGARY (1848)

recognized nations, the Magyars, Szeklers, and Saxons (Germans of Transylvania) had enjoyed for centuries.[71]

Although the Hungarian estates did make some conciliatory gestures toward the leaders of non-Magyars, as shown by the privileges granted to the Eastern Orthodox Church by Act XXVII of 1791, the concept of the political nation continued to be restricted to—in fact became increasingly identified with—the privileged Magyar nobility. Actually, the recognition of the incipient, competitive non-Magyar nationalisms and the numerical weakness of Magyardom added to the momentum of the defensive reaction against the "Germanization" that emanated from Vienna as a by-product of the centralizing efforts of monarchic absolutism. An example of this is the Hungarian resistance to making German the universal language of the monarchy and to its gradual introduction as the language of instruction into the schools of Hungary even before the Diet of 1790. The Diet expressed its concern for the education of youth in Act XV, which provided for the selection of a special ("regnicolar") commission whose task it was to establish the general principles of a system of national education and of the freedom of the press so that subsequent diets could take appropriate legislative action. Act XVI prohibited the introduction of "foreign" languages (characteristically, German was referred to as *lingua peregrina* and Latin, euphemistically, as *idioma latinum*) and stipulated the promotion of the native (*nativa*) Magyar idiom by teaching it in high schools and universities. The same Diet also discussed a project written by an officer of Maria Theresa's guard, George Bessenyei, whose dramatic works, poems, essays mirrored the ideas of Voltaire and the encyclopedists. His pamphlet, entitled *Jámbor szándék* (Benevolent Intention), as well as some of his earlier writings, advocated the propagation of scientific knowledge in the Magyar vernacular as the key to Hungary's happiness; for this purpose it suggested the creation of a Hungarian scholarly association. Completed in 1781, Bessenyei's pamphlet was published by the linguist-poet Nicholas Révai, Stephen Széchenyi's future

---

[71] Gunther E. Rothenberg, *The Military Border in Croatia, 1740–1881* (Chicago-London: University of Chicago Press, 1966), pp. 80f.; Miskolczy, *Ungarn in der Habsburger-Monarchie*, pp. 39ff.; Fran Zwitter, *Les problèmes nationaux dans la monarchie des Habsbourg* (Belgrade: Comité National Yougoslave des Sciences Historiques, 1960), pp. 36, 46; Dimitrije Djordjević, *Révolutions nationales des peuples balkaniques, 1804–1914* (Belgrade: Institut d'histoire, 1965), pp. 13–18; Gábor G. Kemény, *A magyar nemzetiségi kérdés története* (History of the Nationality Question in Hungary), Pt. 1 (Budapest: Gergely, 1946), pp. 11–17; Francis S. Wagner, "Széchenyi and the Nationality Problem in the Habsburg Empire," *JCEA*, xx (1960), 289–93; Radu R. Florescu, "The Uniate Church: Catalyst of Rumanian National Consciousness," *SEER*, xlv (1967), 331–42; Mathias Bernath, "Anfänge der Nationbildung an der unteren Donau," *Südosteuropa-Jahrbuch*, v (1961), 45–60.

tutor, in 1790. It was Révai who distributed Bessenyei's work among members of the Diet.

The new initiatives of the estates indicated, for the first time, their intention rather than ability to legislate in educational matters, which had been and continued to be treated by the administration as being in the realm of royal prerogative.[72] They also marked the beginning of Magyarization throughout the schools and local administrations. Since modern Magyar national self-consciousness began to take shape at the time of the awakening of the non-Magyar peoples in Hungary (an awakening it might even have stimulated), many Magyars assumed that perhaps something should be done to repair the numerical inferiority of their race. Along with voicing rather naïve complaints about foreign speech and new fashions, as did Gvadányi, and the first efforts by the Diet to secure for the Magyar tongue its proper place, as a guaranty of the nation's survival, Samuel Decsy, the author of *Pannóniai Féniksz avagy hamvaiból feltámadott magyar nyelv* (Pannonian Phoenix or the Magyar Language Resurrected from Its Ashes) raised the question in 1790 whether the schools and churches could perhaps be used to "Magyarize imperceptibly."[73]

One of the oldest Hungarian statistical works, printed in 1794, argued, as did a book on the Magyar national idea written in 1939, that "the Magyar was no despot and left the nationalities to enjoy their customs and institutions," and that "nowhere in the world could peoples have a better life enjoying freely their nationality than in the 'sweet Magyar fatherland' which they, too, had praised gratefully not so long ago."[74] Furthermore, the letter and spirit of various laws enacted by the Diet and sanctioned by the monarch were frequently "adjusted" on the local level by the semi-autonomous counties in an extremely nationalistic sense. As early as the last decade of the 18th century the patriotic efforts aimed at embellishing the Magyar idiom and promoting its use in public life instead of German or Latin were thus seconded by a forceful Magyarization campaign in the contemporary press, numerous pamphlets, and the official correspondence of the counties. These writings extolled the alleged virtues of Magyardom, ridiculed the "scandalous" assertion of the non-Magyars that they constituted separate national entities, and advised them to become Magyars since the Magyars were

[72] Kármán, *Ungarisches Bildungswesen*, pp. 79–83, 88f.; Gyula Kornis, *A magyar művelődés eszményei, 1777–1848* (Ideals of Hungarian Culture, 1777–1848), 2 vols. (Budapest: Magyar Kir. Egyetemi Ny., 1927), I, 80–239, Ger. edn., *Ungarische Kulturideale* (Leipzig: Quelle & Meyer, 1930).

[73] Domokos Kosáry, "A Pesti Hirlap nacionalizmusa, 1841–1844" (Nationalism of Pesti Hirlap), *Századok*, LXXVII (1943), 377.

[74] Joó, *A magyar nemzeteszme*, pp. 111–14, 120f., 134.

the only people capable of forming a nation in Hungary.[75] Whereas
Act IV of the Diet of 1805 merely permitted that Magyar along with
the Latin text should be used in official correspondence with the court
and the Hungarian chancery, the county assembly of Pest decided to
keep all its protocols and correspondence with other counties exclusively
in Magyar after January 1, 1806.[76] In a similar manner, 13 other counties
inhabited mostly by Slovaks, Germans, Romanians, and Serbs resolved
to press the Magyarization of other nationalities. Pest county instructed
all communities in which there were no Magyar schoolmasters to employ
teachers who spoke Magyar. Békés county, which had a large Slovak
population, made the teaching of Magyar compulsory in the kindergartens and elementary schools in 1806. These practices were considerably
expanded in the 1830s[77] when tension increased between Magyar and
non-Magyar. It was characteristic of the popular mood that Kazinczy,
the polished architect of the reform of the Magyar language and an
esthetically minded connoisseur of European literatures, dreamed of "ex-
pelling from my fatherland all those who enjoy living on Magyar bread
and air and yet refuse to learn Magyar."[78] Other well educated persons,
somewhat naïvely but sincerely, thought and wrote in the same nationalistic fervor.

It is evident that there was already considerable intolerance toward
the non-Magyar nationalities and that the old-fashioned nationalism
based on the Hungarian estate was rapidly turning into a linguistic
and political nationalism (but without entirely abandoning its feudal
base) before Stephen Széchenyi's advent on the scene. It should also
be pointed out that besides revealing their ardent Magyar patriotism,
members of the Diet of 1790–91, half of whom were freemasons,[79] showed
an honest interest in political, social, and economic reforms. In addition
to the commission dealing with education and cultural affairs, eight
other commissions were elected to come to grips "systematically" with
all major problems of Hungarian life. Their reports (the *operata*, which
filled some 96 volumes and which have not been thoroughly evaluated

[75] E. Arató, "Die verschiedenen Formen der nationalen Unterdrückung in Osteuropa und die Madjarisierung in der ersten Hälfte des 19. Jahrhunderts," *Studien zur
Geschichte der Österreichisch-Ungarischen Monarchie* (Budapest: Akadémiai Kiadó, 1961),
pp. 423ff. For additional examples see Gogolák, *Beiträge*, pp. 198, 254ff.; Valjavec,
Geschichte der deutschen Kulturbeziehungen, III, 334–41, IV, 11–15.

[76] Docs. 36–37, Szekfű, ed., *Iratok*, pp. 276f.

[77] Arató, "Die verschledenen Formen der nationalen Unterdrückung," 426–30.

[78] Cited by Ludwig Spohr, *Die geistigen Grundlagen des Nationalismus in Ungarn* (Vienna:
W. de Gruyter, 1936), p. 112 and n. 43 (after Julius Farkas, *Die ungarische Romantik*,
p. 118).

[79] László Balázs, *A felekezetek egymáshoz való viszonya, 1791–1830* (The Interrelationship
of Religious Denominations, 1791–1830) (Budapest: Medika, 1935), p. 31.

by Hungarian historians as yet) were supposed to serve as a point of departure for the legislation of future Diets. The French revolutionary wars nipped the plan in the bud. But when a new generation some 30 years later resumed the work of reform, it decided to turn to the dusty folios for guidance.[80] Yet along with this systematic updating of the *operata*, the leadership given by Stephen Széchenyi initiated a new approach to the problem of reform at that time; we shall have to consider in some detail the interaction of the two methods in due course.

For the moment, let us say only that the hour of birth of the future leader of the Hungarian age of reforms coincided, figuratively speaking, with the emergence of the "nationality question" in Hungary although he could not possibly have been aware of this in his formative years. His parents' as well as his older brothers' and sisters' homes in Vienna and western Hungary were centers of that multilingual, literary-musical cultural exchange in which members of the intellectual community could freely move under the wings of their enlightened noble patrons regardless of religious, ethnic, or even social background. Indeed there were many such foci of friendly intercommunication and common work between the aristocratic upper strata of late 18th-century Hungarian society in northwestern Transdanubia, Slovakia, and Transylvania, where the closeness of Vienna or the traditions of urban life had deeper roots than in the areas previously occupied by the Turk.[81]

In this cultural interchange the role of German mediation should not be underestimated. The German element in Hungary was particularly strong in the cities and represented, on the whole, a more advanced civilization. Frequently, it was also more willing to assimilate voluntarily than any other ethnic community, with the possible exception of the Jews. But the interplay of the German Enlightenment and Romanticism with the awakening of the different nationalities in Hungary, including the Magyars, was also attributable to the education of the new noble and non-noble intelligentsias in Vienna, at the university, the Theresianum and the Pazmaneum, or, in the case of Protestants, at the German universities of Halle, Göttingen, Jena, and Leipzig. Since the Counter-Reformation, it had become increasingly difficult, and after 1815 all but impossible, for Hungarians to accept the stipends of Swiss or Dutch universities; in the 18th century, their number also decreased at universities in the German lands because the latter were also suspect in the eyes of the imperial authorities.[82]

---

[80] Kornis, *Magyar művelődés*, I, 173ff.; E. Balázs, *Berzeviczy*, pp. 1of.

[81] *Ibid.*, pp. 16ff.; Gogolák, *Beiträge*, pp. 199 and *passim*.

[82] Valjavec, *Geschichte der deutschen Kulturbeziehungen*, III, 40–115; Béla Dezsényi, *Magyarország és Svájc* (Hungary and Switzerland) (Budapest: Teleki Intézet, 1946), pp. 59–75.

However important German cultural mediation might have been in the spheres of education, literature, science, manners, and even the preparation of better food, the disciples and admirers of things German soon began to set forth ideas of their own. J. Kollár, P. J. Safařik, and F. Palacký, who all registered as *Hungari* while they studied in Jena,[83] became leaders of the Slav renaissance. Southern Slav ballads and folk songs had a great impact on early 19th-century Hungarian literati enjoying the hospitality of the Serbian writer Michael Vitkovics in Pest. Indeed, the printing press of that city's university, whose curriculum continued to reflect the influence of its older counterpart in Vienna, began to publish some highly significant works, which testified to the cultural progress made by the various nationalities of Hungary and to the possibilities of their friendly cooperation.[84]

What was Francis Széchenyi's attitude toward the national ferment in his homeland? His significance in young Stephen's education and the Monarchy's cultural life justifies an additional look at his views. In a draft prepared for the committee in charge of educational affairs in 1791, Count Francis put the emphasis on religious tolerance, suggesting that it was the pivot of an unitary system of national education in which Catholics and Protestants alike could teach and learn. He also urged the teaching of modern foreign languages in the schools because he did not consider the knowledge of Magyar and Latin sufficient to enable an enlightened person to communicate with foreigners. In the same year, there appeared the translation of a German booklet on "The Enlightenment of the Common People," which was probably the work of Peter Barany, the secretary of Francis Széchenyi. Written from a conservative standpoint, the opuscule suggested that true enlightenment must rest on Christian principles adding, however, that rulers must not treat human beings like cattle and that popular education was the best preventive medicine against revolution. Barany was also the author of one of the three pamphlets published in 1790 which advocated the political rights of noble ladies on the basis of their ability to educate themselves. In this address to the Diet, written at the suggestion of Count Francis, Barany argued, in behalf of Hungary's mothers, that noble women also had a right to attend a free assembly of a free country.[85]

[83] H. Oncken, *Deutsche Einflüsse in der Nationalitätenbewegung des 19. Jahrhunderts*, p. 615, as quoted by Spohr, *Die geistigen Grundlagen*, p. 111 and n. 31.

[84] For details cf. Arató, *A nemzetiségi kérdés*, I, 135–70. For the role of Calvinist colleges in Hungary in the education and awakening of Czech intellectuals in the early 19th century, see Richard Pražák, *Maďarská reformovaná inteligence v českém obrození* (The Magyar Reformed Intelligentsia in the Czech National Rebirth) (Prague: Statni pedagogicke nakladatelstvi, 1962), Vol. 83 of *Opera Universitatis Purkynianae Brunensis. Facultas Philosophica*.

[85] Kornis, *Magyar művel"dés*, I, 208f., 263, 283f. and n. 1, II, 483f. and n. 3.

Although the tragic events related to the Martinovics conspiracy generated a radical change in Széchenyi's attitude toward the ideas of the Enlightenment, he continued to be the foremost patron of scholars and writers. Michael Csokonai Vitéz, Hungary's greatest lyric poet before the 19th century, condemned by the school board of the Calvinist College of Debrecen in part because in his farewell address to the youth he spoke Magyar "in spite of the bylaws of the school," asked Széchenyi in 1802 to help him obtain a position at a higher institute of learning where he could teach the theory of Magyar poetry. Five years earlier, the scholar Révai, a member of the Piarist Order and a teacher, described his desperate financial situation to Count Francis begging him for assistance.[86] But by far the most important of Francis Széchenyi's contributions to Hungarian cultural life was the foundation of the Hungarian National Museum. His collections of rare coins, coats of arms, maps, statues, paintings, books, and manuscripts were donated to the nation in 1802; it is interesting that in organizing the original Széchenyi Library, Count Francis relied on George Ribay, an expert bibliographer and early pioneer of the idea of the national unity between Czechs and Slovaks and of the identity of their languages.[87]

The foundation of the Hungarian National Museum, an example to be followed in Bohemia within 15 years, was commemorated by the Diet of 1807 in the form of a special law. In Act XXIV of that year the estates expressed their gratitude to the benefactor by saying, symbolically, that he had followed "the vestiges of his forebears of glorious memory."[88] This emphasis on the Széchenyi tradition, which in the eyes of Stephen Széchenyi undoubtedly included his own father's life and deeds, appears to be all the more significant because he himself was very much preoccupied with his ancestors' footsteps, as is shown by his private diaries, letters, speeches, and writings. Among these references, those to his parents, particularly his father, prevail. There is an entire volume of letters to his parents:[89] they reflect his devotion and respect and often end in a request for their blessing.

Francis Széchenyi's life has more than once been compared with and interpreted as a prelude to his son's career. But the parellel should not

---

[86] *Ibid.*, I, 373, 387 and n. 3.

[87] Gogolák, *Beiträge*, pp. 214–18.

[88] The Latin text of Law XXIV of 1807 which enacted the foundation of the National Museum was reprinted in Fraknói, *Széchenyi Ferencz*, p. 262. For the patriotic enthusiasm generated by the munificence of Francis Széchenyi see the contemporary account by Richard Bright, *Travels from Vienna through Lower Hungary* (Edinburgh: A. Constable, 1818), pp. 269f.

[89] Antal Zichy, ed., *Gróf Széchenyi István levelei szülőihez* (Count Stephen Széchenyi's Letters to His Parents), Vol. IX in *SzIM* (Budapest: Athenaeum, 1896), cited hereafter as *Széchenyi szülőihez*.

be exaggerated; the two Széchenyis, Francis and Stephen, were different personalities and had to face different problems. Yet there are certain analogies in their fate and Francis Széchenyi's deep influence on his son is undeniable.[90] Stephen himself explained, in 1819, his father's affection for him, saying, "My father loves me very much because he was very similar to me in his youth." Almost 10 years later, however, he thought that in spite of the similarity which others found in them, his father, who might have been a better man, was more narrow-minded than he. He also asked God to give him more strength than He gave to his father.[91]

Stephen Széchenyi's close friend and aide in the 1840s, Louis Kovács, was of the opinion that besides his patriotism and strong religious feeling, Count Stephen also inherited from his father the latter's melancholic nature and pessimistic outlook. This interpretation of Stephen Széchenyi's personality followed that of Kemény's, but Kovács added an interesting touch to the picture. Agreeing with Ignatius Acsády, that Stephen Széchenyi was a "Werther-like nature full of sentimentalism and morbid sensitiveness," he raised the question why Széchenyi appeared to his contemporaries, in Kemény's words, as a man who "ponders everything carefully, considers people only like blind tools, an apostle of the cold teaching of utilisation, a scourge of enthusiasm, extremely selfish, a clever calculator, a good patriot, but without warm feelings, a man of virtue but without a heart."

With regard to Stephen Széchenyi's sensitive and sentimental nature, Kovács referred to Count Francis. Concerning Stephen's intellectual abilities, however, he pointed to George Festetich who, according to Francis Deák, had an extraodinary intellect, despised the frailties of emotions, and did not refrain from making sarcastic remarks in the presence of high dignitaries. Thus, said Kovács, "Two traits in the count's personality, his sharp sarcasm and his delight in sometimes overcoming ruthlessly the inclination of his heart or to scourge the role of emotions in politics, refer to his maternal uncle, Count Festetich."[92]

We know too little about the laws of heredity and about the ways nature responds to youthful impressions; therefore, the student of history had better rely on dependable data. But it is true that willpower and persistence were not Francis Széchenyi's strong points. Mindful of this, Stephen must yet have known that these were precisely the characteristics that enabled a man to accomplish something for posterity. Was it

[90] Cf. Fekete, *Széchenvi vallásossága*, esp. pp. 57–75.

[91] Viszota, ed., *Naplók*, I, 620 (May 1819) and *ibid.*, III, 225 (July 15, 1828).

[92] Lajos Kovács, *Gróf Széchenyi István közéletének három utolsó éve, 1846–1848* (The Last Three Years of Count Stephen Széchenyi's Public Career, 1846–1848), 2 vols. (Budapest: 1889), I, 241–45, 264f.

perhaps in a moment of analyzing the maternal side of his heritage that at the age of 28 he wrote a Hungarian poem which went—or so it seems—beyond the expression of filial piety required by the occasion, his mother's birthday?

> Lo, Thou hast kept me with prayer between fire and sword,
> Thou hast quickly attended me in sickness,
> Thou hast instructed me,
> Advised me,
> Thou hast planted in my heart the good, which lives
>   and continues in me,
> And *whatever little I shall do in the future* for God,
>   my Sovereign, and my *Fatherland,*
> Is *Thy work.* —
> And thus unto Thee
> May be bestowed along with my gratitude the blessing of God,
> Through which Thy soul shall see the reward of its pains.[93]

Throughout his life, Stephen Széchenyi often felt himself bound by the traditions and "fate" of his family. Family tradition remained a moral obligation and basis of comparison for his inner self. Imaginary or real, this half-conscious tie with the forefathers was always present in his thinking, particularly in critical moments; at times, it even bordered on the limits of self-destruction: less than 60 years after Leopold II had given a warning to the archduke palatine regarding the "dangerous" Széchenyis and Festetichs, a broken man in the mental institution of Döbling accused himself of being a snake, a tool of Satan, murderer of his wife, the poor "Birdie," a killer of his unfortunate children and of his fatherland.[94] Claiming that he was the Antichrist, the great monster of the Apocalypse and Ariman, the principle of evil, this man reproached himself for having started all the misery of Hungary,[95] and summed

---

[93] May 1, 1817. *Gróf Széchenyi István verse anyjához, Gr. Festetics Juliánához.* Megelőzi Széchenyi nekrológja Toldi Ferenc által. (Count Stephen Széchenyi's Poem to His Mother, Countess Julianna Festetich. Preceded by An Obituary Written By Francis Toldi) (Pest: G. Emich, 1860), italics in original.

[94] Letters to his wife and brother Paul, both on Aug. 28, 1849, in Árpád Károlyi and Vilmos Tolnai, eds., *Gr. Széchenyi István döblingi irodalmi hagyatéka* (Count Stephen Széchenyi's Posthumous Papers of Döbling), 3 vols. (Budapest: Magyar Történelmi Társulat, 1921–25), I, 432f. This set, Vols. VII–IX of *SzIÖM*, in *Fontes*, will be cited hereafter as *Döblingi hagyaték.*

[95] Letters to Dr. Görgen, Apr. 21, 27, 1850, *ibid.*, 435 and 435f.; also to his wife, Aug. 25, 1850, László Bártfai Szabó, ed., *Adatok gróf Széchenyi István és kora történetéhez, 1808–1860* (Contributions to the History of Count Stephen Széchenyi and His Times, 1808–1860), 2 vols. (Budapest: 1943), II, 724. Cited hereafter as *Adatok.*

up his nightmares with sarcastic self-mockery: "I, son of the glorious Franci Széchenyi and nephew of George Festetich . . . I did this!"[96]

Such nightmares, however, did not becloud young Széchenyi's rather unsophisticated horizon. *God, King, Fatherland:* these chivalric ideals dominated Stephen's thinking when at the age of 18 he left the paternal roof. His letter of April 11, 1809 mirrors the patriarchal atmosphere of the Széchenyi home. It also reveals the educational goals Francis Széchenyi had set up for his children, which reflected the spirit of the Catholic restoration following the shock of the French Revolution.[97] There is no mention of human rights or liberty in the letter; instead, man's duties toward his parents and fellow men, his loyalty to the throne and obedience to God are strongly emphasized. While clinging to the well established traditional values, young Stephen added a word of his own: *in deeds,* and not only in words did he intend to express his gratitude to his parents; the awareness of having acted honestly and in the right way should be his reassurance, and virtue his loftiest aim. Not the abstract morality of a layman but an active life expressed in good works and leading to the blessed enjoyment of eternal Divinity; "*nothing new* [italics his] according to journals and fashions, no new manners, we stick as our blessed old Christians did to our religion," without paying any attention to the bluffs of cunning illuminati (*geschickte Aufklärer*)—*this* was the starting point of Stephen Széchenyi, imbued with pious religious feeling and mistrusting the ideology of the Enlightenment. Against this background even respect for the law obtained a certain patina from the transcendental ideas of religion. As can be seen from this early letter, young Stephen promised to be a man of action and yet a man of conscience; for the calm of his conscience was to be the essential condition of that "inner silence" toward which he strived in his mature years.[98]

Aside from the positive ideals of Christian virtues and the negative attitude toward the "spirit of the age," the letter also reveals the author's lack of sophistication. The sincere but naïve tone, and the orthographical errors betrayed certain gaps in Stephen Széchenyi's formal education. Indeed, except for the living example of his parents, which should not be belittled, the 18-year-old youth had not too much knowledge beyond the three R's. Even by the rather low standards of contemporary Hun-

---

[96] Széchenyi to Tasner, Sept. 7, 1850, Majláth, ed., *Levelek,* III, 630.

[97] Zichy, ed., *Széchenyi szülőihez,* No. 1/1, pp. 3f. Cf. Nos. 1/3 and 1/6, *ibid.,* pp. 5f., 10f.

[98] Fekete, *Széchenyi vallásossága,* pp. 68ff. Cf. Béla Iványi Grünwald's introduction to *Hitel. A taglalat és a hitellel foglalkozó kisebb iratok* (*Credit.* The Analysis and Minor Works Dealing with *Credit*) (Budapest: Magyar Történelmi Társulat, 1930), pp. 182f. This is Vol. II of *SzIÖM,* in *Fontes;* it will be cited hereafter as *Hitel.*

garian education his learning did not reach the average. His Hungarian was faulty, he had not learned Latin, which was about the only strong side of Hungarian high school education, and his written and spoken German reflected the peculiarities of the Viennese popular dialect.[99]

In a few years Stephen Széchenyi became painfully aware of the shortcomings in his education. And if the bitter words at that time reflected the mood of a certain disillusioned *Sturm und Drang* period and of the inexorable self-examination so characteristic of his scrupulous nature, they still contained an element of truth: "Alas, I entered the world without education, without principles, without friends!"[100]

Széchenyi's complaints about the gaps in the education received in his parents' home seem somewhat harsh if examined against the background of the educational ideals of the Hungarian aristocracy and landed gentry of his time. According to these ideals, education's task was to help unfold a gentleman whose main virtues were humility before God, patriotism, human decency, and charity. Indeed, these were the virtues Francis Széchenyi endeavored to instill in his children and Stephen's later development shows that his father did not fail him.

Yet Stephen was 28 when he began to make up for what he considered a lack of formal education, as indicated by his German grammatical, logical, and prosodical exercises dating from 1819. Ten years later, at the age of 39, the author of *Hitel* renewed his efforts to master the language of Horace and Virgil. Sweating in the heat of 35 degrees centigrade and cursing "the damned dead language," he still continued to cram Latin in order to prevent his opponents from accusing him of championing the Magyar idiom only because of his ignorance of Hungary's official language.[101]

It is worth mentioning, however, that according to his school records young Stephen was a prize pupil. Yet neither the school reports nor the occasional eulogies of his teachers[102] need be taken too seriously. In the Hungarian *gymnasium* of Széchenyi's time, up to the 1830s, the teaching of Latin was at the center of education; geography, natural sciences, arithmetic, even instruction of Magyar were of secondary impor-

---

[99] Padányi, *Széchenyi kulturája*, pp. 51–66; Friedreich, *Széchenyi élete*, I, 14–19. For the general level of Hungarian education see Kornis, *Magyar művelődés, passim*. For the educational goals and value system of the schools in the Austrian Empire of Francis I, see R. John Rath, "Training for Citizenship in the Austrian Elementary Schools," *Journal of Central European Affairs*, VIII (1948), 147–64.

[100] July 17, 1819, Viszota, ed., *Naplók*, I, 653. Cf. *ibid.*, pp. 702f. (Nov. 1819).

[101] *Ibid.*, I, 864–70; IV, 65, 131, June 30, Sept. 23, 1830.

[102] Gyula Viszota, "Gróf Széchenyi István a gymnasiumban" (Count Stephen Széchenyi in the Gymnasium), *Századok*, XLI (1907), 917; Fraknói, *Széchenyi Ferencz*, pp. 302–308.

tance and dealt with only if there was time left over after Latin.[103] Although there was some question of sending him to a public school,[104] Stephen Széchenyi, like many magnate youths, was privately educated in his parent's home, occasionally visiting the gymnasiums of Pest, Sopron (Ödenburg), and Szombathely (Steinamanger) between 1802 and 1808 to take examinations for his three grammar, two humanities, and two philosophy classes.

Because Francis Széchenyi was unable to obtain a qualified teacher from the Piarist Order he hired a young Slavonian German, Johann Liebenberg (Lunkányi), as a tutor for his youngest son. But, as indicated in the contract of 1801, he reserved for himself the spiritual guidance and direction of Stephen's education.[105] Liebenberg's chief merits were his honesty and sober sense about economic matters. After his "school years" Stephen Széchenyi kept him on as the manager of his estates for his lifetime, and it was due to Liebenberg's frugality and constant preaching of economy that the first years of the young master's "independent" management of his estates did not result in bankruptcy.[106] Also, Stephen received French and Italian lessons from an exiled French abbé, as well as instruction in drawing and architecture (!) from the great Hungarian linguist, Nicholas Révai.[107]

Yet none of his teachers left such a deep imprint on Stephen's personality as did his father. In an early letter, 12-year-old Stephen expressed the desire to follow his "Dear, Beloved, and Kind Father's" example:

Although I do not even deserve the catalog of the beautiful Hungarian House of Books because of my tender age, and am unable duly to appreciate its value, yet my Father graciously let me have it; so that I can follow his example at some time in the future, and can promote to my best abilities the happiness of my beloved Fatherland. I shall do my best, and I shall be as good a student as I can, and I shall practice myself in good works, so that in this way I can give pleasure to my Dear Mother as a token of my gratitude for this beautiful catalog of the House of Books.[108]

---

[103] Kornis, *Magyar muvelődés*, I, 470f.

[104] Liebenberg to Francis Széchenyi, Dec. 27, 1803, in Antal Zichy, *Gr. Széchenyi István életrajza* (Biography of Count Stephen Széchenyi), 2 pts. (Budapest: Magyar Történelmi Társulat, 1896–97), I, 12–17, published in Vols. XII and XIII of *Magyar történeti életrajzok* (Hungarian Historical Biographies), ed. Sándor Szilágyi.

[105] Fraknói, *Széchenyi Ferencz*, pp. 302f.

[106] See, e.g., Stephen Széchenyi's letters to Liebenberg in Majláth, ed., *Levelek*, I, esp. pp. 1, 4f., 10–13, 16–19, 25ff., 29f. 33–39, 44–56, 60f., 65.

[107] Cf. Széchenyi's letter of Nov. 29, 1803, in Zichy, *Széchenyi életrajza*, I, 10f.

[108] Letter "To My Dear Beloved Father," Dec. 26, 1803, Pest, facsimile in Zichy, *ibid.*, I, 13. For the catalog in question, see No. 22,122 in Frederic Adolphus Ebert,

The catalog, distributed by Francis Széchenyi among foreign and domestic dignitaries and scholars and his own children, was the list of his books and manuscripts donated to the National Museum. Stephen's thank you note, probably inspired by one of the tutors, was written in a calligraphic hand and, moreover, in good Hungarian. In a decade or so, however, Stephen was to forget almost completely his mother tongue learned in his parents' house; it was not long, either, before he became oblivious of his promise to study diligently. It was not as if his father did not endeavor to discipline him and teach him the principles of Christian humility. While on their estate at Cenk (Zinkendorf), Stephen and his brother Paul had to tutor a couple of pupils from the village school at the order of Francis Széchenyi; also, family tradition has it that Stephen had to kiss the hands of the oldest serf during a visit with his father to the Széchenyi estates in Somogy county.[109] Still, as a 10 to 12-year old boy, he wrote later, "I felt myself very unhappy that I, offspring of a wealthy and well known family, had been forced to chew, digest, and ruminate the Latin *Orbis Pictus* in a narrow, ill-lit, and damp study, while the peasant lads of my age who lived on my place, worked in the garden, enjoyed the fresh air under the open sky, and could admire the great world *in natura et originali*. This indeed, was a true satire on the philosophy of education."[110]

Even in Hungary, however, life was not all bitterness for a young count: "In our midst, quite a few had been chaperoned in their childhood by two hussars who praised all their deeds, thus hoping, even if in vain, for an increase in their monthly salary: if the little count stepped a thousand paces, he was a good walker; if he took an exam at home and his parents held a high office, he certainly would be an excellent student." At the end of this sarcastic description, included in *Hitel*, Széchenyi suggested that after having finished school, his imaginary young count took an office, travelled around the country with relay horses, spent six weeks in Venice and Munich studying outlandish philosophies, and finally, having become familiar with his fatherland and foreign countries as well, began to deliver "speeches about the English

---

A General Bibliographical Dictionary, 4 vols, (Oxford: at the University Press, 1837), IV, 1,808–1,809.

[109] Fraknói, *Széchenyi Ferencz*, p. 303; Friedreich, *Széchenyi élete*, I, 18: Lajos Hőke, "Magyarország helyzete 1820–25-ben" (The State of Hungary in 1820–25), *Hazánk*, v (1886), 6.

[110] Gr. István Széchenyi, *Önismeret* (Self-knowledge) (Budapest: 1875), pp. 6f. This work, written in 1857, was first published (partly) in 1875. It was reprinted in Károlyi and Tolnai, eds., *Döblingi hagyaték*, III, 579–788, together with the second part of the work (pp. 789–834) which had been confiscated by the police in 1860 but was discovered after World War I.

Parliament, or the French Chambers, explaining to his listeners how the agriculture of Gaul was reduced to poverty, and how Britain was going bankrupt because of the steam and power plants. . . ."[111]

These features of self-centered Hungarian provincialism were by no means characteristic of the circumstances under which the Széchenyi children had been raised. Yet the aging parents did have a soft spot in their heart for their youngest son, as can be seen from a letter of Francis Széchenyi's written at the end of his life:

. . . therefore I beg you, forgive me, if I had possibly offended you with my bad example through word or action—if, out of indulgence, I did not reprimand or punish you (when I ought to have done so)—and if I did not instruct you sufficiently so that following the Christian and civic duties some day you might become well liked by and useful to God and your fellow men.—Forgive me and pray to the Lord that he shall not take me to account for this, as he had done with High Priest Eli because of his children.[112]

Regarding it as his father's spiritual testament, Stephen Széchenyi always carried on him this letter as a talisman. Later, with the wisdom of a lifetime, he deplored the fact that he had not been sent to a public school, thus "getting into contact with my schoolfellows most of whom would have occasionally dashed me to earth without mercy; and who, in case I had taken umbrage at this and meditated revenge, would even have honored me with sound blows. . . ."[113] Looking back to his

[111] Iványi-Grünwald, ed., *Hitel*, pp. 345f.

[112] May 16, 1817, cited in Fraknói, *Széchenyi Ferencz*, p. 338. In the same letter Francis Széchenyi reminded his son: "If you had completed your studies in accordance with the intentions of your parents, you could have acquired previously the knowledge for which you want to make up now." This passage can be interpreted as an admission of his own weakness, a reminder of Stephen's unwillingness to study in his early youth, or perhaps as a hint to the external circumstances which caused him to interrupt his studies and join the army in 1809. Even on Francis Széchenyi's Hungarian estates, the atmosphere in which the children were raised was far from provincial, as can be seen from the observations made by an Englishman who brought a letter of introduction from his homeland to Count Francis in 1793. The same traveller was subsequently introduced by Francis Széchenyi to Count Ignatius Festetich who, "like many of his countrymen, let his whiskers grow under the reign of Joseph II and was one of the boldest opposers of his despotic orders, some of which were very oppressive to the great landed proprietors." Townson, *Travels in Hungary*, pp. 38–46.

[113] *Önismeret*, p. 8. According to Széchenyi, he was frail and sickly as a young boy, and was never too strong as a man either. Due to a lack of systematic physical education, he learned to swim at the age of 28 and to skate even later. (*Ibid.*, pp. 7–10.) In evaluating these remarks written in a work which was supposed to serve educational purposes, one must keep in mind that in early 19th-century Hungary systematic physical

youth, he wrote: "My spiritual abilities had developed very slowly, and had matured very late, so that I had great difficulties in studying and learned little; thus my knowledge would have no doubt rightly put me on the sluggard's bench in a public school." He insinuated that because of his social status, he luckily managed to pass his exams "through clever combination and manipulations," adding that the excellent performance suggested by his school records was a big lie. Pointing out the adverse effect of unnecessary pampering of children on the youthful body and mind, old Stephen Széchenyi did not spare religious bigotry either. It occured to him that when he first went to confession he was told that there could be no greater sin than to conceal a vice and yet receive Holy Communion, that it was an ineffable sin to take in any food or even a drop of water before receiving the sacraments. He recalled that he was filled with hundreds of scruples since he did not even know what sin was and to what extent the same sin should be considered as more or less serious due to different circumstances and motives. Finally, he remembered, he had lost his peace of mind and become so perplexed that he confessed innumerable sins never committed, only to avoid omitting one by chance. As to the priests to whom he confessed, he doubted that any of them was able to give him useful advise.[114]

The depth of the impressions of childhood and of the probing mind can be measured by the fact that only a few pages after the above passage, Széchenyi sincerely and passionately professed his Christian and Catholic faith.[115] It is clear that had not young Stephen been highly sensitive and scrupulous by nature, he would not have remembered only the negative aspects of a religious exercise of which he basically approved, and could have overcome much more easily his early traumatic experience.[116] Besides, the elaborate criticism concerning the deficiencies of his early education came relatively late and was magnified by the bitter experiences of a long life. By 1819, however, as said before, Stephen Széchenyi had no more illusions with regard to his own educational background. He went even so far as to suggest that up to the war of 1809 his life was spent in complete ignorance.[117] He learned to look with a critical eye at his parents, too, but he never ignored the importance of their moral teaching.[118]

---

education and sports were practically nonexistent, and it was precisely Széchenyi who introduced a series of sports to Hungary. See László Siklóssy, "Széchenyi and Sport," *Hungarian Quarterly*, VII, 474–84.

[114] *Önismeret*, p. 9.

[115] *Ibid.*, p. 15.

[116] Fekete, *Széchenyi vallásossága*, pp. 66f.

[117] Nov. 1819, Viszota, ed., *Naplók*, I, 702f.

[118] April 19, 1819, *ibid.*, I, 593.

In 1809 Stephen's formal education at the domestic hearth came to an end. Once more there were three Széchenyis in the army, as at the time of Maria Theresa. Although only one member of the family could be called up according to law, all three sons of Francis Széchenyi joined the insurrection of the Hungarian nobility against Napoleon.

For 17 years Stephen Széchenyi wore the uniform of the Austrian Kaiser. Despite his lack of experience in military affairs, he proved himself to be courageous in that short and ill-fated campaign.[119] Appointed lieutenant because of his father's connections he was assigned to the headquarters of the noble levée by the commander-in-chief, Archduke Charles. Soon Baron Voith, Stephen's immediate superior, wrote to Francis Széchenyi about his son's skillful behavior on an intelligence mission, and Emperor Francis expressed his satisfaction to the novice *propter virtutem militarem contra hostem.*[120] But it did not take Stephen Széchenyi very long to grasp that imperial recognition was easily forgotten and dearly won in peacetime.

The life in the field slowly but surely broadened the young officer's horizon. His "ignorance," on which he passed such a harsh judgment in later years, was counterbalanced by an open mind, a desire to learn, readiness to help, and personal charm. He was well-liked by his comrades; one of them, a French royalist officer, was willing to appreciate even ignorance for his sake. Characteristically enough, Széchenyi jotted down the remark by saying that this at least was a compliment which he deserved.[121]

In the years following Stephen Széchenyi's departure from home, his inner development can best be followed in the letters written to his parents. Neither distance nor the hardships of camp life diminished his desire to tread in their footsteps.[122] Unstudied simplicity and a purity in his approach to the complicated phenomena of the world greatly contributed to his personal integrity. When he was in charge of supervising the construction of fortifications, the colonel turned over to him an uncounted amount of money and, after the job had been done, threw out all his accounts, trusting Stephen's honest face and his family's reputation. Surprised by this state of affairs in the army, Széchenyi related that there were some who advised him to rise to the occasion and help himself to a few thousand gulden.[123]

[119] For detailed documentation see Nos. 1/18–28 in Zichy, ed., *Széchenyi szül lhez,* pp. 23–32.

[120] "Because of bravery in action," *ibid.,* Nos. 1/23, p. 27 (n.d.), and 1/20, p. 24 (Aug. 26, 1809).

[121] Note-book No. 1, 8, in Viszota, ed., *Naplók,* 1, 764. Also, entry in Oct. 1814, *ibid.,* 1, 28.

[122] Zichy, ed., *Széchenyi szülőihez,* 1/4, pp. 7f.

[123] *Ibid.,* 1/6, pp. 10f.

The letters, describing an officer's life, reflected the morale of the army which was rather hopeful at first.[124] But the disastrous defeats of the inexperienced and ill-equipped insurrectionary nobility made him realize that this type of army could never stand against Napoleon.[125] Some 20 years later, in his book *Világ* (Light), he put it more bluntly, saying, "even the most gallant man has to prepare for battle first, lest it turn out like the encounter at Győr (Raab)."[126]

After the Treaty of Schönbrunn (Vienna), which was so humiliating for Austria, Stephen spent a short time in Moravia whence he returned to his regiment then stationed in Világos, on the border of Hungary and Transylvania, expressing his joy over returning to his fatherland.[127] This was the first sign of his awareness that his fatherland was Hungary proper and not the Austrian Empire, although there was no sharp distinction between the two concepts in his mind for a number of years. In Világos he also had to realize that in this fatherland of his there were different nationalities, some of them extremely backward culturally.[128] The contrasts of natural wealth and bad management, the combined lack of civilization and social destitution, were to keep his mind busy on a much larger scale when two decades later he was to start the regeneration of all of Hungary; for the time being, the shock came on the personal level. It is no wonder that the longing for his family found repeated expression in his letters. On the whole however, he was satisfied, and even seems to have begun to read, probably the then fashionable love stories, although he did not elaborate on this topic in detail.[129]

One of his favorite pastimes was touring the unknown country. Besides the beauties of nature he tried to observe and compare people, customs, and ways of cultivating the soil.[130] Sometimes, he managed to express his impressions in a concise yet picturesque description, like in the letter reporting about the grape harvest in the fall of 1810.[131] On other occasions a single remark would reveal his synoptic approach to man and his environment: ". . . the number of sparrows is especially enormous, what a blessing for the fruits in Bohemia."[132]

[124] *Ibid.*, 1/5, p. 9 (June 7, 1809).

[125] *Ibid.*, 1/7, p. 13 (June 18, 1809).

[126] *Gróf István Széchenyi, Világ vagy is felvilágosító töredékek némi hiba s előítélet eligazítására* (Light or Enlightening Fragments to Straighten Out Some Mistakes and Prejudices), p. 100 in Vol. 1 of Kálmán Szily, ed., *Gróf Széchenyi István Munkái. II. Sorozat* (Count Stephen Széchenyi's Works. Series II), 2 vols. (Budapest: Magyar Tudományos Akadémia, 1904–1905). This set will be referred to hereafter as *SzIM*.²

[127] July 3, 1810, Zichy, ed., *Széchenyi szülőihez*, II/1, p. 33.

[128] July (?) 21, 1810, *ibid.*, II/2, p. 34.

[129] July 28, Aug. 5, 1810, *ibid.*, II/3, II/5, pp. 36–39.

[130] Aug. 24, 1810, *ibid.*, II/8, pp. 42ff.

[131] Autumn 1810, *ibid.*, II/12, p. 51.

[132] May 27, 1811, *ibid.*, II/13, p. 51.

In 1811–12 he was stationed in Bohemia where, in his opinion, roads were even worse than in Hungary. Still he managed to get to Prague and make the acquaintance of many Bohemian noblemen who invited him to hunting parties, the recurrent theme of which, as we learn from the letters, was money.[133] It was perhaps the sign of a not quite clear conscience that the idea of self-perfection emerged in one of his letters. Characteristically, this concept, so important in Széchenyi's thinking was also associated with the family circle as if it were a spontaneous continuation of the spiritual guidance received from his parents. Responding to his father's admonition to perfect himself, as far as possible, in every enterprise of his, he promised to redouble his efforts in order to make happy his good parents "and this I cannot accomplish otherwise *but through good morals and perfectionism.*"[134]

In early October 1812 Stephen Széchenyi received with enthusiasm, and some justified anxiety, the news about the Hungarian Diet's decision to support the war effort. Shortly thereafter he reported about the rumors according to which the French had lost one important battle in Russia and were retreating in disorder. Although Széchenyi did not know how much credit to give to the rumors which may have referred, in a somewhat exaggerated form, to the sanguinary battle fought on September 5 and 6 at Borodino, he knew that preparations for war were made in the Austrian garrisons of Bohemia. According to him, it was not yet known whether Austria would move against Russia or France. He expressed his doubts about the adequacy of Austrian military power, but added with some resignation, "we soldiers always entertain hopes of war *in the belief invariably to be victorious* even if experience teaches the contrary." Instead of trusting everything to fate and counting on good luck, he stressed the need for developing certain military skills, concluding that "reason must be able to compel change; and should this fail to happen, one still remains great even in defeat."[135]

[133] Nov. 12, 1811, *ibid.*, II/15, p. 55.
[134] Aug. 15, 1810, *ibid.*, II/6, pp. 40f. (italics in original).
[135] Oct. 5, 1812, *ibid.*, II/14, pp. 53f. (italics in original). In the opinion of Antal Zichy, voiced in his Széchenyi biography (I, 50), the news transmitted by Széchenyi was only a false rumor, because at the time Széchenyi wrote his letter there was no French retreat yet. Zichy, however, misdated and misplaced the letter in his edition of Széchenyi's letters to his parents. The whole atmosphere of the letter in question indicates that Széchenyi knew exactly what he was talking about: as a military man he could not possibly have mentioned armed clashes between the French and the Russians eight months before Napoleon had attacked Russia. Besides, at the beginning of his letter, he wrote: "Eben komme von Leutomischel, von Graf *Waldstein* den ich nicht antraf und meine Reise wieder zurück machen musste ohne mit ihn [*sic*] gesprochen zu haben, etc." [Italics in original]. In a letter dated in Hohenmauth, like the one in question, on Oct. 3, 1812 and given No. IV/16 by Zichy, Széchenyi mentioned: ". . . heute gehe noch nach Leutomischel um den Grafen Waldstein einen Besuch zu machen . . . ." In addition to the content of the letter of Oct. 5, this circumstance solves the problem; obviously the letter of Oct. 5 was written in 1812, i.e., two days after the

From this report, the naïve tone of previous letters had disappeared. Instead, one finds an attitude of scepticism, an effort to register facts, to evaluate chances critically, and to reject all kinds of gambles where responsible decisions are needed. These were qualities which anticipated the real Széchenyi. The agitated flow of ideas in the letters, the lack of periods and abundance of questions and exclamations, the whole soliloquy of reflections showed his hand; even the monumental idea of subduing fate by reason or perishing with dignified greatness, though not original, bore the mark of his genius.

The events of the following two years were going to strengthen Széchenyi's realistic outlook. They were the years of the great War of Liberation, and we have more than 50 letters addressed to his parents from this phase of his life.[136] They are particularly precious for, as Francis Széchenyi remarked in his own hand, they bore witness to the fact that his son "had served with 'glory and honor' under the commander-in-chief Prince Carl Schwarzenberg in the war that determined the fate of Europe."[137]

The first three letters of 1813 were written during the armistice between Napoleon and the Allies.[138] In the summer Széchenyi was stationed in Bohemia at the headquarters of Prince Schwarzenberg as one of the latter's orderly officers. He was promoted to second captain but, "being busy all day doing nothing," he found the service rather boring and could hardly wait for something to happen again.[139] Actually, in his next letters he was already able to report to his father about the troop movements of the Allied (Széchenyi called them "Combined") Forces and about the first skirmishes with the French. He had no more reason to complain: Schwarzenberg who liked him very much, drove him "in an un-Christian way;" in the courier service he lost his horse as well as his great coat so that he fell sick. Although the fighting spirit of the combined armies was good and the population of Bohemia seemed to support the allied cause enthusiastically, Széchenyi noticed that the generals did not always see eye to eye and failed to coordinate their actions. Consequently, they suffered heavy casualties; by September 3, 1813 there were more than 8,000 wounded in the hospitals of Prague.[140]

---

planned visit to Waldstein had been mentioned in the letter of Oct. 3, 1812. At that time the fact that the Russians were resisting Napoleon and were not going to surrender probably reached the Bohemian garrisons. (Cf. following note!)

[136] Letters III/1–60, IV/1–4, *ibid.*, pp. 60–149. Letters III/1–2, pp. 6off., should be placed between III/31 and 32 because of errors in their dating. Cf. Friedreich, *Széchenyi élete*, I, 27 and n. I.

[137] Zichy, ed., *Széchenyi szülőihez*, p. 60.

[138] Mar.–July 1813, *ibid.*, III/3–5, pp. 62–67. See n. 136.

[139] July 15, 1813, *ibid.*, III/5, pp. 65ff.

[140] Aug. 18–Sept. 3, 1813, *ibid.*, III/6–8, pp. 67–73.

Two days later he wrote about 14,000 wounded, including French casualties. While commending the example of humanitarian assistance given by the inhabitants of Prague to the victims of the war, he mused that all sacrifices were justified in order to rid mankind of slavery and tyrannical oppression.[141]

Besides the many interesting details observed by a soldier's eye, Széchenyi felt particularly deep sympathy for the sufferings of the civilian population. A passage of a letter written in mid-September shows how the 22-year-old captain saw the great war. Telling his father that he would sacrifice anything to promote the common cause because "it is terrifying what the poor people of Saxony and part of Bohemia have suffered," he went on to describe "the unbearable stench of the wounded and the dead still lying unburied on the battlefield," and the shortage in all supplies caused by the deterioration of the roads.[142]

Széchenyi was deeply shocked by the horrors of modern warfare. The heroic pose which this part of his life has been presented as has left little room for a deeper analysis of his personality which at that time began to undergo a remarkable change. Yet he himself gave repeated expression of this inward metamorphosis: "One may say that this kind of warfare is too stupidly barbaric to please even the most insane person on this earth; the road from Leipzig to this place [Frankfort on the Main] is hideous because there are at least 15,000 corpses and 10,000 horses left on the highways so that one can neither ride nor travel without stepping on dead people. There is no village in the whole region which has not been burned down or pillaged. It is really so horrifying that it is impossible to comprehend it."[143]

Although he was still ready to sacrifice everything for the common good, his letter of November 17, 1813 takes an unexpected turn. Expressing a desire to see the end of the campaign, "this terrible tragedy," he compares his previous self, when he undertook all his enterprises with a certain passion, to his present mood when he acts only out of a sense of duty and iron discipline. "The more one knows this horrible trade, the more one can see that what we refer to as *great* and *noble,* is so *little* and low." Man was striving for outward appearances and honor, to be won from his fellow men, rather than for "a soothing consciousness of which heavenly feeling the unfortunate has no knowledge or foreboding." The greatest merit a warrior could achieve was *"to kill, or have killed, as many people as he possibly can";* he who

---

[141] Sept. 5, 1913, *ibid.*, III/9, p. 74; also Nov. 17, 1813, *ibid.*, III/20, p. 90.

[142] Sept. 16, 1813, *ibid.*, III/12, pp. 78f. Cf. Oct. 13, 1813, III/17, p. 87: ". . . *was die Armee, was wir alle, und die armen Landbewohner leiden ist wirklich unglaublich"* (italics Széchenyi's).

[143] Nov. 6, 1813, *ibid.*, III/19, p. 89; Cf. Mar. 14, 1814, III/47, p. 129.

accomplished this, was loved, honored, and appreciated; and he who finished the "beautiful" job without being ordered to do so, could not help receiving a medal. "War is so much against everything implanted in our hearts by nature since childhood that, indeed, it takes some effort, and a certain strength, to suppress all feelings of mercy and compassion. At long last, I have hardened my heart with great exertion into steel and I now am so dreadfully cruel that I scarcely dare remain alone with myself. I always need someone around to protect me against myself."[144]

This bitter, almost cynical and self-destructive letter was written exactly one month after the battle of Leipzig by a man who had obtained recognition for his daring and who had as yet no literary background in European culture. At the root of this man's disillusionment lay personal experience. His emotional reactions came from a sincere and human effort to find an answer to questions[145] his piercing eye suddenly discovered in a world that up to then he had believed well arranged by religion, patriotic virtues, and paternal care. Stephen Széchenyi, aged 22 and for four years a soldier in the Austrian army, set his foot on the path of self-education. It was to direct him far beyond the sphere of his contemporaries, but it was not to lead him to much personal happiness.

Széchenyi said very little in his letters about his participation in the battle of Leipzig, although for his behavior he was promoted to the rank of first captain, and was decorated with the Prussian Order of Merit and the fourth class of the Russian Vladimir Order.[146] Half jokingly he tried to play down his role in a report given to his father who heard some exaggerated accounts through a letter from Count Ferdinand Zichy.[147] Only once in his later years, on October 28, 1844, did Stephen Széchenyi recall in public his mision to "heroic Blücher" at Leipzig.[148] Subsequent historical writings tended to overstate his importance in the crucial phase of the fighting. It has been truthfully reported that when commander-in-chief Prince Schwarzenberg needed a courier

[144] Nov. 17, 1813, *ibid.*, III/20, pp. 90f. (italics in original). Cf. Mar. 6, 1814, III/44, p. 123.

[145] Cf. the terminology "satisfaction of the conscience" (*die Zufriedenheit meines Bewusstseins*) and "absolution by the inward and worldly judge" (*von den Innern und Aussern Richter frey gesprochen*) in his letter of Dec. 3, 1813, *ibid.*, III/24, p. 97.

[146] *Ibid.*, III/60, p. 144.

[147] *Ibid.*, Oct. 22, 1813, III/18, p. 88 and Dec. 17, 1813, III/28, pp. 103f. Count Ferdinand Zichy, ill-fated commander of Venice in 1848, was the husband of Sophie Széchenyi, that is, he was Stephen's brother-in-law. His letter (Nov. 15, 1813, *ibid.*, III/58, pp. 142f.) described Széchenyi's role as a courier for Schwarzenberg at Leipzig. Cf. Zichy, *Széchenyi életrajza*, I, 67–71.

[148] This occurred during the debate in the chamber of magnates, and Széchenyi expected the enactment of equal taxation in Hungary. Oct. 28, 1844, Viszota, ed., *Naplók*, VI, 122f.

to deliver an important message to General Blücher on the evening of October 17, 1813, Széchenyi volunteered for the task. According to these accounts, not only did this "fiery Magyar" succeed in reaching Blücher through enemy-infested territory but he also forwarded the "invitation" to the decisive battle to the hesitating Crown Prince Bernadotte, making sure, by his confident conduct, the latter's timely arrival on the battlefield.[149]

A sober evaluation of the facts shows that there were many allied representatives, the most important of whom was Sir Charles Stewart, attached to the Swedish headquarters and "charged generally with the military interest of Great Britain in the north of Europe,"[150] who kept on urging the prince royal to intervene more vigorously on the side of the anti-Napoleonic forces. But there is no doubt Széchenyi behaved courageously on October 16, 1813, the first day of the fighting at Leipzig, and that he demonstrated great skill as a voluntary courier to Blücher whom he accompanied to Bernadotte in order to be able to give a full report to the commander-in-chief about his mission. This assumption is substantiated by a draft of a protocol summarizing the agreement reached by the Swedish and Prussian military leaders at Breitenfeld at eight o'clock in the morning of October 18, 1813, shortly before the beginning of one of the decisive battles of European history. The opening sentence of the document—which mentions our hero by name, saying that Field Marshall Schwarzenberg had announced through the Captain Count Zechenyi (*sic*) the intention of the Russian, Austrian, and Prussian monarchs to press their attack against the enemy—indicates both the significance of Széchenyi's enterprise and the confidence of the allied generals in his abilities to accomplish the task.[151]

[149] Freiherr Joseph Alexander von Helfert, *Kaiser Franz und die europäische Befreiungskriege* (Vienna: Prandel & Ewald, 1867), p. 153; M. Thielen, *Erinnerungen aus dem Kriegerleben eines 82 jährigen Veteranen der Oesterreichischen Armee* (Vienna: 1863), pp. 74f. as cited, e.g., in Friedreich, *Széchenyi élete*, I, 29–31. Also Zichy, as quoted in n. 147.

[150] Lt. Gen. Charles William Vane, *Narrative of the War in Germany and France, in 1813 and 1814*, 2d edn. (London: 1830), p. 178. Sir Charles Stewart, subsequently Lord Vane, third Marquess of Londonderry (1778–1854), was the half-brother of Lord Castlereagh. British ambassador until the latter's death, he referred to Széchenyi, whom he visited in October 1840 at his estate in Cenk, as his "old and particular friend." *Ibid.*, *A Steam Voyage to Constantinople, by the Rhine and the Danube, in 1840–41, and to Portugal, Spain &c., in 1839*, 2 vols. (London: H. Colburn, 1842), I, 82f. and 110f.

[151] Kungl. Krigsarkivet, Stockholm, *Kriget i Tyskland, 1813–1814, Nordarméns högkvarter*. Handlingar från diverse personer (The War in Germany, 1813–1814. Headquarters of the Northern Army. Papers from Various Persons), Vol. 31, B.I.N. 12.b. For helping me find the link missing from earlier interpretations of Széchenyi's military career, I am deeply indebted to director Bertil Broomé, of the Royal Military Record Office, Stockholm, and to his aides, especially Mrs. Åsa Schreck, for their efficient assistance. For the problems of the traditional interpretations see Kálmán N. Thurzó, "Széchenyi szerepe a lipcsei csatában" (Széchenyi's Role in the Battle of Leipzig), in *Hadtörténelmi*

Shortly after Leipzig, Széchenyi was ordered to follow the withdrawing French troops. Having crossed Switzerland, he reached French soil by mid-January 1814. His appraisal of the French army is interesting. At the beginning of the campaign he discovered that the French soldiers were poor shots; also, in his opinion, French losses considerably surpassed those of the Allies.[152] But he admitted French tactical superiority in pitched battles, and acknowledged Napoleon's military genius.[153] Among the allied leaders, he highly praised Schwarzenberg, admiring his ability to get along with vacillating monarchs and rival generals. In a few years, he was to reverse his opinion, always maintaining, however, his admiration for Wellington and Blücher. Talking about the excellent troops of *"General Vorwärts,"* he concluded that youngsters of "this respectable nation" were proof "that one can never subjugate a people."[154] His high opinion of Prussian military discipline, however, did not prevent him from recognizing the bravery of the French veterans, great even in their defeat.[155] When, years thereafter, he read the jingoist poems of Friedrich Rückert exhorting the Germans to take revenge on France, he could not help bursting out in indignation, saying that never

---

Közlemények (1914), 334–62. Cf. László Bártfai Szabó, "Gróf Széchenyi István katonai pályája, 1809–1826" (The Military Career of Count Stephen Széchenyi, 1809–1826), in *ibid.* (1928), p. 45 and n. 15. A recent study, Karl Fürst Schwarzenberg, *Feldmarschall Fürst Schwarzenberg* (Vienna-Munich: Herold, 1964), pp. 244f., seems to follow the traditional interpretation, according to which Széchenyi would have reached Blücher's headquarters on the evening of October 17, 1813, whence he proceeded to Bernadotte during the night. In Thurzó's opinion, however, Széchenyi left Schwarzenberg's headquarters on the evening of October 17 and, after spending most of the night on horseback to avoid the French positions, reached Blücher "at dusk," shortly *before* daybreak on October 18. Having transmitted Schwarzenberg's message to the Prussian general, he might have escorted Blücher to Bernadotte to ascertain their definitive agreement, concluded in Breitenfeld during the early morning of October 18, 1813, and to report it back to Schwarzenberg. As Thurzó said, Széchenyi himself has never spoken about his "mission" to the crown prince in public, and Swedish historiography does not mention it either. The essential part of Thurzó's legitimate doubts, however, has been answered by the draft of the Breitenfeld protocol. According to a letter written by Archivist Sören Tommos of the Swedish *Riksarkivet* on Oct. 24, 1967 under the number Dnr 1,065/N5, there might once have been a duly signed document based on the draft of the Bernadotte-Blücher agreement, since there seems to be a reference to it in Lars Tingsten, *Sveriges Krig och Yttre Politik, augusti 1813-januari 1814* (Stockholm: 1924), p. 212, but it cannot be found in either the *Riksarkivet* or the *Bernadotteska Familjearkivet*, the royal dynasty's family archives. Some of the previous anecdotes "perpetuated" probably by the letter of Count Ferdinand Zichy (cf. n. 147) seem to survive. Cf. Denis Silagi, *Der grösste Ungar* (Vienna-Munich: Herold, 1967), pp. 73f.

[152] Sept. 16, 1813, Zichy, ed., *Széchenyi szülőihez,* III/11, p. 78.

[153] Sept. 21, 1813, *ibid.,* III/13, pp. 79f. and Sept. 24, 1813, *ibid.,* III/14, p. 82.

[154] Sept. 21, 1813, *ibid.,* III/14, pp. 8of.; also Mar. 6, and Apr. 16, 1814, III/44 and 51, pp. 124 and 133; Jan. 14, 1814, *ibid.,* III/33, pp. 109f. Concerning Wellington, see, e.g., Dec. 1815, Viszota, ed., *Naplók,* I, 167.

[155] Mar. 13, 22, Apr. 16, 1814, Zichy, ed., *Széchenyi szülőihez,* III/46, 48, 51; pp. 127f., 130, 133.

in his life was he more annoyed than he was by this book of "Teutonic self-conceit" and that a hundred Prussian lads were not worth one soldier of the French Guard.[156]

Széchenyi loved France—the people, the country, Paris. He felt sorry for the French soldiers driven into senseless resistance by Napoleon "during whose lifetime no lasting peace could be obtained."[157] His heart sank at the sight of the devastated villages, although occasionally he himself had been "chased like a rabbit" by French soldiers and peasants over hedge and ditch;[158] but it was a mark of his greatness to be able to put aside unpleasant personal memories when shaping his favorable opinion of the French as a nation.[159]

During the campaign in France he spent most of the time on the road, carrying important messages between Schwarzenberg, Blücher, General Yorck, and the allied monarchs, or trying to establish their whereabouts if they had lost contact with each other.[160] March 3, 1814 he wrote to his father how he had managed to "discover" Blücher's and Bülow's united armies close to Paris, some 38 miles from Schwarzenberg's divisions, each unaware of his ally's movements. More often, he refrained from revealing the character of his mission because he took into account the vigilance of some overpatriotic postmaster who could withhold his letter. Meditating about the usefulness of destroying truthful letters, he noted: "Unfortunate the land where the citizen is not supposed to know of the adverse moments of his fatherland; miserable the soldier, whose courage does not increase in danger."[161]

Sometimes he was in a desperate mood. The hardships of the war began to tell on him. In February he lost his way in a deep morass while on duty; from fear that he might not be able to carry out his

---

[156] Dec. 23, 1820, Viszota, ed., *Naplók*, II, 100. He very early recognized, however, the potential strength of Prussia. Spring 1815, *ibid.*, I, Annex I, 8, pp. 770f.

[157] Jan. 17, 1814, Zichy, ed., *Széchenyi szülőihez*, III/35, p. 11, and Feb. 8, 1814, *ibid.*, III/39, pp. 114f.

[158] Feb. 10, 1814, *ibid.*, III/40, p. 116 and Mar. 3, 1813, *ibid.*, III/42, p. 121.

[159] Sept. 1815, Viszota, ed., *Naplók*, I, 134.

[160] E.g., Jan. 14, Feb. 6, 10, Mar. 3, Apr. 20, 1814, Zichy, ed., *Széchenyi szülőihez*, III/33, 38, 40, 42, 52; pp. 105f., 114–17, 121f. 137. Baron Stein, too, mentioned Széchenyi's courier service: "As soon as the news of the capture of the capital [Paris] was brought to the Emperor Francis by Count Szezeny [*sic*], I hastened to the Emperor Alexander. . . . " Quoted in J. R. Seeley, *Life and Time of Stein*, 2 vols. (Boston: 1879), II, 311.

[161] Feb. 12, 1814, Zichy, *Széchenyi szülőihez*, III/41, p. 118. Széchenyi dreaded despotism. He was on excellent terms with Czar Alexander's brother, the Grand Duke Constantin, who had invited him several times to join his regiment of cuirassiers. He refused, despite his desire to see Russia, for he did not want to serve under a prince who in a moment of anger could dispatch him to Siberia (Nov. 17, 23, Dec. 3, 1813, Mar. 8, 1814, *ibid.*, III/20, p. 91; also III/22, 24, 45, pp. 95f., 99, 126).

task, the idea of suicide again came to his mind.[162] His comrades may not have noticed this; they liked him because, as one of them put it, he was the one "who entertains us in such a pleasant way by his always equally good humor."[163]

Occasionally, he tried to look at himself in an impersonal and detached manner, making an effort to interpret his own life as a series of adventures and tribulations, the outcome of which, no doubt, would enrich his existence.[164] But the affirmative answer to the question of the usefulness of his experience was given on a personal level, exclusively from the point of view of his own individual development. This did not mean that he was not prepared to sacrifice his life for what he thought to be the interest of mankind, namely, for the victory over Napoleon. He abhorred war and created for himself a rather pessimistic "golden rule," preparing himself always for the worst; at the same time, he was always ready to go to battle "to put an end to this terrible war."[165] Characteristically, at this time in his life, the problems of personal happiness and the welfare of humanity often appeared on distinctly separate levels. He was willing to shed his blood for freedom, but could feel very unhappy after the greatest victories; on the other hand, it seemed to him that the ultimate source of personal happiness lay in being left alone with his beloved ones, *procul negotiis*.[166] This was the human voice of a tired soldier who, after having done his duty, was longing for the family hearth. It was not, however, written in the stars of Stephen Széchenyi to enjoy this kind of domestic bliss.

From April 1, 1814 on, he wrote his letters from Paris and its environs. For a short while everything seemed wonderful and possible in beautiful France. In a deep and joyful awe he wrote of "flourishing prospects of the future," of "the transformation of entire states, of the liberated mankind," of the "natural chaos stemming from all these unbelievable circumstances" and of his own bewilderment and fear making it difficult to distinguish between dream and reality.[167] His dreams about the future were somewhat overshadowed by the memory of those who had died for that future. Also, the fate of Napoleon reminded him of the transient glory of what is called human greatness. He admired Napoleon as a great general,[168] and could hardly believe that Bonaparte, "the retired

---

[162] Feb. 10, 1814, *ibid.*, III/40, pp. 116f. Cf. the letter of Nov. 6, 1813, cited in n. 143 above.

[163] Mar. 8, 1814, *ibid.*, III/45, first postscript, p. 127. According to Viszota, ed., *Naplók*, I, p. xxvii, the postscript was written by Prince Schwarzenberg.

[164] Mar. 6, 1814, Zichy, ed., *Széchenyi szüleihez*, III/44, pp. 123f.

[165] Mar. 14, 1814, *ibid.*, III/47, p. 129.

[166] Apr. 16, 20, 24, 1814, *ibid.*, III/51–53, pp. 133f., 136f.

[167] Apr. 12, 1814, *ibid.*, III/50, p. 131.

[168] Apr. 12, 16, 28, 1814, *ibid.*, III/50–51, 55, pp. 131ff., 140; also, end of Sept. 1815, Viszota, ed., *Naplók*, I, 136f.

ruler of the world," would be able to survive his humiliation on a small island.

Paris, "this seductive city," excited his imagination since everything "that is now great and mighty in Europe lives within the walls of the city of Paris"; from there, happiness and tranquillity would emanate into the whole world.[169] Indeed, it was a historic moment full of hopes and Paris was the center of the world.

Yet impressed as he was by the French capital, by its wide streets, numerous squares, palaces, and theaters, Captain Széchenyi felt a peculiar sadness because "we do not have any of this at home and shall never reach this stage; this will always be very sad to me."[170] The cultural inferiority complex, so painfully throbbing in representatives of all backward "peoples of the orient," suddenly broke through with the experience of western urban civilization and helped arouse Stephen Széchenyi's patriotic feelings: "Although Paris may well be the most beautiful and pleasant dwelling place one may imagine with the liveliest of phantasies, there is still something in man's nature that powerfully attracts him to his fatherland, to his place of birth; and so it is with all of us. Even the Russians are longing for their snow and are quite willing to exchange this nice mild climate on the banks of the Seine for the cold deserts of their devilish land; and what about ourselves? What about me who has such a lovely fatherland?"[171] Fatherland? But did not Stephen Széchenyi himself talk of "we Austrians"?[172] Actually, the term "fatherland" had a double meaning for Széchenyi at that time. In a broader sense, he considered himself to be a loyal subject of the Austrian emperor, thus he was an "Austrian." Simultaneously, "fatherland" was also something more personal to him; it meant primarily his homeland proper, the restricted area between Vienna and the German-Hungarian western corner of Hungary, Ödenburg (Sopron), the Neusiedler See (Fertő), Zinkerdorf (Cenk), and his family circle.[173] It was rather a longing for his *Heimat* than a yearning for the *Vaterland* that tormented him; it was the call of his birthplace and not an abstract love of the fatherland that he was aware of.

For the time being, however, Széchenyi was in Paris, and for a moment even toyed with the idea of visiting London. But he had to give up the plan because of his deplorable financial situation. He had "no uniform, no shirt, *enfin,* nothing—even a pair of boots" when he "took" Paris. Besides, he did not want to avail himself of Schwarzenberg's permission to get an advance from the war chest.

[169] Apr. 24, 1814, Zichy, ed., *Széchenyi szülőihez*, III/53, p. 137.
[170] Apr. 26, 1814, *ibid.*, III/54, pp. 138f.
[171] Apr. 28, 1814, *ibid.*, III/55, p. 140.
[172] Mar. 26, 1814, *ibid.*, III/44, p. 124.
[173] Mar. 3, Apr. 20, 26, 28, 1814, *ibid.*, III/45, 52, 54, 55; pp. 125f., 136, 139f.

Telling his father that he was going to need *much* money, he explained that everything was "enormously expensive and the opportunity too great—although I am able to resist it, thank God!"[174] This last remark was not to be taken too literally. Trying to comfort his father that it was better to live in Paris at a high cost than not to live there at all, he referred to the storm which was too vehement to subside in such a short time. Grown coarse in the long war, it would take a while before man can reenter moral life, he wrote, before he could rid himself of his animal and sensual nature which possessed him during the struggle; inclined to stick to blood and cruelty, he despised all forms of moral existence and would need time to adjust to the quiet and social life of a human community which seemed so boring to a hardened warrior.[175]

Széchenyi's sharp self-analysis and careful observation of the psychology of the "mass-man" after a major war made him conscious of the difficulties in restoring peace to a war-torn continent. In spite of his expectations he personally had to leave Paris within a fortnight for Italy. He was to accompany his friend, Prince Alfred Windischgrätz, sent to Italy to give diplomatic support for the restoration of the King of Sardinia.[176] Széchenyi's three letters from May and June 1814 were already dated in Turin whence, due to a change in their original itinerary, he could return to Vienna and to his loved ones.

Five years after he had left his parents' house at the age of 18, his friends still considered Stephen Széchenyi somewhat ignorant. But his lack of culture greatly differed now from the inexperienced naïveté of 1809. Good humored and sociable on the surface, this "new" Stephen Széchenyi was disillusioned from the bottom of his heart; his former unclouded serenity was deeply shattered. Looking for an escape from his frustrations as well as a vent for his dormant drives after the military campaigns, he was ready for debauchery and all sorts of escapades in the flush of the great victory. Yet his mind, touched by scepticism, was susceptible to fresh impressions.

Vaguely aware of the change, he tried to dream himself into a self-constructed idyllic world and endeavored to convince himself that he had every reason to be satisfied. But this self-imposed conviction of happiness was undermined with doubts and questions, as shown by a letter to his father,[177] in which he rejected the childhood vision of blessed happiness expressed in his letter of farewell in 1809. The repudiation

---

[174] Apr. 16, 20, 24, 1814, *ibid.*, III/51–53, pp. 134–37.
[175] Apr. 20, 1914, *ibid.*, III/52, pp. 135f.
[176] May 4, 1814, *ibid.*, III/57, p. 141.
[177] June 1, 1814, *ibid.*, IV/4, p. 148.

of a child's "heated imagination" was but a reflection of the emotional chaos left behind by the European war; it also betrayed a breakdown in the lines of communication between the ideals of the older generation and the real experience of the younger one. In the case of Stephen Széchenyi, the natural reaction to his former conservative education never led to an open breach—he loved and respected his parents too much for that. But the signs of his intellectual and emotional confusion were discernible.[178] It was in this mood that he read Goethe's *Werther,* whose misfortune reminded him of his own,[179] and became acquainted with Byron's poetry. About the same time, he started to keep a diary.

It was in July 1814, shortly after his return from Italy to Vienna that Stephen Széchenyi entered the first item in his diary.[180] Not yet 23, he was going to write his diaries for the next 45 years. They served as a repository of his ever-active mind and became an outlet for his emotional reactions. They were also the ballustrade on the staircase leading up the steep road marked *know thyself.*

[178] In one of his very early diary entries Széchenyi clearly mentions the clash of generations, relating it also to the problem of education. Sept. 1814, Viszota, ed., *Naplók,* I, 20. Also, Note-Book III, 8, Annex VII, *ibid.,* I, 846.

[179] Dec. 12, 1814, *ibid.,* I, 58.

[180] *Ibid.,* I, 3 and n. 2.

CHAPTER III

Stefferl

It takes several things to keep a diary. First, there is the need for discipline; one has to stop daily and jot down the events of the day. This in turn requires a breathing spell of evaluative reflection. Although the diarist may tend to be an introvert, he must be passionately interested in life—in his own to be sure, but in other people's lives as well. This attitude of "no day without a line" develops a certain depth and impartiality of observation while at the same time being personal; it demands perseverance and spiritual alertness.

Writing diaries is the genre of thinkers and ages of reasoning. It is almost unknown in Hungarian historiography. From this point of view, too, Stephen Széchenyi is an exception. There were a few Hungarians like Francis Kazinczy, literary "dictator" of the early 19th century, who kept a diary during certain periods of their lives; Francis Széchenyi was one of the few. But Stephen Széchenyi is the only Hungarian whose life story could be followed, with minor interruptions, on the basis of his diaries.[1]

In addition to his father's example and advice, Széchenyi could have gotten the idea of keeping a diary from many persons in his entourage: statesmen like Metternich and Friedrich Gentz, his superior in the army Prince Schwarzenberg, friends like the Viennese socialite Countess Lulu Thürheim; all followed the fashion of writing a diary.

[1] For an analysis and history of Széchenyi's diaries see the introductions by Viszota in *Naplók*, I, pp. vii-xxx; and by Károlyi in the first two volumes of *Döblingi hagyaték*. Also David Angyal, "Gróf Széchenyi István naplói" (Count Stephen Széchenyi's Diaries) in his *Történeti tanulmányok* (Historical Studies) (Budapest: Magyar Tudományos Akadémia, 1937), pp. 3–51 and *ibid.*, "Gróf Széchenyi István ifjukori naplói" (Count Stephen Széchenyi's Early Diaries), *Századok*, LIX (1925), 337–65; Gábor Halász, "A naplóiró Széchenyi," *ibid.*, LXXV (1941), 278–85, republished as "Széchenyi's Diary," *Hungarian Quarterly*, VII (Winter 1941–42), 435–43; Géza Tasner, *Széchenyi szellemi hagyatéka és Tasner Antal végrendelete* (Széchenyi's Spiritual Legacy and the Last Will of Anton Tasner) (Budapest: 1876).

At the outset, there was hardly any system to his diary entries. Interesting events, amusing stories, obscene jokes, citations, and observations concerning his family and contemporaries all appeared randomly in his "booklets," the writing of which was known to his friends and to his family. Although he sometimes showed or read parts of his notes to those close to him, he never thought of publishing his diaries. He authorized his secretary, Anton Tasner, to use his writings and papers after his death as he pleased but ordered him to destroy all his diaries. Only because of the devoted secretary's insistence did Széchenyi change his mind. In his Supplementary Testament of December 15, 1841 he completely entrusted his diaries, along with all his other writings, to Tasner.[2]

According to Széchenyi's instructions, Tasner deleted from Széchenyi's text words, names, sometimes even lines, which in his judgment could have compromised the reputation of the family or close friends. Occasionally, the deletions can be reconstructed; they seldom confuse the original meaning. Besides these deletions, there are some interruptions in the continuity of those 42 handwritten volumes of diaries preserved by Anton Tasner and sold by his son to the Hungarian Academy of Sciences in 1877. There are no entries from April to June 1815, and for the month of August 1815; i.e., from the period of the campaign against Murat in Italy, and from Széchenyi's "participation" in the events of the Congress of Vienna. There are only a few entries from the period of January 1816 to June 1818, and there is an interruption from August 11, 1818 to April 4, 1819, too. But the latter gap is easily interpolated by a travel diary, written at the same time during his Oriental trip. After August 1819 Széchenyi's notes are again incomplete for several months. But from June 1820 to September 4, 1848, until the date of his transfer to the asylum of Döbling, the diaries are a continuous reflection of his emotions, his physical and mental tribulations. Although he began working again in 1857, the date of the first diary entry in this phase of his life was October 2, 1859. From then on, he resumed the writing of his diary until his last days, stopping only a week before he committed suicide.[3]

Despite these gaps, the diaries contribute much to our understanding of contemporary Hungarian history and give some interesting sidelights

---

[2] B. Szabó, ed., *Adatok*, I, 393; G. Tasner, *Széchenyi szellemi hagyatéka*, pp. 11, 26, 31f.

[3] The diaries written after September 4, 1848 were completely unknown before World War I. Confiscated by the police during a house search on March 3, 1860, they were rediscovered and published by Árpád Károlyi in *Döblingi hagyaték*. After Széchenyi's death in 1860, Tasner, himself ailing, went to work on the diaries in his possession with the help of a servant (!) to "complete" the task of deleting all passages he considered "compromising." G. Tasner, *Széchenyi szellemi hagyatéka*, pp. 82f.

on European events as well. They are invaluable, primary source material on Széchenyi.

Though characteristic and interesting from the very beginning, the diaries became more personal around 1818, when jokes and anecdotes were almost completely replaced by references to his readings, and by intimate problems. Yet the diaries are too unorganized and fragmentary to be an autobiography. Often, particularly in the early years, Széchenyi copied many pages from his favorite readings into the diaries; on other occasions, however, and sometimes on very important ones such as when the Academy was founded, his notes are very laconic if not completely silent. Before he entered public life in 1825 his diaries were, generally speaking, more detailed and contained many rather lengthy deliberations related to religion, the problems of human life, and, primarily, to love. The diaries also preserved copies of some letters, the originals of which would have been otherwise unknown to us. After 1830 Széchenyi became more intimately involved in politics and other related public activities, and had less free time; but he kept up his diaries which by then had become a necessity of life. Since he often wrote merely brief, concise references, intelligible only to one conversant with contemporary social and political conditions, the reading of the diaries must be supplemented by and checked against the context of other data.

The diaries are the most direct means of understanding Széchenyi's personality. They are subjective and candid, revealing his secret and unsocial thoughts; hence, in addition, they are often illogical and unfair, sometimes cruelly so even concerning their author. Therefore the diaries might be interpreted as analogous to subconscious material elicited by psychiatrists during the process of free association. One always has to keep in mind, however, that Széchenyi's *whole* personality is infinitely more than the congealed lava of his frustrated, desperate, or enthusiastic eruptions as retained in the diaries.

Széchenyi's subsequent works reflect the style of the diaries. The frequent digressions and the apparent lack of a logical structure, the emotional vigor and a certain impatient tone, the spontaneous abundance of ideas and the absence of any artificially arranged system—all were present in Széchenyi's later writings and speeches. They bore the imprint of his diaries: they showed the diarist's spontaneity and revealed flashes of genius, but they also revealed his somewhat self-centered frame of mind and betrayed his inclination to indulge in lengthy and perplexing tirades which at times obscured his thoughts about men and society.

Széchenyi himself used his diaries as a measure of self-control and of moral and intellectual growth. In 1857 he advised his older son, Béla, to keep a diary because it would help him make good use of his time and money.[4] He also warned Béla to observe exactly the place and time of events *"in order to be able to be fair to and tolerant of others,"* since one looks at things with a different eye at the age of 17, 27, or 47.[5]

This was the voice of old Széchenyi's wisdom, but there was a restless inquisitiveness and spiritual hunger present in the rather varied notes of Stephen Széchenyi's first scribbling block written in the summer of 1814, part of which he copied into his first regular diary during the autumn of the same year.[6] The little volume in gilt-edged leather-binding had the following inscription in gold: *"Das Gute und Schlechte, welches ich erfahren I."* It started with a citation from Mme de Staël's *De l'Allemagne: "Nulle réflexion, nulle complaisance ne peut faire qu'on s'y amuse de ce qui n'amuse pas. . . ."*[7]

Dozens of other quotations from *De l'Allemagne* were to follow on the first pages of the diary: many of them centered around the problem of the "national spirit" and "natural character" of a country.[8] Széchenyi did not have to bring the book directly from Paris. The French authoress was extremely fashionable in Vienna, and Széchenyi himself met her in person in 1810.[9] Although in December 1821 he called the "woman-writer" "exceptionally superficial," he continued reading her books immediately after they had been published: in February 1823 he read *De l'Amour;* in May 1824 he reread all four parts of *De l'Allemagne,* copying new citations into his diary; and in August 1825 he finished reading the *Lettres sur l'Angleterre.*[10] Between 1814 and 1820 Mme de Staël was an important cultural screen for Széchenyi; in 1820 he read *De la littérature considérée dans ses rapports avec les institutions sociales*[11]

---

[4] "Gróf Széchenyi István intelmei fiához, Bélához" (Count Stephen Széchenyi's Admonitions to His Son, Béla), Károlyi and Tolnai, eds., *Döblingi hagyaték,* I, 538ff.

[5] *Ibid.,* I, 541 (italics in original).

[6] Annex No. I, 8, in Viszota, ed., *Naplók,* I, 747–77; and *ibid.,* I, 3 and n. 2, 747 and n. I.

[7] *Ibid.,* I, 3 and n. I.

[8] *Ibid.,* I, 7f.

[9] He had the edition of 1814. All volumes are marked in Széchenyi's own hand: *"Gelesen."* B. Szabó, ed., *Széchenyi könyvtára,* p. 85, No. 1,030. For Mme de Staël's visit in Vienna (1808) and her influence on contemporary Viennese social life, see Gräfin Ludovika Thürheim, *Mein Leben. Erinnerungen aus Österreichs grosser Welt.* Trl. into Ger. and ed. René van Rhym (pseud.), 4 vols. I (Munich: Müller, 1913), 230–40. See also Mihály Bariska, *Gróf Széchenyi István és a francia irodalom* (Count Stephen Széchenyi and French Literature), No. 4 of the *Bibliothèque de l'Institut Français à l'Université de Budapest* (Budapest: 1928), pp. 55–61. For background cf. the important chapter, "Madame de Staël and Cultural Nationalism," in Hans Kohn, *Prelude to Nation-States* (Princeton, N.J.: Van Nostrand, 1967), pp. 125–32.

[10] Dec. 2, 1821, Feb. 10, 1823, May 22, 1824, Aug. 20, 1825, Viszota, ed., *Naplók,* II, 228, 333, 491–94, 593.

[11] Aug. 1820, *ibid.,* II, 35.

and although at that time he could already be considered a rather widely read person, he still jotted down a number of quotations from the book, remarking: "very interested."[12]

Indeed, Mme de Staël transmitted to Széchenyi a great many cultural concepts, important names, and ideas. Thus the idea of comparing the development of a nation to the life of an individual, so extremely important in Széchenyi's thinking, was taken over by him from Mme de Staël; similarly, he was influenced by her suggestion concerning the possibility of perfecting the human spirit.[13] True, along with Mme de Staël, Széchenyi began to read German romantics (primarily the patriotic works of De la Motte Fouquet and Oehlenschläger), and probed into the last part (*Klugheitslehre*) of Wenzel Immanuel Gottfried's four-volume philosophical work.[14] In a relatively short time these and other lesser lights were replaced in his reading list by the works of Goethe, Tasso, Byron, Alfieri, Shakespeare, Burke, Voltaire, Herder, Rousseau, Franklin, Montaigne, and subsequently Bentham and Adam Smith, giving him new insight into the question of improving man and regenerating a nation.[15] In spite of important critical reservations, certain qualities of these authors—such as Montaigne's scepticism, Voltaire's sarcastic wit or Rousseau's egalitarianism to name but a few—were to exert lasting effect on Széchenyi's attitude toward social institutions, as well as on the way to express his ideas about them.

Despite the fairly rapid expansion of Széchenyi's intellectual horizon and his peculiarly individual way of discovering the unknown land of European civilization, the stimulating effect of Mme de Staël in the initial stage of his cultural "unfolding" between 1814 and 1820 is undeniable. Even when he disagreed with her, as in the case of the suggestion that a nation's "character" shows only when it is free, Széchenyi's reaction was characteristic for both Hungarian conditions and for the trend of development in his own thinking: "It seems to me that peoples reveal their [true] character mostly when they are about to lose their freedom or have already lost it and seek to regain it!"[16]

The endeavor to interpret a nation's history in terms of the development of its national character was to remain an important part of Széche-

[12] Dec. 12, 1820; also Dec. 23, 25, 27, 1820, *ibid.*, II, 95, 101–106.

[13] E.g., May 20–25, 1819, *ibid.*, I, 629. Cf. Dávid Angyal, "Les idées historiques du comte Etienne Széchenyi," *Revue de Hongrie*, III (1909), 407.

[14] July and Aug. 1814, Viszota, ed., *Naplók*, I, 4ff., 10ff., 17ff. The title of Gottfried's work is *Vollständiger Lehrbegriff der gesammten Philosophie, dem Bedürfnisse der Zeit gemäss eingerichtet*, I–IV (Linz: 1803–1805).

[15] Angyal, "Les idées," pp. 411–17, 531–37; Padányi, *Széchenyi kulturája*, 77–145. A complete list of Széchenyi's readings in this period is given in Viszota, ed., *Naplók*, I, 915f.

[16] Dec. 25, 1820, *ibid.*, II, 103.

nyi's philosophy of history, and so was his inclination to relate a country's evolution to the emergence of leaders such as Washington, Franklin, Bolivar, Iturbide in America.[17] Yet it was not in the field of culture or philosophy of history, that young Széchenyi's interest primarily lay in the period of 1815—19. The discrepancy between the increasingly bigoted atmosphere of the parental house and the harsh reality of the Napoleonic wars was a shock to him. A natural reaction followed—and not only on the spiritual level.[18] If there was any single factor dominating his life in the years we are concerned with, it certainly has to be assigned to Eros.

Family tradition had it that when Stephen Széchenyi, or "Stefferl," as he was nicknamed by the Viennese *jeunesse dorée* and intimate friends, visited his sister Countess Frances Batthyány, she ordered her pretty maids to hide while the "savage soul" was staying in the castle. The pious lady then crossed herself after Stephen's departure, blessing God for having relieved her house of the evil; allegedly, she once wrote to a close friend: "If some day Stefferl departs this life and, as I hope, knocks at the gates of heaven, St. Peter will probably keep him waiting for a while sending word in a hurry to St. Ursula to keep her eleven thousand virgins out of the way because Stephen Széchenyi is coming!"[19] In the summer and autumn of 1814 the veteran of the French wars had a true opportunity to pursue pleasure. At the end of August he became completely independent financially, for old Francis Széchenyi partitioned the family estates among his three sons. Cenk (Zinkendorf), the favorite residence of the family, went to Stephen.[20] Trusting the management of his estates to his former tutor, Stephen Széchenyi abandoned himself to the frivolous whirl of the Congress of Vienna. He wrote to Liebenberg when he wanted to make a present of shepherd dogs to Lady Castlereagh or needed Hungarian wines for some friends.[21]

At the beginning of the Congress Stefferl was attached to the suite of the king of Bavaria. The good-looking captain of the Merweldt uhlans escorted the most beautiful women of Vienna. Some of them belonged to the immediate family circle, as did his sister Sophie, Countess Ferdinand Zichy, called by Alexander I *la beauté triviale,* and his sister-in-law

---

[17] May 1824, *ibid.*, II, 493f.

[18] This had been noticed by Kemény. Cf. Angyal, "Széchenyi naplói," pp. 4f.

[19] Falk, *Széchenyi és kora,* p. 16. "Stefferl" is the German diminutive of "Stephen."

[20] For a specification of the assets of the Széchenyi fortune and of the distribution of the estates among the children of Francis Széchenyi, see Fraknói, *Széchenyi Ferencz,* pp. 319–29.

[21] Nov. 1814, Viszota, ed., *Naplók,* I, 41; letters of Sept. 3, Oct. 12, 23, Nov. 3, 1814, Majláth, ed., *Levelek,* I, 1–6.

Caroline, Countess Paul Széchenyi, whom the Tsar dubbed *la beauté coquette;* others, like Julie Festetich Countess Charles Zichy, *la beauté céleste,* and Gabriella Hunyadi Countess Zeno Saurau, *la beauté du diable,* were also relatives or close friends.[22]

Stefferl, brimming with life, widely travelled and "different," was in demand, too. Even his extremely pretty sister-in-law took a liking to him. Described graphically by an expert, Countess Thürheim, the woman who was to become immortal through Széchenyi's feverish, guilt-ridden dreams comes to life again:

> Caroline . . . was one of the most charming and reckless creatures I ever knew. Raven locks surrounded her brown, velvet face; her Caucasian eyes, straight and fine nose, lovely mouth and pearly teeth, that flashed like lightning through the clouds of her easily aroused temper, gave an incomparable charm to this sweet creature. Her character resembled her appearance; for it was rather piquant than pleasant. She was a spoiled child who would brook no contradiction and wished to rule over friend and foe alike. She often hurt others by her impetuosity, but her heart was irreproachable, full of high and noble sentiments.[23]

Had Stephen been firmly determined to ignore Caroline, it would have been hard to resist the charming temptation. But he was, in the words of a Prussian officer, good-natured and mischievous, "a young lion who can be guided by a silk thread."[24] Besides, it flattered his ego to make a new conquest, especially because, "ignorant and ambitious" as he was, to use his own words, he enjoyed himself in the role of a *séducteur*[25] and liked to boast of it. Intoxicated, he once made a remark in society about his other sister-in-law, the wife of his eldest brother Louis, saying that if he wanted it, this woman could be his, too. On another occasion, he bragged of his success with Caroline to Prince Schwarzenberg.[26] The family was shocked and his mother implored him in tears to think of life eternal.[27] To avoid a scandal, Stefferl decided to go to Naples at

---

[22] For the names assigned by Alexander to the beauties of Vienna, see Thürheim, *Mein Leben,* II, 94; also Viszota, ed., *Naplók,* I, 24 and n. 2 and Annex No. 1, 8, p. 758.

[23] Thürheim, *Mein Leben,* II, 270. With two minor corrections, I have used the translation of the quoted fragment in Joseph Östör, "Széchenyi and Women," *Hungarian Quarterly,* VII (Winter 1941–42), 496.

[24] Nov. 1814, Viszota, ed., *Naplók,* I, 50.

[25] Apr. 9, 1819, *ibid.,* I, 586.

[26] Károlyi and Tolnai, eds., *Döblingi hagyaték,* I, 143; Jan. 28, 1823, Viszota, ed., *Naplók,* II, 327; July 29, 1830, *ibid.,* IV, 89f.

[27] Nov. 21, 1814, *ibid.,* I, 45. Cf. his letter to Prince Edward Lichnowsky, Dec. 1 (correct date: end of November), 1814, *ibid.,* I, 52f. and the pertinent notes.

the end of November, but before leaving Vienna, he was asked by Metternich to send him reports about Murat's activities.[28]

Historians disagree on whether or not Széchenyi actually fell in love with his sister-in-law. According to Károlyi, who first read Caroline's letters, carefully put away by Széchenyi but confiscated by the police during the house search of 1860 in Döbling, the whole affair was a platonic one, particularly on Széchenyi's part.[29] Viszota went one step further, admitting that Széchenyi "was at fault, too" because of his unguarded remarks and because of his flirtation, which was far from unusual in the lax atmosphere of the "dancing" Congress.[30]

It is very probable that Caroline loved Stephen Széchenyi. The tender, occasionally beseeching tone of her letters is more than revealing.[31] Stephen Széchenyi did not remain unaffected by this passion either. Apparently his relationship to his beloved brother Paul did not suffer during the crisis and he was able to comfort himself that nothing irreparable had happened. Still his diary entries betray a guilty conscience: "I was in *love* and my love was a crime."[32] As the years went on, his sense of guilt turned into self-flagellation.[33] This is perhaps why Byron and the reading of Alfieri's tragedies struck such a profoundly personal chord in Széchenyi's heart.[34] Hinting at his father's marriage to his former sister-in-law and at his own liaison with Caroline, he could not get the sin of Oedipus off his mind. Referring to "thoughtless and rash actions producing irretrievable roots," he began to suspect the existence of families trying to fight in vain, generation after generation, against the same sin as though they were driven by evil forces. This led him to believe that the sin of Oedipus was more than a fable, since it seems to have emerged repeatedly in some families including his own. Recalling again the similarities between his father and himself, he became "strongly convinced that fatal love can survive from generation to generation in certain families."[35]

In the relationship with Caroline are the beginnings of Széchenyi's terrible guilt complex, as well as his almost superstitious and un-Catho-

[28] *Ibid.*, I, p. xxxviii; also, Dec. 1814; Jan. 28, Feb. 7, 1815, *ibid.*, I, 54, 94ff., 98.
[29] Károlyi and Tolnai, eds., *Döblingi hagyaték*, I, 141ff.; also B. Szabó, ed., *Széchényi család*, III, 97–100.
[30] Viszota gives many references to the whole Caroline problem in *Naplók*, I, pp. cxi–cxxvi.
[31] A dozen of Caroline's letters to Stephen Széchenyi were published in B. Szabó, ed., *Adatok*, I, 2–7.
[32] Apr. 1, 1815, Viszota, ed., *Naplók*, I, 110 (italics in original). Cf. Aug. 9, Dec. 11, 1814, *ibid.*, I, 17, 54f.
[33] E.g., July 21, 1818, May 1819, *ibid.*, I, 196, 636f.
[34] *Ibid.*, I, pp. xciii f.; Zichy, *Széchenyi életrajza*, I, 137f.
[35] May and Aug. 2, 1819, Viszota, ed., *Naplók*, I, 614f., 676f. Cf. Sept. 7, 1820 and Feb. 9, 1823, *ibid.*, II, 62, 331.

lic belief in the power of destiny, which often even embarrassed intimate friends.[36] At the height of the crisis, in the fall of 1814, his suicidal thoughts reappeared, too.[37]

Caroline died of consumption in August 1820. Széchenyi continued to mourn her memory and blamed himself for her untimely death. Year after year he was particularly remorseful around the anniversary of her passing. In April 1830, e.g., he reread Caroline's letters, previously sealed and destined to be burned only after his death. Accusing himself of having assassinated in cold blood "this pure, childlike and ingenuous being who died of a broken heart," he recalled how he had "murdered" Caroline and how he was being destroyed by his apparently unrequited love for another woman, Crescence, his future wife. At the time, he saw in all this imaginary parallel the just vengence of fate. He concluded: "My life is becoming more and more disgusting every day. As I go on developing virtue in myself more and more, I am compelled to feel increasingly what a monster I once used to be."[38]

Thus wrote Stephen Széchenyi who had just proposed to regenerate a nation in *Hitel*. His language did not differ a bit from the self-scourging tone of September 1848, or from his bitter "Confession" written in the Döbling asylum. On both occasions the nightmares about Caroline were to reemerge in the form of unmitigated remorse further reinforced by the vision of Hungary's presumed annihilation and the self-inflicted responsibility he felt for it.[39]

We know from Countess Thürheim,[40] a close friend of the families of both Stephen and Caroline that Caroline was sensitive, flighty, and spoiled—not as innocent as Széchenyi depicted her in subsequent years. Although there is no way of proving or disproving certain aspects of a personal relationship in regard to which more or less strict silence had been kept by those involved, from the historian's point of view the essential issue is clear enough: Stephen Széchenyi never completely recovered from the emotional shock suffered in the years 1815–20.

---

[36] Kovács, *Széchenyi közéletének három utolsó éve*, I, 51f.

[37] Oct. and Nov. 1814, Viszota, ed., *Naplók*, I, 26, 31.

[38] Apr. 3, 1830, *ibid.*, IV, 32f. Cf. Sept. 8, 1820, *ibid.*, II, 63.

[39] Sept. 3, 1848, Károlyi and Tolnai, eds., *Döblingi hagyaték*, I, 389. From the penultimate entry before Széchenyi's transfer to the Döbling asylum. See also the beginning of Széchenyi's "Great Confession," written in Döbling, Mar. 21, 1849, *ibid.*, I, 427.

[40] Thürheim, *Mein Leben*, II, 270–73. There is no question in the present writer's mind as to the basic truth of Lulu Thürheim's account of the Caroline-Széchenyi affair. Some of Széchenyi's diary entries (Aug. 1819, Viszota, ed., *Naplók*, I, 675f., 688), as well as a published exchange of letters between him and Countess Thürheim (B. Szabó, ed., *Adatok*, I, 21–36 and 47ff.), suggest that they were rather intimate friends around 1819–20 and that she knew what she was talking about in her memoirs.

It has been contended by some[41] that Széchenyi would not have been so affected by his unsuccessful love affairs had he not already been neurotic. It is difficult, however, to distinguish cause and effect in Széchenyi's case in spite of the relative abundance of source material. Széchenyi's emotional disturbances and suicidal plans can be traced back to his early youth and even his childhood. But it is important to remember that he lived and created with his emotional problems and neuroses for many decades and apparently suffered a nervous breakdown in 1848 only under very special circumstances; besides his physical sicknesses, the more important of which are all known to us, the crises of his emotional, intellectual, and public life did not by any means always coincide, but overlapped, affected by varying circumstances.

Széchenyi's outward appearance and behavior, at least in his youth, did not reveal the volcanic "aberrations" of his inner self. In this respect his diaries can completely mislead the modern reader. In Naples he continued to be the light-hearted charmer so well known in Viennese society. Some of the tricks were remembered years after he had played them;[42] Italian princesses, and visiting English ladies from the suite of the Prince Regent's wife, became interested in him, and he, in turn, felt that he "could fall in love" with Murat's wife, Queen Hortensia for whom he maintained his sympathy even when she had to go into exile as Countess Lipona.[43]

Amorous adventures were not his only interest though. As an officer of the victorious army he was embittered to see hundreds of Austrian soldiers in rags, begging along the road to Naples: it was at this time that he first thought of resigning his commission.[44] Among the entertainments of court life he found time to learn Italian. On New Year's Day 1815 he began to read the *Gerusalemme Liberata* in the original. In mid-February he started the *Nouvelle Héloïse;* hence Tasso's Italian verses alternated with Rousseau's French prose in the diaries.[45] Besides widening his literary horizon he visited the artistic monuments of ancient Rome and the relics of early Christianity. Several times he burst out

[41] See Béla Grünwald's interpretation in his *Az uj Magyarország. Gróf Széchenyi István* (New Hungary. Count Stephen Széchenyi) (Budapest: Franklin, 1890.)

[42] July 25, 1817, Viszota, ed., *Naplók,* I, 183f.

[43] Dec. 1814, Jan. 1815, Sept. 1, 1825, *ibid.,* I, 65–74, 88ff., 96–99; II, 601. Also Nov. 3, 1815, Zichy, ed., *Széchenyi szülőihez,* IV/26, p. 179. For Széchenyi's impressions during his Italian trips cf. Marianna Takács, *Hogyan látta Gr. Széchenyi István Olaszországot* (Count Stephen Széchenyi's View of Italy), No. 19 of *Pubblicazioni dell'Istituto Italiano della R. Universiteta "Pietro Pázmány" di Budapest* (Budapest: 1940).

[44] Dec. 12, 1814, Viszota, ed., *Naplók,* I, 58f. For Széchenyi's views on the army cf. Aug. 9, 1820, *ibid.,* II, 54–61.

[45] Jan. 8 and Feb. 1815, *ibid.,* I, 75 and 104ff.

indignantly that the petty rulers and princelings of Italy did not give enough financial help to unearth the hidden treasures of its own soil. Boiling with rage, this new proselyte of ancient civilization was quite willing to put the blame on the whole Italian people.[46] The rash and immature summary judgment of an entire nation was a far cry from the appraisal of the craftmanship of Italian laborers given by Széchenyi in the 1840s. Then, however, Italian workers toiled on the suspension bridge, dreamed up by Hungary's reformer for a native land which lacked skilled labor; in 1815 it was a civilized *Austrian* officer looking down on a backward people. Still, in a somewhat peculiar way, this was a sign that the pampered "Stefferl" of Viennese society could occasionally be a moralist, too.

His primary interests, however, did not lie in the past. After having seen the catacombs he admitted frankly in a rather belittling tone that he had no particular respect for antiquity; he could get more excited about the road leading through Mont Cenis Pass than about the Church of St. Mark in Venice.[47] But the potential conflict between old and new cultures, classical and practical ideals, came to a temporary halt due to the influence of an English archeologist, Sir William Gell. An aristocrat like Széchenyi but a scholar of high reputation, Gell left a deep impression on his Hungarian friend who was so anxious to broaden his knowledge. Gell's scholarship and account of his travels in Greece stimulated Széchenyi to consider for a moment the possibility of devoting himself exclusively to scholarly activities.[48]

Yet the "Hundred Days" of Napoleon, and Murat's decision to switch back to his former master, forced Széchenyi to abandon Naples. On March 11 he joined the Austrian army and in early April he was in action against his former host's troops. After the short war in which he again distinguished himself,[49] he had to take a rest, for he had been wounded and become ill during the campaign. He spent the summer in Vienna and on the family estates. He read a great deal—Tasso, La Bruyère, novels, dramatic works, travel books, and German and French poems published in periodicals.[50]

By the time he recovered, peace was restored. On September 9, 1815 he left Vienna for England.[51] In Paris he reported at headquarters to Schwarzenberg in the hope of advancing his military career. Soon, how-

---

[46] Jan. 11, 1815, *ibid.*, I, 81ff.
[47] Jan. 8, 1815, *ibid.*, I, 77f.
[48] Jan. 11, 17, 1815, *ibid.*, I, 80f., 85.
[49] On Széchenyi's participation in the campaign against Murat, see Zichy, ed., *Széchenyi szülőihez*, IV/5–14, pp. 149–59, and *ibid.*, *Széchenyi életrajza*, I, 92–100.
[50] Viszota, ed., *Naplók*, I, 111–31.
[51] Sept. 9, 1815, *ibid.*, I, 131.

ever, he wrote to his father that Schwarzenberg and Metternich, both very busy yet gracious, advised him to be patient since Francis I had rescinded all military promotions now that peace was restored.[52]

For more than 10 years former comrades-in-arms, generals, Metternich, and the kaiser continued to counsel "patience" to Captain Széchenyi who thought a military career was to be the ultimate goal of his life, but never obtained the desired promotion to the rank of major. He himself was inclined to attribute official reluctance to promote him to discrimination against Hungarians. More likely, the coolness toward his military ambitions may have been related to a denunciation which charged that Captain Széchenyi had predicted the dissolution of Austria within a century, as a result of the uneven development of the components of its national life. These rash statements, allegedly made at a dinner in Prague after Széchenyi's recovery from illness in September 1813, were first attributed apparently to the influence Francis Széchenyi presumably had on the views of his inexperienced son; consequently, they were not taken seriously. But they were remembered and committed to paper in December 1814 when, at the Congress of Vienna, Stephen Széchenyi again may have shown signs of his dissatisfaction with Austrian conditions. Thus his presumed opinions were commented on by some of his Prussian friends who, according to the informer of the secret police, were eager to forward them to their monarch.[53]

Disappointed by spending his days vainly in the antichambers of important persons, Széchenyi tried to resign himself to a "secondary role" in life instead of groveling before low-ranking bureaucrats.[54] This disillusioned admission of his frustration was in itself an indication of hope for a more distinguished career.

In any event, Széchenyi asked for a furlough and joined a delegation led by a friend of his to the Prince Regent who was the "owner" of the Austrian regiment to which he had recently been transferred. Széchenyi, however, did not plan his trip to England as a pleasure voyage. In a letter to his father, he expressed the intention to use his trip for studying all aspects of English life, in order to be able to serve his fatherland and satisfy his conscience.[55]

There was nothing new about a Hungarian aristocrat's visit to England. "Anglomania" in Hungary, or the tradition of setting up English customs and manners as examples, can be traced back to the last decades of the 18th century when family ties and relations of friendship between

[52] Sept. 21, 25, 1815, Zichy, ed., *Széchenyi szüloihez*, IV/16–17, pp. 160f.
[53] B. Szabó, "Széchenyi katonai pályája," 43f.; August Fournier, *Die Geheimpolizei auf dem Wiener Kongress* (Vienna-Leipzig: 1913), pp. 310f.
[54] Sept. 21, 1815, Viszota, ed., *Naplók*, I, 132.
[55] Sept. 21, 25, 1815, Zichy, ed., *Széchenyi szüloihez*, IV/16–17, pp. 160f.

English and Hungarian aristocrats became frequent.[56] Indeed, Széchenyi's father was one of those who displayed a keen interest in British institutions. Naturally, during the 25 years following the French Revolution, direct Anglo-Hungarian contacts considerably slackened. Yet exactly during this quarter of a century, English society underwent a tremendous change and Hungarian social and economic conditions, too, became ripe enough to raise the question of Western-type reforms.[57] Under the influence of Stephen Széchenyi the third and fourth decades of the nineteenth century became the high point of Hungarian interest in England, for he "represented England in his books, articles and speeches as the country of freedom, enterprise, public spirit, wealth and general striving for moral improvement."[58]

The two and a half months of his first sojourn in England were a great experience for Széchenyi.[59] He had read several travelogues while still in France, yet the insular country was a surprise which "made life again attractive for him."[60] The day after his arrival the delegation was received by the Prince Regent who, in Széchenyi's opinion, was a fool. But he also realized that in England it was not of the utmost importance to have a wise king on the throne since the constitution limited royal power to doing only good whereas, according to Széchenyi, wrongdoing was entirely beyond its purview.[61]

During the first two weeks, he tried to get acquainted with London and its surroundings, diligently learning English. He felt as though he were in a great marketplace shopping for a lifetime.[62] Intending to become useful to his own country, "since in time we shall have manifold relations with this land," he worked hard, endeavoring to combine his

---

[56] Stephen Gál, *Hungary and the Anglo-Saxon World* (Budapest: 1944), pp. 13f.; *id.*, "A fiatal Széchenyi Angliában" (Young Széchenyi in England), in *Magyarország, Anglia és Amerika* (Hungary, England and America) (Budapest: n.d.), pp. 65–72.

[57] For this period in Hungarian history see Ferenc Eckhart, *A bécsi udvar gazdaságpolitikája Magyarországon 1780–1815* (The Economic Policy of the Court of Vienna in Hungary, 1780–1815), (Budapest: Akadémiai kiadó, 1958); the introductory volume by Sándor Domanovszky, ed., *József nádor élete és iratai* (Life and Papers of Palatine Joseph), 4 vols., Vol. 1 in 2 pts. (Budapest: Magyar Történelmi Társulat, 1925–44), in *Fontes*, and Gyula Mérei, *Mezőgazdaság és agrártársadalom Magyarországon 1790–1848* (Agriculture and Agricultural Society in Hungary 1790–1848) (Budapest: Teleki Pál Tud., Int., 1948).

[58] László Országh, "Magyar utazók Angliában 1842-ben" (Hungarian Travellers in England in 1842), *Angol filológiai tanulmányok*, III, 131.

[59] Oct. 1, 1815, to Dec. 14, 1815.

[60] Oct. 2, 1815, Zichy, ed., *Széchenyi szülőihez*, IV/18, p. 162.

[61] Oct. and Nov. 1815, Viszota, ed., *Naplók*, I, 139, 161. Several times during this visit to England Széchenyi was invited to dinner parties of the Prince Regent, where even his soldier's ears were somewhat shocked by the language of his host. Cf. Oct. 26, 1815, *ibid.*, I, 143.

[62] Oct. 6, 12, 1815, Zichy, ed., *Széchenyi szülőihez*, IV/19–20, pp. 164f.

self-education with goals far beyond the individual sphere. In a way, this was a return to the old ideals instilled in his parents' home, but on a higher, more conscious, level.[63] Yet trying to go beyond the purpose of erudition-for-its-own-sake for the first time in his life, Széchenyi felt a desire to see Hungarian reality, also. The contours of a vision of his backward country were vaguely perceptible in the London fog: after his visit to England, Scotland (and perhaps Ireland), he planned to go back to Vienna, Cenk, and then he wanted to spend the summer in Somogy county in order to get acquainted with "our constitution and laws." By that time his English would be good: "the smallest perfection gives satisfaction because it brings us closer to the *possibility of serving the land* which begot us and of serving the people we love."[64]

His progress in English seemed slow by the end of his third week in England, but he found it worthwhile to sit at home all day long and study Shakespeare, this "English temple of poetry."[65] At first he found the horse races at Newmarket considerably less interesting,[66] but quickly changed his mind when he became familiar with the technique and purposes of horse-breeding in England.

Through his friend Prince Paul Esterházy, recently appointed Ambassador of Austria to England, Széchenyi was received in the diplomatic circles of London, as well as the homes of the English aristocracy. His diary entries of the time reveal a strange mixture of the atmosphere prevalent in Holland House and in the salons of Lady Melbourne and Caroline Lamb, on the one hand, and of his innermost feelings on the other. The encounter with Caroline Lamb resulted in painful reminiscences of another Caroline and in her thumbnail sketch of the impressions Széchenyi made on the sharp-tongued English poetess, who was not so silly as Széchenyi believed she was when it came to taking the measure of a young man's talents: "You don't have principles: [you have] much buoyancy, a very good heart, plenty of wit; you have read fairly much in your life but you don't have much experience. You have a talent for amusing others and for giving a pleasant twist to whatever you say. You are unable to attach yourself; love is constant in you but you very frequently change its object."[67]

[63] Oct. 12, 15, 1815, *ibid.*, IV/20–21, pp. 165–69.

[64] Oct. 15, 1815, *ibid.*, IV/21, pp. 169f. Somogy is a county in the southwestern part of Hungary. There were Széchenyi estates in Somogy. (Italics in original.)

[65] Oct. 15, 21, 1815, *ibid.*, IV/21–22, pp. 167, 171. Also Nov. 3, 1815, *ibid.*, IV/26, p. 179. Cf. Alexander Baumgarten, "Széchenyi and English Literature," *Hungarian Quarterly*, VII (Winter 1941–42), 484–92.

[66] "Horse racing, as one can imagine, is a folly." Oct. 19, 1815, Viszota, ed., *Naplók*, I, 141; Nov. 3, 1815, Zichy, ed., *Széchenyi szülőihez*, IV/26, p. 172.

[67] Nov. 4, 1815, Viszota, ed., *Naplók*, I, 145f.

Whatever the merit of Caroline Lamb's observation preserved by Széchenyi, social life in England undoubtedly refined his taste and manners. More important, his independent-mindedness was stimulated, too. At a dinner party given by Lady Holland in late 1815 he noticed to his surprise a large portrait of Napoleon on the mantelpiece. "Isn't it fortunate to be allowed to show one's sympathies in such a vigorous way," he wrote to his father.[68] During a later visit to England in April 1822, when he himself was more conscious of his own rebellion against the spirit of the Holy Alliance, he noted the attention paid to him by Lord and Lady Holland, explaining: "Carbonaris find and love each other everywhere."[69]

But certain peculiarities of English social life were not to Széchenyi's taste. While himself a good eater and drinker, he was not fond of boisterous festivities; he liked company but did not care for big dinner parties because he abhorred "the abominable drinking-bout that could not be avoided" on such occasions.[70] Yet his imagination was caught by those aspects of English life which showed that "apparently, man has made greater progress here" than elsewhere.[71] His critical eyes discovered that "*proud* and even more selfish Albion"[72] seemed to have come up with a new answer to some age-old problems. Admiring the beauty of the land and the variety of buildings, fields, and scenery, so different from everything he had seen before, he had to admit that he found himself in increasing agreement "with the way of life, with the mores and customs of such a free state." He thought there were fewer unhappy people and there was a greater opportunity for common folk to mingle with the nobility in that part of the world where "even the last of the servants had the same rights and identical claims to the pursuit of happiness as the greatest and richest of men." "This equality," he continued "is a great luck. Hitherto I thought of it only as being *possible;* but now I can see that it is *real.*" But he recognized that numerous circumstances made it undesirable to simply imitate the English: "No other nation can shape itself after this model; I believe it is just the opposite diversity which is the real point one ought to find."[73]

Széchenyi's future greatness was indicated not so much by intuitive understanding of England's "secret," but by early awareness of the prob-

---

[68] Nov. 3, 1815, Zichy, ed., *Széchenyi szülőihez*, IV/26, p. 179.
[69] Apr. 27, 1922, Viszota, ed., *Naplók*, II, 288.
[70] Oct. 15, 1815, Zichy, ed., *Széchenyi szülőihez*, IV/21, p. 166.
[71] Oct. 21, 1815, *ibid.*, IV/22, pp. 170f.; cf. Nov. 3, 1815, *ibid.*, IV/26, p. 178.
[72] Nov. 3, 1815, *ibid.*, IV/25, p. 176 (italics Széchenyi's).
[73] Nov. 1, 1815, *ibid.*, IV/24, pp. 173f.

lematical aspects of its adaptability under different conditions. To find an answer to *this* became one of the great problems of his life.

In addition to domestic institutions, England's secret, or as Széchenyi called it, its "pointe," consisted of the machines. Besides politicians, diplomats, and friends in the fashionable world he also sought the company of manufacturers, mechanical and chemical engineers.[74] These connections and those to be made on subsequent trips to England would be of invaluable help to him in later decades when he was to put various economic enterprises into effect in Hungary.

From his notes and letters one can feel the pulse of the industrial revolution and its indelible effect on Széchenyi. He visited workshops and factories, was fascinated by steam engines, gas pipelines, sawmills, sausage-cutting gadgets, and by the "extraordinary" sight of 40 workers producing 500 pairs of shoes a day in Chelsea. Some of his friends laughed at him and he readily admitted that it was rather peculiar for a captain of hussars to listen at least three hours a day to the theoretical and practical explanations of engineers and even common laborers and to smell of oil in the morning and of perfume in the evening.[75] Sensing that a new world was in the making, he answered those who laughed at him by saying he found comfort in knowing how far one could go by applying oneself diligently and how one could achieve considerable perfection in any field even if one were not endowed with unusual talents. In his opinion, the British were not highly gifted but excelled in practical common sense; as he put it, "The Germans write much, the French talk much, and the English do much."[76] Thus he did not overestimate English ability but trusted the power of human endurance and invention, recognizing in them a way of improving the lot of mankind.

Perfection was the dream and deity of his soul; from it, quiet bliss emanated. The journeys he undertook appeared to him as long field trips.[77] At the end of his first English journey he asked himself whether he was any better or smarter than on the day he left Vienna. No doubt he knew more than before but had he grown wiser? was he nearer to the happiness of serenity or was he still running after an unattainable ideal?[78]

The first effort to draw an ethical balance for a period of Széchenyi's

---

[74] Nov. 3, 1815, *ibid.*, IV/26, p. 178; Nov. 4 and days immediately following, 1815, Viszota, ed., *Naplók*, I, 145, 148, 152.

[75] Nov. 1815 and Dec. 13, 1815, *ibid.*, I, 152, 166.

[76] Nov. 1815, *ibid.*, I, 158; Nov. 3, 1815, Zichy, ed., *Széchenyi szülőihez*, IV/26, pp. 178f.

[77] Oct. 21, 1815, *ibid.*, IV/22, p. 171.

[78] Dec. 13, 1815, Viszota, ed., *Naplók*, I, 165.

life was rather uncertain. But the seeds of critical self-examination were there; in a few years an impulse received from the reading of Benjamin Franklin was going to turn these seeds and Széchenyi's inclination for soul-searching and self-knowledge into a daily practice.

For the time being, however, the answers to the questions raised by himself seemed to be somewhat hazy. They were also mixed with a self-imposed romantic pose of "heroic" resignation to mediocrity. Yet at the end of Széchenyi's train of thought, the tone changed and all of a sudden an inner voice began to speak about "his poor, unhappy fatherland" which he must assist. Abandoning "the great world with all its splendor," he decided to turn "to the plough after the sword" and to invite Apollo now that he became fed up with Mars. He added that the little Amor would be welcome, too. Obviously the slight suffered in his military career and the wound received in the Caroline affair[79] were aching. To assist Hungary was not easy either, at least "not in the present," to use his own words, for he was realistic enough to see that he himself had much to learn yet and the fatherland had to change, too.

His English experiences were to help him in this respect, however. The day before he left England he wrote: "In my view, there are three things to be learned in England, all the rest is nothing: [they are] *the constitution, the machines* and *horse-breeding.*"[80] Széchenyi's selection, of course, can be disputed, although it is undeniable that Englishmen of his time were passionately interested in all three topics mentioned by him. I have already pointed out Széchenyi's interest in the constitution from the point of a foreign observer. As for the horses, he visited the races at Newmarket as well as at Epsom; he was a cavalry officer and throughout his entire life had a weak spot in his heart for horses. Horse-breeding and the problem of modernizing Hungarian constitutional concepts along western lines both were going to appear in his reform program, and will be discussed further, as will the question of Hungary's technical development. A word about this last problem, however, should be added at this point.

As indicated above, Széchenyi, who was impressed by all kinds of technical devices, perceived the significance of England's industrial development. Yet he knew that one man could not specialize in everything without wasting his time, especially if he had no special background in mechanics; hence he decided to concentrate on horse-breeding and

[79] "I thought of God and of a woman whom I might have made unhappy and whose memory weighed mostly on my conscience." Dec. 15, 1815, *ibid.*, I, 170.

[80] Dec. 13, 1815, *ibid.*, I, 166f.

obtaining gas from coal.[81] At this stage he also thought that steam power could not compete with cheap labor in backward countries like Hungary; in addition, he was of the opinion that Hungarians were "a warlike nation . . . of an innate ferocity," unlikely to adjust to a spinning mill. He may have anticipated some of the social problems connected with industrialization in what we would call today "underdeveloped" areas, for he thanked God that there were no factories in Hungary.

Assuming that industrial advancement or "perfection" was, as he suggested, always a consequence of misery which forces many people to earn a living the hard way, he concluded that it was only due to the special conditions prevalent in England that this kind of self-perfection resulted in the production of wealth.[82] Following this line of argument, he decided to concentrate his attention on the "Gaslight Machine" because he found it simple and practical. He even managed to smuggle one gas-engine out of England, and was extremely happy that despite the strict regulations, "the proud Englishman disguised as a customs officer . . . sold the soul of his nation, an engine" to him for a bribe of two pounds.[83]

Széchenyi's economic views, particularly those pertaining to the question of the usefulness and practicability of steam power and industrial plants in Hungary, were to undergo a great modification in the years to come. But it is a significant fact that without any specific preparation whatsoever, he realized at the age of 24 the importance of economic problems in a modern nation's life. is rather naïve racial approach to the puzzle concerning the essence of a nation suggested that in England, where he was treated as a Hungarian, he became increasingly aware of his being different from other Austrian officers and of the fact that the concept of a nation involved a certain community and continuity of factors as well.[84]

He was far from being consistent in this respect, however. Occasionally

[81] Nov. 13, 1815, Zichy, ed., *Széchenyi szülőihez*, IV/27, p. 181. Concerning the use of gas, he gave some thought to the problem how it could be compressed and stored in a bottle so that one could extract it as "fire." Annex No. II, Viszota, ed., *Naplók*, I, 782. The same entry shows his interest in other things, too, like smoke-bells, different types of doors, dishes, pots and pans, and—the water closet.

[82] Dec. 1815, *ibid.*, I, 168.

[83] Dec. 1815, *ibid.*, I 166, 168; Nov. 13, 1815, Zichy, ed., *Széchenyi szülőihez*, IV/27, p. 181.

[84] In his entry of Nov. 21, 1814, Viszota, ed., *Naplók*, I, 45, he referred to "Attila's innumerable horsemen with whom he devastated all countries" as to kinsfolk because, as he put it, he himself belonged to the ancient race of Huns. As proof he added that he could never feel so enthusiastic about the most beautiful Swiss Alps or Italian valleys as he did about the flat deserts of his homeland.

he still thought of himself as of an Austrian,[85] but more and more he resented certain aspects of Austrian institutions. Summing up his three most important things to be studied in England—the constitution, machines, and horse-breeding—he excluded, out of resentment, the study of the English army which he regarded as the best in the world at the time, as compared with the Austrian army which he thought had fallen into irreparable decay.[86] Deeply hurt by the neglect of the Austrian army by those in power, he gradually extended his criticism to the ruling dynasty and, to a certain degree, began to look for the signs of Austria's decline in every corner. It is his fault, he conceded, if in his fulminations against the House of Habsburg he lowered himself to the examination of trousers instead of taking up another subject. But, he added, wryly alluding to the shabby attire of the Austrian army, "trousers are so necessary for a hussar and such a brave nobleman and he does not even have trousers. What else can one then expect from such a government? Amen." In the same breath, he also noted the remark of a Prussian friend according to whom one could produce several thousand scholars with the knowledge of which people were ignorant in the Austrian states.[87]

The tone and the association of ideas were those to be used in his sarcastic attacks on the Bach-system in the late 1850s; but already at this point, a discouraging experience or a fitting remark of a friend made him think about the frightening number of problems in central Europe symbolized by the name of Austria.

In mid-December 1815 Stephen Széchenyi left England with the feeling that the trip had been "indispensable" for him. He was glad to return to the continent, though, because "England is charming but I like our bright sun better."[88] An Austrian officer, but half-conscious of his Hungarian patriotism, he was held an Englishman by two Hanoverian officers on account of his English clothes when he set foot on French soil again:[89] the confusion concerning his "real" identity was to outlive him.

The fruits of Széchenyi's experiences in England, supplemented by his numerous subsequent visits there, were to have a lasting influence on his career. But for the moment, his fresh impressions of the great contrast between England and the continent, especially Austria, only added to his inner instability. On his return trip to Vienna he met

[85] Sept. 1815, *ibid.*, I, 137.
[86] Dec. 1815, *ibid.*, I, 167.
[87] Dec. 1815, *ibid.*, I, 167f., 171.
[88] Nov. 3, 1815, Zichy, ed., *Széchenyi szülőihez*, IV/25, pp. 175, 177.
[89] Dec. 1815, Viszota, ed., *Naplók*, I, 172f.

several friends in Paris. One of them, Prince Windischgrätz, who was to play an important role in 1848, said that Széchenyi would be "a very excellent man" if he stayed with him so Windischgrätz could give "appropriate direction" to Széchenyi's many ideas.[90]

On January 2, 1816 Széchenyi arrived in Vienna. During the following year and a half he kept no diary.[91] With his leave of absence repeatedly renewed by the military authorities, he spent most of his time in Vienna, Cenk, or on his brother Paul's estate in Apáti. In the autumn of 1816 he paid another short visit to England where he bought horses; on his way home, he purchased wines and paintings in France and Frankfort.[92]

We know this much from letters written to Liebenberg, which are the most important sources for this period. The central topic of the letters was money. Besides "his melancholic mood, or rather spleen acquired in England,"[93] he also brought home a number of vague "projects" in the form of sketches in his diaries and gadgets such as the "gaslight machine," and a desire for fashionable amusements, all of which were rather expensive. Foreign wines, horses, new furnishings, and fox hunting in Cenk, cooks and stable boys from abroad, all cost money which Széchenyi borrowed from all possible sources including his father, members of the family, friends and financiers. Sometimes his negotiations with a creditor were humiliating.[94] It might have been in such a mood that he wrote to Liebenberg: "In one word, do whatever you wish, scratch the earth, press the peasants in order to produce the greatest possible sum of money, and stay fresh and healthy."[95]

It seemed as if Széchenyi were going to join the ranks of those spendthrift Hungarian magnates whose depreciated letters of credit were dreaded by financiers all over Europe.[96] Some of his amusements, like horse races, were not useless, as the future was to show. In the spring of 1816 he participated in the organization of the first horse races in Simmering and those on the estates of Count Joseph Hunyady. In addition to many Austrian, Bohemian, and Hungarian aristocrats and Sir Charles Stewart, English minister to Vienna, who was a good friend of Széchenyi's, one of the races was also attended by Emperor Francis.

90 Dec. 1815, *ibid.*, I, 173.

91 There is one entry from Mar. 17, 1816, chiefly about comparing a nation's or people's life to that of an individual, *ibid.*, I, 175.

92 Széchenyi to Liebenberg, Nov. 1, 1816, Majláth, ed., *Levelek*, I, 30f.

93 Széchenyi to Liebenberg, Nov. 8, 1815, *ibid.*, I, 11.

94 Széchenyi to Liebenberg, May 17, 1817, *ibid.*, I, 40.

95 Széchenyi to Liebenberg, Feb. 22, 1817, *ibid.*, I, 38.

96 Due to the feudal law system in Hungary, it was an extremely lengthy and complicated procedure to sue a Hungarian nobleman successfully.

On this occasion, Széchenyi's English jockey won, but shortly afterwards Széchenyi himself fell sick and could not enjoy his expensive laurels.[97]

Horses and horse-breeding became one of the great passions in his life. But the time was remote when this passion could also increase his income. For the present his economic situation continued to be poor. In addition to financial difficulties, he came to a moral impasse. Disillusioned by the war, the Caroline affair, his uselessness as a discharged soldier, and the discrepancies between the free atmosphere of England and the realm of Francis I which seemed to have outlived itself—he felt increasingly frustrated and rebellious. His financial embarrassment became known, and his escapades did not improve his reputation.[98] To avoid the gossip of Viennese society and reduce expenses he decided to rejoin his regiment stationed at Milan in May 1817.

There was another reason for Széchenyi's sudden decision: he was once more in love with a married woman. But unlike the occasion of his first, short "Italian journey," this time it was Széchenyi who lost out. His flirtation with Countess Gabriella Saurau dated back to the time of the Congress of Vienna[99] and flared up after his return from England. In the spring of 1817 Gabriella went to Lombardy with her husband, and Széchenyi used his furlough to follow her. He did not know the itinerary of the Sauraus when, approaching Verona, he unexpectedly became aware of the presence of his "angel."

The description of the unexpected encounter[100] is romanticism at its height. Actually the reveries and effusions in Széchenyi's diaries during the period 1817–19 often reflected the influence of the *Nouvelle Héloïse* and other readings of his. Széchenyi's affection was "romantically" hopeless—and somewhat comical. The former *séducteur* and sophisticated dandy was suffering all the torments of love, but *la beauté du diable* only laughed at him; friends who were aware of Stefferl's fickle nature made fun of him.[101]

Yet there was a tragic element in the writhing of a man nearing his thirties who confessed in the diaries his idle dreams of an unrequited love and accepted his rejection with a stoicism bordering on despair, for even writing Gabriella's name was gratifying to him. In one moment

[97] Viszota, ed., *Naplók*, I, p. II; Széchenyi to Liebenberg, August 1816. Majláth, ed., *Levelek*, I, 23f.

[98] Széchenyi to Liebenberg, June 20, 23, 28, Aug. 29, 1817, *ibid.*, I, 44–47, 56; Friedreich, *Széchenyi élete*, I, 54.

[99] Oct. 1814, Viszota, ed., *Naplók*, I, 28; also pp. cxxvi–cxxix.

[100] May 1817, Viszota, ed., *ibid.*, 177f.

[101] June–Aug. 1817; July 21, 22, 25, 1818, *ibid.*, I, 179–86, 197–201, 209.

he wanted to hate her, and in the next one he decided to win her affection through the achievement of "great and noble deeds."[102] To substitute a lofty aim for the image of the beloved woman and sublimate the earthly desire of her into an action promoting humanity—it was at this point that Széchenyi made the first conscientious effort to transform the motive power of Eros into something more ethical and lasting. After visiting the tomb of Titus Livy and seeing a painting of Paolo Veronese in Padua he started to reflect about the intimate connections of Eros and human creativity. However pleasant the thought seemed to be that only through love did people enter real life, that only through love did they become great and noble, that love caused them to be writers or artists, and that Gabriella could perhaps transform him, too, into the idol of an entire region, the very idea of doing for a woman, out of weakness what he should accomplish as a man with his willpower, hurt his pride and arouse his sense of shame.[103]

Although his infatuation with Gabriella did not last long,[104] it had an influence on him, comparable only to that of Caroline and later on, to that of his wife, Crescence. Its negative effects can be measured by the passionate and helpless outbursts preserved in his diary and by the fact that, when Gabriella died in November 1821, barely one year after the death of Caroline, Széchenyi again accused himself of having brought ruin upon a person so close to him. In later years Gabriella's image, as well as Caroline's, was to appear in his tormenting visions.[105]

But there were some positive aspects to the frustrating experience with Gabriella. After the departure of the Sauraus from Italy in June 1817, and after Széchenyi's return to Vienna in January 1818, he started anew to read extensively.[106] He also tried "work-therapy": in October 1817 he sent a memorial to the monarch about the improvement of horse-breeding,[107] and in late 1818, drawing heavily on his experiences in England, he published his first treatise on the subject.[108]

[102] July 22, 1818, ibid., I, 203.

[103] July 23, 1818, ibid., I, 205f.

[104] On Aug. 12, 1819 he was already referring to it as to "a false dream." Ibid., I, 689.

[105] Nov. 26, 1821 and Oct. I, 1842, ibid., II, 224 and v, 633.

[106] Nov. 5, 1819, ibid., I, 704.

[107] A Hungarian summary of this memorial, written in German on October 4, 1817 in Milan, was published in B. Szabó, ed., Adatok, I, 9.

[108] The title of the treatise was "Über die Zucht und Veredlung der Pferde, mit stetem Bezuge auf die Pferdezucht Ungarns, über Gestütte, Wettrennen u.s.w." It appeared in the November–December issue of the Erneuerte Vaterländische Blätter für den österreichischen Kaiserstaat and some of its main ideas were to reappear in Széchenyi's first Hungarian book, Lovakrul (On Horses). Cf. Viszota, ed., Naplók. I, p. liv.

Reading and work, as well as marriage plans, were but efforts to break through the ring of his frustrations. In October 1817 Széchenyi still ridiculed Liebenberg who had suggested matrimony as a cure for his difficulties, but in July 1818 he seriously considered the alternative. In contrast to his fascination with the abstract sciences was his longing for a simple life to be achieved through marrying a decent girl without ambitions. In his soul, the *biedermeier* picture of domestic happiness reemerged, as amidst the disillusionment of the Napoleonic wars.[109] Beyond these alternatives, however, there loomed a question mark, pointing both to the abyss of physical destruction and to the possibility of a completely new start in life.

First it seemed as if he had gone another step in the direction of the former. In Vienna he fell in love, or at least he thought he did, with Caroline's younger sister, Selina, and decided to marry her. This sentiment, too, dated back several years. As early as 1811 Stephen had the name of Caroline's then 14-year-old sister tattooed on his arm,[110] but the youthful flirtation did not take a serious turn until 1818, at the climax of the Gabriella crisis. Recalling the shock of the Caroline affair, Széchenyi's parents violently opposed their son's planned marriage to Selina; he himself was aware of the awkwardness of the situation. So he decided to go for a third trip to Italy, this time extending his itinerary to include the Balkans and Asia Minor.[111]

Széchenyi made rather elaborate preparations for his Oriental journey which was going to take him away from home for 11 months.[112] He carefully studied a number of English, French, and German travelogues and historical works about the Levant. In addition to his cook, valet, and servant, he took along a philologist and archeologist by the name of Landschulz, and a Viennese painter, Johann Ender, who were to help him understand the works of art and to draw sketches.[113] Through the good offices of Metternich, Széchenyi received permission to make

---

[109] Széchenyi to Liebenberg, Oct. 24, 1817, Majláth, ed., *Levelek*, 1, 64; July 31, 1818, Viszota, ed., *Naplók*, 1, 269. I am using the term *biedermeier* in its original meaning—"bourgeois" virtues and limited desires. Cf. Béla Zolnai, *A magyar Biedermeier* (Hungarian Biedermeier) (Budapest: Franklin, n.d.), pp. 5–10. For its literary-artistic and philosophical implications in early 19th-century Hungary see *ibid., passim*.

[110] July 17, 27, 1819, Viszota, ed., *Naplók*, 1, 638, 663. Also Note-Book 1, 11, Annex No. VI, *ibid.*, 1, 835 (draft of letter to Selina, July 1819).

[111] May 1819 and July 17, 1819, *ibid.*, 1, 636f., 652ff., 657, 659. Also Nov. 1819, *ibid.*, 1, 704.

[112] The details of Széchenyi's journey can be gathered from his diary and the letters written to his parents. Cf. also Antal Zichy, ed., *Gr. Széchenyi István külföldi uti rajzai és följegyzései* (Count Stephen Széchenyi's Accounts and Notes of His Travels Abroad) (Budapest: 1890), Vol. V of *SzIM*.

[113] Ender's sketches and paintings done during the trip are in the Széchenyi Museum, Budapest.

the trip from Italy to Constantinople on an Austrian man-of-war which took the new Austrian internuncio, Count Lützow, to his post.[114]

Széchenyi's party left Vienna in mid-July 1818. The first month of the trip, including a 10-day stay in Rome, was spent in Italy. Széchenyi visited some old friends, like the Schellings in Rome and the Kaunitz family in Frascati (he even thought of marrying Caroline Kaunitz),[115] and met many new ones like Count Apponyi in Florence who represented Austria at the court of Tuscany. More important, he continued reading extensively, filling his diary with literary and esthetic notes. These references, sometimes products of the beginner's rash or personal judgments, or perhaps reflections on the remarks of companions, indicate his broadened horizon. During the first week of his trip, Széchenyi quoted or referred to Shakespeare's *Hamlet,* Byron's *Manfred,* four dramas of Alfieri, Lessing, Plato's *Apology of Socrates,* Schiller's *Die Glocke* and *Wilhelm Tell,* translated parts of Plato's *Phaedros,* and tried his hand at writing poetry in German.[116]

His perception of works of art was highly colored by his moods. For example, when he visited Petrarch's tomb in Arque, he remarked that his poems bored him but was fair enough to admit that he probably did not understand the poet. He also found it rather ridiculous that Petrarch had been singing of his unhappy love while "Laura, as everybody knows, gave birth to seven children in nine years."[117] It was an irony that he himself was to wait more than 10 years for a woman who had borne seven children to her first husband before marrying him.

Széchenyi also tried to get acquainted with contemporary art; he visited the studios of Thorwaldsen and Canova, and attended a concert given by Paganini.[118] Naturally, only the more general changes in his outlook resulting from the Oriental trip can be noted here. At the beginning of his journey, he felt physically and morally sick, and in need of some purpose in his life.[119] He wanted to stand on his own feet, be independent and free, realizing that he was not born to languish at the feet of a woman.[120] The idea of doing something for the fatherland and mankind, not for the love of a woman but as a worthwhile goal in itself, became articulated during this journey. To be sure, he still considered himself an Austrian citizen, despite his many critical re-

[114] Aug. 25, 1818, Zichy, ed., *Széchenyi szülőihez,* v/4, p. 197; Aug. 1, 1818, Viszota, ed., *Naplók,* I, 222.

[115] Aug. 9, 13, 1818, Zichy, ed., *Széchenyi szülőihez,* v/1 and 2, pp. 189–92; also, Aug. 9, 1818, July 17, 1819; Viszota, ed., *Naplók,* I, 286, 656f.

[116] July 17–25, 1818, *ibid.,* I, 190–212.

[117] July 25, 1818, *ibid.,* I, 211.

[118] Aug. 3, 7, 1818, *ibid.,* I, 225, 274–85.

[119] July 12, 17, 1818, *ibid.,* I, 190f.

[120] Aug. 2, 1818, *ibid.,* I, 224.

marks about Austrian conditions, and did not know what form his ideas would actually take. Still, he made up his mind to look "farther, think deeper and bigger than other people." Trusting that he had more than average strength of character and intellectual power, he hoped that he would through his achievements "really become increasingly fashionable [popular, better understood] as the years go by."[121]

Trieste, Padua, Ferrara, Florence, and Rome were the most important stops of the voyage. From Italy Széchenyi went on to the islands of Corfu, Milo, and Tenedos, to Troy, Constantinople, Smyrna, Chios, Athens, Thermopylae, the island of Aegina, and Patras, to return to Italy through Malta and Sicily.[122] After seeing the art treasures of the Vatican and Italy, he had the opportunity of getting firsthand experience of living standards, social, and sanitary conditions in Turkey, Asia Minor and Greece. After leaving the Italian cities and roads where he could read all day long in his comfortable coach, he came to regions where the only possibility for travel was on horseback or mule, and where he had no news from home for many weeks. He had to endure hardships and fell ill several times—a considerable change after his previous emotional tribulations. His mind was kept busy absorbing the abundance of new impressions. He became aware of the seriousness of the "Eastern Question": travelling and being in close contact with diplomats and representatives of many nations, his feeling for and interest in political problems increased considerably.[123] The opportunity to contrast the situation of Austria to that of advanced Western and more backward Eastern countries challenged him. He registered with disappointment that the navy and the diplomatic and commercial representation of Austria in the Near East were inadequate for a great power. In this respect, he admired the British while also recognizing Russian strength in the area.

Stephen Széchenyi seemed to be interested in everything. He read, consulted guides, the local population, and his companions, always raising new questions. He admired the beauty of cities, mountains, harbors, and islands; he noted strange costumes and was fascinated by ingenuity in commerce and production; he wondered about the decline of great civilizations and empires, and analyzed the behavior of Greek and Turkish populations. Describing viticulture on the island of Milo, he asked himself if the same method of cultivation could be advantageous in all lands. In picturesque Tenedos he found the quality of grapes

---

[121] Aug. 13, Oct. 23, 1818, Zichy, ed., *Széchenyi szülőihez*, v/2, 10, pp. 193, 228; Aug. 3, 1818, Viszota, ed., *Naplók*, I, 235f.

[122] For a detailed summary see *ibid.*, I, pp. liv–xcvii.

[123] For this and the following, see Aug. 25, Sept. 10–11, 21, Oct. 24, 26, Nov. 1, 28–30, 1818, Jun. 6, 1819, March–April 1819, *ibid.*, I, 298ff., 329, 333, 350f., 361–64, 373, 394, 440f., 447f., 452, 488, 537.

even better than in Milo and "similar to ours," adding that it would be striking to be able to buy these grapes in Vienna. Not too far from Brussa he noticed good hop vines "which cannot be found in all Hungary." He also observed the peculiar way of growing mulberry trees and marked the great income of the population from the breeding of silkworms. In Smyrna he became interested in the manipulation and shipping of cotton; in Scio he put down the figures of orange and lemon production. Travelling in an unknown land and watching exotic plants and people sometimes brought rather familiar associations. Trying to size up the channel between the Asian shore and the island of Scio, he referred to Lake Balaton at its greatest width. He listened to Turkish music in a village of Asia Minor and he compared the musical instrument with the Hungarian *tárogató* (clarinet); another time, he thought it worth mentioning that he had been called "Magyar" by one Turk. Also, he was often referred to as a traveling *principe d'Ungheria*. Somehow, subconsciously, the fatherland, the *real* one, had been present in his thinking all the time.[124]

He had no particular illusions about this fatherland of his, though. His cosmopolitan background suggested to him that Hungary was a place "where no one in his right mind would want to live."[125] There were a number of other derogatory remarks in his notes about the backwardness of his compatriots. At the same time, he also spoke of "the miserable condition of the Austrian states" in general.[126] Still, whatever he meant by fatherland at this point, he was admittedly fond of it: "Poor little fatherland, how filthy you are! Naturally, I do not entirely know you but still should like to take a close look at you because I love you tenderly, aside from your land and *conceited inhabitants*."[127]

It is obvious from the geographical references[128] that this time he definitely meant Hungary, especially its Transdanubian part. Well aware that in the modern Western sense of the term "there is no nation in Hungary as yet and it will take a lot of trouble to create a public spirit in this country,"[129] he suspected that his beloved "filthy little fatherland" might not even want to make use of his talents because of his "too definite views."[130]

This was perhaps the first time Széchenyi referred to such "firm views,"

---

[124] Sept. 8, 10, Nov. 1, 6, 9, 10, 13, 26, 28, 29, 1818, *ibid.*, 1, 324, 327, 393, 406, 411, 417, 423, 430, 436, 446f.
[125] Draft of letter from mid-1819, *ibid.*, 1, Annex No. III, 8, p. 844.
[126] Aug. 11, 1819, *ibid.*, 1, 686.
[127] Dec. 4, 1818, *ibid.*, 1, 461 (italics in original).
[128] Plattensee, Badacson, Neusiedler See (*sic*).
[129] Aug. 1817, Viszota, ed., *Naplók*, 1, 185.
[130] Dec. 4, 1818, *ibid.*, 1, 457.

although ever since his visit to England, certain political and economic ideas had been fermenting in his mind. While attempting to clarify for himself the issues of the Levantine trade and economic development in general, he suddenly turned to the problem of Hungary, taking up the line of thought he had dropped after his return from England. Accordingly, he suggested that "in Hungary e.g. one ought to double the production of fruits, wines, wool, meat, etc.; demands should be limited and one should not think of [building] factories." In accordance with his initial, crude plan for Hungary's economic modernization, conceived under the twofold impact of the shock experienced in advanced England and backward Turkey, Hungary should be a "land of bread" and not a "land of wheels." It should concentrate on improving its agriculture and not waste energy on industrialization, because "ridiculous is the Englishman who wishes to produce wine and fruits but even more comical is a Hungarian who wants to make steel."[131]

In these first coherent economic ideas Széchenyi considered Hungary to be one link in a chain of nations composing Austria. During the Oriental trip he also realized that the internal tariffs separating the lands of the Austrian Empire had the effect on the state that tight ropes have in preventing blood from circulating in the human body.[132] Thus, out of practical considerations, Széchenyi had become a free-trader, well before he read the works of Adam Smith and other English classical economists. Free trade and no government interference were to be focal points of his economic system; they were also destined to bring him into conflict with Kossuth in the early 1840s.

Some writers interpret the time of the Oriental trip as one of the turning points in Széchenyi's life. There is much truth in this opinion, although there is also some oversimplification in it. Széchenyi himself was inclined to dramatize the change in his thinking during the trip.[133] A few months after he had returned from his long journey he drew up a disillusioned "balance sheet" of his life. In this autobiographical evaluation he called the period preceding his trip to the Orient "the period of incongruities."[134] After his second effort to obtain Selina's hand had failed[135] he decided to formulate principles without illusions. These principles were inspired by an inner voice; they pointed toward the ideal of the active life: "A spiritually and physically active life

---

[131] Dec. 4, 1818, *ibid.*, 1, 460.

[132] Feb. 6, 1819, *ibid.*, 1, 503f.

[133] Nov. 13, 1818; Apr. 19 and May 1819, *ibid.*, 1, 422, 593f., 619.

[134] Nov. 5, 1819, *ibid.*, 1, 704.

[135] *Ibid;* also July 17–Aug. 15, 1819, 1, 652–93. Cf. the draft of Széchenyi's novel describing the story of his love for Selina under the title *Lebensgeschichte des F____*, Note-Book II, 2, Annex No. VIII, *ibid.*, 1, 849–53.

alone can carry us to the highest level of human happiness." Also, Széchenyi admitted sadly, these principles which in his opinion were infallible
were often contrary to those of his parents. Scorning the religious bigots
surrounding his father, and inwardly rebelling against priests and young
weaklings, he declared that prayer is a "holy occupation" only insofar
as it prepares for deeds, purifies and suppresses passions, and thus helps
achieve the independence and purity of the soul in which stage alone
is man capable of directing and raising his soul toward God.[136]

Actually Stephen Széchenyi's outlook became more sophisticated as
well as radical. In a state of inner rebellion he tried to reject his whole
past;[137] up to then he was only "a *vain* child, without education, without
counsel"—he had no principles, knew nothing, so the best part of his
life was spent in dissipation and ignorance until the year 1818.[138] Frequent ironical remarks about the stupidity of monarchs and about the
army indicated that gone was "the divine subordination inhaled in
childhood!"[139] His sympathy toward oppressed peoples was aroused in
Greece;[140] his admiration toward countries with constitutional institutions and respecting individual liberty increased. He was impressed
by England's sea power; but his anglophile sentiments, considerably
strengthened during his two-week stay on Malta,[141] did not weaken his
sense of judgement when he saw that the British were not eager to help
"other merchants," namely the Greeks, get on their feet in their own
land.[142]

It is particularly interesting how early Széchenyi divined the rising
star of America. In the harbor of Messina he visited the battleship *Franklin* and the frigate *La Guerrière*. Afterwards he wrote a "long nonsense"[143] into his diary. He drew a parallel between the foundations
of the United States and those of the Roman Empire, claiming that
just as civilization had once come from Asia to Europe, in the same

---

[136] Nov. 1819, *ibid.*, I, 704f., 709.

[137] In addition to the citations and references mentioned see also the entries of
Feb. 11, Apr. 9, May 9–15, July 29, 31, 1819, *ibid.*, I, 522, 584, 606ff., 620, 665, and 672,
respectively. In most cases these references also show Széchenyi's feeling of guilt over
the "errors of his youth," particularly his relationship with Caroline. Cf. also Feb.
24, Mar. 28, 1819, Zichy, ed., *Széchenyi szülőihez*, v/26, 28, pp. 279, 290.

[138] Draft of letter, July 1819, Note-Book I. II, Annex No. VI, Viszota, ed., *Naplók*,
I, 832 (italics in original).

[139] June 5, 1819, *ibid.*, I, 640ff. Also July 19, 27, 1818, Apr. 7, May 16, 1819, *ibid.*, I,
249, 259, 569f., 624.

[140] E.g., Jan. 5, 1819, *ibid.*, I, 486ff.

[141] Dec. 25, 1818, Mar. 9–Apr. 9, 1819, *ibid.*, I, 478, 533–47. Also Mar. 31, 1819,
Zichy, ed., *Széchenyi szülőihez*, v/29, p. 292.

[142] Dec. 2, 1818, Viszota, ed., *Naplók*, I, 454.

[143] Apr. 9, 14, 15, 1819, *ibid.*, I, 546, 549, 552, 556. Also Apr. 11, Zichy, ed., *Széchenyi
szülőihez*, v/31, p. 295.

way culture and perfection was moving successively to America. But in the Roman Republic everything was on a small scale compared to the United States where everything was being started in hitherto unknown dimensions. Impressed with the freshness of the ideas of Americans as well as with the culture and increasing power of the New World, he pointed out certain difference between Englishmen and Americans with regard to their behavior, appearance, and shipbuilding. He particularly stressed the strong sense of independence of the Americans, which, he thought, would make it impossible for them to imitate the British or to accept any rules or examples as guide lines.[144]

These fragments of a "frontier-theory" on a gigantic scale, written in April 1819, were essentially based on personal experience and sharp observation. They continued to challenge Széchenyi's imagination, and several times in the years to come he was at the point of emigrating or at least visiting *das werdende Land*—"the Land of the Future."[145] As in the case of England, Széchenyi's admiration for America never decreased, although his plan to visit the New World failed to materialize. His enthusiasm must have been generally known, for ladies of Viennese society dubbed him *der Americane* (*sic*).[146] There was a grain of truth in the nickname, for in Széchenyi's eyes George Washington and Benjamin Franklin belonged among the greatest statesmen of history[147] and were ideals to be followed. He was proud that an industrialist from Milan once called him "the Washington of Hungary," remarking: "Oh Lord, if it were only true!"[148] With Franklin, Széchenyi was to experience the influence of his ideas from the early 1820's to the end of his life.

Critical reexamination of old ideals and of the past, as well as searching for new ideas and examples to follow, were but different aspects of Széchenyi's effort to prove himself and stand on his own feet. By the time he returned to Vienna in June 1819 his finances were in order again, thanks to his absence from home and to the management of his father and Liebenberg. Although he was occasionally to face financial difficulties in the years ahead, he never got into similar trouble again—he

---

[144] Apr. 1819, Viszota, ed., *Naplók*, I, 589ff.

[145] May 9–15, Aug. 2, 1819, *ibid.*, I, 612, 676f. Cf. also his statement in *A kelet népe* (p. 305 in the *Fontes* edition):

Let us take a look at the people of the United States. How is it that in such a short time they achieved an admirable progress hitherto unknown anywhere? If they maintain their present rate of progress, how can they fail to surpass all the nations of mankind?

[146] Mar. 6, 1821, Viszota, ed., *Naplók*, II, 135. Of course, Széchenyi occasionally was also critical of American conditions, e.g., the institution of slavery. Cf. Sept. 21, 1825, *ibid.*, II, 609.

[147] Aug. 13, 1839, *ibid.*, v, 305.

[148] Nov. 1, 1840, *ibid.*, v, 415.

had learned his lesson.[149] But from his Oriental trip he brought home more ambitious plans than merely to put his own house in order. He was looking for principles for himself and was striving for self-perfection through good deeds as the beginning of a good life. But these were only preludes to further steps to make, for "only he can please his fellow-men, his country and the author of the world who has reached physically and morally the highest possible perfection." Thus children should be taught to strive to be healthy and good, as God has deemed it proper for man to be. But one can side with either good or evil in this life, Széchenyi adds, as one wishes, and there is no need for another judge; one judges oneself.[150]

In these and other reflections, written partly during the idle hours of the repeated quarantines of his journey, Széchenyi laid down the bases of his philosophical creed. This philosophy was essentially Christian, but highly undogmatic and particularly in this period of his life under the influence of the Enlightenment and Greco-Roman antiquity. By the perfection of the soul he did not mean religious exercises, nor anything beyond the capabilities of man; on the contrary, he wanted to obey the "laws of nature"; while respecting the forms of all religions he saw their essence in helping one's fellow men. His thoughts on what kind of help he believed most useful to his fellow men was characteristic; instead of having help doled out, mankind should be taught through example. Yet to be able to teach, one must know—and know in particular—what makes men happy and satisfied. To be able to set an example it is not enough to be a good man; one must be thought of as *being* a good man. Therefore one must think hard about one's deeds and train oneself to be consistently good. In contrast to his father who was regarded by many as a *Betbruder* (a person always in prayers or, in a derogatory sense, a hypocrite) at the end of his life, Stephen Széchenyi substituted for the religious hero the ideal of the active citizen anticipating the great dream of old Faust: "In a prosperous and productive land, the active citizen has a splendid life because everything he had done for the fatherland is being praised and appreciated. He sees his people happy and raised well above others. In every labor of his and in every sacrifice, he finds pleasure and good luck.[151]

---

[149] July 1, 17, 1819, *ibid.*, I, 647f., 658. The accounts of Széchenyi's trip were in good order. Because they contain exchange rates and prices of varied goods and services in a series of countries, they would be of interest to the economic historian. The accounts were published in Annex No. v, *ibid.*, I, 800–14.

[150] May 9, 1819, *ibid.*, I, 607f. For the concept of perfection see also May 20–25, Aug. 12, Nov. 5, 1819, *ibid.*, I, 637f., 688, 697 and note.

[151] May 9, 1819, *ibid.*, I, 609. Parallel to the thought just cited, Széchenyi, characteristically, quoted a dedication to George Washington written by Alfieri in his

One may risk the opinion that this active but abstract patriotism that as beginning to take shape in Széchenyi's thinking was a psychological reaction to the presence of what seemed to him the "negative hero" in the people surrounding his father at the time. In a fragment of a novel written by Széchenyi in 1820 the tragic end of the hero was: "Becomes clergyman."[152] His "positive hero," however, was the "doer" with whom Széchenyi could identify himself. For he too wanted to be an active citizen, helping to put the future generation one step closer to the light—"this I wish to undertake"—regardless of whether hatred or oblivion would be the reward.[153] His concept of the fatherland was at best vague and poetically romantic, but he began to associate it with the concept of a free people.[154] And after long years of soul-searching and tribulations, toward the end of his *Sturm und Drang* period, an incentive for life seems to have emerged in his soul, namely, the opportunity to serve his country and his fellow citizens.[155] Only a few months earlier, the idea of sacrifice for fatherland, throne, and fellow man was still interwoven with the effort of being worthy of an ideal woman (in this case, Selina).[156] This peculiar interrelationship of love, patriotism, and romatic idealism was to characterize Széchenyi's activities for many years to come. But the emphasis was gradually shifting from personal love to patriotism; without ever denying the primary stimulative role of love, patriotism became second nature for Széchenyi by the mid-1820's.

The signs of his soul-searching and brooding about the future were present in the letters written to his parents at the time. In one of these he said that he knew very little about his fatherland and therefore would spend a few months in it to make up for his lack of knowledge.[157] It was during his visits to foreign lands, primarily England and Turkey, that Széchenyi first began to feel the necessity of studying Hungarian conditions, and it was abroad that he realized his people were oppressed and did not even know what freedom was. It was in this phase of his life that Széchenyi not only became extremely critical of his own education and past but also began to give some thought to the problem of how to improve the education of the individual and how to educate and awaken a nation to consciousness. He shared the article of faith

drama *Bruto primo*. It includes the following sentence: "*L'amor della patria dimostrato coi fatti.*"

[152] Sept. 12, 1820, *ibid.*, II, 65.

[153] May 9, 1819, *ibid.*, I, 610.

[154] May 20–25, 1819, *ibid.*, I, 633f.

[155] Nov. 1819, *ibid.*, I, 710.

[156] Aug. 6, 1819, *ibid.*, I, 681.

[157] Dec. 14, 1818, Zichy, ed., *Széchenyi szülőihez*, V/16, p. 254f. Cf. Mar. 10, 1819, *ibid.*, V/27, pp. 282–89.

of the Enlightenment concerning the unlimited possibilities and effects of education both for the individual and for the nation as a whole. "It is above all the education received in one's formative years which is the basis of a man's happiness and contentment in his maturity and old age,"[158] he wrote, citing also the opinion of an English writer, J. C. Eustace, according to whom free government and liberal education were going to determine a nation's "open and manly" character.[159] At this point, Széchenyi thought that to make a nation great it was necessary to educate the majority of its people. Irked by the fact that his compatriots were "respectable competitors" of the Turks in ignorance and laziness, he realized that the conceit and blindness of the natives (i.e., Hungarians) could be changed only through the education of successive generations. "Education, to name once more the keyword, must prevent us from regressing," he mused, adding, "*a good village school,* that's what a backward country needs most." In his opinion, the aim of education should be to raise "good citizens and honest men." In addition to the principles of religion and duties to king and fatherland, his liberal educational system would put a special emphasis on languages (including the mother tongue which at that time was not evident in Hungary), history, mathematics, and law, regular physical education and the furnishing of sex information. He concluded his ideas on education by saying: "The good education of individuals can be managed; but he who wishes to serve his fatherland and compatriots well must lay the foundation for public schools: 'and that is what I want to do, God willing.'"[160]

Széchenyi never developed his early educational concepts into a consistent system, although there are many thoughts about education in his works.[161] In later years he modified some basic tenets of the first draft of his educational ideas, a draft which so remarkably reflected his frame of mind in the years 1815–20. Later, for political reasons and out of fear of agitation by Kossuth and the younger liberal generation, he opposed the extension of public education as premature: the masses of the people will not sufficiently politically mature. In the opinion of

---

[158] Apr. 7, 1819, Viszota, ed., *Naplók*, I, 574, 576f.

[159] Apr. 9, 1819, *ibid.*, I, 577. John Chetwode Eustace wrote a four-volume work about Italy (*A Classical Tour Through Italy in 1802*, London, 1815), that Széchenyi often quoted. The passage referred to is in Vol. III, 283.

[160] Apr. 9, 1819, *ibid.*, I, 577–87 (italics in original). Cf. May, July, Oct., and Nov. 1819, *ibid.*, I, 617f., 629f., 651f., 734.

[161] Cf. Sándor Imre, *Gróf Széchenyi István nézetei a nevelésről* (Count Stephen Széchenyi's Views on Education) (Budapest: 1904); *id.*, "Széchenyi és a magyar nevelés jövője" (Széchenyi and the Future of Hungarian Education), in *Széchenyi eszmevilága* (Széchenyi's World of Ideas), 3 vols. (Budapest: Franklin, 1912–14), II, 36–64.

Kornis,[162] Széchenyi's standpoint in *A kelet népe* and the following debate with Kossuth, Eötvös, and Vörösmarty, was "a historical paradox," because he, the conservative, wanted to give the people political rights first and then educate them. Compared to Széchenyi's earlier liberal views on education, this contradiction appears as one of the signs of a change which occurred in his thinking, as well as in the conditions of Hungary in the 1830's.

After the preceding years of confusion, from the end of 1818 on Széchenyi seems to have overcome his moral crisis, and to have found a direction for his life. Relapses were to occur again, as when he again wanted to marry Selina on returning from the Orient. But his doubts and frustrations could do less harm henceforth, since his whole outlook had become more ethical and mature. Seeking to establish his personal moral independence, he sometimes rejected views formerly accepted without criticism; at the same time, he managed to get rid of his previous self-centered way of thinking. His feeling of responsibility increased, and repenting his former laxity he began to think about his duties toward others.

Paralleling his ethical development, and to a great extent influenced by it, went a certain religious conversion. After a long interruption, he went to church again. He confessed and received Holy Communion in Sicily before Easter in April 1819.[163] In addition to performing certain formal actions essential to the Catholic faith, he made an effort to clarify for himself his own religious beliefs. Tormented by self-accusations because of his past and trying to size up the problems of good and evil and their influence on man,[164] he necessarily had to determine the role of religion in the perfection of human beings since, from the point of view of the believer, man's perfection or deterioration depended on his approach to or departure from God.[165] Viewed in this light, Széchenyi's entire philosophy of life and whole activity as a reformer was a religious and Christian belief in the perfectibility of man.[166] But the use of the term "conversion" in characterizing Széchenyi's religious attitude around 1818–19 must be qualified. First, Széchenyi had never been a renegade and never intended to leave the Catholic Church; hence his conversion was not a new start but rather a revival of his religious feelings after

[162] Kornis, *Magyar művelődés*, 1, 526–32; *id.*, *A magyar politika hősei* (Heroes of Hungarian Politics) (Budapest: Franklin, 1940), pp. 135f.

[163] Nov. 29, 1818, Apr. 14, 19–21, 1819, Viszota, ed., *Naplók*, 1, 441, 551, 558f.

[164] See the lengthy philosophical dispute with his friend, Sir Robert Gordon, secretary of the British legation in Vienna. Nov. 1819, *ibid.*, 1, 712–15. Cf. Aug. 3, 1819, *ibid.*, 1, 679f.

[165] Philosophical notes, Notebook II. 3, Annex IX. *Ibid.*, 1, 854f. (probably from 1819).

[166] Gyula Szekfű, *Három nemzedék* (Three Generations), 2d edn. (Budapest: 1922), pp. 104f.

a period of indifference and cynicism. Second, even after his conversion, he never became a bigot like his father; his Catholicism was never dogmatic, continued to be colored by deistic and enlightened ideas and even contained a touch of relativity. His approach to religion as an essential human and social problem, although not completely unbiased or always consistent, was basically realistic: he tried to steer a middle course between some extreme views of the official Church and intransigent Protestantism which automatically opposed everything Catholic. He dooked at his own church with critical eyes, preferring the "active citizen" to the priest; he believed everyone should have a religion but should stay in the one in which he had been born.[167]

This did not mean, however, that Széchenyi looked at the problem of religion with indifference or a spirit of complacent appeasement. He was a modern man; his attitude toward religion as a phenomenon of society became pluralistic and tolerant. As far as religion as a private affair was concerned, his personal religious experience was highly dynamic and meaningful. Not unlike great religious thinkers, he also felt that man had to take sides in the worldwide struggle of good and evil. This struggle for the individual's moral independence and freedom[168] was the more dramatic because Széchenyi's comprehension of the relationship of sin and atonement was rather un-Catholic. He never really understood or identified himself completely with the Catholic Church's teaching about divine mercy; believing instead that once man had done wrong, charity was unable to whitewash him—he had to cleanse himself.[169] This sense of personal responsibility for one's deeds was particularly painful to Széchenyi from the late 1840s on, when his mind gradually gave way under the pressure of unresolved guilt feelings for his past actions, both personal and public.

His efforts to achieve the "inner silence" and contentment and balanced harmony (*Harmonisches Sein*), coupled with the doubts and phantoms he faced whenever he "waged a look into his soul" as few people did,[170] are reflected in the diary entry for April 19, 1819. Having brooded fairly long over God, soul, immortality, he wrote after his Easter confession on "this remarkable day," he decided after much hesitation that, given the awareness of our ignorance in these matters, all religions are good if we do not permit ourselves to be misled in our actions and principles by illusions, fallacies, and sophisms, and instead follow the

---

[167] June 26–30, 1819, Viszota, ed., *Naplók*, I, 646. Cf. May, July 27, and Nov. 1819, *ibid.*, I, 613, 637, 622, 700f.
[168] Nov. 5, 1819, *ibid.*, I, 693f.
[169] Apr. 4, 1819, *ibid.*, I, 564.
[170] Apr. 4, 7, 1819, *ibid.*, I, 565f., 574.

voice which never conceals the truth and never speaks to us in flattering terms. Unless his head and heart had been confused and bewildered by training and [adverse] example, which seldom happens, man naturally knows whether his actions are good or bad. All honest men, Széchenyi suggested, can get together "in the religion of their heart and soul"; only the forms in which they worship God, abandon themselves to His mercy, and endeavor to save their soul for the other world are different.

Only the painful vibration of the introductory remarks betrayed that there was something more behind the intentionally "objective" tone of the treatise to come. Soon, however, the wisdom of Rousseau and *Nathan der Weise* was abandoned, and behind the surface of enlightened balance, there was revealed the irrational and desperate isolation of a modern being. After a reference to the Turks whose devout prayers at daybreak were so frequently edifying, Széchenyi's tone changed. All people in the world, he thought, have a religion because being entirely in the dark, they all press for the light. *People are locked up in catacombs; everybody is looking for a way out, but there is none. Who can find the best path? People go astray and search in anguish until at long last the roof crumbles of itself. All our religions are like that and not a single one of them is good. The greatest ordeal which we have to undergo in this life consists of the fact that we cannot know anything and have to remain in eternal doubt. Could it be that life is only an apprenticeship leading toward greater perfection which is going to enable us to know how to love and honor God and how to show Him our gratitude? "But how can our dirty soul, this wavering heart honor and love the Almighty? Why, there are so few people who really and truly know how to love and honor their nearest of kin!" Is it not moving to see that members of the human race on trial are so blind as to condemn one another mutually and to persecute each other because of their religion? And that many who have never done anything wrong in their lives and have always fought against their weaknesses despair of a happier future life and believe they have been condemned for eternity? EVERYTHING IS EVIL AT THE BEGINNING OF EXISTENCE, but can this prevail against God? Does any one believe in this if he is to comprehend the harmony of the universe? Every man can understand that much.* According to his present concepts, continued Széchenyi, he himself had no education at all except for the example given by his parents. His youth was spent in ignorance and indolence yet he was not base and entirely depraved; man can hardly reach that stage. But he was not awake to many of his faults and so he acted more cruelly than bloodthirsty animals who tear to pieces their ilk only to feed or defend themselves—whereas he has ruined in good conscience the earthly happiness of a dear being who loved him. He got used to suppressing all pure sentiments and natural kindness to the extent that he was willing to sacrifice the holiest and dearest feelings of a human being to his youthful vanity and pride. He did not know how he managed to come out of this condition; but it was true that he woke up as soon as he had ventured to wage a look into his soul.

Following such bitter self-accusations motivated by his heartless attitude toward Caroline and his ambitions, self-centered vanity, Széchenyi concluded that the performance of certain religious ceremonial actions was essential to find contentment, since, as he put it, even sun worshippers had to adore a symbol to satisfy their imaginations. Hence he saw the meaning of auricular confession in its humiliating effect on man, for, as he interpreted it, self-humiliation was the victory of self-control and will power, particularly if sincere confession was made (as had been his case) to a depraved priest. But even in the deep self-imposed humiliation of his mind, Széchenyi was left unsatisfied with the form of penance meted out by the Sicilian priest: how could a few *thalers,* and the *dry* [!] recitation of five Lord's Prayers and Ave Marias give absolution for all his sins?! His "inner voice" knew better. Still, he was elated and felt like soaring upward to God. Henceforth, he vowed, he was going to observe the practices of his church; as for his views on God and man's future, he thought of them as of the views of a man prepared to die and not acting like a *Betbruder,* a praying friar.[171]

Thus in the strict theological sense of the word, Széchenyi did not undergo a conversion. He was in no mortal sin and did not have to expiate it; neither did he accept without question or reservation all the doctrinal teachings of his faith henceforth. But if we use the term "conversion" in a broader sense, indicating simply a process of cleansing and religious rebirth then we are not far from the truth, for during his Oriental trip Széchenyi passed through the deepest religious experience of his life. Henceforward, he was not immune to moral crises either; but the roots of his faith and his belief in transcendental values remained essentially unshaken.[172]

[171] Apr. 19, 1819, *ibid.*, I, 591–96 (italics Széchenyi's).

[172] For a detailed and well-documented, modern Catholic interpretation of Széchenyi's religious development in this period, see Fekete, *Széchenyi vallásossága*, Chs. IV–V, pp. 76–115. Fekete called Széchenyi's religious "conversion" a romantic Catholic experience *par excellence* (p. 115); he also pointed out that a tendency for spiritual restoration and striving for "inner silence" in post-Napoleonic Vienna and that, somewhat later, the reading of Lamennais, may have influenced Széchenyi's ethical rejuvenation and religious development. Cf. Ottokár Prohászka, "Gróf Széchenyi István vallásossága" (Count Stephen Széchenyi's Religiousness), *Széchenyi eszmevilága*, I, 48–66.

CHAPTER IV

The Choice of Hercules

The years between Széchenyi's "Oriental trip" (a term referring to the Balkans and Asia Minor, in vogue at the time) and his first appearance at the Hungarian Diet of 1825 are characterized by a peculiar duality. On the surface, he was still the somewhat eccentric dandy whom all Vienna, foreign rulers as well as his own sovereign, knew only as "Stefferl."[1] In February 1822 the Countess John Keglevich, née Countess Adelaide Zichy, recorded how "Stefferl Széchenyi gave an excellent and well-arranged dinner-party" to a select group in Vienna. She wrote: "He lives in the Jägerzeile whither he moved from the Zittiry House after his father's death. His flat is homelike, beautifully furnished and exceedingly diverting. One might imagine it to be the storeroom of some merchant in which wares from all parts of the world have been assembled. We did not have time to get a good look at everything."[2] But behind the bushy eyebrows and domed forehead of the *Amerikaner* who suffered from "anglomania" and looked so different to many Viennese socialites,[3] there were but very few really eccentric thoughts to the careful observer.

Széchenyi returned from his Oriental trip with the desire to do something for his fatherland and fellow men. In subsequent years a sequence of unforeseen events focused his attention more and more intensely on the problems of Hungary.

Four main trends are discernible in the process of transforming the *quasi Österreicher,* as he called himself in 1822,[4] into the Hungarian patriot of 1825 who endeavored to brush up on the long forgotten Magyar of his childhood and claimed to have a better insight into Hungarian conditions than Metternich, his benefactor until then. First, his

[1] Mar. 4, 1822, Dec. 8, 1825, Viszota, ed., *Naplók,* II, 250, 659.
[2] Cited by Östör, "Széchenyi and Women," p. 493.
[3] E.g., Feb. 7, Mar. 6, 1821, Viszota, ed., *Naplók,* II, 127, 135.
[4] Travelling through Ulm he recalled the Austrian defeat by Napoleon, saying, "What a reminiscence for a quasi-Austrian!" Mar. 7, 1822, *ibid.,* II, 253.

acquaintance and friendship with Baron Nicholas Wesselényi opened new vistas to Széchenyi's understanding of Hungarian affairs. Second, in 1823 there was the immediate experience of a nationwide conflict between the crown and the Hungarian constitutional party. Then, in mid-1824 he fell in love with the wife of Count Charles Zichy, née Countess Crescence Seilern, a love which inspired him to stay in Hungary and devote his energy to awakening the nation. Finally, during the Diet of 1825–27 he suddenly took upon himself the political, moral, and financial responsibilities which introduced him to the Hungarian public as the new leader of liberal reform in Hungary. It will be the chief task of this chapter to examine these factors in Széchenyi's development. Before turning to this analysis, however, a few words should be said about Széchenyi's personal circumstances in the period we are concerned with.

The psychological and moral anguish referred to previously continued to torment his soul. Caroline died in September 1820, and in December Francis Széchenyi passed away; in November of the following year Gabriella's death shook him, and in January 1824 his mother died. Besides losing the persons who had been so dear to him, Széchenyi's plans to solve some of his problems through a suitable marriage had also failed to materialize. Not before January 1821 did he completely give up the idea of marrying Caroline's sister, Selina O'Meade.[5] From the end of the same year until about February 1824 he had repeatedly sought the hand of Princess Henriette Liechtenstein who preferred, however, another suitor.[6] Along with "being in love" with Henriette, he was also being looked upon as a possible match for Melanie Zichy-Ferraris, granddaughter of Minister Charles Zichy; but in this case it was Széchenyi who was unable to make up his mind.[7] His reputation, so badly hurt by the Caroline affair, was hardly improved by his inconstancy with other women.[8] No wonder that after a number of failures he thought of completely abandoning his marriage plans, recalling also his mother's prediction made when he was 12 years old that he would never be able to marry.[9]

---

[5] Jan. 12, 1821, *ibid.*, II, 114. Cf. Mar. 3, 1821, *ibid.*, II, 134.

[6] Dec. 2, 1821, Jan. 18, Oct. 28, 1822; Jan. 5, Feb. 14, 19, 20, 1824, *ibid.*, II, 227, 236, 441, 459ff.

[7] Oct. 17, Dec. 2, 1821; Oct. 31, Nov. 13, Dec. 18, 1825, *ibid.*, II, 212f., 227ff., 640, 648, 663. Melanie became the wife of Metternich in 1831.

[8] See Jan. 4, 28, Nov. 18, 1823, *ibid.*, II, 321, 327, 417. Also, his mother's fear of a second Caroline case, Feb. 9, 1823, and Princess (John) Liechtenstein's remark, Jan. 19, 1824, *ibid.*, II, 331, 447.

[9] July 1819, Jan. 18, Dec. 7, 1823, Feb. 14, 1824, *ibid.*, I, 652, II, 324, 423, 458. It seems as if there was a strong tendency on the part of Széchenyi's mother to dominate

Actually, in 1823 Liebenberg advised him to remain single because of his financial situation.[10] Even more depressing from Széchenyi's point of view seemed to have been the impossibility of advancing his military career. Having spent about a year in Vienna after his return from the Orient, he was ordered to join his regiment stationed in Hungary in June 1820. The death of his sister-in-law and of his father, however, made it possible for him to get another leave. Using his connections in Vienna, he repeatedly asked for promotion, and also made several futile efforts to buy the right of promotion from senior officers. The empty promises received from officials, conditions within the army itself,[11] and the necessity of spending a certain amount of time with his military unit in backward Hungary tended to build up new pressures—and, as stated earlier, the suspicion that his promotion may have been denied because of his being a Hungarian continued to linger in his mind.[12] Still, he was unable to take the decisive step for a number of years, partly for reasons of honor as well as ambition. He liked to believe those who predicted that "he was to play a role in Europe,"[13] but was too much of a soldier to admit that this role could be promoted by taking off his uniform once and for all. His immediate plans, nonetheless, pointed far beyond the sphere of a military career. Before rejoining his regiment in Bihar county in December 1820 he outlined a project for five months. It included the intention to arrange his travel notes on Greece, to translate Byron's Childe Harold and finish his own novel, to explore the possibility of coordinating the perfection of the soul with wordly wisdom, to write about horse-breeding and guerrilla warfare, to draw up comprehensive reforms for Austria and a plan for education. Besides, he wanted to read Homer and concentrate *entirely* (italics Széchenyi's) on Hungary's history and law system.[14] Obviously, few items of the ambitious plan were completed.[15] But the scope of the work to

---

the emotions of her youngest son. This, in turn, may have influenced the latter to prove himself as a *séducteur*.

[10] July 16, 1823, *ibid.*, II, 387.

[11] Aug. 9, 1820, July 6, 1821, *ibid.*, II, 56f., 171.

[12] Mar. 19, Oct. 18, 1823, Jan. 5, 9, Oct. 14, 1824, Sept. 11, 1825, *ibid.*, II, 348, 408f., 442f., 516, 603.

[13] Dec. 16, 1823, *ibid.*, II, 429.

[14] Dec. 3, 1820, *ibid.*, II, 91f.

[15] Fragments of the description of his journey in Greece, of his ideas about the perfection of the soul, his thoughts about education and his novel are extant in Vol. I of the diaries and have been referred to in the preceding chapter of this study. Instead of a treatise on horse-breeding, Széchenyi wrote a petition on the subject to the emperor and published, in German and Hungarian, a draft project of rules for the horse races to be introduced in Hungary. In addition to this opuscule published in Debrecen (1821), he published a 15-page pamphlet about fox hunting in Ödenburg (1823). These were his first works in print. For a short summary of Széchenyi's literary activity from 1820 to 1825 see Viszota, *ibid.*, II, pp. cxlix f.

be undertaken showed the rather divergent directions of Széchenyi's interest, the latecomer's haste with which he wanted to learn and do everything at once, and also his indecision about which way to turn first.

One interesting aspect of the plan was that it reaffirmed Széchenyi's intention to make a thorough study of Hungarian history and law and revealed his interest in an overall reform program for Austria. He worked hard in subsequent years to broaden his knowledge of Hungarian private and public law as well as constitutional development. But even while attempting to get acquainted with the Hungarian feudal constitution his approach continued to be comparative. This can be seen from the fact that in June–August 1823 he translated the first eight chapters of the work by Jean Louis Delolme, *The Constitution of England*. He thus coupled an intensive study of Hungarian constitutional law with a concentrated effort to absorb the "British political Bible."[16] Like the *oeuvre* of that other Genevese, Rousseau, whose complete works he inherited from his father and whose ideas he held to be more dangerous than useful, the gospel of English constitutionalism also exerted a powerful influence on Széchenyi's attitude toward feudal practices in Hungary.

Széchenyi never went beyond dropping a few scattered remarks about the necessity of reform in Austria, but even those he did make show two essential features of his evolution as a reformer. They suggested that the point of departure of Széchenyi's whole reform program for Hungary was Hungary's organic connection with Austria, and that in the development of his own thinking, reform came first and nationality merely followed suit. It is interesting that while Széchenyi never for a moment wavered from his idea of building all his subsequent reform plans for Hungary *only* upon his original starting point, that is, on the constitutional basis of the Pragmatic Sanction,[17] in time he would gradually shift the emphasis from the problem of reform to the need of maintaining Hungarian nationality. The development of an enlightened cosmopolite, who vaguely felt that *something* had to be done to improve the international status and domestic conditions of his native Austria and, *within* it, Hungary,[18] into a liberal reformer who wanted

---

[16] For Delolme see Palmer, *Age of the Democratic Revolution*, I, 135f., 145–48. Széchenyi's translation is in Annex No. I, p. 1 of Viszota, ed., *Naplók*, III, 383–442.

[17] Feb. 27, 1823, Sept. 28, 1825, and Fall 1826, *ibid.*, II, 339, 617, and Annex No. XIV, 729.

[18] In January 1821 Széchenyi indicated his willingness to give a year's income for the construction of a bridge between Pest and Buda. The idea of offering a whole year's income for the benefit of the public was to be put into practice in 1825, at the time of the founding of the Academy with the definite aim of promoting Hungarian cultural life. Also, some 15 to 20 years later the realization of the bridge between Buda and Pest, Széchenyi's pet project, was to become the symbol of far-reaching constitutional developments. No such afterthoughts were linked, however, to his enthusiasm

to rejuvenate primarily Magyar nationality and thus broaden the traditional concept of the Hungarian nation through economic and social reforms, was the work of the subtle interaction of a number of factors during the 1820s.

A certain trend in Széchenyi's interests is remarkable in the rapidly growing list of the books he read. Until about 1821 belles lettres, travelogues, and memoirs prevailed; from this point on, however, his interest seems to have shifted from literature to history, philosophy, politics, constitutional law, and economics. Out of the approximately 120 books he read in 1823–25 less than a score were literary works. In addition to Voltaire and Rousseau he was particularly impressed by Montaigne and Franklin.[19] Surmising that his efforts to write poetry or novels were doomed to failure, he felt a strong need to organize his practical experiences, impressions, and spontaneous ideas into some kind of a coherent whole. Besides Széchenyi the patriot, Széchenyi the politician and economist was born in this period of his life.

The process of this threefold birth was not smooth or completely conscious. Széchenyi was aware only of the difficulties of discovering his true calling in life. When analyzing his indecision and hesitations he would sometimes bitterly ridicule himself, saying that he wanted to be a famous soldier and a world traveller, to marry and devote himself to social life, to stay a bachelor and raise horses, to enter the diplomatic service and enjoy his independence leisurely in Switzerland, France, England and Italy; to become the leader of a party, dedicating himself entirely to constitutional law, and to write poems and tragedies—all this, he noted, he wanted to accomplish at the same time and at the age of 29.[20]

On other occasions he prayed devoutly for divine guidance, for inward consolation, silent calmness of the soul, purification from prejudices, and a heart full of unlimited indulgence and love for mankind.[21] These poetic prayers showed profound repentance for the follies of his youth and expressed a desire to revive the ideals of his earlier religious education. He made a vow to visit the shrine at Mariazell in Austria, but his views on religion remained pluralistic and the language of his prayers

---

in 1821: seeing what appeared to him the right solution in a certain situation and having also the necessary means for it, he simply offered them—to help his country! Jan. 4, 1821, *ibid.*, II, 108.

[19] Apr. 21, 1821, Jan. 24, Sept. 29, 1823, Aug. 4, 1825, *ibid.*, II, 152, 325, 404, 573. For a complete list of readings in the period in question, *ibid.*, II, 804–808. Cf. Padányi, *Széchenyi kulturája*, 147–53.

[20] Mar. 27, 1821, *ibid.*, II, 143f.

[21] Dec. 26, 1820, *ibid.*, II, 104. Cf. Mar. 21, 1821 and July 28, 1823, *ibid.*, II, 143, 392f. and Annex No. II, 2, *ibid.*, III, 442f.

reflected the influence of the writers of the Enlightenment and of the "enlightened" clergy.[22]

Many of Széchenyi's prayers and religious qualms bore the imprint of his guilt complex and were more or less connected with his neurosis.[23] Likewise, his development as a Hungarian patriot reflected inner conflicts and tensions. Resenting that he had to leave his beloved Vienna, he joined his regiment in Hungary in the early 1820's almost with a feeling of going into exile. His own Hungarian was bad, but he was shocked that ladies did not speak their mother tongue, and that noblemen were surprised if he went to see them on horseback.[24] He disliked the manners and boorishness of Hungarians, too,[25] and decided that Hungary was a backward, old, and dying country, a "land of vice," without civilization, patriotic feeling, and perhaps even without the hope for resurrection from its agony.[26] He could understand those who would prefer suicide to life in this "pitiful land," in "a desert like this," or would "hate, despise, or persecute" its people if they themselves were not related and bound by the ties of affection to it—as he was.[27]

In spite of these premises he fell in love with the country and its people. This love was a sentimental and irrational affair, to be sure—at least in the beginning: he felt like crying while listening to the music

[22] July 12, 1821, *ibid.*, II, 179. In subsequent years Széchenyi's thinking about religion was influenced by the sermons and works of the great "enlightened" Catholic preacher, Stanislaus Albach. Fekete, *Széchenyi vallásossága*, esp. pp. 43–56, 170–77. For the impact of Josephinism on the clergy see also Meszlényi, *A Jozefinizmus kora*, pp. 88–94.

[23] Széchenyi's overactive imagination, suicidal thoughts, and hypochondria (aggravating his real illnesses) were symptoms of a neurotic condition accompanying him since early childhood. Széchenyi biographies and particularly the works dealing with the last (Döbling) period of his life, stress the importance of this circumstance. See, e.g., Dávid Angyal, "The Closing Years of Count Stephen Széchenyi's Life," *The Oxford Hungarian Review* (November 1922), pp. 269–83; Gyula Viszota, "Széchenyi utolsó négy éve Döblingben" (Széchenyi's Last Four Years in Döbling), Reprint from *Budapesti Szemle* (1934, No. 682); and the series of studies on Széchenyi done in the 1920s and 30s by Charles Schaffer, Professor of Psychiatry at the University of Budapest. According to Schaffer, whose interpretation concerning Széchenyi's psychical frame of mind was also shared by Julius Szekfű (*A mai Széchenyi*, p. 483), Széchenyi was "oversensitive" and *déséquilibré*, his frame of mind being characterized by "exaggerated lability" (Károly Schaffer, "Gróf Széchenyi István lelkivilága orvoslélektani szempontból" (Count Stephen Széchenyi's Inner World from the Point of View of Medical Psychology), *Magyar Szemle*, XVIII (1933), 303f.) and his insanity from 1848 to 1856 was "only a transitory episode" and a "consequence of the depraving effect of *external events*." (*id.*, "Az idős Széchenyi idegállapota" [Old Széchenyi's Nervous Condition], *id.*, XXVI [1936], 243, 247 [italics in original.])

[24] June 1820, Viszota, ed., *Naplók*, II, 41ff.

[25] June 6, July 24, Sept. 14, 25, 1820, Jan. 1, 1821, *ibid.*, II, 37, 39, 54, 68, 72, 107.

[26] July 12, 24, Sept. 14, Dec. 8, 14, 1820, Jan. 1, May 15, June 22, July 16, 24, 28, Nov. 14, 1821, Jan. 19, Nov. 15, 1822, *ibid.*, II, 46, 53, 67f., 92f., 97, 103, 108, 160, 166, 182, 195, 197, 220, 234–37, 315.

[27] Dec. 8, 1820, *ibid.*, II, 93.

of a violin, zither, or simple bagpipe. He became fond of the Magyar tongue which he regarded as the conserving force of Magyar nationality, and his imagination became inspired at the majestic sight of the Hungarian *puszta* well before the poets Nikolaus Lenau and Alexander Petőfi had introduced it into German and Hungarian literature.[28] He also came to like the peasants. Dropping in on a session of a manorial court, he became most indignant that while the noblemen liked to compare their constitutional freedom with that of the English, they completely forgot about the serf. He, however, was attracted by the "coarse folk." Basically he was fond of them, wanted to teach and elevate them to the dignity of mankind, but in the next moment abhorred and repudiated them. Moved by their ignorance, he felt like sacrificing himself for them and like sharing their fate; yet he was often horrified by their unjust blindness, pride and self-conceit.[29]

This ambiguous love-hate attitude was typical of Széchenyi's patriotism: from one extreme to the other. Sometimes he hoped that despite the signs of decline peoples were able to make the greatest efforts under the threat of completely forfeiting their liberty; on other occasions he thought that the alien population of Hungary was increasing every year while the native Magyar stock was becoming almost sterile and that the nobility was ailing both morally and physically.[30] On the title page of one of the notebooks he exclaimed: "Hungary is hardly taken into account among the nations."[31] Széchenyi had ceased to be an indifferent visitor. Yet while he became increasingly attached to Hungary, in moments of depression he also kept on planning to emigrate to France, Columbia, or, most frequently, the United States.[32]

As can be seen from previous references and Széchenyi's subsequent writings, his thinking was not free from racist considerations. He realized early that there were national tensions even in leading circles of the Monarchy among Germans, Czechs, and Hungarians, and he himself was not unprejudiced.[33] But he also noticed that the split of Hungarian society along religious and social lines was just as bad as the jealousy among the different nationalities, especially if one added the problem of the peasant.[34] Referring to the constitutional theory that in Hungary

[28] Aug. 9, Dec. 27, 1820, *ibid.*, II, 54, 105.

[29] Dec. 24, 1820, *ibid.*, II, 101f.

[30] Dec. 25, 1820, Apr. 28, 1821, *ibid.*, II, 103, 156.

[31] Mar. 1, 1822, *ibid.*, II, 247 and n. 4.

[32] E.g., Jan. 15, Mar. 3, Oct. 8, 1821, Jan. 14, Oct. 7, 1822, Feb. 9, 24, 1823, Mar. 21, 1824, *ibid.*, II, 119, 134, 209f., 235, 308, 332, 337, 470. His entry of July 1, 1821 (II, 169) shows clearly the emotional connection between conditions in Hungary and his plans to emigrate.

[33] Nov. 5–6, 1820, Spring and July 4, 1821, *ibid.*, II, 79, 170 and 674. (Annex No. II: "*Die Böhmen wachsen uns über den Kopf.*")

[34] Feb. 13, 1822, *ibid.*, II, 244.

peasants were represented by noblemen, Széchenyi said, "The wolf protects the lamb."[35] He held cherished Hungarian constitutional liberties as rather questionable values precisely because he was sympathetic toward the situation of the peasant.[36]

Some writers have tried to draw a sharp line between Széchenyi's plans for reform and the ideas of the Enlightenment in general, and the French Revolution in particular. It has been suggested, that Széchenyi's precursors attacked Hungarian feudal institutions in the name of human rights, equality, and liberty, while according to Széchenyi's point of departure, it was the interests of the Hungarian "race" that demanded the abolition of feudalism.[37] This school of thought prevailed in Hungarian Széchenyi interpretations up to the most recent times.[38] Its extremist disciples, as it were, have made of Széchenyi a pioneer of Hungarian racism.

Nothing could be more inaccurate. Széchenyi was an enlightened reformer, at least in the first part of his career. Reluctantly and almost in spite of himself he approached Hungarian reality with Western standards, following English constitutional liberalism and French enlightened ideals. He considered himself liberal and enlightened, and it was as a liberal and enlightened patriot that he first appeared in Hungarian political life. He was heavily influenced by contemporary romantic thought, and "romantic" elements played an essential role in shaping his patriotic feelings. But it is an oversimplification to claim that whenever the principles of nationality and liberalism clashed, Széchenyi *always* sacrificed (to use Kemény's language) without hesitation the interests of liberty and progress to those of his affection for his race.[39] To separate "affection

[35] Jan. 18, 1822, *ibid.*, II, 236. Cf. Apr. 29 and July 28, 1821, *ibid.*, II, 157, 198.

[36] Apr. 9, 1823, *ibid.*, II, 353. Cf. June 2, 1823, *ibid.*, II, 373.

[37] Béla Grünwald, *Az uj Magyarország. Gróf Széchenyi István* (New Hungary. Count Stephen Széchenyi) (Budapest: Franklin, 1890), p. 399.

[38] From Sigismund Kemény to and including Julius Szekfű. Szekfű, for example, compiled a list of "racial sins" based on Széchenyi quotations in *Három nemzedék*, pp. 59–68; cf. Bálint Hóman and Gyula Szekfű, *Magyar Történet* (History of Hungary), 2d edn., 5 vols. (Budapest: Kir. Magyar Egyetemi Nyomda, 1935–36), v, 260f. Jászi, in his justifiable criticism of Szekfű's "interpretation" of the liberal era (Oscar Jászi, *The Dissolution of the Habsburg Monarchy* [Chicago: 1929], p. 239 and n. 10), forgot to mention that in this "interpretation" Szekfű abused Széchenyi. Besides making some valuable contributions to modern Széchenyi research, Szekfű was occasionally carried away by his desire to present his theses according to present-day necessities. Sometimes he made almost incredible statements, like this one: "Scientific research has finally proved [?] that Széchenyi had been almost under no influence of foreign political writers." *Három nemzedék*, p. 58.

[39] Zsigmond Kemény, *Emlékirat 1849-ből* (Memorial from 1849) as cited in János Török, ed., *Gróf Széchenyi István politikai iskolája, saját műveiből összeállitva* (Count Stephen Széchenyi's Political School, Compiled from His Own Works), 3 vols. (Pest: Heckenast, 1864), III, 330 (italics added).

for one's own race" from the concept of "love of fatherland," and to match against each other the ideas of political liberty, of intellectual and economic progress, as well as nationality, is highly unromantic, although the effort may be justified both from a logical point of view and in certain historical constellations. At the time of Széchenyi's emergence as a political figure in Hungarian history, however, such an approach would only be an artificial abstraction from the given historical situation; instead of explaining, it would only confuse.

Széchenyi was an enlightened liberal and liberal nationalist in the 1820s, a circumstance obscured a century later when it became fashionable in Hungary to discredit everything connected with liberalism. His romantic patriotism was not a negation of but an addition to his enlightened liberal Christian background, as indicated by his great romantic vision of saving a nation for mankind and thus fulfilling his duty toward God and his fellow men.[40] It can be said that mainly from the 1830s on, he became more of a Hungarian nationalist than a progressive liberal; but then in the 40s, when he turned more conservative toward social reform, he also grew more cautious and "progressive" with regard to the nationality problem. His great personal tragedy of trying to reconcile the ideas of the *Gesamtmonarchie* and full development of Magyar nationality also point to the fact that the glorification of the "Magyar race" was never to him an end in itself.

Széchenyi was not against mixing and assimilation of "races."[41] His approach to the problem was pragmatic, preferring practicability to rash action and doctrinal extremes, and to err rather on the side of caution— an attitude, generally speaking, characteristic of him in all spheres of his public activity.[42]

A moderate and middle-of-the-roader in politics from the very beginning, Széchenyi nevertheless resented the spirit and system of the Holy Alliance. His sympathy lay with the oppressed peoples of Europe, with the Greeks and Poles, and he supported the cause of liberal constitu-

---

[40] Széchenyi was not unique in this respect. In the writings of Herder and Rousseau and later Mazzini, elements of Christian romanticism and enlightened rationalism mingled with ideas of liberal nationalism. For this aspect of Széchenyi's intellectual make-up see Dávid Angyal, "Les idées historiques du comte Etienne Széchenyi," *Revue de Hongrie*, III (1909), 534–37 and IV (1909), 14–17; Gyula Kornis, *A magyar politika hősei*, pp. 131–38.

[41] July 23, 1825, Viszota, ed., *Naplók*, II, 557. Even when he made critical remarks concerning the early Hungarian kings' efforts to infuse foreign blood into the weak Hungarian body, Széchenyi's attitude was moderate and not "isolationist," or racist. Cf. *Politikai programtöredékek* (Fragments of a Political Program), in Viszota, ed., *Széchenyi és Kossuth*, II, 731.

[42] July 4, 1823, Viszota, ed., *Naplók*, II, 383, "Man muss in der Welt Hammer seyn, oder Amboss. Ich bin das Letztere," a remark mirroring both his insight into the realities of politics and the awareness of his own limitations as a political leader.

tionalist movements in Italy and Spain, occasionally even expressing anti-royalist sentiments.[43] Upon the condemnation of Count Confalonieri, leader of the Carbonaris in Milan in 1823, he exclaimed: "A martyr of the people! What a disgrace to the Holy Alliance!" The following day, his mother, discussing his plan to resign his military commission, asked him "only not to talk." In answer to the warning, Széchenyi promised to stay "passive and neutral," because there were "too many traitors and weak people in Hungary" and he would hate to see his "oppressors" triumph.[44]

Somewhat earlier, in July 1821, he made a three-week trip to Transylvania. Officially he was in charge of buying horses for his regiment; unofficially he found a pretext to go for another leave and try to collect information about the fate of the anti-Turkish uprising led by Prince Ypsilanti.[45] On his tour of Transylvania, a world unto itself, (due to its traditions of independence and administrative autonomy, maintained even after the principality had come under Habsburg rule at the end of the seventeenth century), he strengthened his friendship with Baron Nicholas Wesselényi whom he had met a year before in Debrecen. At the time Széchenyi thought he had gained much through this new acquaintance.[46]

The friendship, from which both Széchenyi and Wesselényi profited, made history in Hungary. Wesselényi was Széchenyi's junior by five years. At the time of their acquaintance, he had been the recognized leader of the opposition in the Transylvanian Diet. He understood Hungarian and Transylvanian political life much better than did Széchenyi who some 20 years later tried to recapture the warmth of that first political impulse received from the estranged friend:

I had first met Wesselényi twenty-three years ago in Debreczen. I was fascinated by his ardent patriotism, lofty ideas, and a certain charm of his which affected so many of us. Since with each passing day my heart had become more and more convinced that man's worth

---

[43] July 24, 1820, Feb. 6, 22, Mar. 6, 7, 17, 18, Apr. 2, 3, June 21, 1821, Jan. 13, 1822, Jan. 28, Mar. 15, Apr. 16, July 5, 9, 19, 1823, Jan. 6, Aug. 11, 12, 13, 16, Sept. 28, 1825, *ibid.*, II, 54, 126, 129f., 136–39, 141f., 147f., 166, 234, 327, 347, 355, 384f., 388, 522, 580, 583–86, 618.

[44] Dec. 27, 28, 1823, *ibid.*, II, 434.

[45] *Ibid.*, II, pp. xviii–xxii, cxvii. Concerning his indignation at the treatment of Ypsilanti and his troops, see July 20–24, 1821, *ibid.*, II, 186–95. These entries again indicated both his awareness of the European importance of the Eastern Question and his anxiety that Hungary might get involved in a general conflict in which she would lose her constitution and go completely bankrupt.

[46] Széchenyi to Wesselényi and to the Baroness Wesselényi, Aug. 1, 1821, *ibid.*, II, 198; Sept. 15, 30, 1821, Majláth, ed., *Levelek*, I, 70–73.

should be measured exclusively by his usefulness to fellow men, to the fatherland, and hence to all humanity, Wesselényi, too, felt drawn towards me. A reason for this may also have been the fact that after my numerous travels and experiences, I did not shape my opinions from a vulgar standpoint either. It so happened that very soon we were linked together by the chain of the most sincere friendship and the most tender appreciation; as for myself, this chain has never been weakened. We both were ashamed of the depraved condition of our fatherland and of the backwardness of our race. We both felt an indescribable desire to contribute at least a tiny bit to the nursing of our fatherland and people. I said "nursing," because at the time of our friendship's birth, it was only the "saving" and not the elevation or glorification of our race that had become the order of the day—

. . . Together we traveled through great parts of Germany, France, and England. My knowledge and views were broadened, and I may add that even my soul was widened through the day-to-day contact with the noblest and most faithful mind; I acknowledge this with a feeling of gratefulness never to be altered. I trust—at least my conscience ventures to console me—that Wesselényi did not become a worse man either through my acquaintance and in my company. O! what exciting moments we had lived together when, filled with painful longing, we were sometimes struck by a glimmer of hope suggesting that perhaps we Hungarians would not become the only exiles of civilization and for us, too, the day would come when, displaying our peculiar substance, we also would place ourselves, in a modest way though but still with dignity, into the halo of glory of civilized nations.[47]

Concerning the same period, Wesselényi was somewhat less charitable toward his friend. Acknowledging Széchenyi's wide European horizon and the English lessons he received from him, he pointed out to Sigismund Kemény that early in their acquaintance Széchenyi's thoroughgoing knowledge was restricted to literature, that he had given but few thoughts to politics, that his Magyar was very poor, and that he had no faith in Hungary's future. Adding that Széchenyi, like his father, was a religious enthusiast, Wesselényi felt that he was the one who had aroused Széchenyi's patriotic feelings.[48]

---

[47] Széchenyi, "Wesselényi és Kossuth, I," *Jelenkor*, Jan. 22, 1843, in Viszota, ed., *Széchenyi és Kossuth*, I, 282f. This was the first article in a series of 10 under the title "Wesselényi and Kossuth." The series was a continuation of the Széchenyi-Kossuth debate started with *A kelet népe* in 1841. In the privacy of his diaries, dating from the early thirties, Széchenyi also expressed some harsh opinions about his friend.

[48] Grünwald, *A régi Magyarország*, pp. 205ff.; Falk, *Széchenyi és kora*, pp. 19f.; Zsigmond Kemény, "A két Wesselényi" (The Two Wesselényis), in Csengery, ed., *Magyar szónokok*, pp. 120–28.

Széchenyi *had* learned a great deal from Wesselényi, but if Wesselényi had had an opportunity to read his friend's mind or diaries he perhaps would have presented a more balanced account of the beginning of their friendship. Yet his reminiscences were colored by an acrimonious political controversy in which the estrangement of the two former friends was overshadowed by Széchenyi's struggle against Kossuth. In this struggle, Wesselényi, one of the first and strongest supporters of Kossuth, sided with him against Széchenyi until the revolution of 1848 swept the main protagonists from the political arena, leaving some of the issues, unsolved, to posterity and speculating historians.

In the autumn of 1821, however, Széchenyi and Wesselényi were excited by their new fellowship. Different in temperament and family tradition (many rebellious Wesselényis, including Nicholas's father, had suffered from Vienna's wrath), the two young aristocrats had yet a few things in common. Albeit on a smaller scale than Francis Széchenyi, the elder Wesselényi was the foremost patron of art and literature in Transylvania. From early childhood he taught his son to respect the prominent writers of Hungary, many of whom, including Kazinczy, visited the Wesselényis' home in Zsibó. Young Nicholas, also a superb horseman and hunter, thus came to consider the patronizing of cultural life a patriotic duty. Not quite 18, he visited the *Kaiserstadt*, which was the cultural center of Europe at the time of the Congress of Vienna, and Venice and other cities in northeastern Italy. Enriched by his five-month trip he returned to his estate in late 1814 with an ardent desire to learn more and to strive for physical, spiritual, and moral perfection. His active participation in Transylvanian politics provided him in the following years with an experience Széchenyi never had, leading to the conclusion that the two future heroes of Hungary's age of reform were ready for companionship and a joint scrutiny of the problems of their country's modernization, when Széchenyi invited his friend to join him on his next trip to western Europe.

While waiting for their passports in Vienna and on Széchenyi's estate in Cenk, Wesselényi and his host met many Hungarian politicians, among whom Paul Nagy was probably the most thought-provoking. Together they had long discussions about the future of Hungary, the need for promoting the nation's cultural evolution, the importance of the vernacular and original Magyar literary works, the usefulness of horse races, and other topics. It may well be that some of Széchenyi's subsequent plans for Hungary's regeneration were first formulated in these friendly exchanges. In this sense, they can be said to have been conceived in the minds of both Széchenyi and Wesselényi.[49]

[49] Zsolt Trócsányi, *Wesselényi Miklós* (Nicholas Wesselényi) (Budapest: Akadémiai kiadó, 1965), pp. 28–49.

In one of their discussions Széchenyi warned his Protestant friend, whom he did not wish to shock on the voyage, that he was accustomed to praying on his knees each evening before going to bed. After a debate on metaphysics they agreed that one should pray regularly and devotedly while young and strong, and not merely in unfortunate or dangerous situations. On another occasion Liebenberg and Wesselényi argued about whether Mathias Corvinus or Joseph II had hurt Hungary more. Széchenyi remarked: "It is a deficiency of the Austrian Monarchy and Hungary that they have been linked by God in an outburst of His anger.[50] To see how this harm could be undone or repaired, the two friends set out in March 1822 for a six-month journey in western Europe. The trip, referred to by Széchenyi in his article "Wesselényi and Kossuth," was originally intended to include the United States, but officials were shocked that Széchenyi wanted to use his furlough to visit "the land of freedom."[51] As recently as September 1820 Francis I had indignantly declared in Pest: "The whole world has gone crazy and, having abandoned its ancient laws, is yearning for imaginary constitutions."[52]

By that time Széchenyi, too, was giving more and more thought to the problems of constitutional liberty and free institutions. He went to France and England with Wesselényi, as the latter put it in his request for a passport,[53] primarily to strengthen his knowledge of economics. In France he studied methods of sheep-farming, viticulture, and the handling of wine; in England he concentrated on horse-breeding again. His three-day visit to the Carthusian monastery in La Trappe, France, to which Wesselényi later bluntly referred as a manifestation of Széchenyi's religious bigotry, was a profound spiritual experience. Faced with the problem of complete self-denial, Széchenyi raised the question whether man was really born to be a monk. Full of doubts, he nonetheless conceded that if there were a God, he might be pleased that some creatures underwent unspeakable pains and privations for His sake. To prepare himself as a Catholic before Easter, he also went to confession in the monastery but received no absolution. Although he contritely admitted all of his sins, he was unable to promise with a clear conscience

---

[50] Oct. 11, 20, 1821, Viszota, ed., *Naplók*, II, 211, 214.

[51] Oct. 10, 17, 27, Nov. 8, 1821, Viszota, ed., *Naplók*, II, 211–15, 217, 219. Told by Széchenyi that he planned to visit the United States, Count Bellegarde, president of the war council, protested that this was only a caprice unless the Count was dreaming of a constitution. In Metternich's opinion, Széchenyi's travel plan was "bizarre" and impossible to put into practice. Oct. 20, Dec. 2, 1821, *ibid.*, II, 214, 227.

[52] "Totus mundus stultizat, et relictis antiquis suis legibus constitutiones imaginarias quaerit." Cited by Jászi, *Dissolution of the Habsburg Monarchy*, p. 81. Cf. Cecil Marcus Knatchbull-Hugessen, *The Political Evolution of the Hungarian Nation*, 2 vols. (London: 1908), I, 256f.; Hőke, "Magyarország helyzete 1820–25-ben," p. 4.

[53] Friedreich, *Széchenyi élete*, I, 96.

that he would not commit some of them again; still, the act of confession itself brought him relief.[54]

Széchenyi's second, longer sojourn in England convinced him that England was at the zenith of its power but could rise to even greater heights because of a lack of corruption. It seemed to him that the island was on another planet where God gave less sunshine but more intellectual power to his creatures. There was no question in his mind as to the fact that the century belonged to the British.[55] Besides seeing many of his old friends, Széchenyi was particularly fascinated by a new one, the Duke of Wellington whom he considered an English Cincinnatus.[56] After a visit to the House of Lords and the House of Commons, he exclaimed with enthusiasm "What a Country!"[57] But in addition to English constitutional life, Széchenyi thought he found another reason for England's progress in the public spirit of British society. Henceforth it became his ambition to transplant the "secret" of public spirit to his fatherland and his subsequent reforms aimed at strengthening it in Hungary. "What is impossible for the individual, is easily accomplished by a great many."[58] He tried to explain this "simple" truth to his compatriots over and over again.

After his return from western Europe, Széchenyi still intended to visit the United States, and to leave the military service.[59] When received by the Emperor in February 1823 he asked for the sovereign's approval of his horse-racing project and mentioned his overdue promotion. Francis I consented to the project but told him to be patient about the promotion. So he continued to agitate officials in favor of horse races, not quite sure if it were ambition or conscience which drove him.[60]

---

[54] The description of Széchenyi's Easter confession in La Trappe (Apr. 7, 1822, Viszota, ed., *Naplók*, II, 279f.) is a most characteristic document of his sincere devotion to and tormenting doubts about Catholicism. In the present study, an effort has already been made to point out that the apparent contradiction of the active life and the contemplative life was extremely important for Széchenyi. Cf. Apr. 18–20, 1821, *ibid.*, II, 152.

[55] Apr. 10, 15, May 6, June 28, Aug. 10, 1822, *ibid.*, II, 281, 283, 289, 294, 301.

[56] Apr. 17, May 2, June 28, Aug. 5, Aug. 9, 1822, July 10, 1824, *ibid.*, II, 284f., 289, 293, 300f., 503. Széchenyi's image of Wellington excells in its humanity and intimacy. Little stories mentioned in the diaries about Wellington, Chateaubriand, etc., should be of interest to a historian of the age.

[57] June 28, 1822, *ibid.*, II, 293.

[58] June 6, 1822, *ibid.*, II, 293. ("Ich überzeugt, dass das ganze Geheimniss der Civilisation und des Vorwärtsschreitens der menschlichen Gesellschaft im *Gemeinsinn* liegt.")

[59] Nov. 9, 1822, *ibid.*, II, 313.

[60] From the early 1820s on, Széchenyi took an active part in organizing an association for horse-breeding and racing in Hungary. After the death of Count Joseph Hunyadi in January 1822, he became the leader of this work. Shortly before he left for his trip with Wesselényi, he had handed in his plan for the organization of horse races to the monarch. Cf. Viszota's introduction, *ibid.*, II, pp. xxviii f., cxxix–cxxxiv. Also Mar. 18,

In the spring of 1823 Stephen Széchenyi was also given a taste of political maneuvering in Hungary. It came as a shock, because he saw in this the domestic counterpart of the oppressive international policy of the Holy Alliance. Actually, the two were causally related. At the end of February 1823 Count Antal Cziráky, councillor of the lieutenancy and vice-president of the Hungarian chamber, explained enthusiastically to Széchenyi that old Hungarian constitutional liberties rested on four principles: (1) the election of the king; (2) the Bull of Andrew II; the fact that (3) subsidies and (4) recruits must not be drafted without the Diet's consent.[61] In six weeks, however, Széchenyi saw the same Cziráky as royal commissioner using military force to oblige the resisting magistrates of Sopron to obey two royal decrees concerning taxation and recruiting. He also noted with indignation that similar procedures had been followed in other parts of the country.[62]

The first of the two royal decrees so resented in Hungary had been issued in April 1821. It asked for the balance (28,420) of the 90,000 recruits demanded by the king in 1813 and 1815 but not actually called out because of the end of hostilities. The original request had not been acted on by the Diet, either, but had been connived in because of the war with Napoleon. By now, however, it was peacetime and most Hungarians thought that the demand for fresh troops to be used in Italy should be examined by the Diet. In the spring of 1822 another royal decree ordered that the taxes fixed by the Diet some eight years previously should be paid from November 1, 1822 on—not in paper money but in silver. This "adjustment," the repudiation of its own money by the government, may have been justified by the bad condition of Austrian finances and may have contributed to a somewhat more equal distribution of the financial burdens among the different lands of Francis I. But the decree increased Hungary's contribution to the treasury two-and-one-half times. Several municipalities tried to resist the execution of the decrees, opposing through passive resistance the royal commissioners who, nevertheless, managed to overcome the resistance in most places by occasionally resorting to forcible measures. Sentiment ran high and the pressure on the monarch to call the Diet into session increased. For the time being, however, Francis I could ignore the demand, particu-

---

1821, Jan. 14, 31, Feb. 5–6, 13, 1822, Feb. 6, 10, 1823, *ibid.*, II, 142 and n. 2, 234 and n. 3, 239, 241ff., 243 and n. 2, 330, 332.

[61] Feb. 27, 1823, *ibid.*, II, 338. Cziráky was an expert on Hungarian constitutional law. For the Golden Bull of Andreas II (1222) see Henrik Marczali, ed., *Enchiridion*, pp. 133–43. Concerning the departments of Hungarian feudal government (the chancellery, the chamber, the *Curia* and the lieutenancy or *consilium locumtenentiale*) as developed in the 18th century, see *id.*, *Hungary in the Eighteenth Century*, pp. 327–47.

[62] Feb. 27, Mar. 25, Apr. 16, 1823, Viszota, ed., *Naplók*, II, 339, 349, 354f.

larly because the revolutionary movements in other countries were subdued with relatively small forces and there seemed to be no need for asking further subsidies from Hungary.[63]

Széchenyi, who had sympathized with the constitutional movements abroad and had condemned French royalist intervention in Spain,[64] was deeply disturbed by the turn of events in Hungary. He noticed that the spirit of opposition was spreading in the country. The speech delivered in Sopron by Paul Nagy de Felsőbükk, leader of the constitutional opposition, was on everyone's mind. According to the speech, the word "no" had been inoculated into every Magyar while still in the womb.[65] Even Széchenyi was questioned by his brother, Paul, how he could remain in the service now that soldiers had been transformed into gendarmes. Stephen also noticed a certain resentment because neither he nor his brother had attended the county assemblies of Somogy and Zala, which dealt with the royal decrees.[66]

Could one stay in the military service and still remain an honest Hungarian? What should one do if the monarch himself violated the law, sanctioned by solemn oath, and if flatterers and traitors received rewards while good Hungarians were considered rebels who should be grateful if His Majesty did not hang them? What should one think about an administration which first tried to oppress the nobility for many years in order to cajole the peasants, and then turned to conscription and increasing taxes? As shown by Ypsilanti, Pepe, and Confalonieri abroad, liberty must be bought with blood; patriots had to be prepared for anything and had to be stimulated by the love of virtue not by ambition. Széchenyi began to believe that "recent events in Hungary were the first attack on Hungary's constitution—its virginity has been lost."[67]

Trying to face the problem of where all this would lead, he also listed the arguments of the other side. He thought that both the king and Metternich were convinced they were defending the Hungarian constitution, while they were actually undermining it. Was it at all wrong to abolish such *one-sided* freedom which permitted the nobleman to

[63] Knatchbull-Hugessen, *Political Evolution*, I, 257–60. For a detailed account see Mihály Horváth, *Huszonöt év Magyarország történelméből, 1823–1848* (Twenty-Five Years of Hungary's History, 1823–1848), 3d., edn., 3 vols. (Budapest: Ráth M., 1886), I, 18–131; Hőke, "Magyarország helyzete 1820–25–ben," pp. 8–11.

[64] Mar. 15, 1823, Viszota, ed., *Naplók*, II, 347.

[65] Mar. 25, 1823, *ibid.*, II, 350. Paul Nagy also sharply attacked the high-ranking Hungarian sycophants to the throne.

[66] Apr. 8, 9, 1823, *ibid.*, II, 352f. For the political role of the counties and the functioning of the county "congregations" (assemblies), Marczali, *Hungary in the Eighteenth Century*, pp. 142–48.

[67] Mar. 25, Apr. 9, 16, May 9, 1823, Viszota, ed., *Naplók*, II, 361–64.

thrash the peasant who in turn was free to cry? To the opinion of those who said Hungary proportionally contributed more to the upkeep of the Empire than did the hereditary provinces, he opposed the argument that this contribution was paid totally by the peasants who also made up the army—while the nobility led a parasitical existence. Realizing how flimsy and hypocritical the nobility's attitude was, he decided to clarify the issues for himself by collecting exact data concerning the royal decrees and the resistance of the counties. He read carefully the letters of the primate, the representations made to the throne by the counties, Paul Nagy's speech, an article published in the *English New Times* about Hungary, and the *gravamina* (Hungarian grievances). In short, he made a conscious effort to study the situation in Hungary without preconceived prejudices.[68]

It was a task not easily accomplished. A friend, Count Somssich, suggested in a conversation that all Hungarians should become Germans and receive in turn far-reaching rights including habeas corpus. Széchenyi conceded the noble purpose of Somssich's idea, but pointed to its unfeasibility, saying the Emperor would probably have him hung because he would hate to have coregents, while Hungarians would despise him because: how could Hungarians be turned into Germans?[69] Despite his realistic judgment of Austria's conditions and status in the world, and his own somewhat radical thinking at the time, Széchenyi still thought in terms of the whole Monarchy asking whether the Austrian state was capable of improvement and whether it would be possible to introduce ministerial responsibility in Austria.[70] He also realized how difficult it was to maintain the old institutions while introducing new ones. The effort to carefully balance all the arguments in a heated political debate, and to face historical, economic, social, and psychological realities,[71] was remarkable in a man who had had no public responsibilities and had been involved in deep personal conflicts.

While investigating the main political issues in Hungary, Széchenyi also began to feel the responsibility of putting his own house in order.[72] To increase his own income became from now on, so to speak, a moral and patriotic duty for him. He became aware of the idea that wealth, freedom of a nation, duties and rights of the individual were in some sort of relationship—as indicated by the example of England. The

---

[68] Apr. 9, 16, 22, May 9, July 9, 1823, *ibid.*, II, 353–59, 363f., 369, 386. Also the list of documents sent to him from the archives of Bihar County on July 12, 1823. B. Szabó, *Adatok*, I, 44.

[69] May 10, 1823, Viszota, ed., *Naplók*, II, 365. Cf. June 1, 1823, *ibid.*, II, 371.

[70] Feb. 27, Mar. 25, 1823, *ibid.*, II, 339, 350.

[71] May 9, 1823, *ibid.*, II, 361.

[72] May 11, 1823, *ibid.*, II, 365.

English taught him to pay attention to free economic associations as promoters of both economic and social progress. In November 1822 he bought one share in a steamboat on the Danube although he thought the enterprise was doomed to failure.[73] While his attention centered on Hungarian political troubles, he entered the club of Viennese merchants as a member of the Austrian Agricultural Association. He also wrote a booklet on fox hunting, his first work in print.[74] At the same time, he continued to solicit support for a horse-racing association. In a letter in which he asked Prince Paul Esterházy's support, he came back to the conclusion drawn in England: public spirit and free associations were the preconditions needed by men who wanted to be useful to the fatherland.[75] The propagation and realization of this idea in 1823 marked Széchenyi's emergence as a practical reformer.

Much of his thought was devoted to economic problems and technical innovations. He regretted that because free trade among the different parts of the Austrian Monarchy did not exist, producers had difficulties in selling their products. In May 1824 he noted such deficiencies of the Austrian economy as insufficient foreign trade, idleness of peasants due to the uneconomical *robota* system, and the unfair tariff between the Austrian and Hungarian parts of the realm.[76]

Széchenyi related technical advancement to the problem of ethics. Although he had some doubts concerning man's ability to take advantage of the blessings of technology, he thought that by increasing its physical and moral talents, mankind was being inspired to greater, loftier, and better ideals; the closer it approached perfection the more it would improve itself and the easier it would comprehend how backward it still was in every respect.[77] Thus faith in human progress and the unlimited possibilities of moral and technical perfection, so much in line with the great tradition of the eighteenth century, were amalgamated with Christian ethical teachings in Széchenyi's mind.

Questions of technical, economic, and commercial progress absorbed most of his attention during his next visit to France in the spring of 1825. He was appointed a member of the official delegation led by Paul Esterházy, Austrian ambassador in Paris, at the coronation of Charles X in Rheims. In a conversation with Esterházy they seemed to have agreed that the leading trend of the century was the desire to make quick profits; that this was also behind the English recognition

[73] Nov. 3, 1822, *ibid.*, II, 316.
[74] Apr. 22, May 16, Dec. 26, 1823, Oct. 26, 1825, *ibid.*, II, 357, 368, 433, 637.
[75] Dec. 24, 1823, *ibid.*, II, 432f.
[76] Oct. 23, 25, 1823, May 22, 1824, *ibid.*, II, 410, 495.
[77] June 21, 1824, Viszota, ed., *Naplók*, II, 498f. On new technical inventions cf. June 26, 30, July 10, 1824, *ibid.*, II, 500, 502, 504.

of the independence of South American states; and that Austria could participate in the general economic upswing by building canals and roads and by improving her administrative system. When he wrote the main items of the conversation into his diary Széchenyi first thought of discussing all these matters with Metternich.[78]

Impressed by the favorable economic situation of France,[79] Széchenyi read and asked about the French wool and silk industries, sheep farming, banking system, and jotted down information about highways and bridges.[80] In Bordeaux he collected data on wine production, visualizing the exporting of Hungarian wines by railway 22 years *before* the first railroad was opened in Hungary. Admiring the Canal du Midi, Széchenyi began to understand the zeal of the young Emperor Joseph II who at the sight of this example of human technical know-how had become even more disgusted with the old *Schlendrian* ("good old Austria," half-derogatory, half-joking) and had determined to remake everything at home without mature deliberation. After a tour of picturesque southern France and the Provence (he bought his Franklin in Montpellier), Széchenyi stopped in Lombardy, making calculations of silkworm-breeding and studying agriculture. In Trieste he tried to compute the cost of a railroad to Vienna and the approximate amount of export necessary to cover the expenses.[81]

In many respects this journey confirmed the conclusions drawn from his previous trips. "The century is on the march but, unfortunately, I live in a country that is dragging one leg behind," Széchenyi noted.[82] He became particularly annoyed when on leaving France he again felt the power of the Holy Alliance represented by Austria in northern Italy. Infuriated that his books had been taken away from him by the customs officer at the border, he concluded that people with intelligence and knowledge were considered to be superfluous and dangerous in Austria which appeared to him as an "old" country compared with "young" England or France. Although the population of Lombardy did not seem very unhappy under Austrian rule, he still thought that there was a

[78] May 26, 1824, *ibid.*, II, 541f.

[79] In Châlons sur Marne, he was told by a Frenchman that everybody could easily pay twice as much taxes as asked by the state and that indemnity payments would soon be forgotten. May 16, 1825, *ibid.*, II, 540f.

[80] July 5, 9, 20, 21, 1825, *ibid.*, II, 551–55, 557.

[81] July 23, Aug. 2, 4, 11, 17, 18, 20, 25, 28, 31, 1825, *ibid.*, II, 558, 567f., 573, 584–94, 599ff. To really appreciate Széchenyi's deep insight, qualified by the historical perspective *he* had, into the psychology and inspiration of Joseph II, whose voyage of 1777 his own trip of almost a half-century later paralleled in some respects, cf. the recent study by Hans Wagner, "Die Reise Joseph II. nach Frankreich und die Reformen in Österreich," in *Österreich und Europa*. Festgabe für Hugo Hantsch zum 70. Geburtstag (Graz-Vienna-Cologne: Vlg. Styria, 1965), esp. pp. 221–28.

[82] Aug. 10, 1825, Viszota, ed., *Naplók*, II, 579.

profound difference between a monarchic (i.e., absolutistic) and a constitutional government, and preferred the latter.[83]

In a series of notes on economic matters, Széchenyi censured the heavy export duties on tobacco that resulted in the loss of Italian markets. Measures diverting the importation of cotton from Trieste he decried as "Austrian stupidities."[84] As a landowner he was especially interested in the problems of agriculture. He thought agricultural surpluses could be absorbed and sold by raising the level of domestic consumption and export. Domestic consumption could be stimulated by increasing the speed of circulation of money and by a good banking and credit system, while the chances of export could be improved by building canals and railroads. Interestingly enough, this purely economic line of thought ended suddenly on a depressing political note, namely, that "poor old Austria" would be unable to withstand the competition of constitutional England, adolescent America, and geographically favored France.[85]

How to inject new life into old institutions? this was the question on which his thoughts began to concentrate. There seemed to be a difference between innovation and improvement, but they were difficult to distinguish. Via the noble drive of pushing everything toward perfection at high speed one could easily be misled and make things worse than before. By substituting mediocrity for good, however, and by being afraid of everything that was new, Széchenyi thought, one could never break through the circle of tradition and prejudice. He decided to find the golden mean, and to learn to tell innovation from improvement.

These reflections, which he was to resume and expand in later works, did not mean Széchenyi was sure of himself or his calling. In the same diary entry where he mused over differentiating between innovations and improvements, he also confessed that he woke up every day with another idea. One day he wanted to travel abroad, the next to reform old customs and create new constitutions. Sometimes he wanted to retire to his farm, marry, and get rich. Often he thought he would prefer to spend his life in London or Paris and on rare occasions he even thought of rejoining his regiment. Interestingly enough, in his critical self-appraisal he would sometimes wonder whether this hesitation came from his nerves or the food he ate. The secrets of nature continued to challenge his imagination.[86]

[83] Aug. 11-16, 17, 20, 21-24, 1825, *ibid.*, II, 580-86, 589, 593f. Cf. Széchenyi to Wesselényi, Nov. 27, 1822, Majláth, ed., *Levelek*, I, 74.

[84] Sept. 4, 1825, Viszota, ed., *Naplók*, II, 602.

[85] Aug. 16, 1825, *ibid.*, II, 589.

[86] Aug. 11, 1825, *ibid.*, II, 581ff.

There was no question, however, that by now Stephen Széchenyi was widely read and travelled, familiar with the most important questions of international and domestic issues, and deeply interested in economic and constitutional problems. He was a dilettante with many excellent connections all over Europe, but one who had taught himself to work hard and systematically. He was enthusiastic about liberty and independence and greeted the realization of these principles in the New World, but he was realistic enough to refrain from radical extremes in his own country. A moderate even in his "radical" period, his ideal was a constitutional monarchy; he well understood that the Habsburg state was sorely in need of reform. He also knew that he was a Hungarian and that as a big landowner he had certain duties and responsibilities to fulfill. It was at this point that on his return from France in early September 1825 he received, as a member of age of an aristocratic family, a royal invitation to attend the sessions of the upper chamber of the Diet in Pressburg (Pozsony, Bratislava).[87]

The summoning of the Diet for September 11, 1825 indicated a certain willingness on the part of Francis I to return, at least formally, to the constitutional form of government after an interruption of 13 years. The main reason for doing so was probably the administration's eagerness to obtain legalization for the financial reforms introduced in all parts of the realm, including Hungary, during the preceding decade, a measure which, however, the estates refused to sanction. On the other hand, the Diet provided an opportunity for airing the grievances accumulated, particularly during the years 1821–23, and also offered a chance, mentioned in the royal propositions, to resume working on the necessary reforms, a task begun by the Diets of the early 1790s but abandoned during the French wars.

Circumstances, however, did not favor the long overdue reforms. The representatives in the Diet belonged almost without exception to the feudal ruling classes of Hungary. When they talked of "fencing around" the constitution they meant defending their own privileges and receiving a free hand in the administration of the counties. Only a few delegates had instructions from their constituents suggesting moderate progress or reforms.[88] Demands to modify the tariff system between Austria and Hungary and to increase the importance of the Magyar language in the administration of the country both belonged to the list of long-standing grievances. The *gravamina* policy completely ignored the most urgent

---

[87] For a detailed contemporary English account of the composition, functioning, and procedures of the Hungarian Diet, see John Paget, *Hungary and Transylvania*, 2 vols. (London: J. Murray, 1839), I, 166–83.

[88] Horváth, *Huszonöt év*, I, 141f.

problem in the country: the serf. Opposition in the Diet was limited to legal and constitutional issues, amounting to a squabble with the monarch over the question of who should run the country, heedless of the population as a whole. As Paul Nagy—who in 1807 urged the Diet to lighten the burden of the peasant but was shouted down with *ne stultizet* ("don't be crazy")—bluntly put it in his defense of the noble insurrections, the Hungarian constitution was monarchical and consequently could never be used in a democratic way against the king.[89]

Francis I knew well enough that even the most "radical" members of the Diet represented no danger at all to the crown. He ostensibly called the Diet into session for the coronation of his new queen, Carolina Augusta. By making a conciliatory gesture he wanted to steal the thunder of the opposition, which he could keep under control anyway through the completely subservient Chamber of Magnates. He certainly did not plan to press for constitutional reforms, nor was he eager to call the Diet into session in regular intervals as stipulated by a law of 1790. Metternich, who claimed credit for advising the monarch to give up his rigid position and "return to the constitution," was sure of the "good spirit" of the Diet and foresaw "a great deal of empty talk . . . which never rises to anything higher than mere personal and local interest."[90]

Thanks to a number of yet unforseen circumstances the Diet of 1825–27 has been considered the first in a series of "reform diets," marking the beginning of a new era in Hungarian history. This was due primarily to the work of Stephen Széchenyi, a newcomer to politics. He came with great interest to the Diet, intending to observe people and proceedings carefully. In addition to his by then fair knowledge of Hungarian history and constitutional law he had a broad European outlook and an intimate knowledge of west European governmental practices. He had made up his mind to resign his commission as an officer.[91] At the same time, he felt completely independent of the government and yet had nothing in common with the traditional Hungarian *gravaminal* policy of a priori protesting everything that came from Vienna. Capping all this was a feeling of moral independence and striving after truth and impartiality, spurred on by a desire to do something for his country.

---

[89] Oct. 7, 1825, Viszota, ed., *Naplók*, II, 625f.; Hőke, "Magyarország helyzete 1820–25-ben," p. 7.

[90] Metternich to Gentz, Sept. 28, 1825, Doc. 766, in Richard Metternich, ed., *Memoirs of Prince Metternich*, 5 vols. (London: Bentley & Son, 1880–82), IV, 200, cited hereafter as *Metternich Memoirs*.

[91] He no longer cared for his promotion in the army, although he still wore his uniform. In mid-1824 he had resigned his commission but his resignation was not accepted. Széchenyi to Wesselényi and to Paul Esterházy, Aug. 5 and 7, 1824, B. Szabó, *Adatok*, I, 50f.

Széchenyi's patriotic motivation, increasingly present in his thinking since the Oriental trip, was further stimulated by his love for Countess Crescence Seilern, wife of the president of the Royal Chamber, or Treasury, Count Charles Zichy. His last great romantic passion began in the summer of 1824. Crescence gently but firmly seems to have declined his amorous advances. It was the transfer of her husband to Buda in the spring of 1825 that prompted Széchenyi to make Pest his permanent residence after the Diet and thus be closer to the person who inspired him for the rest of his life.[92]

His ardent courtship rejected by Crescence, Széchenyi decided to change his own attitude following a year of inner struggles. The climax came shortly after the Diet had begun its sessions. He convinced himself that he was "not born for vice" and had no right to intrude into the life of the beloved woman. Feeling that she had already turned him into a better man, he chose the "difficult and rough but noble path" of virtue, anxious "to render his compatriots and fellow men a worthier service than he had done hitherto."[93]

The opportunity to put his intentions into practice was at the Diet; in the first weeks he closely followed its proceedings. There was much talk but little organized work, much confusion and loss of time. The president of the lower chamber, the personalis, had no authority among the estates, which paid little attention to him. The upper chamber, on the other hand, was dominated by its president, the palatine,[94] whose directions were usually given to magnates who knew neither Hungarian nor Latin. The speech from the throne, opening the session of the diet, put good arguments, in Széchenyi's opinion, into the hands of the constitution's defenders. The main question, however, was whether the defense of such an anti-liberal constitution was a noble gesture. After all, 400,000 nobles wanted their privileges to prevail against the wishes of a population of 10 million who were not even represented at the Diet. Széchenyi sarcastically rejected the arguments of those who compared the Hungarian peasant's allegedly favorable situation with that of the Austrian peasants or ventured to refer to the titled landowner's paternalistic attitude toward his serf.[95] Concluding that the peasants could perhaps elect noblemen as their representatives, he warned that all of Europe would applaud a "liberal" king who would try to overthrow the anti-liberal Hungarian constitution. In spite of his enthusiasm for independence,

---

[92] Aug. 24, Sept. 2, 1824, Mar. 13, 1825, Viszota, ed., *Naplók*, II, 513f., 532.

[93] Oct. 20, 22, 1825, *ibid.*, II, 636f.

[94] The president of the king's bench (*tabula regis*), the *personalis praesentiae regiae locum tenens*, presided over the lower chamber (or table). For the personalis and the (count) palatine see Marczali, *Hungary in the Eighteenth Century*, pp. 339, 113, 353, respectively.

[95] Sept. 13, 14, 21, 1825, Viszota, ed., *Naplók*, II, 605f., 608f.

liberty, and constitutionalism, such intimate remarks reflected a realistic appraisal of the basic problems. Concerning the preparation of the list of grievances to be sent to the king, he noticed that whereas there were many speechmakers at the Diet, whom he called "poets from fairy land," there were no businesslike individuals with practical knowledge. Instead of irresponsible speeches he suggested that Hungary should seek to reconcile her interests with the general progress of the Austrian Monarchy, for "the dream of an independent, Hungarian limited Monarchy is not for our age—let us not demand impossible things."[96]

Yet he agreed essentially with the content of the Lower Chamber's answer to the Speech from the Throne and to the royal propositions, which was:

1. The Diet shall be called into session every three years.

2. All officials shall take an oath to the Constitution.

3. The Hungarian Lieutenancy shall suspend the execution of decrees contrary to the law.

4. Official correspondence among the counties shall be permitted.

These basic demands constituted the second part of the address, the first half of which contained a list of grievances. It was assumed that the acceptance of the address by the crown would be a guarantee against further violations of the constitution.[97]

When the answer prepared by the Lower Chamber was discussed in the Chamber of Magnates on October 12, Stephen Széchenyi—still wearing the kaiser's uniform—supported it, saying that His Majesty himself encouraged the estates to be frank with him. Even more important— and a first—he spoke in Hungarian an example followed by other magnates.[98] The shock of those who thought that by abandoning Latin as the official language Hungarians would soon all talk German[99] became even greater when, three weeks later, the same Széchenyi offered a year's income for the establishment of an institution for cultivating the Hungarian language.

The offer came at one of the "circular sessions" of the Diet. Detailed discussion of new legislation and other aspects of the Diet's work was actually done in the circular sessions of the Lower Chamber, where deputies elected their own presiding officer, whereas regular sessions were chaired by the appointees of the throne. The draft resolutions prepared

[96] Sept. 28, Oct. 5, 8, 1825, *ibid.*, II, 617, 621, 629.
[97] Oct. 4, 21, 1825, *ibid.*, II, 619, 636; Horváth, *Huszonöt év*, I, 156–61.
[98] Oct. 12–13, 1825, Viszota, ed., *Naplók*, II, 629 and n. 4, 630.
[99] See Cziráky's remark, Oct. 14, 1825, *ibid.*, II, 633.

in the circular sessions were subsequently submitted to the *regnicolar,* or full session of the Lower Table. As a magnate, Széchenyi attended the circular sessions only as a guest, which is one of the reasons we do not know the exact wording of his improvised interlocution of November 3, 1825; the other being the circumstance that no official protocols were kept of the proceedings of the circular sessions. In his diary he merely noted that he had taken the floor in the circular session and antagonized all his compatriots. The remark shows not only his almost pathological sensitivity to criticism but also the existence of resentment, mainly among those aulic aristocrats of the Upper Table who suspected that with the spread of the Magyar idiom the spirit of political opposition would also be strengthened.[100]

Yet in the circular session itself, Széchenyi's initiative inflamed the imagination of many oldtimers who had fought the lost battles for promoting the national idiom in years past. Some immediately recalled that the up to then unknown captain of hussars was the noble scion of the benefactor of the nation, the founder of the National Museum. More important, Széchenyi's generous offer, a princely sum of 60,000 florins, was matched by others in the very same session, thus laying the foundation for the Hungarian Academy of Sciences.

The realization of the Academy (Acts XI and XII: 1827) meant the victory of a national cause for which many Magyar writers and patriots had been working since the late 18th century.[101] Despite its shortcomings, the new institution took a prominent part in the shaping of modern Magyar literature and cultural life, as well as in the creation of Magyar public opinion. Széchenyi's gesture, made on the spur of the moment, was stimulated by repeated, vigorous speeches by Paul Nagy at the circular session of November 3. In the last of his interlocutions Nagy attacked the alienated magnates who would not support financially the cause of the nation's language. Upon this, Széchenyi stepped forward from the audience and made his offer saying that although he did not belong to the great luminaries of the country, he was well-to-do and ready to prove his devotion to the fatherland.

---

[100] Nov. 3, 1825, *ibid.,* II, 642.

[101] For a critical survey of the circumstances of the Academy's founding, the discussion on the character of the new institution, and its history, see Viszota's introduction to *Naplók,* III, pp. lvii–lxxv. The documents about the founding of the Academy (covering the period 1790–1828) were published *ibid.,* III, Annex No. II, 496–740. For the function of Hungarian as a literary language and its role in molding Hungary into a modern national state, see Dezső Pais, ed., *Nyelvünk a reformkorban* (Our Language in the Age of Reforms) (Budapest: 1955). Cf. Gyula Szekfű, ed., *Iratok a magyar államnyelv kérdésének történetéhez 1790–1848* (Documents Relative to the History of Magyar as the Official Language of the State, 1790–1848) (Budapest: Magyar Történelmi Társulat, 1926), published in *Fontes.*

Széchenyi's pledge was only partly inspired by Nagy's rhetoric. Indeed, his patriotic enthusiasm had deeper roots. As he said in a letter to Paul Nagy in early 1830, he had passed his 33rd year, was far from being inexperienced at the time of his gift, and the money involved was equivalent to his net income of three years. Furthermore, he pointed out that he had planned to assist the development of his country long before he went to the Diet.[102] This allegation, emphatically reiterated in the poetically emotional reminiscences of *A kelet népe* in 1841,[103] appears to be borne out by a Hungarian account written shortly after the session. This summary suggests that in his very first declaration Széchenyi may have put it in such a way that stressed he was making his offer only after mature deliberation.[104] Yet there is no evidence indicating it was exactly the Academy Széchenyi intended to give his generous support to. According to Viszota—and there is much documentary evidence in Széchenyi's diaries, letters, and later works to support the thesis—the most important single personal factor prompting Széchenyi at the beginning of the Diet was his desire to prove his virtue and unselfishness to Crescence.[105] Even so, Széchenyi may have acted under the influence of other less conscious yet powerful components of human decisions. Among them, there may have been a hint dropped by his former tutor, Nicholas Révai, an early proponent of the Academy. The fading memory of the teacher was more than supplemented by the vivid discussions with the robust friend, Wesselényi. Wesselényi, who had no property in Hungary proper and could not get an invitation to sit in the chamber of magnates, attended the Diet of 1825 as the representative of an absent magnate in the chamber of deputies. In two effusive letters, written the day after the event, he described how "my Széchenyi" declared his intention to assist "the sacred cause of nationality and language" and how splendidly "seeds sown in good soil commence to sprout."

[102] Széchenyi to Nagy, Jan. 30, 1830, Majláth, ed., *Levelek*, I, 142f.

[103] Ferenczi, ed., *A kelet népe*, pp. 223f.

[104] "*Le Comte Etienne Széchenyi declara* [*sic*] *sa volonté, mûrement réfléchie, d'offrir*," etc. The account, previously ignored by Hungarian historians, was written in French for Sir Henry Wellesley, British ambassador to Vienna, by the young Count Aurel Dessewffy, subsequently Széchenyi's disciple and friend. It was part of the second installment of a series of reports on the Hungarian Diet, sent by Wellesley to Canning from Vienna on Jan. 1, 1826. Cf. F.O. 7/192, *Public Record Office* (London). Gabriel Döbrentei's account, published in the first Yearbook of the Hungarian Academy, also asserts that Széchenyi used the words, "I am doing this after mature deliberation" in making his offer. For this and other contemporary accounts see, besides the references in n. 101 above, Zichy, *Széchenyi életrajza*, I, 200–203 and Friedreich, *Széchenyi élete*, I, 155ff.

[105] Viszota, ed., *Naplók*, III, pp. lxi–lxv. The circular session was held two weeks after Széchenyi had promised to Crescence to take the path of virtue; soon after the session, he confirmed his decision again. Nov. 22, 1825, *ibid.*, II, 652.

In addition to personal factors, one must take into account other pertinent circumstances in order to comprehend the significance of the moment in which Stephen Széchenyi emerged into the limelight of Hungary's history. In the circular sessions of November 2 and 3, 1825 the discussion centered on the questions of how to improve the education of the youth and promote the knowledge of Magyar, regarded as the "national" idiom. On both days, the debate revealed the frustrations and ambitions of Magyar linguistic nationalism, of those who for some 35 years had tried with very limited success to obtain legal sanction for replacing the official Latin language of the Kingdom of Hungary with the Magyar. Undeniably, there was an anachronism in the Latin oratory of the Hungarian legislative assemblies. The papal nuncio, writing his reports to the Holy See in Italian, had to use Latin in his correspondence with the Hungarian clergy who, like the secular authorities of the kingdom, clung to the language of the Romans as though it were the most important safeguard of both their privileges and the constitution. On the other hand, the protagonists of Magyar linguistic nationalism—writers and politicians—tended to look at the Magyar idiom as valuable per se; the very existence of Magyardom might depend on the preservation of it. Since the late 18th century "Magyarization" was held desirable by many decent Hungarian patriots, both as a defensive measure against real or imaginary Germanization and as a reassurance against the potential threat of the perhaps less self-conscious but certainly more numerous non-Magyars. The reluctance of Vienna and the Hungarian central authorities to yield to the mounting pressure for stepped-up Magyarization frequently added to the zeal of officials in the autonomous county administrations who interpreted the law locally as they saw fit. At the same time, they listed the status of the Magyar idiom as one of their grievances to be aired at the Diet.[106]

Small wonder that after the absence of dietal sessions for 13 years, the estates intended to avail themselves of the opportunity. In the two circular sessions already mentioned, as can be seen from the reports of officials and secret agents prepared for Metternich and Police Minister Count Sedlnitzky, speaker after speaker urged the promotion of Magyar at all levels of public life and private affairs. Demands to use Magyar in the Diet, to publish all laws in Magyar, to examine on the basis of a statute of 1792 the officials of both the central and municipal administrations from the point of view of their knowledge of Magyar, and to Magyarize the administration of justice and the official correspondence of all authorities alternated with the ridiculing of the hiring prac-

---

[106] For further references see George Barany, "The Awakening of Magyar Nationalism before 1848," *Austrian History Yearbook*, II (1966), 26–35.

tices of some magnates who seemed to give preference to Germans over Hungarians or of the inclination of some noblemen to import wives from nonconstitutional (i.e., non-Magyar) lands. Count Joseph Dessewffy, who represented Szabolcs county, intended to exclude from the elementary schools children who did not speak Hungarian in order to force parents to teach their offspring Magyar while they were still in the cradle. Others insisted that members of the clergy, teachers, professors of institutions of higher learning and officers of the army be fluent in Hungarian. There were some who wanted to expatriate German burghers unwilling to learn Magyar and to prevent the admission into the guilds of craftsmen ignorant of Magyar. One deputy was concerned with the inscriptions on coins, while many more expressed the desirability of having a national theater and literary prizes in order to promote Hungarian cultural life. It was in this context that the issue of creating an institutional framework for the cultivation of the language itself was repeatedly raised, and it was only after all this and much more had been said and duly debated at considerable length that Széchenyi took the floor and offered his financial assistance for establishing the institution destined "to propagate the national idiom and to raise sons worthy of a fatherland like ours."[107]

Any proper evaluation of Széchenyi's role must be made with this background in mind. Many signs of politically conscious Magyar linguistic and cultural nationalism were present well before Széchenyi came forward. The endeavor to make Pest the cultural center of Hungary and, indeed, to transform it into a Magyar city, antedated his work. Symbolically the Academy was founded in the year which saw the publication of Michael Vörösmarty's romantic epic poem *Zalán futása* (The Flight of Zalán) that marked the beginning of a true renaissance of Magyar literature. A prominent writer, Andrew Fáy, treated even the establishment of the Academy as a "half-political, half-literary subject," whereas Wesselényi looked at it as a steppingstone to the unification of Transylvania with Hungary proper. It was because of these political considerations that he wanted to have an equal number of Catholics and Protestants on the board of directors of the Academy, since, as he put it, "stupid and dangerous papist humbug" must be counterbalanced by Transylvanian Protestants.[108]

The brief reference to the debates of the circular sessions of November 2 and 3, 1825 is necessary because these two sessions, especially the

[107] Wellesley to Canning, Jan. 1, 1826, enclosure, *F.O. 7/192*, PRO (London); Docs. 61a, 61b, and 62 in Szekfű, ed., *Iratok*, pp. 322–33; Viszota, ed., *Naplók*, II, 739–50, Annex No. xv, and *ibid.*, pp. cxlii f., summary by Michael Platthy.

[108] Dec. 10, 1825, Fáy's letter to Abraham Vay and Wesselényi's undated letter to Abraham Vay, as cited by B. Szabó, *Széchényi család*, III, 525 and n. 170.

second one, served as stimuli to mental processes which had begun to take shape in Széchenyi's mind much earlier, but which were still in need of a domestic impulse to launch him onto the Hungarian scene. Also, the two sessions represented a historic moment in the development of that accelerating force—Magyar nationalism—which, ready to cast off its choking feudal corset, was to be for more than a century to come the foremost ideological leitmotif of Hungary's modernization. Széchenyi was not the creator of this ill-defined force; neither was he to follow slavishly its capricious and sometimes tyrannical path in the remaining 35 years of his life. But the fact that he became the founder of the Academy made him in some ways the molder of what turned out to be cohesive and creative in modern Magyar nationalism. Boiling diffusely after having been throttled for decades, this nationalism, steeped in a feudal constitution and way of life, tried to burst into the open at the beginning of the Diet of 1825. In a nutshell, the discussions that preceded Széchenyi's offer epitomized all the frustrations and tempestuous claims of hurt Magyar resentment toward the policies of Joseph II. They also contained most of the necessary elements of what could become, given certain historical circumstances and appropriate leadership, a program of action for a nation yet to be built. Széchenyi recognized the moment and recognized the force; at the midpoint of his life, he thought he could master both.

In spite of the political overtones of Hungarian cultural nationalism, Széchenyi managed to present the Academy as an apolitical issue to Archduke Palatine Joseph and Chancellor Metternich. His sincerity and dedication engendered an atmosphere of enthusiasm in which even conservative magnates thought it their patriotic duty to support the Academy. At the same time, it was Széchenyi's accomplishment that by lending his assistance to the cause of the Magyar idiom and national culture he at once perceived and made clear that Hungary's rebirth as a nation should follow along national lines.

It turned out that the foundation of the Academy became the only reform measure enacted by the Diet of 1825–27. Therefore its importance can hardly be overestimated in those days when poets, writers, and the best thinkers of the nation accepted Herder's opinion that Hungarians were a dying people. Now, however, they were told by the symbolic action of a cultured magnate that it was still possible to reverse the trend. It is no wonder that Széchenyi, who had not firmly believed himself as to the possibility of regenerating Hungary, suddenly became the center of attention.

He also became the potential center of opposition in the Chamber of Magnates. The possibility of having a Széchenyi as leader of the opposition in Hungary may have attracted Metternich's attention. Shortly before and immediately after the opening of the Diet, the chancellor wrote in an overconfident and rather belittling tone to Gentz about "one of the most tiresome constitutional *divertissements* of the world." Not entirely without justification or humor, he complained: "This Diet not only interferes with my time, my customs, and daily life, but actually forces me to change my language and my dress. I have to speak Latin and dress like a hussar, and the refusal to wear moustaches is the only liberty I take upon this occasion."[109] Under the impression made by the events in the Diet and his conversations with Széchenyi, Metternich soon went to the other extreme, stating on December 11, 1825: "In Hungary I encounter all those things on which during my whole public life, especially during the last ten years, I have made war."[110] Two weeks later British Ambassador Wellesley reported that "Metternich's attention for the last month has been wholly devoted to the affairs of Hungary." He also indicated that the administration wanted "to allay the ferment which prevailed among the Deputies" and that "Clubs had been established at Presburg [sic], and I understand that several young men of the first families in Hungary have signed a paper binding themselves to live entirely in Hungary, and not again as formerly to make Vienna their winter residence."

The excerpts from Sir Henry Wellesley's report suggest that at least one of his informers must have been his friend Stephen Széchenyi. But the ambassador was not only informed about and interested in what was going on at Pressburg, he was sophisticated enough to know that "the spirit which has shewn itself in the Diet has prevailed more or less before at every convocation," and that there was "not the slightest ground for apprehending the disturbance of public tranquillity of Hungary."[111]

Indeed, Metternich and some of Sedlnitzky's secret agents, whose reports he read, somewhat exaggerated the significance of the opposition in the Diet of 1825–27. This opposition had no political party platform or leader in the modern sense. It was unified only as far as the traditional constitutional grievances were concerned; this meant mainly the privileges of the nobility in the government of the country and the role of the Hungarian language in the administration. Only very few deputies and young aristocrats had in mind liberal and progressive ideas concern-

---

[109] Aug. 17, 1825, Doc. 765, *Metternich Memoirs*, IV, 199. Also Metternich to Gentz, Oct. 9, 1825, Docs. 769–771, *ibid.*, IV, 204f.
[110] Metternich to the president of the lower house, Dec. 11, 1825, Doc. 784, *ibid.*, IV, 248.
[111] Wellesley to Canning, Dec. 25, 1825, *F.O. 7/188*, PRO (London).

ing the necessity of reforms similar to those of Széchenyi. The Diet, however, was not the place where these ideas could have been discussed.[112]

The chancellor's irritation partly understandable, from his point of view. He had benevolently sponsored Széchenyi, sent him on foreign missions, provided him with a passport for his trips, and dined him in Vienna; he must have been shocked to hear that his protégé was on the side of the opposition at the Diet. Only a week after the circular session in which he promoted the cause of the Hungarian language, Metternich asked Széchenyi, through Melanie Zichy-Ferraris, to come and talk to him.[113]

This first great political debate between Metternich and Széchenyi is known partly from the two documents published in the chancellor's *Memoirs* under the title "The Opposition in the Diet of Pressburg."[114] The first is Metternich's letter to Personalis Szögyényi, President of the Lower Chamber of the Diet, dated December 11, 1825; the second is Széchenyi's Memorial to Metternich of November 15, 1825, containing also the chancellor's marginal notes. Metternich's letter called the attention of the personalis to what he considered the two oppositions in the Diet—one the traditional old Hungarian opposition, loyal and patriotic, the other representing "the spirit of the age," disorderly, and hating the institution of monarchy. Then, with a sudden turn and "in the strictest confidence," the chancellor gave this characterization of Széchenyi: "I know this young man from the beginning of his career, and I have done a great deal for him. He has quick parts, but, like most of our young people, no solid knowledge—a want which he makes up for by a kind of cultivated instinct. His ambition is boundless; he is not frivolous, but a sort of political spitfire, although he can be deep enough sometimes."

According to both Széchenyi and Metternich their first discussion took place on November 12, 1825, "the day on which the Royal answer to

[112] Horváth, *Huszonöt év*, I, 151–54.

[113] Nov. 10, 1825, Viszota, ed., *Naplók*, II, 642. According to Metternich, it was Széchenyi who had asked for the interview (letter cited in n. 110, p. 250). Although Széchenyi had thought of discussing his ideas with Metternich during his last trip to France, his diary entry seems trustworthy enough. Taking into consideration the two men's psychological attitudes, it is of secondary importance who had first used Melanie Zichy's good services, for both probably wanted "to open their hearts" under the given circumstances: Metternich to warn Széchenyi and Széchenyi to enlist the Chancellor's help on his side. Cf. "Miscellania" I and II, Annex No. I, 4a-b, *ibid.*, III, 447–50. Actually, Széchenyi wanted and hoped so much to obtain official approval of his plans that for a moment he even thought of "sacrificing himself" by marrying Melanie, granddaughter of the influential minister of state, Charles Zichy. Cf. Dec. 18, 1825, *ibid.*, II, 663.

[114] Docs. 784 and 785, *Metternich Memoirs*, IV, 248–59.

the first address of the Diet had been published." To Széchenyi's remarks that the court had shown "ignorance . . . with respect to Hungarian affairs" and that "the Diet would come to a bad end," Metternich declared his readiness "to discuss the Royal resolution. Point for point I brought forward, silencing him so thoroughly that he left me with the remark that I was entirely right. Then he went back to his club, to change his opinions again."[115] Actually, the chancellor failed to convince Széchenyi. Immediately after their conversation, Széchenyi noted that although their views agreed in many respects, they embraced opposite creeds. He also remarked that Metternich was superficial and liked to listen to himself only.[116]

Széchenyi's diary also revealed some other details about his debate with the chancellor. According to his notes, Metternich strongly supported the firm tone of the royal rescript, emphasized his hatred for all kinds of opposition, and claimed that by the energetic intervention in Naples and Piedmont the Hungarian constitution had been saved, too. Therefore, the chancellor concluded, the administration stood on the basis of the 800-year-old constitution and not its opponents. The constitution was excellent and had to be maintained; consequently, Széchenyi need not get involved.

Metternich knew he had nothing to fear from the Hungarian feudal constitution. Admitting that previously he had not interferred with Hungarian affairs, he still insisted that in the last 18 months he had brought himself up-to-date. He gave his opinion about Hungarians in no charitable terms, suggesting that Paul Nagy was under the influence of the most dangerous liberal ideas, that the magnates were "the horror of the nation," and that, generally speaking, "there was an infinitely great amount of intelligence in the land but very little real practical knowledge." Correspondence among the counties would lead to anarchy provoking repressive countermeasures: "For God's sake," he implored Széchenyi, "don't force us to hang people." Initiative for legislation and interpretation of the laws were royal prerogatives, hence, the chancellor said, he was very much in favor of calling the Diet into session every three years. It will be uncomfortable, he added, but very useful and not at all dangerous.

This was Metternich's "platform" for Hungary in 1825, a platform full of half-truths and misrepresentations. The chancellor's tone was cynical and his advice to Széchenyi sounded like a pat on the back. He told Széchenyi not to allow himself to be carried away by applause

---

[115] *Ibid.*, IV, 249f.
[116] Nov. 12, 1825, Viszota, ed., *Naplók*, II, 643f. Also "Miscellania" I and II, Annex No. I, 4a–b, *ibid.*, III, 447–50.

and acclamations but to think of his future. He assured his listener that he could see things better from above than Széchenyi could from below; also, one ought to strive for a position on a higher level.

Széchenyi was not misled by Metternich's caricature of Hungary, nor did he ignore his warning about demagogy. He knew the chancellor abhorred nationalism, liberalism, and constitutionalism, but was also aware that many of his statements concerning the selfishness of the estates and lack of culture and common sense were painfully true. Overestimating the endurance of the views held in common with Metternich, he tried to convince his opponent that misunderstanding and mistrust between the crown and the Diet could easily be disposed of once the basic principles had been agreed on. One of these principles, he thought, was the fact that Hungary was a constitutional monarchy and that the king had taken an oath to the constitution; consequently, laws of the realm could be accepted, done away with, and interpreted only by common action of king and estates.[117]

Trusting that he would be able to convince Metternich, Széchenyi sent a memorandum to the chancellor on November 18 six days after their meeting.[118] His ambition was not completely unrewarded. Despite Metternich's highhanded remarks to the personalis,[119] written a whole month after their first discussion and caused partly by the realization of his failure to divert Széchenyi from his position, the memorandum had a certain influence on the chancellor. On November 21 the presidents of the two chambers, the palatine and the personalis, left for Vienna to mediate between the court and the indignant estates. On the same day, Count Joseph Esterházy, Metternich's son-in-law, asked Széchenyi to see the chancellor.[120] Széchenyi, however, preferred to at-

---

[117] This account is based on Széchenyi's entry of Nov. 12, 1825, *ibid.*, II, 643–47. Széchenyi's authenticity of the entry is confirmed by the short summary of the controversial issues noted on a separate page by him right after the conversation. Annex No. XI, 2, *ibid.*, II, 697f. Széchenyi's notes make it possible to go beyond the interpretation given of the important Széchenyi-Metternich relationship in Western historical literature. Cf. George Barany, "The Széchenyi Problem," *Journal of Central European Affairs*, XX (1960), 258f.; Silagi, *Der grösste Ungar*, pp. 100–103.

[118] Nov. 17, 1825, Viszota, ed., *Naplók*, II, 651. (The entries were usually written the day after the date indicated.) The original draft of Széchenyi's memorandum has been published as Annex No. XII, 1, *ibid.*, II, 691–97.

[119] Cf. Annex No. XII, 4, *ibid.*, II, 700–705.

[120] Nov. 21, 1825, *ibid.*, II, 652. Cf. the chancellor's note to Szögyényi:

The day of my departure from Pressburg I received the letter I now enclose, and I informed him that I should be very pleased to enter into real discussions about its contents. [The second half of the sentence in the original reads: "Von hier aus liess ich ihm *mündlich* sagen, *dass ich sein Schreiben erhalten hätte*, und stets bereit sein würde, mich über dessen Inhalt mit ihm *mündlich* zu besprechen." The italicized parts are either omitted from the English edition, or make no sense in the translation.] Expecting

tend the sessions of the Diet and went to see Metternich only on December 8.[121] In the meantime, on November 28, the palatine returned from Vienna with a considerably more conciliatory royal rescript, the main points of which satisfied both Széchenyi and the estates.[122]

The day before the arrival of the palatine, Széchenyi concluded an "alliance of virtue" with two intimate friends, Wesselényi and Count Michael Esterházy. The main points of this alliance—the text of which was the first coherent Hungarian text in Széchenyi's diary—described its purpose as the promoting of the happiness of their compatriots and their progeny. To achieve this goal, members of the alliance were not to hide anything from each other. They must exert an influence over the education of the youth to increase their civic virtues. Convinced that only the growth of reason, morality, and wisdom could advance the progress of mankind, the three agreed to set an example by their own good conduct, following the old principle of not doing anything without bearing in mind that "God and the present Century's Philosophers keep an eye on you." The alliance was to be based on good morals and dignity; "if other nations are wealthier, let us excel in morality and patriotism."[123]

This document, reflecting the influence of the Enlightenment, is also an interesting contribution to the understanding of how Christian and deistic ideals had been correlated in Széchenyi's thinking. At the top of his philosophical "system" there were the twin moral values of the highest intelligence and highest virtue permeating each other in their ultimate realization, God.[124] It is not easy—and perhaps not even necessary—to draw a sharp distinction between Montesquieu's "political virtue" or John Adams' "positive Passion for the public good," on the one hand, and truly virtuous Christian conduct on the other; such lines of demarcation were not always felt, let alone conceptualized in the

---

him every day—as he said to my commissioner that he would call on me immediately [!]—I marked his letter with marginal notes . . . .

Metternich Memoirs; IV, 250, Viszota, ed., *Naplók,* II, 702.

[121] Dec. 8, 1825, *ibid.,* II, 658ff.

[122] Nov. 28, 1825, *ibid.,* II, 654 and n. 1; Horváth, *Huszonöt év,* I, 161f. In Horváth's opinion the palatine, Archduke Joseph, should be given credit for the second rescript. Without belittling the importance of the palatine's mediation, a thorough analysis of the texts of the rescript and of Széchenyi's memorandum to Metternich results in also establishing Széchenyi's influence on the second royal reply exactly through Metternich. See Viszota, ed., *Naplók,* II, p. lxxxviii; Friedreich, *Széchenyi élete,* I, 163.

[123] Nov. 27, Dec. 6, 1825, Viszota, ed., *Naplók,* II, 653f., 657. The goals of the "alliance of virtue" were also defined by Wesselényi, whose description is more detailed and radical in tone. Friedreich, *Széchenyi élete,* I, 138f.

[124] Angyal, "Les idées," *Revue de Hongrie,* III (1909), 532–37.

eighteenth or early nineteenth centuries in the West, either.[125] In east central Europe, where a proclivity for mysticism and irrationalism tended to overwhelm the rationalistic, spiritual foundations of enlightened ideals, such a distinction would be meaningless. Széchenyi's and his friends' romantic patriotism, too, had multiple intellectual and emotional roots: their synoptic view of the new nationalism, of which they were a part, reflected the sincere belief that to serve God, humanity, and the fatherland concurrently, and to enrich one's own life, was possible, hence morally mandatory, and could be achieved without a basic conflict of loyalties.

It was only natural, then, that Széchenyi, imbued as he was at the time with the ideas of Benjamin Franklin, tried to supplement the idealistic "alliance of virtue" with more practical day-to-day agitation. He rented and furnished living quarters in Pressburg with Count George Károlyi, where younger members of the Diet exchanged ideas. This temporary "club" was the beginning of the subsequent, permanent "casino" initiated by him in Pest after the sessions of the Diet were over. It was this club to which Metternich referred in his letter to Szögyényi on December 11 when he also informed the personalis about Széchenyi's second visit. By December 8, when this visit occurred, Széchenyi was the leader of a small but influential group of the liberal opposition at the Diet. The young magnates and deputies, among whom Széchenyi, Wesselényi, Count George Károlyi, and Count George Andrássy were the most prominent, used to gather informally beginning in the autumn of 1825, first in the apartments of Széchenyi and Károlyi, then in an improvised club rented by them. The group discussed the problem of reforms, the newly established Academy, and among other things, questions as to how transportation and commerce should be developed. They were far from seeing eye to eye on all important issues. Széchenyi endeavored to tone down the oppositional character of the club from the start, trying to make it a meeting place of varying shades of opinion.[126]

If one believes Metternich, there was a "strange disturbance" in Széchenyi's deportment during their discussion of December 8 which lasted three hours. Although the recent royal rescript had changed the political situation, the chancellor commented on Széchenyi's memorandum, adding that he considered him "a man lost through vanity and ambition—one of those who bring unhappiness upon themselves." Upon Széchenyi's assurance of loyalty to the throne and complaint about the

[125] Gerald Stourzh, "Die tugendhafte Republik. Montesquieus Begriff der 'vertu' und die Anfänge der Vereinigten Staaten von Amerika," in *Österreich und Europa*, pp. 248ff., 252.

[126] Viszota, ed., *Naplók*, III, pp. xlii f., lxiii; Ferstl and Steinbach Reports, Annex No. II, 6a and Annex No. V, 3c, *ibid.*, III, 608, 775.

shallowness of the Hungarian magnates which led him to try to animate the Hungarian youth, Metternich asked him whether he would dare to make the same confessions to his friends. When, according to Metternich, Széchenyi said this would be impossible, the chancellor accused him of being a traitor either to him or to his friends and himself, warning that he would sink into the mire; or, if he turned around, he would be branded by the very party that led him astray. In Metternich's opinion, Széchenyi "when quite calm" thought as he did and complained of the extravagance of some of his young friends, still hoping to convert them to his own views. In conclusion Metternich expressed the belief that "the Széchenyi-Károlyi Club belongs to the new Opposition, and that one of its leading men is not at all satisfied with it." The chancellor intended to spare the old constitutional opposition, but suggested "to eradicate" the new opposition "for it spreads like a horrible disease." As a means to this end, he pointed to the Diet's circular sessions where the "new opposition" seemed to be particularly strong.

Parts of Metternich's letter sound like efforts to justify to the personalis his lengthy discussion with Széchenyi for, in his own words, "as this took place at the time when I usually receive visitors, I should not be much astonished if the fact of so long a conversation between Széchenyi and myself would soon be generally known."[127] As to Széchenyi's memorandum of November 16, essentially based on the reasoning of his diary entry of November 12, only the most important aspect of it will be mentioned. Széchenyi had pointed out to Metternich that the estates, rightly or wrongly, saw a threat to the constitution in the absolutist tendencies of Vienna. To eliminate the cause of this fear Széchenyi suggested that the monarch's "sincere constitutional feeling which he affirmed by oath on his accession to the throne" be expressed in the next royal resolution. The basis of his proposal was the assumption, clearly expressed in the closing part of the memorandum, that the king himself was under the law and had to obey it.

As mentioned earlier, the practical side of Széchenyi's proposal had been accepted in the second royal rescript and the estates had apparently won their point. The "concession" of "restoring the constitution," as Horváth called it, was essentially a return to the constitutional compromise between crown and Diet in 1790–91 after the death of Joseph II. This did not solve the problem of reform; the meager results of the long Diet bear testimony to this. Furthermore, Metternich, who probably exerted a moderating influence on the monarch in ironing out the differences with the Diet, in no way accepted the hypothesis of the constitutionalists (and of Széchenyi) that the Hungarian constitution

---

[127] *Metternich Memoirs*, IV, 250–53.

might be endangered by the crown. It is clear from his comments on the memorandum that in his opinion the sovereign was the real safeguard of the constitution; the dangers threatening the constitution did not come from "the smallest trace of want of respect to the Constitution on the part of the King," but had other sources, namely, the irresponsible ideas of those taken in by the "spirit of the age." Széchenyi was correct in saying that their political creeds were diametrically opposed in approaching the basic issue of the moment.

This basic issue, as Széchenyi saw it, was the struggle between the principles of absolute and constitutional monarchy. Concerning the question of what happens if king and law came into conflict, he realized that the Diet could not possibly have its way against the crown since the defendant would be the judge of his own case, as it happened to the peasant in a manorial court.[128] As suggested by this spontaneous association of ideas, Széchenyi intuitively perceived that the constitutional issue could not be separated forever from the problem of social reform, and any such effort must necessarily fail in the long run. Just how much of this perception was due to his readings, experiences abroad, or to the influence of Wesselényi or Paul Nagy, is hard to determine. But in grasping at the very beginning of his political career the frailty of the compromise between court and Diet, he far surpassed in insight Metternich and his Hungarian contemporaries as well. True, he was deeply disturbed by the irresponsible behavior of the dietal youth and by the lack of moderation of some deputies,[129] and he probably said so to Metternich. But he was also aware of the shortsighted attitude of the court regarding Hungarian affairs,[130] and was not misled by the chancellor who attempted to divert him from his plans through a mixture of warnings, paternalistic encouragements, flattering promises, and thinly veiled threats, during their meeting on December 8, 1825.[131] Three days later Széchenyi wrote another memorandum and sent it to Metternich on December 16. In his diary he called it "My Confession."[132]

In the introductory part of his "confession"[133] Széchenyi said that for many years he had tried to reach a higher degree of moral independence. The calmness of his conscience and the inner satisfaction he felt told him that he had succeeded in approaching this goal. Opening

---

[128] Nov. 13, 1825, Viszota, ed., *Naplók*, II, 648f.

[129] Oct. 8, Nov. 16, 1825, *ibid.*, II, 629, 650f. Metternich was wrong in thinking that Széchenyi kept his conversations with him secret from his friends. Széchenyi sent a copy of his memorandum to Wesselényi. Friedreich, *Széchenyi élete*, I, 165.

[130] Dec. 6, 1825, Viszota, ed., *Naplók*, II, 658.

[131] Dec. 8, 1825, *ibid.*, II, 658ff.

[132] Dec. 13–15, 1825, *ibid.*, II, 662. In the memorandum, too, he referred to it as his confession.

[133] Published as Annex No. XII, 5, *ibid.*, II, 705–11.

his heart to the chancellor as to no one else in his life, he pointed out that although he disagreed with some of Metternich's views, he nevertheless had listened to them with respect and in silence during their conversation on December 8, because he was impressed by the chancellor's knowledge. Yet he was reluctant to admit that all opposition to the king would necessarily be unconstitutional, as the chancellor had suggested. Political opposition was important to the life of a healthy nation. As for his own "sad end" predicted by Metternich, he was indifferent. Caring nothing for the opinion of the masses, he did not want to seem insincere or double-dealing. He had his principles on which he intended to rely.

Turning to these principles, Széchenyi put, above all, a strong emphasis on his anti-revolutionary feelings. Saying that he hated all kinds of disorder and the revolutionary slogan, *égalité et liberté,* as well as senseless innovations, he added that he would prefer the old *Schlendrian* to unrest and revolution. Yet he claimed to be a friend of "useful inventions and improvements," and thought that all classes should be equal before the law. While abhorring violence he admitted that in many respects his thinking was "very liberal." Thus he held that mankind's happiness depended on "the highest possible degree of civilization and enlightenment," and expressed his belief in a representative form of government and public discussions as the best means of fighting despotism, prejudice, and ignorance. He was against bias but knew it could not be disposed of overnight. In matters of religion he described himself as having no firm opinion. He was in favor of unlimited tolerance, adding that if he had been born a Turk he probably would wash his feet every day with as much devotion as he now went to church every Sunday. He had a deep respect for both genuine philosophical thinking and practical wisdom. In his opinion nationality could not be achieved in a high enough degree. Patriotism was equivalent to devotion to fatherland and king. Deploring the fact that Hungarian magnates caused much of their own degeneracy, he still remarked that the king also made mistakes in dealing with them. In conclusion, Széchenyi repeated his deep trust in the chancellor, saying that he had kept his innermost thoughts to himself up to now, and he could have done so henceforth, too; yet he thought it more honest to speak about them frankly to Metternich.

The chancellor submitted Széchenyi's second memorandum to the state conference on the day of its receipt. In his report to Francis I, Metternich brushed aside Széchenyi's ideas as those of a visionary and of a real but good-natured fool who, however, could serve as a thermometer indicating the political temperature of the surrounding mass.[134]

[134] Annex No. xii, 6, *ibid.*, ii, 711.

Széchenyi's second memorandum was, of course, not a carefully systematic political program. It was intended as a confession, as Széchenyi
said, and as such reflected with remarkable sincerity his political creed,
unclarified and irrational as it was in many respects. It revealed its
author's desire to find the way of peaceful social reform and avoid revolution; it showed his effort to remain loyal to the dynasty and the empire,
yet to promote Hungary's transformation into a modern national state
with a representative government. If one disregards for a moment
Széchenyi's economic program, which belonged to the essence of his
work, one could say that merely from the political point of view the
memorandum contained the whole Széchenyi problem in a nutshell. Metternich may have forecast Széchenyi's personal tragedy because as a
practicing politician he was aware of the merciless rules of the political
game, and Széchenyi was too scrupulous and conscientious to give direction or submit meekly to rough political storms. But Széchenyi did sense
the coming of the storm, and wanted to prevent it at a time when
Metternich was completely out of touch with Hungarian reality, not
because of a particular antipathy to Hungary or progress, but because
he was not sensitive enough to the historical forces of nationalism, liberalism, and the increasing desire of people to have a say in their government.
"Danger there is none, for ideas do not rise to that"—he wrote on
November 7, 1825 to Gentz about the Diet in Pressburg,[135] and advised
the personalis a month later to "eradicate" the new opposition representing "the spirit of the age." Trying to preserve his ascendancy in the
discussion with Széchenyi, he failed to see the truth in the latter's anxiety
both in 1825 and in the years to come. Comparing the chancellor's
position of 1825 with his reflections about the situation in Hungary
written in 1843 and 1844,[136] one wonders whether his high-handed attitude was justified, and whether his often declared ability to foresee the
future could be substituted for the bankruptcy of the system named
after him.[137]

[135] Metternich to Gentz, Nov. 7, 1825, Doc. 771, *Metternich Memoirs*, IV, 205.
[136] "Der Sprachenkampf in Ungarn." Metternich an den Palatin Erzherzog Josef
in Pressburg (Wien, 29 Nov. 1843). Doc. 1,476, *Aus Metternichs nachgelassenen Papieren*,
ed. Richard Metternich–Winneburg, 8 vols. (Vienna: Braumüller, 1880–84), VI,
672–77; "Über die Ungarischen Zustände." Aphoristische Bemerkungen Metternichs,
niedergeschrieben Ende 1844, Doc. 1,492, *ibid.*, VII, 61–63. It may be noticed that these
writings of Metternich were preceded by two memoranda of Széchenyi's dated
July and December 1843, and proposing certain measures of reform. Metternich's
"Aphoristische Bemerkungen" contained sharp critical remarks concerning Széchenyi's
activity but at the same time also reflected the influence of some of his ideas. Metternich
in person gave a copy of his "Aphoristische Bemerkungen" to Széchenyi. Cf. Viszota,
ed., *Naplók*, VI, pp. xxviii f. Széchenyi's two memoranda of 1843 were published as
Annex No. VIII, 14, 18, *Széchenyi és Kossuth*, I, 728–34, 735–43.
[137] This does not mean that Metternich had no theoretical understanding of the
worsening political situation in the 1840s or that he did not want to take steps to

As for Széchenyi, Metternich's warnings made him only more conscious that he had reached a decisive moment of his life. The grounds on which he rested his "opposition" to the regime consisted of the rather moderate views of an enlightened constitutional monarchist. He held that political opposition was not necessarily subversive or antidynastic; that nationalism and liberalism were irresistible historical forces which, however, could be used in a constructive way for the benefit of the nation and of the monarchy as well; and that reforms, soberly put into practice, were absolute prerequisites to any rejuvenation of the Hungarian constitution and the Habsburg monarchy. Széchenyi knew that his tenets were considered "radical" and impracticable by Metternich and most of his compatriots. But he also thought that there was an important range of agreement between the chancellor and himself, and decided to build on this rather limited basis. Hence his efforts to avoid sharp political conflicts with the court, his concentration chiefly (though not exclusively) on economic problems, and his endeavor to introduce reforms from above with the assistance, or at least tolerance of the administration.

Even so, Széchenyi realized that his activities and connections with members of the Hungarian opposition aroused the suspicion of Metternich and the court party. He paid little heed to this, for he put the mandates of his conscience above everything else. His private life became intertwined with his public activities; friendships, love, and even his most important readings seemed to have had a stimulating effect on him. In his letters to Crescence he pledged himself to proceed henceforth toward virtue. His "alliance of virtue" with Wesselényi and Michael Esterházy required them to confess and correct each other's mistakes.[138] The acquaintance with Franklin's ideas stimulated him to systematic

---

improve conditions in Hungary. But his proposals were half-measures and usually came late. Besides, one should not forget that the "Metternich system" was liquidated in 1848 in Vienna and not by Hungarians: Széchenyi's pathological self-accusations written during the summer of 1848 and during the early Döbling period should not be used to justify the chancellor's "forecasts."

[138] This mutual criticism of each other's weaknesses did not work quite smoothly. In March 1826 Széchenyi noted that his friends' criticism frequently was unpleasant; in time they would understand, he added, that one must not resort to rash actions in Hungary. The last remark indicates that Széchenyi was from the very beginning against a rigid attitude (*Unnachgiebigkeit*) and tried to exert a moderating influence on his friends. A few months later he himself became very critical on hearing that Wesselényi, who often spoke of the emancipation of the human race, of liberty, liberalism, and Christian philosophy, cruelly beat his hunter. Széchenyi drew a rather characteristic conclusion from his friend's brutality: "I am much less worthy than Wesselényi. How often must I, then, without even knowing it, act in an unjust, harsh and passionate manner!" Cf. Mar. 4, Dec. 10, 1826, Viszota, ed., *Naplók*, III, 26, 108.

and severe investigation of his own deeds.[139] His activity in the Diet and discussions with Metternich indicated that in his thoughts the path of virtue was identical with the path leading to Hungary's regeneration; within a decade he was to contemplate an alliance of virtue which would embrace the whole nation.[140] To the exhortation of the chancellor, "I tremble for you," Széchenyi retorted with pride: "I do not tremble. Everything I undertake, I undertake in public and I do nothing clandestinely."[141] Indeed, he felt he had come to the parting of the ways: allegorically yet sincerely, he chose to become a new Hercules who, unlike his classic model, would devote his life to promoting the welfare of his compatriots and to the gigantic task of advancing the prosperity of his Hungarian fatherland.[142]

[139] The first "tables of virtue" in his diaries are from the beginning of 1826. See, e.g., Annex No. xiv, Viszota, ed., *Naplók*, ii, 716, 719ff. Cf. July 2–3, 1828, *ibid.*, iii, 216ff. On Sept. 11, 1829 he wrote: "Gelesen Memoires sur la vie de Benjamin Franklin—2 Theile—Mir war alles schon bekannt—und doch las ich sie mit erneuertem interesse. Das wahrhaft Grosse und Einfache—ermüdet nie." *Ibid.*, iii, 348f. One may mention that Széchenyi and his friends must have been acquainted with the concept of the *Tugendbund*, so fashionable at the time among German youth, especially college students. Whatever the impact of the German example may have been in the rest of the empire, Széchenyi's original inspiration had different roots.

[140] Cf. *Hunnia* (Hungary), written in 1835 but published only posthumously, in Török, ed., *Széchenyi politikai iskolája*, iii, 37. This is but another indication of how Széchenyi transferred the ethical concepts of love and friendship into the sphere of his patriotic feelings. Actually, these spheres had been overlapping in his thinking ever since the mid-1820s.

[141] Feb. 13, 1826, Viszota, ed., *Naplók*, iii, 17.

[142] In 1828 Széchenyi translated a poem, written by John Kiss in 1791, into German prose under the title "Alcides' Wahl." (The allegoric poem of Kiss was also a translation from Robert Lowth's English poem, "The Choice of Hercules." *DNB*, xxxiv, 215.) He often departed, however, from the original. These deviations are highly characteristic of his own philosophy of life, suggesting that virtue consists of promoting the welfare of the fatherland and one's fellow men, that the reward of virtue is real inward harmony, and that this harmony is a link between lovers separated by fate. The idea of comparing himself to Hercules was born in a conversation with Crescence in April 1826. Cf. Apr. 15, 1826, Viszota, ed., *Naplók*, iii, 43 and n. 4. For the text of Széchenyi's translation see Annex No. 1, 8, *ibid.*, iii, 463–75.

CHAPTER V

Regenerating A Nation

The legislation enacted by the Diet of 1825–27 could hardly be considered a great achievement. Francis I did sanction several laws in which he recognized his obligation to abide by the constitution, not to make any changes in conscription practices and taxation without the consent of the Diet, and to call it into session every three years (Laws III–V). These laws, however, were only reinforcements of previous royal obligations (chiefly of those enacted during the Diet of 1790–91) and the necessity of their confirmation in itself was proof that the real relationship between crown and estates did not correspond to the solemn provisions guaranteed by the Hungarian constitution. The dual character of this ancient constitution, as well as its undefined procedures in legislative matters, made it difficult to deal in an efficient way with the great number of far-reaching problems accumulated during the 13-year interruption of legislative activity.

The initiative for new legislation lay with the king. He summoned the Diet, at the beginning of which he submitted the royal propositions containing suggestions for new laws. The two chambers of the Diet had to agree on the text of the law. It was sometimes a matter of several months before such an agreement could be reached, if at all, for neither of the chambers could force its will on the other, and the correspondence between them could be dragged out indefinitely. In case of an agreement between the two chambers, the king might still refuse to give his consent to any piece of legislation he disliked; in effect, he had a veto power. On the other hand, governing by royal decree was considered unconstitutional in Hungary, and could be resisted in extreme cases (as under Joseph II or Francis I in 1823) by civil disobedience. In the Diet there were no political parties in the modern sense of the word. Motions were decided not by direct voting but by giving preference to the *sanior pars* or the "sounder" and more influential party whose votes must be "pondered" or evaluated rather than just counted. This practice, and the frequent necessity of mediating between the two chambers and between the Diet and the throne, gave significant power to the personalis and the palatine, the two presidents of the chambers who, however, were nominees of the king. The personalis and the palatine, respectively, were also presidents of the King's Bench (*Tabula Regia*) and the Septemviral Bench (*Tabula Septemviralis*), the two highest courts of the realm called together the Royal Curia (*Curia Regis*). During the sessions of the Diet, the courts remained closed; in fact, the justices of the King's Bench had a right to sit in person in the chamber of deputies.

On the whole, however, deputies of the "lower" chamber were representatives of privileged classes or corporate bodies, the nobility, the clergy, and the chartered or free royal cities. Unlike their Anglo-Saxon counterparts in Parliament, they had to abide by the instructions of their constituents or be forced to resign. Most members of the "upper" chamber, or "table," on the other hand, attended the Diet because of their high ecclesiastic or secular position or high birth, on the basis of royal invitation addressed to them in person. According to the tradition going back to Werbőczi, the sixteenth century codifier of Hungarian feudal law, members of the two chambers constituted one single legislative body. Sitting separately most of the time since the 17th century, they would nonetheless be called into one "mixed" session chaired by the palatine on certain solemn occasions or when differences of the two chambers had to be straightened out. But in the latter case, the procedures for decision-making were rather ill-defined. If there was no lawful basis for voting by estates (*curiatim*) in the Hungarian feudal tradition, there was no precedent for yielding automatically to a numerical majority either, especially since the chamber of magnates was not based on representation. Also, the presidents of both chambers had various means of persuasion, from intimidation to the dangling of royal favor or promotion to a desired office, which made it difficult to organize, let alone maintain for a longer period of time, even a simple majority opposing the administration.

The Hungarian Diet was a mixture of people representing either themselves or their constituents; some were independent, while others had to stick to the directives drawn up by those in whose name they claimed to speak. The order of procedure, the discussion and work in the plenary and circular sessions, which developed from private conferences, depended largely on precedent and the maneuvering skill of the presiding officer. Agreements, once reached, were frequently disputed, too, because of the unreliability of the protocols. The evaluation of the votes cast, and even the decision of when to put a question to a vote, were not exempt from subjective judgment or conflicting interpretations, either.[1] It was only in the Diet of 1825 that a question was first decided by direct voting; as, however, the decisive vote was given by the representative of the free royal cities, which taken together had but one vote, many members of the Diet, including Széchenyi, considered the decision of the personalis as unconstitutional.[2] Not until the 1830s did the principle of following the will of the majority rather than evaluating the votes cast begin to prevail in the Diet.[3]

The understandable timidity with which the feudal Diet slowly began to move in the direction of introducing democratic voting practices into its undemocratic procedures was but one of the obstacles which stood in the path of Hungary's modernization via gradual reform. The royal propositions suggested the resumption of the work of systematic reform for which the Diets of the early 1790s had prepared numerous and elaborate blueprints. But the conditions which these so-called systematic works partly reflected and partly intended to reform had undergone a radical change since the cannonade at Valmy—the paraphrase Goethe—had opened a new phase in world history. The administration of Francis I and the Diet, none of them eager to press very hard for innovations, concurred in the necessity for adapting the "systematic works" to the changed circumstances. This, however, implied that the task of comprehensive reforms was left for a later Diet. To prepare the work of this forthcoming Diet in an orderly and organic way, the Diet of 1825–27 selected a committee of 77, chaired by the palatine, and we shall have to return to the problem of systematic reform in due time. Here we need to stress only that if the long overdue social and economic reforms were not thrust on Hungary through important legislative measures by an unwilling Diet, neither was the administration made happy by the postponement of measures that could conceivably have simplified if not outright improved the governing of the traditionally reluctant Magyars. The British ambassador was not far from the truth

[1] With regard to the Diet of 1825–27, in addition to works already cited, see also: Lajos Hőke, "Az 1825–27–ki országgyűlés" (The Diet of 1825–27), in *Hazánk*, v (1886), 81–97; Lajos Ralovich, "Az 1825–27–ki országgyűlesrlő" (About the Diet of 1825–27), in *Hazánk*, viii (n.d.), 96–113, 173–89, 262–80; István Iványi, "Az 1827–ki országgyűlés követeinek rövid jellemzése" (Brief Characterization of the Deputies of the Diet of 1827), in *Hazánk*, iii (1885), 76–79. Concerning the structure and procedures of the Diet cf. Jenő Gaál, *Gróf Széchenyi István nemzeti politikája* (Count Stephen Széchenyi's National Policy), 3 vols. (Budapest: Magyar Tudományos Akadémia, 1902–1903), i, 12–16. Also, Ferenc Kölcsey, "Országgyűlési napló, 1832–33" (Dietal Diary, 1832–33), in *Kölcsey Ferenc Összes Művei* (The Collected Works of Francis Kölcsey) (Budapest: Franklin, n.d.), pp. 1,394–1,400. For the high courts cf. Marczali, *Hungary in the Eighteenth Century*, 338ff.

[2] Mar. 9, 1826, Viszota, ed., *Naplók*, iii, 27f. and n. 5.

[3] Mar. 27, 1833, *ibid.*, iv, 371.

in summing up his opinion about the two-year-long Diet, when he said the deliberations of the Diet had been equally unproductive to the crown and to the country.[4]

The British report especially emphasized that the administration failed to receive approval of a settlement concerning the regulation of private debts pending since the devaluations of the currency in 1811 and 1816 which had never been approved by the Hungarian Diet.[5] On the other hand, the Diet, which succeeded in forcing the court to observe henceforth certain formalities of Hungarian constitutional practices, was unable to get concessions on such important "grievances" as the problems of making Magyar the official language of the administration, recognizing the independence of Hungarian finances, and reincorporating the *partium* into Hungary proper.[6] Thus, legislatively the Diet ended in a stalemate. The return to the constitutional status quo of 1790–91 was a reflection of the inertia of both court and Diet; it also suggested the great difficulties in creating a modern nation via a feudal Diet.

Széchenyi clearly recognized both of these facts. Seeing the impotence and reluctance of administration and estates, however, he realized at the outset of his public career that the cooperation of crown and Diet was necessary for thoroughgoing and peaceful reforms in the foreseeable future. He reasoned that the first reforms must be initiated in areas relatively neutral and free from rivalry between the court and the constitutional opposition. Moreover, feudal prejudices had to be overcome by creating favorable public opinion for useful improvements, primarily in the economic field, and by stimulating national pride.

Actually the great symbolic breakthrough leading to the creation of a modern Hungarian national state came with the founding of the Academy. Nationwide public opinion, though limited, was created and led by poets, writers, and the educated members of the nobility, who since the end of the 18th century had demanded and prepared the creation of an Academy for the promotion of national culture. That the Magyar idiom was capable of becoming the unifying literary language of the educated and the vehicle of Hungary's cultural life was proved by

[4] Wellesley to Lord Viscount Dudley, Aug. 20, 1827, *F.O. 7/198, Public Record Office* (London).

[5] Hőke, "Az 1825–27–ki országgyűlés," pp. 90f. The two devaluations placed the Austrian currency first at 20 and then eight percent of its original value.

[6] When the Turks conquered Buda in 1541 the eastern counties of Hungary proper came under the rule of the princes of Transylvania (*Partes Regni Hungariae*). After the expulsion of the Turks (1718) many resolutions of the Hungarian Diet called for the reannexation of the *Partium*, i.e., of the three counties of Zaránd, Kraszna, Middle Szolnok, and the district of Kővár. However, the annexation was not carried into effect until 1848. Cf. Marczali, *Hungary in the Eighteenth Century*, p. 332 and n. 1.

Vörösmarty's romantic epos about the conquest of the country by Árpád.[7] From the cultural point of view, the program of emancipating the Magyar language had already been prepared when Széchenyi's example set the legislative machinery into motion. There was an important difference, however, between the "cultural emancipation" of Magyar and its recognition as the official language of the state. Although a preliminary step toward the realization of the latter, the creation of the Academy meant only the former. The two goals were not identical, as indicated by the fact that Count Cziráky, loyal supporter of the court and adamant opponent of making Hungarian the official language of administration, nonetheless contributed financially to the Academy, whereas Count Illésházy, a leader of the Dietal opposition, paid lip service to the Academy while "forgetting" to support it financially.[8]

The support given by many members of the Diet to the cause of the Magyar vernacular, and hence indirectly to the "revival of the national spirit," was one of the few signs which gave Széchenyi hope that the regeneration of Hungary was possible. He referred to these hopeful signs, as well as to the promise of "a noble creature to assist him with faithful heart"[9] when, looking back in an autobiographical passage of *A kelet népe,* he related how at the Diet of 1825 he had stepped out upon the thorny field of public life. He was seriously determined, he wrote, that he, if no one else, would lay the foundation of his nation's future glory or at least devote all his life to this task. Sixteen years later he also sincerely felt that his participation at the Diet of 1825 was not an improvisation or the result of a momentary excitement but part of a well-calculated and far-reaching plan.[10]

To a certain extent, the complete material of the important Metternich-Széchenyi dispute of 1825 described in the preceding chapter supports Széchenyi's claim. His two memoranda to Metternich reveal an intention to regenerate Hungary with Austrian approval and help. Both, and especially the second, show the ideological basis of Széchenyi's thinking on the questions of social progress, revolution, and nationalism. Throughout his life he was to stick essentially to the principles laid

[7] *Zalán futása* (The Flight of Zalán). Cf. Károly Csahihen, *Pest-Buda irodalmi élete 1780–1830*, 2 vols. (Literary Life in Pest-Buda, 1780–1830), (Budapest: Stephaneum, 1934), II, 155–62, which gives a good account of how Hungarian literary life, decentralized at the beginning of the century, gradually moved to Pest. By the time of the formation of the Academy, Pest had become the focal point of literary activities, thus making feasible Széchenyi's idea of turning Pest into the real social and cultural capital of Hungary.

[8] Hóman and Szekfű, *Magyar Történet*, v, 194–99.

[9] I.e., Crescence who, by then, was his wife.

[10] Ferenczi, ed., *A kelet népe*, pp. 223f.

down right at the beginning of his political career—a remarkable consistency, indeed.

Be that as it may, Széchenyi's effort to be impartial, his pragmatic approach to higher aims and ability to campaign vigorously for the realization of experiments yet untried in Hungary were characteristic features of the first years of public activity. During the Diet of 1825–27 he set up as his maxim "to side with the king when the king is right and to side with the people when the people are right." In years to come this intention was to serve as his guide in matters of political consistency.[11] In the chamber of magnates he supported the lower chamber's resolution against government-by-decree, saying the duty of the Diet was to uphold the law of the land and not just oppose according to preconceived principles anything that had been proposed by the other chamber where the oppositional forces prevailed. Reprimanded by the palatine, Széchenyi controlled himself and gave no answer, noting, however, in his diary: "Noticed that the Hungarian magnates deserve neither constitution, nor liberty."[12] Similarly, in the matter of constitutional grievances, he was in favor of the language used by the estates, pointing out that it was not royal grace but royal duty which upheld the constitution. Again he was reprimanded by the palatine; on this occasion, however, Széchenyi was seconded by another young aristocrat, Count Michael Esterházy, who reminded the president of the chamber that he was addressing himself not to an Austrian archduke but to the Hungarian palatine.[13] Toward the end of the Diet, Széchenyi championed the stand of the estates on taxation, stressing that "if every lawful act must be derived from [royal] grace then I cannot see here any constitution, only an absolute monarchy."[14] Széchenyi was also in favor of the lower chamber's resolutions for the use of the Hungarian tongue, for the right of Protestants to attend foreign universities and be tutors in Catholic families, and for the new principle of Hungarian independence in financial questions.[15] It is no wonder that he was considered by the court party

[11] Jan. 28, 1827, Viszota, ed., *Naplók*, III, 124. Essentially, this was to be Széchenyi's answer in the 1840s to the accusations of being inconsistent and of having abandoned the cause of reform.

[12] Apr. 1, 1826, *ibid.*, III, 35f. and n. 1.

[13] Apr. 26, 1827, *ibid.*, III, 150 and n. 3, 151.

[14] Aug. 15, 1827, *ibid.*, III, 171 and n. 1.

[15] Feb. 7, 28, Mar. 2, 1826, *ibid.*, III, 16, 24 and n. 7, 25 and n. 3, 26. For centuries Hungarian Protestants had been able to send young theologians to German, Swiss, and Dutch universities. Special funds which made this possible, however, were restricted to this purpose only; in the absence of students both capital and interest were lost to Hungarian Protestantism. Following the outbreak of unrest among the German Lutheran youth in 1817, which reached its climax with the assassination of Kotzebue three years later, Francis I ordered the teaching of Protestant theological courses at

as a tool of opposition leaders like Paul Nagy and Wesselényi and as an instrument of the Calvinists.[16]

Széchenyi was under different kinds of pressure. First, he was ordered to join his regiment,[17] then, when he managed to have this order changed, varied rumors were circulated that he had ridiculed the clergy and delighted in delaying the Academy's founding so as to escape paying the sum he had promised.[18] Also, Metternich, having failed to "convince" Széchenyi, began to treat him coldly, upon which Széchenyi remarked with pride: "Metternich's system ceases with his life. Mine will begin only after my death."[19] Believing that "he had spoiled everything in Vienna,"[20] he did not yet want to commit himself completely to the "radical" opposition, being well aware of its shortcomings, too.[21]

Although there can be no doubt concerning his stand on the issue of absolutism vs. constitutionalism,[22] Széchenyi was far from supporting unconditionally the estates with whom he sided in most constitutional debates during the Diet. Following his conscience despite Wesselényi's advice to the contrary, he repeatedly supported the royal proposition against the estates concerning conscription for purposes of taxation of those nobles who cultivated land formerly held (but not legally owned) by serfs.[23] He was indignant toward members of the opposition in the lower chamber who staunchly defended the privileges of the nobility when it came to alleviating the tax burden of the "wretched tax-paying people" (*misera plebs contribuens*), namely, the serfs.[24] On every possible occasion he supported proposals directed at improving the situation of the peasants, attacking the selfishness of noblemen who refused to shoulder the burdens of the country[25] although he knew he could lose many

---

the University of Vienna to prevent the spread of dangerous ideas in Hungary through Protestant youth visiting the West. The Protestant estates endeavored to enlist the help of the counties and the Diet to remedy their grievance. Cf. Hőke, "Magyarország helyzete 1820–25-ben," pp. 1f. See also Appendix No. 1, Doc. No. 2a.

[16] Feb. 7, 1826; July 13, 31, 1827, *Viszota, ed., Naplók*, III, 24, 164.

[17] Dec. 26, 27, 1825, *ibid.*, II, 665; Széchenyi to Wesselényi, Jan. 4, 1826, cited in Friedreich, *Széchenyi élete*, I, 169; also Széchenyi, *Politikai programmtöredékek* (Fragments of a Political Program), in Viszota, ed., *Széchenyi és Kossuth*, II, 729.

[18] Feb. 13, Apr. 6, 1827, Viszota, ed., *Naplók*, III, 128, 145.

[19] Mar. 12, Nov. 26, 1826, Feb. 8, 1827, *ibid.*, III, 30, 105f., 127.

[20] Feb. 13, 1827, *ibid.*, III, 128.

[21] June 7, 1826, *ibid.*, III, 67.

[22] In addition to his memoranda to Metternich and his stand taken in the Diet concerning the most important questions already mentioned, see also his diary entries of Feb. 13, 1826, Feb. 18, Feb. 19, May 24, July 31, 1827, Jan. 1, 1828, *ibid.*, III, 18f., 129f., 167, 188.

[23] July 18, Aug. 1, 1826, *ibid.*, III, 79 and n. 2, 81f. and n. 6.

[24] Dec. 26, 1825, July 21, 1826, *ibid.*, II, 665 and n. 2, III, 80.

[25] Dec. 31, 1825, Jan. 11, 1826, *ibid.*, II, 667 and n. 1, III, 8 and n. 3.

of his friends by doing so.[26] Hence, also, his disillusionment at the end of the Diet: "I had already ruined my case with the court party—now it is the turn of my compatriots! It cannot be otherwise!"[27] But even in his frequent hours of despair he tried to comfort himself by saying that he at least had tried to sow the seed.[28]

Those who thought all opposition was unconstitutional and equivalent to high treason regarded Széchenyi as one of the revolutionary youngsters bent on setting everything aflame.[29] Almost without exception, contemporary police reports described him as a dangerous radical and an enemy of the regime.[30] As his stand against the estates more than once indicated,[31] Széchenyi preserved his independence from all factions. He knew that whereas the chamber of the magnates was completely subservient to the palatine and to the court, many members of the lower chamber would be only too eager to be bribed with rank and position by the administration.[32] He soon discovered that there were "royalists" and "anti-royalists" in the Diet—the former expecting titles, orders, and wealth from the court's favor; the latter flattering the multitude with their affected independence. Both parties were driven by vanity and greed. He also noted that whereas they had an 800-year-old constitution, very few in the Diet had any idea about the meaning of the word "constitution." But he admitted that many irresponsible and superficial young people were going too far. A few months after his discussions with Metternich he mused: "The more I think about everything pertinent to our relation with Austria, the more I believe and become convinced that all violence on our side is damaging."[33]

Széchenyi's pride and independent thinking prevented him from seek-

[26] July 18, 1826, *ibid.*, III, 79: "The righteous and noble man must pay little attention to the judgment of the multitude." And in the margin: "Wesselényi is violent against the court; I [am violent] against the inhumanity of the estates."

[27] Aug. 17, 1827, *ibid.*, III, 172. Also, after the speech from the throne, closing the Diet: "Adulation and flattery, how disgusting!" Aug. 18, 1827, *ibid.*, III, 173.

[28] Oct. 8, 1827, *ibid.*, III, 178.

[29] May 10, 1827, *ibid.*, III, 154.

[30] Some of the police agents' reports are the only sources of certain speeches by Széchenyi in the Diet. Even if there are other sources available concerning his activities, and even if the police reports are often biased against him, they usually contain very interesting material. This is why Viszota included in the footnotes and Annexes of the *Fontes* diary edition the most important reports of the *Polizeihofstelle* unknown before World War I.

With regard to the period of and immediately following the Diet of 1825–27, see also Annex No. v, 2–5, *ibid.*, III, 766–77.

[31] Concerning the regulation of the financial obligations of private persons, Széchenyi again favored the royal proposition against the opinion of the estates. May 17, Aug. 4, 1827, *ibid.*, III, 156, 168.

[32] June 5, 8, 1826, Jan. 8, Mar. 28, 30, 1827, *ibid.*, III, 63f., 67f., 117, 141.

[33] Dec. 31, 1825, May 14, 1826, *ibid.*, II, 667, III, 54.

ing popular or royal favor, which, basically, was the cause of his political loneliness. Oversensitive due to his mental tribulations, he was yet correct in sensing that he was little loved: "Many think I am proud, others that I am a *radical reformer,* still others that I am an *aristocrat.* I feel the grief of being completely isolated. In fact, I have ruined my relations with everybody."[34]

One may wonder why police agents considered Széchenyi "a fomenter of rebellion, one who corrupts the youth, and an extremely dangerous individual."[35] Yet they did; Széchenyi's satirical remarks about himself were no exaggeration. Since his participation in the Diet, he was under constant police surveillance. On the basis of the reports of Count Sedlnitzky shortly before the end of the Diet, Francis I gave further instructions that Széchenyi's activities be observed.[36] A year later, the monarch sent a number of police reports to the Hungarian chancellor, Count Reviczky, warning him about "the doings of Count Stephen Széchenyi and his adherents with regard to the Casino in Pest and different projects of this young man."[37]

The emperor-king's letter, as well as Reviczky's instructions asking for a report, indicated that official circles were concerned not only with Széchenyi's role in the Diet but also with his social activities. Reviczky, in a letter to attorney Francis Steinbach (one of Sedlnitzky's agents) asked for information on the Academy of Science, casinos, and horse races, adding that there were people who saw in all these activities the realization of a coordinated plan, reflecting, "according to some, the so-called spirit of opposition, according to others, the Anglo-Gallic-Teutonic liberalism, and the pestiferous political mentality of the modern age."[38] The Hungarian chancellor did not think this "alien" influence had any chance of establishing itself in Hungary, because, as he said, it was in contradiction to the principles of the ancient monarchic constitution and to the cardinal privileges of the nobility; thus "individuals similar to Count Széchenyi" would be doomed to failure. Just the same, he demanded to know "whether and to what extent" the different projects, associations, and unions directed by "Count Széchenyi and his associates deserved attention from a political point of view."[39]

The administration had good reason to be concerned about Széchenyi's

---

[34] Nov. 22, 1828, *ibid.,* III, 277 (Széchenyi's italics). Cf. Oct. 22, 1827, *ibid.,* III, 180.
[35] Feb. 18, 1827, *ibid.,* III, 130.
[36] On July 10, 1827, Annex No. v, 2a, *ibid.,* III, 766.
[37] Annex No. v, 3a, *ibid.,* III, 772f.
[38] Annex No. v, 3b, *ibid.,* III, 773: "*Sunt qui in his spiritum ita dictum oppositionis, alii qui liberalismum anglo-gallo-teutonicum, pestiferumque moderni aevi genium politicum explorasse contendunt.*"
[39] *Ibid.*

activities. By the time of the official reports and inquiries he had become an open agitator for the cause of Hungary's national regeneration. During and after the sessions of the Diet he proceeded chiefly along three lines. By making possible the institution for cultivating the Hungarian language, he gained a nationwide reputation.[40] He also took a leading part in legislative preparation for the enactment of the laws for the Academy, and, after the Diet participated in the work of the special committee which shaped the organization of the new institution in the spring of 1828. It is not an exaggeration to say that without his constant stimulation the Academy could not have come into existence. As a recognition of his patriotic activity he was elected first vice-president of the Academy. Third, although the primary aim of the Academy was to promote the development of the national idiom through scholarly, chiefly philological and literary, means, Széchenyi intended soon to put a stronger emphasis within the Academy itself on applied and practical sciences.[41] On the other hand, Széchenyi decided to write his first book, *Lovakrul* (On Horses), in Hungarian in order to popularize his mother tongue. Thus gradually the idea of cultural reform pointed beyond its original goal, just as reforms begun in the social and economic fields started to intertwine with the general cultural upheaval of the whole nation.

Naturally Széchenyi's well-intended but somewhat vague and sentimental plan of noble self-realization, motivated as it was by his half-conscious desire to compensate for the frustrations suffered in his love life and professional military career, cannot fully explain the nationwide response to his first public initiatives. To understand Széchenyi's emergence as a national leader one must look beyond the sphere of personal fulfillment and even Széchenyi's endeavors to absorb foreign achievements, however significant these factors may have been and however strongly he himself tended to emphasize them. Even his personality and actions will appear in a different light if viewed against Hungarian reality as it existed in the early 19th century.

---

[40] Count Joseph Dessewffy, e.g., wrote a eulogy in the form of an ode to Széchenyi under the title "A szép példa" (Beautiful Example). The censor ordered the issue of the quarterly *Felső Magyarországi Minerva* in which the "obnoxious" poem had been published confiscated. The Latin text of the order in Falk, *Széchenyi kora*, p. 38. For Dessewffy's ode, see Annex No. III, 1, Viszota, ed., *Naplók*, III, 741–44.

[41] Széchenyi to Count Ignácz Gyulay, Jan. 18, 1829, Majláth, ed., *Levelek*, I, 119. Actually there were many plans, old and new, for how to use the money offered for the "cultivation of the Hungarian tongue." The idea of the Academy emerged only during the discussion of the different plans. Some of these plans wanted to stress the propagation of Hungarian through expanding Hungarian instruction in the schools, others proposed to include the National Museum and a National Theater into the sphere of the Academy, etc. For the varied projects see Annex No. II, esp. 4, 5, and 9a–f, in Viszota, ed., *Naplók*, III, 589–607, 649–72.

Physically, perhaps the most salient feature of this background was the absence of decent—and safe—roads. Spiritually, the often cited slogan, "Outside Hungary, there is no life and if there is, it is not the same,"[42] was but a reflection of the provincialism so characteristic of the static Hungarian world outlook. The basic cause of immobility was the Hungarian feudal structure; politically and constitutionally Hungary in the 1820s was still a feudal state. Its economic life was regulated by feudal and manorial patterns rooted in centuries-old legal practices and traditions, the most complete constitutional formulation of which was Stephen Werbőczi's tripartite code of the early 16th century.

The 20th-century reader may find it difficult to visualize the immense complexity and resilience of that ossified crust of feudal institutions that was abolished in 1848. Traces of them have survived in Hungary well into the present generation. Indeed, Werbőczi's magnum opus was one of the few important ties preserving the legal fiction of a united kingdom at a time when Hungary was divided into Habsburg and Ottoman provinces and the semi-independent Principality of Transylvania. Although the *Tripartitum* never formally became the law of the land, in the eyes of the *populus Werbőczianus* (privileged nobility) it remained the guardian of Hungary's very existence. Yet it was this same nobility that undermined the Hungarian state, a state whose independence became a fiction after the Turkish victory at Mohács (1526) largely because of the nefarious activities of the feudal robber barons, one of whom was Werbőczi himself.[43]

The political reunification of Hungary began only after the last nation-wide feudal struggle against the Habsburgs, led by Francis II Rákóczi, had been defeated in 1711. From a nationalistic viewpoint the greater part of the 18th century was a period of national inertia and centralizing monarchic absolutism which resulted in the large-scale denationalization of the aristocracy *if* usage of the Magyar idiom and anti-Habsburg armed resistance are the main criteria of true Hungarian patriotism. But, paradoxically, during the 18th century the foundations were laid for the Hungarian nation-state—the beginnings of the modernization of agriculture, education, administration, credit and taxation, transportation and the judiciary. All these steps, initiated under a dynasty that was indifferent to the would-be national cause, were necessary to supplement if not predetermine the aspiration for a literature in the Magyar tongue and, ultimately, for independent statehood. In contrast to those who have emphasized the widespread resistance to Joseph II's reforms in Hungary,

---

[42] *Extra Hungariam non est vita, si est vita non est ita.*

[43] Oszkár Jászi, *A nemzeti államok kialakulása és a nemzetiségi kérdés* (The Evolution of Nation-States and the Nationality Question) (Budapest: Grill K., 1912), pp. 263–74.

Oscar Jászi has correctly stressed that some of the most erudite pioneers of the Hungarian cultural revival—including the "father of Hungarian literature," Francis Kazinczy, the writer Joseph Péczeli and the linguist Nicholas Révai—sympathized with the revolutionary emperor. Also, Joseph II intended to reunify Transylvania with Hungary, a goal Hungarian national leaders were unable to achieve before 1848.[44] Finally, one might add, such prominent figures of the age of reforms as Széchenyi, Wesselényi, and Baron Joseph Eötvös often used the epithet "great" when referring to Joseph II.

True, Josephinism, with its administrative centralization and Germanization, provoked nationwide resistance from the feudal classes who were anxious to defend their privileges and display the outward signs of patriotism such as Magyar speech and costume. Indirectly, Joseph II evoked a wave of Magyar "estates-nationalism." At the same time, there emerged a small group of educated noblemen, idealistic bureaucrats and non-noble intellectuals, who were in sympathy with the social content of Josephinian reform. The Hungarian Jacobin conspiracy, influenced by the Enlightenment and the French Revolution, was ruthlessly put down in 1795.[45] For three decades after, Magyar nationalism and ideas of reform were confined almost exclusively to literature and culture.

The spread of enlightened ideas in Hungary traditionally has been traced to the Hungarian Noble Bodyguard established in Vienna by Maria Theresa in 1765. Attention has also been called to the impact of the Seven Years War, during which many Hungarians serving in the army were exposed to more advanced Western conditions. Further, the anti-Protestant policy after the *Carolina Resolutio* of 1731 tended to direct the interest of the Protestant estates of northeastern Hungary to cultural and economic affairs at a time when the loss of Silesia by the Habsburgs, the military campaigns, and the first partitioning of Poland began to have a disruptive effect on Hungary's foreign trade with some of her traditional partners.[46] Thus the socio-economic basis for change, expected first from Joseph II's reforms and subsequently from more radical trends, could have been broader than the number of persons directly involved in the Hungarian Jacobin movement or the ease with which it was suppressed would lead us to believe.

The majority of the nobility, which numbered less than five percent of a population of over 8.5 million (excluding the Military Frontier

---

[44] *Ibid.*, pp. 289, 293ff.

[45] For references see Ch. II, notes 30, 34, 35, 37, 38, above.

[46] Éva H. Balázs, "A reformkori nacionalizmus XVIII. századi gyökerei" (The Eighteenth-Century Roots of the Nationalism of the Age of Reform), *Történelmi Szemle*, III (1960), pp. 319–22; *id., Berzeviczy*, pp. 7–11.

with about 700,000) in 1787,[47] were opposed to sharing their privileges
with the rest of the country. There were only a handful who were willing
to do so. Yet the undoing of these few could not reverse some of the
demographic changes that had occurred since the treaties of Szatmár
(1711) and Passarowitz (1718), the former marking the end of Rákóczi's
fight and the latter the restoration of the last Ottoman-held segment
of historic Hungary. Peace, that great healer of mankind's wounds, was
wonderful to Hungary, laid bare and depopulated by two centuries of
uninterrupted dynastic, Turkish, religious, and civil wars. In less than
70 years the country's population, estimated at about 4.1 million in
1720, more than doubled. In 1790 Hungary (Croatia-Slavonia and Transylvania included) was underdeveloped, with less than a half million
inhabitants in 61 chartered royal cities, the largest of which was Debrecen
with a population of nearly 30,000. Most of the "cities" were merely
large villages; the increase in population chiefly affected the rural areas
which were gradually repopulated, to a considerable extent with foreign,
mostly peasant, colonists. Although there is no reliable data on the relative numbers of different nationalities, it is likely that well over half
of Hungary's people were non-Magyars on the eve of the national awakening of east central Europe.[48]

The expanded population made it possible to augment the proportion
of arable land. It is estimated that between 1720 and the census of
1787 arable land increased from 5 to 20 percent—still a very low figure.
But the next hundred years was to see a rapid extension of agricultural
cultivation until by the end of the 19th century the limit was reached
and Hungary had to face the serious problem of rural overpopulation.
During the first half of this period, the number of peasants, mostly
serfs and cotter-tenants (*zsellér*), continued to grow, the *zsellér* much
faster. Whereas in 1775 the number of smallholding serfs on *urbarial*[49]
land was twice the number of cotter-tenants who as a rule cultivated

[47] Béla Pápai, "Magyarország népe a feudalizmus megerősődése és bomlása idején
(1711–1867)" (Hungary's Population in the Period of the Strengthening and Disin-
tegration of Feudalism [1711–1867]), in József Kovacsics, ed., *Magyarország történeti
demográfiája* (Hungary's Historical Demography) (Budapest: Közgazdasági és jogi
könyvkiadó, 1963), pp. 159, 171.

[48] Recent computations, based on a comparison of 18th- 19th-century population
statistics, have resulted in a revision of previous immigration data. The estimated
number of new immigrants at the end of the 18th century is about one million, a figure
considerably lower than the one used hitherto, which is about 3.5 million. Pápai,
"Magyarország népe," pp. 147–51, 160ff.; Erik Molnár, Ervin Pamlényi and György
Székely, eds., *Magyarország története* (Hungary's History), 2 vols. (Budapest: Gondolat,
1964), I, 367. For a more traditional interpretation see C. A. Macartney, *Hungary, A
Short History* (Chicago: Aldine Publishing Co., 1962), pp. 116–21.

[49] From Magyar *úrbér*—a fee paid to the lord for the use of his land. Lat. *urbarium*,
Germ. *Urbar*. Urbarial land was land held in villein tenure.

only up to one-fourth of the area tilled by the smallholder serfs, the census of 1828 showed these two groups of "bound people" as equally numerous, each numbering about a half million. At the same time, there were only about 100,000 male agricultural laborers working on the large estates (this figure was to increase tenfold by 1895), suggesting that the economic structure of Hungary continued to be basically medieval in spite of the innovations aimed at increasing and improving the produce of agriculture and animal husbandry.

The figures quoted above also indicate that due to the improved demographic situation and the possibility of finding new markets for Hungarian products, especially during the French wars, the nobility attempted to give a decreasing amount of land to the new colonists, keeping an increasing proportion of it as allodial (tax-exempt) land.[50] This was but one sign of the hardening conditions of Hungarian serfdom during the last half of the 18th century. Another was the reluctance of the privileged classes to accept the urbarial regulations forced on them by Vienna. Indeed, it was at this time that the alliance between the court and the peasant masses, so much feared in Hungary during the 1830 and 40s, began to form.[51]

It should be emphasized that on the whole the benevolent absolutism of Maria Theresa and the enlightened efforts of the Josephinian state failed to break the political power of the Hungarian nobility. Its overwhelming majority ignored or sabotaged efforts to transform the Habsburg Empire into an efficient modern state; it was reluctant to admit the necessity of social reforms, particularly those which would have ameliorated the condition of the serf. The same nobility, however, loyally supported the dynasty during the Napoleonic wars, the outcome of which had—or so it seemed at first—a stabilizing effect on Hungarian feudalism. But the restoration of peace on the continent brought complex problems. With the prospect of lasting tranquility before them, statesmen of the empire could again concentrate on remodeling the Austrian state along absolutist-Josephinian lines. The attempt was necessarily bound to come into conflict with the constitutional concepts of the Hungarian estates, some of which were touched on in the previous chapter.

Related to the constitutional issues, and of no less importance, were the economic changes that had occurred in Hungary during the early 19th century. Because of them, the privileged classes were forced to face the problems of modern times in spite of their efforts to disregard the social upheaval wrought by the French Revolution all over Europe.

---

[50] Pápai, "Magyarország népe," pp. 155–58, 169f., 201–10.
[51] For a classic example, see Doc. 38 in Eckhart, *A bécsi udvar gazdaságpolitikája Magyarországon, 1780–1815*, pp. 419–26.

In the 1820s there were some 400,000 noblemen out of an estimated population of 10 million.[52] There was an approximately equal number of city dwellers, but their political and economic power could hardly be compared to that of the nobility.[53] The remaining nine million were peasants, primarily serfs and landless agricultural laborers.[54] About two-thirds of the population were non-Hungarians; the Magyars were far outnumbered by Slavs, Romanians, and Germans, primarily in the northern, northeastern, eastern (Transylvanian), and southern parts of the country (Croatia and the Military Frontier), as well as in the cities. Hungarians, however, constituted the overwhelming majority of the nobility—the political nation (*populus*).

There were no legal differences among members of the nobility. All belonged to what was "one and the same nobility," or, to use Werbőczi's language, "*una eademque nobilitas.*" About five-sixths of the cultivated land was for the personal use of nobles or *demesne* (*terra dominicalis*) and, as such, was completely tax exempt.[55] The balance, the *urbarial* land (*terra rusticalis*), was held in villein tenure and carried the entire burden of rates and taxes. The nobility, constituting one-twentieth of the populace, was theoretically fully represented in the feudal Diet. Hungarian historians have often boasted of this relatively high percentage of "enfranchised" population, pointing to the "democratic and repre-

[52] Sept. 21, 1825, Viszota, ed., *Naplók*, II, 609. According to the last census taken, over the opposition of the nobility under Joseph II in 1787, the population of the lands of the Hungarian crown was 8.5 million. After the death of Joseph II the nobility prevented the administration from taking a census in the first half of the 19th century. In 1837 Hungary's population (including Transylvania) was estimated at 12,990,000. Another estimate put the population figure close to 15.5 million; although the latter figure seems to be exaggerated, it indicates the important divergencies between contemporary statistical data. Cf. Antal Éber, *Széchenyi gazdaságpolitikája* (Széchenyi's Economic Policies) (Budapest: Franklin, n.d.), pp. 21f; Fényes, *Magyarország statistikája*, I, 34.

[53] Hóman and Szekfű, *Magyar történet*, V, 242.

[54] According to the tax conscription of 1828, the number of serfs and that of cotters and landless agricultural workers was about equal in Hungary and Croatia (564, 643, and 587, 288, resp.), the second category outnumbering the first one by 3.8 percent. In 1846, however, the agrarian proletariat, which had constantly increased since the end of the 18th century, had a majority of about 32 percent, compared to the serfs. This process was one of the signs indicating important changes in the feudal structure of Hungarian agriculture. Cf. Pál P. Zsigmond, "A tőkés termelés feltételei a magyar mezőgazdaságban 1848-ban" (Conditions of Capitalistic Production in Hungarian Agriculture in 1848), *Társadalmi Szemle* (Feb. 1948), p. 110. A thin, semi-privileged upper stratum of the peasantry was made up by free peasants who numbered about 250 thousand. Ervin Szabó, *Társadalmi és pártharcok a 48/49-es magyar forradalomban.* Bevezeti Jászi Oszkár tanulmánya (Social and Party Struggles in the Hungarian Revolution of [18]48/49. With an Introductory Study of Oscar Jászi), Vienna: 1921, p. 46.

[55] 25 million yokes out of 30.7 million (1 yoke = 1.42 English acres). Éber, *Széchenyi gazdaságpolitikája*, pp. 66f., 69 and n. 11.

sentative" character of the Hungarian constitution as compared to Western countries in contemporary Europe.[56] Such a comparison is misleading; noble representation in the Diet was far from democratic, and a nobility thus constituted had no mandate to represent the rest of the population.

The nobility was not a monolithic class, socially or economically. Its upper segment consisted of the magnates, members of a few dozen leading families of the realm. Particularly since Maria Theresa's times, they had spent a large part of each year in Vienna, often holding high positions at court, in the army, and in the administration. Most were Hungarian in name, but their education and outlook were cosmopolitan and Austrian, or "supra-national," making it seem to patriots that they had become denationalized and alienated. Inside the family circle they used German or French; at the Diet they spoke in dog Latin; they talked only with their servants or peasants in Magyar (or Slovak, Croatian or Romanian).

Aristocrats who had come of age could sit in person in the upper chamber of the Diet; their widows and orphans were represented by an *absentium ablegatus* (deputy of those absent), who had the right of consultation but no vote in the lower chamber. Magnates were, after the church and the treasury, the greatest landowners, their estates often covering dozens of square miles.[57] The economic power of the aristocracy can be seen in the fact that according to Széchenyi the yearly net income of his Casino's 520 shareholders in the 1830s surpassed 12 million florins.[58] Although this tremendous wealth could not have been easily mobilized due to specific Hungarian conditions, one may note, as an illustration of its magnitude and latent potential, that as late as 1844 Széchenyi would have been glad if the Diet had established a public fund of 60 million for necessary investments. According to the plan, the yearly contribution of the entire nobility would have been only three million florins. One may add that the proposal failed although by then both chambers of the Diet seemed to have committed themselves in principle to the idea of the general and proportionate sharing of tax burdens.[59]

[56] Sometimes even benevolent Western historians appear to follow this deceptive line of argumentation. E.g., Blum, *Noble Landowners*, p. 38 and n. 93.

[57] *Ibid.*, pp. 35–38.

[58] Gr.István Széchenyi, *Néhány szó a lóverseny körül* (A Few Words on Horse Races) (Pest: Heckenast, 1838), p. 175. One florin = 48¢. Cf. a similar calculation based on an estimated 15 million income per year of the Casino's 370 shareholders in 1831. *Id.*, *Világ, SzIM*², I, 231f.

[59] Éber, *Széchenyi gazdaságpolitikája*, pp. 167–85. Cf. Széchenyi's exhortation written in the spring of 1844, *Magyarország kiváltságos lakosihoz* (To Hungary's Privileged Inhabitants), pp. 12f., 27, 30.

Despite the fortunes of many great landowners and their importance in advancing Hungarian agriculture, the aristocracy gradually ceased to be the leader of a nation that was awakening to a new political consciousness.[60] The expensive way of life for many magnates who spent their money in Vienna and fashionable places abroad, caring little for their estates, was only one of the causes for this decline. Another reason was the agricultural crisis following the boom years of the continental blockade and Napoleonic wars, which had stimulated the transformation of the big estates into modern capitalistic enterprises.[61] The years of relative prosperity when agricultural products were in demand and large investments made in the hope of good profits were followed by a period of extremely low agricultural prices when money became scarce and competition stiffer, resulting from the appearance of Russian and American grain on the continental markets. The difficulties in selling agricultural products were felt by the whole landowning class, a class that was becoming more and more insolvent as time went by. They were particularly burdensome for the latifundia, the owners of which found it difficult to abandon high living in order to reestablish the financial balance of their estates. The scandals connected with the financial manipulations of some magnates ruined the credit of Hungarian landowners in the money markets throughout Europe.[62] Those who sincerely wished to improve their farming methods were forced to invest vast sums in their estates to keep up with the demands of changing conditions. This, however, involved the need for new sources of credit and for a change in the credit system regulated by feudal law and characterized by patriarchal and precapitalistic forms of business relations.

At the beginning of the 19th century there were no banks in Hungary. Money was borrowed from rich relatives, other noblemen, charitable foundations, or ecclesiastic and secular endowments. The slow rhythm of economic life permitted relatively equitable terms for repayment. Financial operations were dominated by the direct relationship of socially equal partners. The situation underwent a rapid change during the years of inflation and increased speculation when the rich merchant or financier became the main source of credit for the Hungarian landowner, too.[63]

[60] Hóman and Szekfű, *Magyar történet*, v, 210, 223.
[61] *Ibid.*, pp. 219f.; Blum, *Noble Landowners*, p. 96.
[62] Béla Grünwald, *Széchenyi magánhitelügyi koncepciójának szellemi és gazdasági előzményei és következményei a rendi Magyarországon 1790–1848* (Spiritual and Economic Antecedents and Consequences of Széchenyi's Concept Regarding Private Credit Operations in Feudal Hungary, 1790–1848) (Pécs: 1927), No. 14 of *Történeti értekezések* (Historical Studies), pp. 9–19, 69–78, 144f. (cited hereafter as *Magánhitelügy*); also, *id.*, introduction to *Hitel*, in *Fontes*, pp. 55–60, 71–75.
[63] Grünwald, *Magánhitelügy*, pp. 55–69.

Also, new types of agricultural production were developed; it was at this time that Hungarian lords became the "quantity producers" of the Monarchy's wool industry, and sheep raising became the most important branch of animal husbandry. The preeminence of sheep breeding instead of grain producing in many regions of Hungary, where latifundia played a dominant role, had other far-reaching consequences. It left uncultivated and uninhabited the *pusztas* (arid desert areas) largely depopulated during the Turkish occupation and speeded up the enclosure movement which harassed the peasants and threatened even part of the lesser nobility.[64]

The great latifundia, formed in the 18th century,[65] were one of the major social and economic problems of Hungary up to the end of World War II. Széchenyi himself looked with the eyes of a great landowner at the problem of reform; in his opinion, Hungary's regeneration should have been led by the aristocracy. Although natural for Széchenyi, this approach became problematic by the 1820s.[66]

Despite its historical role, dating especially from the Habsburg accession to the Hungarian throne, the aristocracy became increasingly less important to national revival after the Congress of Vienna. Its outstanding representatives, Stephen Széchenyi and Count Louis Batthyány, who became leaders of national stature, made the diminishing authority of their own class even more obvious. In the century following 1815 the political leadership of the nation fell increasingly to the class of the *bene possessionati*, the medium landowners.[67]

This "class," or rather upper segment, of the untitled nobility consisted of 20 to 30 thousand families, or about one-fourth of all the nobles. It lived in relative economic security on a yearly income per family varying from 500 to 3,000 florins. This was a sizeable sum if one takes into consideration that the yearly salary of an average official in the administration or of a secondary school teacher was about 300 to 400 florins, that of a court councillor in Vienna about 3,000.[68] The *bene*

[64] Blum, *Noble Landowners*, pp. 99ff.; Gyula Mérei, "Mezőgazdasági árutermelés és a parasztság helyzete Magyarországon a feudalizmus válságának elmélyülése idején" (Agricultural Production for the Market and Situation of the Peasantry in Hungary during the Aggravation of the Crisis of Feudalism), *Századok*, xc (1956), 59ff.; György Spira, "A Pest megyei parasztság 1848 előtti rétegeződéséhez" (On the Stratification of the Peasantry in Pest County before 1848), *Századok*, cxii (1958), 640; Iványi-Grünwald, introduction to *Hitel*, pp. 45ff.; Horváth, *Huszonöt év*, i, 394ff., Hóman and Szekfű, *Magyar történet*, v, 224–27.

[65] Macartney, *Hungary: A Short History*, pp. 98f., 110f.

[66] Mályusz, "A reformkor nemzedéke," p. 41.

[67] Hóman and Szekfű, *Magyar történet*, v, 209–13, 227ff.

[68] Salaries, including those of professional people or qualified workers, were often supplemented by fringe benefits such as room and board, a garden plot, firewood, etc. For information concerning prices and wages (frequently set or "limited" by the

possessionati were country gentlemen who lived on their estates most of the year and supervised them according to the methods of their fore-fathers. Unlike the magnates, they lived unpretentiously and usually managed to save some money; they became solvent during the infla-tionary period of the Napoleonic wars. The country gentleman, or "gen-try," was at the center of society. His outlook and way of life left its imprint on the development of modern Hungarian society and had a great influence on literature and the thinking of the bourgeoisie.

The landowning middle nobility achieved a considerable degree of eco-nomic and political independence in the early decades of the 19th cen-tury. Its members had a decisive voice in electing the county officials and deputies to the Diet, who usually came from its own ranks. The Hungarian constitutional opposition drew its strength from (and owed its inflexibility and weaknesses to) this influential part of the nobility. Independent in thought and inclined to contemplation, many of them went well beyond the formal education received in school; they became excellent constitutional lawyers and literati; a few, like Francis Kölcsey, excelled in both fields. Through their influence in the Diet, county con-gregations, and administration, as well as their connections and family relations, they became the real leaders of whatever articulate public opinion there was in a country without newspapers and good roads. In the absence of a strong middle class bourgeoisie in the Western sense, the relatively well-educated and economically stable landowning middle nobility, like the lower boyardom in the Romanian provinces of Moldavia and Wallachia, became the leading political force in Hungary, determin-ing the character and pace of reforms to be introduced during the nine-teenth century.

This generalization about the "national" or "historic" noble middle class, however, must be supplemented by adding that after the boom in grain production, this relatively well-to-do nobility began to feel the same economic squeeze experienced by the great landowners. For this reason, Széchenyi correctly stressed the universal need for easier credit terms and the benefits that would devolve upon the entire nobility from the relevant legislative measures. But his claim that both big and small landowner-debtors had benefited from the devaluation of the currency requires some qualification.[69]

---

authorities), see the recent tentative study by Vilmos Bélay, "Adalékok az ár- és bérviszonyok történetéhez Pest-Budán (1790–1848)" (Data Regarding the History of Prices and Wages in Pest-Buda, 1790–1848), in *Tanulmányok Budapest múltjából* (Studies from Budapest's Past), xiv (Budapest: Akadémiai kiadó, 1961), 363–406.

[69] Széchenyi, *Stádium, SzIM²*, ii, 56; Franz Pulszky, *Meine Zeit, mein Leben*, 3 vols. (Pressburg-Leipzig: C. Stampfel, 1880–83), i, 63. For the lower boyardom cf. Fischer-Galati, "The Origins of Modern Rumanian Nationalism," pp. 5of.

In his subsequent agitation for reform Széchenyi wished to fight the narrow-minded complacency of the country gentlemen by arousing them to help themselves and not to blame the government or extraneous conditions for all their troubles. Well aware of the antagonism that separated the middle nobility from the aristocracy, he did not analyze in public the frequently different roots of the indebtedness of the two classes, perhaps to avoid enhancing the social and psychological gap already existing between them. Yet it is interesting that in his report on the Diet of 1825, the papal nuncio pointed out the conflicting economic interests of magnates and common noblemen (*gentiluomini*) by saying that the former were ordinarily (*ordinamente*) debtors, whereas the latter, like the clergy, were creditors. This circumstance, the nuncio observed, contributed to the multiple causes of the nationwide discontent which forced Francis I to call the Diet into session. Since Vienna seemed to favor the magnates, who were often the debtors of lesser noblemen and did not have much to lose in the devaluation in which the latter had lost their savings, he also expressed his fear that the restive country gentlemen could outnumber the supporters of the administration in the Diet. Indeed, the apprehension of the papal diplomat was not without foundation because by the 1830s members of the middle nobility, too, were finding it difficult to make ends meet. Lack of adequate capital and ability to adjust economic practices to the changing times made many of them susceptible to liberal ideas. A classic example was the puritan Francis Deák who represented the most farsighted layer of the *bene possessionati* which realized that it had a vested interest not only in the maintenance of the social status quo but also in economic progress. The latter, however, implied the need for gradual and moderate reforms.[70]

More than half the entire nobility[71] were so-called *armalistae*. They had been ennobled only in the past hundred or two hundred years and lived quite modestly, frequently in poverty. Many had recently risen from serfdom and tilled their own small piece of land held formerly in villein tenure.[72] There was a marked difference between the way of life and opportunity for social advancement of the *bene possessionati*,

[70] Gyula Mérei, *Mezőgazdaság és agrártársadalom Magyarországon, 1790–1848* (Agriculture and Agrarian Society in Hungary, 1790–1848) (Budapest: Teleki Pál Tudományos Intézet, 1948), pp. 96–116. For the nuncio's report see Pietro Ostini to Cardinal della Somaglia, Nov. 25, 1826, No. 478: "Dieta Ungarica del 1825," *Archivio Segreto Vaticano, Segreteria di Stato, Esteri, 1814–1850*, Rubrica 247, Anni 1825–26, Busta 403, Fasc. 2. Cf. Meszlényi, *A jozefinizmus kora*, pp. 295–300.

[71] For a brief critical evaluation of the historical development, functions, duties, and privileges of the nobility, in English, see Marczali, *Hungary in the Eighteenth Century*, pp. 102–11.

[72] E. Szabó, *Társadalmi és pártharcok*, pp. 42ff.

the middle nobility, and this lesser nobility. Many of the lesser nobility held minor offices in the county administration, became priests, lawyers, doctors, or went into the teaching profession. Some of them managed, through marriage or hard work, to get into the upper strata of the nobility. More often the opposite occurred, namely, poorer members of the middle nobility and even the aristocracy, sank within one or two generations into the lesser nobility. Significantly, writers, publicists, and other prominent members of the great generation of Hungary's age of reforms, like Bartholomew Szemere, Ladislas Szalay, Anthony Csengery, Francis Pulszky, Michael Vörösmarty, and, above all, Louis Kossuth, were of the lesser nobility. Barons Joseph Eötvös and Sigismund Kemény also came from impoverished families.[73] Indeed it was mainly the middle and lesser nobility who favored *polgárosodás*—the achievement of bourgeois status and civilization—one of the magic words (not quite corresponding to *embourgeoisement* because of the peculiarities of the Hungarian setting) which inspired educated and progressive Hungarians of the pre-1848 era.

The lower level of the nobility overlapped with the craftsmen, peasants, and even serfs. But this seeming "democracy of the nobility" was anything but democratic or progressive. It was the product of a rigid social structure and its concomitant, poverty; it was also a constant factor of instability throughout Hungary's age of reforms. A case in point is the role played by the "proletariat of the nobility" or "sandal" nobility which worked, lived, and dressed like the peasants. Uneducated and possessing hardly more than a piece of parchment to prove their noble status, tens of thousands of them lived on urbarial land formerly cultivated by serfs. It is hard to determine their exact number but it was at least equal to that of the *bene possessionati*.[74] In many counties, primarily in the north, "sandal" nobles by tradition had to pay taxes. The administration was anxious to legalize and extend this practice so as to increase its revenue and because exemption of the "sandal" nobility would have decreased the amount of taxable land and at the same time increased unbearably the burdens of the serfs. But when at the Diet of 1825 Paul Nagy proposed to abolish the "abuse" of tax exemption of noblemen

[73] Ignácz Acsády, *A magyar jobbágyság története* (History of Hungarian Serfdom) (Budapest: K. Grill, 1908), pp. 494f. For the sandal nobility see also Mária Takács, *Társadalmi állapotok és törekvések Magyarországon, 1830–1847* (Social Conditions and Aspirations in Hungary, 1830–1849) (Budapest: D. Lobl, 1909), pp. 9ff.

[74] According to Mályusz, "A reformkor nemzedéke," p. 44, it was about 125,000. Horváth on one occasion referred to the "sandal" nobility as "the sandalled, proletarian middle noblemen," in *Huszonöt év*, II, 198, while Lord Chief Justice (*Judex Curiae*) Count Cziráky mentioned "hundert Tausende von adeligen Proletariern" in his "Freymüthige Darstellung der politischen Lage Ungarns in gegenwärtiger Zeit," written in 1838 upon the requests of both Metternich and Kolowrat. B. Szabó, *Adatok*, I, 323.

living on urbarial land, his proposal was met with opposition even from the "liberal" deputies who saw in it a threat to the basic privileges of the nobility. Deputies of some eastern counties in the Tisza River (Theiss) region, where the greater part of the constituents would have been adversely affected by the acceptance of Nagy's motion, would have voted for the general taxation of the nobility rather than approve of a principle in conflict with Werbőczi's constitutional theory of "one and the same nobility," all members of which presumably shared the same rights and privileges.[75] Hence the question was referred to a dietal commission and postponed until 1836, while the sandal nobility themselves became more and more restless and were used alternately by administration and opposition to promote their political aims.

In the early twenties the administration tried to line up the minor nobility to break the resistance of the counties. Two decades later the conservatives, supported by Vienna, exhorted the same group with the slogan "We shall not pay taxes!" to regain the majority in the elections from the liberal party. This maneuver was based on the assumption that the sandal nobility would fight to the last ditch for the *primae nonus*,[76] which defined the privileges of noblemen, because only these privileges distinguished them from the peasant masses with no political entity in the constitutional sense. On the other hand, the miserable social and economic conditions of the sandal nobility made it susceptible to the agitation in favor of the emancipation of the underprivileged classes. Already in the "cholera" uprising of the peasants in 1831, some members of the sandal nobility shared the ungenteel feelings of the lowest classes; in the second half of the 1840s Kossuth and the liberals succeeded in swinging them to their side by exploiting their hatred for Austria and resentment of the aristocracy and the well-to-do.[77]

In addition to the deep gulf separating the privileged and underprivi-

---

[75] Horváth, *Huszonöt év*, I, 172ff. The problem was also connected with the tax exemption of serfs in the personal service of great landowners, and was thus part of the controversy between magnates and the rest of the nobility. Mályusz, "A reformkor nemzedéke," pp. 48–52.

[76] Art. IX of Book I in Werbőczi's *Tripartitum*, summing up the cardinal privileges of the nobility, namely, freedom from arrest without due process of law; the right to recognize no other overlord but the crowned king; free exercise of their rights and the use of their property; exemption from taxation and duties; and the right to resist the king without incurring a charge of infidelity if the latter infringed on the liberties of the nation. Cf. Knatchbull-Hugessen, *Political Evolution*, I, 62–66. (The Diet of 1687 abolished the *ius resistendi*.)

[77] Dominic G. Kosáry, *A History of Hungary* (Cleveland-New York: 1941), p. 188; E. Mályusz, "A helytörténeti kutatás feladatai" (Tasks of Local History), *Századok*, LVIII (1924), 556–60. The ambivalence of the impoverished nobility's social role, including its revolutionary potential, was first noticed by Palatine Alexander Leopold in 1795. Mályusz, ed., *Sándor Lipót iratai*, p. 818; Eckhart, *A bécsi udvar gazdaságpolitikája, 1780–1815*, p. 223.

leged classes, there were important splits within the ruling society. Aside from the sandal nobility, perhaps the most important division within the nobility was caused by the suspicion and jealousy with which the common nobility looked at the aulic aristocracy. It was suspected with some justification that Vienna preferred magnates in filling positions. Thanks to their connections, they were said to be treated more leniently in lawsuits involving debts than were lesser noblemen whose estates were distrained without mercy. This widely held opinion, and resentment of the magnates' influence, aided the defenders of a feudal legal system which shielded the entire nobility against all "enemies"—primarily creditors. Such a circumstance was to be a major stumbling block to magnate Széchenyi when he stressed the necessity of changing this same legal system.[78] Aristocrats, in turn, looked down on the rest of the nobility, pointing out their backwardness, outmoded views, and the rather limited scope of their imagination in international questions. Széchenyi himself was not free from this same aristocratic haughtiness, which was to evidence itself in his handling of Kossuth.

Another important factor in 19th-century Hungarian life was the Roman Catholic Church which wielded a tremendous economic and political power. According to church registers dating from 1819, well over half the population (4,935,000) were Roman Catholic; along with the Uniates (625,000), the two churches recognizing the authority of the pope claimed approximately 60 percent of the people. The two Protestant denominations, the Calvinists (1,198,000) and Lutherans (820,000), represented approximately 22 percent, the Eastern Orthodox church (1,365,000) 15 percent, whereas the number of Jews was around 120 to 130 thousand, and that of Unitarians about 40 to 50 thousand. Since the late 18th century all religious denominations had enjoyed a degree of autonomy and were not officially discriminated against, except the Jews, and even here there was some progress. The Catholic clergy, considered the first estate of the realm, had great advantages and privileges. Their high prelates sat in person in the upper chamber of the Diet along with the male members of aristocratic families, a privilege extended to Eastern Orthodox, but not Protestant, bishops in 1792. The Catholic Church was also represented in considerable numbers in the lower chamber by the deputies of the different chapters, although they had only one vote.

Roman Catholicism continued as the dominant religion according to law in the first half of the nineteenth century. Excepting non-Catholic institutions, the Church all but controlled the educational system, and the leaders of the hierarchy held important political positions. The arch-

[78] Mályusz, "A reformkor nemzedéke," pp. 41–59.

bishop-primate of Esztergom had a key role in performing certain constitutional functions at the coronation of the king or election of the palatine; in some cases he could substitute for the apostolic king. He even had the right to grant nobility in certain parts of his diocese, exercising the full power of both the executive and the judiciary over these "ecclesiastic" noblemen. Moreover, each member of the Catholic clergy was regarded as belonging to the nobility; yet he was exempt from the jurisdiction of the secular authorities and had to be judged, eventually, on the basis of the relevant provisions of canon law. The primate and the archbishop of Eger (Erlau), in addition to being members of the upper chamber, were perpetual lords-lieutenant of three counties, thereby exerting direct secular control over local events in their dioceses. Besides, members of the clergy held several seats, ex officio or as nominees of the primate, on the highest courts of the realm and were spokesmen of the delegations taking the messages of one chamber to the other in the Diet. Frequently they were the leaders of deputations representing the whole Diet before the monarch.

The political influence of the church was supplemented by the enormous revenue of the spiritual lords, which rivalled that of the richest magnates. Because of its holdings the Hungarian Catholic Church was one of the richest in the world.[79] The church understandably had a vested interest in maintaining the status quo; furthermore, as an integral part of the nobility it was one of the pillars of feudal Hungary throughout the 19th century and after. But whereas in an earlier age the Catholic clergy was loyal to the dynasty and often also anti-Magyar because of

[79] Marczali, *Hungary in the Eighteenth Century*, pp. 109, 247–300, 338ff. To illustrate the wealth of Roman Catholic high prelates with an example from a later period than the one from which Marczali took his (1783), there is the case of Ladislas Pyrker, Bishop of the Zips (Spiš, Szepesség). Upon his elevation to the Patriarchal See in Venice in 1820, which represented a yearly income of 20,000 florins, Pyrker was granted an additional 15,000 per year by Francis I as a compensation for the loss of revenue caused by his acceptance of the ecclesiastic promotion. Aladar Paul Czigler, ed., *Johann Ladislaus Pyrker. Mein Leben*, Vol. 10 of *Fontes Rerum Austriacarum, Series I, Scriptores* (Vienna: Böhlau Nachf., 1966), pp. 95, 103, 301. Cf. Fényes, *Magyarország statistikája* (Hungary's Statistics), 3 vols. (Pest: Trattner-Károlyi, 1842), II, 79–83. For the (round) figures pertinent to church membership see L. Balázs, *A felekezetek egymáshoz való viszonya*, pp. 18f.; and Johann von Csaplovics, *Gemälde von Ungarn*, 2 vols. (Pesth: Hartleben, 1829), I, 288f. Csaplovics estimates Orthodox believers (for 1821) and Jews considerably higher (1.5 million and 165,000, respectively). According to the data collected by Fényes, which refer to a somewhat later period but are also relevant to the 1820s, almost all the Calvinists were Magyars, 60 percent of the Lutherans were Slovak, less than 25 percent were German, and less than 20 percent Magyar. Among the Catholics about 40 percent were Magyar, 20 Slovak, 15 each Croat and German, and 7 Serb. Over half of the Uniates were Ukrainians (Ruthenes), less than 40 percent Romanians, and more than 10 percent Magyars. The Orthodox population was split almost evenly between Romanians and Serbs, the balance being slightly in favor of the former, although the church leadership itself was in the hands of the latter. *Ibid.*, I, 52f., 90.

Magyardom's close affiliations with Protestantism, especially its Calvinist form, the church's later preeminence in and identification with the Hungarian state, and its tradition of proselytizing, caused it to play a role among non-Magyars, which at the time of competing nationalisms in central Europe remind one of an established national rather than universal church.

Still, there is the danger of sweeping generalizations. Although in their attitude toward Protestantism the Catholic clergy were motivated by the religious rather than Magyar national point of view, the latter was identified even in the 18th century with the interests of Catholicism in situations where followers of an "alien" religion spoke an "alien" language. In the case of the Orthodox Serbs and Romanians, the church tried to both Magyarize and Catholicize; where this approach was doomed to failure it gave its support to the Uniate or Greek Catholic Church.[80] Similarly complex is the question of the real power of the church at a time when religious tolerance was embraced by the fast-growing number of educated people and the officials of the state.

Any evaluation of the strength of the institutional church must take into account its relationship with the state and other denominations. As for the former, the church endeavored to recover the ground lost under Joseph II after his death, but with only limited success. Joseph II's successors and most of their influential advisors, including Metternich, were Josephinists insofar as they jealously protected the emperor-king's right of appointing the high prelates of the church and of supervising their activities at home and their connections with Rome. Even a loyal Catholic like Francis I would consider the church a necessary tool for implementing his policies rather than a spiritual power claiming independence from the royal will. The difference in viewpoints could only result in repeated conflicts between the Habsburg monarchy and the Holy See.[81]

Yet it was not just the rights of the "apostolic" king, elaborated with such thoroughness by Francis Kollár, a Hungarian-Slovak Jesuit scholar with regard to Hungary in 1762, which was opposed by the pope.[82] In the application of the *placetum regium,* which made the publication

[80] Marczali, *Hungary in the Eighteenth Century,* pp. 223ff., 285–88; cf Albert M. Ammann, S.J., *Abriss der ostslawischen Kirchengeschichte* (Vienna: Herder, 1950), pp. 633–59.

[81] Ferdinand Maass, "Der Wiener Nuntius Severoli und der Spätjosephinismus," *Mitteilungen des Instituts für Österreichische Geschichtsforschung,* LXIII (1955), 484–99; *id.,* "Die Verhandlungen des Wiener Nuntius Pietro Ostini über die Beseitigung der josephinischen Kirchengesetze (1832–1836)," *ibid.,* LXVIII (1960), 485–505.

[82] A. F. Kollar, *Historiae diplomaticae iuris patronatus apostolicorum Hungariae regum libri tres* (Vienna: G. L. Schulz, 1762); Gogolák, *Beiträge,* p. 152; Meszlényi, *A jozefinizmus,* pp. 15f.; L. Balázs, *A felekezetek egymáshoz való viszonya,* pp. 9f.

of papal bulls dependent on the sovereign's approval, and the regulation of ecclesiastic affairs without consultation with the papacy, Maria Theresa anticipated the more emphatic assertion of the rights of the state in the religious domain, which was an essential part of Josephinism. But in addition to this expansion of the interest of the state in a sphere traditionally dominated by the church, the Church also had to face the spread of the spirit of the Enlightenment among members of the clergy, itself "contaminated," in the words of a Catholic writer, by Josephinian and revolutionary ideas, and indifferentism. These trends were closely interrelated, in the view of the more conservative representatives of the church, since, in addition to violating dogmas upheld by the Holy See the administration also refrained from filling vacancies in the wealthiest dioceses for a number of years even after the Napoleonic wars, in order to collect their revenues to which it was entitled by law in such cases.[83] These two factors could only weaken the influence of the church after Joseph II's death, at a time when other denominations seemed to have strengthened their positions.

Indeed, Act XXVI of 1791 restored to Lutherans and Calvinists the complete religious freedom that had been severely curbed by Joseph II's predecessors. The law, and the royal resolution on which it was based, emphatically referred to the international treaties of Vienna (1608) and Linz (1647) in recognizing the rights of Hungarian Protestants. It granted them free practice of their faiths, making no distinction between private and public worship, and specified their right to send students to foreign universities. Although they did not obtain full equality with Catholics in every respect—since they continued to be disadvantaged in the case of conversion, or mixed marriages, and their prelates did not become automatically members of the upper chamber of the Diet— their civil rights were fully acknowledged within Hungary proper, in spite of the repeated protests of the Catholic high clergy.[84]

In certain areas, the gains made by the Eastern Orthodox Church

---

[83] Between 1799 and 1820 the archiepiscopal see of Esztergom (Gran) was occupied for only one year (by a foreigner, Archduke Charles Ambrose of Este); in the first quarter of the 19th century the archbishopric of Kalocsa was vacant for five years, as was the bishopric of Besztercebánya (Banská Bystrica), whereas the bishoprics of Győr (Raab) and Vác (Waitzen) were vacant for six, that of Nagyvárad (Oradea) for 10 years. In 1800 eight dioceses, including the archbishopric of Esztergom and comprising more than half of Hungary's Catholic population, were without spirtual leadership. Two years later the revenue which flowed into the coffers of the treasury from six of the seven diocesan sees still vacant was just under 630,000 florins, almost half of it coming from the archbishopric of Esztergom. *Ibid.*, pp. 24f.; Meszlényi, *A jozefinizmus*, pp. 92ff., 113–16, 120–27, 214–18, 224, 234.

[84] Johann Mailáth, *Die Religionswirren in Ungarn*, 2 vols. (Regensburg: Vlg. Manz, 1845), I, 72–90. For the English text of Act XXVI: 1791, cf. Townson, *Travels in Hungary*, pp. 170–80.

were more spectacular than those of the Protestant denominations. Act XXVII of 1791 gave the nonunited Greeks, as the law called them, the right to acquire landed property and to hold public offices, and recognized their autonomy in matters of education. The Diet of the following year seated their metropolitan and bishops in the upper chamber, since the administration wanted to counterbalance the concessions obtained by the Magyar and Protestant, or potentionally oppositional elements, with those given to the overwhelmingly Serbian and Romanian followers of Eastern Orthodoxy, whose privileges and rights were granted by the dynasty rather than derived from international agreements or the Hungarian constitution.[85]

Thus there were important differences even in the status of the "acatholics," to use the language of contemporary documents. Officially the church persisted in referring to Protestants as heretics (*heretici*), whereas the adherents of Eastern Orthodoxy were only schismatics (*schismatici*). The law, which spelled out the ancient rights of Protestantism in Hungary, specifically excluded the kingdoms of Dalmatia, Croatia, and Slavonia (excepting, however, seven Protestant communities in the last province), where, according to the municipal statutes still on the books, Lutherans and Calvinists were not allowed to own property or hold public or private offices.

Despite the surviving discriminations against the acatholics and the fact that Roman Catholicism continued as the state religion of Hungary, the authority of the Church vis-à-vis the state and its relative strength among the other Christian denominations had been on the decline since the end of the eighteenth century. In the same period growing Magyar nationalism and its vehicle, the budding Magyar literature cultivated by and appealing to both Catholic and Protestant clergymen, tended to obliterate religious differences, differences which appeared to be out of place in a time when all patriots were supposed to unify their talents for the sake of the fatherland. Yet another factor tending to promote the spirit of reconciliation among the different religious faiths was the fear of atheism and immorality associated with the anti-clerical and revolutionary aspects of the Enlightenment and the era of the French wars. In a pastoral letter, included as a preface to his book on the significance of Christian moral teachings in the betterment of imprisoned persons, Alexander Rudnay, Bishop of Transylvania, called the attention of his priests to the ethical principles in the Ten Commandments and the Gospels, and acceptable to Catholics, Protestants, Unitarians, and even Jews and nonunited Greeks of their free will. But it is only fair

[85] Keith Hitchins, "The Early Career of Andreiu Şaguna (1808–1849)," *Revue des Etudes Roumaines*, ix–x (1965), 56.

to point out that the Eastern Orthodox Church was not one of the "received" churches. It was merely "tolerated," which meant that its parish priests got no state assistance; in fact, the tithe of Orthodox parishioners was given to the Roman Catholic priest or Protestant pastor instead.[86] Appointed primate of Hungary in the very year of the publication of the book (1819), Rudnay began the construction of the great basilica at his archiepiscopal see in Esztergom. A close friend of Anton Bernolák, who was a pioneer of the Slovak literary renascence, Rudnay openly declared himself a Slav and frequently gave his sermons in Slovak: for this and his loyalty to the court he was considered a promoter of Panslavism and a reactionary by Magyar nationalists. His patronage of the Slovak cultural revival[87] and in many ways enlightened and ecumenical approach to the problems of the age are examples of the interesting parallels and interactions that prevailed in both Magyar and non-Magyar national renaissances in early 19th-century Hungary even within the Roman Catholic Church.

The first three estates of the realm—the Catholic clergy, magnates, and common nobility—had more than adequate representation in the Diet. Townspeople, who according to Hungarian constitutional terminology constituted the fourth estate, were underrepresented. Although the number of citydwellers was greater than that of noblemen, the 50-odd free royal cities, each represented by two deputies like the noble counties in the lower chamber, had but one vote together. Representation for the cities was an issue for several decades, but no changes were made before 1848. The cities wanted an equal vote with the counties, that is, with the nobility. The Diet did not altogether refuse to increase the number of votes given to the cities, if only they would liberalize their administrations and enfranchise a greater number of their inhabitants. The fulfillment of this request would have brought about important changes in city life. The extension of the franchise within the cities would have taken the government of the cities out of the hands of an oligarchic magistracy responsible virtually to no one.[88] However, the cities were more directly controlled by the central authorities (*dicasteria*) than

---

[86] L. Balázs, *A felekezetek egymáshoz való viszonya*, pp. 32–44.

[87] Gogolák, *Beiträge*, pp. 237ff.

[88] For the development and role of this highly authoritarian urban patriciate see Dénes Oszetzky, *A hazai polgárság társadalmi problémái a rendiség felbomlásakor* (Social Problems of the Hungarian Bourgeoisie in the Period of the Dissolution of Feudalism), No. 3 of the *Publications of the Historical Seminar* of the Péter Pázmány University (Budapest: 1935), pp. 51–57, 76f., 82. Concerning the conditions of obtaining the *jus concivilitatis* in the cities of the 18th and 19th centuries, see *ibid.*, pp. 34f. In 1829 there were only 1,673 burghers in Pest, with a population of 50,000, out of which 22,198 paid taxes (*ibid.*, p. 102 and n. 128). Although the proportion of full-fledged burghers varied from city to city, they constituted, generally speaking, only a fragment of the whole populace.

was the rest of the country; in *oeconomicis,* or questions of the budget, they were supervised by the Hungarian chamber, or royal treasury, and *in politicis,* they were under the council of lieutenancy.[89] Liberalization of city government thus would have weakened this dependence on the crown, which almost became an insurmountable obstacle after the 1830s. Then the "new" opposition obtained a precarious majority in the lower chamber of the Diet, while in the upper chamber the balance of power remained with the administration because of the overwhelming majority of loyal magnates and clergy.

Most Hungarian cities in the first half of the 19th century were made up of farmers. As late as 1840 burghers, artisans, craftsmen, shopkeepers, and merchants were in the minority even in such cities as Pest (population 64,000), Debrecen (50,000), Pozsony (35,000), and Szeged (33,000)[90]—which indicates the economic backwardness of the country and retarded development of the bourgeois middle classes. It is true that between the lower bourgeoisie and the noblemen who had their mansions and spent some part of the year in the cities, there was an important segment of upper middle class people who belonged to the so-called *honoratior* class which consisted of professionals—priests, lawyers, doctors, educators, and writers—or to the small group of well-to-do merchants. But the upper middle class was numerically weak and tried to adjust its outlook and way of life to the traditions of the nobility. Due to the reluctance of Hungarian noblemen to enter a business career, commerce and industry were dominated by non-Magyars, Germans, Greeks, Jews, Armenians, and Serbs whose rapid assimilation and Magyarization began only in the second quarter of the century.[91]

One of the most important causes of the slow development of the bourgeoisie was Hungary's industrial backwardness. Despite the country's mineral resources, in 1841–42 only about one-tenth of the Monarchy's industrial plants were in the lands of the Crown of St. Stephen, although these lands constituted almost half the empire's total territory. The actual output of Hungarian industry was even less, because most of it was handicrafts.[92] There was no class of industrial workers in Hungary during the first half of the 19th century.[93] Low-yield agriculture and animal

---

[89] *Ibid.,* pp. 64ff.; Horváth, *Huszonöt év,* II, 178–82, 331–38, 430–40.

[90] Hóman and Szekfű, *Magyar történet,* V, 242.

[91] Cf. Zoltán Trócsányi, "Uj életformák" (New Ways of Life), pp. 260f., in Gyula Miskolczy, ed., *Az uj Magyarország;* Pápai, "Magyarország népe," pp. 208, 212–15.

[92] Mihály Futó, *A magyar gyáripar története* (History of the Manufacturing Industry in Hungary), I (Budapest: Magyar Gazdaságkutató Intézet, 1944), 177–81.

[93] E. Szabó, *Társadalmi és pártharcok,* pp. 51f. For scarce data concerning wages and living conditions of the industrial proletariat in the period in question, see Gyula Mérei, *Magyar iparfejlődés 1790–1848* (Hungarian Industrial Development, 1790–1848) (Budapest: Közoktatásügyi kiadó, 1951), pp. 144–54, 210–15.

husbandry and the lack of capital and credit, resulted in a mediocre commerce and foreign trade, as well as a poor financial balance.[94] Hungary's bad economic situation had become very irritating by Széchenyi's time. Partly because of the increase in population and consumption, partly because of the shock of the war years, debasement of currency, inflation, and problems of economic reconstruction, more people began to think about issues previously left to a small number of experts and government officials.

It was an old grievance of the estates that Vienna's tariff policy, inaugurated during the reign of Maria Theresa, discriminated against Hungarian products and retarded the country's industrial development. The policy regarded Hungary essentially as a foreign country. Prohibitive duties prevented Hungarian agricultural producers from selling their produce abroad, thus supplying Austria with cheap food and raw materials for its industry. In order to protect the Austrian producers export duties were levied on Hungarian agricultural products going to Austria. Industrial goods imported from Austria into Hungary were almost duty free, whereas the same items, if exported from Hungary to Austria, were subject to considerably higher duties. Simultaneously, prohibitive tariff barriers prevented Hungarians from buying industrial products from countries other than Austria. Although this system underwent frequent and at times important changes after Maria Theresa, its basic principles remained unchanged.[95] In 1829 the commercial subcommission of the Diet asked in vain for the abolition of the internal tariff between the Austrian and Hungarian parts of the Monarchy on the basis of the principles of free trade; mercantilistic ideas, fear of heavy losses for the treasury, and the legal problem of the Hungarian nobility's tax exemption prevented Austrian statesmen from yielding to such demands.[96]

The repeated refusal of the Diet to take over a greater part of the Monarchy's financial burdens lay at the root of the Austrian attitude, articulated by Joseph II, that so long as Hungarian noblemen refused to pay taxes and duties, Hungary must not be given equal treatment with the other provinces of the realm in matters of customs duties and state-financed industrialization.[97] Thus, as a noted Hungarian historian

---

[94] Éber, *Széchenyi gazdaságpolitikája*, pp. 23–41.

[95] Gyula Mérei, "A bécsi kormány gyáriparpolitikájának alapelvei Magyarországon 1790 és 1815 között" (Principles of the Viennese Court's Policy Relative to the Manufacturing Industry in Hungary, 1790–1815), *A gróf Klebelsberg Kunó Magyar Történetkutató Intézet Évkönyve* (Yearbook of the Count Kunó Klebelsberg Hungarian Historical Institute), v (Budapest: 1935), 177–91. Cited hereafter as *Klebelsberg Évkönyv*. The classic study of the problem is Rudolf Sieghart, *Zolltrennung und Zolleinheit. Die Geschichte der österreichisch-ungarischen Zwischenzoll-Linie* (Vienna: Vlg. Manz, 1915).

[96] Éber, *Széchenyi gazdaságpolitikája*, pp. 190–94.

[97] Mérei, "A bécsi kormány gyárpolitikája," p. 175. Cf. also Kolowrat's and Gebler's opinions, cited by Sieghart, *Zolltrennung und Zolleinheit*, p. 11.

explained, the rigid insistence on the nobility's tax exemption had dug the grave of Hungarian economic independence, turning the country into the colony of Austria.[98]

But the advocates of retaliatory measures in economics were not very farsighted either. By their discrimination against Hungarian commerce and industry they delayed the rapid development of a strong bourgeoisie whose economic activities sooner or later could perhaps have overcome feudalism in Hungary and which could have given support to the idea of the empire as a whole. By trying to strengthen the *Gesamtstaat* through exclusively financial measures, the advocates of retaliation overlooked the important political factors involved and, exactly at the time of the first stirrings of Magyar nationalism, unintentionally supported particularistic tendencies in the sensitive field of economics. They also indirectly laid the groundwork for the acceptance of Friedrich List's ideas and of Kossuth's Protective Industrial Union. When in the early 1840s Baron von Kübeck, Count Ficquelmont, and others would have liked to reverse the trend and counterbalance the Prussian-led *Zollverein* by an unified Austrian *Zollgebiet*, it was already too late: Hungarian separatist and independence movements began to use against Vienna the very same internal customs frontier once established to fortify the *Gesamtstaat*.[99]

Hungary's dependence on Austria was not restricted to economic affairs. The standing army, created in the early 18th century to replace the noble levée, the governing bodies which included the Hungarian royal court chancery, the Hungarian royal chamber (or *camera*, i.e., treasurey department), and the central administrative organ in Buda presided over by the palatine, the Hungarian council, of lieutenancy—all were subordinated to the imperial authorities. Until the 1830s the activities of the Diet were all but exhausted by voting the taxes and recruits needed for the permanent army, at the expense of the serf. Whatever autonomy Hungary preserved during the first quarter of the 19th century, was maintained in the more or less self-governing noble counties.

Emphasis on independent statehood, written into the feudal constitution but of little practical value, and lack of flexibility in Austro-Hungarian economic relations complicated a situation made difficult enough by nationalistic undercurrents and an extremely rigid social structure. The constitutional opposition never failed to point to the unfair economic policies of Vienna as the source of all troubles in Hungary and as a justification of mistrusting the court; thus nationalistic slogans and

[98] Ferenc Eckhart, *A bécsi udvar gazdaságpolitikája Magyarországon Mária Terézia korában* (The Economic Policy of the Court of Vienna in Hungary during the Reign of Maria Theresa) (Budapest: Budavári Tudományos Társaság, 1922), p. 265.

[99] Julius Miskolczy, "Gesamtstaatsidee und Wirtschaftspolitik in Ungarn 1790–1848," *Klebelsberg Évkönyv*, VI (1936), 189–204; *id.*, *Ungarn in der Habsburger Monarchie*, pp. 20–33, 63ff., 71–79; Sieghart, *Zolltrennung und Zolleinheit*, p. 107.

"gravaminal policy" prevailed where there were ample reasons to pay some attention to the social problems of the country.

In Francis Pulszky's memoirs there is a fine description of the behavior of the common nobility, the dominating class of the nation. His account is the more interesting because his family lived in northern Hungary where there was a mixed Hungaro-German-Slovak population and where city life, uninterrupted by Turkish occupation, had centuries-old traditions. Pulszky relates how the educated youth of the 1820s and early 30s got acquainted with the new Hungarian literature represented by Daniel Berzsenyi's and Vörösmarty's poems, the two Kisfaludy brothers' dramatic and epical works, the "Aurora" yearbook, and Francis Toldy's study on Hungarian literature. These works—even Széchenyi's *Hitel* which came somewhat later—were read in German translation because bookdealer Wigand in Kassa (Kaschau, Košice), who supplied the whole of northern Hungary with reading material, had no Magyar book in stock: "The books were given from hand to hand. Many of us learned only on this occasion that Hungarians, too, had a literature of their own and that there were Magyar books worth reading."[100]

Actually, Magyar language and literature were taught as one elective subject in the College of Eperjes (Prešov) where Pulszky studied but students were merely required to translate German and Latin authors into Magyar. Pulszky also mentions the case of a natural scientist who was highly esteemed abroad and frequently visited by foreigners. He was not, however, supposed to display his foreign decorations because, according to the chancery, it was not becoming for an individual who lived in the countryside and was not even a nobleman to wear medals.[101] Finally, Jews, in the view of Pulszky's father, which was "strongly reminiscent of medieval times . . . but generally shared by the Hungarian nobility," were of an inferior race. Only landowners had a respectable standing in society; noblemen avoided the company of magnates because they depended on court favor through their offices and family relationships; magnates were a separate class, addressing each other by the intimate pronoun "thou" and despising other nobles although the law declared: "Neither shall the Lords [magnates] have more, nor shall the servitors [common noblemen] have less liberty."[102]

Officials in the administration were considered gentlemen, but officials of the royal chamber, such as accountants or tax collectors, were not given full respect because many of them were aliens and not noblemen.

---

[100] Pulszky, *Meine Zeit*, I, 35, 46.

[101] *Ibid.*, pp. 57f.

[102] Paraphrased after Art. II, Book I of the *Tripartitum: Neque habent Domini plus, neque servientes minus de libertate.*

Those who accepted an appointment in the central administration were not held to be good patriots, since patriotism could be reconciled only with the elective offices in the administration of the noble counties. Lawyers and physicians were associated with the society of gentlemen even if they were non-nobles because they knew the intimate secrets of a family. Yet they were not quite equal socially, being dependent on the public, and lacking "complete" independence. Merchants, even of noble extraction, were regarded "only" as burghers.

The upper stratum of the community of burghers consisted of merchants, priests, professors, and houseowners in the cities. Another section of citydwellers were the craftsmen, addressed as "Master." Intermarriage among these various levels of society were practically nonexistent. Occasionally a nobleman would marry the daughter of a prosperous burgher, but the marriage of a noble landowner's daughter into a non-noble family was an unheard-of calamity. Officers of the army were treated as the social equals of noblemen. If a common nobleman spent a great deal of time in the company of magnates, received the title of a chamberlain, or married his daughter to a magnate, he was likely to be ridiculed. In short, concluded Pulszky, society was sharply divided into different classes which communicated with each other but were not integrated. It was to Széchenyi's credit, he added, that the integration of Hungarian society was attempted through the casino movement. "Yet even the casinos brought only the gentry county magistrates, the *táblabirós,* the magnates and the higher officials into daily contact; the wholesale merchants in Pest, who did not feel at ease in this company, founded their own casino whereas the real petit bourgeois (*Spiessbürger*), however rich they might have been frequented neither but remained faithful to their cafés."[103]

In his reminiscences Pulszky, no uncritical admirer of Széchenyi, expressed his appreciation of the latter's efforts to integrate the disparate strata of early 19th-century Hungarian society by starting meaningful social intercourse. At the same time, Pulszky's description reminds one of the complex nature of Széchenyi-style reform which had to overcome psychological and politico-historical blocks even among members of the "respectable" segment of Hungarian society at which it was aimed in the first place.

In the case of the casinos and horse races Széchenyi's creative imagination succeeded in proving that modest beginnings may produce significant results, if they are directed with consistency and purpose. Both casinos

---

[103] *Ibid.*, 1, 63ff. For the concept of the Magyar *táblabiró*, translated as "gentry county magistrate" in the excerpt just cited, cf. Marczali, *Hungary in the Eighteenth Century*, pp. 130–42 and C. A. Macartney, *Hungary* (London: Ernest Benn, Ltd., 1934), pp. 183ff.

(Széchenyi preferred the Italian name to "club" in order to avoid alluding to the political clubs of the French Revolution) and horse races served the purpose of association and concentration, and both were set up on the English pattern. In addition to strengthening the public spirit, however, casinos as well as horse races were to fulfill important economic tasks.

The first casino was the Széchenyi-Károlyi club in Pressburg, established shortly after the beginning of the Diet in October 1825. The club "belonged to the new opposition," according to Metternich's letter to Personalis Szögyényi. In the view of the police, the original purpose of the club (or as the reports called it, "reunion,") was to concentrate the oppositional forces of the Diet. In fact, leading members of the opposition, like Wesselényi, George Károlyi, and others were patrons and frequent guests of the club. Soon, however—and this was probably due to Széchenyi's moderating influence—its visitors began to come from different segments of the political spectrum, and the atmosphere of the club became more neutral, even apolitical. In the opinion of one deputy, the club was visited not only because one could find good patriots there but also because one could have "a real good time there, one could smoke a pipe, exchange ideas, read different papers, and if one would stay longer, one could even have supper. . . ."[104]

As early as November 1825 Széchenyi intended to establish a club in Pest. Called the Casino of Pest, it was inaugurated on St. Stephen's day, August 20, 1827. Starting with 175 subscriptions for a three-year period in June 1827[105] the Casino, like similar institutions abroad, was to be a place where people of good standing and educated men from all walks of society could gather for friendly discussion and for the reading of "varied political newspapers . . . and useful economic, scientific, and artistic periodicals." Széchenyi hoped the Casino and its restaurant would stimulate Hungarian magnate families to spend part of the year in Pest and help it become the center of Hungarian social life.[106] In a letter written in the fall of 1827 to a burgher in Pest, Széchenyi wrote that in the Casino everybody was welcome regardless of his birth, class, or party affiliation.[107]

Thus in Széchenyi's mind the Casino had several functions. It was

[104] Cited in Viszota, ed., *Naplók*, III, pp. xlii f. It is noteworthy that according to an Englishman who visited Pressburg in 1793, "The casino and other coffee-houses would be admired at Paris or London . . . ." Townson, *Travels in Hungary*, p. 440.

[105] Viszota, ed., *Naplók*, III, 452ff., "Miscellania," Annex No. I, 4c. One share cost 100 florins.

[106] Annex No. v, 1, *ibid.*, III, 764ff. (first protocol of the Casino).

[107] Gaál, *Széchenyi nemzeti politikája*, I, 273. See also the chapters written on the Casino and on horse races in *Világ*, SzIÖM², I, 219–326.

a step toward bringing together socially the nobility, the merchants, and the professional classes. It lured the alienated magnates to spend at least part of their income in Hungary and participate in the country's life. It was an effort to make Pest the capital of Hungary, a place where people could exchange ideas, get accustomed to reading, and learn about foreign countries. Members could keep their own wines in the cellar, and the Casino would occasionally send samples to prospective foreign customers on request. The Casino received generous donations from Széchenyi and other magnates, soon overcame all initial difficulties including the suspicion of the authorities, and became a successful national enterprise. The police reports also emphasized that the main goal of the Casino was to promote the national spirit, but they did not overlook its importance in the field of commerce. They mentioned that Széchenyi was able to win over everybody for his purposes, "intended to turn Hungary into a second England," and that there was a possibility that in political discussions loyal shareholders would occasionally be overwhelmed by the opposition-minded. As no unlawful practices could be reported, however, and as the authorities did not believe in Széchenyi's consistency and the Casino's ability to survive the many personal frictions among its members, no administrative measures were taken to suppress its activity.

Mainly because of Széchenyi's efforts the Casino in Pest was firmly established. He recruited new members, made them pay their membership fees, assisted the new institution financially, repeatedly found new accommodations for it, and used his connections with the palatine, Metternich, Chancellor Reviczky,[108] and others to get patronage for the Casino and other enterprises. He participated in the preparation of the statutes and the direction of the Casino which from 1830 on became known as the "National Casino." Soon there were casinos in other parts of the country, too. In 1831 there were only three of them besides the one in Pest, but in 1833 the number was 23 in Hungary proper and five in Transylvania. In that year the king, seeking a way to prevent them from spreading asked for a report on the activities of the casinos. The palatine, however, advised the court that the casinos were private associations, the suppression of which would arouse nationwide protest, so it was decided to keep them only under close surveillance.

The anxiety of official circles stemmed from secret reports that stressed the importance of casinos in forming a nationwide public opinion. According to this line of thought, opposition forces used the casinos to disseminate their subversive and dangerous ideas. In a report prepared

[108] Széchenyi to Reviczky, Sept. 24, Dec. 22, 1828, Majláth, ed., *Levelek*, I, 91f., 114ff.; Széchenyi to Gyulay, Jan. 18, 1829, *ibid.*, I, 117–20.

by Police High Commissioner Leopold Ferstl about the participants of the Diet in 1832–36, and submitted by Sedlnitzky to the monarch, Széchenyi was treated in a rather hostile manner. He was described as one who belonged to the "ultra left," was extremely ambitious, and was longing for popularity. Conceding that he was "enterprising and steadfast," considered by the liberals as "a great patriot," and that he had "a straight character, susceptibility for doing good, as well as fine manners and much experience," the report went on to say that Széchenyi, "imbued with Wesselényi's evil principles and idolizing, at the time, Paul Nagy," was "one of the most exalted" among the young magnates and was, as leader of the magnate opposition, censured by the palatine at the Diet of 1825–27. After the Diet, the report suggested, Széchenyi transferred his "reunion" to Pest where he reorganized it on a broader basis so that it became, upon his instigation, a model "imitated in all significant places of Hungary." Naturally, there was no direct or organizational link between the National Casino in Pest and the other casinos. Széchenyi wanted earnestly to avoid giving the authorities a pretext for intervening. But the example set by him was effective enough; it was true that the casino movement was, in the words of a police report of 1839, his "masterpiece," and that he was its "soul." It was also true that in a few years the casinos began to rival the county congregations in directing and educating public opinion.[109]

Contemporary visitors from abroad praised the National Casino's hospitality with which foreigners were "admitted gratuitously to a participation in all the privileges enjoyed by the regular members." According to Miss Julia Pardoe, writing in the late 1830s,

> The Library, although yet in its infancy, contains many valuable books of reference; and in the reading-room Englishmen will find the Quarterly, Edinburgh, and Westminster Reviews, the Athenaeum, Galignani's Messenger, and all the best Continental journals.
> The ball and billiard-rooms are both extremely handsome; and

---

[109] May 4, 1836, Annex No. 1, 8b, Viszota, ed., *Naplók*, IV, 707. In addition to the official correspondence and secret reports referred to before, see also Annex No. 1, *ibid.*, IV, 659–709. For a detailed analysis of the casino movement, see Viszota's introductions to *Naplók*, III–V, esp. pp. xl–lvi, xlvi–li, and xxxiv–xxxix, resp. Also the three essays, "Első kaszinóink és Metternich" (The First Casinos and Metternich); "A jurátusok kaszinói" (The Casinos of the Law Students); and "A szegénylegények klubjai" (The Clubs of the Poor Fellows), in Sándor Takács, *Hangok a multból* (Sounds from the Past) (Budapest: Athenaeum, n.d.), pp. 160–250, 268–76; Friedreich, *Széchenyi élete*, I, 185f.; István Barta, *A fiatal Kossuth* (Young Kossuth) (Budapest: Akadémiai kiadó, 1966), pp. 41f., 99, 199; B. Szabó, *Adatok*, 331f. (Police report of Jan. 27, 1839 re Széchenyi's "*Meisterwerk*," the Casino.) Actually casinos continued to be important meetingplaces of the landed gentry, well-to-do farmers, and commercial circles in Hungary until World War II.

the Casino known as the "National," for which only nobles or members of the learned professions are eligible, occupies the whole of the first floor; the one above being called the *Kaufmannsche Casino,* and composed of merchants and respectable individuals connected with the commerce of the city; while the basement serves as a *restaurant,* said to be the best in Pesth, whence dinners are provided in very good style all over the house.[110]

It is interesting that in January 1828 Széchenyi proposed to cut in half the prohibitive membership fees of the Casino, but the motion was blocked. In June 1829 he proposed to admit merchants and favored even the admission of Jews. But his proposal was rejected after a heated discussion by a vote of 50-6, Széchenyi being supported only by Wesselényi and four other members. Széchenyi's opponents argued that a rapprochement with the Jews was impossible in Hungary "because experience showed that the magnates did not even want to communicate with the nobility and the burghers." This argument, put forward by "liberals" and constitutionalists like Count George Károlyi and Michael Platthy, provides insight into the social problems Széchenyi had to face at the beginning of his career.[111]

[110] Julia Pardoe, *The City of the Magyar or Hungary and her Institutions in 1839–40,* 3 vols. (London: G. Virtue, 1840), III, 2f.

[111] Viszota, ed., *Naplók,* III, pp. l, and lv. Széchenyi's attitude toward the admission of Jews into the Casino deserves a word of explanation. He was far from being completely unbiased (or consistent) toward Jews, as indicated by remarks in his diaries and letters. (See e.g., his note of June 22, 1825, concerning Alexander Humboldt or, rather, James Rothschild, *ibid.,* II, 545f.) His public attitude, like in most questions of national importance, was pragmatic regarding people of the Jewish faith. He mistrusted persons of Jewish extraction and disliked Jews as an ethnic group; he also feared that Hungarian nationality might suffer from a mass immigration of Jews. He opposed the complete emancipation of the Jews in 1844, emphasizing, however, his sympathy with the sufferings of the Jewish people, his faith in the equality of all men before God, and his appreciation of the efforts of Hungarian Jewry made in the interest of progress and Hungarian nationality. (Cf. his two speeches of Oct. 1, 1844, and also his speech of Aug. 10, 1844, at the Diet. Török, *Széchenyi politikai iskolája,* II, 386–92.) In shaping one's judgment, one has to keep in mind that Széchenyi was just as afraid of and disliked the fact that the majority of cities in Hungary was German, and that Hungarians were outnumbered by Slavs and Romanians in many parts of the country. In his opinion, Hungarians had to strive for moral and cultural supremacy, hard to achieve, however, if they had to absorb at once a vast number of varied cultural and ethnic groups. Some of his most intimate friends, particularly in the last years of his life, were Jewish; also, he could be very "broadminded" if, as seemed to be in the case of Casino membership, this would help to promote his cause, which he always identified with that of the country. As many other facts about Széchenyi, his "aristocratic" anti-Semitism, which was not without hypocrisy, had been grossly misrepresented in the "interest" of Hungarian racism between the two world wars.

For the traditions of "bourgeois" anti-Semitism among the burghers and merchants of Hungarian towns, see Eckhart, *A bécsi udvar gazdaságpolitikája Magyarországon, 1780–1815,* pp. 337–41.

Along with the Casino, Széchenyi also openly used the horse races to promote the idea of "concentrating" national forces.[112] His passion for horses and efforts to introduce horse races into the Monarchy and Hungary proper dated back to earlier years. The first horse races were held in the spring of 1826, during the Diet in Pozsony. Despite the initial opposition of officials in Vienna, Széchenyi carried his point, and from June 1827 on there were yearly horse races in Pest. The organization of horse races paralleled the strengthening of the Casino, whose members were asked to offer prizes for and participate in the races. In return, the latter attracted members and guests, Austrian and foreign, to the Casino. The supporters of the horse races gradually brought into existence between 1828 and 1830 an Association for Animal Husbandry which elected Széchenyi as its first (temporary) president. The association, which encouraged horse-breeding and animal shows, was transformed into the Hungarian Economic Association in 1835, subsequently expanding into all important branches of agriculture.[113]

Intensification of Magyar nationality, promotion of public spirit, and concentration of the patriotic forces: these were the guiding principles of Széchenyi's activities following the Diet of 1825–27. Academy, horse races, and National Casino were instrumental for these purposes. The latter two particularly indicated his serious effort to stimulate agricultural production as well as domestic and foreign trade. In order to get better acquainted with the possibilities of Hungarian foreign trade, he made a special trip to Fiume (Rijeka) and Croatia in July–August 1828, investigating the chances of developing the port of Fiume and the lines of commerce from Pest through Croatia to the Adriatic Sea. Although he did not share the exaggerated hopes of many for Fiume's possibilities, Széchenyi did believe existing conditions for exportation could be improved considerably and that the development of Fiume was a prerequisite to the commercial growth of Pest.[114] He wrote to Chancellor Reviczky that Pest and Fiume should be "centers and places of concentration,"

[112] Széchenyi to Reviczky, Dec. 22, 1828, Majláth, ed., *Levelek*, I, 115. The first horse race in Hungary was organized in Somogy county by Count Joseph Hunyadi in 1815. Klára T. Mérey, *A feudalizmus válságának megnyilvánulása a somogyi mezőgazdaság és a jobbágyság helyzetében, 1815–1836* (The Manifestation of the Crisis of Feudalism in the Conditions of Agriculture and Serfdom in Somogy County, 1815–1836) (Pécs: 1959) p. 13 (No. 23 of *Dunántuli Tudományos Gyüjtemény, Series Historica* 11).

[113] Cf. Blum, *Noble Landowners*, p. 137. For a detailed summary of Széchenyi's participation in the organization of the first Hungarian agricultural societies, see Viszota's introductions to *Naplók*, III–V, esp. pp. xl–lvi, li ff., and xxxix–xliii, respectively.

[114] Aug. 8–11, 1828, Viszota, ed., *Naplók*, III, 239–44. Fiume had belonged to the Hungarian Crown since Maria Theresa, as *Corpus Separatum* (1776). For its commercial importance before Széchenyi see Marczali, *Hungary in the Eighteenth Century*, pp. 76–82.

because "Pest is Hungary's heart, just as Vienna is the head of the *Gesamtmonarchie.*"[115]

Academy, horse races, and National Casino did not absorb all of Széchenyi's energies. He vigorously supported the efforts of Count Maurice Sándor, who was famous as a jockey, to build a permanent bridge between Pest and Buda; he soon became the driving force behind this enterprise, too.[116] In February 1826 he took part, along with several aristocrats and deputies to the Diet, in the foundation of the first Hungarian fire insurance company.[117] Gradually, no important undertaking was initiated without his participation; on the other hand, no enterprise was too little or unimportant for the man[118] who conscientiously tried to follow the example set by his idol, Benjamin Franklin.

By the end of the 1820s Széchenyi's plans were indeed conscious efforts to introduce reforms in Hungary. An interesting evidence of this is his didactic epistle written to Countess Francis Hunyady née Julie Zichy in November 1829. Characteristically, Széchenyi asked the countess not only for contributions but also to copy his letter and show it to her family and intimate friends. In one passage of the letter he "unsnarled the riddle" of his endeavors. Hopefully, he said, the countess did not believe he was going to spend the best years of his life in watching a few horses race or in organizing a smoker. To him, the smell of a pipe was just as unpleasant as the odor of a stable; only with great self-denial could he bring himself to withstand the stench of such establishments as horse races and the Casino. Yet, he maintained, these means were both innocent and sufficiently abundant to lure his compatriots out of their bear's dens, to gather them in one place, and to acquaint them with one another and with educated foreigners. "While I am talking about the horse, the sheep or the cow, I keep on rasping, step by step and very gently, the prejudices of our compatriots. I can assure you that I have already caused some of them quit spitting on a rug; also, I have clipped, rather considerably, the wings of a few who were somewhat too big for their breeches."[119]

---

[115] Széchenyi to Reviczky, Dec. 22, 1828, Majláth, ed., *Levelek*, I, 115.

[116] The first exchange of letters between Count Sándor, Széchenyi, and the English engineer Sir Marc Isambart Brunel concerning the bridge occurred in 1828–29. See Annex No. IV, 1–4, Viszota, ed., *Naplók*, III, 759–64. Also, Sept. 3, 1828, Jan. 29, 1829, *ibid.*, III, 251, 287; and Széchenyi to Wesselényi, Sept. 4, 1828, in Majláth, ed., *Levelek*, I, 84f.

[117] Friedreich, *Széchenyi élete*, I, 186f.

[118] See Széchenyi's first public discussion concerning the outside appearance and printing of *Felső Magyar Országi Minerva* with the periodical's editors. Annex No. III, 1–6, Viszota, ed., *Naplók*, III, 741–59.

[119] Széchenyi to Julie, Nov. 28, 1829, Majláth, ed., *Levelek*, I, 134f.

The letter revealed Széchenyi's intention to be the teacher of his nation. In this process of educating an entire country he assigned a special role to an aristocracy considered by many as an alien and "denationalized" class in contemporary Hungary. In his letter "To Julie" he set up high moral standards for his own class, saying that "the higher someone was born, the richer, the more intelligent, and the more independent he is—the greater are his duties to his fellow men and to his fatherland." Warning that birth, title, and wealth gave no right to be considered a better and nobler man, he held that "the best man is the greatest, noblest, and most outstanding man." Man's greatest fortune lay in developing his soul, for man was created to think; besides his stomach, he also had to give nourishment to his heart and mind. He pointed out that it was man's duty "to further by every possible means true enlightenment and real civilization," and added with emphasis that Hungarians must do this in Hungary *because this was the post assigned to them.* In an emotional appeal similar to the one launched by Mazzini in his essays on *The Duties of Man* some 15 years later, Széchenyi summed up the mission of Hungarians by stressing their duty "to contribute to the embellishment and perfection of the Universe" through the improvement of their own homeland. He found Hungary an ugly country, an aristocracy which should have been a stimulating force, corrupt. Still, Hungary had to be assisted and not despised by the leading families that had the means to do it. In Széchenyi's opinion, Hungary's regeneration was primarily the task of the aristocracy, which ought to spread "the spirit of noble enlightenment" so that both peasant and prince shall recognize their mutual duties, the former's task being to work industriously and to obey, the latter's to give a good example and respect the rights of the neediest peasant. Having thus confirmed the rather paternalistic principles of *suum cuique* (to each his own), he then emphasized the importance of nationality as the basis of all improvement and progress. To the idea of "developing and ennobling nationality" he assigned a broad meaning which included widening of one's knowledge, cultivation of the mother tongue, refinement of morals, and the embellishment of Hungary's heart which he, probably for the first time, called by the name "Budapest."[120]

Széchenyi's patriotic work began to bring results. Despite the suspicion of the court and jealousy of many fellow magnates, he soon achieved a national reputation. Although his relationship with Archduke-Palatine Joseph was far from cordial at the beginning, the palatine's Protestant wife openly praised him because he was "so perceptive to everything noble and great;" the city of Pest conferred honorary citizenship on

[120] *Ibid.*, pp. 130–34. Italics Széchenyi's

him; poets and writers began to dedicate their works to him; county congregations sent their greetings; he received letters from burghers and merchants; also, he was expected to build a permanent (as opposed to the existing pontoon) bridge and theatre. "How many shoulders would be needed to achieve all this," he sighed in a letter to Wesselényi.[121] Even the fairly factual report to the inquiry of Chancellor Reviczky emphasized that Széchenyi, after resigning his commission,[122] "devoted his life to the regeneration of the Hungarian nation," and that he also had the necessary intellectual and physical abilities to achieve his goal.[123] Giving a short summary of Széchenyi's life, the report enumerated his close connections with Wesselényi (*"Omnium pessimus"*) and other liberal magnates, mentioned his reform plans for transforming Hungary into a second England (*"Anglomaniae suae omnia subordinare, et ex Hungaros Anglos formare sibi arroget"*), but firmly stressed that "Count Széchenyi does not go along with the demagogic liberalism of the present age . . . is devoted to the ancient constitution; he also respects, loves and highly praises His Highness and the supreme benevolence of His Majesty, and which is rather amazing in such a man, he is also very religious. He goes frequently to church, attends sermons, and prays devoutly also at home."

The report mentioned Széchenyi's affection for Crescence.[124] Actually Széchenyi ascribed all his successful actions, including his own transformation, to the beneficent influence of Crescence. His diaries and letters are full of references suggesting that it was Crescence who had started him on the hard path of virtue and self-knowledge.[125] He felt she was the primary cause of the ennoblement of his soul, as well as the regeneration of a whole people, and that she was "the Amphitrite who gave a drink to the eagle."[126] She was the one who gave him, as a motto,

---

[121] Széchenyi to Wesselényi, Feb. 8, 1830, Majláth, ed., *Levelek*, I, 144. Cf. Jan. 20, Sept. 20–21, Oct. 17, Dec. 12, 1828, Mar. 22, Dec. 24, 1829, Viszota, ed., *Naplók*, III, 191, 259, 264, 282, 309, 376. Concerning Széchenyi's influence on contemporary Hungarian literature, see István Skala, *"Gróf Széchenyi István és a magyar romanticizmus"* (Count Stephen Széchenyi and Hungarian Romanticism), *Heft des Collegium Hungaricum in Wien*, No. XI (Budapest: 1932), 17–94; Gyula Kornis, *Széchenyi és a magyar költészet* (Széchenyi and Hungarian Poetry) (Budapest: Franklin, 1934).

[122] This happened in February 1826. Feb. 13, 1826, Viszota, ed., *Naplók*, III, 19. Cf. *ibid.*, III, p. xxiv.

[123] Annex No. 3c, *ibid.*, III, 774: *"est illi corpus laboriosum, fatigiorum patiens, et in quibusvis Artibus gymnasticis exercitatum, ingenium excellens, satis eloquentiae, animus gloriae appetens, in coeptis firmiter perseverans, ab impedimentis et obicibus non abhorrens, imo haec vincere solitus. . . ."*

[124] *Ibid.*, pp. 775f.

[125] For detailed documentation see Viszota's introduction, *ibid.*, III, esp. pp. xxii–xl, lviii f.

[126] This mythological symbol became the seal of the Hungarian Academy. Jan. 26, 1826, Feb. 18, Mar. 10, 1829, Apr. 15, 1830, *ibid.*, III, 14, 212ff., 292, 297–305, IV, 36f.

the slogan "self-perfection and Hungary's welfare,"[127] and it was she to whom he dedicated his works and opened his heart concerning his plans for the future.

Preoccupied with the organization of the Academy, the National Casino, and horse racing, he gave much thought to the new bridge to be built between Pest and Buda and to a planned visit to the New World.[128] But this time plans for a visit did not arise from a need to escape, as was the case previously.[129] Instead, his favorable impressions of Americans he had met during his Oriental trip, strengthened by his reading of Franklin and Jefferson, stimulated Széchenyi to think of going on to the United States after another trip to England in late 1829. In England he intended to study the problem of parliamentary reform and the model of a suspension bridge; he wanted to go to America, since, to him, it was "the land where the rights of mankind are the most equal, [and] where the constitution is the best." Now that he had devoted his life to such a noble enterprise, he regarded it as his duty "to go to the fountain from which this essence of justice springs."[130]

This passage from Széchenyi's "Code of Conduct," composed in 1829, is of interest for three reasons. First, it shows, generally speaking, that the "American experiment" had a great appeal to early 19th-century liberals and reformers, even in central Europe, well before the time of Alexis de Tocqueville. Second, it indicates the broad foundation of Széchenyi's approach to the problem of reform in Hungary. The reform movement initiated by him has traditionally been described as having been confined chiefly to the field of economy. This presentation had its origin in a brilliant propagandistic oversimplification of Kossuth. In his polemical *Felelet Gr. Széchenyi Istvánnak* (Reply to Count Stephen Széchenyi) written in 1841, Kossuth drew a historical parallel between the two leaders of the reform movement in the early 1830s, Széchenyi and Wesselényi. He suggested that, "The former wanted to lead to public liberty through public enrichment; the latter to public enrichment through public liberty. According to the former, 'let us only be rich,

---

[127] Oct. 1–3, 1829, *ibid.*, III, 360. Cf. Dec. 8, 1829, *ibid.*, III, 370, where to the ideals of self-perfection and Hungary's welfare he added a third one in case the former two would fail: "If everything is shaking, Faith remains."

[128] Jan. 8, 1827, Sept. 16, Oct. 17, 1828, *ibid.*, III, 118, 257, 264. Cf. Nov. 27, 1826, *ibid.*, III, 106f. According to this earlier program, "we want" people decorated with civic virtues because "on them depend the happiness of a nation" and "real moral independence." This aim was not to be achieved through secret societies, for "The light of civilization is burning and no mortal will extinguish it ever more."

[129] *Lebens Regeln* (Second variant), Annex No. 1, 10b, *ibid.*, III, 492.

[130] *Lebens Regeln und Rath eines treuen Freundes. 1829*, Annex No. 1, 10a, *ibid.*, III, 486.

freedom will follow suit;' in the opinion of the latter, 'let us only be free, opulence will come by itself thereafter.' "[131]

Kossuth's comparison of Széchenyi and Wesselényi was after the Revolution of 1848 transfered and applied by Sigismund Kemény to the Széchenyi-Kossuth controversy of the 40s. Thus a myth was created, which, although containing an essential element of truth, was a distortion because it ignored the political perspectives inherent in Széchenyi's reform in its original conception. Furthermore, it separated Széchenyi's efforts to transplant Western ideas into Hungarian soil from their background in the Western, primarily Anglo-Saxon, world. In this way Széchenyi's contemporary liberal political opponents, perhaps not always consciously, tried to justify Kossuth by playing down Széchenyi's role as a politician. On the other hand, Széchenyi's conservative interpreters, like the historian Szekfű, attempted to present him as the Hungarian national prophet par excellence in order to discredit "international" and "doctrinaire" liberalism presumably imported by Kossuth and others to Hungary where it supposedly had no roots and future whatsoever. The importance of this aspect of the Széchenyi-Kossuth problem can hardly be overestimated, because some of the old battles related to it have been fought over and over again during the last century of Hungary's intellectual evolution.

Third, Széchenyi's intention to study carefully the English parliamentary reform movement and the operation of American democracy, although the latter failed to materialize, nonetheless adds another dimension to his economic reforms. True, he wanted "to secure and develop to a nobler level" Magyar nationality, but at the same time he also wished to transform his fatherland in some magic way "from an outmoded, half feudal, half constitutional imbroglio into a representative system purified from false lustre and suitable to human beings." This vision, reasserted in *A kelet népe,* implies that Széchenyi did not reverse the double socio-political purpose of his very first reforms, namely, the reconciliation of "the two great national interests, the prosperity of our race and constitution without tears and without human sacrifices." Thus peaceful reformation to him meant the foundation of national, economic, *and* constitutional progress.[132]

Széchenyi's interest in the developing West was not utopian, unrealistic, or artificially isolated from the problem of central Europe and Hungary. He soon realized the European significance of the Italian, Polish, and German national movements for unification.[133] While not particularly

---

[131] Ferenczi, ed., *A kelet népe,* p. 424.
[132] *Ibid.,* pp. 219, 238ff.
[133] July 28, 1828, Viszota, ed., *Naplók,* III, 234.

biased in favor of the Germans, he told the Grand Duchess of Mecklenburg, sister of the wife of Czar Nicholas I: "If I were a German, my heart would bleed at the sight of dismembered Germany because I would think [in terms of] one God, one love, and one Germany."[134] himself a nationalist, he recognized the interdependence of economic matters with national and international politics, as illustrated by his reaction to the preliminary steps taken in the direction of the German *Zollverein:* "The German powers have concluded a trade agreement under Prussian leadership. Austria has again missed the boat, which is imprudent. This treaty is the A [alpha leading] to the rest."[135]

This entry, written in September 1829, may serve as a warning to those who underestimate the feasibility of achieving national goals through economic means or overemphasize Széchenyi's "failure" to see the inadequacy of his methods compared to the presumably more efficient political steps favored by the younger liberal opposition in the 1840s.

Széchenyi's vigor in initiating reforms and keen interest in domestic and international events did not mean, however, that he achieved the balanced serenity advocated by his cherished model Benjamin Franklin. His feverish activity was the result of a heroic endeavor to bridge the abyss of his mental conflicts. He was often unhappy because of his affection for Crescence, which he tried to sublimate into a chivalrous service destined to promote the moral perfection of Crescence, himself, and Hungary. Crescence's apparent indifference, occasional illnesses, and Széchenyi's own depressing visions related to previous morbid passions often made him see Hungary as a country in deadly danger and agony. In such periods of despair he found evidence everywhere that Hungary was a corpse; still, thinking of his "saint," Crescence, he decided he would not easily give up his efforts.[136] Sometimes, he happily noted the words of peasants reported by friends, that "Count Stephen Széchenyi is a famous man"; one week later, however, he again believed that the Hungarian aristocracy had been completely Germanized and all his work was in vain.[137]

In the introductions to the edition of Széchenyi's diaries Viszota collected convincing material to prove the connection between Széchenyi's mental instability and his frustrated passions. Without questioning the close relationship between Széchenyi's personal feelings and his interpretation of Hungarian reality, one may mention yet another, sociological aspect of Hungary's "to be or not to be" question in the first decades

[134] Aug. 18, 1829, *ibid.*, III, 342.
[135] Sept. 8, 1829, *ibid.*, III, 351.
[136] Dec. 3, 1827, *ibid.*, III, 183.
[137] Oct. 17, 24, 1828, ibid., III, 264ff.

of the 19th century. In an earlier chapter, reference has been made to Herder's prediction about the expected vanishing of Magyars from the arena of European history,[138] and to the rather considerable effect of this prediction on the Hungarian mind. The danger of being absorbed by neighboring populations was increasingly felt in a country which still remembered Joseph II's efforts at Germanization and in which the ruling Magyar element was far outnumbered by other nationalities, whose national consciousness had been stimulated by the same Herder who had predicted the decline of the Magyar. The vision of "the death of the nation" was particularly repulsive to the educated middle nobility. This landed gentry, or at least its politically articulate segment was, unlike the rather alienated and cosmopolitan aristocracy, a stronghold of Magyar nationality. Efforts to centralize and modernize the administration of the Monarchy were a menace to its political influence, whereas the restlessness of the serfs represented a threat to the economic bases of its very existence. The feeling of decline which prevailed among members of this class was also reflected in the pessimistic outlook of the patriotic literature in the decades preceding Széchenyi's emergence. The tenor of this retrospective literature was that Hungarians had had a glorious past but the present generation was being punished because of the "vices of its forebears" and its own deviation from the national and moral virtues of the early Hungarian heroes.[139]

This "national pessimism" was to a certain extent reversed by Széchenyi's influence on contemporary literature, but by no means did it vanish completely from the thinking of his generation. Actually, he himself noted in 1820: "Every day I am more convinced that Herder is right; the Hungarian nation will soon cease to exist."[140] While keeping these and other pessimistic remarks mostly to himself in his diaries, he did refer to the influence of Herder's prediction on Hungarians in the prefaces to *Világ* and *Stádium,* in 1831.[141] Thus, perceiving Hungary's death agony was not just Széchenyi's personal idiosyncrasy, although this can be documented too—it was a nightmare shared by his entire generation. The gloomy outlook of many leaders of public opinion representing the politically conscious middle nobility, in turn, is one of the explanations for the mixed reaction with which Széchenyi's works were received. True, his habit of belittling the past, his enthusiasm for foreign examples, and his satirical remarks about Hungary's backwardness deeply hurt the national pride, this mirror of the insecurity of Magyardom's

---

[138] See Ch. II, p. 19.
[139] Cf. Skala, *Széchenyi és a magyar romanticizmus,* pp. 7–16.
[140] June 20, 1829, Viszota, ed., *Naplók,* III, 320.
[141] *Világ* and *Stádium, SzIÖM²,* I, 13f., II, 23., resp.

"collective psyche." At the same time, however, he seemed to hold up an alternative to the phantom of national death without destroying the traditional class structure of Hungarian society. Indeed, Széchenyi's alternative seemed to promise a noble and leading role in Hungary's modernization to the landed gentry in general and to the aristocracy in particular. Hence the ambivalent reaction of shock and enthusiasm to his very first book published in Hungarian, *Lovakrul*.

Written in the second half of 1827, the study was published in February 1828.[142] Many features of Széchenyi's characteristic approach to reform were present in the booklet. Its meaningful motto became famous in Hungary, and Széchenyi often returned to it during his political debates in later works: "The little acorn, if sound, will become an acorn-bearing oak in time, but let no one trample upon it."[143]

The book was dedicated to the memory of the late Count Joseph Hunyady, initiator of horse-racing in the Habsburg Monarchy. It summarized the author's views on horse-breeding and was a result of many years of domestic and foreign, primarily English, experience. Evaluating also the opinions of foreign experts on the subject, Széchenyi made a series of proposals to improve Hungarian horse-breeding. The proposals included, among others, the establishment of horse races, annual prizes for the races, training places for the horses, a permanent Society for Horse-breeding, a national horse register, annual horse markets—measures gradually introduced during the next decades for the modernization of animal husbandry. He supported his ideas with a detailed survey of horse-breeding conditions in England, France, Mecklenburg, Bavaria, Naples, and even Russia.[144]

The application of European standards and statistics to illustrate the backwardness of animal husbandry in the Monarchy and, more specifically, in Hungary and Transylvania,[145] was somewhat unusual coming from a Hungarian magnate. But Széchenyi went even further. Digressing often, he engaged in more general comments under the pretext of writing on horses. As he said in the postscript, he did not want his book to be "too boring or smell like a stable."[146] Actually, the ideas disseminated throughout the book went considerably beyond the confines of an economic dissertation. Above all, Széchenyi called the attention of his compatriots to the importance of economic questions in a nation's life, emphasizing that economics should not be mixed up with patriotic enthu-

---

[142] Viszota, ed., *Naplók*, III, pp. lxxvi f.

[143] References concerning *Lovakrul* will indicate the page numbers of the *editio princeps:* Gróf István Széchenyi, *Lovakrul* (Pest: Trattner és Károlyi, 1828).

[144] Pp. 164ff., 178–98.

[145] Pp. 14f.

[146] P. 239.

siasm but approached with sober calculation and systematic work: "Magnanimity and Patriotism should not be confused, for God's sake, with Economics and Commerce. . . . A Thrifty patriot or a well-to-do Merchant-patriot is more useful for the Public Good than a poor and helpless Patriot with a *bel esprit*."[147]

Széchenyi reminded his readers that they lived in a calculating and speculating century and that profit-making was not shameful but an important lever of successful economic enterprise.[148] Referring specifically to profit-making as the secret of successful horse-breeding in England,[149] he also pointed out that the main thing was not to expect help from the government but "to help ourselves!"[150] He was against restrictions in economic and commercial matters, opposing government interference because, as he put it, "Reason held in chains by the mold of Prejudice and custom will never reach heavenly Heights. Anything in the World can attain full Perfection only in the Delight of liberty."[151]

When he advocated the admission of foreign competitors to domestic horse races,[152] he also encouraged profiting from foreign experiences in all branches of the economy. At the same time, he warned against the use of foreign methods without adapting them to Hungarian conditions: "the [horse-] Breeder shall refrain from all *manias;* he should be neither Anglo- nor Arabomaniac. He shall steer a middle course. . . ."[153] Stressing the importance of avoiding frequent changes in the laws and constant vacillations in economic and commercial matters, he put a particular emphasis on the usefulness of concentrated efforts and free associations,[154] for the freedom of association, in his opinion, most successfully promoted the good of mankind, and was the "fountain-head of all Noble, True, Beautiful, and civil Fortune."[155]

Free associations were, according to Széchenyi, the best means of developing and educating a "nation's soul." The "spirit of association" appeared to be a moral concept in his presentation, inspired and stimulated by Christian love of one's neighbor.[156] Just as the perfection of oneself gave impetus to lifting one's soul freely toward the Divinity,[157] he considered the associations to promote human progress as moral bodies

---

[147] P. 177.
[148] Pp. 7f., 10, 26f., 149f., 210 (wrongly: 310—misprint!).
[149] Pp. 43, 45ff.
[150] P. 232. Also, pp. 52, 167, 176.
[151] Pp. 192f, 205.
[152] Pp. 183f.
[153] Pp. 221ff. Cf. pp. 97f.
[154] Pp. 198, 232ff.
[155] P. 81.
[156] Pp. 234f.
[157] P. 147.

giving a highly ethical and Christian interpretation to the Latin adage "The voice of the people is the voice of God" (*vox populi, vox Dei*).[158]

Thus in his *On Horses* Széchenyi submitted, along with an economic theory of laissez-faire, a moralizing and peculiarly individual philosophy built on the same Christian, deistic, and humanitarian elements present in his earlier thinking. By now he had made public his thought, for he intended "to stimulate the Multitude to Ponder, to Judge and Doubt with cold blood, in a word, to Think."[159]

The reaction of "the multitude," however, did not come immediately, and when it did it was far from unanimous. First the publication of the book passed unnoticed; even friends were slow to read it. Crescence expressed a hope that his next work would be in German so she could read it,[160] but Wesselényi was boasting that his friend had learned to write in his mother tongue so quickly.[161] Soon another friend, Francis Ürményi, former keeper of the crown, praised his courage for having "written with a Hungarian heart and demonstrated the weak sides of many prejudices."[162] Other favorable reviews and opinions followed suit. In a letter written to the editor of the *Journal des Cours* in Paris, Széchenyi particularly emphasized the responsibilities of the landowners, "the surest guarantors of order and public tranquillity," both with regard to horse-breeding and necessary improvements in all fields of "public prosperity and general well-being."[163]

Naturally there were many who disliked Széchenyi's onslaught on prejudices, or such statements as "flattery must not be substituted for patriotism." Others may have been shocked by his attacks on mediocrity and alienated patriots, or by his emphasis on nationality.[164] Some may have been suspicious of foreign examples he favored and of innovations in horse-breeding and elsewhere, since Széchenyi also mentioned the need for a new law of exchange.[165] All these may explain the partly unfavorable echo of the book recorded by Széchenyi in his diaries. He was accused of having made his homeland and compatriots ridiculous; the translator of his work tried to dissuade him from publishing it abroad,

[158] Pp. 236f.

[159] P. 241.

[160] Mar. 10, 1828, Viszota, ed., *Naplók*, III, 199.

[161] Friedreich, *Széchenyi élete*, I, 197f. One of the foremost literati, Gabriel Döbrentei, helped Széchenyi polish the manuscript. For Wesselényi's book on the same topic (1829) and the overlapping ideas in the two works, see Trócsányi, *Wesselényi*, pp. 83–86.

[162] Cited in Zichy, *Széchenyi életrajza*, I, 240ff.

[163] Sept. 14, 1828, Majláth, ed., *Levelek*, I, 88. Along with a previous letter written in April of the same year, Széchenyi sent his book to the editor, remarking that "Loyal to the king but jealous of liberty and independence" are words engraved in every Hungarian's heart. *Ibid.*, p. 82. Cf. *Lovakrul*, p. 168.

[164] *Lovakrul*, pp. 19, 24, 49f., 114f., 209.

[165] *Ibid.*, p. 38.

saying that most people in Hungary disapproved of it and that although the lesson was good, one had better keep it within the family.[166]

True, *Lovakrul* was published in German in 1830, and three years later, its Danish version appeared in Copenhagen. When Hans Christian Andersen visited Pest in 1840 the question was put to him if any Hungarian work had been translated into Danish. His answer was: "I knew but one:—'Szechenyi on Horse-racing' "; and added that "it had been just translated by one of my dearest Danish friends." But this was a decade later when Széchenyi was at the height of his popularity and when, as Andersen noticed, "Szechenyi's portrait was to be seen in all the booksellers' shops, and it ornamented our cabin in the steamer, which carried us higher up the Danube."[167] In mid-1828 Széchenyi was told by an intimate friend, the Countess Sophie Esterházy, that in the opinion of many a respectable Hungarian, he did wrong by having written his book and that he was going to cause more damage than good. Upon the remark of the countess that he was detested, Széchenyi noted with resignation: "Thus my era is about to begin. Nonetheless, 'The strong resist, the weak despair.' "[168]

This became the motto of his second book—*Hitel*.

[166] May 1, Nov. 6, 1828, Viszota, ed., *Naplók*, III, 204, 267.
[167] Hans Christian Andersen, *A Poet's Bazaar*, 3 vols. (London: R. Bentley, 1846), III, 243f.
[168] July 7, 1828, Viszota, ed., *Naplók*, III, 219f.

CHAPTER VI

Triple Pyramid

The greatest of Hungarian epic poets, John Arany, referred to Széchenyi's three major works, *Hitel* (Credit), *Világ* (Light), and *Stádium* (Stage), as "a triple pyramid on the borderline between being and non-existence." In his powerful ode, dedicated to "Széchenyi's Memory" and written after the latter's suicide had stunned the country, the poet expressed the deepest feelings of the generation of 1848. This generation saw in Széchenyi the great awakener. Its wounds still fresh from the tragedy that started as a glorious revolution in 1848, it was anxious to expiate symbolically the guilt presumably committed by abandoning the path of caution advocated by him.

Arany indeed caught admirably the mood of the nation in 1860. Poetic metaphors, however, ought to be treated with great care by the historian, although they may reveal in the language of symbols a most significant core of so-called historical truth. In this sense Széchenyi's three books can be considered a landmark in the evolution of Hungarian political consciousness, bound together by the same inspiration and determination to act.

Besides reflecting the "collective unconscious," to use a Jungian term, of the generation of Hungarian 48ers, Arany's imagery and reverence for Széchenyi had other roots. Of peasant stock, Arany represented, along with the lyricist Alexander Petőfi, that populist realism which assured the victory of the "people" in a literature hitherto written mostly by noblemen for members of their own class. In the 1840s the reception of the peasantry into the political nation, let alone the political nation's identification with "the people" as such, had not yet been achieved It is the ethos of the Hungarian peasantry which makes Arany's poetry so exquisite. Yet there is nothing left to chance in his writings which include some of the most accomplished translations into Hungarian of masterpieces of world literature, from Greek tragedies to Shakespeare and Scottish ballads. Why did a learned poet, one of the finest and most alive artists in the Magyar idiom, compare Széchenyi's works to pyramids, structures traditionally built by rather than for downtrodden people, the faceless masses?

Széchenyi appealed to the landed aristocracy, to which he assigned a leading role in Hungary's renewal. Yet landowners, and the landless gentry, many of whom were distinguishable from the peasants only because of their privileges and perhaps their ideology, constituted less than 5 percent of the people. Even if one adds the "fourth estate," which in Hungary meant the populace of the free royal cities—and we know Széchenyi envisaged the inclusion of this politically underprivileged class into the national life—90 percent of the people of Hungary are still unaccounted for. This 90 percent, submerged under the more or less privileged apex of society, was without political existence in Hungarian constitutional law. It was made up of peasants, most of whom were "bound people," or serfs. The serfs represented not just the overwhelming majority of the people, they were the base of a social pyramid whose stability depended entirely on their production. Or in the words written in 1804 by the erudite economist-landowner Gregory Berzeviczy, Széchenyi's most important forerunner in Hungary, it was the peasantry that "carries all public burdens and is the political foundation of the country in general because, more importantly, Hungary is an agricultural country."[1]

What sentiments did the peasantry evoke in Széchenyi, the *grand seigneur,* aside from the romantic nostalgia with which he observed it in the years of his military service and travels, and aside from the sympathy he approached any manifestation of human misery with? What place did he assign to it in his "system" of nation-building and how realistic was his appraisal of its conditions?

There can be no doubt that to Széchenyi the "ennoblement" of his nation implied the granting of constitutional status to the peasant masses. This did not necessarily mean complete—let alone immediate—emancipation; it signified, as a first step, an acknowledgment of a moral responsibility for human beings. This is why at the Diet of 1825–27 he castigated the selfishness of the landowning classes, declaring, "my conscience tells me to avoid all reasonings and, knowing the situation of my serfs, to consider it my obligation to relieve it; all landowners have the same duty, and if a good thing can be done today let us not postpone it till tomorrow . . . ."[2]

[1] Cited by Ignácz Acsády, *A magyar jobbágyság története* (The History of Serfdom in Hungary) (Budapest: K. Grill, 1908), p. 438.
[2] Dec. 26, 1925, Viszota, ed., *Naplók*, II, 665 and n. 2.

In a letter to Liebenberg, Széchenyi instructed the director of his estates to increase the value of his lands without hurting the serfs and to negotiate a contract with them to the benefit of both parties. Accordingly the peasants would get the greater and more fertile part of his lands; tenure of land would be granted for several years to increase their security. They would be given mulberry trees for planting along the roads and on bad soil. Suspicious peasants would be persuaded to accept the arrangement for their own benefit, but in no way would be forced into changing the status quo. To overcome the reluctance of Liebenberg and his other employees Széchenyi repeatedly reminded them to observe "the real benefit of the serfs" and to set an example even at the price of a temporary loss of income, stipulating, "Let us rather strive for the public good than merely for our own profit."[3] In another letter asking the lord lieutenant of Baranya County to look into the complaints of peasants on one of his estates, Széchenyi insisted that he ordered Liebenberg to act in accordance with his liberal ideas (*"Sie kennen meine liberalen Ideen"*) and to keep in mind the well-being of his serfs the more since he himself had neither wife nor children to support.[4] At the end of 1829 he spoke with some of his serfs of the possibility of letting them pay an absolute indemnity for changing their plots into freeholds.[5]

These intentions were very much in harmony with the train of thought which prevailed in Széchenyi's three major works, but they were out of step with the surrounding feudal world. It was only in 1832 that a Transylvanian landowner consented to the emancipation of his serfs for an absolute indemnity, and the better known similar agreements reached by the liberal leader Stephen Bezerédy were concluded in 1838–40.[6] In fact, it was only in 1840 that manumission compensation was made possible by legislative action on a voluntary basis, but the serf's right to emancipation for compensation was not recognized by the Diet before the revolutionary events of 1848.

Széchenyi himself seems to have retreated from the highly idealistic stand taken during the first years of his activity as a practical reformer. Evidence recently found suggests that from the late 1830s on, he connived at, perhaps even encouraged, certain questionable legal maneuvers advo-

[3] Széchenyi to Liebenberg, Nov. 8, 1828, Majláth, ed., *Levelek*, I, 106–109.
[4] Széchenyi to Count Somssich, Sept. 4, 1827, B. Szabó, ed., *Adatok*, I, 71f.
[5] Oct. 24, Nov. 10, 1829, Viszota, ed., *Naplók*, III, 364f.
[6] Cf. Elek Csetri's review of *Annuarul Institului de Istorie din Cluj, 1958–1959* (Yearbook of the Historical Institute of Cluj, 1958–1959), in *Századok*, XCIX (1965), 273; Emil Niederhauser, *A jobbágyfelszabaditás Kelet-Európában* (The Emancipation of Serfs in Eastern Europe) (Budapest: Akadémiai kiadó, 1962), p. 135; Acsády, *Magyar jobbágyság*, p. 482.

cated by his stewards Liebenberg and Tasner and which were not to the advantage of his serfs. Whether or not the shift was brought on by a more conservative attitude in public matters, with his increasingly burdensome family obligations, or simply the passing of youthful idealism, the fact remains that in some of his personal affairs there appeared to be a discrepancy between principles and practice.[7]

The above merely confirms that great men sometimes act in small ways, especially when their money is involved, and Széchenyi was no exception. Significantly, some of the petitions submitted by his serfs resorted to an argument *ad hominem,* holding the writings of Széchenyi the reformer against the actions of Széchenyi the landlord. This, however, occurred in the 1840s, by which time Széchenyi's great books had acquired an independent life of their own and were, as often happens, beyond the control of the author. But in the late twenties these books were yet to be written. There is no reason to doubt that while working on them Széchenyi sincerely desired to put into practice his humanitarian principles and apply the idea of laissez-faire to the relationship of lord and peasant. To be sure, he intended to maintain the traditional structure of property rights, at least initially; and even with this limitation his gestures were extremely progressive in their context.

The situation of the peasant need not be described in great detail. Contemporary accounts as well as recent studies in English make it superfluous to enumerate all the feudal dues and services owed by the serf to his lord or the contributions required from him by the state.[8] Contemporary and modern authors emphasize the difficulty of analyzing the topic adequately, due to the wide diversity in the forms of land tenure in the varied provinces of the Habsburg Monarchy,[9] and due to "the nature of the soil, the facility of communication, the religion of the people, and above all, the character and conduct of the landlord

---

[7] Lóránt Tilkovszky, "A tagositás és legelőelkülönözés Széchenyi István pölöskei uradalmában (Land Reallotment and Redistribution of Pastureland in Stephen Széchenyi's Estate in Pölöske)," in *A Göcseji Múzeum jubileumi emlékkönyve, 1950–1960* (Commemorative Volume of the Museum at Göcsej, 1950–1960), ed. by I. Szentiványi, pp. 239–55.

[8] Blum, *Noble Landowners,* pp. 50–85 *passim.* Also Paget, *Hungary and Transylvania.* I, 285–316; B. G. Iványi, "From Feudalism to Capitalism: The Economic Background to Széchenyi's Reform in Hungary," *JCEA,* xx (1960), 273ff. For Hungarian summaries concerning the conditions of the peasantry before Széchenyi's emergence cf. Acsády, *Magyar jobbágyság,* 337–448; Éber, *Széchenyi közgazdaságpolitikaja,* 56–69; and Homan and Szekfű, *Magyar történet,* v, 229–40. Cf. the comparative study by Laszlo Revesz, *Der osteuropäische Bauer.* Seine Rechtslage im 17. und 18. Jahrhundert unter besonderer Berücksichtigung Ungarns (Berne: Schweizerisches Ost-Institut, 1964),

[9] Blum, *Noble Landowners,* p. 45.

himself."[10] Moreover, the disparity of cultural background and variety of traditions of the heterogeneous nationalities reduce the validity of more generalized statements. With the increase of the population mentioned in the previous chapter, the lot of the peasant deteriorated in less fertile regions such as northern Hungary with its overwhelmingly Slovak and Ruthenian population. In Transylvania, Romanian and Magyar serfs alike suffered from the fact that semi-autonomous Transylvania managed to postpone any serious consideration of the urbarial regulations, introduced in Hungary proper and the Banat of Temesvár in the second half of the 18th century, almost until the revolution of 1848. On the other hand, there were many well-to-do free peasants, mainly Croats, along the southern military frontier; in the privileged "Saxonian" (German) settlements of Transylvania; and in the free heyduck and Jazygian districts of the Trans-Theiss region and of the Hungarian Great Plain, as well as in the rich lands of the Bácska (Bačka) and Bánát, with their mixed population of Serbs, Croats, Germans, Romanians, and Magyars.[11] Széchenyi himself was well aware of these divergencies, as indicated by his description of the misery of Romanian peasants[12] or by the comparison he made in the summer of 1830 between "a cultivated and intelligently civilized German peasant" and his Magyar counterpart.[13]

In spite of the difficulty of comparison, the unreliability of available statistics, and the conspicuous absence of impressive, positive legislation favoring the peasant masses before 1848, not only conservatives but even some radical members of the younger liberal generation such as Daniel Irányi tended to maintain that the Hungarian peasant was better off economically than his brother in the neighboring Austrian provinces.[14] A number of foreign observers as well as modern historians, both Hungarian and non-Hungarian, seem to agree with this judgment.[15] According to Jerome Blum, "The *Robot* burden of the Hungarian peasant was lighter than it was in most of the German-Slav lands. The peasant

---

[10] Paget, *Hungary and Transylvania*, I, 293.

[11] Mérei, "Mezógazdasági árutermelés," pp. 608–14.

[12] See Ch. II. Also, an English observer's remarks, stemming from 1814, about having visited in the course of one afternoon "the dwellings of four distinct nations, each expressing their ideas in their native tongue" on the estates of old Count Francis Széchenyi. Bright, *Travels from Vienna through Lower Hungary*, p. 571.

[13] June 28, 1830, Viszota, ed., *Naplók*, IV, 60f.

[14] Daniel Irányi and C. L. Chassin, *Histoire politique de la révolution de Hongrie, 1847–1849*, 2 vols. (Paris: Paguerre, 1859–60), I, 40.

[15] Hippolyte Desprez, "Les paysans de l'Autriche," *Revue des deux mondes*, Nouvelle Série, XX (1847), esp. 336f.; Iványi, "From Feudalism to Capitalism," pp. 274f. and n. 10–12, 280; István Hajnal, "Az osztálytársadalom" (Class Society) and Trócsányi, "Uj életformák," in Miskolczy, ed., *Az uj Magyarország*, pp. 186 and 259f., respectively; Niederhauser, *A jobbágyfelszabaditás*, pp. 122f.

with a full *session* performed annually 52 days of *Robot* with work animals or 104 days of *Handrobot*. Peasants with part *sessions,* down to one-eighth, did proportionate amounts of *Robot*. Cotters were responsible for eighteen days and landless peasants twelve days each year. In addition to their *Robot* work most of these peasants, or members of their families, worked for hire."[16] A contemporary observer—the Baron de Langsdorff, son-in-law of the French ambassador to Vienna in the 1830s, who was on good terms with Széchenyi and well acquainted with circumstances in central Europe—went even further, stating that the situation of Hungarian serfs compared rather favorably to that of French *métayers*.[17]

Admittedly, Langsdorff's remarks referred to conditions that had already been slowly improving, thanks in part to Széchenyi and to the spread of liberal ideas. But the improvement was perhaps more in the atmosphere than in the economic and legal realities. As we shall see, the arguments used by Széchenyi's opponents after the publication of *Hitel* were very similar to the complacent views voiced by many a Hungarian nobleman to justify the status quo well before Széchenyi. Széchenyi himself brushed aside with a humanitarian zeal and sarcastic contempt the reasoning of those who in 1825 continued to uphold the injustice done by the privileged 400,000 to the "ten million not even mentioned in the Diet." Conceding that the Hungarian peasant might be happier than his Austrian counterpart, he concluded that the horse must also be happier than the donkey because it is being treated better and gets oats for food. He found little comfort in the paternalism of a landlord helping his peasants rebuild the house consumed by fire or replace the dead oxen; to such rationalizations he retorted that the American sugar planter also fed his black slaves well, not because of his love for them but because of his love for his own self. Holding that any attempt to change social conditions rooted in ignorance, destitution, and inequality must be based on respect for human dignity and self-esteem, he thought the opinions of some of his countrymen belonged to the realm of the Tunguz or Bashkir.[18]

As can be seen, Széchenyi's indignation reflected ethical considerations and was not much influenced by the relative position of the Hungarian peasantry in eastern Europe. He knew that Prussia had abolished serfdom while preparing for the Wars of Liberation and that country after coun-

---

[16] Blum, *Noble Landowners*, p. 183.
[17] Emile Langsdorff, "La Hongrie. –La Diète et les Réformes sociales," *Revue des deux mondes*, Nouvelle Série, XXIV (1848), 968–74. According to the diaries Széchenyi saw M. Langsdorff, then Secretary of the French Embassy in Vienna, on May 30 and June 8, 1837, and on June 24, 1838. Viszota, ed., *Naplók*, V, 82, 85, 190.
[18] Sept. 21, 1825, *ibid.*, II, 609.

try was accepting the Code Napoleon; what mattered was *his* homeland's refusal to move. This is why he had but little patience with the hypocritical complacency of his contemporaries. True, deputies in the Diet often came to the defense of the "wretched taxpayer" against exaggerated demands of the crown, and county congregations sent many petitions asking for the reduction of the serf's tax burdens. Such complaints often gave a realistic picture of the misery of the lower classes. Throughout the early decades of the 19th century deputies and counties competed with each other in describing the unbearable burdens of the peasantry every time the administration wanted to raise the amount of the military contribution (the tax paid to the treasury). These accounts, however, kept a remarkable silence about the questions of the lord-peasant relationship, the *robot* and other feudal services and about the cost of county administration, the so-called *cassa domestica,* in brief, about essential factors contributing to peasant destitution.[19] The cost of long Diets, road construction, and other public works in the counties, as well as the considerable increase of the county bureaucracy, taken together put a considerably heavier burden on the taxpaying part of the population, chiefly the peasants and in certain counties the lesser nobility living on urbarial land, than was the case in the previous century. Already in 1817 contributions to the *cassa domestica* in the city of Miskolc and in Borsod county were more than twice as high as the corresponding share of military contribution against which the estates protested in such eloquent terms.[20] At about the same time, authorities worried over a mass emigration of serfs from Transylvania, caused, in the language of a royal rescript, by the "oppressive and inhuman treatment" suffered at the hands of the landlords. Five years later, in 1823, there were still reports about the mass exodus of peasants from Transylvania to Moldavia.[21]

Officials of the autocratic regime of Francis I were right in pointing out what some of their latterday successors still refuse to see: that the emigration of desperate people can "very seldom and very insignificantly" be stopped by "prohibitions and punishments" alone; much safer is the road, so they said, which leads to securing the existence of the inhabitants of the state. The reminder, which rings so loudly through the fog of

---

[19] István Barta, "Kölcsey politikai pályakezdete" (The Beginnings of Kölcsey's Political Career), *Századok*, XCIII (1959), 266–69.

[20] Hóman and Szekfű, *Magyar történet*, v, 236f. Cf. E. Szabó, *Társadalmi és pártharcok*, pp. 49f.

[21] Royal rescript of Feb. 6, 1815; also the *Conclusum* of the *Staatsrat*, dated Sept. 4, 1815, Docs. 36 and 37 in Eckhart, *A bécsi udvar gazdaságpolitikája Magyarországon, 1780–1818*, pp. 414–19; Acsády, *Magyar jobbágyság*, p. 418.

a century and a half, brings us to the dilemma to which Széchenyi reacted so passionately. Almost by instinct, he felt that even his brand of gradual and peaceful economic reform was certain to clash with the entire feudal system. He realized that if no changes were made, all the costs of internal improvements such as road-building, land reclamation, and public works would have to be paid for by the peasant unless taken over by the state, which, in turn, led to the same vicious circle, because in Hungary state revenue depended almost entirely on the peasant's production.

The rapid progress of the West and the spread of individualism and humanitarian ideals had left hardly any impact on the lord-serf relationship in Hungary where everything seemed to have remained in the same old order. It was Széchenyi's own father who had intended to repudiate in a special treatise the "groundless" allegations claiming that the Hungarian serf was a slave whose property was subject to his master's whim and who had to be pitied for all the contributions exacted from him by the state, the county, the priest, and the military. Hungarian psychopolitical reality serves as an explanation for the government's successful endeavor to prevent Paul Nagy from being reelected to the Diet between 1807 and 1825, after he had in vain raised his voice in support of the peasant. It is also a key to understanding the mentality of prominent literary figures such as Kazinczy, Berzsenyi, or Alexander Kisfaludy, all of whom sharply condemned the economist Berzeviczy for having exposed, in strong colors and to the alleged detriment of the nation, the conditions of peasant life. But unlike some of the radical pamphleteers of the Martinovics circle, Berzeviczy and Paul Nagy, too, stopped short of demanding the abolition of serfdom. The poetic genius of Joseph Katona was needed to dramatize the misery of the loyal serf in the touching figure of Tiborc; but his tragic play *Bánk Bán* (Banus Bánk) was performed only posthumously in the 1830s. The other masterpiece, Michael Fazekas's *Ludas Matyi*, a comic epic poem whose hero, Matthew the Gooseherd, succeeds in getting even three times with the lord who once had whipped him, had to be published anonymously in 1815 to become the popular literary expression of the dreams of the downtrodden.[22] Articulate public opinion, reflecting the convictions of the privileged, thus refused to see that, in the words of a noted historian, the life of the serf had been deteriorating ever since Werbőczi's times, with the exception of the 18th century; in Szekfű's opinion, the period of

[22] *Ibid.*, pp. 411f., 429–40; R. R. Palmer and Peter Kenéz, "Two Documents of the Hungarian Revolutionary Movement of 1794," *Journal of Central European Affairs*, xx (1961), 431, 435ff., 441f. For Francis Széchenyi's paternalism toward his peasants, cf. Bright, *Travels from Vienna through Lower Hungary*, pp. 548–54.

"feudal nationalism" preceding Széchenyi's emergence was perhaps the most hopeless in the whole process of this decline.[23]

The causes of deteriorating peasant conditions must not be confined to the feudal mentality and influence of the ruling classes, although these factors tend to give a specific flavor to the Hungarian situation. The basic socio-economic changes began to develop during the century before Széchenyi, with the establishment of a permanent army which, from the point of view of the lord, became an important consumer. Aside from the horrors of forcible recruitment for a lifetime, affecting only the families of those directly involved, the whole peasantry suffered from the increasingly burdensome military contribution, which was the direct tax paid exclusively by the peasant for the maintenance of the army. The continually growing military contribution was one of the main economic considerations, in addition to her piety, which motivated Maria Theresa to impose the urbarial legislation on her reluctant Magyar estates. In the last half of 18th century, the enlightened self-interest of the Habsburg Monarchy made the protection of the serf's ability to produce and pay taxes mandatory even in Hungary, where de facto as well as de jure, the absolutist state became a third party directly interested in the affairs of lord and peasant. Since the state was not only an interested but powerful party, the gradual extension of urbarial regulations to Slavonia, Croatia, and the Banat of Temesvár introduced a new element that was, on the whole, favorable to the peasantry in the tradition-ridden Hungarian world. In spite of the fact that the Transylvanian estates were able to evade any kind of urbarial legislation until the Diet of 1846–47, and in spite of the often successful endeavors of their Hungarian counterparts first to "elude" Maria Theresa and later to sabotage the pertinent ordinances of her successors, the beginning of land surveys and the setting up of standards governing the mutual obligations of serfs and landowners, however defective they were, nevertheless marked a significant step on the road toward Hungary's economic modernization.

The basic measures of the urbarial legislation remained in force until the revolution of 1848. The main categories of labor or *robot* owed by the peasant to his lord have already been mentioned in the passage cited from Jerome Blum's study. One may add that the average size of a full *session,* or land unit held in villein tenure, was 24 yokes (a little over 34 acres) of arable land in Hungary. But it could vary from 12 to 40 yokes (17–57 acres) depending on local circumstances. One of the important innovations introduced by the urbaria was the legal

---

[23] Hóman and Szekfű, *Magyar történet,* v, 240. Cf. Mérei, *Mezőgazdaság és agrártársadalom,* pp. 9f., 131–88; Revesz, *Der osteuropäische Bauer,* pp. 29–95, 128–200, 252–311.

distinction between the two main parts of the manor—the lord's domain, or demesne, supervised directly by him or his stewards, and the urbarial land, of which he continued to be the only legal owner but which was held by his serfs in villein tenure. In this latter part of his estate, once its size had been established by the urbarial survey, the lord's property rights were restricted so that he could neither diminish it nor dislodge his tenants without special reasons or permission. Even if such permission were granted the land had to be given to other peasant tenants or replaced by land of comparable value from the demesne.

Urbarial land was the basis for taxation by the state, whereas the demesne or allodial domain of the lord continued to be tax exempt. In the opinion of some historians, protection of the "tax base,"—in other words, the peasant—was less determined under Francis I than under his predecessors in the previous century. The change in Vienna's attitude has been attributed to the impact of the French Revolution and to the need for "order" and noble support during the Napoleonic wars.[24] The worsening conditions of peasant life, however, cannot be ascribed exclusively to political factors, change in ruler, or the increasing clumsiness of the bureaucracy of the Josephinian state under Francis I. Though all of these played an important role, the process was complicated by demographic and economic trends unfavorable to the peasant.

In addition to his customary right to a certain amount of land in permanent tenure, the hereditary serf also had the right to pasture his cattle on common meadowland or mast his hogs in the common woods. For these rights, similar to rights in other parts of feudal Europe, the Hungarian serf owed the landlord a certain rent, made up of labor, produce, and, to a much lesser extent, money. In addition to the *robot* already mentioned and other forms of *corvée,* such as road construction, free transportation (*Vorspann*), or mail delivery, the serf paid a tithe to the Church, and a "ninth" (*nona*), often another tenth part of his produce, to his lord. Sanctioned by the *urbarial* legislation some of these main obligations such as the *robot* could be commuted into their monetary value, a regulation originally in favor of the serf but subsequently "reinterpreted" as a means to force him to do extra work beyond the *robot* for minimal compensation.

In the 18th century, during the great drive to repopulate the country and bring more virgin land under cultivation, the usufruct of land reclaimed with the work of the peasant was often given to him for

---

[24] Eckhart, *A bécsi udvar gazdaságpolitikája Magyarországon 1780–1815*, pp. 211–35. For the motivation and significance of the agrarian reforms under Maria Theresa and Joseph II, cf. William E. Wright, *Serf, Seigneur, and Sovereign* (Minneapolis: University of Minnesota Press, 1966), esp. pp. 155–64.

a number of years without making him liable for the customary feudal dues. In a way, even a serf could be a part-time freeholder, at least while the terms of the original agreement lasted or until the proprietor changed his mind. According to the law, such land made arable by clearing forests or draining swamps, once it had been in the hands of urbarial peasants, had to be added to already existing urbarial holdings. In practice, the efforts of the landowners to incorporate recently reclaimed areas into their own demesne were frequently successful, because in many cases the serfs themselves refrained from reporting their temporary "free" holdings to the urbarial commissions in order to avoid being taxed by the state. Having benefited first from such an ambivalent situation, they were yet the ones to lose out in the long run because land not entered into the original urbarial register *a priori* belonged to the lord's demesne unless the contrary could be proven, which was much more difficult in most instances. True, sometimes the land ameliorated by urbarial peasants and repossessed by the lord was left in the hands of those who made it usable or it was given to other peasants. The point, however, is that in such cases the agreement between lord and peasant was a private contract to which the state was no party and whose terms could be changed as circumstances changed.

Naturally the very existence of urbarial regulations had an influence on the conditions of that growing part of the peasantry which was not in hereditary serfdom. While there was much underpopulated land available that could be made fertile with relatively little investment by the unsophisticated methods of the time, newly settled colonists, cottagers, contractual serfs, sharecroppers, and tenant-taxpayers were sometimes able to get better terms from the landowner than from his own urbarial peasants or hereditary serfs, since wasteland could be put to use only if there were people around willing to till it. Because of the shortage in capital and lack of agricultural machinery the landowner needed the serf almost as much as the serf needed him if the landowner wished to benefit from his allodial land. Other signs of the primitive conditions of Hungarian agriculture were that one-third to one-half of the fields lay fallow every year while the rest were cultivated with the simple tools of the peasant; crop rotation was unknown; where manure was used as a fertilizer it was used mostly on meadows; livestock was left without shelter in the open air the year round.[25] Last but not least, ignorance of fodder plants, lack of storage facilities, and the absence

[25] For the different types and problems of peasant farming in Hungary in the period from the urbarial regulation of 1767 to the revolution of 1848–49, see in addition to works already mentioned the comprehensive essay by J. Varga, *Typen und Probleme des bäuerlichen Grundbesitzes in Ungarn*, No. 56 of *Studia Historica* (Budapest: 1966).

of transportation caused years of abundance to be followed by periods of epidemics and famine.

It was only in the early years of the 19th century that modern methods of farming and animal husbandry began to be introduced on some of the larger estates. This was also the period of the boom in cereals, when Hungary's agricultural products found a market for a number of years, with the result that the focus of Hungarian production started to shift from self-supply to a market economy.[26]

The agricultural boom was not an unqualified blessing to the peasantry. A market economy and incipient capitalism stimulated the increase in production and lowered its costs. Given Hungary's primitive socio-economic conditions, this meant primarily an endeavor to enlarge the area under the direct cultivation of the large estates and tighten the conditions of peasant farming. Land reallotment and "allodization" (which meant the repossession—frequently illegally—of land previously regarded as urbarial), as well as "curialization"[27] of peasants (their transfer from the category of urbarial serfs to that of cottars or tenant holders), were subtly assisted by the increase in population and the concomitant fragmentation of urbarial holdings, forcing the peasant either to accept the increasingly severe terms of the lord or to abandon the land. Indeed, the complaints about abandoned urbarial land multiplied in the 1820s; frequently such land was given in usage to impoverished members of the lesser nobility, which, however, posed other problems referred to in the preceding chapter.

Within one generation of the solemn but carefully circumscribed confirmation of the serf's right to move away from his lord[28] in Act XXXV of 1791, "freedom of movement" became tantamount in most instances to subjection to growing arbitrariness. It was only in the next two generations that land reclamation and public works began on a large scale. With the gradual disappearance of agricultural reserve land by the 1820s, landowners started to try to cut back even those privileges granted when there was an abundance of land and a shortage of labor. Cottars or settlers on tax-exempt noble estates were required to pay as rent, instead of the customary "ninth" which originated in the 14th century, a fifth, seventh, or eighth (*quinta, septa,* or *octava*) of their produce, which thus more than offset the allodial peasant's privilege of being free from the military tax and the tithe.[29]

[26] Iványi, "From Feudalism to Capitalism," p. 272. As pointed out by Iványi, the first, and to my knowledge, most comprehensive and pertinent, study is Mérei's *Mezőgazdaság és agrártársadalom.*

[27] From the Latin *curia,* in Hungary the residence of the lord of the manor.

[28] Acsády, *Magyar jobbágyság,* 416f.

[29] Varga, *Typen und Probleme,* pp. 72f.

With the passing of the boom in cereals and the arrival of one in wool production, the larger estates began to specialize in sheep-breeding rather than grain production. Perhaps the worst aspect of the enclosure movement that aggravated the lot of the peasant in this second phase of the agricultural boom was the effort to split up the common meadows into plots for the use of the peasants and an area exclusively for the landowner. Even where such a separation of rights, traditionally held in common, failed to be imposed, the large herds of the estate owner tended to overcrowd the communal meadows and woods to the point where the peasant was being starved out in one way or another.[30]

It is difficult to see how the effects of the beginning capitalistic transformation of the Hungarian agriculture could have been avoided. What made them particularly unfortunate for the peasant was that he had to suffer from the consequences of the new trends and the old forces which blocked their free unfolding. The law of aviticity, or entail, that was enacted in the mid-14th century, vesting ownership of land in the family rather than the individual nobleman, still made it possible for members of a noble family to reclaim the lost parts of their original estate any time they were able to rebuy it from the new owner or his descendants. During the cereal boom and in the inflationary period many landowners used their profits to reacquire estates lost to the family rather than modernize the ones they still had in their possession. Also, the law of aviticity stipulated that estates devolve upon the crown after the extinction of a noble family. Obviously, none of these provisions encouraged the development of capitalistic commercial relations since a creditor could never be entirely sure of his property rights vis-à-vis the noble debtor protected by feudal law. Moreover, since the established legal and economic relationship between lord and peasant, which with but few exceptions was confined to the so-called market towns and other privileged cities or districts, made it impossible for peasants to own land, one may well conclude that the existing feudal order prevented the evolution of the incipient market economy into a full-fledged capitalistic system.[31]

As a result of this distorted development, which hurt the entire country but put the greatest burden on the peasant, even efficient methods of management and the introduction of labor-intensive plants such as tobacco, corn, or potatoes could cause further hardship to the tiller of the soil. In many respects this was still a medieval society where miners, craftsmen, charcoalburners, vine-dressers, and peddlers were

---

[30] *Ibid.*, pp. 61f.
[31] Iványi, "From Feudalism to Capitalism," pp. 273f., 276f.

often categorized as "industrial" or "censual" peasants and would pay
a fee (*census*), collectively or individually, like the citizens of the "peasant towns" or "market places," for the landlord's permission to ply their
trade and go about their daily business. Similarly mills, distilleries, and
inns had to be licensed by the landowners who also had a right to
charge tolls on bridges and authorize the production and sale of potash,
bricks, or wine. The life of thousands of families could change overnight
if the ruler decided to donate, or the treasury to sell, one of the leniently
managed royal or state estates to a private person who might order
a new land survey resulting in an increase of the allodial estate at the
expense of urbarial holdings. This in turn would lead to collecting the
same dues from proportionately smaller full *sessions* or their subdivisions.
If the serf wanted to demur or to appeal the decision of the manorial
court he needed a lawyer who knew that in order to turn, wheels of
the bureaucratic machinery in Buda or Vienna had to be greased just
as did the creaking wheels of the carriages which brought his clients
on winding roads from faraway dark villages in Transylvania or the
poverty-stricken dust of the Great Plains. Few were the instances when
a county official would take the side of those exploited by his peers,[32]
but it is part of the whole truth that there were, as always have been,
such decent men in Hungary, too.

The conflict between the deteriorating conditions of peasant life and
society's indifference to them seems to have reached its climax in the
late 1820s. In spite of the confusing ambiguities and gaps in the available
data some of the main trends of the half-century spanning the urbarial
statistics of 1775 and the tax conscription of 1828 are clearly discernible.
One of them has already been mentioned in the previous chapter: the
group of cottar tenants or peasants with less than one quarter of a
session of land, half as strong numerically as the group of serfs with
holdings above the limit just indicated in 1775, increased threefold in
size and became slightly more numerous than the more well-to-do urbarial peasantry. The total of the two groups was about one million
in 1828.[33] Despite arbitary procedures and lawlessness aimed at restricting peasant holdings, over five million yokes of arable land were entered
into the urbarial registers in the period—land that could not be taken
away from the peasantry as a whole; yet the amount of land was twice

---

[32] See the case of Deputy Lord Lieutenant Boér in Torda County. Eckhart, *A bécsi
udvar gazdaságpolitikája Magyarországon, 1780–1815*, pp. 249ff. and 415–19, doc. 37, *ibid.*
Of the 24 urbarial lawsuits still pending in early 1835 one originated in 1821 and the
rest in 1825–27. Cf. No. 9/1835 (Jan. 6, 1835), *MKA*, HHStA (Vienna).

[33] Varga, *Typen und Probleme*, pp. 131f.; Pápai, "Magyarország népe," p. 202. The
data include only heads of families.

as high in the allodial estates under the direct management of the owner.[34] The entire area under cultivation was estimated at 30.7 million yokes in round figures,[35] and of course the share of the peasantry in pastures and forests was considerably smaller than their share in arable land. The holdings qualified legally as urbarial included neither plots below one-eighth of a full *session* nor those of cottars, settlers, or "gardeners" cultivating, for example, tobacco fields, nor cleared woodland or "remanent" fields (*terrae remanentiales*). (Originally the latter might have been clearings, tracts obtained by the drainage of swamps, or simply "surpluses" remaining after a newly ordered survey succeeded in "correcting" the alleged or intentional errors of a previous urbarial conscription.)

Thus a rather sizable portion of the cultivated land, which was in fact in the peasant's hands, continued to be legally part of the lord's demesne. Even so, the very existence of the separate category of urbarial land was a potentially dangerous limitation of property rights from the point of view of the landowning classes. Although neither hereditary nor contractual serfs could become individual freeholders of land before the 1840s, urbarial land kept growing, along with the increase in population and cultivated territory. In the two decades from 1828 to 1848 the urbarial area clearly recognized as such doubled, reaching the 10-million mark by the latter date.[36] This also showed, *a posteriori*, that the process was historically irreversible and could be solved only by a revolutionary change in property ownership.

There were no signs of or demands for such a change in 1828. The feudal legal system was firmly entrenched in the private and public domains, despite the indirect pressures beginning to develop in economic relations. The economic burdens of the peasantry appeared to be more crushing than ever. In the year mentioned, the total value of taxes paid by serfs in Hungary and Croatia was estimated at 52.5 million florins, a sum that did not take into account the tithe, the church tax, and other minor dues, but did include the military tax paid to the state which amounted to 25 million.[37] The magnitude of these figures can be grasped if one knows that the value of Hungary's entire agricultural export to Austria in 1827 was appraised at 35.6 million florins, or that a decade or so later the entire yearly income of 1,550,000 tax-paying serfs, counting 80 florins per family of five or six, was said to be 124 million florins.[38]

Széchenyi and all the financiers in Europe knew that many Hungarian

---

[34] Niederhauser, *A jobbágyfelszabadítás*, p. 124.

[35] Acsády, *Magyar jobbágyság*, p. 456.

[36] Varga, *Typen und Probleme*, pp. 124–28.

[37] Acsády, *Magyar jobbágyság*, p. 456.

[38] Éber, *Széchenyi gazdaságpolitikája*, pp. 27, 67f.

magnates were up to their ears in debt. We have also indicated that a large segment of the lesser nobility became increasingly insolvent in the post-Napoleonic period. But the indebtedness of most of the peasantry defies any description. According to a contemporary prize-winning study of Hungarian serfdom, if *robot,* public works, *Vorspann,* the right of the lord to double the labor demanded from the serf in the case of urgent work, are combined, there were hardly more than 100 free days for the serf. "Taking into consideration that there are about 50 days in a year when no work can be done outdoors . . . the tiller of the soil obliged to *robot* has hardly 50 days for himself, which is excessively little, indeed."[39] The inequities of the system were increased by the tax exemption of those serfs in the personal service of landowners and who were frequently better off.[40]

The disproportion between income and burdens of the economically weakest classes of society may have been comparable, as some held, to the onus carried by peasants in other countries, mainly the Austrian provinces. Even if this had been the case, the peculiarities of Hungarian municipal autonomy, which combined both political and juridical functions in the administration of the counties, makes any comparison meaningless. An organic part of this antiquated system of local self-government was a cobweb of seignioral courts which had jurisdiction, with certain exceptions, in cases in which noblemen were not implicated. In each manorial estate the lord had primary jurisdiction over his serfs. It is therefore unrealistic to evaluate the economic aspects of Hungarian serfdom without taking into account this built-in extra-economic authority of the landowner, which under normal circumstances and at least locally, was a powerful controlling factor in the peasant's daily life.

The gap between Austria and Hungary, from the point of view of the overall development of society, was paramount. Whereas Western countries were far ahead of Austria in commerce and industry, in Austria and Bohemia trade and industry contributed a considerable share to the national income by the beginning of the 19th century. In Hungary, however, the lack of industry, weakness of trade, and absence of a strong bourgeoisie meant that, around 1830 society remained essentially dependent on the work and productivity of the peasant.[41] Hence to raise

---

[39] Quoted *ibid.*, pp. 62f.

[40] Mályusz, "A reformkor nemzedéke," p. 47.

[41] Hóman and Szekfű, *Magyar történet,* v, 229f. It might be interesting to quote from a report of the U.S. Legation in Vienna, dated 1840: "It is supposed that one fifth of the whole population of Bohemia [estimated by the same report at about four million] is engaged in manufactories of one kind or another, and we can therefore calculate upon a large product in that line," July 14, 1840, Mr. Mühlenberg to Mr. Forsyth, Doc. 246, *Sen. Docs.,* 2d Session, 27th Cong., p. 70.

the problems of agriculture and the serf meant to touch upon the most crucial point of national life.

This is exactly what Széchenyi did by publishing *Hitel*. Fully aware of the implications of his work, Széchenyi was "a courageous and purposeful apostle of the spirit of the age who emerged not from the midst of the masses but came from the most prominent circles of great landowners and magnates, and who was not only talented but also had the authority to give due emphasis to his words and receive attention in society."[42]

Thus the historian of Hungarian serfdom pointed to Széchenyi's dependence on the "spirit of the age," which he identified with the contemporary liberal reform movement. The implication was that Széchenyi's reforms were not the outcome of a mass movement and that their success was due largely to their aristocratic origin. This interpretation, based on facts, has nevertheless some problematic aspects. It is true that Széchenyi's emergence, considered in its total historical context, seems to be more a specific case of the general history of European cosmopolitanism and liberal ideas than merely an outgrowth of Hungarian homespun philosophy. Yet one does not necessarily have to agree with the exaggerated claims of Julius Szekfű or his disciples concerning Széchenyi's "uniqueness" in Magyardom's history to see, as has one of Szekfű's earliest critics, that virtually all of Széchenyi's practical plans for reform were taken into consideration in varying degrees and pondered by Dietal commissions between 1790 and 1830.[43] During the reign of Francis I, however, these earlier reform plans gradually petered out and fell into oblivion, first because of the reaction to the French Revolution and because of the reluctance of the administration to heed the necessity of reform in Hungary.[44] Hence a feeling of frustration and general dissatisfaction had spread among all classes of society as a result of the regime's mistrust of any progress or reform; so much so that, in the opinion of one noted author, "At the time of Széchenyi's emergence conditions in Hungary were similar to those under Maria Theresa. It was not only the opportunity for gradual conservative reform which had disappeared irrevocably; public spirit was even more obsessed by despair and backwardness."[45]

According to this analysis, the work of the Dietal commissions in 1828–1830 was retrogressive compared to that done more than 30

[42] Acsády, *Magyar jobbágyság*, p. 459. Cf. Iványi-Grünwald's introduction to *Hitel*, p. 249.

[43] Mályusz, "A reformkor nemzedéke," pp. 17–22, 26, 30f., 38, 72–75.

[44] *Ibid.*, pp. 28–31. For Széchenyi's forerunners in Hungary and a criticism of some of Mályusz's extreme views, see Iványi-Grünwald's introduction to *Hitel*, pp. 222–49.

[45] *Ibid.*, p. 32.

years before; this was the main reason why Széchenyi's program appeared "new" and "radical" to his contemporaries.[46] Although the last words of the statement are true, it is unconvincing to say that Széchenyi's reform was doomed to failure in the 1820s and 30s because it allegedly relied exclusively on the aristocracy and neglected the lesser nobility.[47] Aside from its deterministic overtones, such an interpretation appears to have a certain appeal to Hungarian historians because it tends to assign the blame for the absence of political or social progress in the first three decades of the 19th century overwhelmingly to Vienna. But it is difficult to go along with statements comparing conditions under Maria Theresa to those in the 1820s or attributing the "nearly unchanged existence" of feudal social conditions in Hungary to the invariably anti-Magyar economic policies of the court of Vienna, as has been done recently.[48]

What failed to change was the feudal legal-constitutional order. I have tried to show, in part through Széchenyi's eyes, both its persistence and cruel rigidity in human relations. Even in political affairs, below the surface of an increasingly anachronistic feudal outlook, there began to develop the new force of Magyar nationalism, powerful undercurrents of which, after the 1790s could not be ignored for long. Still very weak under the great queen, and predominantly feudal under her three successors, this new factor on the Hungarian scene commenced to acquire features pointing toward the modern rather than medieval world. The budding concern with the assimilation of non-Magyars, the care for a Hungarian literature in the vernacular, the pressure for establishing Magyar as the official language of the state, and the idea of "Magyarizing" through education all but prepared the public for a considerable expansion of that "estates nationalism" which served as a vehicle for Hungarian patriotism before Széchenyi.

Through examples from both political and literary fields I have attempted to suggest that the social content of Hungarian patriotism continued to be meager and was subdued when not in line with traditional thinking. But I have also suggested that capitalistic practices succeeded in penetrating the precapitalistic Hungarian world and that the new economic forces were on a collision course with the feudal structure. To say that Vienna or the Hungarian estates could be in complete control of either Magyar nationalism or liberal capitalism is somewhat unrealistic. Moreover, the Hungarian estates had as much to do with conditions

---

[46] *Ibid.*, pp. 34–38.

[47] *Ibid.*, pp. 39, 60 and n. 67.

[48] Eckhart, *A bécsi udvar gazdaságpolitikája Magyarországon, 1780–1815*, p. 349. For a qualification of this view by Zs. P. Pach, see the postscript in *ibid.*, pp. 428f.

of backwardness in Hungary as had Vienna or certain historico-geographical conditions. If it is impossible to ascertain the exact proportion of responsibilities in such a case, it appears to be nevertheless fair to state that prior to Széchenyi's appearance, it was the *kaisertreu* administration which, on the whole, granted a minimum of protection to the serf.[49]

Naturally this means Vienna was not only a source of evil but an important, though only potential, social force, which could under certain conditions be used for gradual reform of either the "liberal" or "conservative" type. Such a working hypothesis lay at the core of Széchenyi's pragmatism. His aristocratic concept of reform may have needed corrections as to the role of the lesser nobility, in particular after the 1830s. He may have overestimated the political weight of the aristocracy and the importance of its participation in Hungary's regeneration. Such "miscalculations" could have and eventually did result in serious political mistakes, but they could not irreparably damage his reform plans. A careful study of the social forces in Széchenyi's time indicates that the sine qua non of any peaceful reform was the support of Vienna. Széchenyi was right on this crucial point and he was theoretically correct in thinking that an enlightened and energetic administration could have mustered enough forces to put reforms into practice, precisely because of the disunity of the ruling classes. But the administration was weak and distrustful of Széchenyi's plans.

In previous chapters I have tried to describe the genesis of the idea in Széchenyi's mind that he, "if no one else," would initiate Hungary's regeneration. I stressed the complex background of his decision by referring above all to his critical attitude toward Hungarian conditions. The roots of this criticism lay in the intellectual and emotional experience of progress manifested in the Western world, primarily England. His firsthand experience dating back to the Napoleonic wars and supplemented by frequent travels in subsequent years, by familiarity with the writings of English classical economists and Bentham, and by acquaintance with the methods and limitations of the Hungarian constitutional opposition in and out of the Diet, convinced Széchenyi that reforms in his fatherland must be based on economic modernization. Stimulation of the economy, however, was blocked by the country's feudal structure. Consequently he decided to attack feudalism as the main cause of "rot-

---

[49] For a German assessment of the *Staatskonferenz*, dated Sept. 25, 1822, which shows how urbarial regulations were evaded in Hungary, see Doc. 38 in Eckhart, *A bécsi udvar gazdaságpolitikája Magyarországon, 1780–1815*, pp. 419–26. For the significance of the administration's role in protecting the elementary rights of the serf against his lord, see the speech made by Francis Deák in the Diet on Aug. 1, 1833, in Manó Kónyi, ed., *Deák Ferencz beszédei*, 2d edn., 6 vols. (Budapest: Franklin, 1903), I, 28f.

tenness" in Hungary, an attack that was intensified by an impassioned appeal for Hungary's moral and cultural rebirth along national lines.

Széchenyi's criticism of and devotion to his homeland had common origins. His intention to improve himself and to do something for mankind can be traced to his early youth. Often the desire for self-perfection and to be useful to his fellow men were strongly motivated by a romantic effort to prove himself worthy of a beloved woman. But the determining factor—to prove himself through hard work for his country—was Széchenyi's firm belief in a system of values. This system of values was founded on the ideals of righteousness and justice and the assumption that nations as well as individuals could fulfill their divine purpose only through constant attention to bettering themselves. Thus the achieving of "inner calm" so often mentioned in his writings was exactly the opposite of contemplative seclusion; in the event it was the result of good works done for that most tangible unit of organized human society—the nation.

It is to be expected that these elements of Széchenyi's thinking should appear in his three major books on reform. He wrote them, in one breath, so to speak, within a period of a little over three years to strengthen his agitation for reforms. He wanted to break away from the piecemeal discussion of the "systematic works" of Dietal commissions compiled in numerous Latin folios during the preceding decades. Without losing sight of larger aims, he started on a small scale. Horse races and the National Casino were not suppressed by the government, he wrote in early 1830, because they were not thought to be important enough. In order to lend respectability to the cause of reform, however, people must learn gradually that casinos and races were not the ultimate goals.[50] Realizing that the medicine he intended to administer to his nation was strong, he decided to proceed step by step. Three months after the publication of *Hitel* he wrote Wesselényi that he had started to work on the continuation of his book, but that "for many reasons and that the Dose should not be too great" he did not wish to release it at once.[51]

Széchenyi began work on *Hitel* shortly after the publication of *Lovakrul*. According to a letter of March 19, 1828 the title of his new work was to be "On People or On the Foundations of Happiness."

[50] Széchenyi to Baroness Forray, Feb. 23, 1830, B. Szabó, ed., *Adatok*, I, 99. Concerning the tremendous paper work being done by the Dietal commissions Széchenyi wrote: "I cannot help wondering enough about the nine Latin volumes containing not one single *foundation stone*—not half an ounce of philosophy!—I am horrified." Széchenyi to Wesselényi, Oct. 5, 1831, in Majláth, ed., *Levelek*, I, 200 (italics in original).
[51] Apr. 17, 1830, *ibid.*, I, 162.

He thought also of calling it "The Foundations of Inner Calm." By the end of the same year, however, under the impact of a personal experience, he settled on the final title—*Credit*.[52] In January 1829 a diary entry noted that the main cause of troubles in Hungary was the lack of credit, because "from the Throne down to the beggar nothing else but the word keeps states together!"[53] This first formulation of the basic idea of the book, published exactly one year later, indicated the broad moral connotations of the work. Indeed, to Széchenyi, lack of credit was inseparable from what we nowadays call the "credibility gap."

The message of *Hitel* was primarily economic, and can be summed up as follows. The Hungarian landowner was condemned to starvation despite his numerous herds, filled pits for storing grain, fertile lands, and tax exemption. He was sunk in debt despite the fact that he did not carry any burdens of the country while many hands worked for him without being paid. The cause of this ridiculous and sad situation was the lack of credit.[54] The lack of capital and credit was due to the antiquated legal system which gave no security to the creditor.[55] Outmoded farming methods and feudal institutions such as common use of land-forest-pasturage, guilds, *limitatio, robot,* and tithe prevented the landowner from modernizing his farm and laying the foundation for his spiritual and material well-being.[56] Bad roads and undeveloped trade were additional sources of backwardness. But unlike those who blamed the country's geographic situation or the internal customs, Széchenyi pointed rather to the bureaucratic interference with commerce, the low yield of production, lack of communication, low level of domestic

---

[52] A Viennese banking firm which refused to give him a loan of 10,000 florins reversed its position after a bitter letter from Széchenyi. Nov. 19, 1828 and Jan. 3, 1829, Viszota, ed., *Naplók*, III, 274f., 283. Cf. Viszota's introduction to *Naplók*, IV, esp. lxx f. and his articles published in *Budapesti Szemle*, 1909 and 1916: "Széchenyi Hitel cimü művének második kiadása" (The Second Edition of Széchenyi's Credit) and "Széchenyi Hitel cimü művének keletkezése" (Genesis of Széchenyi's Credit).

Besides Viszota's contributions, at this point I refer only to two valuable works, namely Iványi-Grünwald's introduction in the *Fontes* edition (pp. 5–264) and Kautz's analysis in the Academy edition, *SzIM*², I, pp. iii–lxvii. It would be impossible to list all the studies done on Széchenyi's three major works within the limits of the present study. For short summaries of *Hitel* in English see Paget, *Hungary and Transylvania*, I, 209–16; Knatchbull-Hugessen, *Political Evolution*, I, 278ff.

[53] Jan. 29, 1829, Viszota, ed., *Naplók*, III, 287f. For Széchenyi's personal financial motives and the problematic sides of their generalization in a strictly economic sense, see György Spira, "Egy pillantás a Hitel irójának hitelviszonyaira" (Glancing at the Credit Conditions of the Author of Credit), *Történelmi Szemle*, VI (1963), 344–54.

[54] *Hitel*, pp. 283–86, 299f., 314f., 394. All references to *Hitel* are based on the edition in *Fontes*.

[55] *Ibid.*, pp. 301–305, 341.

[56] *Ibid.*, pp. 332–54. The *limitatio* was an official list of prices for victuals and industrial ware, fixed by the counties. Marczali, *Hungary in the Eighteenth Century*, p. 72.

consumption, uncertainty of export tariffs, and dishonest commercial practices as the basic causes of economic misery.[57] As a cure, he suggested mutual enlightenment, education, publicity and discussion, a national bank, improvement of quantity and quality of production, export premiums, and "above all, the sanctity of credit."[58]

The peculiar mingling of moral, educational, political, and economic topics, as a means to improve the country's economic backwardness, was but one of the signs that for Széchenyi economics was organically connected with the social patterns and political conditions in his fatherland. A truism today, this idea was far from acceptance by his compatriots. At the time of the publication of *Hitel* neither the concept of political economy nor its classic representatives in England were even known in Hungary. It was Széchenyi who first called attention to "this nameless science yet in its childhood; which, however, is in our judgment to develop amazingly in the future."[59]

Széchenyi went far beyond the sphere of political economy in a chapter called "What to Do and Where to Start."[60] He drew a line between "credit in the strict sense" and "credit in a broader sense," and at once overstepped the orthodox concepts of economics to present a challenging sequence of thoughts of his own. "Credit in the strict sense" could essentially be realized, in Széchenyi's opinion, by introducing a modern mercantile code and law of exchange (*cambio-mercantile jus*) to be strictly enforceable on the privileged noblemen.[61] Besides mentioning briefly the need for establishing a national bank,[62] the proposal for a new and efficient mercantile code was actually his only tangible proposal for institutional changes. But this single issue involved a series of other legal and political problems closely connected with the nobility's prerogatives and with the law of aviticity, or entail.[63]

As for the noble prerogative, Széchenyi tried to prove that the acceptance of a severe mercantile code did not necessarily infringe upon the liberties of noblemen. Siding with Bentham, he held that antiquated old laws should not despotically bind a new generation which had infinitely more experience than its forebears.[64] Besides questioning Hun-

[57] *Hitel*, pp. 354–82.
[58] *Ibid.*, pp. 382–91.
[59] *Ibid.*, p. 393.
[60] *Ibid.*, pp. 394–451.
[61] *Ibid.*, pp. 349, 419–51.
[62] Which Széchenyi called it; but he actually thought of a "land bank," that is, a financial institution for providing cheap loans to landowners. *Ibid.*, pp. 385–88.
[63] In this part of *Hitel* Széchenyi relied heavily on arguments put forward in the *Book of Fallacies* by Jeremy Bentham. Cf. Iványi-Grünwald's introduction, *ibid.*, pp. 104–28, 188, and the important footnotes on pp. 424–27, 430–33, 435, 470f., 473, 483.
[64] *Ibid.*, pp. 484ff.

gary's old glory, Széchenyi also claimed that by encouraging extravagance the feudal laws actually had a very detrimental effect on the old families whose support was their alleged purpose. By admitting, furthermore, that he did not think the "conservation" of completely indebted and irresponsible magnates was necessary or useful for the public good, Széchenyi openly advocated the rights of the creditor, of the financier and merchant in a country where tradition, law, and national pride had always been on the side of the debtor of noble blood. From this point of view—as well as that of stressing the importance of a money economy instead of a subsistence economy (e.g., by substituting pecuniary redemption for services in kind in the lord-serf relationship and by satisfying the creditor with the actual money value of a mortgaged land instead of handing it over to him *in natura*)—Széchenyi prepared the way for capitalism in feudal Hungary.[65]

As to the law of aviticity dating back to 1351, which entailed the land of a nobleman to the most distant member of the family and upon whose death the ownership reverted to the crown, Széchenyi took a cautious position. He did not call for its abolition, at least not yet in *Hitel*. Throughout the work he argued from the viewpoint of a land-owner, going out of his way to prove that it was in the best interests of the landowner to get rid of the feudal system which had brought him poverty and prejudices instead of making him free and a real owner of his property. Yet the law of entail was the main obstacle to the free buying and selling of land, preventing non-nobles from acquiring landed property. Without its abolition, or, to put it differently, without changing the whole structure of Hungarian private law, no efficient law of exchange could have been introduced with binding force on the nobility.[66] Széchenyi's opponents were quick to see the implications of the problem, and in *Stádium* Széchenyi himself drew the logical conclusion by proposing the abolition of the law of entail.

Before examining the book's final conclusions in the socio-economic field, let us look briefly at Széchenyi's concept of "credit in the broader sense."[67] Unlike the concrete restricted economic interpretation of "credit in the strict sense," this phrase had wide connotations in Széchenyi's mind, stretching from the sphere of religion to the world of his innermost speculations about man's destiny. To Széchenyi it meant mutual trust and the sanctity of the given word. Accordingly, mutual trust and uprightness are the foundations of throne and family. The

---

[65] Cf. Iványi-Grünwald, *ibid.*, pp. 131f.
[66] Iványi-Grünwald, *ibid.*, pp. 62, 70, 229f.
[67] *Ibid.*, pp. 395–419.

ability to believe is the chain linking humanity to God Almighty who, in the realm of "virtue without witness" is perfect and eternal supreme Truth. Mutual trust and honesty, however, depend on the citizen's civic virtue which in turn rests on the firm foundation of nationality. In his words, "first one has to be and only afterwards can one develop into a good, honest and virtuous man"[68]—the implication being that nationality is a moral category and *a priori* a condition of a country's development. When examined closely nationality is, said Széchenyi, "a human being's natural property interwoven with his veins and with the secret recesses of his soul that cannot be annihilated without annihilating our self-respect . . . ."

Disregarding his own experience, Széchenyi used scornful language against cosmopolitans, praising the patriotic virtues and stressing the importance of domestic literature because "one of the main attributes of healthy nationality is the national language."[69] But he went beyond this linguistic approach to the concept of nationality and proposed concentration and free association of forces as a means of strengthening national bonds. "Sacrificing part of everybody's natural liberties in order to achieve social freedom"—this principle of the social contract theory is, according to *Hitel,* a necessary working condition of strong societies and countries.[70] Association results in discussion, exchange of ideas, and elimination of mistrust among different social strata, thus constantly augmenting "the entire nation's *decorum* and real strength."[71] Concentration of social forces must be founded upon human wisdom in order to last; hence the deepest cornerstone in the sequence of thoughts departing from "credit in the broader sense" is "the educated head." From this "little root" both happiness and misery can spring for mankind: "The real power of a nation lies in the number of its scientifically educated heads. Their number is the most interesting part of a country's statistics. Public strength consists not of fertile plains, mountains, minerals, climate, etc., but of reason being able to make sensible use of them. There is no more genuine weight or strength than that of the human brain. More or less of it is more or less happiness for a nation."[72]

This "educated human brain" is a highly spiritualized concept in

---

[68] *Ibid.,* pp. 395–99.

[69] *Ibid.,* pp. 399–407.

[70] *Ibid.,* pp. 408f. and n. 3. For Rousseau's influence cf., e.g., Apr. 21, 24, 1821, June 1, 1823, Viszota, ed., *Naplók,* II, 152f., 371f.; also the "Publisher's Preface," written probably by Liebenberg (Lunkányi), in *Stádium, SzIM²,* II, 9f.

[71] *Hitel,* pp. 410–13.

[72] *Ibid.,* pp. 413f. The term "science" in Hungarian, as in German or Russian, includes the humanities.

Széchenyi's thinking. It is the creative force in a nation's life, determining its rank among other nations, for the greater the public intelligence of a nation the more independent, free, and strong it is. Also the educated brain is a *morale pondus* carrying certain "ethical weight" and setting normative standards: the public weal must be promoted by everybody according to his intellectual and financial abilities. The patriot of birth and means can do much to spread public intelligence and increase the fatherland's strength; the landlord can have an influence on the spiritual and physical well-being of his serfs whereas the latter's good morals have little bearing upon the lord's as a human being.[73]

Taking the educated mind as a *morale pondus*, Széchenyi builds "concentration," "nationality," "civic virtue," "credit in a broader sense," upon it as upon a cornerstone. Only after this spiritual system of values does he add as a superstructure "the real subject of the present work," namely, "credit in a stricter sense," which is "the foundation of agriculture, crafts, manufacturing, mills, and trade."[74]

It is not a simple task to give the right impression of *Hitel*. It is an involved work, difficult to read, each page brimming with ideas. Even by trying to separate artificially its basic economic content from its speculative basis one can only describe the bare skeletons of a number of provoking thoughts. Széchenyi did not challenge the legal foundations of Hungarian feudalism in the book. He did attempt to convince the reader that feudalism is morally wrong, makes no sense in the modern world, and hurts even those who are supposed to benefit from it. To say that the peasantry were the most numerous part of the fatherland and thus should be given consideration, or to ask "whether, suppose we were peasants, we would work as diligently in *robot* without looking right or left as if we labored for a certain sum of money which could be earned in six or sixteen days depending on us,"[75] meant to ignore the constitution and the social patterns of a country in which the nobility *was* the nation, physical labor and commerce were looked down upon, and where birth, religion, rank, and wealth usually determined one's place in society for a lifetime. By presenting the law of entail as a primary cause of perpetuating the country's poverty and by interpreting the privileges of the nobility as moral and economic wrongs, Széchenyi put the axe to the roots of Hungary feudalism. His sarcastic remarks about road-building and communication were illustrations of the inefficiency of municipal administration. To side with the creditors against the debtors representing the majority of the noble class was equivalent

[73] *Ibid.*, pp. 414–18, 442.
[74] *Ibid.*, p. 419.
[75] *Ibid.*, pp. 347–50.

to demanding the transformation of the legal system and throwing open the gates to capitalism.

Széchenyi exposed the inefficient forced labor of the serf not only as unfair to the peasant, useless to the privileged, and a farce as a domestic public works system, but also as a national disaster which criminally wasted the country's valuable resources. While conceding that a change in the system of export and transit duties would be both possible and desirable, Széchenyi nevertheless belittled the problem of the internal tariff barrier between Hungary and the Austrian provinces. Thus he pulled the ground out from under the protagonists of traditional gravaminal opposition to the government. Reminding the reader to be fair to the interests of other parts of the Austrian Empire, Széchenyi undertook to demonstrate that the alleged harm done to Hungary by the internal tariff could even be turned into profit by improving the methods of agriculture and the quality of raw materials. This again was an argument to support his thesis, according to which, instead of expecting everything from the government, one should develop and rely on the nation's own latent and squandered forces. Instead of blaming the administration for all their troubles Széchenyi thought people should look around at home and find the sources of backwardness and misery, "because whereas one could not give orders to someone else . . . one could command oneself."[76]

Széchenyi's suggestions were presented in the form of "advices" which could be put into practice on a voluntary basis and without damage to the country's legal system or constitution.[77] He did not propose an elaborate program for reforms (the plan for his next book). From a strictly legal standpoint his work was a moderate and realistic approach to the issue of Hungary's regeneration. In fact, however, because of its implications and the language used in it, *Hitel* was a violent attack on practically all aspects of old Hungary. True, ideas of equality before the law or freedom of press were mentioned only "with inexplicable good feeling" as promoting forces of England's "amazing development"[78] but Széchenyi drew a fine distinction between "innumerable *real* noblemen and mere Hungarian nobles," sarcastically questioned the nobility's services to the country in the past, and stressed the necessity of "the nobility's ennoblement" in the present.[79] He said, "where there are duties, there must also be rights; and where rights, liberties, and privileges

<hr>

[76] *Ibid.*, pp. 280, 329f. For the foregoing summary cf. pp. 278, 298, 301–305, 339–45, 347–50, 352–55, 359, 361f, 367f., 379f., 389ff., 421f., 435–40, 446f.

[77] *Ibid.*, pp. 448–51.

[78] *Ibid.*, pp. 360f.

[79] *Ibid.*, pp. 462–65, 470–73 (italics in original).

can be found, there must certainly also be duties."[80] He sharply censured magnates who forgot their mother tongue, squandered their wealth, and were reluctant to shoulder the burden of improving domestic conditions in proportion to their economic means. He did not refrain from concluding: *"we, well-to-do landowners are the main obstacles to the progress and greater development of our fatherland."*[81]

Advocating a deeply ethical and idealistic type of utilitarianism Széchenyi believed that "the highest degree of truth and justice must also be the greatest benefit to all."[82] Therefore, he advised the nobility, "it would be wiser to do voluntarily and with lofty goodwill now what time and the spirit of the age will force you to do sooner or later anyway"—meaning by this the contribution to the tax burdens of the country.[83] He held that a representative system of government must be based on public intelligence;[84] hence he did not talk about a complete political emancipation of the serf. Yet his description of the abuses of peasants made one blush and might well have served as a model for similar sketches in Joseph Eötvös's novels and Alexander Petőfi's poems.[85] He visualized a country with better roads, more cultivated land, vigorous commerce, cleaner cities, greater culture, loftier patriotism, and more civic virtues. He dreamed of less mud, dust, reeds, uncontrolled waters, useless plains, brushwood, selfishness, vanity, sycophancy, haughtiness, prejudice, ignorance and rowdyism—than he thought to have actually found in Hungary at the time.[86] He wanted his compatriots to respect each other without mutually investigating each other's religious beliefs and without persecuting or despising someone because he was a count, baron, officeholder, merchant, burgher, or peasant.[87] He was yearning for a country where, according to the laws of nature and supreme justice, everybody, or at least the greatest part of the population, would have enough to eat and the possibility of advancing economically, mentally, and morally, "developing their immortal human dignity on the basis of a sounder philosophy purified by Christianity."

To realize his vision of a nation where all parts of the populace would have their mutual rights and duties, Széchenyi proposed to heighten considerably domestic consumption as a prerequisite of economic welfare.

---

[80] *Ibid.*, p. 456. Cf. pp. 461f.
[81] *Ibid.*, p. 460. Cf. 319f. and n. 2, 457f., 469f., 477, 489 (italics in original).
[82] *Ibid.*, p. 478.
[83] *Ibid.*, pp. 462f.; cf. pp. 458, 480f.
[84] *Ibid.*, p. 474.
[85] *Ibid.*, pp. 472f.
[86] *Ibid.*, p. 468. Cf. pp. 487f.
[87] *Ibid.*, p. 456.

In order to achieve this goal he demanded the improvement of the lot of the toiler of the land by asking the landowning classes to help shoulder the burdens of the country.[88] As an ultimate aim, to be accomplished by the country's regeneration, he launched the idea of "emancipating all our compatriots through participation in civil rights."[89]

Forty years after the French Revolution this program for the gradual transformation of society through economic stimuli may seem modest compared to western European developments. The liberal economic doctrines on which *Hitel* was based had long been known in the West from the works of the English classical economists often referred to in Széchenyi's book.[90] Also, one may conclude from a careful study of Széchenyi's diaries that his thinking was more radical than his proposals indicated. The book was not a systematic treatise on political economy. But perhaps precisely because of this, it was extremely effective. Had it been written as a scientific work, it probably would have missed the mark in Hungary. As a propaganda pamphlet, though, it was exactly what the public at large could absorb. Despite its stylistic shortcomings— he jumped "from one subject to another in a bewildering fashion" and appealed "rather to the imagination than to the intelligence"[91]—*Hitel* was a peculiar mixture of Franklin's common sense, Bentham's utilitarian dialectics, and Christian teachings of the necessity for man's effort to improve himself and become more like his Creator. Széchenyi's "Christian perfectionism," as it was sometimes called,[92] was deeply rooted in Platonic thought and drew inspiration from the optimistic belief in progress of the 18th century. This idealistic "system" rested on the immovable values of supreme justice and the rewarding "inner calm" of one's conscience.[93] It was also characterized by a peculiar romantic flavor derived from Széchenyi's indebtedness to Mme de Staël and Herder's philosophy of history.

Elements of this "system" were present in Széchenyi's thinking and can actually be traced in his writings for a number of years before the publication of *Hitel*. His study *Lovakrul* had already advocated calculation in economic matters, a new law of exchange, the observation of foreign examples, sensible and economically sound patriotism, and the elimination of exclusive Hungaro-centric thinking.[94] In his first book

[88] *Ibid.*, pp. 478ff.
[89] *Ibid.*, p. 482.
[90] For example, *ibid.*, p. 349.
[91] Knatchbull-Hugessen, *Political Evolution*, I, 279.
[92] Cf. Iványi-Grünwald, Introduction to *Hitel*, pp. 166f., 204ff., 235, 240ff., 245f., 253.
[93] *Ibid.*, pp. 462, 464, 466, 487.
[94] See the passages in *Hitel*, pp. 279f., 328, 351, 360–63, 430, 465, 490f.

Széchenyi also stressed Christianity's civilizing effect on moral and social conditions. Reading the arguments put forward in *Hitel* in favor of free discussions and the usefulness of opposing views[95] one cannot help recalling Széchenyi's memoranda to Metternich. Suggestions concerning the aristocracy's duty to participate in Hungary's advancement were often mentioned in Széchenyi's letters, as in the one to Countess Julie Hunyadi. Other varied problems, like the connection with Fiume, the importance of internal consumption, the clash between new and old ideas, the difference between simple complaining and a real desire to improve things, the significance of education, the role of women's patriotic feelings in furthering cultural development, and the issue of Magyarizing social life in Hungary[96] had either been elaborated on previously in his diaries or were continuations in public of a chain of thought started in the intimacy of his notes and letters, primarily those written to Crescence.[97] Sometimes a notion written down 10 years earlier, like the idea that the center of civilization has been moving from Asia to Europe and from Europe to America, would suddenly reemerge in *Hitel*.[98]

The book was a challenge to friend and foe alike. The censor who read parts of the manuscript warned Széchenyi in March 1829 that however useful his book would be he would be stoned because of it.[99] In the closing part of the work, Széchenyi himself raised the question: "How can a born Hungarian magnate say such things and how can he expose his compeers to mockery, hatred, and ridicule all over the fatherland? What is his intention? To overthrow the good old order with his dangerous principles and to cause general confusion?"[100] In reply to this and similar objections he would point out that sincere patriotism does not refrain from attacking backwardness, prejudices, and ignorance; that devotion to the fatherland is not equivalent to blindness; that truth is preferable to self-deception. Instead of an uncritical admiration of past glory, Széchenyi reminded his nation: "The *Past* has slipped from our grasp forever but we are masters of the *Future*. Let us not

---

[95] *Ibid.*, pp. 296f., 382–85.

[96] *Ibid.*, pp. 276, 290, 305–15, 321–27, 378f. Cf. also the dedication of the work "To the Ladies of Nobler Spirit in Our Fatherland."

[97] See, e.g., his long letter to Crescence, Mar. 10, 1829, Viszota, ed., *Naplók*, III, 296–305. In this letter Széchenyi expressed, among other things, his intention "to be an honest comedian and a noble mystifyer," ready to deceive people in order to be able to be useful to them. Concerning the role of Crescence cf. Viszota's introduction to *Naplók*, IV, esp. pp. 191–95. Iványi-Grünwald also emphasizes the influence of the Franciscan preacher Stanislaus Albach, Hiltel, pp. 196–206.

[98] *Ibid.*, pp. 371f.

[99] Mar. 3, 1829, Viszota, ed., *Naplók*, III, 295.

[100] *Hitel*, p. 467.

bother then with futile reminiscences but let us awaken our dear fatherland through purposeful patriotism and loyal unity to a brighter dawn. Many think: 'Hungary *had been;* I like to believe: she *will be!'* "[101]

The concluding phrases of *Hitel* sound like the death knell of the fruitless "policy of grievances," but they heralded a new era and became the winged words of the Hungarian age of reforms. In five months more than two thousand copies of *Hitel* were sold in the country where in the words of Paul Nagy "The best Hungarian books could count only on some two hundred customers." By 1832 Széchenyi's work was published in four Hungarian and three German editions. According to the preface of the third Hungarian edition and a letter of Döbrentei, Széchenyi had begun to work on the second part of *Hitel* in mid-1830. The second part was to announce his program for reforms and was later incorporated into *Stádium.*[102]

The echo and aftermath of *Hitel* must not be separated from the origins of *Világ* and *Stádium. Hitel* acted as a catalyst on contemporary Hungarian society. The more educated and the young people especially thought the book was epoch-making. Members of the old-fashioned nobility, of course, maintained that counts had better stick to horses and leave issues of nationwide interest to abler hands. These circles were happy to hear that Count Joseph Dessewffy, respected member of the moderate constitutional opposition, who eulogized Széchenyi after the foundation of the Academy of Sciences, was to write an "Analysis" (*Taglalat*) as an answer to Széchenyi.[103] In the opinion of the conservatives, *Hitel* was a dangerous and subversive work, "a *Satire* on Great Hungarian Landlords and Magnates," "a blasphemy on the entire Noble Nation," inciting peasants and serfs to rebellion.[104] To present Széchenyi as a dangerous social reformer seems today almost incredible; yet that was the violent reaction to *Hitel* of segments of the nobility.[105]

Whereas defenders of the ancient privileges attacked Széchenyi for having exposed the weak spots of the nation to the eyes of strangers, the younger generation read *Hitel* as the gospel of a new era and re-

[101] *Ibid.,* pp. 487f., 490ff. (italics in original).

[102] Viszota, ed., *Naplók,* IV, pp. lxx f.; Sept. 18, 1830, *ibid.,* IV, 122; Horváth, *Huszonöt év,* I, 239; Széchenyi to Gabriel Döbrentei, July 2, 1830, Majláth, ed., *Levelek,* I, 166.

[103] Pulszky, *Meine Zeit,* I, 46f. Cf. n. 40, p. 144, in Ch. V of this study.

[104] Cf. the anonymous pamphlet against Széchenyi: *Gróf Széchenyi István azon munkájának, mellynek neve Hitel kivonása, csekélly észrevételekkel* (Extract of Count Stephen Széchenyi's Work Called *Credit* with a Few Remarks), in *Hitel,* esp. pp. 683, 690f. (italics in original). For a detailed evaluation of the reception of *Hitel* see Iványi-Grünwald's introduction, pp. 250–59; also Horváth, *Huszonöt év,* I, 213–16.

[105] That this type of reaction was to be expected is obvious from the benevolent report of censor Friedrich Drescher who gave the *Imprimatur* to the book. Jan. 20, 1830, Viszota, ed., *Naplók,* IV, 9–12.

garded is author as the new leader.[106] Széchenyi closely followed the
reactions to his work, writing down good and bad alike in his diaries.[107]
To some, he was a traitor to the fatherland. Metternich lectured him
upon receiving his work, saying that the administration was not shy
of light but feared fire. There were rumors that copies of the book
were burned in several counties, and suggestions to take up *Hitel* as
a special *gravamen* in the Diet. Still others held that he wrote only
to get attention, that he had turned into an aulic sycophant and would
soon receive a high position.[108]

Whatever Széchenyi's personal feelings may have been, and he was
very bitter at times,[109] there can be no doubt that *Hitel* provoked a
sharp antagonism within the public. Henceforth, national life was to
center on political questions rather than literary debates, as it had in
previous decades.[110] Only a few months after *Hitel* was published a
discussion between Dessewffy's *Taglalat* and Széchenyi's counterattack
in *Világ* captured the attention of the public.

Count Joseph Dessewffy, a literate and widely read leader of the constitutional opposition in the Diet, was far from holding extreme "reactionary" views. Although a magnate by birth, he was not a great landowner;
on the contrary, he had experienced the financial reverses the entire
noble class had faced because of the devaluation of currency and the
agricultural crisis. To him, impoverishment of landowners was not a
consequence of outmoded Hungarian feudalism, but a result of an unfortunate combination of shortsighted Austrian politics and the sinister
forces of capitalism.

In his "Analysis of Credit,"[111] Dessewffy censured Széchenyi for the

[106] Horváth, *Huszonöt év*, I, 214f. In his letter to Széchenyi, a Catholic priest dubbed
him "Creator of Hungarians", Sept. 3, 1833, Viszota, ed., *Naplók*, IV, 408.

[107] E.g., Feb. 8, 10, 18, 20, 26, June 12, 17, July 4, Oct. 20, Nov. 26, 30, 1830,
Jan. 9, Mar. 17, 1831, *ibid.*, IV, 17f., 20–23, 47, 71, 145, 161, 165, 176, 184. Széchenyi
to Wesselényi, Mar. 14, 1830, B. Szabó, ed., *Adatok*, I, 101.

[108] Feb. 28, Mar. 1, Apr. 2, May 1, Oct. 25, Nov. 22–23, 1830, Jan. 31, 1831, Viszota,
ed., *Naplók*, IV, 24, 32, 41, 146f., 158f., 176. Subsequently Metternich seems to have
made another interesting remark (Oct. 29, 1830, *ibid.*, IV, 150): "Votre livre Vous a
fait dans l'opinion publique Hongroise beaucoup de tort—mais aussi a-t-il était fait
pour offenser—car il n'y a rien qui blesse autant que les vérités."

[109] Cf. Széchenyi to Wesselényi, May 10, 1830, Majláth, ed., *Levelek*, I, 163: "That
I shall be covered with mud, crucified, and burned because of *Hitel;* that it will be said
it had been written by someone else—that I wrote it in German and with the heart
of a German and someone else translated it into Hungarian;—or, that I wanted to
become County Administrator and Knight of the Leopold Order, etc. etc.,—My
Friend! I was prepared for all this. . . . "

[110] Gyula Farkas, A *"fiatal Magyarország" kora* (The age of "Young Hungary")
(Budapest: Magyar Szemle Társaság, 1932), p. 10.

[111] Gróf Jósef Dessewffy, A *"Hitel" czimü munka taglalatja* (Kassa: 1831), republished
in the annex of *Hitel* in the *Fontes* edition (pp. 497–647). My references are to this
edition.

lack of organization of his work and for his exaggerations. Criticizing Széchenyi's brilliant one-sidedness in his attack on the old regime, Dessewffy said that problems beyond the influence of the Hungarian landowner, like devaluation of the currency and the increase of grain supply on the international markets, should not be oversimplified. These factors, Dessewffy rightly emphasized, had a considerable bearing on economic conditions in Hungary. To Széchenyi's "anglomania," he opposed examples relevant to the problematic sides of the credit system and capitalism in England.[112] Also, Dessewffy spoke about the tariff question as an independent economic problem, pointing out the unfavorable effects of Vienna's policy on Hungarian economics, whereas Széchenyi saw the close connection between tariffs and the nobility's refusal to share the burdens of taxation, and objected to the idea of blaming all the problems of the country on a single cause.[113]

Similarly, Dessewffy defended the legalistic-constitutional standpoint of the feudal estates on the vital issue of the lord-serf relationship. Although Széchenyi did not clearly say so in *Hitel,* his book implied that this issue belonged to the sphere of public law. Dessewffy invoked the principle of the sanctity of private property, firmly supporting the traditional concept according to which the feudal rights of the lord were based on his right to unrestricted and exclusive ownership of the land. According to this view, all aspects of the problem were in the realm of private law. Holding that urbarial burdens were less heavy in Hungary than, say, Moravia and that the central authorities always sided with the peasant, he accused Széchenyi of having proposed the abolition of the *robot* and all other feudal services without compensation. This, he stated, was a direct violation of the property rights of the landowning classes and a great injustice to the nobility.[114] In Dessewffy's opinion the nobility had to be protected because its political and economic strength was the guaranty of the evolution of nationality and of the maintenance of the constitution. Hence the law of entail should be strictly observed and the validity of a new mercantile code limited to the cities and merchants. The political and military organizations of the nobility, as represented by the counties and the noble insurrection, had been of great value to the country in the past and were great assets in the present. Consequently it would be unfair to command the nobility to sacrifice its age-old rights voluntarily.[115] In this respect, Dessewffy's attitude was typical of the nobility's general reaction to *Hitel.*

---

[112] *Taglalat,* pp. 505ff., 532ff., 536, 549f., 569–75, 588f., 616f., 621.
[113] *Ibid.,* pp. 571ff.; Éber, *Széchenyi gazdaságpolitikája,* pp. 195–99.
[114] *Taglalat,* pp. 552f., 557–64, 580f., 614f.
[115] *Ibid.,* pp. 550f., 592ff., 607f., 618, 623f., 629–32, 637–40.

Despite Dessewffy's basically critical attitude toward Széchenyi's ideas, his ironical and didactic tone, and his occasional personal gibes,[116] he never once questioned his opponent's patriotic intentions. But to Dessewffy belittlement of the nobility seemed like a "blasphemy on the whole nation" before the entire world. Still, he did not think that the matter of Széchenyi's book should be taken up as a national "grievance."[117] Furthermore there were important areas of agreement between him and Széchenyi which were only too easily overlooked by contemporaries in the heat of the debate. Thus, according to Dessewffy, noblemen should pay toll on new roads, should take over half of the burdens of the cost of county administration (*cassa domestica*), and should contribute half of the expenses of the deputies to the Diet. He proposed pecuniary commutation of feudal services, based, however, on mutual agreement. He also supported the idea of enabling talented non-nobles to hold office, adding that all public offices should give personal nobility to the officeholder.[118]

Such concessions intimated that even defenders of noble privileges admitted the necessity for some reforms, without however endangering the old constitution and the feudal order. This single qualification was the difference between Széchenyi and many of his Hungarian opponents in the early 1830s; but this was precisely the difference between old and new. To overcome the crisis threatening the landowning classes Széchenyi, by implication, proposed the revamping of the Hungarian legal system. He wanted to "ennoble" and save the noble classes by searching for new ways in a new historical situation. Dessewffy, typical representative of an important trend in contemporary Hungarian society, was also aware of the crisis. Far from being merely selfish in the vulgar sense of the word, he sincerely believed in the possibility of solving the critical

---

[116] Once he called Széchenyi the "Hungarian apostle," *ibid.*, p. 564; cf. pp. 570f., 621, 628.

[117] *Ibid.*, p. 633. At least on one occasion Dessewffy conceded that *Hitel* was "an immortal work" (p. 590).

[118] *Ibid.*, pp. 577f., 626, 637, 640f. It is interesting how Dessewffy tried to refute Széchenyi's accusation that the peasants were unrepresented in the Diet. Saying that peasants were even less represented in the other hereditary provinces, he put forward the usual argument based on the feudal constitution, according to which the nobility represented the peasants as well as their own class. To support his thesis, however, Dessewffy went one step further, pointing out that nobles living on other noblemen's land were landless and constituted the majority of the nobility. Dessewffy interpreted the Hungarian constitution as "a fortunate combination of aristocracy and democracy, that is, of landed and landless nobility, the latter's interests being almost identical with those of the people of the country [i.e., peasants], particularly since the last Diet" (pp. 630, 632). Thus in a characteristic way this typical representative of the middle landowning class did not close his eyes to certain economic and social facts, but tried to use even the miserable condition of the lowest nobility to prevent the "radical" curtailment of noble privileges.

problems of Hungary through strengthening the old feudal order—which meant turning back the clock. That there was no real chance of doing this any more was made clear to everybody by Széchenyi's *Világ*.

Ignoring lesser criticisms[119] Széchenyi decided to write a sharp and quick counterattack. He was irritated by some of Dessewffy's ironical remarks, but knew his opponent had the reputation of being moderate and progressive. In addition to revealing a more thorough knowledge of local conditions, Dessewffy was correct in pointing out that the political independence of Hungary and agricultural overproduction on international markets were important factors and had to be taken into consideration in evaluating domestic economic conditions. But Dessewffy's argument amounted essentially to telling the nation that its fate depended completely on others and that by forcing Vienna to accept a more favorable tariff policy toward Hungary, all troubles could be cured without resorting to social and economic reforms. Széchenyi was optimistic about the possibility of competing successfully with foreign agricultural products. He believed it would be premature to raise the issue of complete Hungarian independence before creating an economically sound basis for the social development of the entire Hungarian nation, including all classes of society. But even if this were not the case he still had to refute Dessewffy's arguments, because they were apt to lull the nation to sleep, whereas Széchenyi's efforts were directed toward awakening her, with drastic methods if necessary.

Within a few months he wrote *Világ* (Light or enlightening Fragments To Set Right Some Errors and Prejudices), 3,250 copies of which were published in July 1831.[120] According to many authorities *Világ* is Széchenyi's best, most effective work, because of its brilliant force and convincing argumentation.[121] It must be said, however, that in its content the book does not bring forth any basically new ideas.[122] It is partly a refutation of Dessewffy's arguments, partly a forceful explanation of the suggestions in *Hitel* and of Széchenyi's activity as a practical reformer. The problems treated in the book overlapped with those raised in *Hitel,* which preceded it, and with those of *Stádium* which was soon to follow. Hence the three books can be considered essentially as portions of a single, tripartite work, in which *Hitel* was intended to break ground, *Világ* to annihilate the arguments of the opponents and create the emo-

---

[119] Cf. Kautz's introduction to *Hitel* in *SzIM²*, I, p. xxxv and Iványi-Grünwald's introduction to *Hitel*, pp. 255–58; also Annex, *ibid.*, pp. 681–92, 696–99.

[120] *Világ vagy is felvilágosító töredékek némi hiba's előitélet eligazítására*, 2d edn. (Budapest: 1904), in *SzIM²*, I, 1–356. Subsequent references will be to this edition.

[121] Horváth, *Huszonöt év*, I, 217; Gaál, *Széchenyi nemzeti politikája*, I, 339; Kautz, Introduction to *Világ* in *SzIM²*, I, p. li.

[122] *Világ*, p. 340.

tional atmosphere for *Stádium* which was to bring the concrete program. As a polemical work written in a hurry *Világ* was an unsystematic poorly proportioned work, and Széchenyi was aware of its shortcomings; but he knew the book's success depended on the speed of his reaction and therefore decided not to wait.[123]

According to Széchenyi, the essence of his work was "to show the public Hungary's backwardness in everything" because this confession was the prerequisite of all progress. He endeavored to prove that "Hungarians were a youthful people full of vigorous energy and . . . capable of achieving anything if they would develop their Public Intelligence and Nationality." He wanted to convince his readers that the raising of public intelligence and nationality depended greatly on the unification of Buda and Pest into one capital city where the creative forces of the nation could be concentrated.[124] In Széchenyi's words, his "rhapsodic opuscules" *On Horses* and *Credit* were intended to provoke the exchange of ideas, to unify his fellow countrymen, to broaden their minds, and to further the development of Magyar nationality.[125] If in *Hitel* he admittedly wrote "in vinegar, nitric acid, and stronger poison . . . *to arouse our somnolent* compatriots *a little bit,*" the "moral diagnosis or pathology" of *Világ* was hardly more charitable.[126] Around 1820, Széchenyi said, Hungary had been "split into some five political factions, six religions, 10 different nationalities, 52 municipalities, altogether 73 separate units, disregarding the Jazygian and Cumanian districts, royal cities, etc."[127] To make the consequences of this typical feudal pattern more explicit, Széchenyi presented an appalling description of the selfish rivalries among the different social strata and suggested that the country was reeking from its own decomposition.[128]

Two aspects of this description were particularly striking. First, Széchenyi scornfully pointed out the failure of the alienated magnates and ignorant nobility to live up to their Christian and patriotic duties. Second, he stressed that the majority of the city population were non-Magyar, and that among the peasants the increase of the Hungarian element was slower than that of other nationalities. Again minimizing the Hungarian past, partly to justify his belief in the nation's youth and

---

[123] Széchenyi to Wesselényi, Dec. 22, 1830, Oct. 5, 1831, Majláth, ed., *Levelek*, I, 188f., 200.

[124] *Világ*, pp. 1f. Cf. also pp. 70, 309, 335.

[125] *Ibid.*, pp. 226, 344.

[126] *Ibid.*, pp. 8, 59 (italics in original).

[127] *Ibid.*, p. 43.

[128] *Ibid.*, pp. 43–50. It is interesting to see the influence of this analysis on Wesselényi's *Szózat a magyar és szláv nemzetiség ügyében* (Admonition Regarding the Magyar and Slav Nationalities), which was published in 1843.

hopeful future, Széchenyi ridiculed the "unfortunate idea" that backward Hungary was "the Garden of Eden on earth." More emphatically than in *Hitel* he warned that noble privileges were not identical with real liberties, that the nobility as a whole fell far short of being free and independent since, in his view, *"only intellectual standing . . . gives real supremacy in this world; hence poverty,* at least at the present, means servitude."[129]

To the concept of liberty he referred in dithyrambic words as "this most beautiful gift of the gods" and "supreme good" abused by noblemen and tried to give it a Christian interpretation with a deep social content.[130] After an illustration of how feudal social conditions prevented investors from establishing factories and able foreign craftsmen from settling in Hungary, thus frustrating the industrial development of the country, Széchenyi concluded that "either the *Primae Nonus* [which formulated] noble privileges must be restricted or else the same privileges must be extended in a modified form to all inhabitants of our fatherland. . . ."[131] Asking "Where is the Hungarian Nation today?" he answered that she could not be found anywhere in Hungary, because the term *nation* had no meaning.[132] To Dessewffy's charge that he wanted to abolish all feudal services without compensation, Széchenyi said he did not want to rob or ruin the nobility, a great part of which had nothing else to live on but these services.[133] At the same time, however, he insisted that besides taking over part of the peasants' financial burdens, the nobility must also help them to rise socially, because "Hungary will be neither happy nor of exalted position until the people [i.e., the *plebs*, the peasantry] are admitted to the ranks of the nation [i.e., *populus* in the terms of the constitution]."[134] With the suggestion that the "spirit of associations, the soul of factories, and social liberties were interrelated with certain little chains," Széchenyi broadened the Hungarian-nation concept restricted previously to the privileged. By insisting on the elimination of "feudal filth" he intended to strengthen the bases of the social pyramid.[135]

The constitution, too, was to be "free and capable of being broadened and reformed." Széchenyi conceded that Hungarians, having a constitution, did possess a framework of liberty. But they could progress consider-

---

[129] *Világ*, pp. 52f., 60f., 120f., 137, 279f. (italics in original).

[130] *Ibid.*, pp. 247–82, esp. 247–50.

[131] *Ibid.*, p. 271. Also, pp. 256–60, 267–71, 280f., 286. For the *Primae Nonus*, or Pt. I, Art. 9 of Werbőczi's *Tripartitum*, see Ch. V, n. 75 in this study.

[132] *Ibid.*, pp. 206, 267.

[133] *Ibid.*, pp. 89, 200.

[134] *Ibid.*, p. 84f., 341.

[135] *Ibid.*, pp, 277f., 341f., 346.

ably faster on the path of civilization, he added, if the spirit of liberty could be supplemented by the spirit of competition.[136] Thus he substituted the dynamic outlook of capitalistic free enterprise for the static constitutional and economic categories of the earthbound Hungarian feudal structure. Stable agricultural production and an increase in both exports and domestic consumption were closely related and dependent on better allotment of land, security of property owners, efficient enforcement of the law, reorganization of economic and financial matters—in a word, on reforms.[137] He foresaw the lesser nobility's pauperization, brought on by the repeated subdivision of their small holdings and their reluctance to go into the professions, commerce, or crafts. He also warned that it was in the interest of the country to grant the peasant the right to own land.[138] Inspired by the English public spirit, Széchenyi suggested a combined effort of all social strata, stressing the interdependence of nationwide progress, healthy utilitarianism, and a more liberal constitution.[139] He thought concentration of the centrifugal forces dominating the country's life could not be accomplished by the administration: the spirit of free association should be developed in complete freedom and by voluntary contribution. This, however, depended primarily on the participation of independent landowners to whom the country looked for leadership in combining the split forces of the fatherland.[140]

As for the aim of this concentration of patriotic efforts, *Világ* elaborated in detail on the purposes and social implications of horse races, the Academy of Sciences, and Casino, as well as the usefulness of a permanent bridge between Buda and Pest, a National Theater, and a public fund for financing some of these projects. In answer to Dessewffy and other critics Széchenyi stressed that all of his practical reforms were simply means toward harmonizing the different economic, social, and religious interests in the center of the country for common enterprises. As he put it, his purpose was not to initiate "one railway, one factory, the regulation of rivers, one Hungarian theater, or one bridge," but to stimulate the creation of "workshops for discussion" concerning where and how to start working for Hungary. It seemed to him very important not to let means and ends become confused; therefore, he did not insist that the order of reforms proposed by him was unchangeable or that precisely these reforms were the strongest cornerstones of Hungary's regeneration. He knew perfectly well that a permanent bridge between

[136] *Ibid.*, p. 222.
[137] *Ibid.*, pp. 110–13.
[138] *Ibid.*, pp. 49, 341.
[139] *Ibid.*, pp. 208–13, 223.
[140] *Ibid.*, pp. 228f.

the two parts of the capital would be economically justifiable only if there were good roads leading to it on both sides of the Danube.[141] While stressing intellectual power as the fountainhead of liberty, competition, and the progress of civilization, he yet warned that the country's "physical and mechanical progress"—or economic welfare, must be preceded by its moral development.[142] He risked ridicule of his preaching tone because, to him, the "science of morals" was the beginning of everything, the only thing that could lead people to the idea of divinity, the ultimate goal of human existence. If only the practical science of ethics could be planted in the hearts of people, there would be no more need of utopian theories, *Hitel*, or *Taglalat*. Hence, according to Széchenyi's system of values, peoples and nations were also governed by moral law, just as a morally independent individual rested his case on the clearness and inner calm of his conscience.[143]

Széchenyi's ethical approach to all problems of life and society explains his efforts to mediate between government and nation. His attitude during the Diet of 1825–27 and disputes with Metternich indicated that he could not side wholeheartedly with either the administration or the feudal opposition in Hungary. In *Hitel* he had already reminded his fellow countrymen not to blame the government for everything. This was more than just a tactical maneuver to avoid political conflicts with Vienna, although this was important for him, too. A true disciple of Franklin, Széchenyi wanted Hungarians to help themselves because such actions, though limited at first, could regenerate the entire life of the nation.

The concept of individual moral and educational progress and effort was one of the most important aspects of his initiatives. It went beyond the profit motive and was the basic reason for insisting on careful financial planning as a guaranty of the success of all his enterprises. In *Világ*, too, Széchenyi tried to pave the way for cooperation of government and nation, reminding both parties in a conciliatory tone to forget the grievances of the past, which were meaningless to the future. He was inclined to see a certain improvement in the administration's policy toward Hungary and made a new effort to prove that the redressing of Hungarian economic grievances, primarily in the field of tariff policies, depended on giving up part of the nobility's privileges and on alleviating the burdens of the peasant.[144] Real consistency under Hungarian political circumstances required an independence of spirit and ability to steer

---

[141] *Ibid.*, pp. 65ff., 74f., 80f., 166, 202, 212f., 226, 229–36, 240ff, 329f.
[142] *Ibid.*, pp. 220, 223, 236, 238, 268.
[143] *Ibid.*, pp. 172, 174, 246.
[144] *Ibid.*, pp. 70–78, 106ff., 180, 214ff.

a "sober and fair middle road" between the excessive demands of both public and administration. A lonesome giant among modern Hungarian politicians, Széchenyi questioned the nation's infallibility, declaring that just as one should be able "to live and die for the nation's rights," one should also feel a moral obligation to stand up for one's "lawful monarch" even against the "unbridled people and one's compatriots" if the king had a just case.[145] This attitude of always supporting the right cause even though, to paraphrase Horace, the world might crumble, appeared as a high moral standard in Széchenyi's earliest writings. It was to give a tragic shade and a mark of heroic greatness in the later part of his career.

Under the impression made by the July Revolution in France and the Polish uprising of November 1830, Széchenyi became more convinced of the necessity for changing the law of entail and of making concessions to the lower classes.[146] Fearful of an alliance between the peasantry and the lesser nobility, he urged the initiation of an era of more practical knowledge, of noble-minded and not merely privileged representatives, of patriots and not just supporters of the administration or people. Thinking that "Magnates and Noblemen standing between King and Cotter had a real mission ordered by God," he dreamed of a Hungary where the sovereign could feel secure although many of Europe's kings had lost their thrones and become wanderers.[147]

In *Világ* Széchenyi put special stress on the cultivation of the Hungarian language. He said in the introduction that "Public intelligence and Nationality" were cornerstones of his "system," the former being developed through and carried by the latter. Like many of his compatriots he thought the future of the nation was in close correlation with the development of the Hungarian language, hence his emphasis on the Academy in which he saw a key to Magyar cultural life. For similar reasons he supported the idea of creating a Hungarian National Theater. Elaborating on the idea of education he attached great significance to the attributes "Christian and national," for "Christianity" to him meant a common basis for all Christian churches in the country, whereas "national education" was equivalent primarily to the fostering of "education in the Magyar tongue."[148]

It is important to understand the defensive character and moral connotations of Széchenyi's nationalism in order to grasp the difference

[145] *Ibid.*, pp. 168ff.
[146] Cf. his conversations with the palatine, Oct. 29, Dec. 15, 1830, Viszota, ed., *Naplók*, IV, 149, 167f.
[147] *Világ*, pp. 181ff.
[148] *Ibid.*, pp. 128, 160, 176, 236f., 328–31.

between his program of "Magyarization" and the subsequent, coercive and jingoistic efforts to transform all non-Hungarians into Magyars. Széchenyi was the first to protest against such methods, but the younger, liberal nationalist generation drew much of its inspiration from his works while failing to accept his Christian and humanitarian principles. Széchenyi did not deny that he encouraged "the Magyarization of our German fellow countrymen" and that he was deeply concerned with the non-Hungarian population's rapid rate of increase. He would have been delighted if non-Hungarians could have been "Magyarized" on the basis of the Hungarian population's moral and intellectual supremacy. But he knew that Hungarians first had "to learn almost everything and teach only very little, cleansing Hungary first of all its dirt so it would become acceptable and in time worthy to be imitated." He warned that the voluntary acceptance of Magyar nationality by non-Hungarians did not depend on the spread of external folklore and customs. His advice was to abolish prejudices, be unselfish and generous patriots, and remember that while "being Hungarians . . . the ennoblement of our nationality must be based only on . . . justice . . . because we are also human beings at the same time."[149] A firm believer in the regenerating force of the mother tongue, he proposed that Magyar be accepted as the official language of all nationalities in the kingdom, partly as a substitution for dead Latin, but partly also as a means toward maintaining Magyar nationality. As he saw it, Hungary was "an Asiatic colony in the heart of Europe," and her peculiar national virtues could be maintained in the interest of mankind only through developing the Magyar idiom. All other nationalities had powerful kinsmen beyond the state borders whose very existence guaranteed the survival of their race. Hence, promoting Hungarian was, in his eyes, a sacred duty and a national self-defense; a loyal Catholic, he would have been happy to see the Hungarian translation of the Gospel "in every hut, hovel, cottage, and room."[150]

At the Diet of 1830 more members used Magyar in the discussions, and Széchenyi noted with pride: "They are carried ahead by the 'spirit. . . .'"[151] While "rejoicing in silence" at the first fruits of his work he pointed out as early as June 1830: "All my establishments are gaining ground—yet they turn against the German language."[152] A few days later, explaining his ideas to Baron Langenau, Austrian

[149] *Ibid.*, pp. 8, 46, 54, 64.
[150] *Ibid.*, pp. 329f., 333f., 338.
[151] Dec. 17–18, 1830, Viszota, ed., *Naplók*, IV, 169f. Cf. Széchenyi to Wesselényi, Dec. 22, 1830, Majláth, ed., *Levelek*, I, 188.
[152] June 12, 1830, Viszota, ed., *Naplók*, IV, 46.

military commander of Buda, Széchenyi stressed that Hungary's welfare was closely connected with Austria's. Linking the country's ability to pay taxes with its military potential, he expressed his desire to increase both. To the question how this could be accomplished, his reply was that "through practical intelligence," adding that this meant Hungarian schools and the abolition of Latin from public life. Whereas Széchenyi had no qualms about abolishing Latin, he revealed his fears of Hungary's "Austrianization."[153]

Three elements of this conversation are of some interest. First, there was the necessity of substituting Hungarian for Latin, "the dead tyrant," which hampered the modernization of the country's administration and legislative activity. As Széchenyi put it, the works of Adam Smith could not be translated into Latin.[154] By emphasizing the need for educating the population with an eye to achieving Hungarian cultural supremacy, Széchenyi also thought of establishing a widespread Hungarian school system thus touching on a sore spot of subsequent decades. In order to understand this, one must turn to the third aspect of his attitude, namely, to his defensive reaction against the danger of Germanization, as the *other* alternative to Latin at the time.

Many educated Hungarians had an inferiority complex about German culture, which was related to the non-Magyar character of the urban populace. Some of the important urban centers, such as Pressburg (Pozsony, Bratislava), Ödenburg (Sopron), Kaschau (Kassa, Košice), Ofen (Buda), or even Pest, were still culturally German cities. A remark made by Széchenyi in mid-1832 reveals his sensitivity to the issue: he was worrying about Hungary which he feared was stone-dead (*"mausetot"*) because it was "drowning in the German intelligentsia."[155] Less than one week after his conversation with Baron Langenau, Széchenyi mused over a talk he had with a German peasant during a short stay in Slavonia. He knew that in order to "Hungarize" or create a Hungarian world, the positive aspects of Magyardom must become preponderant. But he rather doubted that the latter would ever catch up with let alone surpass Germandom. After all, as Hungarians tended to gain ground, the German intelligentsia expanded, too, perhaps even faster. The slogan *extra Hungariam* was ringing in his ears and the poorly cultivated fields of Hungary appeared before his spiritual eyes while he tried to listen to the intelligent explanations of the German farmer who told him he wanted to live like a human being and not like an animal. Széchenyi noted with some sadness that only a superior economy

153 June 22, 1830, *ibid.*, IV, 51.
154 Sept. 18, 23, 1830, *ibid.*, IV, 121, 131.
155 July 22, 1832, *ibid.*, IV, 281.

and culture could inspire imitators. Yet he wondered how he could raise his savage, ignorant, cussing, and barbaric compatriots to the level where "Hungarization" would be meaningful and not repulsive to non-Magyars.[156]

Széchenyi's anxiety to Hungarize via spiritual means cannot be divorced from his attempt to bring into being a better and more prosperous Hungarian nation. The firm stand he took against Kossuth in his later years sometimes causes us to forget his kind of nationalism, especially his worries about German cultural supremacy. Still, in addition to his profession of creed in *Világ* and in his diaries, some of his letters bear testimony to the direction of his train of thought in this part of his life. To his friend Wesselényi he once complained that in Pest "there is much Germandom and little Magyardom."[157] He also thought it extremely important that the Hungarian element in the western regions bordering Austria be strengthened. In a letter to the Bishop of Győr (Raab) he referred to the family residence, Cenk (Zinkendorf), as "the first Hungarian Community in the West and thus, so to speak, a Defense Post of our Hungarian Fatherland." There, he continued, a good priest was needed who besides being "an honest man must also be an enlightened and moderate Hungarian with immaculate conduct and behavior."[158] He did not wish to see Magyar nationality submerged in the surrounding German and Slav seas. In an argument about the principles of liberty and nationality he pointedly asked his opponent, who insisted that liberty was more important than nationality, "But if you want to achieve liberty, on the basis of what nationality do you hope to accomplish it? Slav or German?"[159]

The question itself shows that Széchenyi, especially in the later part of his career, saw a certain contradiction between the quick extension of constitutional liberties and the aggravating nationality problem. On October 3, 1844 he said in the Diet: "We live under circumstances at the present when Magyardom is in direct connection with the nobility and aristocracy, and let us admit that any kind of democracy here would hurt the Magyar nationality."[160] Yet one must remember that in Széchenyi's romantic vision the unfolding of national character was still a cohesive factor promoting the mutual understanding of different peo-

---

[156] June 28, 1830, *ibid.*, IV, 60f.

[157] Széchenyi to Wesselényi, June 15, 1832, Majláth, ed., *Levelek*, I, 226.

[158] Széchenyi to Bishop Sztankovits, May 17, 1838, B. Szabó, ed., *Adatok*, I, 309.

[159] Oct. 5, 1845, Viszota, ed., *Naplók*, VI, 266.

[160] Quoted in Gyula Miskolczy, *A horvát kérdés története és irományai a rendi állam korában* (History of and Documents concerning the Croatian Question in the Period of the Feudal State), 2 vols. (Budapest: Magyar Történelmi Társulat, 1927–28), I, 351, in *Fontes*.

ples. In 1832 he wrote into the album of Sir John Bowring, writer, politician, and translator of Hungarian poetry into English:

All noble-minded people are joined together by the angel of nationality, although they may speak a different language and may have different fatherlands.

Therefore I salute you as a congenial soul of the Magyar.

Devote yourself to your nation, devote yourself to mankind as you have done hitherto, and your temples will be wreathed with unfading evergreen laurels.[161]

The positive and humanitarian approach to the problem of nationality helped Széchenyi conceive at an early stage its significance in the Austrian Empire. It enabled him to appreciate other peoples' efforts to develop their national entities. It also made him resent all aggressive and exaggerated demands whether they originated in domestic quarters or were imported from abroad. After reading *Sollen wir Magyaren werden?*, a pamphlet published anonymously in German which contained a violent attack on forcible Magyarization, Széchenyi remarked: "Bitter, but mostly true!"[162] As shown by this remark, the gulf separating Széchenyi from other Hungarian nationalists, which became obvious only some 10 years later, was already present in the early 1830s. At this point one may simply say that even in its most romantic period Széchenyi's patriotism was never blind or inhuman.

Adherents of reform, in the words of a contemporary reviewer, regarded Széchenyi's *Világ* as "the herald of the pillar of fire" and "the dawn of the morning star," leading Hungarians to the promised land and to salvation. Many who were still hesitant after having read *Hitel*, became under the impact of *Világ* convinced supporters of the reform movement. Defenders of the old regime ceased to attack Széchenyi openly henceforth, seeing how mercilessly he had torn to pieces the arguments of his opponent.[163] Széchenyi indeed wanted to annihilate completely

---

[161] Oct. 10, 1832, Viszota, ed., *Naplók*, IV, 312.

[162] May 25, 1833, *ibid.* 380. Historians who frequently payed lip service to Széchenyi's "ideal patriotism," continued to scorn the pamphlet, ignoring Széchenyi's own words. Cf. Szekfű, *Iratok*, p. 139; Miskolczy, *A horvát kérdés*, I, 168ff. For the pamphlet see Stanislaus Hafner, "Sprache und Volkstum bei den Slawen im Vormärz," *SOF*, XXIV (1965), 146f.

[163] This can be seen from the clumsy defense of Dessewffy's criticism of Széchenyi, written by József Ponori Thewrewk, first under pseudonym right after the publication of *Világ* in July, 1831, and published in the following year in Orosz, ed., *Széchenyi mint iró*, (pp. 9f.) and also in Orosz's "opinion" about *Világ* in the same volume (p. 405). Paraphrasing Leibnitz, Thewrewk characteristically interpreted the saying *extra Hungariam* by suggesting that just as the present world is the best one of all possible worlds, so for the Hungarian his fatherland is the best and most perfect of all conceivable

the opposition to reforms, but his sarcasm directed against Dessewffy was often tactless and personal.[164] Dessewffy's three sons, who came to the defense of their father in a pamphlet entitled "A Few Words on Credit, Analysis, and Light," demonstrated that Széchenyi had overstepped the limits of self-defense. But they treated him with great respect, saying in conclusion: "May God help in furthering and broadening through *Világ* the good of the country and the scope of its author's purview for the steady public benefit of the fatherland."[165]

On July 3, 1831 Széchenyi noted in his diary that he had completed *Világ*. The next sentence of the same entry mentions the outbreak of cholera in Hungary. Two months later, he resumed his work on *Stádium*.[166] This sequence of events is significant, for between the two dates occurred the most violent peasant uprising in Hungarian history since the Dózsa rebellion of 1514.

The jacquerie came on the heels of the defeat of the Polish upheaval by Russia and paralleled the influx of immigrants into upper Hungary. Leading noble families in northern Hungary and Transylvania, many of them bound by traditional friendship to their Polish counterparts, competed with each other in offering shelter and help to the refugees. These arrived in great numbers despite the preventive measures taken by the imperial authorities. But whereas the nobility, at least its propertied part, identified the cause of Poland with its own fight for constitu-

---

fatherlands. Thewrewk, *Töredék-Észrevételek a Világ czimű munkára* (Fragmentary Observations Concerning the Work Called *Világ*), pp. 111f. (Cf. Silagi, *Der grösste Ungar*, pp. 33, 146.) Thewrewk's pamphlet and Orosz's *Vélemény a Világ czimű munkáról* (Opinion About the Work Called *Világ*) constitute the first monograph on Széchenyi; both were published in *Széchenyi mint iró*. See also Horváth, *Huszonöt év*, I, 217–20.

[164] E.g., *Világ*, pp. 94f.; also the chapter "Reason and Heart," *ibid.*, pp. 184–201. Széchenyi himself very soon regretted his "unkind" attack on Dessewffy. Cf. the draft of his letter to Count Waldstein, Sept. 27, 1831, Viszota, ed., *Naplók*, IV, 219. A decade later, during his debate with Kossuth, Széchenyi was reminded that he, too, used to be "tactless."

[165] Cited in Gaál, *Széchenyi nemzeti politikája*, I, 341f.

[166] July 3, Sept. 6, 1831, Viszota, ed., *Naplók*, IV, 192, 208. As early as May 10, 1830 Széchenyi wrote to Wesselényi that "in a short time," the continuation of *Hitel* would be in print under the title *Birói Zálog* (Mortgage). On the 2nd of July he said in a letter to Döbrentei that the work would be "soon" published. But in December he already thought it "more useful to the public good," if he first settled the matter of *Taglalat*. In October 1831, i.e., after the publication of *Világ*, he promised a new work for winter, "the skeleton of which is ready—its material has long been ready—it just has to be put together." Referring to his numerous literary plans, as he had done in previous December, Széchenyi added in English and German: "And here I am a regular Scribler!—Gott ist gross, und die Wege, die er uns gehen lässt, unbegreifbar." Actually, Széchenyi used his first notes written for *Birói Zálog* in *Stádium*. See Széchenyi to Wesselényi, May 10, 1830, Sz. to Döbrentey (*sic*), July 2, Sz. to Wesselényi, Dec. 22, Sz. to Wesselényi, Oct. 5, 1831, Majláth, ed., *Levelek*, I, 164, 166, 188f., 201. Cf. Viszota, ed. *Naplók*, IV, p. lxxi.

tional freedom and openly manifested its sympathy toward the Poles in county assemblies and even at the subsequent Diet of 1832–36, the destitute Slovak, Ruthenian, and Romanian peasants of northern Hungary saw in the undoing of the Polish landlords by "the good Tsar" an example that ought to be followed closer home.[167]

In the summer of 1831 cholera hit the northeastern counties of Hungary and then spread to the rest of the country. The disease attacked some 530,000 people, almost half of whom are said to have died. The heaviest losses occurred in the areas neighboring Galicia where the peasant's condition was the most miserable. Commenting in December 1830 on the Polish revolution, which he thought was well organized, Széchenyi immediately associated the events in Poland with the social conditions prevalent at home. In the absence of timely concessions by the landowners he foresaw an alliance of the peasants with the impoverished nobility. Still before the outbreak of the epidemic, in early June 1831, he expressed increasing concern with the inadequacy of the Hungarian representative system, remarking sardonically: "[The nobles] wish to hurry to the aid of the Poles and do not assist their own peasants! They are chattering about liberality and are flaying their own serfs."[168]

Széchenyi's fears were more than borne out by the "cholera uprising" in which an estimated 45,000 peasants, joined in many cases by members of the sandal nobility, participated. In addition to widespread social dissatisfaction, the violence of the outburst was made worse by primitive conditions, superstition, and a complete breakdown of communication and administration. Rumors that lords, doctors, Jews, and Catholic priests had poisoned the wells resulted in mob violence against the well-to-do, the clergy, and the nobility. For a moment, there may have been some gloating in Vienna over the object lesson taught to liberal Magyars by the people who, as Metternich put it, were hanging the friends of Poland.[169] But there was no doubt about the outcome; the military soon quelled the riots without mercy.[170]

---

[167] Endre Kovács, *A lengyel kérdés a reformkori Magyarországon* (The Polish Question n Hungary During the Age of Reforms) (Budapest: Akadémiai Kiadó, 1959), pp. 67–200.

[168] Dec. 15, 1830, June 7, 1831, Viszota, ed., *Naplók*, IV, 167f., 190.

[169] Cited by E. Kovács, *A lengyel kérdés*, p. 112.

[170] For the cholera uprising cf. Pulszky, *Meine Zeit*, I, 48–54; Horváth, *Huszonöt év*, I, 266ff., Hóman and Szekfű, *Magyar történet*, v, 285f. and, more recently, Lóránt Tilkovszky, *Az 1831. évi parasztfelkelés* (The Peasant Uprising of 1831) (Budapest: Művelt Nép, 1955). For a contemporary account see János Balásházy, *Az 1831dik esztendői felső magyarországi zendűléseknek történeti leirása* (Historical Description of the Rebellions of 1831 in Upper Hungary) (Pest: Trattner és Károlyi, 1832); also, Pyrker, *Mein Leben*, pp. 158–61. Cf. Roger E. McGrew, *Russia and the Cholera, 1823–32* (Madison and Milwaukee: University of Wisconsin Press, 1965).

Besides harsh repression the administration also resorted to other methods to prevent the reoccurrence of a mass upheaval of the peasantry. Citing as examples Bohemia, Moravia, Silesia, and Galicia, urgent instructions were sent in October 1831, to the royal cities and the counties to prepare the ground for the establishment of communal granaries, "this in Hungary yet alien institution," but the measure, as the official correspondence of subsequent years was to show, never got beyond the stage of planning.[171] Hardly more successful were the endeavors to get at the heart of the problem with the help of the clergy. Ordered by Francis I to find out "in a proper way" (*auf so eine schickliche Art*) the real causes of the people's restlessness, but without revealing that this was the only purpose of his canonical visitation, the bishop of the Zips (Szepesség) reported that the populace was very superstitious and that it expected the abolition of serfdom. In his sermons, the bishop added, he praised the villages that remained calm during the uprising. Peasants known to have sympathized with the rebellion were admonished to repent. But efforts to discover a conspiracy in Zemplén County brought no result since the authorities were unable to find further copies let alone the authors of a subversive appeal posted in a church of Sátoraljaujhely.

Directed against the nobility and clergy, the appeal in question described the misery of the peasants. It was anti-feudal in tone, giving the impression that the insurrection was not hostile to either king or citydwellers; moreover, it solicited the support of the military.[172] In the absence of documentary or other evidence the incident appears to have been an isolated phenomenon in the confusion and fear which surrounded the cholera and the peasant movement. But it aroused, understandably, the interest of officials who were also eager to learn about the mood of the non-Catholic population in whose midst the revolutionary ferment seemed to have originated. Hungarian Chancellor Reviczky and Baron Ignatius Eötvös, who was in charge of suppressing the jacquerie in Hungary, wrote of an altogether unreliable Ruthenian clergy (*"in jeder Hinsicht unverlässliche russniakische Geistlichkeit"*), without making any distinction between Uniate or Eastern Orthodox. In a report on the Romanians the Transylvanian chancery referred to alleged intrigues (*"Umtriebe"*) of the Orthodox clergy and Russian influence in the Orthodox church and suggested that the Uniate church and the work of proselytizing be promoted. Pointing out that ever since Catherine

---

[171] *Österreichisches Staatsarchiv* (Vienna), *Abt.: Haus-, Hofund Staatsarchiv, Minister Kolowrat Akten* (cited hereafter as *MKA*), No. 2,429/1831. Cf. No. 1,752/1835, *ibid.*
[172] *Ibid.*, No. 2,803/1831; Nos. 144, 1,318 and 1,476/1832; No. 1,656/1836. Cf. Tilkovszky, *Az 1831. évi parasztfelkelés*, pp. 148–52.

the Great had given financial assistance to the construction of an Orthodox church in Kronstadt (Braşov, Brassó) believers were permitted to
mention in their prayers the name of the reigning tsar as their patron,
the chancery advocated the printing of prayerbooks in Hungary rather
than their importation from abroad (Russia). A *Stimmungsbericht* for
January 1832, submitted by the governor of Dalmatia, made mention
of the activities of Russian emissaries directed presumably by the consul
of Russia in Cattaro (Kotor). Since the Peace of Adrianople (1829),
which strengthened the position of the tsarist empire in the Danubian
Principalities and the Balkans, Austrian officials could not quite overcome
the suspicion, however ludicrous, that Russian help might somehow be
flowing to rebellious subjects ready to rise against their lawful monarch.
Anxious to avoid contributing, in the Bucovina, to the Orthodox population's alleged preference for the Russian government, afraid of liturgic
books containing prayers for the tsar rather than the emperor-king, and
worried about any individual's conversion to Orthodoxy, especially in
the military frontier region, the administration thought in early 1831
of creating a General Synod for the Orthodox Church of Austria to
be presided over, in true Josephinian form, by a civil servant.[173] The
attempt to follow the Russian pattern and drive out fire with fire was
eventually abandoned. Yet the plan in itself shows that Hungarian liberals were not the only ones in the Habsburg realm obsessed in the
second quarter of the 19th century by Russophobia. There can be no
doubt, however, that the memory of the horrors of the rebellion of
1831, kept alive by peasant unrest throughout the rest of the decade,
continued to remind the feudal classes in Hungary of their shaky position.

During the cholera epidemic many magnates, including Széchenyi's
two brothers, went abroad with their families. Stephen Széchenyi stayed,
warning his serfs in an open letter to take measures of precaution against
the epidemic and promising to help them.[174] In letters to friends he
expressed the hope that perhaps the cholera, the jacquerie, and the
panic caused by the crumbling of the feudal constitution would at long
last wake up the blindest opponents of reform to the necessity of sober
concessions. He noted with bitter irony that if the emancipation of all
inhabitants of the country could be achieved at the cost of 300 to 400
thousand lives the cholera would have been worth it.

Yet the opponents of reform were quick to point out that according
to some reports rebellious peasants in a few places had referred to *Hitel*
and *Világ*. They urged beheadings and hangings rather than leniency,
saying that "everything would be all right in Hungary, if only Stephen

---

[173] *MKA*, Nos. 724, 966, and 2,803/1831; Nos. 467 and 478/1832; No. 569/1834.
[174] To the Serfs of Czenk (Zinkendorf), July 24, 1831, Majláth, ed., *Levelek*, I, 189ff.

Széchenyi's Plague did not spread . . . that was the cause of the revolts in Upper Hungary."[175] Széchenyi, however, held that "if we do not do something in the near future, surely the thresher, scythe, and ax will do it, and not only what is necessary but plenty more." Perhaps alone among Hungarian politicians—if one ignores Wesselényi who was in Transylvania at the time—he tried to put the question of social reform on the agenda. Trusting that the administration would support such a move, he suggested that the table of magnates give leadership to the work of "calm reformation." But his friend Wesselényi disagreed, questioning Vienna's goodwill. It was at this point that the first, two great leaders of Hungarian liberalism realized that they had come to the parting of the ways.[176]

But Széchenyi continued to work in his own way on the "calm reformation," for which he intended to set forth the program in *Stádium*. But when in February 1832 he ventured to read a few passages to George Andrássy, the latter became horrified, called Széchenyi's new book a burning torch which no one could extinguish or control and which no decent censor in his right mind should permit to go into print.[177] Shocked, but persistent, Széchenyi first thought of giving the title *Reformatio* or *Regeneratio* to his work. Rumors concerning the "dangerous" influence of his previous writings, however, made the authorities more cau-

---

[175] July 27, 1832, Viszota, ed., *Naplók*, IV, 283. Cf. Oct. 5, 25, 1831, Jan. 19, 28, Feb. 2, 4, 10, 1832, *ibid.*, IV, 222, 226, 238–42; George Andrássy to Széchenyi, Sept. 6, Oct. 12, 1831, Wesselényi to Széchenyi, Oct. 26, 1831, Michael Esterházy to Széchenyi, Jan. 14, 1832, B. Szabó, ed., *Adatok*, I, 125, 137, 142, 156; Széchenyi to Wesselényi, Oct. 20, 1831, Majláth, ed., *Levelek*, I, 202.

Recent Hungarian research has found evidence that Széchenyi's works were read in the villages and even translated for Transylvanian peasants into Romanian: "*libri, sed praeprimis libelli, novalia non tantum leguntur, sed nonnulli novalium articuli prout et liber Hitel translati sint in idioma Valachicum* . . . ." Cited by István Barta, "A magyar polgári reformmozgalom kezdeti szakaszának problémái" (Problems of the Initial Phase of Bourgeois Reform in Hungary), *Történelmi Szemle*, VI (1963), 33f. and n. 33 and 34. On July 17, 1831, there was a mob riot in Pest, which may have been led, perhaps even organized, by students and radical intellectuals. In this prelude to the peasant uprising, an inflammatory leaflet was found, the authors of which could not be identified by the investigating officials. One of the suspected ringleaders, a lawyer who admitted having read the revolutionary appeal, defended himself by saying that on the basis of the "democratic principles" expressed in it he assumed that "some German" must have borrowed "these principles from the work entitled *Hitel*." (" . . . *principia haec aliquis Germanus ex opere Hitel intitulato desumpserit*") István Barta, "Az 1831. évi pesti koleramozgalom" (The Cholera Movement of Pest in 1831), in *Tanulmányok Budapest Múltjából* (Studies from the Past of Budapest), XIV (Budapest: Akadémiai kiadó, 1961), 461f., 469 and n. 82.

[176] Széchenyi to Wesselényi, Aug. 26, Oct. 5, Nov. 8, Dec. 5, 1831, Jan. 5, 1832, Majláth, ed., *Levelek*, I, 193, 200, 203ff., 208f., Wesselényi to Széchenyi, Oct. 26, Nov. 29, Dec. 18, 1831, B. Szabó, ed., *Adatok*, I, 142, 147–50; Aug. 26, 1831, Viszota, ed., *Naplók*, IV, 201ff.

[177] Feb. 2, 1832, *ibid.*, IV, 240.

tious, especially since *Stádium* proposed a series of reforms which, according to many contemporaries, affected not just by implication as did *Hitel* or *Világ* but explicitly the social system of Hungary. Hence *Stádium* was suppressed in the spring of 1832 and was published anonymously in Leipzig in November 1833.[178]

Széchenyi did not easily give up the fight for his work. A few days after the publication of the book was prohibited he wrote: "I work diligently and with self-reliance. If my wings are clipped, I shall walk on foot. If my feet are cut off, I shall move along on my hands. Should they be torn out, too, I shall crawl on my belly."[179]

It was in this mood that he decided to change the original motto of the book, "Man's worth is measured only by his usefulness," to "Again and again—incessantly." Yet despite his influence with official circles (and he tried to use the best connections he had), the publication of *Stádium* was stopped in June 1832 by the lieutenancy after 11 sheets had been printed. Instead of appearing on the eve of the Diet of 1832–36 the printing of the book was considerably delayed. Even so, it had a great impact on members of the Diet and deeply affected the thinking of the adherents of reform in subsequent years.

Széchenyi's experience with preliminary censorship was not unique. Introduced under Joseph II and "developed" under Francis I to an all-encompassing degree,[180] its constitutionality was often questioned in Hungary. Yet it had been practiced since the 16th century, and the estates tacitly accepted it. Indeed, one section of Act XXVI of 1791, which restored the privileges of Protestants, specifically mentioned the selection and responsibility of censors, whose task it was to examine religious books before sending them to the printer, and whose names had to be submitted to the lieutenancy.[181]

The system of censorship was an organic part of Austrian government before 1848. Most high-ranking officials, including the kaiser and Met-

[178] Cf. Gyula Viszota, "A Stádium megjelenésének története," (History of the Publication of "Stage") in *SzIM²*, II, pp. v–xxxiv; Gyula Kautz, "Gróf Széchenyi István 'Stádium' czimü munkájának méltatása," (Appraisal of Count Stephen Széchenyi's "Stage"), *ibid.*, II, pp. xxxix–lii; Viszota's introduction to *Naplók*, IV, esp. p. lxxii. Also the Latin letter of the palatine to Chancellor Reviczky and the petitions of the censor to the palatine and the lieutenancy (June 1832), in B. Szabó, ed., *Adatok*, I, 159–62. For the aftermath of the investigation, Oct. 24, 1834, July 6, 10, Sept. 7, 1835, Reviczky reports, *ibid.*, I, 214f., 227, 229–39.

[179] June 26, 1832, Viszota, ed., *Naplók*, IV, 273.

[180] Julius Marx, *Die Österreichische Zensur im Vormärz* (Munich: Oldenbourg, 1959), p. 55.

[181] Marczali, *Enchiridion*, p. 771; and Townson, *Travels in Hungary*, p. 174. For the origins and practice of censorship in Hungary, cf. Egyed Schermann, *Adalékok az állami könyvcenzura történetéhez Magyarországon Mária Terézia haláláig* (Data Concerning the History of the Censorship of Books in Hungary up to the Death of Maria Theresa) (Budapest: Stephaneum, 1928).

ternich, regarded it as a sometimes perhaps unpleasant and clumsy but basically useful and perfectly legitimate tool of paternalistic absolutism. In spite of occasional blunders and the resentment of liberals, who naturally condemned it altogether, one may say that many censors were educated and scholarly persons willing to give a benevolent opinion about the work submitted if no question of religion, good morals, or loyalty to the dynasty and the state (the two were held to be identical) were involved. Such benevolence was especially probable if the author had an aristocratic patron or was himself a member of the reliable higher nobility, as was Széchenyi. In the "negotiations" preceding a work's publication the censor would occasionally seem harsher than he actually was in order to justify his salary, on the one hand, and avoid being reprimanded by his superiors on the other. The censor of *Stádium,* for example, reported a number of changes allegedly suggested by him and accepted by Széchenyi. Yet we know from the manuscript that the report was exaggerated and served the purpose of playing it safe. In such circumstances, of course, the censor had to be sure his author was both able and willing to compensate him financially if he lost his job.

At the time the printing of *Stádium* was stopped, Wesselényi's book "On Misjudgments" (*Balítéletekről*), of which six sheets were ready, was also prohibited. In both instances the material in print was supposed to be destroyed, and the censors received a strict warning to submit important works for approval to the higher authorities before giving the go-ahead to the printshop. In vain Széchenyi petitioned the president of the lieutenancy, the Archduke-Palatine Joseph; all he obtained was the sum payed by him to the printer. The lieutenancy, however, ordered the "guilty" censor to reimburse the treasury for the sum refunded to Széchenyi, whereas Széchenyi, in turn, had to make up for the censor's losses to save him from financial ruin.[182] Since the ruse failed to work in the case of *Stádium,* Széchenyi sent the manuscript, with the help of Liebenberg,[183] to Otto Wigand's publishing house in Leipzig, where it was printed in 1833, as was Wesselényi's book a year later. By November 1833 copies of *Stádium* were smuggled back to Pressburg where anyone interested could read it. The authorities made only a halfhearted effort to confiscate the copies. Széchenyi himself noted that his book was being sold openly both in Pressburg and Vienna, which, apparently, Metternich did not mind.[184] Széchenyi's delight must have been great, indeed, because he succeeded in taking his revenge on the establishment by describing in an anonymous preface the tribulations of a fictitious

---

[182] Friedreich, *Széchenyi élete,* I, 286–89.
[183] Lóránt Tilkovszky, "Lunkányi arcképéhez," *Soproni Szemle,* XIII (1959), 361f.
[184] Széchenyi to Tasner, Nov. 24, 1833, Majláth, ed., *Levelek,* I, 338; Nov. 3, 4-5-6, 7, 1833, Viszota, ed., *Naplók,* IV, 427.

Hungarian author who was prevented by the unlawful action of the authorities from publishing his work. In such a case, it was suggested,

> . . . the manuscript is being submitted to the Council of the Royal Lieutenancy where it is being read or not read by almost every member of the Council, frequently including even the junior clerks. Finally, after six months of perhaps a year, the book is being discussed in a plenary session; in the meantime, the author plays the role of some sort of a criminal who is supposed to kowtow to his judges,—and who are they sometimes—to solicit their favor and to keep them in a good mood so his book can be sent to the printer. If the manuscript is rejected, that is the end of the matter; if it obtains approval, nothing has been gained yet because the manuscript proceeds to the Chancery where it begins to swing again in a circle just depicted in order to go to the Cabinet where it falls into oblivion at long last.

Making fun of the bureaucracy was, naturally, only a sidelight of minor significance in the story of *Stádium*. But how characteristic it was of Széchenyi, who was able to discover only a donkey's long ears, as he once said to Wesselényi, whereas his friend saw the devil's horns behind every action of the Viennese administration. How characteristic it was of him to thumb his nose at the authorities, as he did in his last years, when he succeeded in making the Bach regime the laughing-stock of the public at such tragic cost to himself.

As it was, the first edition of *Stádium* did not conceal its author's name; it was only the editor-smuggler of the manuscript who was to remain unknown. The maneuver further increased the public's interest, already aroused by Széchenyi's earlier writings. Soon *Stádium* came to be regarded, in the words of the historian of the period, as "the manual of Hungarian radicalism."[185] One may add that it was also the most systematic and logical of Széchenyi's works.

Dedicated "To Hungary's Representatives," *Stádium* proposed "Twelve Laws"[186] as initial steps toward enacting new legislation at the forthcoming Diet of 1832–36. The book actually spelled out only nine of the "laws," submitting the first phase of the suggested new legislation—hence the title which in Hungarian means "stage."

[185] Horváth, *Huszonöt év*, I, 277.

[186] *Stádium*. Irta Gróf Széchenyi István 1831-ben. Kiadta Z**** 1833-ban (*Stage*. Written by Count Stephen Széchenyi in 1831. Published by Z**** in 1833), 2d edn., *SzIM²*, II, 1–260. Subsequent references will be to this edition, published by the Academy. The Twelve Laws were summed up by Széchenyi on pp. 39–42 in this edition. At one point Széchenyi thought of giving the title *A törvényekrül* (About Laws) to his new book.

The "Twelve Laws" suggested by Széchenyi can be summed up as follows. The first law would have established a new commercial code and court, envisaging complete legal equality between nobles and non-nobles in credit operations, and permitting no appeals against the court's decisions to higher authorities. The second intended "to abolish for ever" the law of entail (*jus aviticitatis*); once a transaction had been concluded by common consent, neither the seller nor his family had any right to cancel it. The third law would have terminated the exchequer's right to inherit land after the extinction of a family, adding, however, that upon any exchange of landed property resulting from sale, inheritance, or will, a one-percent transfer duty (*laudemium*) had to be paid to the treasury. The fourth law stipulated that "in Hungary everybody had a right to possess personal and landed property of his own (*jus proprietatis*)"; but whereas noble land continued to be exempt from taxation, non-nobles had to pay a land tax. The fifth law declared the equality of all before the law, explaining that henceforth the *primae nonus,* summarizing the privileges of the nobility, would be extended to everybody. At the time of reelection of officials every three years, according to law six, taxpayers should elect two special "legal defenders," one noble and one non-noble, to represent them in the county administration. The seventh law demanded proportional participation of all in the expenses of county administration and the Diet. Law eight declared that tolls and tariff duties should affect everybody equally and should be determined by the Diet. The ninth law would have abolished all monopolies, guilds, price limitations "and other such nuisances to public diligence and competition." Law ten stipulated that "in Hungary laws, orders, and sentences shall be binding only if [published] in the Magyar tongue." According to law eleven Hungarian municipalities would receive the royal word through the lieutenancy. Finally, law twelve would introduce public trials.

Essentially, the Twelve Laws contained the program of the whole Hungarian "Era of Reform." Their enactment would have transformed the feudal constitution and prepared the way for the complete emancipation of the serf.[187] Having elaborated in detail on the first nine laws in *Stádium,* Széchenyi planned to commence the second part of his book with the tenth law.[188]

As can be seen, even in his most radical work Széchenyi avoided

[187] Cf. István Barta, ed., *Széchenyi István válogatott írásai* (Selected Writings of Stephen Széchenyi) (Budapest: Gondolat, 1959), pp. 183f.; *id.,* "A magyar polgári reform-mozgalom," p. 314.

[188] *Stádium,* p. 258. His book *Hunnia* (Hungary), written in 1835 but published posthumously, consisted of the justification of "Law Ten"; he never elaborated on the problems involved in laws eleven and twelve.

discussing openly Hungary's administration because to do so could have brought him into conflict with Vienna. Concentrating primarily on laws attacking feudalism, he emphasized the necessity of developing the country's productive capacity and general welfare because these goals were also in the government's interest. Hence the utilitarian principle of usefulness to all was prominent throughout the whole book, particularly in those parts where Széchenyi tried to convince the nobility that they themselves would benefit most from the abolition of the feudal system.[189] In this respect, he vigorously reiterated the statements made in *Hitel* and *Világ*.

On the one hand, *Stádium* was indeed a logical continuation and a program for action based on the principles set forth in Széchenyi's earlier works. On the other, it was a timely warning to attempt "a mild reformation without convulsion" because of "the twofold sad lesson" that had just excited the country.[190] The defeat of the Polish revolution, conjuring up the nightmare of the extinction of a nation and reviving Herder's ghost, and the horrors of the cholera uprising overshadowed the entire work. In a powerful introductory exhortation Széchenyi reminded his fellow countrymen: " 'To keep a nation for mankind,' " this and no lesser question is put to us now, and its happy solution depends on us. Let us respond—for God's sake—to this decorum. Young and old, noble and non-noble, Catholic and non-Catholic shall extend their hands to each other, and shall not sacrifice the good and even the existence of our fatherland for their vain passions and pusillanimous feuds."[191] Referring to the Polish events and cautioning that the nation's very survival depended on the solution of the problem of the peasant, Széchenyi remarked bitterly that it was not enough to intervene with sincere enthusiasm for oppressed foreign nations and that liberal slogans were rather ridiculous on the lips of those who trespassed the law and rode roughshod over people at home.[192]

The proposals in *Stádium* were long overdue. Széchenyi correctly recognized that the main issue of the moment was "the fate of the landless nobility and that of the toiler of the land and their relationship to the government, county, and, in the latter's case, to the landlord." Therefore he wanted to secure "the civil existence of all inhabitants of Hungary,"[193] partly through giving the right to hold property to the peasant, partly through persuading the lower strata of the nobility to take up some gainful employment.

[189] *Stádium*, pp. 43, 89f., 113f., 184, 234, 243, 249, 253, 257f.
[190] *Ibid.*, pp. 30, 43.
[191] *Ibid.*, p. 1.
[192] *Ibid.*, p. 180.
[193] *Ibid.*, pp. 37f.

Above: Stephen Széchenyi's birthplace, the Wilczek Palais,
Vienna, Herrengasse. (Engraving, ca. 1737.) Cf. Chapter II,
22, n. 44.

Left: Archway and grillwork,
1967. Photograph courtesy of
Mr. Karl Dworak, Vienna.

Right: Count Stephen Széchenyi, Lieutenant of the 1st Uhlaner Regiment, 1812.

Below: After a watercolor portrait by John Ender (1793-1854), showing Széchenyi during his and Ender's Oriental trip in 1818-19. In lower left corner is "Graf St.[efan] Széchény"—in Francis Széchenyi's hand. In the lower right corner is the phrase, "tâchez d'être heureux!"—words of Selina O'Meade, noted in Stephen Széchenyi's hand.

After a copy by Anton Weinwurm, jr., of an oil painting done in 1835 by
August Schöfft (1809-1888). It shows Széchenyi as a champion of steam
shipping and navigation on the Lower Danube.

GRÓF **SZÉCHENYI** ISTVÁN

Composite lithograph drawn by John Schindler in 1835, after the original painting by Anton Einsle. At the lower left is Széchenyi's remark (in German): "I have no objection against the multiplication and publication of this lithograph." At the lower right is the censor's mark—"*Admittitur.*"

A drawing of the construction of the Chain (Suspension) Bridge.

Széchenyi's bridge linking the twin cities of Buda (Ofen) and Pest. Built by Adam and Tierney Clark. On the right bank of the Danube is the Royal Castle. A mid-19th-century engraving.

VILÁG

VAGY IS

FELVILÁGOSÍTÓ TÖREDÉKEK

NÉMI HIBA 'S ELŐITÉLET ELIGAZITÁSÁRA.

IRTA

GRÓF SZÉCHENYI ISTVÁN.

PESTEN,

Füskúti Landerer Nyomtató Intézetében.

1831.

A facsimile of the title page of *Világ* (Light, or Enlightening Fragments to Straighten Out Some Mistakes and Prejudices).

Opposite page: Formal portrait of Stephen Széchenyi, by Francis Schrotzberg, 1844.

Opposite page (lower): Formal portrait of Stephen Széchenyi's wife, née Countess Crescence Seilern, by Francis Schrotzberg, 1844.

The cylinder mill of Pest. In the foreground is Széchenyi on horseback.

The Széchenyi mansion at Cenk (Zinkendorf).

In accordance with his philosophy of history, Széchenyi tried to examine carefully the present stage, or phase, of development reached by the Hungarian nation, so as to be able to present a balanced program of action corresponding to the principle of the "golden mean."[194] Despite the "radical" appearance of the "laws" proposed in his book, his program was essentially conciliatory and conservative, aimed at safeguarding the leading role of the aristocracy. But in using the term "aristocracy," he reinterpreted it according to its original Greek meaning. Instead of a "debased oligarchy," he was in favor of the "true principle of aristocracy," urging that the leadership of the country be assigned to "the best people" who would be selected not on the basis of birth or genealogical tables but "always and everywhere" on the basis of "reason, justice, and virtue," regardless of whether these were "ornaments of the immortal soul of the prince or lowest of serfs, of the very old or very young." Accordingly, a nation's progress should be secured by the leadership of an intellectual élite and by the directing force of moral quality rather than the "precedence of chance."[195] He held that not all people were mature enough for the freedom of the press and for government by a responsible ministry, adding that a really free republic must be based on intelligence and not belie its principles by having "thousands of helots, Roman slaves, and American Negroes crying to heaven."[196] Yet it was his deep belief that people could and should be educated for representative government.

Széchenyi wanted to promote this education for responsible citizenship step-by-step, as shown by his detailed analysis of laws seven and eight. By suggesting in the former that the nobility share the burdens of Hungary's domestic administration, and in the latter that they contribute to the establishment, under the auspices of the Diet, of a nationwide system of communication, flood control, and water regulation, he intended to move in the direction of general and proportional taxation.[197] But law seven said nothing about the military tax payed to the state, which constituted about half of the financial burdens of the peasantry, because Széchenyi knew that half a loaf is better than none and perhaps also because he purposely abstained from issues involving the relationship of Hungary with Austria. At the same time, the vision of a unified communication system and large-scale land reclamation incorporated in law eight was more than an economic project. It revealed his intention

---

[194] *Ibid.*, pp. 33, 35.
[195] *Ibid.*, pp. 131f. Again Wesselényi's *Szózat* was strongly influenced by these ideas, although by 1843 he supported Kossuth against Széchenyi.
[196] *Stádium*, pp. 33, 36f.
[197] *Ibid.*, pp. 212–15.

to concentrate on a capital enterprise where he had a good chance of getting the support of the administration, of proving the senselessness of feudal restrictions, of educating the public to share the responsibilities and expenses of an undertaking which involved the resources of the entire country, and—last but not least—of demonstrating the necessity of surrendering private to public interests.[198]

Even this brief reference to some of Széchenyi's proposals should remind us how cautious one must be in evaluating the legal aspects of his activities as a reformer. It has been said that he wished to begin his reforms in the realm of private law and economic relations.[199] To be sure, Széchenyi was not a trained lawyer; his outlook, unlike that of most Hungarian politicians, was not primarily legalistic. But in the decade preceding the publication of his major writings, he made a determined effort to acquire a substantial knowledge of Hungarian constitutional law and legal practices. He knew very well that one of the salient features of Hungarian feudal law was that private and public law could not be neatly separated. In fact, legal scholars traditionally defended the private interests and privileges of the nobility by identifying them with the constitutional liberties of the noble nation. The obverse of this statement is, of course, that any breakthrough in the domain of private law could present a serious challenge to the whole structure of the feudal constitution. It is not quite clear, however, to what an extent Széchenyi wished to press the issue of the legal destruction of feudalism in *Stádium.*

In harmony with Széchenyi's previous thinking, the strongest case for equality before the law was made in the first three proposals of *Stádium,* which intended to establish legal safeguards for capitalistic commercial transactions and credit operations. True, in a later phase of his career, Széchenyi decided to modify his seemingly uncompromising views on the law of entail and on the rights of the treasury to inherit, acquire, and donate land.[200] But this does not change the fact that the arguments set forth by him in 1831 were taken over and expanded by Kölcsey, Deák, Kossuth, and others during and after the Diet of 1832–36 in their attacks on one of the cornerstones of Hungarian feudalism. Also, Széchenyi's insistence that his noble compatriots were no real proprietors of the land—of which they had only the usufruct, whereas its real ownership was vested in the king—broke with centuries of Hungarian legal scholarship while relying on foreign sources rejected in Hungary. Again the new generation of liberal constitutional lawyers and politicians sided

[198] *Ibid.,* pp. 225–29.
[199] Tamás Vécsey, "Széchenyi és a magyar magánjog" (Széchenyi and Hungarian Private Law) (Budapest: Magyar Tudományos Akadémia, 1895), pp. 10f.
[200] Ferenczi, ed., *A kelet népe,* p. 399.

with the contention put forward in *Stádium*[201] in its endeavor to lay down the legal and socio-economic foundations for a new interpretation of what the concept of the Hungarian nation ought to be.

Laws four, five, and six of *Stádium* were most important from the point of view of the lord-peasant relationship. The first of these suggested the extension of the right to own property, even allodial or demesne land, to all non-nobles, including serfs. This proposal, related to Széchenyi's concern with the increase of both domestic consumption and production, was a step pointing beyond the feudal order. But it must keep in mind that the law as formulated in *Stádium* was only permissive, that it assumed the voluntary agreement of the parties involved and the ability of the peasant to pay a fair price to the lord. At no point did Széchenyi propose the compulsory redemption of land or the immediate and complete emancipation of the serfs with, let alone without, indemnification of the landowners. Moreover, ownership of land would not have made noble and non-noble equal in the eyes of the state, because the former's demesne would have been tax-exempt as before whereas the latter's purchased property would have been taxable.

Similarly, the principle of egalitarianism incorporated in the fifth law of *Stádium* was subject to qualifications. True, Széchenyi referred to the relationship between the nobleman and the tiller of the soil as being against the laws of nature. He also condemned the manorial courts and demanded the enactment of new civil and penal codes to secure the personal safety of all citizens and to protect them against arbitrary actions. But he himself insisted only on the immediate proclamation of the principle of equality before the law, whereas its full application would have to be put into practice cautiously. Although he thought educated people of the upper strata of society deserved harsher punishment for the same crimes than their lower-class counterparts, he nevertheless stressed the need for maintaining corporal punishment in cases involving non-nobles. If one adds that according to law six the task of the "legal defenders" was chiefly to protect the taxpaying peasants against the arbitrariness of the landowners, one may conclude that as far as the conditions of serfdom were concerned, the main thrust of *Stádium* was directed against the existence of abuses rather than against the system itself.[202]

However great the impact of Széchenyi's most radical and systematic book might have been on the evolution of Hungarian liberalism before

[201] Márton Sarlós, *Széchenyi István és a feudális jogrend átalakulása* (Stephen Széchenyi and the Transformation of the Feudal Legal Order) (Budapest: Közgazdasági és Jogi Könyvkiadó, 1960), pp. 25–37.

[202] *Ibid.*, pp. 11–25.

1848, his proposals were geared to existing political realities as he understood them. He refrained from analyzing the legal and political ties connecting the Austrian and Hungarian halves of the Habsburg realm and treated only perfunctorily their economic relations. His criticism of the constitutional structure of Hungary, despite the sharp attacks on some of its outdated legal aspects and despite the explicit wish to include the majority of the people into the nation-building process, nonetheless stopped short of suggesting a meaningful political solution to the problem. The emphasis on the urgency of changing the relationship of lord and peasant was justified chiefly on humanitarian grounds and by economic reasoning, without visible concern for the serf's civil rights or political representation. Thus it is fair to point out that from a strictly legal standpoint the carefully planned reforms suggested in *Stádium* reflected Széchenyi's desire for "a sober and quiet reformation." Frequently accused of inciting the peasants to rebel against their masters,[203] his ideas embodied the principle of gradual progress rather than revolution.

Still these ideas seemed to be "radical" to many contemporaries, due to an interplay of factors, both personal and impersonal, some of which have already been mentioned. The circumstance that Széchenyi abandoned the traditionally legalistic approach to Hungary's basic problems, gave equal attention to humanitarian considerations, and, whenever possible, focused on cold economic facts, was a novelty on the Hungarian scene. It was also unusual that the social criticism voiced in *Stádium,* as in *Hitel,* came not from an impoverished nobleman or a bitter intellectual but from someone whose forebears were high prelates of the church, royal chamberlains, and loyal supporters of the dynasty, whose father was a patron of art and literature and a founder of many a charitable institution both in Hungary and Austria, and who himself was not only widely read and travelled, but who had demonstrated his ability to straighten out his own financial affairs and his willingness to sacrifice part of his wealth for the public good.

Likewise, unorthodox was the multilingual, former cosmopolite's attitude toward the function of the Magyar vernacular in Hungary's political life. In 1825 he initiated the foundation of the Academy of Sciences for cultivating the Hungarian idiom. But in law ten of *Stádium* he went much further by specifying that in order to be valid, not only laws, orders, and sentences, but even petitions, contracts, agreements, and accounts must be written in Magyar after the first day of 1835. It is true that *Stádium* failed to elaborate on the tenth law, but that

---

[203] Kemény, "Széchenyi," 454–62.

was not necessary in this particular instance. Laconic as the statement was, it threw Széchenyi's authority behind that radical linguistic nationalism[204] which shocked those who regarded Latin as a shield of the ancient feudal constitution and which he himself wanted to nip in the bud before long.

It will be remembered that in his first book, *On Horses,* Széchenyi protested against confusing patriotic wishful thinking with economics. Yet as the father of modern Magyar nationalism he tried to drive home in all his major works the idea that to promote Hungary's economic welfare was both a lucrative proposition from which all would benefit *and* a sacred patriotic duty to which all must devote their best talents. Speaking of the immensity of the task set forth in law eight of *Stádium,* which visualized the creation of a unified communication and flood control system for Hungary, he intimated that only the awakened *soul of the nation*[205] could be equal to it. To awaken the "nation's soul," he argued throughout his book that the "unification of interests" (*érdekegyesítés*) of toilers and landowners was not only possible but necessary in order to build a true nation. To make the peasant producer interested in improving the quality and quantity of his work by allowing him to become the owner of his land and to abolish the worst aspects of the feudal economy, Széchenyi persisted, would at once heighten the value of the nobleman's estate and transform him into its proprietor, in theory as well as in fact. Indeed, this was the central economic theme of *Stádium,* to which Széchenyi kept returning from different angles.[206] That there could be a community of interests between lord and peasant from a national and economic standpoint, was one of Széchenyi's new discoveries for his fatherland, as was his attempt to demonstrate the obsolescence of noble privileges and serfdom on the basis of economic arguments. Thus, Széchenyi was one of the earliest champions of that policy of liberal reform which saw in the "unification of interests" of all social classes one of the main roads leading to Hungary's transformation into a modern national state.

One of the ingredients that made *Stádium* look so radical at the time was Széchenyi's emotionally charged and highly individual style. To achieve his purpose, he resorted to the most critical tone in scourging

[204] Sarlós, *Széchenyi,* p. 38.

[205] Italics in original.

[206] As early as 1828 it was reported about Széchenyi that he intended to make Hungary flourish and her people united: ". . . *omnes ejus conatus eo directi sint, . . . ut Hungaria efflorescat, et gens uniatur.*" He himself spelled out the idea in the concluding part of *Világ* (p. 219 above). Cf. Barta, "A magyar polgári reformmozgalom," pp. 332f. and n. 28. See also the introduction by Antal Mátyás to the recent edition of *Stádium* (Budapest: Közgazdasági és Jogi Könyvkiadó, 1958), pp. 15–22.

the abuses and corruption of the "vampire" feudal classes, which kept the taxpaying peasantry on the level of "a vegetating animal."[207] He held a mirror before the eyes of the nation, which reflected "spiritual as well as physical darkness and filth," saying that it was "the most heartless of all cruelties to imprison the spiritual talents of a man" and that physical annihilation was a merciful deed compared to the "mutilation of a fellow man's immortal part." He did not hesitate to compare the rule of free and proud Hungarian noblemen to sheer despotism: "Where man is the despotic master of his fellow man, there the meadow is covered with a winding sheet instead of flowers and all of nature is mourning."[208] Charging that the lot of the peasantry had deteriorated in comparison with preceding centuries to the point where it could justly be called "the wretched taxpaying people" (*misera plebs contribuens*), he grimly warned that this was not a problem of a small sect but "a question of nine million, who are loyal serfs, and how loyal! who are brave soldiers, and how brave! who, in short, are patiently carrying all the burdens and whose greater part is the last guarantee, hope, and preserver of Hungarian nationality!"[209] He flatly stated that the concept of a nation was incompatible with the coexistence of a privileged few and an underprivileged peasant majority; therefore, the foremost task of nation-building in Hungary must consist of "placing all inhabitants in the common rights of mankind which means securing everybody's political existence."[210]

Shrugging off the constitutional doctrine of the Holy Crown as a myth "which is de facto not true either in the physical or the moral sense,"[211] Széchenyi wanted to see Hungary "at long last not merely de jure but also de facto as a *regnum per se et pro se existens, et independens*,"[212] in mutually advantageous interpendence, however, with the other provinces of the Austrian Empire.[213]

It has been said that in *Stádium* Széchenyi used inflammatory dialectics in support of his thesis, arguing both rationally and emotionally.

[207] *Stádium*, pp. 44f., 133–46, 165f., 173, 178–81, 193–96, 254f.
[208] *Ibid.*, pp. 16, 108ff.
[209] *Ibid.*, p. 47. The term "miserable taxpaying people" was first used in a law of 1571.
[210] *Ibid.*, p. 70.
[211] *Ibid.*, pp. 74f. and n. 1. Concerning the "Doctrine of the Holy Crown," see Marczali, *Hungary in the Eighteenth Century*, pp. 110 and n. 2, 155 and n. 1, 329; also, Ferenc Eckhart, *A szentkoronaeszme története* (History of the Idea of the Sacred Crown) (Budapest: Magyar Tudományos Akadémia, 1941). In brief, according to the theory, the Holy Crown of St. Stephen, which was the symbolic owner of all the land, was also a corporate body of which the king was the head and all nobles, individually, were members.
[212] *Stádium*, p. 68: "An independent kingdom existing by itself and for itself." This was an allusion to Act X of 1791. Cf. Ch. II, 27 in this book.
[213] *Ibid.*, pp. 251ff.

At his best when criticizing the old order, he was also brilliant in showing the usefulness of his ultimate goals. But Széchenyi was inclined, at least in his published works, to touch rather lightly on the difficulties of putting his proposals into practice, thus raising unjustified hopes among the masses.[214] His correspondence and diaries leave no doubt that he was far from unconcerned with these difficulties; yet it was exactly the agitating style of his major books that was held against him in the great dispute with Kossuth, when Széchenyi seemed rather to overemphasize the importance of manner and tactical considerations in politics.

By the 1840s, however, the political atmosphere of the country had changed. A considerable part of the public tended to belittle the importance of international affairs while debating the issues of Hungarian national development. A decade earlier, Széchenyi had to use persuasive language to substantiate his claim that "the improvement and ennoblement of our domestic conditions depend on us."[215] To justify the claim, the restricted class concept of the privileged had first to be replaced by the reality of a whole nation as visualized by Széchenyi. This is why he made it clear in *Stádium* that he intended to lay a cornerstone weighing 10 million (people) and not merely a few hundred thousand.[216] Thinking of his nation, he planned to erect a pyramid capable of withstanding the corrosive forces of tempests that were bound to come.

[214] Horváth, *Huszonöt év*, I, 277.
[215] *Stádiun*, p. 257.
[216] *Ibid.*, p. 18. Széchenyi also used the term "pyramid" in a symbolic sense. See p. 219 and n. 135 in this chapter. For the source of Arany's image of the "triple pyramid" cf. Vilmos Tolnai, "Adatok Széchenyi és Arany viszonyához," (Data on the Relationship of Széchenyi and Arany) *Philológiai Közlöny*, LV, 29–33.

CHAPTER VII

"Sublime Fatherland"

Stádium was Széchenyi's last great reform work. His next major book, *A kelet népe,* written and published in 1841, was not an organic continuation of his ideas about reform, although it marked an important turning point in his political career. During almost a decade separating the two books, Széchenyi concentrated on promoting the nation's material welfare. Most of his political and literary activities, though not all of them, went to support his economic enterprises.

As early as 1830 Széchenyi dictated the following lines, resembling a political testament, to his young friend Count John Waldstein:

There are but three ways of advancing Hungary's development: nationality, communication [between the different classes of society], and finally commercial links with other nations.

I urge you to take these to heart. The first one, you shall promote according to your best abilities, and you shall adorn it with true nobility. The second one shall materialize through the development of our capital, Budapest. You ought to do your utmost in order that Budapest should cease to be a dead end, and to achieve this goal the Danube has to be opened up for navigation and commerce.[1]

Széchenyi made this statement during a trip to the Lower Danube, undertaken shortly after the publication of *Hitel,* with the purpose of exploring the possibilities of shipping to the Black Sea through the "Iron Gates." On the trip, in mid-July 1830, he became very ill and was tortured by forebodings of death. In his pain the notion of suicide re-emerged in his mind. But he was buoyed by the conviction that despite the errors of his youth "he had been born for virtue," that he must not abandon "his recently established new school in Hungary,"[2] and

---

[1] July 17, 1830, Majláth, ed., *Levelek,* II, 8f.
[2] July 15, 1830, Viszota, ed., *Naplók,* IV, 84. On July 13, 16, and 19, he wrote his last will. B. Szabó, ed., *Adatok,* I, 104ff.

that thanks to Crescence whom he "adores and respects like a sister of angels" he was able to lift his soul to God.[3]

His "new school in Hungary" truly began to bear fruit. The charter of the Academy of Sciences was finally approved by the king and began to function in 1831. During the same year Széchenyi began to agitate for a Hungarian National Theater to be built in Pest to further the cause of nationality and embellish the capital, the population of which was overwhelmingly German at the time. Elected a member of Pest County's Committee for Advancing the National Idiom, chiefly by assisting Hungarian dramatic art, Széchenyi was asked to submit a plan for a national theater.[4] Therefore, he wrote simultaneously with *Stádium* an elaborate pamphlet, *Magyar játékszinrül,* which he published in the spring of 1832.[5] In it Széchenyi suggested that a joint stock company be created for the construction of the theater, an idea he continued to press for in subsequent years. Though his support helped make the opening of the Hungarian National Theater possible in 1837, it did not come into being according to his original plan.[6] In his pamphlet on the theater Széchenyi again emphasized that the nation's creative energies should be concentrated in "Buda-pest," whence they would permeate the entire country.[7] And he again attacked the outmoded feudal financial structure. Parts of his work sounded like a satire on the Hungarian nobility, although he was well aware of the resentment this could provoke.[8]

Horse races, the National Casino, the Academy of Sciences, and the National Theater were to promote Magyar nationality and a concentration of the nation's resources in Budapest by creating a Hungarian public opinion in the capital. Although the first two gave some indirect assistance to commerce, Széchenyi's plan to regulate the Lower Danube and make the entire river navigable was much more important commercially. By establishing regular steamship service between Vienna and

---

[3] Sept. 14, 1830, Viszota, ed., *Naplók,* IV, 117f.

[4] Széchenyi to Wesselényi, Jan. 5, 1832, Majláth, ed., *Levelek,* I, 210.

[5] *Magyar játékszinrül* (On the Hungarian Theater) (Pest: Füstkuti Landerer, 1932).

[6] Just as with the idea of the Academy, that of a permanent Hungarian theatre dated back to 1790, the period of national reaction to Joseph II's efforts at Germanization. On different occasions, the Diet took up the matter of the national theater. In 1807 it was even included among the "grievances" of the country (gravamina). For a summary of the story and Széchenyi's role, see Viszota's introduction to *Naplók,* v, pp. xliv-lxiii; Ferenc Szabolcs, *A nemzeti játékszin eszméje a magyar és német irodalomban* (The Idea of the National Theater in Hungarian and German Literature) (Budapest: Kir. Magyar Egyetemi Ny., 1938), esp. pp. 38–72. Also András Fáy, *Gróf Széchenyi István pestmegyei működése* (Count Stephen Széchenyi's Activities in Pest County) (Budapest: Wodianer, 1925), Postscript by Dezső Rexa.

[7] *Magyar játékszinrül,* pp. 17ff.

[8] Apr. 9, 1832, Viszota, ed., *Naplók,* IV, 257.

Constantinople, Széchenyi hoped to expand the commercial connections of the Habsburg Monarchy with the Balkans, the Middle East, and even southern Russia. Budapest, centrally located on this line, was to become the focal point of Hungarian trade and to develop its own connections with the rest of the world through the Black Sea ports. Instead of merely an insignificant extension of Viennese commercial and banking interests, Budapest was to be an independent Hungarian commercial and industrial emporium with its own port, shipyard, and permanent bridge binding together the western and eastern halves of the country.

Széchenyi never forgot that in order to realize his vision he needed the assistance of the administration and Austrian capital. He even tried to raise money for "his" enterprise in England; in 1834 he placed an advertisement in English papers containing the "Outlines for the Extension of the Company for the Navigation of the Danube, &c". In the advertisement he described his project to the English public:

> In the year 1830, a Company was formed in Austria at the head of which were the first Banking firms of Vienna including Messrs Shuller et C°., Sina, Geymüller, Friesenhof, Benvenuti & c° for the purpose of navigating the River Danube by Steam Boats. The Austrian Government sanctioned the undertaking by granting a Charter, in virtue of which the Proprietors obtained the exclusive privilege of not only navigating the Danube, but also all other navigable Rivers within the Austrian Dominions for a period of 15 years. The Company was formed by the issue of 200 Shares of £50 each, all of which were taken. The Directors immediately ordered a Steam Vessel of 60 horse power to be constructed under the superintendance [sic] of an Englishman, Mr Andrews, upon the most approved principles, and the Engines were procured from the Manufactor of Messrs Boulton & Watt of Soho.
>
> The Vessel was named "Francis 1st" (in compliment to the Emperor of Austria) and commenced running between Vienna, Raab, Pest & Semlin, in the year 1831.[9]

To be sure, Széchenyi was not the initiator of steam navigation on the Danube. Originally he had subscribed to only one share of the steamship company. But after his first trip on the Danube from Pest to Con-

---

[9] Annex No. II, *ibid.*, IV, 710. For Széchenyi's activities with regard to the regulation of the Danube see Viszota's Introductions to *Naplók*, Vols. IV–VI, esp. pp. x–xiv; iv–ix; lix–lxix, resp.; Sándor Lipthay, *Gr. Széchenyi István műszaki alkotásai* (Count Stephen Széchenyi's Technical Constructions) (Budapest: 1896), pp. 44–70. Also the great number of letters and reports published in Majláth, ed., *Levelek*, I–III and B. Szabó, ed., *Adatok*, I–II, as well as his *Ueber die Donaudampfschiffahrt. Aus dem Ung. von Mich. Paziazi* (Buda: 1836). This was a series of 22 articles, originally published in the Hungarian periodical *Társalkodó* (1834–38). For excerpts in English cf. Henry Hajnal, *The Danube* (The Hague: M. Nijhoff, 1920), pp. 130–36.

stantinople his interest in the company considerably increased. From that time on, he encouraged the company to build more ships and extend its lines to Hungarian waters, including later on even the Theiss (Tisza) River. He helped the company to place its shares both in Hungary and abroad, and endeavored to get concessions and privileges for it from the authorities. He urged sending Austrian consuls to the ports of Viddin and Russe (Roustchouk), Bulgaria, and demanded more reasonable customs and quarantine regulations. He also proposed to supply coal free of charge to the steam boats on the Lower Danube for a number of years, arguing that whereas the Monarchy's interests demanded the establishment of regular ship service, the company's investment would not pay off immediately. Moreover, he pointed out that the trade stimulated by the navigation lines would bring new life and industry to the Monarchy's unused mineral resources along the southern borders.[10]

These suggestions were important. Obsolete Austrian quarantine regulations, which had annoyed Széchenyi in some of his earlier voyages, were a real nuisance preventing the development of foreign trade. Shortly after the establishment and gradual expansion of American diplomatic and consular missions in Central Europe during the period 1819 to 1838, a move motivated chiefly by the commercial interests of the United States, American representatives began to complain about their difficulties. According to the report of a tobacco agent submitted to the Department of State in early 1838, ". . . I have had occasion to speak with Prince Metternich, Count Kollowrat, and the Baron Eichoff [sic], on the subject of the quarantine regulations, which have so long served as an insuperable barrier in the way of commerce between this empire and the new world; and I am happy to be able to inform you that all these distinguished and enlightened gentlemen are as surprised at, as they were ignorant of, the existence of such absurd and fatal regulations. They all see the importance of their being immediately revised, and are anxious to have the subject come up from Trieste for consideration."[11]

[10] Széchenyi to Benvenuti, Jan. 5, 1832, Széchenyi to Archduke Palatine Joseph, July 19 and Sept. 16, 1833, Széchenyi to Baron Ottenfels, Sept. 17, 1833, Majláth, ed., Levelek, I, 212f., 253f., 305–308, 312f. Cf. July 14, Aug. 1, 1830, Viszota, ed., Naplók, IV, 82, 93. For the first Austrian efforts to use steamships on the Danube see Hajnal, The Danube, pp. 122–25; A. Hoffmann, "Die Donau und Österreich," SOJ, V (1961), 39ff.

[11] Niles to Murray, Feb. 14, 1838, Sen. Doc. No. 246, 27th Cong., 2d Sess., 1841–42, p. 21. For the first (apparently unheeded) effort to call the British government's attention to the desirability of increasing England's commerce with the Habsburg state, see the private letter written by I. Irving to the Earl of Aberdeen soon after the conclusion of the British-Austrian commercial treaty of 1829. Enclosed with the letter, dated Mar. 4, 1830, was a memorandum of one Mr. Freeland, "a respectable merchant

American representatives, no doubt, did their best to convince the Austrian authorities of the necessity of modernizing the system of imperial customs and quarantine regulations. Yet it was about two years before the "immediate" changes, the reasonableness of which was apparently recognized by the leading statesmen of the empire, were put into practice.[12] The example indicates the bureaucratic obstacles blocking any attempt at reform in the realm of the Habsburgs even when there were no major political issues involved and when officials seemed to agree that the Monarchy too was to benefit from the changes.

Széchenyi, as we have seen, had called attention to outmoded quarantine regulations years before American agents raised the issue. Despite his illness and many adverse circumstances which affected his first trip on the Lower Danube, undertaken in the company of Count Waldstein and hydraulic engineer Beszédes, he also reported with great enthusiasm to Chancellor Reviczky and Archduke Palatine Joseph on the possibilities of "utilizing" the Danube. A comprehensive plan of river regulation, flood control, irrigation, and improved communication—this was Széchenyi's great vision for Hungary and the whole of Danubian Europe. It was the suggestion of an empire-builder who planned for generations[13] and dreamed of a commonwealth of nations. Even on his first trip he thought of winning over Count Kolowrat, influential leader of the Monarchy's domestic affairs by telling him that if the Elbe or Moldau Rivers could be linked with the Danube, the latter's regulation would be most advantageous to Bohemia.[14] Similarly, in 1833 Széchenyi wrote to his

---

of Trieste," which stressed that "The Austrian Government was too deeply committed by a long course of fostering measures towards the Manufacturing Establishments in its Proper States, to admit of a free, or of comparatively free, foreign competition." Hungary, however, which had neither manufactures nor refineries, could give certain advantages, especially if its production and connection with the Adriatic Sea would be improved. At the present, it takes sixty days, and costs ten pounds per ton, to transport hemp from Neusatz (Novi Sad, Ujvidék) to Trieste. The modification of the tariff was also necessary, since Hungary's "raw produce, wool, for instance, pays a duty on admission into Austria, and the cloth, manufactured from it, must again pay a duty on being exported to Hungary." *Aberdeen Papers*, cxcvi, Add. MS 43,234, Folios 288–96, British Museum, London. For a critique of the Austrian "prohibitive system" by leading Austrian officials in the years 1840–41 cf. Adolf Beer, *Die Österreichische Handelspolitik im neunzehnten Jahrhundert* (Vienna: Vlg. Manz, 1891), pp. 16–20.

[12] For detailed references see George Barany, "The Interest of the United States in Central Europe: Appointment of the First American Consul to Hungary," *Papers of the Michigan Academy of Science, Arts, and Letters*, xLVII (1962), 275–79.

[13] Széchenyi to Archduke Palatine Joseph, Aug. 24, 1830, Majláth, ed., *Levelek*, i, 173. Cf. same to Reviczky, Aug. 13, 1830, *ibid.*, i, 169. For modern plans to enhance the commercial value of the Danube, see Stephen Gorove, *Law and Politics of the Danube* (The Hague: M. Nijhoff, 1964), pp. 8–11, 149–52, 155, and the July 1968 number of *Österreichische Ost-hefte*, x, esp. pp. 209ff., 226f., 242f., 245.

[14] July 1, 1830, Viszota, ed., *Naplók*, iv, 65f. Legislation for the construction of the Elbe-Moldau-Danube Canal was passed some 70 years later, in 1901, so that it was

friend Baron Ottenfels, internuncio of the Monarchy in Constantinople, about the significance of the Danube as an international waterway, asking him to use his influence with Metternich in favor of the project. In this letter he also stressed that the private company to be established for the exploitation of Danubian trade could promote Bohemian and Styrian products, thereby arousing interest in the project both in the Monarchy and in Germany and helping the administration obtain "a foothold in countries where we have little influence at the present."[15]

---

more than a century before the plan materialized. Actually, official plans aimed at linking the Monarchy's waterways with each other and with the German lands antedated Széchenyi. This, however, does not detract from the value of either his initiative or his willingness to work for putting into practice what was indeed a task for several generations. For earlier suggestions about connecting the Danube and Theiss Rivers, and improvement of communications with the Adriatic port of Fiume, see Docs. 207 and 208 in Domanovaszky, ed., *József nádor*, IV, 617–44 (Reports of Palatine Joseph). Cf. Beer, *Österreichische Handelspolitik*, pp. 38, 434f., 568 and n. 9.

[15] Széchenyi to Ottenfels, Sept. 17, 1833, Majláth, ed., *Levelek*, I, 313f. It is interesting to notice, in this context, the following, somewhat overoptimistic, excerpts from contemporary reports of the U.S. Consulate at Vienna:

> . . . It appears to me that it would be highly advantageous for the American manufacturers to make purchases in Hungary direct, which would enable them to compete with effect in the East India markets, for which at this moment generally the wool is purchased, and as the cloths are not of the very super-fine, the competition were easier. But should the United States manufactories not be sufficient, the wool may be made up into cloth in Bohemia, where labor is so very cheap and where they have excellent manufactories for the fabrication of middling fine cloths, which are the very sort for the East India market, now much in demand in England, and in the manufacture of which Hungarian wool is much consumed. The Hungarians might undertake these speculations themselves were they acquainted with the sea trade; but they are not, and as Austria has no communication with the East Indies, it would be a great advantage for the merchants of the United States to avail themselves of these circumstances. The same may be done with the metallic produces of Austria, particularly quicksilver, to which I have alluded in my former reports. In return to these articles may be brought cotton, the consumption of which article augments every year in this country, single manufactories of which order at once from the Viceroy of Egypt one and a half million of pounds.
> . . . A great undertaking is begun to open the navigation of the Danube between Semlin and Orsawa, by removing the rocks called the "Iron Doors," which, though in the territory of Turkey, yet this expensive work is carried on by the Austrian military, and will shortly open the navigation to the Black Sea: now a 3d small steam vessel runs between this and Semlin, and so, in time much may be expected, as there is a talk of connecting the Rhine with the Danube, and thus one could travel to Trebizund, and from thence there are, as you know, three easy ways to India. This by an enterprising nation, and under the direction of another more commercial government, would lead to great results, but, alas, it will hardly be of any great account. It might probably be very beneficial if some spirited persons were to profit of this occasion by forming a company of steam vessels, and so take out a patent for the Black Sea. They are here, and still more on the Black Sea, very unskilful in ship-building, and know very little of steam engines.
> . . . The Danube is already navigable to the Black Sea, and only a few rocks more are to be blown to make the navigation very convenient. Should the Danube

This time Metternich had no objections. As French diplomats suggested, Metternich, worried perhaps that the Prussian-led *Zollverein* could exclude the Habsburg states, especially Bohemia, from the German markets, wanted to have another outlet besides the Elbe River for Austrian products. Improvement of Danubian navigation, especially if supplemented by a revision of some tariff regulations, could also help the states of southern Germany, strengthening their ties with Austria rather than Prussia. At any rate, the chancellor thanked the palatine for the information (supplied by Széchenyi) with regard to the Danube regulation and emphasized the importance of the undertaking from the point of view of Hungarian, Austrian, German, and world trade. He also stressed that the political conditions were never more favorable for an enterprise of such common usefulness. Agreeing with Széchenyi that besides overcoming the physical obstacles hampering the utilization of "that invaluable waterway," he added that the royal commissioner (in this case, Széchenyi) would need administrative and financial assistance to be able to fulfill his task.[16] At the request of the palatine, Széchenyi accepted in the spring of 1833[17] the "special mission" of regulating the navigation on the Lower Danube "flowing by the Turkish-Serbian and Wallachian provinces."[18]

It would lead us far beyond the scope of the present study if we tried to give a detailed account of Széchenyi's activities connected with the regulation of the Lower Danube. Including his exploratory journey of 1830, he made at least 10 major trips to the Lower Danube between that date and 1846, occasionally spending weeks and months on the spot in planning, directing, and supervising the road-building, construction work, and blasting of rocks in the narrow passages between Belgrade and Viddin, called the Iron Gates. The technical director, and Széchenyi's right-hand man at the Lower Danube was Paul Vásárhelyi, a

---

be brought into communication with the Rhine, a great flux of trade is expected to this part of Europe.

Schwarz to McLane, Aug. 15, 1833 and Apr. 10, 1834, Schwarz to Forsyth, Mar. 10, 1835, *House Ex. Doc. No. 71*, 31st Cong., 1st Sess., pp. 16, 21, 26.

[16] Oct. 5, 1833, B. Szabó, ed., *Adatok*, I, 186f. Cf. Beer, *Österreichische Handelspolitik*, p. 568 and n. 8. For the French reports see de Brussière to de Broglie, Mar. 18, Ste-Aulaire to de Broglie, Apr. 11, 1833, Vol. 418, *Correspondance politique, Autriche;* and La Rochefoucauld to de Broglie, July 12, 1835, Vol. 422, *ibid.*, Archives du Ministère des Affaires Etrangères (Paris).

[17] Széchenyi to Archduke Palatine Joseph, June 25, 1833, Majláth, ed., *Levelek*, I, 237, June 24, July 2, 1833, Viszota, ed., *Naplók*, IV, 383f.

[18] *"Regulandae in inferiori Danubii provinciae Turcico-Servias et Valachias alluente navigationis":* the expression was used by the palatine in a letter to the lieutenancy. In it he supported Széchenyi's request for a passport to England. Nov. 12, 1833, B. Szabó, ed., *Adatok*, I, 191.

Hungarian engineer, who also assisted him in the regulation of the Theiss River in the 1840s. As Széchenyi foresaw, the funds of the treasury were insufficient to accomplish the entire task along the Lower Danube. Despite his efforts, work stopped in 1837, to be resumed only toward the end of the century. Even so, he laid the groundwork for subsequent decades, and more important perhaps, he called the attention of future Austro-Hungarian statesmen to the Monarchy's vital interest in the Balkans.

One may only speculate to what an extent, had Széchenyi received from the administration all the assistance he needed, his efforts could have speeded up the economic evolution of the Balkans at a time when the political atmosphere was, if not "more favorable than ever," as Metternich intimated, at least less adverse to the Habsburg state than after the revolutionary period of 1848–49. At that time, Hungarian circles suggested that Austria-Hungary disengage itself from German and Italian affairs in order to live up to its "mission" in southeastern Europe. Using some of Széchenyi's ideas as a vehicle, one of the proponents of such a foreign policy, Baron Sigismund Kemény, proposed the reopening of the Oriental question to forestall the national movements in the Balkans from extending to the South Slav and Romanian population of Hungary. This essentially anti-Russian concept of the Monarchy's mission in the Balkans, also advocated by Count Julius Andrássy, was closely related to the idea of Magyar domination over the non-Magyars within the Hungarian "political nation."[19]

Although Széchenyi expected the strengthening of "Hungarismus" in Hungary proper and the increase of the Monarchy's influence on the Balkan peninsula as a result of his work on the Lower Danube, the idea of domineering was far from him. But it is true that it was difficult to draw a line in such a case, as he himself was to soon realize.

There were other sides to Széchenyi's "special mission" besides its economic and technological aspects, which contribute essential features to our portrait of him. His talent for organization enabled him to put to work the Austrian and Hungarian civilian and military authorities. He used all his connections—in the administration, with the steamship company, in the diplomatic corps, and in England—to further his aims.

[19] Zsigmond Kemény, "Még egy szó a forradalom után" (Yet Another Word after the Revolution), in *Báró Kemény Zsigmond Összes Művei* (Complete Works of Baron Sigismund Kemény), ed. Paul Gyulai, XII (Budapest: Franklin, 1908), 206–398; Imre Gonda, *Bismarck és az 1867-es osztrák-magyar kiegyezés* (Bismarck and the Austro-Hungarian Compromise of 1867) (Budapest: Akadémiai kiadó, 1960), pp. 23–27, Domokos Kosáry, "Kemény és Széchenyi 1849 után" (Kemény and Széchenyi after 1849), *Irodalomtörténeti Közlemények*, LXVII (1963), 160–68. Cf. George Barany, "Hungary: The Uncompromising Compromise," *The Austrian History Yearbook*, III (1967), Pt. I, 245f.

It was not an easy task to provide his enterprise with money, machinery, supplies, and skilled labor in those rugged and backward regions of old Hungary. Most of the time Széchenyi managed to do it, but he sometimes complained bitterly that the "moral obstacles" hampered his work[20] and hindered his efforts more stubbornly than the rocks in the straits. Afraid that in the long run the bureaucratic imbroglio involving the emperor-king, the palatine, the Hungarian chancery, the *Hofkriegsrat,* and the estates might let him down "out of jealousy, vindictiveness, prejudice, stupidity, and laziness,"[21] he yet decided to swallow his pride and continue to cool his heels in the waitingrooms of the great in order to prepare what he envisaged to be the future of the Austrian Monarchy.[22]

Another remarkable thing about Széchenyi was the tact and diplomatic skill with which he secured the cooperation of all interested parties, including the Sublime Porte, Serbian and Romanian princes, and Russian generals. His correspondence and contacts with this international body are most interesting. He carried his point by "proving" that besides Austria, it was rather the party in question that had a vital interest in accomplishing his project. From Prince Miloš of Serbia he bought breeding boars and brood-sows for the palatine, emphasizing the importance of steamboats "intended for the conveyance only of swine."[23] To Prince Alexander Ghica he pointed out that his protection of the steamship company would invigorate commerce between the Romanian provinces and the lands of the Habsburgs.[24]

Széchenyi also had to obtain the support or at least benevolent neutrality of the Russians who had most to say in the regions of the Lower Danube since the Peace of Adrianople (1829). Part of the negotiations were carried on by the Austrian and Russian ambassadors to Constantinople; as a result of instructions given by the governor-general, Count Kiselev, Széchenyi found a friendly reception upon entering Wallachian territory in the summer of 1833.[25] In a letter addressed directly to the commander-in-chief of the Russian forces then occupying the Romanian

[20] Széchenyi to Reviczky, Jan. 23, 1835, B. Szabó, ed., *Adatok,* I, 220, same to Benvenuti, Aug. 25, 1833, Majláth, ed., *Levelek,* I, 289.

[21] Széchenyi to Baron Puthon, July 12, 1833. *ibid.,* I, 244.

[22] Dec. 6, 1833, Viszota, ed., *Naplók,* IV, 433. Cf. Beer, *Die Österreichische Handelspolitik,* pp. 25ff., showing also the bureaucratic obstacles blocking the development of the Adriatic port of Trieste, an alternative to Danubian shipping.

[23] Széchenyi to Miloš Obrenović, July 11, and Aug. 17, 1833, Majláth, ed., *Levelek,* I, 241, 285; "Outlines for the Extension of the Company for the Navigation of the Danube," Annex No. II, Viszota, ed., *Naplók,* IV, 711; Széchenyi to Schedius, July 19, beginning of Sept., and Sept. 26, 1833, B. Szabó, ed., *Adatok,* I, 182, 184, 186.

[24] Széchenyi to Alexander Ghica, Sept. 13, 1834, Majláth, ed., *Levelek,* I, 504.

[25] Széchenyi to Baron Ottenfels, Aug. 2, 1833, *ibid.,* I, 261f.

Principalities, Széchenyi stressed the community of interests of all parties concerned, as the opening of the Danube to steamships would be "an incalculable gain to both Hungary and Wallachia," saying that "it would be an entirely new source of riches for both the Austrian Monarchy and the great Empire of All the Russias."[26]

In 1834 Széchenyi spoke of his work on the Lower Danube with Russian Ambassador Pozzo di Borgo in Paris. For a moment he thought he had won Russian support for his project.[27] But he noted a few months later that the Russian envoy in Constantinople, who in public was in favor of making the straits at the Iron Gates navigable, said entirely different things to Turkish officials in private conversations.[28] Not quite sure of the Russians, Széchenyi feared even more the secret opposition of the English government, whose commercial interests might have been damaged by the improvement of the continental route through the establishment of the Vienna-Constantinople line. Consequently he advised the Austrian internuncio to try to obtain the benevolence of the Russian government by pointing out this presumed opposition of the British in the negotiations in the Ottoman capital;[29] in England he himself intended to use the opposite side of the same argument.[30]

The purpose of Széchenyi's official trip to England in early January 1834 was to obtain technical information for the Lower Danube enterprise.[31] But he used the opportunity to lobby for his project by visiting important members of the government, leaders of the opposition, and Nathan Rothschild.[32] He handed over copies of the "Outlines for the Extension of the Company for the Navigation of the Danube" to the Duke of Wellington; Lordchancellor Lord Brougham, Chancellor of the Duchy of Lancaster; Lord Holland; Prime Minister Lord Grey; Secretary of State for Foreign Affairs Lord Palmerston; First Lord of the Admiralty Sir James Graham; Sir Robert Peel; Chief Secretary for Ireland E. J. Littleton; and Secretary of State for War and Colonies E. G. Stanley.[33] A few weeks later Sir James Graham, who seemed to have been won over by Széchenyi, nonetheless protested on behalf of his government against the project.[34] Thus Széchenyi's previous suspicions appeared to

[26] Széchenyi to Kiselev, July 31, 1833, *ibid.*, I, 260f.
[27] Jan. 3, 1834, Viszota, ed., *Naplók*, IV, 441.
[28] Sept. 19, 1834, *ibid.*, IV, 494.
[29] Széchenyi to Baron Stürmer, Aug. 11, Sept. 21, 1833, Majláth, ed., *Levelek*, I, 273, 315ff.
[30] Mar. 19, 1834, Viszota, ed., *Naplók*, IV, 462.
[31] According to an official letter addressed to Ambassador Paul Esterházy, which Széchenyi copied into his diary on Jan. 19, 1834, *ibid.*, IV, 445.
[32] Mar. 15, 18, 1834, *ibid.*, IV, 461.
[33] *Ibid.*, IV, 462. For the text of the "Outlines," see Annex No. II, *ibid.*, IV, 710–13.
[34] Apr. 11, 1834, *ibid.*, IV, 472.

be wellfounded; in spite of his valiant efforts it was not easy to play off Britain and Russia against each other.

Széchenyi had less reason to fear the British than he had thought at the time. He the "anglomaniac" would have preferred American steamers to English because "we know that the United States of America lead the way in river navigation." But besides the public's mistrust of American ships and the long waiting period from order to delivery, he also assumed even in 1835 that "the English would have been against our dealings with Russia and Turkey, if we had placed the order elsewhere. . . ."[35]

He was of course right in taking for granted that trade and politics went hand-in-hand in those days, too. Besides, the British were rather sensitive in that new phase of the "Eastern Question," which began in 1833 with the treaties of Unkiar Skelessi and Münchengrätz. They suspected, erroneously, that the first treaty had turned the sultan into a vassal of the tsar and that the second had sanctioned a deal in which Austria and Russia agreed on dividing the Ottoman empire. In fact, the treaty of Unkiar Skelessi, which gave some advantages to Russia, did not place Russia in a privileged position vis-à-vis England, and at Münchengrätz Metternich succeeded in undermining the Russian position by making the Europeanization of the Oriental question an integral part of the Russo-Austrian alliance.[36] Among the great powers immediately interested in the Balkans and the Near East, Austria was the weakest, especially if one keeps in mind that Prussia had no direct interest in the area and the July Monarchy had yet to overcome on the domestic and international scenes the handicaps related to its very birth. Still, the split that developed between the three conservative east European powers—Russia, Prussia, and Austria on the one hand, and their liberal counterparts, England and France, on the other, due to their differing views on Belgium and Portugal—gave Austria a certain maneuvering possibility in an area where the maintenance of the status quo, symbolized by the preservation of the Ottoman empire seemed to be of paramount importance to all. In a sense, Austria held the balance of power in that conflict of interest which eventually contributed to the Crimean War but which began to take shape first in the 1830s.[37]

In this initial period of steam shipping, Russian and Austrian com-

---

[35] Cited in Hajnal, *The Danube*, pp. 134f.

[36] Philip Mosely, *Russian Diplomacy and the Opening of the Eastern Question in 1838 and 1839* (Cambridge: Harvard University Press, 1934), pp. 7–30; Nicholas V. Riasanovsky, *Nicholas I and Official Nationality in Russia, 1825–1855* (Berkeley-Los Angeles: University of California Press, 1959), pp. 238–46, 260–63).

[37] Vernon John Puryear, *International Economics and Diplomacy in the Near East* (Stanford: Stanford University Press, 1935), p. 7.

panies coordinated their services on the Danube and the Black Sea; indeed, Austrian vessels held first place throughout the decade in the carrying trade of Odessa, outdoing both Russian and British shipping in that most important port of export in southern Russia.[38] Due to the rapid economic growth of its southern provinces in the early 19th century, Russia's export of grain from Black Sea ports increased "until it constituted from a third to a half of all Russian exports." In time this circumstance became "a major motivating factor" in Russia's policy toward the Straits and the Balkans.[39] But in the 30s such pressure had not yet materialized. Whatever competition there was with Russia's foreign trade in the Black Sea ports came not from *outside* sources, in the strict sense of the word, but from the Danubian Principalities which owed their exemption from restrictive Turkish commercial regulations to the very Treaty of Adrianople that gave Russia control over the mouth of the Danube and hence also over Danubian trade. Moreover, England was the best consumer of grain and other Russian products, and British merchants dominated the Russian markets. Not until the mid-1840s, when Greece, Turkey, and Turkey's Danubian provinces became better customers of Great Britain than Russia, did British officials show serious concern over Russian quarantine regulations, neglect of the maintenance of the delta region, and hence unfair interference with Danubian commerce.[40] A British investigation in 1837 found that "Russia was doing everything to facilitate navigation" in the Danube delta.[41] Aware of the inconsistencies of Russian policies, Széchenyi himself acknowledged both the help given to him personally during his negotiations in the Principalities and the Russian mediation, which assisted the Austrian steamship company in settling a dispute with Turkish authorities concerning the regular boat service between Constantinople and Smyrna.[42]

Political rather than economic controversies lay at the roots of that potentially dangerous conflict which involved Great Britain and Russia in the 1830s. Or, as has been pointed out, it was the British Whig government's, especially Palmerston's, close identification with the liberal movement all over the continent that seemed to represent a challenge

---

[38] *Ibid.*, pp. 110f., 130ff.

[39] Cyril E. Black, "Russia and the Modernization of the Balkans," in Charles and Barbara Jelavich, eds., *The Balkans in Transition* (Berkeley-Los Angeles: University of California Press, 1963), p. 149.

[40] Vernon John Puryear, *England, Russia, and the Straits Question, 1844-1856* (Berkeley: University of California Press, 1931), pp. 82-97; Puryear, *International Economics*, pp. 108f., 127-39.

[41] *Ibid.*, p. 137.

[42] Hajnal, *The Danube*, pp. 55, 133.

to the absolutist regimes of eastern Europe even in their own spheres of influence, namely, the German lands and Central Europe. It has also been said, however, that the Eastern Question tended to "cut across the two *blocs* which had formed in Europe and in a short space dissolved them."[43] Ideologically bound to Nicholas I, "the policeman of Europe," and resentful, not entirely without justification, of Palmerston's personality and methods, Metternich did his best to bring about this result. His first aim was to split the Anglo-French entente of the early 1830s because he regarded France as a hotbed of revolutionary conspiracies. But he also knew that Austria's long-term interests required a counterbalance in the Balkans in order to offset the overwhelming power of friendly Russia. Russia had imposed the principle of free navigation on the Danube on Turkey in the Peace of Adrianople, and became the mistress of that great river as a consequence of the same treaty.[44] In view of the strong and adverse Anglo-French reaction to Münchengrätz, Metternich repeatedly and emphatically assured Britain that the tsar did not wish to seize Constantinople. Although he could not completely allay Palmerston's suspicions, his good offices contributed to a certain relaxation of the tension between the two power blocs by 1834–35.[45]

Mistrusting both Russia and Austria, Palmerston refused to give serious consideration to Metternich's overtures aimed at forming an essentially anti-French coalition, only to return to the idea some five years later at the time of yet another crisis in the Near East.[46] Viewed against this background, British reluctance to give unqualified support to Austrian projects on the Lower Danube becomes more understandable. Although Széchenyi did not elaborate on his conversations with Sir James Graham, it is quite probable that the latter's "protest" may have been an expression of England's interest in the Danubian area and of British resentment of any unilateral action, rather than of a determination to obstruct Széchenyi's efforts. British opposition to the development of Danubian shipping was neither absolute nor unchangeable, as shown by a report of Sir Frederic Lamb to Palmerston. According to the English ambassador at Vienna, impediments to the navigation of the Danube should continue, but "if we succeed in obtaining a favourable commercial

---

[43] Charles Webster, *The Foreign Policy of Palmerston*, 2 vols. (London: G. Bell & Sons, 1951), I, 3, 221.

[44] Puryear, *International Economics*, pp. 5ff., 134f., 185, 189ff.; Puryear, *England, Russia, and the Straits Question*, pp. 131ff.

[45] *Ibid.*, pp. 15–27, 106f.; Webster, *Foreign Policy of Palmerston*, I, 342–46. Cf. Lamb to Palmerston, Aug. 5, 1836, *F.O.* 7/257, Public Record Office (London).

[46] Harold Temperley, *England and the Near East, The Crimea* (Longmans, Green and Co., 1936), pp. 8off.

Treaty, the reverse will be in England's interest."[47] In another report written in July 1837 the envoy expressed the view, based on the project of the convention of commerce and navigation, that the political importance of the treaty might outweigh its commercial value. Lamb predicted that the British-Austrian agreement then under consideration could be the link between the heterogeneous parts of "this Great Central Empire." He also added that it could contribute "to the establishment of a liberal administrative system in this Country, by which both its external strength and its independence of all Neighbouring States can not fail to be increased."[48]

Palmerson certainly disagreed with the optimistic second half of his ambassador's proposition. Evaluating the desirability of replacing in Serbia the influence of Russia with that of Austria, he asserted that "The Austrian Govt. is always so alarmed at the Progress of Political innovation, and at the appearance of Representative Institutions in any Country at all neighbouring upon Austria, that there can be no doubt that [crossed out: "all"] the Influence of Austria in Servia would be employed to prevent the progress of Improvement in the Govt. of that Country."[49]

Palmerston's disillusioned view of Austrian resistance to change, expressed in rather scornful language in some of the foreign secretary's dispatches (sent through the post to make sure Metternich read them),[50] was nevertheless close to reality. This can be seen from the definition of Austria's "mission," given by the Austrian chancellor in reply to British protests against the treatment of the Republic of Cracow by Russia, Prussia, and Austria. Indignant because of Palmerston's intention to send a British consul to the Polish city-state Metternich questioned England's right, based on the multilateral agreements reached at the Congress of Vienna, to interfere with the decisions of the three "creative and protective" powers of the East. Austria, said Metternich, was a great power placed in the center of the continent where it was promoting a conservative and peaceful policy. In order to fulfill its role effectively, it was necessary *"que l'Autriche ne soit point troublée dans les principes mêmes de son existence."*[51] In a confidential letter explaining that Aus-

---

[47] Lamb to Palmerston, May 14, 1837, *F.O. 7/264*, PRO (London). In a letter dated Dec. 11, 1967, J. T. Ward, author of the recent biography *Sir James Graham* (London-New York: Macmillan, 1967), has kindly informed me that he found no reference to a meeting or discussion between Széchenyi and Sir James Graham in the latter's correspondence. In his words, "it seems likely that Graham would not have cause to write about the matter."

[48] Lamb to Palmerston, July 3, 1837, *F.O. 7/264*, PRO (London).

[49] Palmerston to Lamb, Oct. 7, 1837, *F.O. 7/263*, PRO (London).

[50] Webster, *Foreign Policy of Palmerston*, I, 357.

[51] Metternich to Hummelauer, May 9, 1836, *F.O. 7/260*, PRO (London) (Italics in original).

tria's interests were identical with those of England in the Orient, the chancellor elaborated, in the spirit of Francis I's legacy, on what he considered to be the fundamental principles of the Habsburg empire's existence:

> *Un grand Etat placé au centre de l'Europe, servant ainsi de lien entre l'occident et l'Orient (sic), comme entre le midi et le nord, doit, s'il veut remplir la tâche que la Providence lui a imposée, tenir éloigné de lui tout mouvement désordonné, puisqu'un tel mouvement n'a jamais de limites connues ni même applicables. Un état dans cette position centrale doit rester immobile, car son mouvement ébranlerait tout autour de lui.*[52]

The Whig government in England, especially Palmerston, were supporters of both a strong Central Europe and the liberal movement.[53] Vienna's reluctance to go along with reforms that might smack of an intention to abandon the "policy" of immobility and Austria's (as well as Prussia's) submissiveness to Russia, an attitude Palmerston tried to change by proving that Russians were not ten feet tall,[54] left relatively little room to the British for maneuvering. This can be seen from Palmerston's meddling with Serbian affairs, an effort that showed him at his worst.[55] Surely the foreign secretary failed to make adequate diplomatic preparations to promote the two objects his government had in view with respect to Serbia, namely, that Serbia "should form a barrier against the further encroachments of Russia," and that Serbia "should afford an opening for the extension of the commerce of Great Britain." It is also true that to achieve these ambitious goals Palmerston had to attempt to obtain the assistance of Austria, a country he suspected of trying "to keep things stationary" in Serbia and of coming perhaps to an understanding with Russia about dividing Serbia. The most important aspect of Palmerston's Serbian adventure, however, was not its failure but rather the endeavor to find an alternative to both the ascendancy of Russian and Austrian influence in Serbia. While pointing out to Lamb that Austria's predominance would be essentially defensive and hence preferable to Russia's, which would be used for offensive purposes directed against countries beyond Serbia, he nevertheless stressed that the

---

[52] Metternich to Esterházy, Dec. 1, 1836, *ibid.* (italics added). For a French description of the Austrian "mission of immobility" cf. Ste-Aulaire to Thiers, Mar. 16, 1836, Vol. 423, *Correspondance politique, Autriche,* Archives du Ministère des Affaires Etrangères (Paris).

[53] Webster, *Foreign Policy of Palmerston,* I, 3, 221ff., 236f., 369.

[54] Palmerston to Lamb, Dec. 8, 1837, *F.O. 7/263,* PRO (London).

[55] Webster, *Foreign Policy of Palmerston,* II, 576–79.

rise of Austrian influence "would not be unattended with Evils although of a different Nature from those which would follow the Dictation of Russia." Austrian and British interests coincided only insofar as both countries needed a bulwark against Russian atttck. But with respect to "the principles of political Improvement," he added, "the views and interests of Great Britain would differ from those of the Cabinet of Vienna."

The Servia of Prince Miloš Obrenović was not the best place for introducing,[56] in Palmerston's words, "progressive improvements." The foreign secretary wanted to render persons and property more secure, increase the authority of the law, call into full activity the industry of the population, and properly develop the natural resources of the country. Moreover, Palmerston did not wish to disturb the political status quo in the Balkans, which meant "keeping Servia as She is, with respect to political Dependence." Still, the attempt to give the Servian people "an Interest in maintaining their present political Position" and to open to them "for that purpose such a Prospect of internal Prosperity, as may render them unwilling to be incorporated with the Russian Empire" should not be casually dismissed as a mere reflection of England's undoubtedly increasing strategic and commercial interests in the Near East.[57] The idea that an increase in commerce of Great Britain with Servia, the second object mentioned in Palmerston's instructions, "can evidently be attained by no other means than by the gradual Improvement of the Country," and the repeated emphasis on the need for "encouraging [Palmerston crossed out: "furthering" and then also "promoting" in order to find the proper word] improvement in Servia" show how purposefully the foreign secretary wanted to apply British trade as a lever to enhance the political stability of southeastern Europe.

More successful,[58] and in the long run also more significant, than his experiment in Servia, was Palmerston's effort to cooperate with Austria against Russia in the question of Danubian trade and navigation. Here the commercial interests of both countries seemed to require the confirmation of the principle of free navigation against any potential Russian restrictions. The negotiations, which began in 1836 and led to the conclusion of a treaty two years later, were aimed at broadening the provisions of the Austrian-English commercial agreement of 1829. The correspondence relevant to the protracted discussions of the new

---

[56] L. S. Stavrianos, *The Balkans since 1453* (New York: Rinehart, 1958), pp. 251ff. The citations in this and the preceding paragraphs are from Palmerston to Lamb, Oct. 7, 1837, *F.O. 7/263*, PRO (London).
[57] Stavrianos, *Balkans since 1453*, pp. 319ff.
[58] Webster, *Foreign Policy of Palmerston*, II, 579ff.

treaty—made particularly difficult not only by the intricate Austrian commercial system of prohibitions customarily mentioned in this context but also by British unwillingness to grant full reciprocity to Austrian carrying trade, instead of the treatment given to "most favored nations"—clearly reveals Great Britain's growing determination to stimulate the economic evolution of the area exposed to Russian penetration in accordance with Britain's own liberal policies.

The widening of the British political horizon created some favorable conditions for the national awakening of the peoples of eastern Central Europe. Ambassador Lamb, more conservative than Palmerston and more sympathetic to Metternich's policy, tried to convince the leaders of the Austrian government of the beneficial political results of "a revisal of their commercial system." Sir Frederic, an old friend of Széchenyi's and the brother of Prime Minister Lord Melbourne, reported on one of his conversations with the chancellor:

I have represented to Prince Metternich that the unity and vitality of their Empire are attached to it [the revisal of the Austrian commercial system], that in the East they are menaced by the advancing civilization of Russia, to which no solid resistance can be opposed unless it be met by another civilization, that it is for Austria to put herself at the head of this, to begin by Hungary, and extend it gradually along with Commerce and wealth throughout the whole of the Countries bordering on the Danube, as far as the Black Sea.—That the Commerce by the Danube will at the same time give to Bavaria and Wurtemberg a community of interests with Austria, and counterbalance the ascendancy which Prussia has acquired over them.[59]

According to the envoy, Metternich was "not insensible to these reasonings," which he also strived to convey to other "leading Persons in the State" in order to "overthrow," as he put it, "their confidence in their present System." Lamb, who claimed to have succeeded in proving the inadequacies of the Austrian commercial system, was cautious enough to add: "Whether they will have vigour to change it is another question, and one which is yet doubtful."[60] There is little doubt, however, that Széchenyi would have been pleased with the language used in the ambassador's report.

The parallelisms between the English ambassador's report and some of Széchenyi's ideas may well be sheer coincidence. But we know that the British kept a close watch on the progress made on the Lower Dan-

[59] Lamb to Palmerston, Dec. 29, 1837, (no. 93), *F.O. 7/266*, PRO (London).
[60] *Ibid.*

ube, relating it to the prospects of trade with Britain. In one of the enclosures attached to Lamb's account of the "Difficulties in the way of concluding a Commercial arrangement with Austria according to the instructions of V^t Palmerston," the representative of the Board of Trade in the negotiations, John McGregor, reported:

> Count Sekcheniyi [sic] has just arrived here from Pesth, in order to further arrangements to remove completely the obstructions at the Eisen Thor [Iron Gates] in the Danube, and he and all leading Hungarians are very anxious to have a commercial intercourse with England, to enable them to have a demand for their own Commodities and to be supplied with our fabrics. I wish much that Prince Esterházy were here at present.
> The Steam Navigation of the Danube from Ulm downwards to Vienna will be in operation it is stated in June.[61]

Indeed, the intricate negotiations concerning the commercial treaty to be concluded between Austria and England reveal some of the most fascinating and significant aspects of the history of Central Europe in the 19th century. Historians who have reproached Széchenyi for giving preference to Danubian navigation instead of attending the sessions of the Diet tend to underestimate the relationship of economics and political evolution in the modern world. This connection must be grasped in order to be able to comprehend the goals of British policy toward Austria and the underdeveloped area of southeastern Europe.

As stated in Palmerston's instructions to Lamb, the Board of Trade wanted to include certain articles of British manufacture in the list of commodities on which Austrian import duties were to be lowered. Accordingly, "the insertion of British cotton goods, woolens, and hardwares in that List would be of great importance; and such a reduction of Duty on these Commodities, as might permit them to be consumed in the States of Hungary, and in the Southern Provinces of Austria, would be the only means of extending our intercourse with those Provinces."[62]

[61] McGregor's report of Apr. 30, 1837, enclosed with Denis Le Marchant to Palmerston, May 11, 1837, *F.O.* 7/269, PRO (London). Széchenyi first met McGregor during his visit to England in early 1834. Jan. 25, 1834, Viszota, ed., *Naplók*, IV, 446. He had dinner in ambassador Lamb's home in Vienna in August 1832 and May 1840; the latter, in turn, visited Széchenyi in Hungary in the fall of 1836. Aug. 10, 1832, Oct. 19, 1836, May 18, 1840, *ibid.*, IV, 287, V, 29, 385. A few weeks before Lamb's report to Palmerston Széchenyi noted in his diary that the British ambassador was extremely friendly to him. Sept. 28, 1837, *ibid.*, V, 118. For other contacts cf. Apr. 4, 1834 and Nov. 1, 1836, *ibid.*, IV, 470 and V, 31.

[62] Palmerston to Lamb, Sept. 30, 1837, *F.O.* 7/263, PRO (London). Cf. Office of the Committee of Privy Council for Trade to Backhouse, July 24, 1837 and Board of Trade to Palmerston, Aug. 1, 1837, *F.O.* 7/269, PRO (London).

Opposed by bankers and entrepreneurs in Vienna,[63] the reduction of import duties would also have meant a considerable loss of revenue to the Austrian treasury that it could hardly afford. Hence Kolowrat, who was basically in favor of better commercial relations with England and actively participated in the discussions, offered a gradual change of the tariff system, insisting, at the same time, on complete reciprocity for Austrian carrying trade with British shipping. This proposal prevented the parties from making progress for many months. As Lamb remarked in a report on the arrival of an American tobacco agent in Vienna, the Austrian government "feels that there are facilities for treating with the United States which do not exist with us. They have no Navigation Law. They have no Manufactures, and thus the two main difficulties in framing a Treaty with England are avoided."[64]

In reply to some of Kolowrat's strong reservations about the British proposals, McGregor accepted the extension of the principle of reciprocity with English ships, in addition to all vessels under the Austrian flag carrying Austrian products or goods imported from Austrian ports, also to Austrian ships arriving from the ports of the Danube and the Ionian Islands, then administered by Britain, confining the clause of the "most favored nation" vis-à-vis Austria only to direct trade between different parts of the British empire and England's foreign commerce with other countries.

Explaining his obligation to abide by the main provisions of the British Navigation Act of 1833, McGregor reminded Kolowrat that ". . . with England *the policy paramount to all others,* is that of *maintaining Naval supremacy:* & this policy on the part of England is even of the highest importance to Austria, in the event of a general war in Europe. . . ." As an example he referred to the role played by the British fleet in the Napoleonic wars, suggesting also that some of the privileges preserved for British commercial navigation served the purpose of making available a permanent pool of sailors in time of war. In offering extended benefits to Austrian shipping, McGregor expressed the hope that ". . . Austria would sufficiently relax her *Anti-commercial system* to create an *International* Commerce *forward,* &, *vice-versa,* through Hungary, *to* & *from*

---

[63] Webster, *Foreign Policy of Palmerston,* II, 580. For the fears of Austrian business circles about British competition, see Beer, *Österreichische Handelspolitik,* pp. 311–16.

[64] Lamb to Palmerston, Dec. 29, 1837 (no. 91), *F.O. 7/266,* PRO (London). Actually, as seen from a French report, both American (Niles) and British (McGregor) negotiators complained about the "impossibility" of negotiating with the Austrians. Louis de Ste-Aulaire to Molé, Feb. 2, 1838, Vol. 425, *Correspondance politique, Autriche,* Archives du Ministére des Affaires Etrangères (Paris). For the motivation of American diplomatic and consular relations with Austria cf. Barany, "The Interest of the United States in Central Europe," pp. 275–81.

the Black Sea, & thus, by the material interests created by such *Commerce & Intercourse,* bind the Countries lying below the Austrian dominions south to the Balkan, & north to the extremities of Wallachia, in the consequent bonds of friendly alliance, & of possible amalgation [*sic*] with *Austria;* which as the friendly & natural Ally of England would at the same time give far greater political power to both Empires."

Adding that, "Without such relaxation, however, in the *Tariff,* as would open the *Media* of Commerce with Austria, placing the Ports of the Danube for Austrian ships upon the same footing, could not be attended with any beneficial results," and the British government could not bear "the responsibility of so far deviating from the Navigation Laws of 1833," McGregor resorted to yet another argument "to admit of Trade to a reasonable extent with Hungary." Its implications were unmistakable:

Exclusive of the desirable political Union which relations of material Interests, the only secure bond of political Alliance, would establish, there are new *resources* developing their *productions* in other Countries, to which our Merchants & Manufacturers are directing their views of profit.

For example, the South of Russia has within the last eleven years become a valuable pasturing Country for Merino Sheep. The Wools of that Country are much the same in quality as those of the Merino sheep of Hungary, & other Austrian Dominions. . . .

Fully aware of the economic disaster which the loss of the English market would mean to Hungarian and Bohemian landowners, and of the political consequences such an event would have in Austria, the representative of the Board of Trade pointed to the favorable duties at which goods for consumption, including colonial wares, cotton and woolen manufactures, and products of iron, steel, and brass could be imported into Russia, making it possible for the English merchant to reap "a *double profit* in trading with Russia for *Wools.*" McGregor supported his argument by saying that whereas there was scarcely a bag of the wools of southern Russia imported into England in 1824, and the imports of 1829 amounted to 153,614 lbs., by 1835 they were over 5.2 million lbs. Quoting other items of Anglo-Russian trade, such as flax, hemp, bristles, tallow, hides and skins, McGregor suggested that all of these could be furnished by the Austrian dominions provided they would purchase more British manufactured goods.

Despite the emphasis on economics, the British kept on stressing "the great Political Consequences of such an Alliance, as bearing upon the power & security of both Empires," and indeed granted important concessions to Austria in the final version of the treaty without yielding, however, in the matter of complete reciprocity.[65] Envisioning an expansion of English influence via trade with Austria as a stimulus to resisting Russia, they wished to maintain the international balance of power while opening up southeastern Europe economically.

This British political concept was not necessarily harmful to the peoples of Central Europe and the Balkans, especially to those who albeit restless were still under Ottoman rule. Neither was it against the principles of Széchenyi who indirectly through his work on the Lower Danube and directly through his close connections with all negotiating partners exerted an influence on the outcome of the negotiations—as the recurrent references to Hungary's economic evolution, and to him personally, suggest.

Metternich used the new commercial agreement with England to negotiate a more favorable arrangement with Russia. The treaty, signed in July 1840, confirmed the freedom of navigation on the Danube, simplified the Russian quarantine regulations in the delta, and imposed on Russia the obligation to clear the Sulina channel of the obstructions to shipping.[66] It is interesting that Article VIII of the convention referred

[65] All the direct citations follow the orthography of the draft of McGregor's reply, bearing no date, to Kolowrat's letter of Nov. 14, 1837. An English translation of Kolowrat's letter, along with McGregor's answer and his letter of Nov. 1, were enclosed in Lamb to Palmerston, Dec. 29, 1837 (no. 93), *F.O. 7/266*, PRO (London). Besides the ones already cited see McGregor's report on his interviews with Metternich and Kolowrat, dated Apr. 27, 1837, and enclosed in Denis Le Marchant to Palmerston, May 11, 1837, *F.O. 7/269*, PRO (London). For the interpretation of the treaty and the political-military implications of the training of sailors in the British commercial fleet, see Lord Beauvale (Sir Frederick Lamb) to Palmerston, Sept. 8, 1839, and Beauvale to Metternich, Sept. 7, 1839 (enc.), *F.O. 7/282*, PRO (London). Cf. No. 398/1938, *Minister Kolowrat Akten*, Staatsarchiv (Vienna) (cited hereafter as *MKA*). For the text of the treaty and the explanatory declarations see *British and Foreign State Papers*, xxvi (1837–1838), 677–87. For details and pertinent documentation see Alfred Francis Pribram, *Österreichische Staatsverträge. England*, 2 vols. (Vols. 3 and 12 in *Veröffentlichungen der Kommission für Neuere Geschichte Österreichs*, (Innsbruck-Vienna: 1907–1913), ii, 631–714. J. H. Clapham, in *The Cambridge History of British Foreign Policy*, ed. A. W. Ward and G. P. Gooch, 3 vols. (New York: Macmillan, 1922–23), ii, 467ff., emphasizes the anti-Prussian aspects of the treaty. For other evaluations, see Webster, *Foreign Policy of Palmerston*, ii, 580f.; Puryear, *International Economics*, pp. 141ff.

[66] *Ibid.*, pp. 143ff. The text of the "Convention entre l'Autriche et la Russie, concernant la Navigation du Danube" was published in *British and Foreign State Papers*, xxviii (1839–1840), 1,060–63, Cf. No. 1,716/1840, *MKA*, Staatsarchiv (Vienna), with the official Latin, French, and German texts. Concerning British interest in and reaction to the negotiations, relative to the new Austro-Russian treaty and Russia's alleged obstruction of the navigation in order to protect the trade of Odessa against the competition of the Principalities, cf. Palmerston to Beauvale, May 20, Aug. 6, 1840, *F.O. 7/288* and *F.O. 7/289*, PRO (London), Beauvale to Palmerston, July 18 (no. 99), Aug. 25, Oct. 24, Nov. 1, 1840, *F.O. 7/291A* and *F.O. 7/291B*, PRO (London). For

to "goods shipped from Vienna or Hungary on the Danube"; though carelessly formulated, the phrase nevertheless intimated, perhaps for the first time in the text of an international treaty concluded by the Habsburg state in the modern era, that Széchenyi had succeeded in putting his fatherland on the map.

From a political point of view the high hopes attached to the Anglo-Austrian treaty of commerce and navigation in Britain failed to materialize while Metternich was in power. The date of expiration of the convention with England—1848—also marked the end of his system. After the revolutionary turmoil that shook the Habsburg Empire, however, the community of political and economic interests, anticipated and promoted by the treaty of 1838, began to reassert itself in spite of the assistance given by the tsar to Francis Joseph in 1849, and the fact that Austria supported, de facto if not de jure, the British against the Russians in the Crimean War. The Treaty of Paris (1856), which ended that conflict, eliminated Russia's control of the estuary of the Danube and placed its navigation under the auspices of a European commission. By entrusting police and quarantine regulations, as well as the improvement and maintenance of the riverbed and the mouths of the Danube, to an international body, and by admitting Turkey to the European concert, the treaty could—and did—apply the general principles accepted by the Congress of Vienna for the navigation of rivers specifically to one river—the Danube.[67] It thus gave validity to the British view emphasized since the early 1830s, namely, that free navigation on the Danube was a European question.[68] The efforts to transform the Danube into an international waterway, to bring thereby European civilization to Hungary, and to link the whole underdeveloped area of southeastern Europe to the advanced western parts of the continent and to England, make of Széchenyi a statesman of truly European significance. Indeed, he was recognized as such by his foreign politician friends, one of whom, Sir Charles Stewart, third Marquess of Londonderry, represented England in Vienna until his half-brother Lord Castlereagh's death. No liberal or Russophobe, he wrote a special "Report to Prince Metternich of the Navigation of the Danube" after his trip to the Near East in 1840–41. In it he expressed his admiration for the "Herculean project" designed to unite "the commerce of your Empire with that of the City

---

the difficulties hampering the evolution of Austro-Russian trade relations cf. Beer, *Österreichische Handelspolitik*, pp. 432–49.

[67] For details cf. Hajnal, *The Danube*, pp. 69–81; Gorove, *Law and Politics of the Danube*, pp. 24ff.; Puryear, *England, Russia, and the Straits Question*, pp. 131–38; Anderson, *Eastern Question*, pp. 134, 137, 140–48.

[68] Hajnal, *The Danube*, p. 56.

of the East" and for "the singular public spirit, talents, and abilities of Count Stefan Zecheny [*sic*]. . . ."[69]

The British conception of enhancing the political stability and gradually lifting the economy of southeastern Europe through trade was not an unqualified, let alone unselfish, blessing in disguise for the Ottoman Empire and its people. History shows that few if any, bold and forsighted programs are in that category, and Metternich knew this. He refused to imitate the Anglo-Turkish commercial convention of 1838 which served as a model for a Franco-Turkish treaty signed at the end of the same year. Although British trade increased considerably throughout the Ottoman Empire in subsequent years, some aspects of the treaty, such as the export tariffs, were not to the advantage of Turkish merchants. Since the Austrian chancellor wished to maintain rather than weaken Turkey, he was trying to safeguard Austria's privileges on the basis of existing agreements, rather than by the duplication of the convention of Balta Liman, until a better agreement could be worked out.[70]

Initially Turkish officials were extremely suspicious of Széchenyi's activities along the Danube border. But soon his "personal diplomacy" began to bear fruit. The commanding pasha of Orsova, who first threatened to give order to shoot at Széchenyi's workers, became such a good friend of his that he even asked Széchenyi to write a "strong" letter to him so that he could ask for more favorable directives from the Porte.[71] Appreciating the pasha's loyalty to existing orders and at the same time his benevolence, Széchenyi carefully avoided embarrassing him. He insisted that the "ticklish situation" be trusted only to people who will refrain "from the use of *any means* while pursuing steadfastly our goal." Even in diplomacy, certain moral principles were far more important to him than the achievement of a cherished project in which he had invested so much of his time, money, and health. Offering to resign as royal commissioner if his warning were not respected,[72] Széchenyi thus showed that in his opinion, "credit in the broader sense," the sanctity of the given word, dignity and mutual appreciation of each other's interests, were guidelines which ought to dominate the relations

[69] Vane, *Steam Voyage to Constantinople*, I, 132–45, 342f. Cf. Ch. II 51, and n. 150 in the present study.

[70] Puryear, *International Economics*, pp. 117–30, 139ff. Cf. Beer, *Österreichische Handelspolitik*, pp. 396–418.

[71] Széchenyi to Archduke Palatine Joseph, July 19, 1833, Széchenyi to Baron Ottenfels, Aug. 2, 11, 1833, Széchenyi to Archduke Palatine Joseph, Aug. 16, 1833, Széchenyi to Baron Ottenfels, Aug. 27, 1833, Majláth, ed., *Levelek*, I, 249, 262–65, 272f., 278, 294f.

[72] Széchenyi to Archduke Palatine Joseph, Aug. 16, 1833, Széchenyi to Baron Ottenfels, Aug. 27, 1833, Majláth, ed., *Levelek*, I, 279, 294. Cf. his letters to the palatine and to Baron Ottenfels, July 19, Aug. 2, 1833, *ibid.*, I, 249, 264f. (italics in orig.).

of classes and peoples, and the domain of international affairs as well. Small wonder that whereas he was respected and admired by many, he was also considered a dilettante by more sophisticated professionals.

While aware of the international importance of regulation and navigation of the Danube Széchenyi also realized the domestic political implications of the issue. He attempted to convince the palatine and Austrian officials that the development of Danubian trade and the growth of the Hungarian economy would have a favorable impact on the country's ability to share the burdens of imperial defenses and finances. Moreover, the "concentration of forces" in Pest would increase the political significance of the capital, which in turn would diminish the influence of the semi-independent counties.[73] Thus Széchenyi's term "concentration in Pest" implied, as he himself suggested, the transformation of the old "municipal constitution" and the weakening of the decentralized feudal administration of Hungary. If put into practice without reservation, Széchenyi's conception was more revolutionary from the institutional point of view than the policies of most members of the liberal opposition, including Kossuth in the 1830s and 40s, who considered municipal politics the center of the nation's political life. Here lay one of the essential differences between Széchenyi and the vast majority of Hungarian patriots with regard to domestic politics. Although he never fully developed his concepts of what (at that time) would have meant a genuine constitutional revolution, he resented the fact that "now it is not the Diet which gives orders to the counties but [it is] the Diet [which] receives orders from fifty-two counties."[74] Unlike most of his contemporary Hungarian politicians, Széchenyi was neither a product of, nor did he thrive on, the political atmosphere of the counties. This, to be sure, was a source of weakness in his later career when he tried to block Kossuth, whose main strength was in the counties dominated by the liberal opposition. Yet even in the 1830s Széchenyi refrained from launching an open and all-out attack on county administration, albeit he often derided it in his writings. Presumably he did not wish to raise a large constitutional issue that inevitably would have involved Hungary's entire administration system, hence also its connections with the rest of the Habsburg domains. Whereas Kossuth continued to defend county autonomy up to the Spring of 1848, Széchenyi in a sense was the precursor of the "centralists" of the 1840s. This small but important group, which included Baron Joseph Eötvös, his brother-in-law August Trefort, the legal scholar Ladislas Szalay, and others, was to challenge more consistently than Széchenyi the political monopoly of the nobility in the counties and

[73] Oct. 29, 1830, Viszota, ed., *Naplók*, IV, 149. Cf. June 22, 1830, *ibid.*, IV, 376.
[74] May 7, 1833, *ibid.*, IV, 376.

in the Diet with the purpose of setting up a government responsible to a truly representative parliament.[75]

Since the autumn of 1830 Széchenyi had been on friendly terms with Archduke-Palatine Joseph, prominent in Hungarian politics for 50 years. Their friendship, which was to develop into close political cooperation in the next 15 years, began with what Széchenyi called a "general confession" (*General Beichte*), in the course of which he breifed the palatine about his ideas.[76] Still, at the time of his designation as royal commissioner in charge of the work on the Lower Danube in 1833, he had doubts. Suspicious that the administration wanted only to remove him from the Diet in order to walk out on him later,[77] he nevertheless accepted the commission because he was keenly aware of the limitations of Dietal work and the social and cultural ramifications of Danube navigation.

Both factors should be remembered even if Széchenyi's appointment as royal commissioner was the result, as may well be the case, of Vienna's successful attempt to divert a potential troublemaker's boundless energies from Hungarian domestic politics to an economic enterprise useful to the Monarchy as a whole.[78] As to the inefficiency of the Dietal machinery in the cause of reform, Széchenyi's exasperation was paralleled by that of Francis Kölcsey, whose beautifully written "Dietal Diary" is a moving and melancholic document reflecting the frustrations of a poet-leader of early 19th-century Hungarian liberalism.[79] With regard to the socio-economic connotations Széchenyi attached to the task of regulating the Danube, some of his scattered observations made well before he was offered the position of royal commissioner are most revealing. "Steamboats cannot stand the smell of feudalism" he wrote in the summer of 1830. Watching the boats towed by laborers who earned 1½ to 2 cents per day or no wage at all if weather conditions were adverse, he noted disapprovingly that it was going to be difficult to compete with this kind of labor since "the steamboat is not for barbarians *id est* 'my compatriots' but for civilized people."[80] Translating his program for reforms into the language of steamship navigation, he added that

[75] For references see George Barany, "Hungary: The Uncompromising Compromise," *The Austrian History Yearbook*, III (1967), Pt. I, pp. 238f. and n. 11–13.

[76] Oct. 29, 1830, Viszota, ed., *Naplók*, IV, 148ff.

[77] July 8, 1833, *ibid.*, IV, 386.

[78] Lóránt Tilkovszky, "Ismeretlen Széchenyi-levelek" (Unknown Széchenyi Letters), *Valóság*, II (1959), 92f.

[79] See for example, his remarks on censorship and freedom of the press, on phrase-mongering and noise-making instead of a meaningful debate in the entries of Jan. 15, 19, 24, 1833, in Kölcsey, "Országgyűlési napló," pp. 1,252f., 1,260–63, 1,270f., in *KFÖM*; also his "Farewell to the Estates" of Feb. 9, 1835, *ibid.*, 1,171ff.

[80] Aug. 1, 1830, Viszota, ed., *Naplók*, IV, 93 (italics Széchenyi's).

steamboats must be preceded by property ownership by the middle class, by tenants unwilling to leave their fields to pull boats, by education, by a degree of morality, and by a desire for a better existence worthy of a human being—all of which, in his words, excluded the slightest trace of the stench of the feudal order.[81] This, to be sure, was the outline of a dream to be realized by generations to come; it is even moot whether its full implications have ever been given a chance in Hungary.

Széchenyi's preoccupation with the problems of Danube navigation did not entirely prevent him from participating in the work of the Diets of the 1830s. From Constantinople he sent to Wesselényi two proposals for the Diet of the fall of 1830. He wished to extend the Dietal journals to cover the sessions of the upper table, a suggestion resisted by the majority of that chamber. Furthermore, he proposed that the Diet of 1831 be held in Pest instead of Pressburg because "the acceptance of this single motion would mean that we have accomplished the progress of another half century."[82] Yet the journals of the upper chamber were first established during the Diet of 1843–44, whereas Széchenyi's desire to move the Diet to Pest materialized only in 1847–48.

Actually, the Diet which convened in early September 1830 accomplished very little. It crowned Ferdinand V and decided to postpone the "systematic works" for reform until the next Diet. It also voted the recruits requested by the administration in view of the situation in France. Széchenyi arrived from his first Danubian journey during the discussion of the demand for new recruits and participated in the debate. The opposition of the lower chamber put forward the old grievance of having alien commanders in Hungarian regiments and asked for a separate grading of Hungarian officers. Although Széchenyi thought that he himself had been handicapped by his Hungarian birth during his military career, he nevertheless supported the administration with regard to a unified, common training program for all officers in the army. In pleasing Metternich he thus shocked the traditionalist members of the opposition who had already looked askance at him because of the publication of *Hitel*. Some said that he was running for office, others that he was a renegade and sycophant.[83] Feeling increasingly isolated, Széchenyi remarked only that he did not mind being "virtuous without witnesses."[84]

[81] June 25, 1830, *ibid.*, pp. 54f.
[82] Széchenyi to Wesselényi, Aug. 24 and Oct. 6, 1830, Majláth, ed., *Levelek*, I, 172, 179.
[83] Nov. 7, 14, 22, 23, 26, 27, 1830, Viszota, ed., *Naplók*, IV, 152 and n. 3, 154 and n. 4, 155, 158f., 161 and n. 4, 162.
[84] Nov. 23, 1830, *ibid.*, IV, 159.

Yet at the end of the Diet, during the drafting of the new laws, he firmly sided with the opposition, which wanted to insert into the text certain expressions safeguarding the nation's constitutional rights with respect to the throne.[85] As a result, the court made some concessions to the demands of the Diet. Széchenyi, "even during the short period of his presence at this Diet, too, a significant influence, was enthusiastically greeted upon his arrival by the young magnates of the opposition, and enjoyed, especially in these quarters, universal respect." While acknowledging the fact that Széchenyi supported the royal propositions in the matter of recruits, the police report, from which the quote is taken, nonetheless characterized him as belonging to "the left side of the opposition" and as being "the focal point of all exalted young magnates."[86] On the other hand, Chancellor Reviczky's report to the king commented favorably on Széchenyi's election to the vice-presidency of the Academy. Referring to the talents "demonstrated in his well-known work 'On Credit,' " the Hungarian chancellor had high praise for Széchenyi's unselfishness and independence from popular trends. Although he kept Széchenyi under strict observation during the Diet, Reviczky added, he failed to discover anything doubtful in his private life, whereas in public Széchenyi was one of the most zealous and active supporters of the administration.[87]

Among the concessions obtained by the Diet was the recognition of the principle that the text of the coronation oath and charter could be changed. On the question of recruits the administration agreed to justify its request to the estates. This, in the opinion of the conservative Lord Chief Justice Count Cziráky, was equivalent to admitting the estates' right to interfere with the issue of war and peace and to intrude in the domain of foreign affairs hitherto considered to be a royal prerogative.[88] Also, the lower chamber began to send its messages to the chamber of magnates in Hungarian instead of Latin; this practice, begun in October 1830, was a step toward introducing Magyar as the legislative language. The same tendency was strengthened by the passing of Act VIII of 1830 which stipulated that henceforth the lieutenancy was to communicate in Hungarian with counties using that idiom. Similarly, the language of the judiciary was to be Hungarian "within the confines of the kingdom," and no one ignorant of the language could be admitted

---

[85] Dec. 17, 18, 1830, *ibid.*, IV, 168ff.

[86] "Charakteristik der ungarischen Landtags Deputirten vom Jahre 1830," Annex No. 1, 1832/1, *ibid.*, IV, 665ff.

[87] Jan. 26, 1831, B. Szabó, ed., *Adatok*, I, 111f.

[88] "Freymüthige Darstellung der politischen Lage Ungarns . . . ," *ibid.*, I, 325. For an evaluation of the results of the Diet of 1830 see Horváth, *Huszonöt év*, I, 250–55.

to the bar. More important, the knowledge of Magyar became a prerequisite for holding public office.[89]

The new law was restricted to Hungary proper and had no validity in Croatia or Transylvania. At the same time, however, relations between the Hungarian and Croatian estates were also disturbed by an impassioned discussion of religious issues, since many Hungarians wanted to extend Act XXI of 1791 to Croatia. This law, which declared the emancipation of Protestants, was ignored in Croatia where the Catholic clergy opposed the granting of property rights to Protestants. Hence the deputies of Croatia, insisting on the country's autonomy within the lands of the Hungarian Crown, refused to make any liberal concessions and denied even the competency of the Hungarian Diet to raise the Protestant issue in Croatia. Interestingly, in this struggle for freedom of conscience the deputies of Slavonia, which was the eastern half of the area between the Drava (Drave), Danube, and Sava (Save) Rivers and was divided into three countries (Szerém, Verőce, and Pozsega), sided with the Hungarian liberals, opposing on an important issue the views of the Croatian estates. Thus the alignment of political forces foreshadowed in the Protestant issue the parties opposing each other on the nationality question in subsequent years.[90]

In the chamber of magnates the champion of religious freedom was Wesselényi who for the first time participated in the Hungarian Diet.[91] Eventually it was he and not Széchenyi who became the real leader of oppositional forces at the Diet. Széchenyi supported without reservation the views of the opposition in the issues of religion and the Hungarian language, but did not want to commit himself to any single faction or party. His plans for reform, as well as his inclination to refrain from extremes, caused him to reject emphatically his friend's open defiance of the government. Wesselényi approved of Széchenyi's ideas in general and considered the privileges of the nobility obstacles to progress. Yet his approach to reform was more legalistic and less flexible than Széchenyi's. He advocated just as vigorously as Széchenyi the modernization of Hungary. In certain respects he went further, as shown by his demands for a free press, ministerial responsibility, national independence

[89] For a Latin text of the law see Szekfű, ed., *Iratok*, p. 399. Cf. Miskolczy, ed., *A horvát kérdés*, I, 111ff.

[90] *Ibid.*, I, 115–22. The southern parts of Croatia and Slavonia were under military administration. The Military Frontier Region, originally established as a defense measure against the Turks in the early 16th century, had no elected representatives in the Diet. See the comprehensive studies by Gunther E. Rothenberg, *The Austrian Military Border in Croatia, 1522–1747* and *The Military Border in Croatia, 1740–1881*.

[91] Although his estates were in Transylvania he had recently bought some land in Hungary proper. Being a magnate by birth enabled him to receive a royal invitation to the upper chamber. Horváth, *Huszonöt év*, I, 224–31, 253.

protected by firm constitutional guarantees, and a cautious formulation of the emancipation of the Jews. Steeped in the Hungarian tradition, he believed in the necessity of gaining the support of the landed gentry and the feasibility of infusing his ideas of reform into the political life of the counties. Like Széchenyi, he intended to shape a new nation that included the peasant masses. But to him the municipal structure of the Hungarian constitution was a shield against administrative absolutism and therefore he regarded it as the political basis of the process of nation-building. Unwilling to make any concessions where the constitutional rights of the nation were at stake, he relentlessly exposed abuses committed by the administration, going so far as to oppose, in his *Balítéletekről* (On Misjudgments), the theory of passive resistance, to the execution of unconstitutional measures.[92] Thus when Széchenyi had nearly finished *Világ*, in which he gave some credit to the administration for having improved its policies toward Hungary,[93] Wesselényi shocked his friend by refusing to allow the conscription of recruits from his estates.[94] In the fall of 1830, after an argument between Wesselényi and Michael Esterházy, his partners in the "Alliance of Virtue," Széchenyi began to doubt the future of their alliance. By June 1831, upon hearing about Wesselényi's violent attack on the administration at the county congregation of Szatmár, he thought his friend did more harm than good to the cause of liberal reform.[95] He was still anxious to discover "more liberalism" in his compatriots.[96] But whereas in 1826 he deplored the lack of sufficient "republican seriousness" in the younger generation of magnates,[97] less than five years later, after the publication of *Hitel* and *Világ* and especially after the cholera uprising, he insisted that even Wesselényi give the benefit of doubt to the government.

Yet besides the realization of the danger of another *jacquerie* and the agreement on the need for the unification of forces, the two friends sharply disagreed on the means to be used to achieve their goals. Széchenyi admonished Wesselényi to stand firmly by the king in the hour of emergency, stressing the monarch's benevolence and the administration's willingness to make liberal concessions. He also urged Wesselényi to come to Pest and help work out a common plan of action for the public good *in centro*, at the heart of the country, and not *in partibus*, on the periphery, from his Transylvanian seclusion. He warned his friend not to defy the government but to postpone the confrontation

---

[92] *Ibid.*, I, 282ff.; Trócsányi, *Wesselényi*, pp. 122–50.
[93] Cf. Ch. VI, p. 221 of this study.
[94] Apr. 3 and 24, 1831, Viszota, ed., *Naplók*, IV, 186f.
[95] Oct. 29, 1830, June 22, 1831, *ibid.*, IV, 149, 191.
[96] June 7, July 14, 1831, *ibid.*, IV, 190, 192f.
[97] Nov. 10, 1826, *ibid.*, III, 100.

of forces until they had gained strength, because, he wrote, "You want to be the hero of a tragedy . . . whereas I wish to succeed."[98]

But Wesselényi failed to see any benevolence in the government. He thought trust in it was dangerous to the country, if not harmful to Széchenyi himself. He said: "You want to use the Government as a tool but this is exactly their purpose with regard to you; you are too weak to achieve your aim and we all are too weak for it; but the Government is very strong and very smart." He interpreted as ill will what Széchenyi considered merely stupidity and ignorance of the bureaucracy. Furthermore, he refused to admit that any reasonable concessions could be expected from the upper table which reflected the separate vested interests of the magnates. The nation's will could only be represented by the lower chamber whence all healthy movements must start. He resented Széchenyi's urging him to come to Pest and refused to see any objectionable violence in his own methods consisting merely, as he put it, of attending congregations and of telling the truth without disguise or flattering, "as becomes a man." After this exchange of letters, they both felt that their views concerning the promotion of the country's progress were diametrically opposed. Pledging each other their personal friendship, their close political collaboration ended on a bitter note.[99] For another decade they continued to stand shoulder to shoulder on important issues or in moments of emergency, but they were never able to see eye to eye as they had in their years of youthful enthusiasm and planning.

Because of cholera, the Diet originally summoned for October 1831 did not convene until December 1832. In the meantime, in February 1832, Széchenyi formed an association for constructing a permanent bridge between Buda and Pest. Accompanied by George Andrássy, he made another trip to England in late summer, also visiting Germany, Belgium, and France. Together they published a "Report of Count George Andrássy and Count Stephen Széchenyi to the Bridge Society of Budapest upon their Return from Abroad."[100]

Besides collecting technical information and plans for the bridge construction, Széchenyi made inquiries into nearly everything connected with

[98] Széchenyi to Wesselényi, Nov. 8, 1831, Majláth, ed., *Levelek*, I, 204. Cf. p. 231 of the preceding chapter.

[99] Wesselényi to Széchenyi, Oct. 26, Nov. 29, Dec. 18, 1831, B. Szabó, ed., *Adatok*, I, 142, 147–50. Széchenyi to Wesselényi, Nov. 8, Dec. 5, 1831, Jan. 5, 1832, Majláth, ed., *Levelek*, I, 205, 208f. Also, Apr. 13, 1833, Kölcsey, "Országgyűlési napló," *KFÖM*, p. 1,345; Trócsányi, *Wesselényi*, pp. 118–21.

[100] "Gróf Andrássy György és gróf Széchenyi Istvánnak a Budapesti Hid Egyesülethez irányozott Jelentése midőn külföldről visszatérének" (Pozsony: 1833). The pamphlet, written by Széchenyi in late December 1832, was translated into German by Michael Paziazi.

his present or future enterprises. He visited factories and shipyards, was interested in road-building and steam mills, studied new inventions such as concrete-mixing and Roman cement. He had long conversations with engineers and industrialists, and frequented scientific institutions. He tried the new railroad between Manchester and Liverpool, but usually travelled by stagecoach to economize. His diaries of the time are interspersed with production figures, calculations, and sketches of gadgets and practical devices. Besides investigating the most important industrial centers in England and on the continent, he also wanted to gather information about American technology. From F. B. Ogden, United States Consul in Liverpool, he asked for data subsequently used in the report to the Bridge Society. Part of the questions to the consul pertained to the ways of fund-raising for purposes of building bridges: is it done by government or private companies? In the former case, "in what way are the taxes laid on the public?" In the latter, how do private firms get back the money invested? Do they have a right to collect tolls, and are these "stipulated for a certain number of years, or forever?" Széchenyi also wanted to know the number of piers holding the Delaware Bridge, the width and cost of each of its spans, whether there were any police regulations limiting "the number of cattle—persons, or wagons etc. going at the same time on a bridge p. ex. the Schoolkile or the permanent bridge in Philadelphia? And if you may go as fast on them as you please, —or be obliged to slaken your pace?"[101]

However naïve some of the questions may seem to us today, they reflected the manifold aspects of a real problem in an underdeveloped country where a dredging machine brought by Széchenyi from England caused quite a sensation. We have it on the authority of Princess Melanie, Metternich's third wife, who attended the "social event" with her husband, that "Stepherl" Széchenyi's "ingenious" machine, dubbed "Cavafango," which was to clear the riverbed of the Danube near Vienna, attracted "the whole court, at least all the archdukes." Széchenyi's diary entry from the same day adds a touch of frivolous irony to the successful demonstration of the excavator's operation in the presence of prominent personalities, including, besides the chancellor and

[101] Nov. 3, 1830, Viszota, ed., *Naplók*, IV, 348. The citations follow Széchenyi's original orthography in the diary. The two bridges mentioned in his inquiry may have been the Delaware River Bridge built by Lewis Wernwag at New Hope, Pa., in 1821, and the Permanent Bridge over the Schuylkill River, constructed by Timothy Palmer in 1801–1805. The dispatches from Consul Ogden, included in the General Records of the Department of State in the National Archives, Washington, D.C., (R.G. 59), do not mention Széchenyi's request. The records of the United States Consulate at Liverpool, England (R.G. 84) contain no communications from Ogden prior to September 1831.

the archdukes, Kolowrat, who gave him the permission to import the equipment: "There were very many women, and real pretty ones at that."[102]

Széchenyi's inquiry to the American consul revealed his great interest in the financial side of bridge construction. Besides the embellishment of the future Hungarian capital and its importance, from a commercial point of view, his fight for the bridge at the Diet of 1832–36 also became a symbolic fight for abolishing the nobility's tax exemption. As a result of his lobbying at the county congregation of Pest, in the municipal council of the city, as well as at the Diet where he received considerable help from the palatine, Széchenyi overcame the combined resistance of the defenders of feudal privileges and the burghers of Pest who had such vested interests in the status quo. In the spring of 1836 the Diet passed a law (1836: XXVI) ordering the construction of a permanent bridge and creating a National Committee to start negotiations with financial circles and entrepreneurs. Another law (XXV) enacted the principle of the right of expropriation. Széchenyi played a prominent role both in these negotiations and in the organization of a joint stock company which finally accomplished the task. Although the law itself declared that the paying of tolls by noblemen on the bridge would not establish a precedent and Metternich told Széchenyi that he had defeated his own purpose, still its passing was considered by friend and foe alike as a victory of the reform movement over feudalism.[103] In a letter to engineer George Rennie, son and associate of the builder of London's Waterloo Bridge, Széchenyi summed up the issue:

A child can see that we are in a great want of good roads, and that we ought rather to begin with making roads than with the construction of a bridge of so difficult and expensive execution. But in our country all those are exempted from a toll, who could pay it, and the

[102] Mar. 28, 1835. "Aus dem Tagebuche der Fürstin Melanie." *Aus Metternich's nachgelassenen Papieren*, ed. Richard Metternich-Winneburg, 8 vols. (Vienna: Braumüller, 1880–84), VI, 10; Mar. 28, 1835, Viszota, ed., *Naplók*, IV, 534f. Also Nov. 28, 1833 and Mar. 17, 1835, *ibid.*, 431, 532. Count Mitrovszky to Chancellor Reviczky (Mar. 23, 1835), B. Szabó, ed., *Adatok*, I, 223.

[103] Besides the relevant sections in Viszota's introductions to *Naplók*, IV–VI, see for details his *A Széchenyi-hid története az 1836: XXVI. t.c. megalkotásáig* (History of the Széchenyi Bridge until the Enactment of Law 1836: XXVI) (Budapest: Magyar Tud. Akadémia, 1935). Cf. also Széchenyi's apology for the bridge, handed to Metternich in January 1836, Metternich's aide mémoire ("Gespräche zwischen dem Grafen Stephan Széchenyi und dem Fürsten Metternich am 21. und 23. Jänner 1836"), as well as Count Majláth's report in Annex No. 1, 1836, 1/a-c, Viszota, ed., *Naplók*, IV, 696–703. The financial group constructing the bridge was headed by the Viennese banker Baron George Sina, and the technical work was directed and supervised by two English engineers, Adam and Tierney Clark.

whole weight of upholding communication lies on the poor. The making of better roads is therefore not the thing we must begin with, but the very first thing to pass over is to establish the principle of a general toll, to be paid by everybody. And this we carried by a law, which orders that everybody shall pay on the bridge between Buda and Pest. We consider this bridge as a medium to get by and by to the roads too.[104]

It is interesting that the archconservative lord chief justice, who refused to vote any subsidies for a national theater because he did not want to build a theater "on the ruins of our constitution," went out of his way to prevent the Diet from enacting the bridge law, and after his failure pledged himself never to walk over the bridge but rather to cross the Danube by boat.[105] As for Széchenyi, he was literally trembling for "his bridge" during the decisive debates in the Diet[106]; he continued to regard the work on the bridge as a symbol of his lifework for Hungary up until his collapse in late summer 1848.

The Suspension (Chain) Bridge, or the "Széchenyi Bridge," as it is known today, was in many respects the archetype of the pattern of Széchenyi's creative genius. Designed for the promotion of commerce and communication, the bridge was to be a permanent link between Buda and Pest, separated hitherto completely during the weeks of ice drift in winter. Hence the bridge also served the practical aim of creating a modern urban center by uniting the two halves of Hungary's future capital. Saying that "our country would grow in strength by welding together the sections of Buda and Pest and—by developing everything Beautiful, Great, and Glorious in the heart of the fatherland under the protection of the deity of Nationality," Széchenyi ascribed to the material usefulness of the bridge a high moral and national function.[107] It was significant that the breakthrough in the nobility's tax exemption came for the sake of establishing a capitalistic enterprise: Viennese and domestic capital, English iron and technical know-how, Italian skilled workmen, and Hungarian laborers had been put to work shoulder to shoulder by Széchenyi to achieve the first great accomplishment of capitalism in Hungary.

The bridge, Danube regulation, and the National Theater were on

---

[104] Széchenyi to Rennie (in English) Nov. 11, 1837, Majláth, ed., *Levelek*, II, 437.
[105] Zichy, *Széchenyi életrajza*, I, 371; Apr. 26, 1836, Viszota, ed., *Naplók*, IV, 657.
[106] Jan. 11, 1835, Apr. 23, 27, 28, 29, 30, 1836, *ibid.*, IV, 515, 656f.
[107] Quoted in Hóman and Szekfű, *Magyar történet*, V, 229f. The pontoon bridge, which connected Buda and Pest, was usually assembled in March and disassembled in early December, depending on weather conditions. Cf. Csaplovics, *Gemälde von Ungarn*, I, 167ff.

the agenda of the Diet of 1832–36. It was primarily Széchenyi's agitation which directed public attention to these issues. The Diet convened in the spirit of reform advocated by Széchenyi. The same international and domestic factors—the July Revolution, the defeat of the Polish uprising and subsequent influx of émigrés into Hungary, the country's economic backwardness and the cholera revolt which aroused public interest in Széchenyi's books and activities—greatly increased the expectations of those in favor of change before the Diet. One should add that the legislation enacted by this lengthy Diet fulfilled only in part the hopes of the pleiad of liberals attending it.[108]

Yet the Diet of 1832–36 was the first "Reform Diet" in the true sense of the word.[109] For the first time, a number of new deputies brought fresh blood into the ranks of the traditional opposition, which had previously tried to defend chiefly the privileges of the nobility against Vienna. Among them were the poet Francis Kölcsey, deputy of Szatmár county, his colleagues Edmund Beőthy from Bihar, Gabriel Klauzál from Csanád, Stephen Bezerédy from Tolna, Gabriel Lónyay from Zemplén, and Ladislas Palóczy from Borsod, joined later by Francis Deák, deputy of Zala. Though under the influence of Széchenyi's ideas, they stood even closer to Wesselényi, whose emphasis on the nation's constitutional rights had a greater appeal to the legalistically minded liberal nationalists of "Young Hungary."

These men, including Kossuth who was not a deputy but a representative of absent magnates in the lower table and thus had no vote,[110] were born between 1790 and 1805. One of them, Palóczy, was Széchenyi's senior by eight years. They, along with some younger men such as Count

---

[108] For a detailed evaluation of the Diet of 1832–36 see Horváth, *Huszonöt év*, I, 288–461, II, 3–32; Hóman and Szekfű, *Magyar történet*, V, 286–99. For contemporary accounts cf. Deák's report in Kónyi, ed., *Deák beszédei*, I, 267–313; Lajos Hőke, "Az 1830. és 1832–36-iki országgyűlések" (The Diets of 1830 and 1832–36), *Hazánk*, V, 161–87; and above all, Lajos Kossuth, *Országgyűlési tudósitások* (Dietal Reports), 5 vols. (Budapest: Akadémiai kiadó, 1948–61), published as Vols. I–V of *Kossuth Lajos Összes Munkái* (Louis Kossuth's Collected Works; cited henceforth as *KLÖM*) in *Fontes*.

[109] As early as 1839 Julia Pardoe used the term "Reform Diet" in her book, *The City of the Magyar or Hungary and Her Institutions in 1839-40*, III, 231. She also frequently referred to the "Liberal Party throughout the kingdom." Even before Miss Pardoe, a French analysis of the laws enacted by the Diet of 1832–36 called the latter "*un véritable parlement de réforme.*" "Mémoire sur la Hongrie et sur les loix rendues par la dernière Diète—1832–36," No. 11 (May 1837), p. 149, in *Mémoirs et documens (sic)*, Vol. 51, *Autriche, 1830 à 1847*, Archives du Ministère des Affaires Etrangères (Paris).

[110] This was the first time that the future leader of the Hungarian revolution of 1848–49 attended the Diet. Some Hungarian and non-Hungarian works refer to one Louis Kossuth, a namesake of his, who was present at the Diet of 1825–27, also as a representative of absent magnates. Cf. Lajos Kossuth, *Ifjúkori iratok. Törvényhatósági tudósitások* (Papers of Youth. Municipal Reports), *KLÖM*, VI (Budapest: Akadémiai kiadó, 1966), ed. István Barta, p. 5 and n. 1.

Ladislas Teleki, the Barons Joseph Eötvös and Sigismund Kemény, Ladislas Szalay, and Francis Pulszky, all born before 1815, played a leading role among the members of that noble "Generation of the Age of Reforms," which had so much to do with the preparation of Hungary's internal transformation that occurred in 1848.

The emphasis here is on the epithet "noble" and the substantive "reform," marking the social background and aim of this group, to which one may with some elasticity apply the term "generation." It is important to keep in mind that none of those belonging to it were professional revolutionaries, although many of them toyed with radical ideas in their youth; most supported and some even directed the revolutionary events of 1848–49. It was this generation of the age of reforms that made the difference between the historical situations that obtained on the Hungarian domestic scene after the French Revolution of 1789 and the July Revolution of 1830. Without it, the seeds sown by Széchenyi would have perished.

In order to understand this cross-fertilization of minds, one may recall that even in Hungary, many of Széchenyi's ideas were not entirely new. I have already referred to Gregory Berzeviczy as being perhaps the most significant advocate of economic reform in Hungary prior to Széchenyi. Among Széchenyi's precursors in the sphere of modern political thought one should not ignore Széchenyi's father's secretary and friend, Joseph Hajnóczy, one of the executed leaders of the Martinovics conspiracy. At the time Stephen Széchenyi was born, this great legal scholar attempted to formulate a new concept of Hungarian nationhood based on the extension of the nobility's privileges to the lower classes and on the emancipation of the serfs. He too dreamed of unifying the interests of all segments of society, and was in favor of general taxation on the basis of both human rights and natural law. Inspired by British, American, and above all French political thought, he was also sharply critical, like Széchenyi, of the Hungarian feudal constitution. But unlike Széchenyi, Hajnóczy wrote his major works in Latin and became a radical republican, embracing in his later works an increasingly democratic and nationalistic political philosophy.[111] Isolated and premature, Hajnóczy's and his less erudite associates' ideas were of no consequence in his homeland where the issue of reform was shelved for another generation.

It was different with Széchenyi. He came at a time when budding Magyar nationalism, frightened and subdued during the French revolutionary and Napoleonic periods, was about to regain its momentum,

[111] Bónis, *Hajnóczy*, pp. 5, 68, 72–82, 90–93, 100–103, 120–23, 173–78, 183–87, 204f., 208f., 238–45, 262–93.

and when the essentially conservative and politically influential middle landowning class began to worry about its economic security. Széchenyi's activities were calculated to bring about both a national and an economic rebirth. His writings, especially *Hitel,* had such a stunning impact on the public because the author could not be accused of being unmindful of the problems of the large estate owners, as was the agricultural expert John Balásházy, whose study, which won the award of the National Casino in the year preceding the publication of *Hitel* (1829), intended to assist the small farmer by following a line of argumentation resembling that of Széchenyi.[112] The international crises and domestic social tensions of the years 1830–31 further heightened the impetus of Széchenyi's agitation.

It was in this strained atmosphere that the county assemblies began a nationwide discussion of the report of the Dietal committee, to which Act VIII of 1827 assigned the task of revising the outdated suggestions for systematic reform originally initiated by the Diet of 1791.[113] Széchenyi, as we have seen, did not think very much of such a time-consuming and, in his view, impractical approach to the problem of Hungary's regeneration. Historians, too, tended to contrast rather than bring in harmony his initiatives with the "systematic works," an obvious euphemism for delaying all meaningful reforms under the pretext of acting on them systematically and in accordance with established political and legal procedures.

Yet Széchenyi himself attended at least some of the sessions of the delegations established by Sopron and Pest counties for the evaluation of the revised "systematic works" (*operata regnicolaria*) proposed by the Dietal commission. At his suggestion, on November 6, 1832 the deputies of Pest county were instructed to initiate at the forthcoming Diet the creation of a national fund of three million florins to develop the country's transportation system. Although the Diet of 1832–36 failed to consider this proposal,[114] Széchenyi was to return to the proposal in subsequent years; more important, the attempt shows that he did not ignore any channel that could be used for furthering his projects once he had formulated them.

Less direct but not necessarily less meaningful was Széchenyi's influence in the debates of other county assemblies over the systematic works. In early 1830, stimulated largely by the appearance of *Hitel,* county

---

[112] Lóránt Tilkovszky, "Balásházy János élete és munkássága" (The Life and Work of John Balásházy), *Századok,* xcvi (1962), 414f.

[113] Cf. Ch. V, p. 137 in this study.

[114] Fáy, *Széchenyi pestmegyei működése,* p. 24.

after county began to urge the chairman of the Dietal commission, the palatine, to make the results of its investigation available to the countries Due to the increasing pressure the *operata* were printed during the short autumn session of the Diet of 1830 and distributed among the municipalities by the end of the year. In the following spring came the formation of county committees which first discussed the new proposals. In the absence of a free press, this discussion provided the opportunity to articulate new ideas and political views reflecting widespread awareness of the revolutionary events in western Europe and Poland. Although the work of the county committees was interrupted in the summer of 1831 by cholera and the peasant rebellion, which caused the postponement of the Diet until 1832, public excitement did not subside. After resumption and completion of the debate in the delegations, the county assemblies had to approve the suggestions made by the committees. By the fall of 1832 this, too, had been accomplished, and the opinions of the different counties were given as instructions to the deputies representing them in the Diet. Formulated as amendments to the original reports of the Dietal commission, they were also submitted to the palatine, who was to preside over the forthcoming Diet.[115]

The labors of the Dietal commission in charge of improving the ancient systematic works between 1828 and 1830 did not give much encouragement to those advocating meaningful reforms. There were fears that the same "spirit" of immobility that was characteristic of the *operata* and everything related to them for some 40 years was to prevail this time, too. Such anxieties and the debates provoked by them may have contributed to the writing of *Hitel* and *Stádium*,[116] although Széchenyi's motivation was both more personal and complex, and his major books were stimulants rather than products of the decade that followed the Diet of 1825–27. It was in this 10-year period, which includes the Diet of 1832–36, rather than in the relatively short time span spent on discussing the systematic works and preparing for the Diet,[117] that the new opposition organized its forces, formulated the major goals of its program, and obtained considerable influence in both the counties and the Diet. These were the formative years of Hungary's great reform generation, whose leaders were to dominate the country's political life for about a half century.[118]

[115] Barta, *A fiatal Kossuth*, pp. 151ff. Barta's recent study contains a comprehensive analysis of the discussion of the systematic works and a meaningful documentation of their relation to Széchenyi's agitation. Cf. *ibid.*, "Széchenyi és a magyar polgári reformmozgalom kibontakozása" (Széchenyi and the Unfolding of the Bourgeois Reform Movement in Hungary), Történelmi Szemle, III, 224–40.

[116] Barta, "A magyar polgári reformmozgalom," 339, 341.

[117] *Ibid.*, 339–42.

[118] Joseph Eötvös died in 1871, Francis Deák in 1876.

It was also during the same epoch, that old-fashioned "estates" nationalism, still prevalent in the Diet of 1825–27, was gradually replaced by something radically different, which yet claimed and in some respects preserved the heritage of its antiquated predecessor. Using the linguistic-literary movement as its spearhead, modern Magyar nationalism, as the squaring of the circle can be called, appeared under the auspices of a liberal ideology, the strength of which was clearly demonstrated in the debates over the *operata*.

Inspired by English, American, and French rationalistic doctrines, or rather by the composite model abstracted from them, this liberal ideology appealed to all those who resented the economic or socio-political legacy of feudalism or who through reading and travel were impressed by the more elastic social structure, the more efficient economy, and the freer cultural climate of advanced Western countries. The two groups overlapped, of which Széchenyi was the classic example.[119] He and his works turned out to be prime molders of Hungarian liberalism which, in the absence of a politically articulate or economically independent bourgeoisie, was noble by social background, aggressively Magyar if not outright separatistic or oppressive by intention, and moderately progressive by the very definition of its anti-feudal political and economic endeavors.

The discussions following the publication of the revised systematic works, which constituted a prelude to the Diet, revealed many features of incipient Hungarian liberal nationalism. The nine *operata,* each of which was considered separately by a special committee delegated by the county assembly that finally discussed it, dealt with economic matters, public law and politics, *urbarial* affairs, legal problems, public education and science, churches, military affairs, taxation, and mining.

The majority of the counties seem to have been concerned above all with the *operatum commerciale* and wanted to put it on top of the agenda at the forthcoming Diet. In connection with the debates, which touched on a wide variety of subjects, most counties echoed the complaints of previous decades, attributing the economic ills of the country to its "colonial" dependence on Austria. Demands for complete reciprocity between the two halves of the Monarchy, changes in customs and tariff policies and their control by the Diet, construction of roads and canals, regulation of the Danube, building of a bridge connecting Buda and Pest, encouragement of industrial and trading enterprises, and establishment of financial institutions, alternated with suggestions

[119] Barta, "A magyar polgári reformmozgalom," pp. 322–26; István Fenyő, "A polgárosodás eszmevilága utirajzainkban 1848 előtt" (Ideas of Embourgeoisement in our Travelogues before 1848), *Irodalomtörténeti Közlemények,* LXVIII (1964), 603–12.

for the introduction of the French metric system, the limitation of the immigration of Jews (to get rid of their competition) and the abolition of all restrictions on the immigration of Jews (to further the increase of commercial capital).[120]

Many of the proposed economic measures showed the impact of Széchenyi's activities which, naturally, was felt less in the debate on the *operatum publico-politicum* or in the sphere of public law and politics. Efforts to reassert the nation's sovereignty and redefine the very concept of the nation were manifest in suggestions to limit the veto power of the king and the upper table, to elect the presiding officers of the Diet, to separate the three branches of government, to give more votes to the royal cities, to eliminate the deputies of absent magnates, and to give representation to the peasantry, although this last mentioned proposal was supported by only a few counties. Many more, however, insisted on establishing Magyar as the official language of the Diet, on transforming the lieutenancy and other administrative organs into governing bodies responsible to the Diet, on making the counties and cities more independent from central controls and politically more democratic by extending somewhat the suffrage and by sharing more equally the burdens of taxation. Most of these stipulations were conspicuously absent from the original report submitted to the counties by the Dietal commission. The original, however, intended to legalize preliminary censorship, an attempt overwhelmingly rejected again but which continued in practice.

Those parts of the systematic works which dealt with taxation and mining provoked few new ideas. Many counties had little experience or interest in mining, and those which were affected by it refrained on the whole from challenging the age-old royal prerogative in the exploitation of mines. The discussion of taxation was highly technical, focusing on the abolition of abuses rather than the nobility's tax exemption, which was raised elsewhere. Similarly conservative was the treatment of military affairs, since the overwhelming majority of the nobility wanted to maintain the noble levée and resisted the proposal of the Dietal commission, which suggested that young noblemen obtain their basic military training on a two-year tour of duty as recruits in the imperial army, after which they would serve in the special detachments of the nobility, called *banderia*.[121] Although there were numerous sugges-

---

[120] For most of the data in this and the next seven paragraphs I am indebted to the detailed analysis of Barta, *A fiatal Kossuth*, pp. 153–73.

[121] From the Italian, *bandièra* (flag), hence "military unit under its own flag." Usage of the term goes back to the 14th-century Italian inspired reorganization of the Hungarian military establishment under the kings of the Anjou dynasty.

tions for improving the organization of the noble insurrection and making the nobility less dependent on the regular army than was the case during the cholera uprising, no important changes in Hungary's outdated military system proved to be feasible before 1848.

Church affairs appear to have caused less controversy in the preliminary debates than one would expect by recalling what happened at the subsequent Diets. True, there were voices demanding the abolition of monastic orders, the Dietal control of religious foundations, training of the clergy, the abolition of celibacy, and impediments blocking a person's conversion from one faith to another. These were signs not just of anti-clericalism among certain segments of the nobility but also of increasing religious indifference. Naturally the two trends may overlap to a certain extent. But they are not to be confounded. Half of the noble counties, altogether 26, were represented by Protestants in the Diet of 1832–36,[122] although less than one-fourth of the people were Protestant and the Catholic Church continued as the established church. This, too, shows that by the second quarter of the 19th century nationalism, the secular creed, had begun to take precedence over religious beliefs in the minds of educated and politically articulate Hungarians.

The impulse of Magyar nationalism was especially strong in the deliberations on education and science. Most liberals disputed the validity of the administration's claim that the direction of education was a royal prerogative; they also wanted to curb the influence of the clergy in it. Advocating a secular educational system to be controlled by the Diet, they pressed for the widespread usage of Magyar as the language of instruction. Some counties did not wish to permit the teaching of any subjects in the non-Magyar vernaculars of the kingdom except at the elementary level; others wanted to set up minimum requirements of education stipulating that illiterates be refused admission to the crafts and permission to marry, or that daughters of better families remain single until they learn perfect Hungarian. As silly and blind as some of these ideas may seem in retrospect, they were meant quite seriously as certain developments of Magyar, and other, nationalisms have taught us since the end of the last century. The desire in the early 19th century to create a unitary state-sponsored system of education implied a certain liberalization of the rigid feudal structure. The elevation of the masses through education, even if through exclusively or predominantly Magyar education, was part of Magyardom's nation-building process—as was the attempt to assist the talented poor (as Nógrád and Zala counties demanded) ; to forge "the citizens of different background,

122 Kölcsey, "Országgyűlési napló," *KFÖM*, p. 1,382 (May 28, 1833).

language, and custom," even the Jews, into "one moral body," as Baranya
county suggested; or to weld them, "regardless of religious distinctions,"
as Temes county put it, "into one indivisible unity, recognizing only
the prospering of the fatherland as [being in] their self-interest." Somewhat
naïve and certainly controversial from the beginning, this vigorous
Magyar nationalism coincided with the national awakening of Hungary's
non-Magyar peoples, and even stimulated it. Increasingly resented by
the ethnically conscious segment of the clergy and the educated elements
of Slavs, Romanians, and Germans, the liberal nationalism of the
Magyars nevertheless contained a good deal of idealism and was meant
to serve as a vehicle for the democratization of society as a whole. Unfortunately idealism and a desire for social progress are seldom clearly
understood or taken at face value, however sincerely they may be felt
by those who themselves are suspicious of the motives of the administration in power. This is one of the reasons why they cannot be relied
on as universal panaceas for the ills of underdeveloped countries yearning
for "national" independence before having achieved nationhood, especially if their population is multi-ethnic, as was that of 19th-century
Hungary. Kossuth and the liberal leaders of Magyardom were to learn
this bitter lesson the hard way, as were others in different parts of the
world at a much later date.

Whatever the merits and demerits of such speculations, and one could
argue about them at considerable length, the discussion of public education and science revealed the liberal reformers' concern with the selection
and financial situation of teachers, the modernization of the methods
of education, the introduction of modern languages and physical education, the publication of textbooks, and the education of girls. There
were demands for greater emphasis on Hungarian and world history,
and for a change in the Academy's charter, one provision of which
prevented this "work-shop of universal national culture" from penetrating the spheres of religion and political science. Frequently echoing
Széchenyi's terminology, these endeavors interpreted the promotion of
human progress as a sacred patriotic duty, and intended to use education
and science as modern tools for the furthering of social reform, the
goal of which was a more civilized, affluent, equitable, and free society.

The *operata* dealing with *urbarial* and legal affairs were crucial to
liberal reform. In *urbarial* affairs the Dietal commission's report went
beyond the *urbarial* contracts customary since Maria Theresa, insofar
as it proposed to give the serf the right to dispose freely of the usufruct
of the *urbarial* land tilled by him. Under the influence of the writings
of Széchenyi and to a lesser extent, Balásházy, as well as Wesselényi's
agitation, many county committees began to pay attention to the country's economic needs, the most pressing of which appeared to be the

reevaluation of the lord-peasant relationship. In May 1831 the county committee of Pest went on record in favor of making it possible for the serf to become the free owner of his *urbarial* plot and to redeem his feudal servitudes, including the *robot*. Because of the cholera uprising the proposal was not considered until January 1832. But it was approved, printed, and sent to the rest of the counties whose majority agreed with its tone and general principles. The one major stumbling block, which seemed to have caused some second thoughts even to people otherwise willing to discard outdated feudal methods of production, was the question of the *robot*. Its sudden and complete abolition could have presented serious problems to the agricultural economy of a country which suffered from a chronic shortage of capital and whose heavily indebted ruling nobility could hardly afford any other kind of labor but that of its dependent serfs, however obvious its deficiency might have been to those willing to look.

The serf's property rights, the abolition of the law of entail and manorial courts, considered in the discussion of urbarial affairs, loomed large in the debate on the *operatum* (which focused on Hungary's legal system). Széchenyi's idea of extending the nobility's privileges—expressed by Werbőczi's famous *Partis Primae Titulus Nonus* to the peasant masses, because, in the language used by Nógrád county, this was their natural right and was also the way of advancing a people toward nationhood—was feasible only if the serf could own property, acquire an education, and hold any public office. This implied, as Temes or Zala counties suggested, again in line with Széchenyi's argumentation, that ancient laws must not tie the hands of the present generation but should be changed so that "noble and non-noble patriots" might share equally both the burdens and opportunities of the fatherland. Equality before the law was perhaps the most significant of the demands for the modernization of the Hungarian civil and penal codes. These codes also included, in addition to the ones already mentioned, proposals for restricting the jurisdiction of ecclesiastic courts, equality of all religious denominations, abolishment of capital and corporal punishment, and, above all, legal safeguards for the peasant, enabling him to become in fact a free Hungarian citizen, a part of the nation.

It is obvious in retrospect that Hungarian feudalism, based as it was on social and economic inequality and on the political supremacy of a privileged class, could not possibly have absorbed all these ideas overnight. Those familiar with the history of Central Europe in the last century and a half may even doubt that Hungarians ever understood, let alone honestly wished to implement, the great legacy of their Age of Reforms.

Yet great legacy it was. According to István Barta's computation, more than one-third of the counties (19) gave definitely progressive instructions to their deputies for the Diet of 1832–36, and only about a dozen were firmly controlled by conservatives reluctant to go beyond changes suggested by the preliminary report of the Dietal commission. The balance of the counties, whose stand shifted according to the issue involved, had no clear-cut profile that could be labeled as either "liberal" or "conservative"[123]—in itself a warning not to use the labels carelessly or too frequently.

It is also essential to bear in mind that the pressure for liberal reform began in earnest before the cholera uprising. Although the uprising stunned the country and tended to polarize public opinion, it nevertheless appears to have helped rather than hindered those in favor of change. In calling attention to the urgency of reforms lest the nobility resign its leading role in shaping Hungary's future, the "party of reform," as it was dubbed before the term "liberal" became fashionable, cautioned against giving Vienna another opportunity to revive the old alliance of the court and the peasant, making thereby the country and its privileged classes even less independent than they had been before.

This two-pronged appeal to the politically articulate nobility's common sense and national pride, which Széchenyi and Wesselényi so often used in their agitation and which was to reach its perfection in Kossuth's rhetoric, drew its strength from two sources. One was the fear of the privileged propertied class of a radical social revolution and the other the sincere desire of the "generation of reform" to improve the human condition by creating a better Hungarian nation. The reality of the first was driven home by the Polish revolt and the related Hungarian events in 1830–31, and again by the insurrection in the Republic of Cracow in 1846. Also, some Austrian officials, including Metternich, were not above using thinly veiled threats when the noble Magyars seemed to be too restless. Of equal importance was the other factor, which may be referred to as the basically enlightened and socially concerned inspiration of Hungarian liberalism. Because of the blunders of the protagonists of Hungarian liberalism in their policies toward the non-Magyar population of the kingdom; the abuses committed against the underprivileged, especially the non-Magyars, by the regime that claimed its name after 1867; and the vilification by Hungarian and non-Hungarian opponents for more than hundred years, the achievements and moral strength of early Hungarian liberalism are easily forgotten. Still, to ignore the Western inspiration, integrity, and high political standards of many 19th-century Hungarian liberal leaders would prevent getting to the heart of the movement that brought Hungary to life and accomplished Magyardom's evolution into a nation, in the modern sense of the word.

[123] Barta, *A fiatal Kossuth,* p. 173.

To attribute to a liberal ideology the original impulse, which started the fascinating metamorphosis of aristocratic Hungarian patriotism through the stages of gentry chauvinism, and populist ethnocentrism into proletarian Magyar nationalism, while some of its essential ingredients remained unchanged for 150 years, seems an exaggeration only if one forgets the complex background and nature of the political and intellectual fermentation that took place in the county assemblies and casinos in the 1830s. Széchenyi's *Hitel* was part of this fermentation, and in some respects even generated it. Its concluding section cautioned that Hungarians must not stand pat in a changing world but must move forward, lest they be pushed back by superior forces. To Széchenyi as well as other liberals, advancement through reforms appeared to be a feasible alternative to revolution.[124] Interestingly, one of the earliest explanations given by Kossuth in parentheses for the readers of his Dietal Reports immediately after the opening of the Diet in December 1832, derived the meaning of the yet alien political term "liberalism" from the concept of "truly moderate liberty."[125] That Kossuth was sincere in his belief that moderation was an integral part of true liberalism can be seen in the recently discovered text of one of his first public speeches. Although its tone seems immoderate to contemporaries, even in this speech, "given with unthinkable audacity . . . as though he had held the torch of sedition in his hands," as the aging literary dictator Kazinczy put it in a letter written in 1831,[126] Kossuth insisted on "the development and guaranteeing of liberal institutions on the basis of the established rights rooted in the foundations of society" precisely in order to avoid "the licentiousness of the monstrous years of the last century" and the repetition of "the bloodstained events of 1830."[127]

Along with progressive ideas about the need for radical reform, incipient Hungarian liberalism contained an element of ambivalence, or a strain of conservatism. In this context the terms "liberal" and "conservative" were supplementary, at least until World War I. But to assume, as Marxist historiography tends to do,[128] that the victory of liberal ideas was foredoomed because liberalism's champions preferred gradual reform to revolution in order to save their nation from unnecessary sacrifices, is just as ahistorical as was the endeavor of some historians between the two world wars to obliterate the legacy of liberal democracy in Hungary.

Some serious limitations of Hungarian liberalism became obvious in

---

[124] Barta, *A fiatal Kossuth*, pp. 37–45, 98–108, 116ff., 127–36, 150–53.
[125] Kossuth, *Országgyűlési tudósitások*, I, 12 (Dec. 19, 1832: c.).
[126] Viszota, ed., *Széchenyi és Kossuth*, I, pp. xiv. ff (Kazinczy to László Bártfay).
[127] Barta, *A fiatal Kossuth*, pp. 35–40. For the entire speech cf. Kossuth, *Ifjukori iratok* in Barta, ed., *KLÖM*, VI, 215–19.
[128] See even Barta, *A fiatal Kossuth*, p. 166.

the very first Diet at which it appeared in strength. As Kölcsey, a leader of the liberal opposition, noted, deputies favoring freedom of the press immediately asked for restrictions when their own speeches were reported in a way they disliked. Complaining about the lack of unity of the opposition, Kölcsey pointed out that the conflicting interests of nobles, burghers, and peasants should be compromised in the interests of the nation as a whole.[129] He recorded with resignation that the deputies of the cities, "like most people," wanted to be liberal at the expense of others: they were ready to abolish the landlord's prerogative to license the peddlers and shopkeepers of the countryside, but were not eager to abolish the regulations restricting trade in the towns.[130] He also deplored the human frailties of some of his colleagues—their craving for limelight, talkativeness, yearning for office, and reluctance to speak up for principles disapproved by those in power[131]—all of which made it difficult for the opposition to close its ranks when the pressure of the administration and its supporters increased.

Széchenyi, too, often expressed his dissatisfaction with the Diet which in his words "fell asleep." He often thought that there was much theory and little practical work done.[132] To some extent this is why he engaged in feverish activities outside the Diet, trying to push his other enterprises, the Academy, Casino, and Economic Society. Sometimes he was away from Pressburg for many months directing the work at the Lower Danube or collecting information abroad. Yet besides "his" projects he kept an eye on the procedures of the Diet and participated in the debates on the most important issues, exerting a decisive influence on their outcome.

Kölcsey spoke with great warmth of his first encounter with Széchenyi. Himself a prominent writer, he complained to the founder of the Academy about some bureaucratic procedures that seemed to menace the creative activity of writers working for the new institution. He also remarked that many people did not seem to comprehend Széchenyi's ideas about the extension of constitutional rights to the entire people, the construction of a bridge between Buda and Pest, or the appearance of steamships on the Danube. Comparing the rhetorical abilities of Wesselényi, whose speeches revealed a strictly logical construction, with those of Széchenyi, the father of modern Hungarian political oratory said: "Széchenyi's speech is marked by effusion and digressions, its most characteristic feature being its capriciousness. Flitting from one subject to

[129] Jan. 15, 21, 29, 1833, Kölcsey, "Országgyűlési napló," *KFÖM*, pp. 1,252f., 1,266f., 1,277f.

[130] Apr. 13, 15, 1833, *ibid.*, pp. 1,343, 1,346f.

[131] Mar. 7, May 11, Aug. 19, 1833, *ibid.*, pp. 1,316f., 1,364f., 1,444ff.

[132] Dec. 9, 1833, July 13, Aug. 1, 1834, May 20, Dec. 3, 1835, Viszota, ed., *Naplók*, IV, 434, 484, 486, 555, 622.

another, he makes you laugh and then again serious for a moment. What a successful popular orator!"[133]

Although Széchenyi was not without vanity, nothing could have been further away than an appeal to the mass audience. But Kölcsey was right in sensing that he introduced a new style into Hungarian political debates. Széchenyi seldom prepared for his speeches, improvised most of the time on the spur of the moment; his language was closer to that of conversation than the solemn tone, sometimes bordering on mannerism, which was customary in the speeches made in the Diet or county assemblies. In the Diet he tried to mediate between the administration and the opposition. He wished to encourage what in his opinion were the government's good intentions by urging moderation on the radical wing of the oppositional forces organized by Wesselényi in the spring of 1833.[134] At the same time, he endeavored to convince the conservatives to make concessions to the causes of progress and Magyar nationality. In the debate on the royal propositions, suggesting that the Diet take up first the *urbarial* question,[135] Széchenyi vigorously supported the administration. The majority of the deputies, in accordance with the instructions of the counties, proposed to start discussion of the *commerciale* in order to take care of Hungary's economic grievances. After lengthy deliberations they were willing to join together the proposals concerning *urbarium* and commerce and military contribution and to submit them simultaneously to the king. Wesselényi favored this procedure, which would have made it possible for the Diet to include in its resolutions some of the old grievances, such as the tariff question, but Széchenyi emphasized that no grievance of the nation could be more urgent than the situation of the peasant. Unlike Wesselényi, he also rejected the idea of reproaching the government for having postponed the Diet during the cholera epidemic, concluding that an essentially good proposal need not be rejected just because the administration must always be opposed.[136] He carried his point, basically because Wesselényi agreed with him on the vital importance of improving the peasant's lot. According to a copy of an intercepted letter written by Széchenyi in early 1833,

[133] Dec. 18, 20, 1832, Jan. 21, Feb. 1, 1833, Kölcsey, "Országgyűlési napló," *KFÖM*, pp. 1,201, 1,204ff., 1,266, 1,282f.

[134] Zsolt Trócsányi, "A 'Wesselényi védelme' szerzőségének kérdéséhez" (On the Question of the Authorship of 'Wesselényi's Defense'), *Századok*, XCVI (1962), 840.

[135] The royal propositions suggested the following agenda: (1) settlement of the *urbarium;* (2) reorganization of the judicial system; (3) regulation of military contributions; (4) commerce; (5) settlement of Dietal allowances; (6) reimbursement of Dietal expenses advanced by the treasury.

[136] See Széchenyi's speech of Jan. 22, 1833, in Kossuth, *Országgyűlési tudósitások*, I, 114ff. Also: Feb. 9, 1833, *ibid.*, pp. 160f., 164f. Cf. Dec. 20, 1832, Jan. 22, Feb. 9, 14, 1833, Viszota, ed., *Naplók*, IV, 359, 361–64.

it was Wesselényi who ultimately succeeded in making the order of procedure suggested in the royal propositions acceptable to the opposition, and the palatine thanked him for his endeavors.[137]

Indeed, Wesselényi, unyielding defender of Hungarian constitutionalism, has often been misunderstood and misrepresented by his opponents. His political tactics were not by any means consistently suitable and some of his rash actions deterred even friends such as Széchenyi, whose fury bordered at times on hatred in condemning his friend's "haughtiness," "histrionics," "madness," and "dangerous irresponsibilities.[138] Yet despite his many shortcomings, this Herculean daredevil of Hungarian political life was not a barbarian, as he is sometimes described, but a widely read, warmhearted protector of downtrodden people. He was not even disloyal to the dynasty. A remarkable excerpt from his speech in the debate of the royal propositions on January 22, 1833 is highly characteristic of his outlook on the problems Hungarian liberals must face. Recognizing the dynasty's efforts to alleviate the peasant's misery, efforts that were obstructed by the estates, Wesselényi turned to the reign of Maria Theresa, who had attempted to obtain the Diet's cooperation, saying:

. . . many other subjects distracted the Country's attention and time so that there was nothing done concerning the *Urbarium* and the peasant's lot. Following her Christian duty, Maria Theresa had thus been so to speak forced to further this cause outside the Diet. True, she did it illegally but to the commanding good of mankind which is the law of all laws. It was then that the Sybil appeared to our nation the first time offering her 9 books. But we found them too expensive, rejected them and thus three of the books were thrown into the flames . . . .

In the last quarter of the past century Joseph, adornment of his age and a Great Man on the throne, by an unlawful act which yet deserves blessing, abolished serfdom, this dirt of humanity. In 1790, the Estates of the Realm approved of this action and started consultations with regard to the conditions of the peasantry. It was then, that the Sybil appeared the second time offering again but her six books. We again found them too expensive and they again fell prey to death.

We should have abolished Serfdom, eliminated all its remnants, and washed off its filth in order to save the peasants from the burdens

[137] Széchenyi to his brother Paul, Annex No. 1, 1833/2, *ibid.*, IV, 667.
[138] E.g., Dec. 25–26, 1831, Mar. 18, Apr. 24, Dec. 14, 1832, Feb. 1, 9, Apr. 30, 1833, Feb. 12, 1835, *ibid.*, IV, 235f., 253, 259, 357, 362f., 375, 524.

of despotism and insecurity which pressed their person and landholding as a consequence of their old situation [rooted] in serfdom; instead, we clumsily abandoned the laudable work, turning it into the object of committee work lasting some 42 years.

Today the Sybil reappeared with her last three books. Let us not turn her down and let us not cause her to throw these too into the flames because, by heaven, the flames reducing them to ashes may as well consume our own person and property and that of our progeny.[139]

A careful reading of Wesselényi's speech, recorded by Kossuth, shows some of the features that made the leaders of the "generation of the age of reforms" so remarkable. Wesselényi, the champion of constitutionalism, was willing to approve even arbitrary actions of the dynasty on the basis of Christian humanitarianism and enlightened principles, provided that they would ameliorate the conditions of the serf. But he scrupulously preferred legislative action to absolutistic measures. In fact, he repeatedly cautioned his peers against giving the peasantry the impression that the court was its liberal protector and the nobility its real enemy. Suspecting that the administration wanted to drive a wedge between nobleman and serf by making urbarial affairs the first item of the agenda of the Diet, Wesselényi, Kölcsey, and other liberal leaders decided to attack the problem directly and accept the challenge, since there was no patriotic duty higher than the need for securing a civil constitution for 10 million oppressed people. Or to again paraphrase Kölcsey, the administration desired the enactment of the urbarium for the urbarium's sake, whereas Wesselényi, and his friends, intended to build a nation with the help of the new urbarial regulations. This "trifle" naturally made quite a difference between the chiefly economic aims of the administration and the primarily political goals of the opposition.[140]

Kölcsey knew that as far as the royal propositions were concerned Széchenyi took the side of the court party opposed by Wesselényi. Impressed by the vigor of Széchenyi's eloquence and the impact of his personality on the majority of deputies, Kölcsey yet referred to Széchenyi and Wesselényi by the Homeric epithet, "the two marshals of the people."[141] Indeed, the two fought together for a number of important issues, al-

---

[139] Kossuth, Országgyűlési tudósítások, I, 124ff. Both Wesselényi and Széchenyi recognized the greatness of Joseph II. With regard to Széchenyi, cf. Hunnia (Hungary), in Török, ed., Széchenyi politikai iskolája, III, 44, 60; also Ch. V, 146.

[140] Jan. 5, 6, 8, 11, 14, 23, 1833, Kölcsey, "Országgyűlési napló," KFÖM, pp. 1,229f., 1,232, 1,234, 1,240f., 1,243ff., 1,247, 1,269.

[141] Jan. 21, 22, 1833, ibid., pp. 1,265f., 1,269. Cf. Ilias, I, 16, 375.

though Kölcsey could not help noticing the element of discord that disturbed their personal relationship.[142]

Leaving aside the personal factor and the increasingly obvious differences in the choice of both methods and eventual goals, too, no amount of cooperation between Széchenyi and Wesselényi could have overcome the basic difficulties inherent in the very makeup of the feudal Diet. A brief analysis of the most significant issue, namely the urbarial question, shows that the legislation enacted by the Diet lagged far behind the original intentions of many liberal patriots. The reasons for this were many. On the one hand, most deputies were reluctant to give up any economic privileges of the nobility or, even if inclined to do so, were bound by their constituents' instructions to the contrary. On the other hand, the administration, posing as the defender of the serf against his lord for tactical reasons and for filling the coffers of the treasury, would not go beyond minor economic favors. It trimmed even the meager concessions offered by the estates in the sphere of civil rights or with regard to the possibility of an absolute indemnity, which would have permitted some serfs to become free landowners. Rejection of the more progressive parts of the estates' urbarial proposals "under the pressure of powerful oligarchs," as Paul Nagy put it, intimated that Vienna was perhaps more interested in maintaining the division among the nation's social strata than in improving the conditions of the serfs. The government also resorted to other maneuvers. Several times during the Diet it succeeded in having the originally progressive instructions changed in the county congregations by stirring up the venable "sandal" nobility, thereby causing the abdication of a number of deputies who refused to represent the retrogressive views of their constituents at the Diet. Francis Kölcsey, one of the liberal leaders in the lower table was one of those forced out of the political arena in early 1835.

The protracted discussion of the urbarial question, the abridged protocols of which filled 14 folio volumes, resulted in measures of limited importance. Laws IV–XIII of 1836 permitted pecuniary redemption of feudal services on the basis of voluntary agreement, but the serf was not allowed to redeem the land held in villein tenure. Manorial courts were not abolished but the lord could not sit in judgment over his own serf. If the serf moved to another lord he had the right to sell the usufruct of the land he had tilled hitherto. The estates also agreed that the ex-

---

[142] Mar. 11, Apr. 13, 1833, Kölcsey, "Országgyűlési napló," *KFÖM*, pp. 1,320f., 1,345.

[143] Horváth, *Huszonöt év*, I, 372–411; Blum, *Noble Landowners*, pp. 209f.; Ludwig Wirkner, *Meine Erlebnisse* (Pressburg: C. Stampfel, 1879), pp. 76–90; Hanns Schlitter, *Aus Österreichs Vormärz, III: Ungarn* (Zurich, Leipzig, and Vienna: Amalthea Vlg., 1920), p. 5.

penses of the Diet should henceforth be paid by the nobility and that "sandal" nobles on urbarial land should be taxed. The positive aspects of this law, however, were marred by the circumstance that it became a constant irritant among the lower nobility, with them alternately blaming the administration and the liberal opposition for the "infringement" on their ancient privileges.[144]

Széchenyi approved of and energetically fought for the pro-peasantry measures[145] although the results obtained fell short even of his program of gradually improving the conditions of the serf. He realized that while making some minor concessions the estates upheld the feudal system as a whole. Yet he appreciated small steps in the right direction, particularly because the concessions obtained from a reluctant Diet and a no less cautious government were the first pieces of enacted legislation favorable to the serf since Maria Theresa.

In the long and heated debate over the Protestant grievances concerning mixed marriages, conversion, and the "voluntary" approval of the children's Catholic education (reversalis), as well as over the proposal to make Magyar the "diplomatic language" of Hungarian legislation and administration, Széchenyi sided unreservedly with the liberal majority of the deputies against the conservative high clergy and magnates in the upper table.

According to many contemporaries such as Kölcsey, the religious issue was second in importance only to the urbarial question, the former affecting three million Protestants and the latter 10 million taxpayers.[146] Protestants objected to certain parts of Law XXVI of 1791, the purpose of which was the confirmation of their rights on the basis of previous domestic legislation and international treaties. In practice, however, some Catholic clergyman violated, if not the letter then the spirit of the law; and the official interpretation, which maintained the right of the crown to arbitrate disputed cases, appeared to favor the Catholic Church. This raised a constitutional issue, since the liberal members of the Diet could not fail to point out, in accordance with Act XII and other legislation enacted in 1790–91, that "the power of creating, repealing,

[144] Horváth, Huszonöt év, I, 411–23; Hóman and Szekfű, Magyar történet, v, 289f. For the far-reaching political and social implications of the blunder committed by the administration when it rejected the progressive but still conservative proposals of the urbarial bill passed by the Diet, thus giving a valid argument to the opposition, see Max Freiherr von Kübeck, ed., Tagebücher des Carl Friedrich Freiherrn von Kübeck von Kübau, 2 vols., Vol. I in 2 pts. (Vienna: Gerold, 1909), I, Pt. 2, p. 753 (Jan. 26, 1837). Cf. the French ambassador's remarks about the Austrian government's "Machiavelism" toward the peasant, Ste-Aulaire to Molé, Oct. 7, 1836, Vol. 423, Correspondance politique, Autriche, Archives du Ministère des Affaires Etrangères (Paris).

[145] E.g., May 6, 1833, Oct. 15, 26, 1835, Viszota, ed., Naplók, IV, 376, 610, 612.

[146] Kölcsey, "A vallás ügyében" (In the Matter of Religion), III, KFÖM, p. 1,110.

and interpreting laws" was not an exclusive royal prerogative but also one of the basic rights of the nation represented in the Diet.[147] This is why, in the words of Kölcsey, himself a Protestant, "the sons of Luther and Calvin looked on in silence, while the followers of [Cardinal] Pázmány's creed rivaled each other in speaking up in their behalf."[148]

Though somewhat exaggerated, this observation showed the great change in the atmosphere of the lower table where liberal Catholics Edmund Beőthy or Francis Deák, supported by the majority of the estates, half of whom were Protestant, led the fight for the liberty of conscience against the Roman Catholic clergy who had a dominant influence in the upper table. In the latter, Széchenyi repeatedly proposed that the lower table's resolution granting full equality to Protestants be submitted to the monarch without discussing the painful issue in the house of magnates. When his motion was voted down he strongly condemned the bigotry of certain prelates of the Catholic Church, adding that he wanted it to go on record for posterity "that Stephen Széchenyi had opposed this decision with all his power."[149] The debate in which Széchenyi competed with Wesselényi in championing the Protestant cause failed to bring any results due to the resistance of the majority in the upper table, which rejected the bill of the table of deputies six times. In their seventh message to the upper table the deputies proclaimed their intention to suspend "the request of the nation" and declare the objectionable practices illegal if the magnates continued their opposition to the lower table's resolution.

The inconsiderate usage of the "second veto" in the religious issue greatly increased the resentment against the upper table; this mistrust was to bring bitter fruits in subsequent years. The defeat of what he regarded as the cause of the freedom of conscience also disappointed Széchenyi. For many months he abstained from the Diet, dropping in only occasionally to see whether his compatriots were still asleep. At times he would ask someone else to make a motion in his stead, such as in the case of the proposal to move the Diet to Pest.[150] His depression over the situation may have been one of the factors motivating him

[147] See Kölcsey's argument "A vallásról vallásra szabad általmenetel tárgyában" (In the Matter of Free Conversion from One Religion to Another); and "Üzenet a fő RR.-hez a vallás tárgyában" (Message to the Magnates in the Matter of Religion), *KFÖM*, pp. 1,111–16. Also Beőthy, in Kossuth, *Országgyűlési tudósítások*, i, 88ff.

[148] Feb. 4, 1833, Kölcsey, "Országgyűlési napló," *KFÖM*, pp. 1,284f.

[149] Speech of Mar. 9, 1833, Kossuth, *Országgyűlési tudósítások*, i, 226f. Cf. Mar. 27, 28, 1833, *ibid.*, pp. 255f., 261, 267, 269, 272f. Also Feb. 21, Mar. 4, 9, 26–29, 1833, Viszota, ed., *Naplók*, iv, 364ff., and n. 6, 369ff. For a conservative Catholic interpretation see Meszlényi, *A jozefinizmus*, pp. 346–64.

[150] July 3, 1833, *ibid.*, iv, 384.

to accept the royal commission for supervising the works on the Lower Danube. Knowing that his absence from the Diet might seem desirable to the opponents of reform, he yet thought that at least he could spend his energies in creative work for the tangible benefit of Hungary.

More successful were the opposition's efforts in the language question. In several speeches, Széchenyi sarcastically denounced Hungarian circumstances where legislative matters were discussed in German at home, debated in Magyar at the Diet, submitted in Latin to the throne, translated into German for the councillors who ignored both Latin and Magyar. Then the royal rescript, he said, drafted in German by the councillors, would be sent back in Latin translation to the Diet which in turn again would debate it in Magyar to enact finally a Hungarian law in Latin.[151] In another fiery plea, Széchenyi repudiated the idea of any compulsion as "prejudicial and fruitless because the might of reaction usually exceeds in strength the action," adding, however, that for some 40 years the Magyar vernacular demanded its "natural rights," hence there could be no question of "rashness." Reminding his listeners that the flow of history could not be forcibly stemmed, he suggested a substitution of living Magyar for dead Latin in public life, for "either there will be a more Magyar world than today in the course of a generation's lifetime, or the Magyar must perish."[152] This rigid either-or, reflecting the inferiority complex of Széchenyi's generation which dated back to the Herderian trauma, must be remembered when making our judgment on the vigorous campaigns for Magyarization and its excesses in subsequent years. As for Széchenyi, he was not only "the father of Hungarian reform," as Michael Horváth dubbed him, but also the father of modern Magyar nationalism, which is sometimes overlooked.[153] His patriotism, as I have tried to show, was a lofty and humanitarian feeling. Yet in matters of reforms and nationalism it is hard to draw the "correct" demarcation line at the "right" time. Széchenyi was to find out about this only too soon after distressing experiences of his own.

Act III of 1836, which was passed by the Diet largely because of Széchenyi's forceful agitation and above all because of the palatine's willingness to compromise, still was defensible from a constitutional point of view.[154] Laws still were to be published in two languages, namely Latin and Magyar, but the Magyar was to be the authoritative text (1§).

[151] Speech of Jan. 21, 1833, Kossuth, *Országgyűlési tudósítások*, I, 108f.

[152] Speech of Feb. 20, 1833, *ibid.*, I, 185f. and 186f. Cf. Jan. 21, Feb. 21, 1833, Nov. 30, Dec. 18, 29, 1835, Viszota, ed., *Naplók*, IV, 361, 364, 622, 628ff.

[153] Horváth, *Huszonöt év*, II, 249.

[154] For the text of the law see Szekfű, ed., *Iratok*, p. 482. For pertinent documents see *ibid.*, Docs. 82–121, pp. 399–485.

The new act permitted lawsuits to be carried on in Magyar before the high courts, stipulating that in such litigations the decisions of the courts should also be handed down in the same tongue (2§). Henceforth, preambles and conclusions of official documents could be issued in Magyar (3§). Birth, marriage, and death registers were to be kept in Magyar in places where the language of parish preaching was Hungarian (4§). Finally, the law stipulated the establishment of a chair for the Magyar tongue in the Romanian seminary at Arad (5§).

On the whole, the new law was moderate, as shown by the permissive rather than mandatory language used in it. Correctly executed, it would have defended Magyar nationality without encroaching on the rights of other ethnic groups. Still, it was strongly resented by non-Magyars for a number of reasons. It was enacted at a time when the latter had already begun their own national renaissance and were as oversensitive as the Magyars, who prided themselves on their "historic" rights based on the unity of all lands belonging to the Crown of St. Stephen. Especially vigorous was the opposition of the Croats, who alone among the non-Magyar nationalities had a vote in the Hungarian Diet and who were recognized as having a "historical" entity, constitutionally speaking. They protested against the new law in the Diet, then after its enactment, in a petition sent directly to the court. Although the new law did not affect Croatia, outspoken Croatian objections to it stemmed from fears aroused during the Dietal debates over the issues of religious freedom, judicial reorganization, and tax distribution. The Croats felt that their religious privileges and internal autonomy were threatened by Magyar Calvinism, called the "Hungarian creed" and liberalism, which many thought identical.[155] Against Hungarian liberal and progressive representatives the Croats found their protectors in the Catholic high clergy, the conservative magnates of the upper table, and the administration at Vienna, whose "meddling" in Hungarian "domestic affairs" was rejected however by Hungarian liberal patriots. The exaggerated demands of the latter tended to strengthen Croatian separatism and contributed to the reevaluation of the traditional Hungaro-Croatian collaboration against Viennese centralization and Germanization of the late eighteenth century.[156]

As indicated previously, Széchenyi sensed quite early the dangers of the nationality question.[157] Still, in September 1834 he began to write the second part of *Stádium* under the title *Hunnia nyelve* (The Lan-

---

[155] For the interchangability of terms and the importance of the "superstructure of religious animosity," see the observations in Pardoe, *City of the Magyar*, II, 155–65; also the police reports of Aug. 27 and Sept. 8, 1840, in B. Szabó, ed., *Adatok*, I, 361ff.

[156] Miskolczy, *A horvát kérdés*, I, 114–53.

[157] See Ch. VI, p. 222-26 in this study. Cf. Wagner, "Széchenyi and the Nationality Problem in the Habsburg Empire," pp. 287–311.

guage of Hungary).[158] The book, the final title of which became *Hunnia* (Hungary) was to justify and elaborate on "law ten" proposed in *Stádium*.[159] A year later, at the time of the discussion of the language question in the Diet, Széchenyi still thought "*Hunnia* will not be superfluous . . . ."[160]

Hunnia was another eloquent plea for Magyar nationality and language. Széchenyi, who wrote a great part of this work in the form of a petition to the monarch, put a special emphasis on his personal loyalty to the dynasty and on his patriotic motivation—"two qualities which had already been reconciled by my forefathers and thus are in my blood." Stressing that Hungarians were a loyal people, he urged the sovereign to grant them their language. This would remove the basic causes of mistrust between nation and king, so often abused by "unfortunate councillors" implying that all Hungarians were rebels. *The greatest treasure of Hungarians is their national idiom; this is the only safeguard of their entity as a nation, for no nation can exist without a national language. Hungarian progress depends on loyalty to the dynasty and on the promotion of national characteristics predetermined, however, by the free development of the language.* The main cause of the country's degeneration, according to *Hunnia,* lay in the "unnatural contempt for our national idiom." This "national crime," however, had been and was being committed not by foreigners but by native Hungarians.[161]

The weak points in Széchenyi's romantic nationality and language concept can be seen fairly easily. The importance of *Hunnia* is *not* the fact that Széchenyi went out of his way to prove the necessity of "introducing among 'Magyars' instead of the dead Latin tongue the living Magyar idiom."[162] He had already done this in earlier works and public speeches. But it is significant that even in his tirades against the use of Latin he never for a moment abandoned his humanitarian principles for the sake of jingoistic glorification of the Magyar. He firmly believed that there must be one official language for legislative and administrative purposes in Hungary, and proposed that this official language should be Magyar, adding categorically, however, "It is not our intention to go beyond that."[163]

[158] Sept. 14, 1834, Viszota, ed., *Naplók,* IV, 493.
[159] Cf. Ch. VI, 235 of the present study. The book was first published by János Török, ed., *Széchenyi politikai iskolája,* III, 1–62. My references are based on this edition. The choice of title reflects the influence of the widely held belief, subsequently refuted, that Magyars were descendents of Attila's Huns.
[160] Nov. 2, 1835, Viszota, ed., *Naplók,* IV, 614.
[161] *Hunnia,* pp. 4f., 12, 38, 40–47, 56–62 (italics added).
[162] *Ibid.,* pp. 4, 9f., 57f.
[163] *Ibid.,* pp. 20f., 31.

Széchenyi warned his readers that they need not try to make up overnight for what their forebears had neglected to do for eight centuries.
Debased Magyardom could not be repaired through miracles, but only
through considered action. He suggested that the Magyar tongue be
given "neither greater nor smaller sphere" than Latin had in the country's political life and education. Scrupulously stopping at this point,
he advised that each should be allowed to exercise freely his religion,
language, customs, and national traditions. He insisted that Magyardom
should conquer sympathizers by "ennobling our customs, broadening our
intelligence, cleansing our constitution from the feudal tripe, and by
incessantly developing and embellishing our mother tongue." Cautioning
against going beyond this, he paraphrased a French author: "He who
wants less or more than that, either forgot the rights of nationality or
attacks the truths of humanity."[164] He also advised that the attachment
of other nationalities to their own tongue and cherished traditions should
not be belittled. Significantly, he pointed out that Austria was "an empire
of many languages and different nationalities" whose existence was due,
in addition, to divine providence, to the "patient mildness with which,
generally speaking, its rulers avoided attacking any nation's genius in
open or by force." On principle, he said, and according to the letters
of the treaties binding Hungary to Austria, Hungarians were still independent; regarding the facts, however, the country was about to share
the lot of other provinces where absolutist government increasingly replaced the rule of law.[165]

This was a realistic approach, in line with his family's tradition, but
it also reflected Széchenyi's new Hungarian nationalism. It implied a
careful evaluation of the relative strength of the varied nationalities
in the empire without giving up any real interests or opportunities for
the Magyar. In Széchenyi's opinion, non-Magyars were closer to the
fountainhead of civilization than Hungarians, and did not face the danger of losing their mother tongue because their kinsmen beyond the
borders were more numerous. "Fatherland is based not on lifeless earth
but upon living people"—thus the survival of non-Hungarians seemed
to be secure because of their numerical strength. The potential Magyar
advantage, Széchenyi held, was their constitution, which incorporated
the principle of representative government. Hence Magyars could become
the "main nation" of the empire by developing their constitution and
by being an example to other parts of the realm, especially since neither
Slav nor German had as yet achieved progress in this direction.[166]

[164] *Ibid.*, pp. 13f.
[165] *Ibid.*, pp. 14-17, 19.
[166] *Ibid.*, pp. 17f., 22f., 28-35.

Whereas Széchenyi readily admitted the importance of German diligence and perseverance, as well as progress in literature and social life, he reminded his compatriots not to replace Latin with German as the official language and not to submit to the Austrian political system, but rather to stick to their representative form of government.[167]

In *Hunnia* Széchenyi set forth a number of ideas which were to inspire generations to come. At least on one occasion the Hungarian demand for granting a constitution to the non-Hungarian peoples of Austria was going to shake the realm of the Habsburgs when formulated in Kossuth's well-known speech on March 3, 1848. The Hungarian architects of the Compromise of 1867, too, followed in Széchenyi's footsteps in their effort to shift the center of the empire to Hungary. One emphatic message conveyed by *Hunnia* failed, however, to inspire Széchenyi's nation:

Therefore, let us respect the language and way of life of any people no matter how minute their sphere of existence is; for even the smallest distinct human quality represents a link in the chain the grades of which uplift mankind toward perfection. Let us respect not only everybody's earthly property but also the greatest treasure of his soul, his "loyalty to the fatherland and nation!" Only in this case can we, people of another kind, expect with some justification tolerance and indulgence toward the treasures of our own.[168]

There is but one more thing to remark about *Hunnia*, namely, that Széchenyi finally decided not to publish it. Only in 1858 did he give permission for its publication as a protest against the absolutist regime then prevailing in the empire. But the book was confiscated in the printshop at the order of Governor General Prince Albrecht and was published posthumously. Before the revolution of 1848, however, Széchenyi himself prevented the publication of his work not because, as has been suggested, he was satisfied with the language law of 1844,[169] but because he had realized as early as October 1835 that the book might have become outdated.[170] Although the language law of 1836 did not substitute Magyar for Latin, as was Széchenyi's aim, it did eliminate most obstacles to the trend. In the heated political atmosphere toward the end of and after the Diet, Széchenyi did not wish to inflame the language debate any further because by that time he had a better understanding of the

[167] *Ibid.*, p. 25.
[168] *Ibid.*, pp. 20f.
[169] Cf. Károlyi's introduction to *Döblingi hagyaték*, I, 163f.
[170] Széchenyi to Tasner, Oct. 17, 1835, Majláth, ed., *Levelek*, II, 133.

implications of the nationality problem in the monarchy, particularly in the Hungarian half. This was a primary motive for his unexpectedly vehement attack on Kossuth and his supporters a few years later. In the diaries and even in *Hunnia* Széchenyi revealed not only his ardent nationalism but his contempt for the "scatter-brained" extremists who intended to push for Magyarization by force.[171] Before long he was to dramatize this attitude by taking a public stand against them, since he feared they could provoke both a violent social revolution and a war between different ethnic groups in Hungary.

The antagonism of the ruling classes toward social reform came to the fore during the Diet of 1832–36. Although the opposition had a majority in the lower table, most of the proposed progressive measures were obstructed by the solid bloc of royalist and clerical conservatives in the chamber of magnates, where Széchenyi and Wesselényi had little support. Kölcsey repeatedly warned the magnates not to use their power in the upper table as a second veto (the first one being that of the king) against the nation's will as represented by the chamber of deputies[172]; his views were shared by moderates like Deák or Széchenyi.[173] But the dignified warning, forcefully reformulated by Kossuth less than a decade later, was to horrify Széchenyi and many other aristocrats: "If this nation has a destiny—and she certainly has one—it will come true with and by them if they like it; without and even against them, if necessary."[174]

Széchenyi himself noticed the alienation of the lesser nobility from the magnates.[175] In most major issues, such as urbarial, language, religious questions, the union of Transylvania and Hungary,[176] and the

---

[171] *Hunnia*, p. 55.

[172] Mar. 4, May 21, June 4, 1833, in Kossuth, *Országgyülési tudósitások*, 1, 214f., 400f., 436f.

[173] See Deák's speech of May 25, 1833 about the mutual relationship of the two chambers of the Diet. Kónyi, ed., *Deák beszédei*, 1, 13ff. The identification of the "nation's will" with the liberal majority's intentions in the lower table can be challenged. Besides the highly unrepresentative character of the Hungarian feudal Diet, the peculiarities of the system of voting in the Diet made any talk about the majority of the nation sound questionable. Supporters of the government, as well as conservative foreign observers, did not fail to point out that the representatives of the chapters and towns, taken together, outnumbered those of the counties even in the lower chamber, but that they had only two votes. If one adds the magnates, whose overwhelming majority were conservative, to the number of the opponents of liberal reform, one may indeed conclude, as did the British ambassador, that those claiming to speak in the name of the nation constituted only a minority of the representatives in the Diet. Cf. Beauvale to Palmerston, Nov. 12, 1839, *F.O. 7/282*, PRO (London).

[174] "Hivatás" (Calling), *Pesti Hirlap*, no. 14 (Feb. 17, 1841), republished in Ferenczi, ed., *A kelet népe*, p. 139.

[175] *Hunnia*, pp. 5f.

[176] Feb. 15, 1833, in Kossuth, *Országgyülési tudósitások*, 1, 169.

constitutional problem of Ferdinand V's title[177] he supported the opposition as a matter of principle against the archconservative majority of the chamber of magnates. Yet he hated radicals and derided "the sordid chaps," sneering even at Wesselényi who, in his opinion, was willing to accept their support but was too vain to try to influence them.[178] Széchenyi's disdain of the middle nobility, which, as Wesselényi and subsequently Kossuth correctly realized, was becoming the leading political force of the nation, contributed heavily to his failure in political leadership. His misjudgment of the political forces limited for him the possibility of successfully moderating between a suspicious administration and an increasingly bitter opposition. He honestly tried to overcome these difficulties. Toward the end of the Diet he again supported the government against the deputies in the matter of taxation. He wanted to please the palatine, who had helped him in most of his major enterprises such as the Academy, National Theater, bridge, and Danube navigation. But he worried about losing his influence both with the supporters and opponents of the administration.[179] Such an overpessimistic attitude was not justified—not yet. But there was validity in Széchenyi's doubts about the feasibility of his policy of the "golden mean," or "*juste milieu*" as contemporaries called it.

The conflict between Vienna and the Diet took a sharp turn when early in 1835 the government decided to impeach Wesselényi and another deputy who supported him in the Diet. The reason was Wesselényi's outspoken criticism of the administration at the Transylvanian Diet and at a county congregation in Szatmár in December 1834. Since the rights of freedom of speech and parliamentarian immunity were involved, the procedure was unconstitutional. In the nationwide storm of indignation that followed, Széchenyi used all his influence on both sides of the issue. In the Diet he defended in a moderate tone the principle of freedom of speech, supporting Deák's thesis that there was a difference between criticizing the government and committing high treason. Behind the scenes he urged Wesselényi, deputy Balogh, and other leaders of the opposition not to push things too far. At the same time, he pleaded with the palatine and high officials in Vienna to drop the whole case.[180]

---

[177] June 1, 1833, Viszota, ed., *Naplók*, IV, 559. As emperor of Austria, a title created in 1804, Ferdinand was the first; as king of Hungary, he was the fifth to bear that name since the Habsburgs came to the Hungarian throne in the early 16th century.

[178] Apr. 30, 1833, *ibid.*, IV, 375. Cf. Feb. 14, May 7, 1833, *ibid.*, IV, 363f., 376.

[179] Apr. 11–13, 16, 1836, *ibid.*, IV, 650–54.

[180] Feb. 12, 27, Mar. 3–6, June 22–30, July 1, 6, 1833, *ibid.*, IV, 524, 527, 529, 567–74, 576f. Cf. Viszota's introduction, pp. xv f. and xlvi, *ibid.* For the Transylvanian Diet of 1834–35 and Wesselényi's role in the county assembly of Szatmár in December 1834, see Horváth, *Huszonöt év*, I, 433–54, II, 55–61; and Trócsányi, *Wesselényi*, pp. 203–91.

While not quite fruitless,[181] Széchenyi's efforts did not bring the desired results for Wesselényi who was subsequently sentenced imprisonment for three years. To the bottom of his heart and among friends, Széchenyi severely disapproved of Wesselényi's actions.[182] He may have had some doubts about the language reportedly used by Wesselényi, but there was no question in his mind concerning the essence and tenor of his friend's philippics. Still, he would have kept on writing petitions for him; but Wesselényi preferred using his own legalistic defense instead of Széchenyi's more diplomatic version.[183]

In official circles "independence" was interpreted as unreliability; Széchenyi's attempt to save Wesselényi from prosecution and his close ties with members of the opposition were watched with misgiving. In his presence Metternich and Princess Melanie often inveighed against *"la Jeune Hongrie,"* meaning Wesselényi and the young liberals. The chancellor and his circle treated Széchenyi as a "repentant sinner" rather than a reliable go-between.[184] In early 1834, on the occasion of one of his official trips to England, a letter of recommendation was sent from Vienna to Ambassador Paul Esterházy, asking him to assist Széchenyi in collecting some necessary data. At the same time, however, another letter secretly instructed the envoy to keep a close eye on Széchenyi and George Károlyi, lest they publish in the English press the speeches given in the Hungarian Diet in support of the Polish upris-

---

For Széchenyi's efforts in behalf of his friend, see also *ibid.*, pp. 343–50, 360ff., 404, 406, 430, 434, 437.

[181] July 1, 1835, Viszota, ed., *Naplók*, IV, 574. Actually the proceedings against Balogh were stopped by a royal decree in October 1835. Cf. Ferenczi, ed., introduction to *A kelet népe*, p. 5.

[182] See the entries of Mar. 3 and 13, 1835, Viszota, ed., *Naplók*, IV, 528, 530. They were a prelude to what was to come on a large scale in the Kossuth debate: "Wesselényi . . . has never followed my advice . . . he ruins and smashes everything I have sown and cultivated for such a long time. . . . How painful! I have conceived with him the first idea of pulling Hungary out of the dirt! Our intent was so pure. . . ." Cf. Mar. 15, 1836, *ibid.*, IV, 646.

[183] Wesselényi's petitions drafted by Széchenyi (a) and by himself (b) were published in Annex No. 1, 1835/4a–b, *ibid.*, IV, 675–82. For details see Zsolt Trócsányi, "Wesselényi Miklós fogsága" (Nicholas Wesselényi's Imprisonment), *Századok*, XCIV (1960), 794–810, and XCV (1961), 281–98; also, Trócsányi, "A 'Wesselényi védelme' szerzőségének kérdéséhez" (On the Question of the Authorship of "Wesselényi's Defense"), *ibid.*, XCVI (1962), 836–40. See also István Barta, "Ki irta Kölcsey 'Wesselényi védelme' cimű munkáját?" (Who wrote Kölcsey's Work [entitled] "Wesselényi's Defense?"), *ibid.*, XCV (1961), 720–28; Barta, "Zárószó a vitához" (Postscript to the Discussion), *ibid.*, p. 841. These studies, the first of which is part of Trócsányi's new Wesselényi biography, suggest that "Wesselényi's Defense," previously attributed to Kölcsey and listed among his works, was actually written by several prominent attorneys and politicians, including Peter Benyovszky, Deák, and Kölcsey, although Wesselényi himself contributed to and remained in control of the work as a whole.

[184] Nov. 25, 1833, July 22, 1834, Viszota, ed., *Naplók*, IV, 430, 485.

ing.[185] Metternich was usually cool toward Széchenyi's projects and frequently lectured his former protégé, pointing to the dangerous paths he was taking, his anti-governmental speeches, and the casinos which turned into political clubs. Occasionally, the chancellor would also show Széchenyi reports which denounced him as a characterless radical and a dangerous enemy of the regime.[186]

Széchenyi answered the accusations in a detailed letter in defense of his position. He referred to his 17-year service in the army, after which, as he put it, he decided to lead a useful life, unlike many other Hungarian magnates, "who are purloiners of God's time and people's money." At the beginning of his public career, he continued, he often loyally opposed the government without ever being against or endeavoring to undermine the regime. Although many saw only an offended captain of hussars in him, he actively began to support the government from 1830 on, acknowledging even publicly in *Világ* that he had recognized a change for the better in its policies. Stressing his moderating role and the value of an independent man's services to the administration, Széchenyi then expressed his horror of anarchy and weak government. As for Wesselényi, Széchenyi held that clemency and benevolence could achieve more than a show of force. Declaring that Hungary's welfare could only be promoted simultaneously with that of Austria, Széchenyi stated that he had confidence in the government and would never work against its interests, but rather would always be willing to give his opinion if asked. In conclusion, he came to the main point: offering his services as a mediator between the "Austrian Government and Hungary." Unselfish mediation, he stressed, could eliminate much misunderstanding between nation and government. This is why he regarded it as his mission "to play the role of a go-between in a narrow sphere but in an extremely independent position."

These were the highlights of Széchenyi's apologia to Metternich, written on April 30, 1835. Some of the chancellor's caustic marginal remarks on it suggested that the author was a hypocrite; the palatine thought too that Széchenyi wanted to use this way to propagandize his ideas, and that his vanity was sufficient explanation for the self-imposed role of mediator. While there was some truth in the palatine's suggestion, there are several things yet to be said about this "Confession of 1835,"

---

[185] Metternich based his second set of instructions on a report from Chancellor Reviczky. Annex No. 1, 1833/10, *ibid.*, IV, 670. Esterházy showed both instructions to Széchenyi who faithfully copied them into his diary. Jan. 19, 26, Feb. 27, 1834, *ibid.*, IV, 445, 447, 455.

[186] Dec. 6, 1833, Jan. 14, Mar. 16, Apr. 21, 26, 28, May 2–3, 1835, *ibid.*, IV, 433, 516, 532, 541f., 544–49. For a summary of the charges, Széchenyi's written answer, and the comments on it, see Annex No. 1, 1835/7a–e, *ibid.*, IV, 683–94.

which was very much in line with Széchenyi's other writings and thinking
at the time. The apology revealed a cautious reevaluation of the first
10 years of Széchenyi's public career. The reevaluation somewhat overemphasized Széchenyi's collaboration with the government, and thus was,
if not untrue, at least historically incomplete. But the apologia was sincere, insofar as Széchenyi became increasingly aware of certain radical
trends in the reform movement and decided not to support them.

Another root of Széchenyi's emphasis on loyalty was his fear that
a sudden reaction of the government to a careless move of the opposition
would annihilate the tender firstlings of his work. The reasons for this
anxiety were not merely imaginary. The Wesselényi incident and the
fact that he himself was under permanent surveillance were sufficient
proof. He knew that Metternich and other officials disliked the idea
of having an "independent" mediator between government and nation.
From a logical point of view, Chancellor Reviczky was right in raising
the question in his comments on Széchenyi's apologia, that if the count
sincerely trusted the government, why did he want to mediate? Metternich himself had rejected Széchenyi's suggestion in their debate of
1825, remarking that this was the role of the palatine. But Széchenyi
was aware of the ferment in Hungary and did not belittle it, as did
most Viennese officials. He also knew the Magyar frame of mind, which
mistrusted everything and everybody connected with Vienna. He sincerely
believed that this potential source of trouble was not understood by
the leaders of the administration and could not be controlled by people
who conceived of him as a revolutionary and who blamed him for the
peasant upheaval of 1831.[187]

The fermentation of the country's political life continued during and
after the Diet of 1832–36. Although the legislation enacted was not
very impressive the discussions in the Diet and the deputies' reports
to the county congregations after the Diet animated the atmosphere.
But if the new laws failed to give a true picture of the nationwide
increase in strength of the party of reform, they at least meant a break-
away from the almost 50-year-old Dietal practice of taking up reforms
only "systematically." Ever since the Diet of 1790–91 had decided to
propose legislation for reforms, subsequent Diets were obsessed by the
idea that these had to be dealt with "organically" as a whole, and
that no individual measures should be enacted "*per excerpta*," or separately, taken from the context of the nine Latin codices containing the
voluminous reports of the Dietal commissions in charge of different areas
of reform. The Diet of 1832–36 at long last recognized that this "method"

[187] See Ch. VI, p. 230ff. in this study.

did not suit the demands of progress. Largely under the influence of Széchenyi's agitation, such as in the case of the bridge, the Diet chose to act on issues not foreseen in the "systematic works."[188] On the other hand, the reluctance of the opponents of reform to break with outmoded traditions made the enactment of thorough and far-reaching reforms in the Diet extremely difficult, if not practically impossible. This was another reason why Széchenyi wished to widen the social basis for reforms outside of the legislative body.

His endeavors were greatly assisted by the circumstance that events related to the Diet of 1832–36 reached in a relatively short time a much wider public than they had before. This was primarily due to the activities of the "Dietal youth" attending the sessions of the Diet in great numbers. Traditionally, the Dietal youth consisted of law students who wanted to get acquainted with Dietal proceedings. In most cases, they were hired by the counties or, less often, by members of the upper table to copy official documents and to prepare the records of the proceedings. Often, they represented absent magnates or their widows and consequently had a right to sit in the chamber of deputies. Although such an *absentium magnatum ablegatus* could not vote and would very seldom take the floor, he still was a member of the Diet and enjoyed certain privileges; thus he was closely affiliated with the Diet. Moreover, the Dietal youth constituted a Magyar audience in German Pressburg, whose burghers were partly disinterested in and partly hostile to the Hungarian feudal legislature, members of which occupied, without compensation, much of the city's best living quarters.

This audience was not silent. Patriotic and noisy, it often interfered with Dietal proceedings by booing "reactionary" members of the Diet and by encouraging progressive deputies. Imbued with French liberal ideas, the law students drafted programs for a modern parliamentarian democracy with a responsible government and popular representation, thus going well beyond Széchenyi's *Stádium*. After the Diet of 1825 police reports and petitions of the municipality of Pressburg continued to complain about the turbulence of the Dietal youth and their excesses against peaceful burghers. Part of the complaints were undoubtedly justified. The behavior of the law students, who would occasionally hamper rather than promote legislation, left much to be desired. At the same time, many talented leaders of the Hungarian liberal era came from the ranks of the Dietal youth, had high moral standards, and were sincerely devoted to the causes of Magyardom and progress.[189]

---

[188] Horváth, *Huszonöt év*, ii, 30ff.

[189] For the outlook and activities of the Dietal youth cf. Horváth, *Huszonöt év*, i, 303ff.; Hóman and Szekfű, *Magyar történet*, v, 297; Géza Ballagi, *A nemzeti államalkotás*

The Diet of 1832–36 was attended by about 1,500 law students. Many liberal counties sent 15 to 20, or even 30 to 40 scribes with their deputies to further the cause of reform at the Diet and to inform the public at home. Some of the *jurati,* as the students were called, were widely read and well educated and often came from or had close connections with leading noble families in the counties. They became powerful opinion-shapers at a time when the publication of Dietal records was incomplete and delayed, and when politics were banned from the country's only newspaper by an unconstitutional censorship. Whenever the censor of *Jelenkor* (Our Age) thought he had discovered a passage smacking of liberalism, he deleted it, exclaiming "Here are the principles of Count Széchenyi."[190]

Besides Széchenyi, the Dietal youth had other sources of inspiration, although he was held in great respect and was honored several times with ovations and torchlight parades. Francis Pulszky, one of the leaders, described the somewhat confused outlook of this young liberal intelligentsia:

. . . The idea of a revolution was rejected by every one of us. In fact, we liked to demonstrate our loyalty but at the same time, we bemoaned the fate of [Francis II] Rákóczi, cursed the Germans, were enthusiastic about the *Paroles d'un Croyant* by Lamennais, shouted stormy *Vivat!* [long-live] after the speeches of some of the bolder deputies, gave torchlight serenades to Count Széchenyi, who always cautioned us to be moderate and prudent and whom, because of this, we respected but did not like. Above all, we kept on studying the history of the French Revolution.[191]

In the words of the poet Petőfi, the bible of "Young Hungary" was indeed the history of revolutions, especially the French Revolution. The

---

kora, *1815–1847* (The Period of the Formation of the National State, 1815–47), Vol. IX of *A magyar nemzet története* (History of the Hungarian nation), ed. Sándor Szilágyi (Budapest: Athenaeum, 1897), pp. 419–30; Pulszky, *Meine Zeit,* I, 103ff., 111–22; Dániel Kászonyi, "Egy régibb kor férfiai" (Men of a Previous Age) and "Egy régibb kor ifjai" (Youth of a Previous Age), *Hazánk,* IV (1885), 519–54, 562–84; Sándor Takács, "A jurátusok kaszinói" (Casinos of the Law Students), "Jurátus-csaták Pozsonyban 1844-ben" (Skirmishes of Law Students in Pressburg in 1844), and "Idősb Andrássy Gyula az 1847–1848. évi országgyűlésen" (Count Julius Andrássy, Sr., at the Diet of 1847–48), in *Hangok a multból* (Voices of the Past) (Budapest: Athenaeum, n.d.), pp. 203–50, 334–51, 366–70, resp.
[190] "*Adhuc principia Comitis Széchenyi.*" Feb. 25, 1832, Viszota, ed., *Naplók,* IV, 247.
[191] Pulszky, *Meine Zeit,* I, 113.

leaders of the *Jugend-Verein,* several times reorganized but under constant police surveillance, formed an association for human rights, supporting the cause of the oppressed and the outcast of society, such as Poles and Jews. One of the brilliant young patriots, Ladislas Lovassy, who was subsequently sentenced to 10 years in a secret trial and went insane in jail, was the first to come out openly for the emancipation of Jews at a meeting of the law students' casino during the Diet of 1832–36.[192] Lovassy, his brother Francis, and other leaders of the young liberals gave active assistance to Polish refugees, some of them, like John Tormássy, supporting the fight for a free and democratic Poland. Inspired by the writings of Heine, Börne, and some of the Polish revolutionaries, these radical republicans condemned the Holy Alliance, the Austrian administration's failure to help the Poles, and even the conservative wing of the Polish leadership. No wonder that the secret police and Metternich associated them with Young Italy and French and Swiss revolutionaries, suspecting the existence of a Europewide conspiracy to overthrow legitimate rulers such as that of the Habsburg Monarchy. Among the charges brought against the leaders of the Dietal youth in a secret trial held immediately after the end of the Diet, the contacts with Polish revolutionaries were prominent.[193]

Popular sovereignty and the liberation of the peasants were also among the goals of these young liberals. Admiring personal courage and enthusiastic about constitutional rights, they lionized Wesselényi. When their idol was prosecuted they organized nationwide protests and demonstrations of sympathy in his support.

The younger generation of the county nobility served, in a broader sense, as the social basis for the Dietal youth. Closely affiliated with this core of "Young Hungary" were the college students, Hungary's budding intelligentsia, who were often of non-noble background. The youth of Pest was a particularly important segment of this nationalistic and socially progressive part of the politically active populace. Under Joseph II Buda became the seat of many government offices including the lieutenancy. At the same time, the Hungarian University was trans-

---

[192] Sándor Takács, "A pénzkirályok nálunk" (The Lords of Money in Our Midst), *Hangok a multból,* p. 359 and n. 9, 10. Violent opponents of Jewish emancipation were primarily the overwhelmingly German mining towns and the burghers of Pressburg and Pest, incidentally, the centers of the most educated and well-to-do segment of Hungarian Jewry. A proposal to grant Jews full citizenship was first made in the Diet during the debate on religious freedom in April 1833 by Alexander Császár, deputy of Temes county, which was later seconded by Simon Dubraviczky, deputy of Pest county. Kossuth, *Országgyülési tudósítások,* I, 297, 456.

[193] Kovács, *A lengyel kérdés,* pp. 181–200.

ferred to Pest; in subsequent decades the foundation of the National Museum, Academy, and National Theater all contributed to making Pest the literary and cultural center of the country, while the Casino and Széchenyi's other enterprises tended to stimulate the city's economic development. Small wonder, that the youth of Pest increasingly felt like being in the focus of Hungarian national life.[194]

The radicalism of the Dietal youth actually became an important factor in Hungarian politics. Young Louis Kossuth, partly also created by it, contributed to its influence. Himself a representative of two absent magnates, he became the editor of the *Országgyűlési tudósítások* (Dietal Reports). The reports, dictated by Kossuth to a number of law students who also took care of their distribution, made history in Hungary. Out of the reports Kossuth forged a mighty weapon which he masterfully wielded for the advancement of the reform movement. Besides Széchenyi's *Hitel,* his Dietal Reports were probably the most efficient stimuli of public opinion. They were read in casinos, country houses of the nobility, offices of county administration, and influenced even the supplemental instructions sent to the deputies during the Diet.[195] After the Diet, the Dietal Reports were in fact continued under the title of *Törvényhatósági tudósítások* (Municipal Reports). Assisted by a well-organized group of local correspondents, Kossuth informed the public about the county congregations following the Diet, thus keeping alive interest in the cause of progress and reform.

Széchenyi watched the growing excitement in the country with a feeling of uneasiness. Averse to demagogy and to uncontrollable and capricious masses in general, he feared that in a fit of reaction the government might again abandon the constitutional ground which it had just barely accepted in 1825. Although police agents often charged him with courting popular favor, he actually did his best to calm the Dietal youth, stressing the necessity for dignified behavior.[196]

In his memoirs written in exile half a century later, Kossuth com-

---

[194] For an analysis of the role and composition of "Young Hungary," see László Révész, "Das Junge Ungarn, 1825–1848," *Südostforschungen,* xxv (1966), 72–119.

[195] Introduction to Kossuth, *Országgyűlési tudósítások,* I, 7.

[196] Even Sedlnitzky's agents had to admit occasionally that there was a difference between the "dangerous machinations and aims" of Széchenyi and those of Wesselényi. But the difference was interpreted as a tactical maneuver. Jun. 17, 1837, Sedlintzky's report to the *Staatskonferenz,* B. Szabó, ed., *Adatok,* I, 282. In regard to Széchenyi's dignified and rather reserved attitude among the youth, a good example is given in the different eyewitness reports describing the torchlight serenade honoring Széchenyi on May 10, 1834. Cf. Wirkner report, Annex No. 1, 1834/4b, Viszota, ed., *Naplók,* iv, 672; Kászonyi, "Egy régibb kor ifjai," 563f.; Palatine Joseph's report, B. Szabó, ed., *Adatok,* I, 201. As for Széchenyi, he only remarked: "Remarkable serenade, with fifty torchlights. It will make me many more enemies," May 10, 1834, Viszota, ed., *Naplók,* iv, 478.

plained about the great personal antipathy which Széchenyi had felt toward him at the beginning of his public career. According to Kossuth, he had never given Széchenyi any cause for hatred; rather, he had "watched every word of his with religious awe, venerating him as the regenerator of our fatherland." Kossuth also intimated that Széchenyi did not read his Dietal Reports, thus suggesting that whereas he never forgot the "respect and appreciative recognition owed by all Hungarians to my great opponent," Széchenyi's attacks on him were characterized "from the very first moment" by "impassioned hatred bitter as gall," as he put it, "heavens knows why!"[197]

We know, however, from a police report dated April 15, 1833 that in an intercepted letter written to Helmeczi, editor of *Jelenkor,* Széchenyi mentioned both Kossuth and the Dietal Reports as "dangerous means of oppositional propaganda."[198] There is also evidence that the Dietal Reports were sent to Széchenyi when he was in Orsova, on the Lower Danube.[199] There can be no doubt that Széchenyi was one of the first who had realized the far-reaching political implications of Kossuth's talents as an agitator. Just as in the case of Wesselényi, Széchenyi thought Kossuth's agitation would ultimately result in the wrecking of his own, budding reform plans. If he disapproved of the actions of Wesselényi, who was his friend and social equal, he would certainly fight tooth and nail this yet unknown plebeian.

One may add that Széchenyi must also have been aware of the malicious rumors about Kossuth's private life, spread by Count Charles Andrássy, who at a meeting of some leaders of the opposition objected to the selection of Kossuth as editor of the protocols of the Diet, since, as he put it, "Kossuth's person was suspect . . . ."[200] Although Széchenyi may not have put much stock in the rumors, as has been suggested recently,[201] he did resist Kossuth's effort to become, with Wesselényi's

---

[197] Annex No. XI, Viszota, ed., *Széchenyi és Kossuth,* I, 770–73; Annex No. XI/II/b, *ibid.*, II, 1,082ff. Cf. Kossuth, *Ifjukori iratok,* in Barta, ed., *KLÖM,* VI, 381. Written by Kossuth in early 1833 under the title *A magyar fő rendek 1833-ban* (The Hungarian Magnates in 1833), this recently discovered fragmentary work, which remained unpublished and hence unknown to contemporaries, referred "to the immortal Count Stephen Széchenyi," who was the first to make "the charming sounds of our vernacular heard in the assembly of the dignitaries of our fatherland."

[198] Annex No. I, 1833–35, Viszota, ed., *Naplók,* IV, 669.

[199] Annex No. XI, Viszota, ed., *Széchenyi és Kossuth,* I, 771 and n. 2.

[200] Dec. 30, 1832, Kölcsey, "Országgyűlési napló," *KFÖM,* p. 1,221.

[201] Barta, *A fiatal Kossuth,* 62f. and n. 59. The rumors, some of which continue to survive in the Western literature on Kossuth, were mainly related to two accusations. According to one of them, Kossuth had had illicit relations with Countess Etelka Szapáry, wife of Count Charles Andrássy. Related to this is the other accusation, namely, that due to this relationship, Kossuth was able to use the money of the Countess

help, a member of the National Casino. Commenting on the latter's friendly recommendation given to Kossuth, he expressed his fear that Wesselényi was going to destroy the fruits of *his* hard labor.[202] Consequently, Széchenyi resolved to ask Kossuth personally to quietly withdraw his application, explaining that his presence would give the Casino an unfavorable political reputation. Kossuth agreed but deeply resented Széchenyi's behavior.[203] In his words, Széchenyi told him: "You do not even imagine what an important person you are taken for 'up there' [in Vienna]; they are very suspicious and afraid of you, this is a fact, I know it that's the trouble." Széchenyi may have said this to make his suggestion more palatable or perhaps to influence Kossuth to be more careful in his reports. In any case, when the Municipal Reports, established and edited by him after the end of the Diet, were suppressed, and Pest county protested against the ban, Széchenyi anticipated an increase in Kossuth's influence and a political crisis.[204] Shortly thereafter, in the fall of 1836, he noted with apprehension that Kossuth had been proposed as a corresponding member of the Academy.[205] A month later he remarked that Kossuth ought to be imprisoned, adding in despair: "I am finished and so is Hungary."[206]

In a sense, Széchenyi's forebodings proved essentially to be right. Soon after the Diet, Vienna decided to crack down on the leaders of the Dietal youth and intimidate the opposition. Count Reviczky, the favorite of the late Francis I, was removed and the Hungarian chancery was taken over by Count Fidel Pálffy, Kolowrat's nephew, whom Széchenyi previously had characterized as "worse than an Austrian minister."[207] Upon the appointment of this typically "alienated" aulic magnate who did not speak Magyar and with whom he had clashed a number of

---

to pay off his gambling debts. Whereas recent Hungarian historiography appears to have proven that the first accusation was without any foundation, there is evidence that the charges of gambling and inappropriate use of some money was not entirely groundless, even if Kossuth managed to repay his debt before he could be accused of embezzling funds. It seems, however, that his enemies in Zemplén county, perhaps for political reasons, as Barta said, succeeded in trumping up the charges and forcing Kossuth to forego whatever plans he might have had in county politics, thereby launching him, at least indirectly, on a very different career. *Ibid.*, pp. 59–80.

[202] May 28, 1836, Viszota, ed., *Naplók*, v, 6.

[203] May 29, 1836, *ibid.*, v, 6f. Cf. Kossuth's letter of the same date, cancelling, "due to a certain condition," his application for Casino membership, and the account of his first personal encounter with Széchenyi in his Memoirs. Annex Nos. I and XI, *Széchenyi és Kossuth*, I, 665, 772f.

[204] Aug. 18, 1836, Viszota, ed., *Naplók*, v, 18. For the pertinent documents see Kossuth, *Ifjukori iratok*, in Barta, ed., *KLÖM*, VI.

[205] Sept. 4, 1836, Viszota, ed., *Naplók*, v, 22.

[206] Oct. 9, 1836, *ibid.*, v, 28.

[207] Dec. 14, 1835, *ibid.*, IV, 624.

times during the Diet of 1832–36,[208] Széchenyi commented: "I can see now how everything is going up in flames and falling into ruins!"[209]

For months Széchenyi watched stunned and uneasily the secret arrests and illegal trials of many leaders of the youth, the prosecution of Wesselényi, other oppositional deputies, Kossuth, and the appointment of archconservatives to offices both in Hungary and Transylvania. He also noted that the national opposition to Vienna had stiffened, and that this made a rapprochement between administration and nation extremely difficult, if not impossible. Filled with apprehension and disillusioned that the purport of his lifework was in danger, he thought that a period of reaction and reprisals had begun and that order would be reestablished with the help of 300,000 Russians.[210] Even before the end of the Diet of 1832–36 he had feared that the Diet would be dissolved and a 10-year "provisional" government by decree proclaimed.[211] Subsequent events showed that this fear had some foundation and that the Széchenyi-Kossuth antagonism lay deeply embedded in domestic and international political tensions.

This antagonism, which became a most important factor in the *Vormärz,* was undoubtedly strongly motivated by personal factors. True, Kossuth wrote about Széchenyi in his Dietal Reports with the respect due to the recognized hero of the national rebirth. Up to 1841 he did his best, and repeatedly tried to obtain Széchenyi's friendship. Yet in his very first report on the session of the chamber of magnates in January 1833 Kossuth, characterizing the participants of the discussion, mentioned "the eccentric Széchenyi" as one of "many others making up a respectable line." In the preceding sentence, however, he wrote about Wesselényi's "precise judgment, vigorous logic, and weighty diction" as

---

[208] The bridge, Hungarian language, amelioration of the serf's conditions, constitutional rights of the nation—in short, everything Széchenyi stood for—were violently opposed by Pálffy. Cf. Feb. 10, Oct. 28, Nov. 7, Dec. 12–15, 1835, *ibid.,* IV, 524, 613, 616, 625ff. Also Széchenyi to Wesselényi, June 15, 1832, Majláth, ed., *Levelek,* I, 227. This letter shows that already during the lifetime of Francis I there were rumors of Reviczky's dismissal and, more important, of Pálffy's candidacy as his successor. The ominous undercurrent, that Vienna's policy toward Hungary might take a sharp reactionary turn, seems to have been constantly present.

[209] July 19, Aug. 14, 1836, Viszota, ed., *Naplók,* v, 12, 17.

[210] May 25, June 1, Aug. 26, 30, Nov. 6, 25, 1836, Feb. 16, 27, Mar. 2, 6, 7, 8, 9, 10, June 16, July 3, Nov. 25, 1837, *ibid.,* v, 5, 7, 20f., 32, 39, 56f., 59–63, 89, 95, 133. The British ambassador, who sympathized with the measures taken by the administration, nevertheless stressed the illegality of the secret proceedings. In his "report upon affairs of Hungary and Transylvania; disturbed state of those Countries," he indicated that out of 300 members of the bar, 289 refused to have anything to do with the trials. Lamb to Palmerston, Apr. 21, 1837 (no. 30), *F.O. 7/265,* PRO (London). For details and the connections between the political trials of Wesselényi, the leaders of the Dietal youth, and Kossuth, cf. Trócsányi, *Wesselényi,* pp. 317–425.

[211] June 27–29, 1835, *ibid.,* IV, 570f.

qualities which were increasing his influence daily, and would enable him to become "before long one of the leaders of the upper table."[212] While emphatically praising Wesselényi on different occasions,[213] Kossuth repeatedly referred to Széchenyi as "the eccentric," comparing his speeches to a pile of ideas similar to "a collection of precious treasures scattered all over a luxurious palace.[214] Széchenyi's forensic performance *was* uneven. Brilliant, witty, full of ideas, he was able to capture the attention of his audience. But, as Kölcsey said, he would often digress from his subject, get involved in a rather intricate sequence of thoughts through which the listeners could hardly follow him without losing the main thread of the oration.[215] Still, Kossuth praised Wesselényi and hurt Széchenyi's vanity precisely at the time when Széchenyi had become increasingly convinced that his friend had chosen the wrong method of political opposition. Széchenyi, of course, was well aware that in fashionable society he was still considered as "eccentric Stefferl," a term he disliked very much in his mature years.[216] He would have been more than human if he had not resented the rather embarrassing epithet assigned to him before the whole country by Kossuth, an upstart, whose personal integrity had been questioned by some of those attending the Diet.[217]

---

[212] Kossuth, *Országgyűlési tudósítások*, I, 112.

[213] E.g., Dec. 29, 1832, *ibid.*, I, 36.

[214] Jan. 22, 1833, *ibid.*, I, 114, 116.

[215] It is difficult to make a sound judgment today of the real effect of Széchenyi's rhetorical abilities. Only a fragment of Széchenyi's *oeuvre* as a public speaker is extant. Many of the 120 speeches are but short interlocutions. At the dawn of modern Hungarian political oratory, most great speakers like Paul Nagy, Kölcsey, Wesselényi, and others were influenced by Cicero's Latin style. Széchenyi, however, followed the English parliamentarian practice. His speeches were usually improvisations, the more eloquent parts of which were often interrupted by conversational asides or dry and objective argumentation. Thus his rhetoric was characterized by the virtues of a really great orator as well as by rudimentary mistakes. Cf. Ferenc Kelemen, *A magyar politikai szónoklat története a mult század első felében* (History of Hungarian Political Oratory in the First Half of the Past Century) (Budapest: 1937), pp. 10ff. Also Falk, *Széchenyi és kora*, pp. 114f. and Langsdorff's account in Doc; 8a, App. I, p. 456 of this study.

[216] June 12, 1830; Sept. 14, 1831, Viszota, ed., *Naplók*, IV, 47, 213. Even his family name, often distorted by foreigners, irritated him for blocking his fame (or so he thought). Cf. Dec. 23, 1833, Jan. 6, 1834, Nov. 26, 1847, *ibid.*, IV, 438, 443, VI, 680. In this last entry, e.g., he remarked: *"Mein Name Sze, che, nyi ist nicht gemacht um bekannt zu werden."* Also July 20, 1821, *ibid.*, II, 181.

[217] The probability that Széchenyi took offense at the epithet "eccentric" in the Dietal Reports is also supported by Wesselényi's testimony reported by Kossuth's secretary, Antal Vörös, Doc. 1,761, Annex No. IX, Viszota, ed., *Széchenyi és Kossuth*, I, 743ff. The value of this evidence is somewhat limited by the fact that it came from a person who himself was deeply involved on Kossuth's side in the controversy, and that it completely ignored the political connotations of the issue, which are even more important than the personal factors. Viszota's introduction, *ibid.*, I, pp. xiii–lxi, contains much valuable data as to how the casino movement and the Dietal youth were

After 1834, when Kölcsey was forced to resign his seat as deputy and Wesselényi departed to the Transylvanian Diet, whence he returned as a proscribed person, the direction of the opposition passed gradually into the hands of Francis Deák. Széchenyi recognized Deák's talent, but felt somewhat humbled by his superior legal erudition.[218] Despite this initial jealousy, frankly admitted by Széchenyi in his diaries,[219] and despite his inclination to look upon Deák as a provincial pettifogger[220] Széchenyi nonetheless respected Deák. He frequently asked his advice and tried to obtain his support on important issues. Appreciating Deák's sober caution toward extreme moves and his willingness to compromise where it could be done without detriment to constitutional principles, Széchenyi regarded Deák, especially after their successful political co-operation at the Diet of 1839–40, as the potential focus of a constructive center party. He wrote in his diary, more to himself: "Away with all envy, my compatriots. Let us yield precedence to him!"[221]

Wesselényi, Széchenyi, Deák, and Kossuth, those most remarkable representatives of Hungarian political thinking in modern times, were all active participants in the Diet of 1832–36, as was "the child with the ardent soul" (Kölcsey's term), Joseph Eötvös. To contemporaries and to the popular mind, they were but different shadings of the reborn Hungarian national genius. Yet there were very important differences in their outlook and temper, which were obvious to the careful observer. Széchenyi, more universal and less legalistically minded and more familiar with the international balance of power and the weight of economic forces, stood somewhat aside from the others, who relied on constitutional abstractions and were perhaps less afraid of experiments pointing toward modern parliamentary democracy. As to temper and political tactics, Deák, the most balanced and stable but also the least daring of them, was probably considerably closer to Széchenyi than to Wesselényi and Kossuth. Yet it so happened that in the early 1840s Deák seemed to form a common front with the other two, joined also by Eötvös and Count Louis Batthyány, in opposing Széchenyi, who gave increasing support to the administration.

---

used increasingly for the political purposes of the liberal and national opposition, and also as to the origins and early development of the Széchenyi-Wesselényi and Széchenyi-Kossuth antagonisms.

[218] Oct. 16, Nov. 25, 1835, Viszota, ed., *Naplók*, IV, 610, 621.

[219] Apr. 12, 1836, Mar. 30, Dec. 25, 1839, Jan. 28, 1840, *ibid.*, IV, 651, V, 263, 344, 352.

[220] Cf. the draft of Széchenyi's unpublished polemical articles during the bitter discussion following *A kelet népe* and his Academic Address of 1842. Annex No. x/2-3, in Viszota, ed., *Széchenyi és Kossuth*, I, 749-53.

[221] Apr. 30, 1840, Viszota, ed., *Naplók*, V, 380.

Actually, Széchenyi tried to enlist official support for his projects or at least to make them palatable for *gutgesinnt* circles from the beginning of his career. In his public statements, made partly for tactical reasons but also because he chose to think that the government had improved its policy since 1830, Széchenyi emphasized his loyalty, the constructive character of his critical attitude, as well as his independence from both administration and parties. Yet Kossuth was right in pointing out in his recollections that during the Diet of 1832–36 Széchenyi, far from being a "man of the government," was generally considered as being one of the leaders of the opposition.[222] Széchenyi's maneuvering possibilities were helped by the fact that there was some room for cooperation between the administration and the liberals in the Diet. After his arrest in 1837, Kossuth himself referred to the:

Dietal documents and records as genuine proofs of the fact that whenever the Government made a proposal to promote the welfare of the taxpaying population involving the sacrifice of the nobility, it always obtained its goal in the Diet with the help of the [party] wrongly termed opposition against those who opposed even that His Majesty should call himself Ferdinand V and who protested that the Hungarian constitution would come to its end if noblemen would have to pay tolls on the permanent bridge to be constructed between Buda and Pest.[223]

In the case of the bridge, where Viennese capital was involved, and in the case of the solution of the urbarial question, which was also desired by the government, legislation was enacted with the support of the progressive forces, while it was delayed for many months by the staunchest conservative adherents of Vienna. But such action required the cooperation of moderates on both sides, the administration and the loyal opposition. Once the feelings of partisanship ran high, the delicate work of Széchenyi was in danger, because extremists on either side could force his moderating hand.

Suspicion and misunderstanding at both ends of the political spectrum placed certain limits on Széchenyi's endeavors. Young radicals occasionally would accuse him of having given in to Vienna because he had suggested that they trust the "paternalism" of the government.[224] At the same time Sedlnitzky's report on the participants of the Diet of 1832–36 still depicted Széchenyi as belonging to the "ultra-left" and

[222] Annex XI, Viszota, ed., *Széchenyi és Kossuth*, I, 771.
[223] June 8–9, 1837, Kossuth's voluntary testimony, Annex No. II, *ibid.*, I, 677.
[224] Sabbas Vukovits to Sigismund Ormos, June 12, 1833, B. Szabó, ed., *Adatok*, I, 225.

as being the one "who, besides Wesselényi, could and partly did cause at present the greatest embarrassment to the high Government."[225] These contrasting views of Széchenyi show that he tried to walk a tightrope and that his attitude must have been ambivalent in the eyes of many, to say the least. Friends loyal to the dynasty, like Paul Esterházy, would question his right to interpose himself between government and nation. Irked, Széchenyi could only say: "Of my own volition [because] that's what I want, and I can be hanged [for it]."[226]

Yet the decade 1830 to 1840 was on the whole the most successful and perhaps the happiest period of Széchenyi's life. To be sure, he was frequently sick, having almost constant gastric, liver, and bilious troubles. His recurring mental conflicts and moral struggles, often interrelated with his physical ailments, did not make life easier, either.[227] But his "manifold wonderful activities" (*"Wunderbar viel Thätigkeit"*),[228] and feverish involvement in numerous enterprises helped him overcome the neurosis mentioned in his diaries alternately as pusillanimity (*"Kleinmüthigkeit"*), mental sickness (*"Seelenkrankheit"*), spleen or melancholy.[229] He enjoyed being overwhelmed with work,[230] occasionally even complaining that the administration would not utilize him enough, hence he was determined to impose himself upon it.[231] Gradually, however, he could not help noticing that he was increasingly respected by officials, in Viennese social circles as well as in the Diet. There were many signs that he was increasingly popular in the country at large. Several counties instructed their deputies to thank him for his patriotic activities; they were joined by the clergy.[232] On one occasion, he noted: "Universal respect. I begin to enjoy life!"[233] For a moment, he thought

---

[225] Annex No. 1, 1836/8a–b, Viszota, ed., *Naplók*, IV, 706–709. Sedlnitzky's report, submitted on Aug. 14, 1836, was based on Police Commissioner Leopold Ferstl's character sketch, dated May 4, 1836.

[226] Jan. 28, 1836, *ibid.*, IV, 637. For Széchenyi's moderate stand in the discussion of the case of the arrested leaders of the Dietal youth, see his speech in the county congregation of Pest, made on Aug. 30, 1836, in Kossuth, *Törvényhatósági tudósitások*, in Barta, ed., *KLÖM*, VI, 730f.

[227] Cf. Viszota's documentation in the introduction to *Naplók*, IV–VI, esp. pp. xxv–xxxv; vi ff., xc f., x–xxvi, resp. As a characteristic example I refer to the entry of Sept. 4, 1832, *ibid.*, IV, 296f. Viszota, however, fails to point out that Széchenyi, like many of his prominent contemporaries, including Wesselényi and Vörösmarty, was infected with venereal disease. Cf. Trócsányi, *Wesselényi*, p. 392.

[228] July 1, 1833, *ibid.*, IV, 383 (italics in original).

[229] E.g., Dec. 17, 1837, May 21, 23, 26, 28, 1838, Feb. 9, 12–13, 1839, *ibid.*, V, 140, 185f., 240f.

[230] June 24, July 4, 1833, *ibid.*, IV, 383, 385.

[231] Aug. 31, 1831, *ibid.*, IV, 206.

[232] E.g., Feb. 20, 1832, Jan. 9, 10, 13, 14, 1835, *ibid.*, IV, 245, 514ff.

[233] Jan. 27, 1835, *ibid.*, IV, 520. Cf. Feb. 18, 1835, *ibid.*, IV, 525, with its built-in qualifications and doubts.

this was the high point of his life and perhaps a good time to die.[234] This remark in itself suggested that his satisfaction was not without worries or qualifications. While supervising the work on the Lower Danube he expressed his anguish that official circles would take umbrage at the signs of his growing popularity, regarding them as so many sins committed by him against the government.[235] Similar doubts emerged in his mind at the end of the Diet, when the youth thanked him in a demonstration of sympathy for his Dietal activity. Commenting on the torchlight serenade, he noted in his diary: "In Vienna, one will dislike this very much."[236] Tormenting himself almost pathologically, he jotted down views like that of the Baron Albert Prónay, in whose opinion "Stephen Széchenyi fancies that he is administering baptism to the Hungarian nation and it does not dawn upon him that he may administer extreme unction to it."[237]

The nation thought just the opposite. After a visit to the National Museum, founded by his father whose portrait on the wall caused his heart to flutter, Széchenyi remarked that in Hungary, where people had so many prejudices, it was impossible to win respect in one's lifetime. Although yearning for his compatriots' esteem he believed he would be recognized by them only after his death. These thoughts were committed to paper in 1826.[238] In less than a decade unknown people were glad to have caught a glimpse of "the great Stephen Széchenyi" wherever he appeared. Non-Hungarian skilled laborers working on his projects knew him as "the master builder of the land" (*"Landes Baumeister Csicsinyi"*). Counties asked his permission to have his portrait painted, elected him to the *nobile officium* of a county-court judge (*táblabiró*); others sent a silver cup or a golden pen "to the Incomparable Patriot and to the great Hungarian Writer Count Stephen Széchenyi." Cities entered his name on the register of electors and there were motions in the Diet to perpetuate his merits by enacting a special law. Upon the occurrence of a vacancy, several deputies promoted his candidacy as keeper of the crown. Although he may have desired the recognition earlier and the proposal was accepted with unanimity in one of the circular sessions, Széchenyi himself asked for the withdrawal of the motion. He did not wish to embarrass the palatine and the administration by encroaching on the royal prerogative to select the candidates. It was

[234] Jan. 21, 1835, *ibid.*, IV, 518.

[235] Nov. 8, 1834, *ibid.*, IV, 503.

[236] May 5–7, 1836, *ibid.*, IV, 638. Cf. Sedlnitzky's reports to the monarch, May 13, Aug. 14, 1836, Annex No. 1, 1836/7–8b, *ibid.*, IV, 705–709; and B. Szabó, ed., *Adatok*, I, 267.

[237] Oct. 4, 1835, Viszota, ed., *Naplók*, IV, 607.

[238] Apr. 12, Nov. 13, 1826, *ibid.*, pp. 42, 100f.

on this occasion that Széchenyi, deeply moved, first used the term "Sublime Fatherland" in a solemn address, instead of the official style and title of the Diet, "Illustrious Estates and Orders." He wanted to make it clear that he intended to thank the entire nation and not just the representatives of the feudal classes for the honor they intended to bestow on him.[239]

[239] May 1, July 31, 1832, Sept. 3, 4, 1833, Sept. 2, 1834, Feb. 24, Mar. 16, 20, Apr. 7, 12, June 25, Aug. 1, Sept. 22, 23, Oct. 3, Nov. 6, Nov. 11, 1835, *ibid.*, IV, 261, 285, 408f., 492, 527, 532, 538f., 569, 588, 604f., 607, 616, 618; B. Szabó, ed., *Adatok*, I, 232, 274ff. (Speech of Sándor Bölönyi Farkas, Sept. 24, 1835 and letter of the city of Buda, dated Mar. 3, 1837); June 26, 1833, Apr. 13, Nov. 12, 1835, Kossuth, *Országgyűlési tudósítások*, I, 498f., IV, 345 and V, 222f. Kossuth, *Törvényhatósági tudósítások*, in Barta, ed., *KLÖM*, VI, 809, 1,014; Széchenyi to Tasner, Nov. 12, 1835, Majláth, ed., *Levelek*, II, 171. Cf. Friedreich, *Széchenyi élete*, I, 400–408. It is noteworthy that the petition of the Graeven regiment (cf. Ch. II, 17), promoted by Széchenyi's uncle, Count George Festetich, repeatedly used the epithet "Sublime Fatherland." See Grünwald, *A régi Magyarország*, pp. 201–207.

CHAPTER VIII

No More Agitation

In December 1834 Count Charles Zichy died suddenly, leaving behind
Crescence with seven small children and the eighth on its way.[1] Zichy's
death brought a great change in Széchenyi's life; in February 1836
he married the woman of his dreams. A year later, she gave birth to
his first son, and for the first time Széchenyi wrote in his diary: "[I
am] happy, very happy. Much happier than I thought it possible!"[2]

Here then was Count Stephen Széchenyi, 45 years old, happy and
at the height of his popularity. To most of his compatriots and to many
foreigners he was "the great patriot." After a decade of longing for
Crescence, he had reached the threshold of personal happiness, although
the lurking ghosts of his former mental conflicts were neither completely
defeated nor banned from the family nest blissfully surrounding him.
But if, at the outset of his career, his patriotic feelings had been strongly
motivated by personal factors, like family tradition, ambition, and romantic love, a decade of experience in literary and public activities
had taught him to put the duties to his fatherland above all, including
the domestic hearth. Events of the next 25 years eloquently and tragically
proved that he never hesitated when he had to choose between the
conflicting demands of family happiness and devotion to country.

Nor did he shy away from sacrificing the popularity he had achieved
in the country during the first decade of his public life. Whatever ambition and claim he may have had for name and reputation, he was ready
to sacrifice it to put into effect the absolutely necessary reforms in a
peaceful and lawful way, which he felt could happen in Hungary only
if initiated by popular men who respected both government and country.
The idea of being the honest broker in the midst of divisive forces
that he thought should be carefully controlled, caused him to urge Met-

---

[1] Dec. 19, 1834, Viszota, ed., *Naplók*, IV, 510; Dec. 17–20, From the Memoirs of
Countess Keglevich, B. Szabó, ed., *Adatok*, I, 217.

[2] Feb. 5, 6, May 1, 1836, Viszota, ed., *Naplók*, IV, 639, 649, 658.

ternich and the administration to use *his* popularity before it was too late.[3] Incidentally, the already mentioned, malicious report on Széchenyi's "ultraradical" and "dangerous" activities, submitted to the king after the Diet of 1832–36, suggested that he be detached from the "ultraliberal opposition party" and that "his otherwise in some respects noble character" be utilized "for promoting the fatherly intentions of His Imperial and Royal Majesty."[4] But Széchenyi's concept of creating a third force between government and radical opposition was turned down in rigid terms by Metternich.[5]

To understand why the chancellor failed to sympathize with Széchenyi before the *Vormärz*, a fact deplored by some historians,[6] it may be useful to point out that Metternich himself wholeheartedly supported the administration's strong-fisted policy toward Hungary in the 1830s. This was so not only because of Metternich's personal inclinations but also because of his insufficient grasp of the dynamic nature of modern political trends and his trust in the stability of an international order, the establishment of which was to a large extent his own work. In a well-known comparison of Bismarck and Metternich, Heinrich von Srbik stressed more than 40 years ago that both statesmen had a negative view of the function of a parliamentary opposition and that both were blind to the need for educating political parties for responsibility. In this parallel, which appeared in the concluding chapter of the second volume, the last to be published during his lifetime, Metternich's biographer also referred to Széchenyi's conversations with the chancellor in 1825. Claiming that there had been an essential identity of views between Metternich and Széchenyi on many important questions of the day, and that from the early 1840s on, their rapport had become one of confidence (*Vertrauensverhältnis*), Srbik nevertheless intimated that Széchenyi at a relatively early stage of his public career seemed to have a better understanding of the conditions under which modern constitutional government works.[7] The more complete documentation of this

[3] Jan. 16, 1836. Széchenyi's representation to Metternich concerning the bridge, Annex No. 1, 1836/1a, *ibid.*, IV, 696. Széchenyi was aware that his "writing to Metternich & Co." could "break his neck" politically if it were known in Hungary. Jan. 16, 1836, *ibid.*, IV, 634; also Metternich's comments, Annex No. 1, 1836/1b, *ibid.*, IV, 702.

[4] Sedlnitzky report, Annex No. 1, 1836/8a, *ibid.*, IV, 709.

[5] See his comments (and Count Majláth's) on Széchenyi's bridge proposal, the principles of which were far-reaching. Annex No. 1, 1836/1b–c, *ibid.*, IV, 701ff.

[6] Arnold Whitridge, *Men in Crisis. The Revolutions of 1848* (New York: Scribner's, 1949), pp. 240–43, 254f., 257, 262–67. Cf. Béla Menczer, "Metternich und Széchenyi," *Der Donauraum*, v (1960), 78–86.

[7] Heinrich Ritter von Srbik, *Metternich, der Staatsmann und der Mensch*, 3 vols. (Munich: Bruckmann, 1925–54), I, 469, II, 193, 554. For more complete citations cf. George Barany, "The Széchenyi Problem," *Journal of Central European Affairs*, xx (1960), 252f., 258f., and pertinent notes.

relationship by Julius Viszota, an important source for any correct interpretation of Austro-Hungarian history in the first half of the 19th century confirms Srbik's favorable opinion of Széchenyi.

As for the link between the Austrian chancellor's views on Hungarian domestic politics and international affairs, one must recall that ever since the July Revolution—and, more specifically, since the agreements of Münchengrätz and Berlin (1833)—the cornerstone of Metternich's foreign policy was Austria's conservative alliance with Russia and Prussia, which granted the right of mutual intervention to the sovereigns of the three powers against any internal or external enemy.[8] This confirmation of the principles of the Holy Alliance, to use a broad generalization, may be explained to some extent by the change in the chancellor's order of priorities in his fight against the revolutionary "disease," which he considered his life task.

If one is to believe a secret and confidential report sent by Sir Robert Gordon from Rome in 1819, the English envoy never had an interview with Prince Metternich "without my attention being forcibly drawn to this point [i.e., Russia] by His Highness, who discovers the existence of a Russian Agency and intervention in every quarter and every passing event in Europe." According to the same letter, Metternich claimed to be in possession of evidence of a conspiracy headed by La Harpe, and intended to get Francis I to write about it to Alexander I.[9] Besides the tsar's liberal ideas, the chancellor also feared Russia's overwhelming military power, which could be used, as he said in a letter to Esterházy, anywhere in the world.[10] For about a decade Metternich continued to stress that the Russian empire was "on the confines of civilization, not presenting any resemblance to the other states of Europe, differing from them by its religion, mores, and spirit of its inhabitants, and by all the material conditions which constitute the individual existence of states . . . ." At the end of 1828 the chancellor observed that "the new emperor [Nicholas I] managed to spread about him a system of fear, a regime of fear befitting Russia . . . ." At the same time, he thought of Great Britain as the only possible counterbalance to "the ceaselessly invading march of the colossus of the North . . . ."[11]

[8] Algernon Cecil, *Metternich*, 3rd edn. (London: Wm. Collins, 1947), pp. 254f., 276; H. du Coudray, *Metternich* (New Haven: Yale University Press, 1936), pp. 271–76, 280. For the origins of the "doctrine of intervention," see Paul W. Schroeder, "Austrian Policy at the Congresses of Troppau and Laibach," *Journal of Central European Affairs*, XXII (1962), 140 and 151f.

[9] Sir Robert Gordon to Aberdeen, Apr. 22, 1819, Folios 110–13 in *Aberdeen Papers*, CLXXXI, MS 43,219 (British Museum).

[10] Metternich to Esterházy, Feb. 15, 1819, cited by G. de Bertier de Sauvigny, *Metternich et son temps* (Paris: Hachette, 1959), p. 198.

[11] Metternich to Esterházy, Dec. 18 and 2, 1828; Metternich to Vincent, Jan. 27, 1826; both cited *ibid.*, pp. 199ff. For Metternich's fear of Russia see also Enno E.

The Russo-Turkish war of 1828–29 did not improve Austria's position vis-à-vis Russia. Still, the shock waves of the revolutions in France and Belgium, which had their repercussions in both Italy and eastern Europe, caused the Austrian government to do everything in its power first to aid the suppression of the Polish insurrection and then to capture those Poles who succeeded in making their way to Galicia or Hungary. Indeed, the conventions signed at Münchengrätz and Berlin in 1833, involving the internal security of Russia, Austria, and Prussia, were in a sense the logical extension and formal approbation of a close cooperation regarding Polish affairs and subversive activities, which had begun earlier and was to continue for years to come.[12] "Thus does their joint possession of Poland act as a tie between the three Powers," remarked Sir Frederic Lamb subsequently, and he was not far from the truth.[13]

The British ambassador also noted that "the game is not equal," since, in his words, "the attitude of Hungary cripples the freedom of action of Austria and imposes upon her the necessity of keeping upon terms with her powerful neighbour." Earlier in the same report, the envoy stated that

in the year 1831 when it was expected that Austria might have to employ the greater part of her force in the West of Europe, Russia offered to assemble an army of 50,000 men on the Frontier of Hungary for the purpose of keeping that country quiet. —The community of feeling between Hungary and Poland has imposed this necessity upon Russia, who before the Polish insurrection is supposed to have been looked to by the Hungarian Malcontents for support.[14]

The information, sent to Palmerston in 1837, did not agree with the facts in all its details. Yet it reflected a certain psycho-political reality which, imponderable though it may have been in 1830 and 1831, became quite tangible a few years later. Above all, it suggested that Metternich's reliance on the Russian alliance had multiple roots, including the mutual interest of the two countries to keep both Poland and Hungary "quiet."

Undoubtedly the conservative turn in the Austrian chancellor's thinking should be related, in the first place, to the establishment of the July Monarchy in France. Henceforth, Metternich could never bring himself

---

Kraehe, "Raison d'Etat et idéologie dans la politique allemande de Metternich (1809–1820)," *RHMC*, XIII (1966), 188–94; W. L. Blackwell, *The Beginnings of Russian Industrialization, 1800–1860* (Princeton, N.J.: Princeton Univ. Press, 1968), p. 244.

[12] P. S. Squire, "Metternich and Benckendorff, 1807–1834," *The Slavonic and East European Review*, XLV (1967), 156–62. Cf. Ch. VI, 227f. For Metternich's own interpretation see No. 2661/1833 (Nov. 8, 1833), *MKA*, HHStA (Vienna).

[13] Lamb to Palmerston, Apr. 21, 1837 (No. 30), *F.O. 7/265*, PRO (London).

[14] *Ibid.*

to trust that country completely, although he subsequently accepted Louis Philippe's regime as the least of many evils that could emanate from the traditional center of European revolutions. It is very probable that the chancellor's growing support of the movement of Roman Catholic restoration and the papacy was part of his attempt to find ideological allies against the "dangers" of a liberalism embraced by France and England, especially by the latter's Whig government. To be sure, Metternich's new interest in the Jesuits and Catholicism was motivated by his opposition to the Josephinian trends as represented by Kolowrat domestically.[15] Personal factors such as the influence of the chancellor's third wife, Melanie Zichy-Ferraris, and that of her even more bigoted mother must not be ignored either.[16]

Naturally, it is easy to exaggerate, as Srbik contended, the importance of personal considerations in the process of policy-making. Yet it is undeniable that Metternich's marriage in 1831 to "the vigorous Magyar lady," his junior by 32 years, made him a member of that Magyar aristocracy which was accustomed to discussing politics. In fact, Stephen Széchenyi himself became a member of the chancellor's family circle after 1831, not because of Melanie's previous affection for him but rather because his brother Paul was the chancellor's brother-in-law.[17] Since Paul's wife, Emilie, and her younger sister, Princess Melanie, frequently visited each other, the chancellor could not have helped getting involved in Hungarian affairs.

In fact, Hungary was very much on Metternich's mind in the year of his marriage to Melanie. Even before the cholera uprising,[18] and apparently without being directly connected with it, there was much unrest among the Hungarian and Romanian peasants of Transylvania. Besides the usual factors contributing to an increase in the serf's economic burdens, such as the incorporation of urbarial land into the lord's allodial property, collection of the tithe from uncultivated fields and excessive demands of *robot* and corvée, to name but a few, there were other

---

[15] Winter, *Der Josefinismus*, pp. 273f., 279, 286ff., 350ff.

[16] Srbik, *Metternich*, I, 244f., 310f. For Metternich's growing interest in and changing views of Roman Catholicism and the papal curia after 1815, see Erika Weinzierl-Fischer, *Die Österreichischen Konkordate von 1855 und 1933* (Munich: Oldenbourg, 1960), pp. 13–22 (*Österreich Archiv*). According to "a well informed friend" of Baron Kübeck, the Russian court had granted, under rather unclarified circumstances, a loan of 400,000 rubles to Melanie's financially hard-pressed family. After Melanie's marriage to Metternich, the loan was reclassified as a gift to her parents. Kübeck, ed., *Tagebücher*, I, Pt. 2, p. 382.

[17] Paul Széchenyi's second wife, Emilie Zichy-Ferraris, whom he married in 1823, was Princess Melanie's older sister. László Bártfai Szabó, *Gróf Széchenyi István és kortársai* (Count Stephen Széchenyi and His Contemporaries) (Budapest: Kir. Magyar Egyetemi Ny., n.d. [1926]), pp. 103f.

[18] Cf. Ch. VI, 228ff.

circumstances that tended to create a tense atmosphere similar to the one at the beginning of the *jacquerie* a few months later in eastern Slovakia. One circumstance was the conscription of raw recruits in large numbers at the beginning of 1831, a measure necessitated by the international situation. In Transylvania recruiting appears to have been coupled with a campaign to convert the nonunited Orthodox Romanian and Serbian populace to the Uniate church en masse under the slogan that whoever refused to embrace the one true (Greek Catholic) religion would be conscripted into the army. The harshness of recruitment and forcible proselyting, however, coincided with the appearance of Russian troops beyond the Carpathians. The result was the spread of rumors among the Orthodox clergy and peasantry, according to which the patron of all true believers, the Orthodox tsar, who had crushed the Catholic Polish landlords, was going to liberate his co-religionists from the yoke of their oppressive Magyar counterparts. The growing excitement among the serfs, in turn, caused panic among members of the nobility; in many instances, they began to move from the countryside to the urban areas and requested the noble "insurrection" (levée) be summoned. While keeping an eye on neighboring Poland, the administration preferred increasing the number of troops in Transylvania to arming the nobility. It also stopped the recruitment. The two measures brought the situation under control just before the outbreak of even greater unrest among the peasants of Upper Hungary.[19]

As in the latter movement, the "malcontents" of Transylvania, who looked to Russia for help, were mostly Orthodox peasants. Groundless and hopeless as their dreams were, they mirrored the Russophobia of the Magyar nobility, which was very real.

Széchenyi and other Hungarian noble reformers, as we have seen,[20] attempted to use the sad events of 1831 to justify the need for immediate reform. The administration, however, could exploit the "great fear" of the nobility of *both* peasants and Russians to keep the initiative in its own hands by threatening potential opponents with the nightmare of a rebellion of serfs and by strengthening its ties with the tsarist empire. In his Hungarian policy, Metternich needed both levers. Knowing that in a critical confrontation with the Magyar opposition, which he tried to avoid, he could not rely on a revolutionary force inherent in any

---

[19] Lóránt Tilkovszky, "Román jobbágyok mozgalmai Erdélyben és a Tiszántulon 1831-ben" (Movements of Romanian Serfs in Transylvania and the Trans-Theiss Region in 1831), *Századok*, XCI (1957), 773–84. For the unrest among Romania peasants in the Danubian principalities and the role of Russia, cf. Radu R. Florescu, "British Reactions to the Russian Regime in the Danubian Principalities, 1828–1834," *Journal of Central European Affairs*, XXII (1962), 33f.

[20] Cf. Ch. VI, 230f.

peasant movement, he had to be able to fall back on Russian help in order to make sure that he could control the unruly Hungarians in any emergency.

The chancellor's policies had severe limitations. Russophobia was not an attitude confined to Hungarians alone, or to men who opposed the government. In 1831 Transylvanian officials searched for Russian emissaries, as did their colleagues in other parts of the Habsburg monarchy, to explain Russian sympathies among the peasants.[21] Such is the natural inclination of bureaucrats in an authoritarian regime, who may have learned how to obey but not how to distinguish, seeking to blame "subversive elements" and "conspiracies" whenever complex social conditions lead to crises difficult to prevent, let alone solve.

The problems Metternich had to face would have taxed the ingenuity of a much more efficient and sophisticated administrative apparatus than he had at his command. On the basis of the agreement reached with Russia at Münchengrätz, the Austrian chancellor agreed to a close cooperation between the two countries' secret services, to control on an international scale the activities of Polish émigré organizations, centers of political subversion and revolutionary propaganda in general. This was one of the consequences of the change in the political atmosphere,[22] the improvement of which was one of the chancellor's long-range goals. At the same time, but on a different level, in the areas touching on religion and politics, Austro-Russian relations tended to be strained. After the uprising of the Poles in 1830–31 the domestic policy of Nicholas I became increasingly anti-Polish, hence also anti-Catholic. By the end of the decade, this trend culminated in forcing the Uniate Church of the Ukraine and White Russia to sever its connections with Rome and return to the Eastern Orthodox mother church.[23]

This reversal of a historical process that might have been just as politically motivated initially as was the tsar's action more than two centuries later, was embarrassing to the chancellor because in the Habsburg lands with an Orthodox population an opposite trend prevailed. Although, as shown by the example of the highly sensitive Military Frontier Region, the official attitude toward the followers of the Greek Ortho-

---

[21] Tilkovszky, "Román jobbágyok," pp. 775; Tilkovszky, *Az 1831, évi parasztfelkelés*, pp. 153f.

[22] Squire, "Metternich and Benckendorff," pp. 16off.; Squire, "The Metternich-Benckendorff Letters, 1835–1842," *The Slavonic and East European Review*, XLV (1967), 368–90.

[23] Riasanovsky, *Nicholas I and Official Nationality*, pp. 225, 229f. According to the relevant imperial ordinance, quoted by a Russian author, the Uniate Church was a tool for the "guileful politics of the Polish republic." Translation and citation from J. H. Billington, *The Icon and the Axe* (New York: Knopf, 1966), p. 159.

dox Church was to adjust to the changing military, international, and domestic conditions, on the whole, the direction of change pointed to diminishing rather than augmenting the privileges granted the Orthodox church and its followers.[24] With the notable exception of the reigns of Joseph II and Leopold II, a strange combination of the interests of the state as interpreted by Austrian, Croatian, and Hungarian military and civilian authorities, of political Catholicism, and of intransigent Magyar nationalism, led especially after the Napoleonic wars to efforts aimed at converting large segments of the Orthodox populace in the Kingdom of Hungary if not directly to Catholicism then at least to the Uniate church. It so happened that while the papacy protested against the persecution of Catholics in Russia and Metternich used the controversy as a pretext to frustrate the tsar's plans to marry his daughter, the Grand Duchess Olga, to the Archduke Stephen, son of Palatine Joseph,[25] Hungarian Catholic prelates persisted in their proselytizing activities which they claimed to be highly successful. In a memorandum dealing with the situation of the Orthodox church in Hungary, the eloquent Bishop of Csanád, Joseph Lonovics, suggested that "the maintenance and extension of the union [between the Catholic and Greek Catholic, or Uniate, Churches] is in the interest of the government not only for religious but also for political reasons . . . ."[26]

The controversies related to the strengthening of the Uniate church

[24] Rothenberg, *The Military Border in Croatia, 1740–1881*, pp. 8, 13f., 25, 28–33, 37, 57–61, 71, 81f., 87, 90, 98, 103, 125, 136f. Cf. Nicolas Zernov, *Eastern Christendom* (London: Readers Union, 1963), pp. 172f., 195ff.

[25] Constantin de Grunwald, *Tsar Nicholas I*, tr. Brigit Patmore (New York: Macmillan, 1955), pp. 202–26. The real cause of Vienna's refusal of the tsar's marriage proposal was the fear of establishing a junior branch of the Habsburg dynasty in Hungary. After the death of the old palatine, fairly popular among Hungarians and consequently mistrusted and dubbed "Rákóczi" in court circles, his son, the Archduke Stephen was expected to follow him. With the help of a Romanov father-in-law or brother-in-law tsar, whatever the case might be, he could easily have gotten out of hand under certain circumstances, a possibility Metternich did not discount, however remote. The example of Louis Philippe could not be entirely ignored. For broader aspects of the conflicting interests of Russia, Austria, and the Holy See, cf. Friedrich Engel-Janosi, with the collaboration of Richard Blaas and Erika Weinzierl, *Die politische Korrespondenz der Päpste mit den österreichischen Kaisern, 1804–1918* (Vienna-Munich: Herold, 1964), pp. 13–28, and the pertinent documents (Vol. II of *FKgÖ*); Eduard Winter, *Russland und das Papsttum*, 2 vols. (Berlin: Akademie Verlag, 1960–1961), II, 185–279 (*QSGO*, VI); Amman, *Ostslavische Kirchengeschichte*, pp. 504–18.

[26] P. 10 of the memorandum, dated Jan. 3, 1845. Enclosed with Lonovics's letter to *Staats- und Conferenzrath* von Justel, *Kabinettsarchiv, Separatkonferenzakten*, 17s/1845, HHStA (Vienna). For a concise survey of the problems of the Uniate church in the Habsburg monarchy see Helmut Rumpler, "Politik und Kirchenunion in der Habsburgermonarchie," *ÖOH*, VI (1964), 302–20. Cf. Keith Hitchins, "Andreiu Şaguna and the Restoration of the Rumanian Orthodox Metropolis in Transylvania, 18 6– 1868," *BS*, VI (1965), 2–7.

in the Habsburg and its absorption in the Romanov empires, the protection of Armenian Catholics in Russia and of Orthodox Christians in Greece and Turkey, the efforts of the tsar to subdue the unruly Poles and of the latter to obtain papal support against him, involved the delicate triangle of St. Petersburg-Rome-Vienna. Given the large proportion of her Orthodox and Slavic population, Austria's interests overlapped with those of the curia in most religious issues. Military and political considerations, however, prompted the Austrian chancellor to follow a cautious course, mediating and thereby controlling, if possible, the disputes. Disturbed also by the tensions between the Holy See and Prussia, and by the vicissitudes of the Eastern Question, Metternich yet went on assuring, with a straight face, foreign envoys that Russia was a trustworthy member of the European concert, that the tsar was a firm supporter of the status quo, and that his promises should be relied on.[27] Essentially he was right, although Sir Frederic Lamb, for one, did his best to convince Metternich that the opposite was true, and that some action was warranted to safeguard Austrian interests against the encroachments of its dangerous neighbor.[28] The same British ambassador, who often endeavored to deflect the chancellor from his set course, was realistic enough to recognize the cause of Austrian perseverance in the principles of the alliance with the tsarist empire:

It is neither fear of Russia, nor liking to [sic] Russia that makes Prince Metternich cling so closely to her alliance, it is the fear of needing her support arising from His want of Confidence in the stability of the existing state of things in Europe. —This feeling of insecurity applies not only to the west of Europe but to the dominions of which the Austrian Empire is composed. —He cannot own this but I know it beyond the possibility of a doubt. He reasons thus. "If revolt were to take place in Hungary, in Poland or Italy, support from France would be out of question nor could it be expected from England. —The popular Party there would raise a cry of encouragement to the revolters and

---

[27] Lamb to Palmerston, Aug. 5, 1836, *F.O. 7/257*, PRO (London). Stating that a partition of Turkey would be undesirable from the Austrian point of view, Lamb added: ". . . if to her untractable Hungarians and Transylvanians and Poles were to be added a population of Servians and Bosnians, in exchange for a portion of her present civilized subjects, I am at a loss to conceive how any regular Government could be carried on." The shift of Austria's influence and power from the German and Italian lands to southeastern Europe, which the British discussed in terms of possible concessions to France at the time, materialized about 30 years later as a consequence of the national unification of Germany and Italy, leading essentially to the results anticipated by the English diplomat. Cf. Lamb to Palmerston, Mar. 5, 1837 (No. 18), *F.O. 7/264*, PRO (London).

[28] Cf. Ch. VII, 260.

probably furnish them with aid which no ministry either Whig or Tory would be strong enough to prevent or discountenance.[29]

Repeatedly in his subsequent reports written in the spring of 1837, the ambassador of England, in his evaluations of Metternich's policy, linked the administration's difficulties in Hungary to the general European situation. Warning his government confidentially that "With the uncertain futurity of France, with the disturbed aspect of Hungary, it is evident that this country [the Habsburg Monarchy] has a most difficult game to play," he attributed the chancellor's "vacillation of conduct" vis-à-vis England "not to want of good will, but to weakness of position." Knowing that from England, Austria was "separated by principles as fatal in her mind to her unity and Power as is the physical preponderance of Russia," Lamb yet agreed with Metternich that the Austrian empire was both "the chief counterpoise to the military ascendancy of Russia" and "the main Dike against the possible outbreak of Republicanism and conquest from France." While thus conveying some of the chancellor's pet ideas to his government, the ambassador nevertheless made some valid observations concerning the way in which Metternich tended to look at the world:

Placed between two great dangers, one in the East and one in the West, he has always overlooked the one which appeared to him to be the least urgent, in order to provide against the other. —Until he shall feel the West of Europe to be secure he will not turn his main attention to the East. —Till then he will not sacrifice his relations with Russia unless to withstand such an attack by her upon the Turkish Empire, as should threaten its existence, a case which he is convinced will not occur.

The chancellor, Lamb predicted, would seek to temporize and apply palliatives in the East, recommending that Britain do the same. In this policy, he said, Metternich was motivated "not by indifference, but partly by the embarrassment of his situation, and partly by a conviction that there is no real danger to Turkey as long as England and Austria shall be combined in her support. —This is probably true . . ." concluded the ambassador, stressing that in Metternich's mind the imminence of danger in western Europe—meaning by this France—outweighed the dangers of Russian encroachments on Turkey.[30] He even went so far

[29] Lamb to Palmerston, Aug. 5, 1836, confidential (No. 13), *F.O. 7/259*, PRO (London).
[30] Lamb to Palmerston, Apr. 21, 1837, confidential (No. 32), *F.O. 7/265*, PRO (London).

as to visualize a situation in which the chancellor's subservience to Russia might increase,[31] referring again to "the state of Hungary and France," which might explain Austria's reliance on Russia in spite of the hostility of its educated classes and the army to the realm of the tsar.[32]

Sir Frederic Lamb's analysis proved remarkably accurate, as shown by Metternich's correspondence with Nicholas I, which coincided almost to the hour with the reports sent by the envoy to Palmerston.[33] Using the sickness and expected death of the Archduke-Palatine Joseph as a pretext,[34] Metternich accused the latter of having been soft and characterless in his policies during the 42 years of his "government" in Hungary. Suggesting that the "old constitutional opposition" had ceased to exist and that the four Hungarian factions attacking royal authority consisted of separatists, Protestants (*"luthériens calvinistes"*), demagogues, and prejudiced weaklings, Metternich assured the tsar that the Austrian government was prepared for all eventualities. Referring to the Polish revolt of 1830–31 the chancellor stressed the difference between Poland and Hungary—the latter had no national army, no national bank, and no historic leaders of the stature of Prince Adam Czartoryski. He also informed Nicholas of the recent trial for high treason organized by the court against the "clubs of young people," adding, however, that the main culprits could not be touched because of their parents' connections with the palatine, who allegedly refused to obey Vienna's "most positive orders." But Metternich was confident that it would be impossible for the "parties of opposition" to lead the government astray from the path followed.

In his reply, Nicholas indicated that he would abide by the "engagements contracted at Münchengrätz and confirmed at Berlin relative to the right of intervention which will serve everywhere as sufficient guaranty to the social order. . . ." The tsar's formal promise that *"at all events* Austria can count on Russia,"[35] was to materialize only in 1849;

[31] Lamb to Palmerston, Apr. 29, 1837, *ibid.*
[32] Lamb to Palmerston, May 14, 1837, *ibid.*
[33] This exchange of letters, which took place between Apr. 11 and May 13, 1837, was published in Erzsébet Andics, *A Habsburgok és Romanovok szövetsége* (The Alliance of the Habsburgs and Romanovs) (Budapest: Akadémiai kiadó, 1961), Annex, Docs. 1a–c, pp. 187–96. Originals in the *Staatsarchiv* (Vienna), *Staatskanzlei III, Russland, Varia*. For Metternich's fear of an international conspiracy of revolutionaries and his role in the political trials in Hungary, see Gyula Miskolczy, *A kamarilla a reformkorszakban* (The Camarilla in the Era of Reforms) (Budapest: Athenaeum, n.d.), pp. 105ff.
[34] The Archduke-Palatine recovered and lived until January 1847. For the source of Metternich's attack on the palatine and his remarks about the opposition, see the secret report to Sedlnitzky—"corresponding completely," in Metternich's words, to the chancellor's "own sentiments"—in Schlitter, *Aus Österreichs Vormärz, III, Ungarn*, pp. 78f., n. 5.
[35] Italics in original.

by that time, however, Metternich had been swept away by the revolution, which in turn was overwhelmed by the concept of foreign policy that survived the chancellor. But in 1837 the Russian answer contributed to Metternich's misjudgment of the political forces in Hungary. Relying perhaps too much on external help, he underestimated the strength of the domestic opposition—a source of danger should an international crisis arise.

For the time being at least, Széchenyi's efforts to obtain the enlightened assistance of Vienna's absolutistic government for Hungary's national rebirth failed. His attempts to introduce liberal and progressive reforms in a conservative way were frustrated by an overconfident administration at a time when the appeal of the essentially aristocratic system advocated by him seemed to have gained ground even among the middle nobility, and when the adherents of French liberal democracy based on popular sovereignty had as yet no organized party or national leader in the country. But instead of grasping the historical opportunity, Vienna refused to help Széchenyi and tried to intimidate the country by starting a wave of terror after the Diet of 1832–36. Thus the supporters of reform were further antagonized, or, as Szekfű put it, "Széchenyi had already been defeated when Kossuth, an unpretentious lawyer and silenced editor, was in prison studying English."[36] In fact, the administration's full support was an absolute must for the success of the Széchenyi-type paternalistic reform, which was, theoretically, still feasible in the mid-1830s.

Before turning to the Diet of 1839–40, which dramatized both the adverse results of the government's shortsighted policies toward Hungary and the inherent possibilities of Széchenyi's concept, we should look briefly at his activities in the social and economic areas. Immersed in different enterprises previously initiated or still in the process of being put into practice, such as the suspension bridge, Széchenyi cautiously but with great vision pioneered the road for Hungary's further spiritual and material ascendancy. An amateur diplomat, if necessary, he was a true cultural ambassador of Magyardom. The Academy had hardly begun its work when in early 1834 Széchenyi presented in person copies of its first yearbook to the French and Bavarian Academies. He gave one copy to Ambassador Lieven in London for the Russian Academy, while sending others to the Royal Society in Edinburgh and the Asiatic Society in Calcutta. Through William Vaughan, who was a foreign mem-

---

[36] Hóman and Szekfű, *Magyar történet*, v, 299. Cf. Gyula Szekfű, *A magyar állam életrajza* (Budapest: Dick Manó, n.d.), pp. 183–92. Szekfű's latter work was originally published in German: *Der Staat Ungarn, eine Geschichtsstudie* (Stuttgart-Berlin: Deutsche Verlagsanstalt, 1917).

ber of the American Philosophical Society, and whose brother John was the Society's librarian, he transmitted the Academy's periodical *Tudománytár* (Depository of Science) to Philadelphia. Along with the Royal Society in London, as early as 1833, the American Philosophical Society was the first foreign cultural institute to which the yearbooks of the Hungarian Academy were sent.[37] The scope and purpose of broadening Hungary's cultural ties with the outside world as conceived by Széchenyi, as well as his style, can best be judged from an excerpt of a letter written to Pierre Du Ponceau, President of the American Philosophical Society, in June 1833:

. . . For what could be sweeter than to be at least in spiritual connection with people from whom location, distance, and especially the isolated situation of our country seem physically to separate us, if not forever yet perhaps for a long period of time, and for whom we nonetheless bear as much affection and such an inexplicable sympathy despite these hindrances, as for only very few people in other countries.

The qualities of the soul do not recognize time. Although the angel of Light has taken up quarters but a short time ago in the rugged wilderness of America, yet it has lent its radiance to those, who languishing for centuries under more adverse circumstances, like us, had hardly been able to extricate one leg from the disgusting feudal confusions debasing mankind and particularly our fatherland. Under more fortunate circumstances we ought to blush on account of such backwardness which, however, has not completely suppressed, thank heavens, all [vestiges] of our nationality. The national quality upon which our existence has been based is still alive; some time in the future, we shall be able to stand our ground among the ranks of advanced free generations.

At long last, even we woke up from our ancient lethargy on the tombs of our magnanimous forefathers. True, we are often split because of immature vainglory and hotheaded rivalry, which further

[37] Jan. 6, Feb. 17, Mar. 9, 18, 1834, Viszota, ed., *Naplók*, IV, 442f., 453, 459, 461. Cf. Viszota's introduction, *ibid.*, IV, pp. xii f. and lx. Also Dóra F. Csanak, "Az Akadémiai Könyvtár története a szabadságharcig" (History of the Library of the Hungarian Academy 1826–1849), *Magyar Könyvszemle*, LXXV (1959), 52f. For further details see Francis S. Wagner, "The Start of the Cultural Exchange between the Hungarian Academy of Sciences and the American Philosophical Society," *The Hungarian Quarterly*, V (1965), 90–96. Under the date of Jan. 6, 1834 there is a brief note in the *Registre* of the French Academy about Széchenyi's personal presence at the session of the *Académie des Sciences*. Accordingly, he gave to the French *Institut*, on behalf of the Hungarian Scholarly Society the statutes and plans of that institution, along with several brochures. In his diary Széchenyi mentioned that the session was presided over by the famous scientist, Louis Joseph Gay-Lussac, upon whose request he gave a brief address to the session. Széchenyi also noted that according to the Baron de Prony, a French engineer, he was *"un charmant Hongrois dont il est impossible de prononcer le nom."*

diminish and weaken our small number and feeble ranks, but we hope and believe, trusting the one living God, that the future generation will be united by that national spirit which, preferring honor and glory to all goods of life including life itself, is deeply rooted in our nation's soul and is increasingly developing day by day.

Our Academy whose Vice President I am, sends its greetings to the learned Societies of that Country where the divine residence of Sacred Liberty stands in hitherto unknown purity amidst the miracles of great nature. Fare you well in the halo of your true greatness.[38]

Széchenyi's letter to the president of the American Philosophical Society revealed some of his innermost thoughts about the interdependence of what he deemed "national quality," human dignity, true liberty, and the maturity of a people to achieve them. He was deeply concerned with finding out the "laws" of this correlation. His subsequent fight with Kossuth, motivated as it was by a fear of revolutionary anarchy and a desire for peaceful progress even if peaceful progress meant a slowdown of the coveted social change, sometimes obscures his sincere and emotional attachment to the cause of liberty. Yet this was the root of his admiration for America and England. To those who thought England's greatness depended on its financial power, he answered that money was only the *visible instrument* of its evolution. More basic and imperceptible was the intelligent use of financial means. The peculiarity of the mechanism of domestic consumption, he held, was determined by the freedom and maturity of a people. He also added that any confused ideas about this intimate relationship could lead to disaster.[39]

In reality, Széchenyi did not overlook the great moral significance of revolutionary sacrifices in forging the national unity of a people. During a visit to a monument in Niš built of the skulls of those who defended the city in the Serbian revolution of 1809 against the Turks, he concluded in respectful awe that such experience and schooling might well be the common ground on which Serbian unity could be built. Serb society, he believed, was more cohesive and less prejudiced than its Hungarian counterpart, perhaps because "such a bitter fountain of blood shed for independence sooner or later will and must bring forth freedom and happiness for Serbia." The lesson from the Serbian example seemed

[38] Széchenyi to Pierre Du Ponceau, June 10, 1833, Majláth, ed., *Levelek*, II, 15f. Széchenyi's letter was an answer to Pierre Du Ponceau's letter of Jan. 5, 1833, acknowledging the receipt of the Academy's first yearbook and announcing that the yearbooks of the Philosophical Society, dating back to 1770, had been sent to the Academy. My efforts to locate Széchenyi's original letter in the archives of the American Philosophical Society have so far failed.

[39] Oct. 23, 1832, Viszota, ed., *Naplók*, IV, 329f., italics in original.

all the more painful since, in the language of symbols used by Széchenyi, the blood shed for the independence and self-preservation of his fatherland may not have been pure enough because "it poured for the privileges of an effeminate class and not for the universal freedom of the land. This is why it cries for vengeance and confers no blessing."[40]

Széchenyi's opinion of Serbia, formulated in 1830, became even more favorable when he learned that the Serb Legislative Assembly [Skupština] of 1827 had ordered the translation of the Code Napoléon, while the Hungarian Dietal commission was still lost in the Latin "systematic works." Lamenting the absence of practical common sense among his compatriots, Széchenyi was afraid that only a dreadful reminder similar to the one he saw in Niš could force Hungary to catch up with the outside world.[41] The same inclination to atone for past sins through tragic sacrifices explains his bitter remark about the potential usefulness of the peasant uprising of 1831,[42] or his advice a year later that the Hungarian legislation acquaint itself intimately (*"innig"*) with the "spirit of revolution and reforms" in England and France so that it could comprehend "the transition from the feudal system *id est* barbarism to the present stage and civilization."[43]

In fact, Széchenyi devoted all of his energy to laying the groundwork for the transition from feudalism to modern society. On Aug. 1, 1834, when the Diet seemed to have gotten hopelessly lost in the endless debates of the urbarial question (*"Landtag schlaft ein"*), Széchenyi gave a detailed report to the palatine on the progress of Danube regulation, also asking permission to begin the preparatory work for a port and dockyard in Pest and Buda.[44] Besides luring foreign capital to Hungary for the development of new industries,[45] he also encouraged the training of Hungarian workers under the guidance of foreign, chiefly English and Italian, technicians and skilled laborers.[46] Occasional accusations to the contrary,[47] he made considerable efforts to supply his enterprises with domestic raw materials while also giving much thought to developing those branches of heavy industry that could use the natural resources of Hun-

[40] Sept. 27, 1830, *ibid.*, IV, 134.

[41] Oct. 1, 1830, *ibid.*, IV, 138f.

[42] See Ch. VI, 230.

[43] Oct. 23, 1832, Viszota, ed., *Naplók*, IV, 331.

[44] Aug. 1, 1834, *ibid.*, IV, 486. To the Archduke Palatine, Majláth, ed., *Levelek*, I, 453. For details see Viszota's introduction to *Naplók*, V, pp. lxix–lxxiii.

[45] While promoting such major enterprises as the Steamship Company or the Bridge Association, he did not refrain from useful initiatives on a smaller scale. Cf. his petition of May 23, 1837 to the lieutenancy, B. Szabó, ed., *Adatok*, I, 281.

[46] To the Chief Justice of Szeged. Feb. 14, 1836, Majláth, ed., *Levelek*, II, 248.

[47] See the sculptor Stephen Ferenczy's letter to his brother, Oct. 8, 1838, B. Szabó, ed., *Adatok*, I, 320f.

gary.[48] As has been said before, he tried to prove in his attacks on the feudal structure that even the landowners, who had a vested interest in its maintenance, would benefit economically from its abolition. Similarly, he insisted that while technical innovations might temporarily hurt or even economically ruin those engaged in the outmoded crafts, they were absolutely indispensable for the general welfare of the public, and would in the long run create new possibilities for employment.[49] In order to prepare society for technical progress, Széchenyi proposed at a meeting of the Hungarian Economic Society (which had gradually developed from the horse races and Society for Animal Husbandry) to include in its plans for expansion the establishment of a model farm and an endowment for promoting agricultural and polytechnical instruction.[50] Simultaneously, at the county congregation of Pest he suggested the creation of a polytechnical university at Pest.[51]

It is remarkable that the same man who had the least illusions about Hungarian economic conditions and the most doubts concerning the nation's ability to survive, became the prime mover of the first successful capitalistic enterprises in Hungary. Széchenyi's practical leadership in his fatherland's economic development can be appreciated only if one takes into account how often he was frustrated by official lack of comprehension and by his own compatriots. It is also amazing that he never let his frustrations interfere with the scrupulous thoughtfulness characterizing the preparation and execution of his enterprises. He realized that "In a country like Hungary, where everything is new and untried, 'Success' is absolutely needed, since a failure would be more than a stop, it would cause 'retrogradation.' "[52] He wanted by all means to avoid "retrogradation" as a possible source of a national catastrophe. He de-

---

[48] Széchenyi to Baron Sina, Sept. 16, 1838, *ibid.*, I, 320; Sept. 7, 1832, Viszota, ed., *Naplók*, IV, 299. But he refused to risk the success of his enterprises by applying yet untried domestic materials. This is why, in the case of the suspension bridge, he preferred English iron to Austrian or Hungarian, as shown in a letter to William T. Clark, July 4, 1839, Majláth, ed., *Levelek*, II, 665.

[49] Cf. the 20th article of the series on Danube navigation, published in *Társalkodó*, July 29, 1836. Also cf. Antal Zichy, ed., *Gróf Széchenyi István hirlapi cikkei, 1823–1848* (Count Stephen Széchenyi's Newspaper Articles, 1823–1848), 2 vols. (Budapest; Athenaeum, 1894), I, 159–68. (*SzIM*, VII.)

[50] Mar. 17, 1839, police report on the general meeting of the Economic Society, B. Szabó, ed., *Adatok*, I, 336f. Széchenyi to Casimir Batthyány, Mar. 18, 1839. Majláth, ed., *Levelek*, II, 640f. Mar. 17–18, 1839, Viszota, ed., *Naplók*, IV, 255 and n. 4, 6. Cf. Viszota's introduction, *ibid.*, v, pp. xxxix–xliii.

[51] Mar. 13, 1839, *ibid.*, v, 253 and n. 1. At the Diet of 1832–36 the estates proposed establishing vocational schools in the major cities and the foundation of a technical institute in Pest. The proposal, however, was rejected by a royal rescript in rather evasive language. Horváth, *Huszonöt év*, II, 23ff.

[52] Széchenyi to Richard Tattersall, Apr. 20, 1837, Majláth, ed., *Levelek*, II, 406.

sired "success" because, as he had written to Wesselényi in his warning of November 8, 1831, he did not wish to be "the hero in a tragedy."[53] The understanding of this inner drive to escape an impending catastrophe, partly internal, partly external, is an important key to the interpretation of Széchenyi's lifework and tragic end.

One of the most telling examples of his vision of an economically sound industrial development was his initiative to establish a modern milling industry in Hungary. He first saw a steam mill in Birmingham, England on October 19, 1823. Although he did not think it significant, he did jot down some pertinent technical data and production figures.[54] But in subsequent years he began a careful investigation of the English, American, Swiss, German and north Italian milling industries. In addition to corresponding with the leading firms and experts, he used the information volunteered by a Hungarian officer, Lazarus Mészáros, then stationed at Milan. Through this correspondence and his connections with Széchenyi, Mészáros became a member of the Academy; in 1848, he became minister of defense in the government of Count Louis Batthyány.[55] Following up the leads furnished by Mészáros and after meticulous technical and financial planning, Széchenyi formed a joint stock company mainly with domestic capital.[56] The company managed

[53] Széchenyi to Wesselényi, Nov. 8, 1831, *ibid.*, I, 204.

[54] Oct. 19, 1832, Viszota, ed., *Naplók*, IV, 323f.

[55] Mészáros had read Széchenyi's letter asking Pest county for permission to build a steam mill, published in *Társalkodó*, 1837, p. 211, and called Széchenyi's attention to the cylinder mill built by a Swiss firm at Melegnano. Upon reading Széchenyi's letter republished by B. Szabó in *Adatok*, I, 282, I became convinced that this letter must be identical with the letter published by Majláth in *Levelek*, II, 1, under the incorrect date of June 7, 1827, instead of 1837. A recent one-volume edition of Széchenyi's selected writings (Budapest: 1959; p. 58), edited by Stephen Barta, also seems to have overlooked this error. There are but minor orthographical and a few very slight textual differences in the two versions printed by Majláth and B. Szabó, negligible differences which probably stem from some editorial work. Széchenyi's diaries and Viszota's detailed study on the development of the cylinder mill at Pest in the introductions to *Naplók*, Vols. V and VI, pp. lxxiii–lxxxii and lxxiii, resp., seem to support my assumption, based primarily on the consideration of certain logical historical chronology which prevails also in Széchenyi's individual development and public career. In addition, there is a conclusive philological proof to decide the issue. In the second half of botn variants of this important letter (i.e., in the one published in *Társalkodó* in 1837 and ih the one allegedly written in 1827), Széchenyi applied the same argument for thn need for success in Hungary that he used in his English letter to Tattersall, written on April 20, 1837. Whereas it is unlikely that he used the same idea in similar phrasing in two letters separated by a decade, this should be only natural in an interval of but seven weeks, especially, if the idea were thought to be important enough by Széchenyi from the point of view of educating the Hungarian public. Finally, it is improbable that Széchenyi would have undertaken the promotion of steam mills more than five years before he saw one in England.

[56] The Swiss Holzhammer firm, which supplied the patents and technical assistance to the enterprise, held half of the shares as royalty, according to the original contract. Viszota, *ibid*, V, pp. lxxiv f. Cf. Jenő Gaál, "Gróf Széchenyi és a pesti hengermalom

to overcome the resistance of the miller guild and prove that cylinder mills could be profitable in Hungary.

To put Széchenyi's entrepreneurial genius in proper perspective, it will suffice to sum up the main ideas expressed in his letter to the estates of Pest county in June 1837. In it, he indicated his intention to found a corporation to operate a steam mill in Pest or Buda. He stressed that he was not thinking of a single mill, but of a model, in the hope that other steam mills might spread all over the country, making it possible to replace grain with flour in Hungarian foreign trade. He pointed out that such a development would benefit farmers and at the same time give an opportunity to otherwise resourceless people to make a living as millhands, as coal miners in the Mohács region, or as carpenters preparing wooden staves to hold the flour. To assure the success of the new enterprise, Széchenyi asked the abolition of price controls in the flour business. Without such action, success or profit would be in danger; yet, he insisted, "in our land, at least for the time being, the failure of enterprises would be most detrimental not only to the entrepreneurs but also to the general public because the latter would be deterred from the most useful enterprises by the ones that failed due to miscalculation and error."[57] Such failures, he feared, would discourage the public which would relapse for many years into its old apathy.

Obviously, Széchenyi's views on Hungary's industrialization had changed considerably since he first visited England. At that time, he did not believe in the need for or feasibility of Hungary's industrial evolution. Some 15 years later his books *Hitel* and *Világ* tended to brush aside the "senseless" opinion of those who thought that it was impossible to have factories in Hungary. In the 1830s he himself began to look for ways and means to diversify the Hungarian economy. All his life, however, he emphasized the necessity of gradual industrialization in a backward country, holding that success depended on developing agricultural production first.[58] By pointing to the organic connection

---

társaság" (Count Széchenyi and the Cylinder Mill Company of Pest), *Értekezések a társadalmi tudományok köréből*, XIII (1909), 593–638. It is interesting that among the data contained in this study, delivered originally as a lecture at the Academy on Feb. 8, 1909, the author included the letter mentioned in the previous note (pp. 601f.). In an asterisk remark on p. 602, he referred to the opinion of "qualified men," according to whom the dating of the letter by Majláth was erroneous, since the correct date was "probably" 1837. In spite of this, the erroneous—and anachronistic—dating "survived," as I have tried to show occasionally causing some farfetched conclusions. Cf. Miklos Szucs Nicolson, "Count István Széchenyi (1792 (*sic*)-1860): His Role in the Economic Development of the Danube Basin," *Explorations in Entrepreneurial History*, VI (1953–54), 175.

[57] Széchenyi to Pest county, June 7, 1837, B. Szabó, ed., *Adatok*, I, 282.

[58] *Hitel*, p. 358; *Világ*, p. 274. Széchenyi to Pest county, Feb. 27, 1835. Majláth, ed., *Levelek*, I, 602f.

between these two major branches of the economy, he put his finger on one of the problematic aspects of the modernization of Hungary and the rest of east Central Europe, and perhaps of other underdeveloped regions, as well. In spite of being a latecomer to Hungary and east Central Europe, the industrial revolution, when it finally arrived, had not been preceded by an agricultural revolution comparable to the one that paved its way in western Europe. It may well be that this is one of the really important features distinguishing the east European version of the industrial revolution from its west European counterpart, as some Hungarian historians seem to contend.[59] Be this as it may, Széchenyi was certainly anxious to anticipate and avoid, as far as possible, any lopsided development of the economy in the process of modernization. His cautious attitude was determined perhaps less by the mentality or "class limitations," to use Marxist phraseology, of the great landowner, which he undoubtedly was, than by the fact that unlike some 20th-century planners in underdeveloped countries, he, "the great patriot," was both free and willing to think in terms of economic realities rather than national prestige.

It would be preposterous, of course, to suggest that Széchenyi or any other talented individual could singlehandedly have changed overnight either the physical setting or the socio-economic environment into which he was born. Regardless of the political coloring of the regime in power, such long-range changes could be controlled or "engineered" only under certain, historically rare, conditions. Able and sympathetic leadership, the diligent efforts of several generations, and reasonable stability in domestic and international affairs are some of the essential components, a fortunate combination of which might result, if not in a miracle, at least in a favorable atmosphere for successful reform and progress. Evidently Széchenyi could not expect such a historic opportunity, if there is such a thing, to execute his plans. As Franklin's disciple, he also knew that man himself can greatly contribute to his own betterment. This is why he continued to work relentlessly—in some fields, with tangible success.

In the founding of a milling industry, besides participating in the preparation of blueprints for the first cylinder mill in Pest, the selection and purchasing of the site for the buildings and its machinery, and the recruitment of the technical personnel, Széchenyi also presided over most of the sesssions of the board of shareholders after their first meeting in December 1838.[60] His speech, given in early January 1842, at the

---

[59] Lecture given by Iván T. Berend at the University of Colorado, Boulder, Colorado, Feb. 13, 1967.

[60] J. Gaál, "Széchenyi és a pesti hengermalom," pp. 608ff.

fourth general meeting of the shareholders, and held shortly after the new enterprise became operational, is of particular interest. In it Széchenyi stressed the significance of substituting step by step, as he put it, flour for grain in Hungary's export trade so that it can supply Vienna, Prague, and even compete with the grain of Odessa on the world market. After a brief survey of the immediate financial and technical tasks, he emphasized that the new mill had to be strengthened by making it profitable. Ridiculing the "soft-headed" dreamers who wished to promote the cause of mankind without considering the demands of certain priorities, he advocated the establishment of a vigorous and businesslike enterprise which would be able, in due time, to pursue higher goals, too. These included the recognition of the need to provide the public, especially the "poorer class," with the best food at the cheapest possible price. Thus the new mill should put an end to profiteering, and stabilize, as time went on, the price of flour in periods of good and bad harvests alike, and regardless of road conditions, by securing the supply of the needy. The other "nobler aim" for which Széchenyi was striving was to raise the quality of the products to be exported and thereby augment the value of Hungary's soil.[61]

The triple task, set forth by Széchenyi, reflected the thoughts of a man who obviously believed in the soundness of the free enterprise system but intended to operate it as a responsible patriot with a social conscience. This anticipation of "welfare capitalism," even in its rudimentary form, may have been beyond the purpose and grasp of most of his compatriots. But the idea itself shows Széchenyi's vision, courage to adapt his methods to local conditions, and his considerable organizational ability.

Indeed, the milling industry became by the end of the 19th century Hungary's most important export industry and played a key role in the rapid development of the food-processing industry. The latter, in turn, was the main stimulus to Hungary's industrialization.[62] Other by-products of Széchenyi's cylinder mill at Pest were, besides the "discovery" of Mészáros, the first careful investigation of domestic fuel (coal) resources for the planned mill[63] and in 1841 the auxiliary machine shops. A few years later, in 1845–47, the machine shops were enlarged to become

[61] For Széchenyi's speech, cf. *ibid.*, pp. 617–20, 623–26.

[62] T. Erényi, "Die Hauptrichtungen der Entwicklung der Gewerkschaftsbewegung in Ungarn," *Etudes historiques*, publiées par la Commission Nationale des Historiens Hongrois, 2 vols. (Budapest: Akadémiai kiadó, 1960), II, 231. I.T. Berend and Gy. Ránki, "Das Niveau der Industrie zu Beginn des 20. Jahrhunderts," in V. Sándor and P. Hanák, eds., *Studien zur Geschichte der Österreichisch-Ungarischen Monarchie* (Budapest: Akadémiai kiadó, 1961), pp. 280–86 (*Studia Historica*, No. 51).

[63] Széchenyi to Hunter & English, Sept. 20, 1837, cited in Futó, *A magyar gyáripar*, I, 182. Also letter mentioned in note 57 above.

the first factory of the Hungarian machine industry, the *Pesther Maschinenbau und Eisengiesserey Gesellschaft*. Széchenyi's interest in stimulating certain branches of incipient Hungarian industries led to his participation in the Association for Factory Founding (*Gyáralapitó Társaság*),[64] initiated by Kossuth at the end of 1844 to obtain the co-operation of those who like Széchenyi refused to support the National Protective Union (*Országos Védegylet*), which had been founded a few months earlier. As shown by its very name, protectionist tendencies and political agitation were dominant in the Protective Union, and the same trends prevailed in the National Industrial Union (*Országos Iparegyesület*), which had come into being in 1841. In all three associations Kossuth's influence was strong; this was one reason why Széchenyi soon resigned his post as vice-president of the Association for Factory Founding.[65] The other was his awarnesess of Austrian disapproval of Hungarian protectionism[66] which he rightly thought ineffective anyway, at least economically. Thus the Széchenyi-Kossuth antagonism, the origins of which were political but which was motivated by personal antipathy from the beginning, was to cast its shadow on economic matters. This meant that Széchenyi's authority was seriously questioned in a field where up to the early 1840s his leadership seemed to have been generally recognized, if not completely unchallenged.

It is worth taking a brief look at some of these challenges, because they shed interesting light on the behavior of both Széchenyi and the newly emerging entrepreneurial class in Hungary. After the enactment of legislation by the Diet of 1832–36, which prepared the ground for the building of railroads in Hungary, there developed a rivalry between two major financial groups for the right to construct a line connecting Vienna with Pest. Széchenyi, for reasons to be detailed in connection with the Diet of 1839–40, supported the Viennese banker Baron George Sina who was also the main financier of the suspension bridge. His chief competitor was Solomon Rothschild of Vienna, who allied himself with several prominent Hungarian businessmen.[67] The appearance of this new Hungarian bourgeoisie, the most enterprising representatives of which were frequently of German, Jewish, Greek, Serb, Swiss, French, or Italian background, was but another sign of advancing capitalism

[64] Cf. Viszota's introductions to *Naplók*, v and vi, pp. lxix ff. and lxiii f.; also to *Széchenyi és Kossuth*, ii, cxx–cxxviii. Cf. Jan. 22, 1841, Viszota, ed., *Naplók*, v, 440 and n, 2; *id.*, "Széchenyi, Kossuth és a Gyáralapitó Táraság," *Budapesti Szemle*, cxxxix (1909), 136–41.

[65] Gyula Mérei, *Magyar iparfejlődés, 1790–1848* (Hungarian Industrial Development, 1790–1848) (Budapest: Közoktatásügyi kiadó, 1951), pp. 220–27, 253ff.

[66] Széchenyi to Lunkányi, Nov. 27, 1844, cited by Tilkovszky in "Ismeretlen Széchenyi-levelek," p. 94.

[67] Mérei, *Magyar iparfejlődés*, p. 165.

in Hungary. Whether dealers in grain, tobacco, wool, hides, and wine, mediators between the merchants on the Balkan Peninsula and the commercial circles of Austria and Western countries, or organizers of new enterprises in their adopted country—this new Hungarian capitalist class demonstrated its vigor in the competition for the charter of the first railroad in Hungary. Eventually both groups were given permission (in the 1840s) to build their respective railroads, and Széchenyi, too, modified his original views on the matter.

Of a different nature was a challenge which revealed a subtle change in Széchenyi's liberal views on the relationship between lord and peasant. As I attempted to show in the preceding chapter, the urbarial legislation enacted by the Diet of 1832–36 was only a watered down version of the progressive reforms suggested by the liberal opposition.[68] Although they represented a step forward, the new laws had a number of provisions that were either ambiguous or outright damaging to the peasants. Act VI of 1836, which defined the conditions under which the lord might recover cleared woodland, was unfavorable to the serf. The same law also permitted the separation of allodial pasture from the communal meadow on the request of one landowner or the majority of serfs. In many cases, the serfs would have benefited from the separation of their holdings from the lord's share, especially, if the latter's cattle or sheep were about to crowd out peasants' livestock from the area held in common. Yet the law also stipulated that under no circumstances was the landowner to be prevented from using the grassland he needed, leaving the arbitration of disputes to the manorial courts. The stipulations of Act X of 1836, which provided for the commassation of land where one landowner or the majority of peasants requested it, gave similar advantages to the lord.[69]

Still, the serfs could appeal the decisions of the local courts, and their case was not always hopeless in the 1830s, particularly in counties dominated by the liberals. In Sopron county, where Széchenyi and his brothers had most of their estates, this resulted in an interesting situation. As we know, Széchenyi directed the managers of his estates in the late twenties to let his serfs have the better part of the land,[70] if necessary, to reach a friendly agreement with them on the separation of his privately managed holdings from theirs, a desired goal for the sake of improving the quality and quantity of production. Despite the objections of the director of his estates, who had a firsthand knowledge of the financial implications of his costly innovations and magnanimity, but who was

[68] See Ch. VII, 289ff.
[69] Mérei, *Mezőgazdaság és agrártársadalom*, pp. 189–206.
[70] See Ch. VI, 186f.

also aware of Széchenyi's wish to help transform the serf into a peasant freeholder, Széchenyi insisted on proving the feasibility of his liberal ideas to both fellow landowners and his own reluctant stewards. Even so, it took years for the voluntary agreements to be signed, since the serfs mistrusted any proposals coming from their lord, from past experience, and from an intimate knowledge of the true intentions of his representatives.[71]

The decade following the Diet of 1825–27, which saw so many new trends and challenges to the established socio-economic order on the Hungarian political scene, also caused a change of heart in Széchenyi. True, he himself was instrumental in bringing about the incipient shift in the outlook of his compatriots. But his own attitude toward the outside world, seemingly so carefree and exuding youthful energy, though undermined with anguish below the surface, began to undergo a gradual change. To those asking how he was to live without income after the foundation of the Academy, he was reputed to have replied that his friends would support him. In justifying his generosity to his serfs, he stressed that he had no family to take care of.[72] Previously, he had not minded being regarded as a center of the new opposition, challenging cautiously but firmly even Metternich during their private conversations. His major books, in which he refrained from attacking the administration, advocating a sober middle course instead, nevertheless reflected a liberal ideology. By the second half of the 1830s, however, he was a married man with obligations to a large family. Yet he had even less time than ever before for his estates, which continued to be the main source of his income, due to his involvement in public affairs and anxiety to supervise in person his enterprises. Assuming, correctly, that peaceful reform depended to a very large extent on the government's active assistance, he sometimes forgot that the government also had a stake in the same cause. Having received some help for his projects, such as the works at the Iron Gates and the suspension bridge, he became increasingly anxious not to "look bad" in Vienna at a time of growing polarization of political forces in Hungary.

The ambiguity of his position carried over into the sphere of his private affairs precisely because he was such a prominent public figure. His relationship with the peasants on his estates is a telling example. If he wanted and had to be magnanimous to obtain the voluntary coopera-

---

[71] Loránt Tilkovszky, "Az elkülönözés és tagositás Széchenyi István cenki uradalmában" (The Separation and Commassation of Land in Stephen Széchenyi's Estate in Cenk), *Agrártörténeti Szemle*, III (1961), 33–40.

[72] Kemény, "Széchenyi," p. 357. Széchenyi to Count Somssich, Sept. 4, 1827, B. Szabó, ed., *Adatok*, I, 71f.

tion of his serfs for the sake of introducing progressive measures in his domains prior to the Diet of 1832–36, the new legislation gave him a lever he could use against them should they prove too stubborn in defending their own interests. Liebenberg, who was ennobled upon Széchenyi's recommendation by the Diet and Magyarized his name to Lunkányi, strongly advised his master to avail himself of the lever. After the promulgation and explanation of the new urbarial laws to the peasant deputations in Sopron county, the first such public meeting having been arranged by him on Széchenyi's family estate in Cenk, Liebenberg persisted in his complaints about the "ultraliberal," "Lutheran," and "have-not" county magistrates, who themselves had no serfs to worry about and allegedly continued to inquire about the grievances of the peasants, encouraging them to start urbarial lawsuits against their lords.[73] He also reported that landowners in Sopron and neighboring counties were gleefully watching how the separation and commassation of land was going to be effectuated on Széchenyi's estates, since it was he who had started the whole trouble. Knowing how sensitive the issue was, Liebenberg offered to find some loopholes so Széchenyi's image as a liberal would not be hurt. One of them was to conclude a sham contract between himself and Széchenyi, stipulating that Liebenberg become Széchenyi's tenant for a number of years on those estates where the unpopular measures were to be put into effect. Széchenyi rejected this, saying that he had never advocated "that kind of stupid liberalism, according to which you take something out of one's pocket in order to put it into the other's." Referring to the abolition of feudal dues without compensation as "outright spoliation," Széchenyi instructed the director of his estates to protect his "just rights" and disregard the opinion of those who would accuse him of having reversed himself.[74]

In spite of the unyielding tone of his master's letter, written at the end of 1836, Liebenberg was afraid, with some justification, that Széchenyi's liberal inclinations would ultimately lead him to make concessions detrimental to his own interests just to save face before the public. This is why he repeatedly advised Széchenyi to get busy on the Lower Danube and not visit his estates in the critical spring of 1837. Széchenyi followed the advice, giving Liebenberg a free hand in dealing with his serfs in 1837 and in subsequent years. He continued to urge his steward to reach an agreement, whenever possible, without litigation with the peasants. But the evidence shows that he knew Liebenberg and some of his other employees were not above questionable manipula-

[73] Tilkovszky, "Az elkülönözés és tagosítás Széchenyi cenki uradalmában," pp. 40–43.
[74] Széchenyi to Lunkányi, Dec. 11, 1836, cited ibid., pp. 44f.

tions, which included tampering with justice; in fact, Széchenyi seems to have occasionally connived at such practices.[75]

By proxy and in his private affairs, Széchenyi thus began to oppose the liberals years before he took a public stand against them in national affairs. He was still considered as one of the leaders of Hungarian liberalism at the Diet of 1839–40, but his nonpolitical public activities appeared to absorb most of his energies. Besides the major projects already known to us, there was a wide variety of these other activities, ranging from embellishing the capital-to-be to the foundation of a rowing club at Pest or a mulberry association in Sopron and Vas counties.[76] In addition to the series of articles on navigation of the Danube, he wrote other small works, in part to popularize his more practical endeavors. From 1834 to 1837 he worked on *Pesti por és sár* (Dust and Mud of Pest), fragments of which, however, were not published until shortly before his death.[77] Parts of this work are interesting, such as the suggestion to build durable, hygienic houses and to develop a national style in architecture, or Széchenyi's poetic, and prophetic, vision of turning Lake Balaton into a great resort and recreational center.[78] Of the other two booklets written in this period, the first was directed against Marshal Marmont, who in his travelogues belittled Hungarian horse-breeding, and against some of Széchenyi's critics at home, whereas the second advocated domestic silk production.[79]

Yet no amount of "organic work," to borrow a term from the vocabulary of late 19th-century Polish history, could blot out Széchenyi's worries about the political situation in Hungary. The prosecution of Wesselényi, the leaders of the Dietal youth, and Kossuth failed to produce the results Vienna expected. True, the Diet convened in June 1839 in the conspicuous absence of Wesselényi and Kossuth. But prior to its opening, when the administration began to proceed against the deputies, who

---

[75] *Ibid.*, pp. 45–58.

[76] Cf. Viszota's introduction to *Naplók*, v, pp. lxxxii–lxxxv.

[77] For the fragmentary work, Széchenyi began to write a new preface, but that, too, remained unfinished and was published only after World War I, in Károlyi and Tolnai, eds., *Döblingi hagyaték*, III, 839.

[78] *Pesti por és sár*, pp. 77f., 88–96, 101–107, in János Török, ed., *Gróf Széchenyi István fennmaradt munkái* (Count Stephen Széchenyi's Extant Works), 2d edn., 2 pts., (Pest: Heckenast, 1872).

[79] Gróf István Széchenyi, *Néhány szó a lóverseny körül* (A Few Words on Horse Racing) (Pest: Heckenast, 1838); Széchenyi, *Selyemrül* (On Silk) (Pest: Trattner-Károlyi, 1840); August Frédéric Louis Viesse de Marmont, duc de Raguse, *Voyage du m. le maréchal duc de Raguse, en Hongrie, en Transylvanie, dans la Russie méridionale, en Crimée et sur les bords de la mer d'Azoff; à Constantinople et sur quelques parties de l'Asie Mineure; en Syrie, en Palestine et en Egypte*, 5 vols. (Paris: 1834–35; Vol. v published in Brussels, 1859). The remarks resented by Széchenyi appeared in Vol. I, 40ff.; Gyula Viszota, "Gróf Széchenyi István és Sopron vármegye" (Count Stephen Széchenyi and Sopron County), *Budapesti Szemle*, CXII (1902), 54–62.

had publicly protested the illegal arrests and trials, the opposition answered by setting up the same persons as candidates for the forthcoming Diet. In Pest county the liberals succeeded in electing Count Gideon Ráday as deputy even though he was being prosecuted. Elsewhere similar efforts were frustrated by the administration but the resulting bitter political struggles stirred up nationwide excitement.[80]

In the rising storm of national protest the *Staatskonferenz*, weakened by the endless bickering of Kolowrat and Metternich, became hesitant. Although the information sent by the Austrian chancellor to the tsar exaggerated the palatine's Magyar sympathies and somewhat overstated the absence of a strong hand in Hungary, it is true that the resistance of many of the 52 more or less self-governing counties could not be ignored. Moreover, the necessity of summoning the Diet to vote fresh conscripts for the army made it difficult to maintain indefinitely the policy of overt terror, especially because Metternich had been anticipating new trouble in the Near East and France since the spring of 1838.[81] The chancellor also knew that the dispute between the Prussian state and the German Catholic hierarchy might have repercussions in Austria, Hungary, and Transylvania.[82]

Characteristically, both Metternich and Kolowrat asked Chief Justice Cziráky's opinion on the Hungarian situation on the same day. The staunch conservative lord chief justice replied with a stinging denunciation of "the mischief started in 1825" and recommended a strong-fisted policy. In places, his description of Hungarian political life sounded like a threat of the Last Judgment. Speaking of the "aroused passions of partiality" agitating Hungary, of the "democratic fever" and "revolt against all authority" eroding the rights of the king, he cautioned the administration that strong dams must be built against the threatening flood. Cziráky, who had pledged never to cross Széchenyi's bridge, proposed to muzzle the circular sessions which had a considerable influence upon the legislative work of the last Diets. It will be recalled that whereas the two chambers of the Diet were presided over by royal appointees, the palatine and the personalis, the circular sessions elected their own

[80] Horváth, *Huszonöt év*, II, 101–105.

[81] Metternich to Apponyi, Docs. 1,318–23, 1,325 and Metternich to Sainte-Aulaire, Doc. 1,324, in Metternich-Winneburg, ed., *Aus Metternichs nachgelassenen Papieren*, VI, 264–76.

[82] Report to Emperor Ferdinand, Doc. 1,336, *ibid.*, VI, 284ff.; Maas, ed., *Der Josephinismus*, V, 497–553, Docs. 60–68; Srbik, *Metternich*, III, 157f. According to a French diplomat, Metternich commented on the dispute between Berlin and Rome by saying: "Je fais le mort." The chancellor was worried lest "difficulties" similar to the Cologne affair occur in Hungary any day. Langsdorff to Molé, Feb. 17, Mar. 23, 1838, Vol. 425, *Correspondance politique, Autriche*, Archives du Ministère des Affaires Etrangères (Paris).

officers. According to the chief justice, however, discussions chaired by elected officers reflected a "purely democratic form" and hence were incompatible with the aristocratic Hungarian constitution. He held that in the developmental trend since the Diet of 1790 there had been a continuous and systematic push of the "democratic element," concluding that it was high time to wake up.[83]

During the proscription of radical patriots Széchenyi was overcome by the fear that the administration might revert to absolutistic government. "We might wind up in a dictatorship," he wrote in mid-1837,[84] and a year later he jotted down Metternich's alleged opinion, according to which "Count Széchenyi had done so much damage that six such *characters* (?) cannot make up for it."[85] Knowing that anybody advocating liberalism, nationalism, or constitutional government was mistrusted in Vienna, Széchenyi was afraid that archconservatives led by Cziráky might get a free hand in Hungarian affairs. Shortly before the Diet he warned his brother Paul (hoping that his words would be relayed to Metternich) that Cziráky's "obscurantism and his mad intention to turn loose the epoch of Maria Theresa once more on Hungary" might lead to the most dangerous reaction. He ended the letter by imploring Paul Széchenyi: "Think of me! God save us from this evil! Amen! All extremes are venomous!"[86]

Excessive though Széchenyi's fears may have been, they were not imaginary or without foundation. To the inquiries of French diplomats, who kept a close eye on the arrests and trials of the Dietal youth, Kossuth, and Wesselényi, Metternich replied that the administration wished "to intimidate rather than punish," and that he recommended a policy of "salutary terror" (*terreur salutaire*) to "enlighten" the public.[87] When asked about the convocation of the Transylvanian Diet in March 1837, but two years after the previous assembly proved to be unmanageable

---

[83] November 1838. "Freymüthige Darstellung der politischen Lage Ungarns in gegenwärtiger Zeit," in B. Szabó, ed., *Adatok*, I, 323ff. At the request of Ferdinand V, Cziráky elaborated on his proposals in the form of an aide memoire in early 1839, *ibid.*, p. 330. Cf. his memorandum of Aug. 31, 1836, recommending a cure for "Hyperhungarismus," in Szekfű, ed., *Iratok*, pp. 482–85. In 1791, as a student at the University of Pest, Cziráky is alleged to have been among those promoting the patriotic trend condemned by him later. Cf. Géza Ballagi, *A politikai irodalom Magyarországon 1825–ig* (Political Literature in Hungary Until 1825) (Budapest: Franklin, 1888), pp. 597f.

[84] June 9, 1837, Viszota, ed., *Naplók*, v, 85; on Sept. 26 and 27, 1837 Metternich, Pálffy, Széchenyi, and the engineer of the suspension bridge, Clark, dined at Sina's. *The Diary of Philipp von Neumann*, ed., 2 vols. (Boston: Houghton & Mifflin, 1928), II, 69f.

[85] Aug. 15, 1838, Viszota, ed., *Naplók*, v, 197. Italics and question mark Széchenyi's.

[86] Széchenyi to Paul Széchenyi, Apr. 8, 1839, B. Szabó, ed., *Adatok*, I, 338.

[87] Ste-Aulaire to Thiers, July 3, 1836, Vol. 423, *CPAu*, AMAE (Paris); Ste-Aulaire to Molé, Jan. 14, Mar. 2, 21, Apr. 10, 24, May 2, 18, 1837; Vol. 424, *ibid*.

and had to be dissolved, the chancellor explained that Hungary must be taught an object lesson.[88] Indeed, it seemed as though the strong-man methods of Royal Commissioner Archduke Ferdinand d'Este, who was given extraordinary powers to subdue Transylvania, were to bring results. In the spring of 1837 the nuncio wrote that Hungary and Transylvania were in a state of sedition and that anti-Catholic agitation and demagoguery were rampant. Reporting the illness of the palatine, whom he mistrusted, the papal envoy was even more alarmed by the possibility that the Archduke Joseph could be succeeded by his son Stephen who, in the nuncio's words, was "infected" by the spirit of liberalism and Hungarian nationalism.[89] Yet deprived of its leader, Wesselényi, the Transylvanian opposition proved to be impotent.[90] Hungary, too, appeared to have calmed down somewhat, in the French ambassador's opinion, by the time the well-liked palatine regained his strength in the fall of 1837.[91]

Still, creation of martyrs and persecution tended to unite rather than weaken the ranks of the Hungarian opposition. Due to the clouds appearing both on the international and domestic horizons, the *Staatskonferenz* saw fit to improve the general political atmosphere before the beginning of the Diet. At the end of 1838 Count Anton Majláth took over the Hungarian chancery from the hated Pálffy, and somewhat later Count George Majláth became lord chief justice instead of Cziráky, who had been transferred to Vienna. Since Personalis Somssich had also been removed, both high courts of the realm involved in the political trials received new presidents.[92]

The conciliatory gestures aimed at strengthening the administration's position at the forthcoming Diet were supplemented in the spiritual realm by the appointment of a new archbishop of Esztergom.[93] In the fall of 1837, with the archiepiscopal see vacant for over six years, the nuncio raised the issue by calling Metternich's attention to the dangers of leaving the Hungarian Catholic hierarchy without leadership at a time when controversial theological trends and the need for resisting

[88] Ste-Aulaire to Molé, Mar. 30, 1837, Vol. 424, *ibid.*

[89] Altieri to Lambruschini, Mar. 17 ("Sullo Stato attuale della Ungheria e Transylvania") and Apr. 14, 1837, Anno 1837, Rubrica 247, Busta 409, *Segreteria di Stato Esteri, 1814–1850*, Archivio Segreto Vaticano.

[90] Trócsányi, *Wesselényi*, pp. 333, 337.

[91] Ste-Aulaire to Molé, Sept. 11, 22, 1837, Vol. 424, *Correspondance politique, Autriche*, Archives du Ministère des Affaires Etrangères (Paris).

[92] Wirkner, *Meine Erlebnisse*, pp. 107ff.; Ballagi, *A magyar nemzeti államalkotás kora*, pp. 469ff. Cf. No. 947/1838, *Kabinettsarchiv, Staatskonferenzakten*, Staatsarchiv (Vienna).

[93] Ste-Aulaire to Marshall Soult, June 14, 1839, Vol. 426, *Correspondance politique, Autriche*, Archives du Ministère des Affaires Etrangères (Paris); Kübeck, ed., *Tagebücher.* I, Pt. 2, pp. 802f.

liberal innovations demanded firmness. In this context the papal envoy also referred to the approaching Hungarian Diet. The chancellor, however, remained noncommittal. Without denying the validity of the nuncio's arguments, he spoke about the immense difficulties of finding an appropriate person for such a high position, which was of great consequence not only to the church but also to the state. As Metternich put it, the primate could under certain conditions be more important than the palatine because "such is his dignity and national authority."[94] Having this in mind, no doubt, and perhaps also the enormous revenues of the archbishopric of Esztergom, collected by the royal treasury whenever the archiepiscopal see was vacant, the chancellor resumed discussion of the matter with the nuncio in the spring of 1838 by suggesting the candidacy of the archbishop of Salzburg, a young member of the Prince Schwarzenberg family. Although it was not unusual to transform foreigners into Hungarian ecclesiastic dignitaries (one Prince Schwarzenberg was bishop of Győr in the early 19th century), under the given circumstances the papal envoy could not help raising objections to the plan for sending a member of the Austrian Catholic hierarchy to Hungary, a country where he had no previous contacts or experience before. After dropping Schwarzenberg's candidacy it took yet another year before the administration and the curia finally settled the issue by elevating a rather reluctant Bishop Joseph Kopácsy to the archiepiscopal see of Esztergom.[95]

The maneuvers related to the appointment of the primate of Hungary were characteristic of the half-measures taken by a weak administration. Wesselényi's final condemnation to three years imprisonment in early February 1839, because, to quote the French ambassador, "It was very important for the imperial government that justice be done before the reunion of the Diet this coming spring,"[96] upset the effect of Vienna's previous acts of goodwill. It is true that Wesselényi's sentence was suspended soon after his arrest and that he was allowed to take the waters at Gräfenberg, Bohemia (partly in an attempt to save his eyesight before going competely blind). This belated leniency, due primarily to Deák's personal intercession in Vienna,[97] did not change the fact that barely one year after his heroic rescue work in the spring 1838 inundation of Pest, the "shipman of the flood" was declared guilty in a political

[94] Altieri to Lambruschini, Oct. 13, 1837, Anno 1837, Rubrica 247, Busta 409, *Segreteria di Stato Esteri, 1814–1850*, Archivio Segreto Vaticano. For Cardinal Lambruschini's reply, approving the nuncio's initiative, see *ibid.*, Lambruschini to Altieri, Oct. 27, 1837.

[95] For details, cf. Meszlényi, *A jozefinizmus*, pp. 364–83.

[96] Ste-Aulaire to Molé, Feb. 11, 1839, Vol. 426, *Correspondance politique, Autriche*, Archives du Ministère des Affaires Etrangères (Paris).

[97] Ede Wertheimer, "Franz Deák in Wien im Jahre 1839," *Pester Lloyd*, Mar. 31, 1900, pp. 2f.; Trócsányi, *Wesselényi*, pp. 430–35.

trial that most Hungarian patriots believed unconstitutional. To impeach, let alone condemn, a person for high treason because of words spoken in a county congregation was a flagrant violation of the freedom of assembly. Moreover, Wesselényi's undoubtedly harsh censure of the administration was interpreted by the majority of his judges as being an offense to the monarch, whereas, according to the Hungarian constitution, or in any constitutional country, as Deák stated tersely, "government and king are not identical."[98]

Liberal public opinion was further incensed by the administration's refusal to recognize the validity of Count Ráday's election as Pest county's representative in the Diet.[99] Thus a fresh grievance was added to the long list of violations of freedom of speech. The rescript relative to the Ráday-case was "most respectfully put aside"; although the county congregation "yielded to force" and declared itself unwilling to oppose the royal decision, it nonetheless instructed the other deputy of Pest county to raise the issue as a "national grievance" and not to take up any other item of the agenda before the constitutional rights of the county had been restored. Because the majority of the lower table supported Pest and because the administration would not give in, the Diet began with a political tug-of-war, during which the lower chamber refused to consider the royal propositions.[100] After three months the impasse ended with Ráday's resignation of his mandate; Széchenyi was instrumental in persuading Ráday and the opposition to accept the face-saving solution.[101] But having dropped the Ráday case involving the freedom of election, the chamber of deputies raised the question of freedom of speech and demanded the impeachment of the judges who had condemned Wesselényi, Kossuth, and the leaders of the Dietal youth. The opposition, led by Deák, was unwilling to compromise on the constitutional issue, which became the focal point of the debates for nearly a year.

[98] *Ibid.*, pp. 411–27; Kónyi, ed., *Deák beszédei*, i, 166f.

[99] Posterity is indebted to Julia Pardoe for a colorful eyewitness account in English of one of the elections for the Diet, held in Pest shortly after Ráday had been disqualified by the administration. Cf. *The City of the Magyar*, ii, 147–74. Miss Pardoe wrote: "I never knew the full meaning of the word *noise* until I attended the Pesth election," *ibid.*, p. 254.

[100] The three royal propositions showed a lack of imagination. Two of them dealt with military problems (recruits and food supplies), the third with Danube regulation. All fell far short of the suggestions made by Aurel Dessewffy in January 1839. Cf. "Fragmente aus einem Aufsatz über den bevorstehenden ungarischen Landtag," in *Aus den Papieren des Grafen Aurel Dessewffy*, gesammelt und herausgegeben durch einige seiner Freunde und Gleichgesinnte, 2 vols, in 1 (Pesth: Landerer & Heckenast, 1843), i, 81–85.

[101] Mar. 8, Aug. 3, 4, 5, 6, 30, Oct. 19, 1839, Viszota, ed., *Naplók*, v, 251, 302f., 309, 321f.

The problem of religious freedom, unsolved by the previous Diet because the resistance of the chamber of magnates, again contributed to the political tension. On the eve of the Diet of 1839 the bishop of Nagyvárad (Oradea) issued a pastoral letter forbidding his clergy to bless mixed marriages without adequate assurance (*reversalis*) that the children would be brought up in the Catholic faith. This was far more than an internal affair of the church. The public, including liberal Catholics, reacted with indignation to this reopening of the "Cologne Affair" in Hungary, which was contrary to the practice followed by the clergy since 1790 and which involved the secular jurisdiction of municipalities.[102] As Széchenyi, himself a Catholic, put it: "Should the Diet not include as part of its deliberations and perhaps not even discuss this question, which has stirred half the country into a revolutionary upheaval?"[103]

The Diet of 1839–40 witnessed an important shift in the balance of political forces. In the chamber of magnates the conservative majority still prevailed. But the membership of the aristocratic opposition, which had no real leader since Wesselényi had been removed from politics, increased to about 40, and, more important, was reorganized by Count Louis Batthyány around a "Casino of the Opposition." The group's program was independent of both Széchenyi and Wesselényi. It reflected Széchenyi's economic reforms, but it was more radical, paid greater attention to constitutional issues and the problem of national independence. Furthermore, its stress on the gradual elimination of all privileges and emancipation of all classes and religious denominations showed the influence of French liberalism.[104] This liberal group included young Baron Joseph Eötvös and Count Ladislas Teleki; although it continued to be a minority in the chamber of magnates its intellectual potentialities outweighed its numbers in subsequent years. Also, Batthyány became a national leader of great significance. His authority was one of Kossuth's political assets; in the early 1840s Széchenyi feared the radicalism of Batthyány more than that of Kossuth.

Another sign of the changing times was the emergence of a party of young conservatives. Hitherto, with the exception of Széchenyi, Wesselényi, and a few others, the upper table simply followed the instructions of the administration in a political showdown. Among the young

---

[102] Horváth, *Huszonöt év*, II, 105–108; Ballagi, *A magyar nemzeti államalkotás kora*, pp. 492–500; Anton Springer, *Geschichte Österreichs seit dem Wiener Frieden 1809*, 2 vols. (Leipzig: S. Hirzel, 1863–65), II, 37–41. For an apologia of the Catholic clergy's standpoint see Meszlényi, *A jozefinizmus kora*, pp. 344–416; Pyrker, *Mein Leben*, 197f., 219–22, 263ff.

[103] Falk, *Széchenyi és kora*, p. 118.

[104] Hóman and Szekfű, *Magyar történet*, V, 319f.

men taking their seats at the Diet of 1839–40 was Count Aurel Dessewffy, the oldest of the three sons of Széchenyi's opponent in the *Hitel-Taglalat-Világ* debate,[105] Baron Samuel Jósika, prominent in Transylvanian politics, and Count George Apponyi, who was to become Hungarian chancellor in a few years. Inspired by Széchenyi, these men were in favor of economic reforms from above. Supporting the government without being servile to it, they advocated a strong and efficient, but Hungarian, administration that would approach the country's problems with an open mind. Out of this group there developed "the party of cautious progress."

The reorganization of the liberal forces, the waning of the "old" opposition and the debut of intelligent young tories considerably extended the arch of political life hitherto sustained primarily by the chamber of deputies. In the latter, Deák's leadership was unchallenged. But the numerical supremacy of the liberals, so marked in the lower table in the previous Diet, was somewhat lessened, since the instructions of many representatives were partially favorable to the administration. The prevalence of an essentially moderate leadership in the chamber of deputies and the takeover by a new generation in the chamber of magnates meant that modern party politics and parliamentarian tactics could make their first appearance in the feudal Diet of Hungary.[106]

Széchenyi attended the meetings of the aristocratic oppositional party but maintained his freedom of action by setting up "conditions"[107] which suggested that he did not want to commit himself to the new party. Although he supported the opposition in all major issues during the Diet and was still considered one of its leaders, his emphatic "independence" from the opposition as a party was the first step toward his political alliance with the conservatives in the years to come.

Yet during the Diet of 1839–40 Széchenyi still referred to the young conservatives, whose talents he recognized, as "Royalists" and "Purists" in his diaries. In his intimate thoughts, supporters of the government were still "the other side," and votes for resolutions of the opposition

---

[105] See Ch. VI, 213–27. For a sample of the ideas of the talented leader of the young conservatives, who died unexpectedly after the Diet of 1839–40, see his perceptive but fragmentary essay, cited in n. 100 above.

[106] Horváth, *Huszonöt év*, II, 110–35; Falk, *Széchenyi és kora*, 105–108; Pulszky, *Meine Zeit*, pp. 206ff., 225; Zoltán Ferenczi, *Deák élete* (Deák's Life), 3 vols. (Budapest: Magyar Tudományos Akadémia, 1904), I, pp. 246–51; Trócsányi "Wesselényi fogsága," pp. 809f.; Árpád Kerékgyártó, *Tiz év Magyarország legujabb történelméből, 1840–1849*) (Ten Years from Hungary's Most Recent History, 1840–1849) (Budapest: Franklin, n.d.), pp. 1–10; "Aus dem Tagebuche der Fürstin Melanie," in Metternich-Winneburg, ed., *Aus Metternichs nachgelassenen Papieren*, VI, 306. Also the police report of Dec. 24, 1839, in B. Szabó, ed., *Adatok*, I, 356.

[107] June 10, 1830, Viszota, ed., *Naplók*, V, 287.

he registered as "for us." Police agents reported that "Kossuth's spirit" prevailed in literary circles and the Academy, which, founded by Catholics, was allegedly dominated by Protestants and turned into a "political club" by Széchenyi. They continued to describe him as the main supporter of "liberal," "democratic," "Protestant," and "oppositional" ideas. Reflecting the emotional undercurrents that cut across religious, national, ethnic, and social categories, this confusion between stereotyped traditions and current political trends seemed to be one of the major psychological blocks which prevented the peaceful evolution of events in the Hungarian pre-March.[108]

More than anybody else, Széchenyi felt the palpitation and ambivalence of this great period of Hungary's modern history. On the one hand, he did his best to convince Ráday not to go to Pressburg, asking him repeatedly that he resign after the Diet had opened its sessions; on the other hand, he tried to prevail upon the palatine "not to completely neglect the opposition,"[109] because this could result in yielding the leadership of the reform movement to more radical elements.

Actually, moderation was not much appreciated at the beginning of the Diet, when feelings ran high. Louis Batthyány, with whom Széchenyi often clashed, called him a "waverer" and "inconsistent," and Széchenyi answered in kind, saying that Batthyány was an "agitator without a plan."[110] Even the moderate Deák, who used his popularity with the Dietal youth to promote dignified behavior, often irritated Széchenyi because the latter tended to regard Deák's patient consistency and legal scruples as mere pettifogging. Despite these frictions, the personal relations of Széchenyi and Deák were correct.[111] However, their friendship suffered from Széchenyi's struggle with Kossuth in the 1840s; but it outlasted the storm and became a source of hope for Hungarians during the absolutistic era of Bach in the late 1850s.

His efforts to cooperate with Deák and patch up his quarrels even with Batthyány did not dispel Széchenyi's misgivings about the radical trend in the country's political life. It is important to realize that Széchenyi's deep anxiety had been there long before Kossuth's emergence, and the latter forced him only to stand up publicly against the movement

[108] July 24, Aug. 23, 26, Sept. 4, 1839; Jan. 11, Feb. 20 and 21, 1840, in Viszota, ed., *Naplók*, v, 300, 307f., 311, 347f., 358; police reports of Jan. 27, Apr. 12, 1839, Aug. 27, Sept. 8, 1840, in B. Szabó, ed., *Adatok*, I, 331f., 341f., 361ff.; also, Viszota's introduction to *Naplók*, v, pp. xv, xxvi f.
[109] Aug. 6, 1839, *ibid.*, v, 303. Cf. n. 101 above.
[110] Aug. 5, Sept. 5, Nov. 21, 1839, Jan. 25, Feb. 24, 28, 29, Apr. 1, 1840, *ibid.*, v, 303, 311, 333, 351, 359, 361f., 370.
[111] June 22, Aug. 6, 29, Sept. 13, Oct. 25, Nov. 20, Dec. 17, 18, 23, 25, 1839, Jan. 28, Feb. 22, 26, Apr. 27, 30, Aug. 20, 1840, *ibid.*, v, 292, 303, 309, 314, 324, 332, 341–44, 352, 359f., 378ff., 398.

that he himself had begotten. The question as to who should try to control the trend started by him loomed very large in his mind from the very beginning of the Diet. First, control should come from someone else, for how could the same person do two apparently clashing things—namely, initiate movement and restore order?[112] The raising of the question was characteristic enough, yet a few months later Széchenyi seemed to have gone even further, as though he had found the person who should shoulder the fatal task when he wrote: "This frenzy of the year 1825 will cost me my life."[113]

Shortly before the Diet, Széchenyi thought that the slightest provocation or blunder could lead to disaster due to the explosive political atmosphere. He equally dreaded a conservative reaction led by the Cziráky-group and an outburst of nationwide anger. This is why, almost simultaneously with the letter in which he cautioned his brother Paul concerning Cziráky's suspected plans, he also strongly disapproved of Joseph Katona's masterpiece, *Bánk Bán*. Performed in the new National Theater at Pest, this greatest of all Hungarian tragic plays, to paraphrase the literary historian Paul Gyulay, focused on early 13th-century national resentment of German influence at court: Széchenyi was unable to understand how the administration could consent to the presentation of such evil "nonsense" on the stage.[114]

To defeat such "dangerous tendenicies" Széchnyi set out to prove that he was not courting popular favor, that even a just, popular cause may not always be in the best interests of a nation if pushed too far and too fast. When upon his entering the county congregation of Pest in November 1837 he was received with thundering *"Éljen!"* (Long live!)-exclamations, he turned around and left. At the same congregation it was argued that the constitutional right to freedom of the press was violated by the censor who had prevented the publication of news concerning the arrested Dietal youths. Széchenyi took a public stand against unlimited liberty of the press. Recalling that although his personal integrity had been questioned by the suppression of his book *Stádium,* he expressed doubts as to how the freedom of the press could be reconciled with the feudal constitution still in force. Instead of demanding complete freedom of the press for a nation not yet ready for it, Széchenyi told his audience first to abolish the law of aviticity and the privileges of the nobility. Conceding that the freedom of the press greatly con-

---

[112] July 6, 8, 1839, *ibid.*, v, 296f.
[113] Dec. 21, 1839, *ibid.*, v, 343.
[114] Mar. 23, 1839, *ibid.*, v, 259f. In the play, the hero, Bánk, who is palatine and viceroy, while King Andrew II is on his crusade in the Holy Land (1217), kills Queen Gertrudis of Merania as the cause of the country's enslavement by German knights. Cf. Ch. VI, 191.

tributed to the progress of nations, he yet warned those citing the British example that in England the writ of habeas corpus applied to all, whereas in Hungary the *Primae Nonus* restricted the same privilege exclusively to a few noblemen.

On the occasion mentioned, Széchenyi succeeded in impressing his listeners with his witty speech; they laughed at some of his eccentric examples and the issue was shelved.[115] But the problem of how to win over both excited people and a stubborn administration to a moderate stand remained and continued to torment Széchenyi. At times, he thought there was no human warmth in his personality to attract people,[116] and that in order to be understood and liked, he ought to "take up decisive colors."[117] He knew that the palatine and Vienna expected him to prove his loyalty by supporting the administration.[118] Reluctant to give up his principles, which were essentially identical with those of the opposition, he decided to defend them at the Diet while working simultaneously for a compromise acceptable to both sides.

In his first speech on the Ráday affair he frankly admitted that he wished the whole affair had not happened at all. He said that although some people had begun to raise doubts of his patriotism, he had tried to eliminate the whole question from the agenda. Now, however, that the case had come up before the Diet, he supported the lower table's resolution to consider the issue on the basis of the principle involved. Without taking a firm stand on the merit of Ráday's election, Széchenyi thought it dangerous from a constitutional standpoint, if the Diet were prevented from discussing any question, because, as he put it, public opinions, "this triumph of Christian religion," stood higher in the 19th century than the will of monarchs or any other power.[119]

On realizing Vienna's indignation over his address of June 20, Széchenyi explained his standpoint in a major speech a few days later in the form of a "profession of creed."[120] Although he had tried to explain his views in some detail, Széchenyi felt he had been misunderstood. Comparing the present circumstances with those of 1825, he admitted that he himself might have contributed to the current excitement. In 1825 he had had a beautiful dream of Hungary's national development; at the present, he thought that perhaps it would have been better

---

[115] Nov. 14, 1837, Viszota, ed., *Naplók*, v, 129f. and n. 8, the latter containing the German translation of Széchenyi's speech as reported by a police agent.

[116] Aug. 22, 1839, *ibid.*, v, 307.

[117] Oct. 23, 1837, Jan. 14, 1840, *ibid.*, v, 122, 348.

[118] June 19, 22, 1839, *ibid.*, v, 290, 292.

[119] June 20, 1839, *ibid.*, v, 290f.; n. 3, p. 290 of the work, contains the German version of Széchenyi's speech as reported in *Informations Protokoll*.

[120] July 2, 1839, *ibid.*, v, 294f. n. 7 contains the speech as reported by *Informations Protokoll*. Cf. n. 118 above.

to abide by the old order. It would have been desirable if nation and government had found a common language in 1825. Due to certain events, which wise people received with moderation but some others with passion, the present situation seemed to be similar to that of 14 years before. Hence, Széchenyi summed up his political creed as follows: (1) Above all, he considered himself a Magyar. His main purpose was to promote the national interest of his country without, however, suppressing any other nationalities living in Hungary. (2) He pledged his loyalty to the ruling dynasty. He regarded Hungary's ties with the dynasty as the cornerstone of national existence. No friend of absolutism, he would still prefer it to anarchy. (3) As an old soldier, he had always been, and remained, in favor of order. Whereas there could be order without liberty, there was no liberty without order.

Having laid down the principles of his creed, Széchenyi demanded the quick solution of the Ráday affair, which was keeping the greater part of the country agitated. If the government could disenfranchise a deputy, it would mean the law had been overthrown. Furthermore, Széchenyi insisted on discussing the grievance in order to find a solution for the constitutional problem, and not mere palliative measures.[121]

At first, it seemed as if Széchenyi were repenting his own initiative regarding reforms since 1825. The repeated emphasis on "order," the warning against anarchy and exaggerated chauvinism, shown also in his personal diaries,[122] suggest the seriousness of his position. Yet a careful analysis of the speech reveals that despite an important change in tone and some inconsistencies, Széchenyi still stood on the ground of constitutional opposition, as he had in 1825. At that time, in the discussions with Metternich and in the memoranda given to him, Széchenyi stressed

[121] In 1840 Julia Pardoe, in *The City of the Magyar*, III, Annex pp. 429f., published the English translation of a Széchenyi speech under the title "Speech of Count Stephen Széchenyi in the matter of Count Gidion Ráday in the Chamber of Magnates, on the 2nd of July 1839." This speech, however, is not identical with Széchenyi's speech of July 2, 1839, as recorded by the *Informations Protokoll* in *Naplók*, v, n. 7. On the basis of a comparison of the texts, I am inclined to think that the speech in Miss Pardoe's book is an English version of Széchenyi's first speech in the Ráday affair, held on June 20, 1839. The German version of this speech as reported by the *Informations Protokoll* was reprinted by Viszota in *ibid.*, v, 290. This raises the interesting question of whether the only Széchenyi speech ever published in toto in English, and for all practical purposes unknown in Hungary for a century, is more authentic than the German version recorded in the third person and published only in 1937. This is not completely excluded, although the Pardoe version obviously underwent some editorial polishing. Miss Pardoe, who often saw Széchenyi at the time of the Diet, must have received the text or the English draft of the speech from Széchenyi's inner circle, or perhaps from Széchenyi, who used to supply foreign friends with material on Hungary. Cf. June 8, 1837, *ibid.*, v, 85.

[122] Cf. n. 112, 113, 114, 115, 118 above.

[123] Cf. Ch. IV, 124-34.

the need for opposition;[123] now in the Diet he emphasized order. But, de facto, he defended the right of freedom of speech and the constitutional claim of the Diet to examine any question pertinent to the nation's life. He placed the authority of public opinion above that of the monarch and government, declaring:

. . . I honour our most gracious Monarch. I honour the Government. But that either the King or the Administration has the power to limit or to control the confidence of others, I deny.

On this subject the judgment must be pronounced by a higher voice —the voice of public opinion, before which we must all alike bow down.[124]

As in 1825, Széchenyi's constitutionalism was still "diametrically opposed" to the adminstration's official views. Whereas he and the opposition distinguished between king and government, Széchenyi was snubbed by the otherwise moderate palatine, who interrupted one of his speeches, declaring, "Sovereign and government are identical."[125] Comparing the substance of Széchenyi's "political creeds" of 1825 and 1839, there is one essentially new element in the latter, namely, the emphatic attention given to the nationality problem. In this respect, the Diet of 1839–40 did not calm Széchenyi's previous anxieties. The language law enacted by the Diet[126] replaced Latin with Magyar as the official language of all legislative and administrative activities in Hungary proper. This was a victory for Magyar nationalism and was welcomed as such by Széchenyi. But the law was much more unfavorable to non-Magyars than the law of the previous Diet had been. Henceforth all ecclesiastic authorities had to correspond with secular authorities in Magyar; priests were required to know Magyar, and within three years birth registers too had to be kept in that tongue. True, Croatia was still exempted from the law, chiefly because of the resistance of the chamber of magnates. But the law hurt all other non-Magyar nationalities, and the bitter debates in the lower table left no doubt that if the deputies had their way, this exemption too would soon be abol-

---

[124] Pardoe's text, in *City of the Magyar*, III, Annex p. 430. Cf. n. 121 above.

[125] July 24, 1839, Viszota, ed., *Naplók*, v, 299f. Bariska, *Széchenyi és a francia irodalom*, pp. 23f., correctly stresses that the distinction between monarch and administration was intimately related to Montesquieu's thought, and that occasionally Széchenyi would even name his source. More important, however, is the way in which Széchenyi and many other Hungarian constitutionalists used Montesquieu's and other French writers' ideas. Note, e.g., the peculiar echo of Rousseau's concept of "general will" in Széchenyi's reference to the power of public opinion in the passage quoted in the preceding paragraph.

[126] Law VI of 1840, published in Szekfű, ed., *Iratok*, pp. 51of.

ished.[127] To be sure, the attitude of the Croatian representatives toward the language question was rigid, because they opposed the introduction of Magyar as the official idiom even in Hungary proper. The Croat stand on the religious issue was also irksome to Hungarian liberals.[128] Since the Diet failed to work out a modus vivendi between the Hungarian and Croatian deputies, the debate and acceptance of the new language law made things worse than they had been before. Very few, however, grasped the dangers involved as early as did Széchenyi.

The Diet also enacted a new urbarial law, which permitted individual serfs, as well as entire communities, to pay a fixed sum as manumission compensation, thus opening the way for serfs to become free landowners. The law was initiated in the chamber of deputies and Széchenyi vigorously supported it in the house of magnates.[129] True, the great expectations concerning voluntary agreements between landlords and serfs failed to materialize, causing the liberal opposition to demand new legislation in subsequent years.[130] Yet even in its permissive form, the enactment of the principle of manumission compensation tended to undermine feudalism.[131] Similarly, a series of new commercial and exchange laws, in the acceptance of which Széchenyi was instrumental,[132] restricted somewhat the economic privileges of noblemen, stimulating trade and also paving the way for putting into practice the principle of equality before the law.[133]

In addition to the legislation already mentioned, Széchenyi participated in the discussion of a number of other questions, including the National Theater, construction of the permanent bridge, Dietal records, representation of cities, and the Danube regulation.[134] He followed with particular care the first Hungarian railway legislation. Actually, the twin laws concerning the right of expropriation and the obligation of noblemen to pay tolls on the permanent bridge, which had been enacted by the Diet of 1832–36, were the legislative prerequisites of railroad building in Hungary. But it was only the fear of a Vienna-Lemberg (Lvov) railway, with its implication of competition from Galician grain in

[127] Miskolczy, *A horvát kérdés*, I, 228.

[128] For details, see *ibid.*, I, 224–55. Cf. Ch. VII, 293f.

[129] Horváth, *Huszonöt év*, II, 165ff; Jan. 14, 15, Mar. 9, 1840, Viszota, ed., *Naplók*, v, 348f., 364.

[130] Acsády, *A magyar jobbágyság*, pp. 482–89.

[131] Miskolczy, *A kamarilla*, pp. 180–85.

[132] Mar. 13, Apr. 17, 1839, Apr. 1, 1840, Viszota, ed., *Naplók*, v, 253, 270 and n. 3, 370 and n. 4.

[133] Horváth, *Huszonöt év*, II, 167f.; Kerékgyártó, *Tiz év*, p. 21; Ödön Kuncz, *A magyar kereskedelmi- és váltójog* (Hungarian Commercial and Exchange Law), 3d edn. (Budapest: Grill, 1937), p. 36.

[134] For a summary cf. Viszota's introduction to *Naplók*, v, xiii ff. and lxi f.; Friedreich, *Széchenyi élete*, I, 431–38.

Austria, that induced the Diet of 1839-40 to pay serious attention to the building of roads. Of the two competing projects Széchenyi favored the one promoted by the financial group of Baron George Sina, financier of the bridge. Sina planned to build his line along the right bank of the Danube, but the majority of the Diet supported those who proposed to construct the railroad on the left bank of the river. Széchenyi mistrusted Sina's rivals and was afraid that the country would be unable to carry the burden of two competing railway systems, which might also diminish the income of the steamship company just born, and of the bridge yet to be built.[135] Without going into the details of railroad lobbying, venomous traces of which can be followed in Széchenyi's diaries,[136] two things may be mentioned at this point. First, in subsequent years, the problem of railroads was more and more closely related to domestic politics, hence became a part of the Széchenyi-Kossuth struggle, which at times tended to dominate public life. Second, Széchenyi himself modified his views as the years went by: the outcome of his mature ideas was his Proposal on the Organization of the Hungarian Communication System, submitted to the Diet of 1847-48.[137] This plan, written by Széchenyi's aid, Louis Kovács, but inspired by Széchenyi and published under his name was an overall plan to build a unified system of roads, canals, and railways in Hungary. It was corroborated by data gathered from all over the world, and it had a great influence on the construction of the Hungarian communication system in the second half of the 19th century. One of its interesting aspects was that Széchenyi, the pioneer of private enterprise, suggested that the state take over the direction and financial management of the country's communication system.

An unpopular proposal was Széchenyi's suggestion to determine by law the minimum size of noble land.[138] By keeping a necessary minimum in the hands of one member of the noble family, Széchenyi intended to preserve the economic viability of the lesser nobility, saving, as he saw it, this stronghold of Magyar nationality from "the *inescapable de-*

[135] Cf. Adolf Fenyvessy, *Az első magyar vasút története* (History of the First Hungarian Railroad) (Budapest: Magyar Tudományos Akadémia, 1883), *Értekezések a nemzetgazdaság és statisztika köréből* (Studies in the Fields of National Economy and Statistics), éd. Béla Földes, 1/9, pp. 3-90.

[136] E.g., Nov. 30, Dec. 6, 7, 1839, Feb. 27, Mar. 21, Apr. 22, 1840, Viszota, ed., *Naplók*, v, 336, 338, 360, 367, 375.

[137] *Javaslat a magyar közlekedési ügy rendezéséről* (Proposal on the Organization of the Hungarian Communication System)(Pozsony: 1848). The *Proposal* was submitted to the Diet in January 1848. (At that time, Széchenyi was president of the department of communication of the lieutenancy.)

[138] "A Minimum kérdése" (The Question of the Minimum), originally published in *Társalkodó*, June 5, 1839 (No. 45), reprinted in Török, ed., *Széchenyi politikai iskolája*, III, 63-76. Cf. Feb. 26, Mar. 13, Apr. 16, Dec. 23, 1839, Viszota, ed., *Naplók*, v, 246, 253, 269 and n. 3, 343.

cline caused by the infinite subdivision of its landowning."[139] He also stipulated compensating those noblemen who would lose their land, enabling them by this protective device to go into the professions or business. Although the motion at first had some support in the county congregation of Pest, which had preceded the Diet, it failed to carry. Even so, the plan stirred up resentment against Széchenyi among the masses of the lesser nobility, who looked upon the land not only as a source of income (constantly decreasing), but as the basis of their social status and way of life. Viewed from a different angle, Széchenyi's scheme, aimed at fixing the least amount of noble landholding, showed that by the end of the 1830s he had definitely ceased to advocate the idea of abolishing without qualifications the law of aviticity or entail, which he seemed to have proposed in *Stádium*.[140]

Széchenyi's scruples about diluting Magyar nationality also caused him to take a stand against the complete emancipation of Jews. The liberal majority of the deputies proposed that the Jewish population be granted those civil rights which the nonnoble part of the populace enjoyed. But the original bill of the lower chamber was watered down due to the combined resistance of the heavily German cities, the chamber of magnates, and the administration. Still, Law XXIX of 1840 was the first positive legislative act favoring the Jews since 1791. It considerably improved the situation of Jewish citizens born or "legally resident" in the country, since it permitted them to choose their domicile (except in the mining centers), to own real estate, pursue freely any trade, craft, or profession.[141]

Anti-liberal historians between the two world wars used to emphasize the numerical increase of Jews in Hungary during the first half of the 19th century. They pointed to Széchenyi and Deák, both of whom urged the closing down of Hungary's northeastern (Galician) frontiers to immigration, while granting gradually, full citizenship to those Jews already in Hungary.[142] One could add that Deák's attitude was probably a reflection of the cautious pragmatism so characteristic of him in approaching any complex and emotionally charged problem, whereas we know from some of Széchenyi's diary entries[143] that he was far from unbiased regard-

[139] Török, ed., *Széchenyi politikai iskolája*, III, 67 (italics in original).

[140] Ch. VI, 235, 239.

[141] Mar. 9, 1840, Viszota, ed., *Naplók*, v, 364; Horváth, *Huszonöt év*, II, 168; Kerékgyártó, *Tiz év*, pp. 22, 29f. Géza Ballagi, "Az 1839/40-diki országgyűlés visszhangja az irodalomban" (The Echo of the Diet of 1839–40 in the Literature), *Értekezések a Társadalom Tudomány Köréből*, x (1890), 71–80. Even in 1848 complete emancipation was blocked by the opposition of the towns. Cf. Pulszky, *Jellemrajzok*, p. 20.

[142] Szekfű, *Három nemzedék*, esp. 232–41; Hóman and Szekfű, *Magyar történet*, v, 378f.; Kosáry, *A History of Hungary*, pp. 322ff.

[143] Sept. 13, 1837; Dec. 6, 7, 1839, Viszota, ed., *Naplók*, v, 338; Széchenyi to Benvenuti, June 25, 1840, Majláth, ed., *Levelek*, III, 54.

ing the Jews, especially after his marriage to the extremely bigoted Crescence, who did not always exert a wholesome influence on her husband. It appears to be true that Széchenyi often succumbed to the popular antisemitism, shared and propagated especially by the nobility of the northeastern counties, which attributed the abject poverty of their serfs to the unrestricted immigration of Galician Jews. In the late 1820s Kölcsey's—and even young Kossuth's—thinking was also tainted by such vulgarizations,[144] although they both knew about the multiple roots of peasant destitution and about the far from blameless Jewish innkeeper-usurer's role as a buffer between lord and serf. Kossuth was soon to join the liberal advocates of the emancipation of the Jews in Hungary; but Széchenyi, who, along with Wesselényi, was willing to admit Jews to the Casino in 1829, and who resolutely condemned the anti-Jewish excesses committed in Pressburg by the mob in the first days of the revolution of 1848,[145] never retreated from his reservations about their emancipation.

He was indeed afraid, and said so in public, lest instead of assimilating Jews, Magyars themselves should be absorbed by them.[146] Aside from anti-semitic prejudice, which he would not publicly admit, Széchenyi's nationalism was not free from ethnocentric racism. Since, however, racism was both more naïve and less discredited at the time, Széchenyi was not ashamed of openly defending the Magyar "race," especially because he had serious doubts that large segments of the non-Magyar population could be rapidly assimilated into Magyardom. He was certainly less optimistic, and in this respect, more realistic, than either Eötvös or Kossuth. Any sober treatment of Széchenyi's stand on the so-called Jewish question therefore must try to examine this stand in the light of his general views on the nationality problem. Such a synoptic approach, carefully avoided by those who regarded him as the archetype of 20th-century Magyar racists, would show that Széchenyi's opposition to the immediate emancipation of Jews was strongly motivated by his fear of German supremacy. In this context, the speech he gave at the county congregation of Pest shortly before the Diet, is of particular inter-

[144] See Kölcsey's speech "A szatmári adózó nép állapotáról" (On the Condition of the Taxpaying People in Szatmár), *KFÖM*, pp. 1,038, 1,043f.; Kossuth's fragmentary "Értekezés az éhinségek okairól" (Dissertation about the Causes of Famines), in Kossuth, *Ifjukori iratok*, pp. 179f. Explaining, with rare sincerity, why he refrained from burning the fragment, old Kossuth remarked, in his own hand, that he wanted posterity to see on the basis of this example the results of the "terrible" educational system of his youth and the "underdeveloped" stage of his intelligence at the age of 26. *Ibid.*, p. 183. Cf. István Barta, "Kölcsey-problémák" (Kölcsey Problems), *Századok*, xcvi (1962), 193.
[145] Széchenyi to Tasner, Mar. 21, 1848, Majláth, ed., *Levelek*, iii, 603f.; György Spira, *1848 Széchenyije és Széchenyi 1848-a* (Széchenyi of [the Year] 1848 and [the Year] 1848 of Széchenyi) (Budapest: Akadémiai kiadó, 1964), p. 60.
[146] See his speeches of Aug. 10 and Oct. 1, 1844, in Török, ed., *Széchenyi politikai iskolája*, ii, 385–92.

est. According to a police report, Széchenyi justified his opposition to emancipation by suggesting that any fair answer to the question must be based, in descending order, on considerations for one's own race, for the class concerned, and finally for mankind. With regard to the first consideration, he thought it "sadly true" that Magyardom, which in his opinion had alone sustained the constitution hitherto, was increasingly on the wane, whereas the Germans were demanding preponderance. Looking at the city of Pest, he frequently asked himself whether he was in Hungary. He reminded his audience that before assisting other nations such as the Poles—for whom he had a soft spot in his heart, but whose resurgence he doubted—one first must strengthen oneself, since Magyar had not even been recognized as the diplomatic language of the realm. While he conceded that Jews were diligently learning Magyar, he still suspected them of doing this only "out of affectation," in order to achieve emancipation. Yet he doubted that Jews could be quickly transformed into Magyars through emancipation because they were too German-minded and could hardly mingle with an Oriental race. If one gave them the right to own land, he would not know what would happen to the Magyars. To the argument that in England Jews possessed all civil rights, he countered that there the number of Jews was very small, whereas in Hungary emancipation would mean the same as if the planet Jupiter were to collide with the earth, since the latter would be swallowed up by the former.[147]

The inclination to measure Magyardom's strength by the spread of the Magyar vernacular, overemphasis of the significance of the constitution (which he himself so often derided), fear of German cultural supremacy as a pretext for refusing civil rights to Jewish people, abandonment of the linguistic argument in the special case of the Jews, questioning the Jews' sincerity by denying the worthiness of emancipation as a goal valuable per se for society as a whole, and the implied threat that by making Jews full citizens Magyardom could lose its land—this line of argumentation was surely an epitome of anti-semitic hypocrisy. Even if Széchenyi believed in what he said, this speech, elements of which were to reemerge in his own subsequent public announcements on the topic, and in the arguments of those who intended to acquire the aura of respectability at a much later date,[148] showed Széchenyi at his worst.

[147] Apr. 20, 1839, Viszota, ed., *Naplók*, v, 271f. and n. 4. (Police report, Ger.). Cf. however, Deák's report on the results of the Diet of 1839–40, submitted to the congregation of Zala county on July 27, 1840. Kónyi, ed., *Deák beszédei* I, 538f.

[148] It is illuminating that the only Hungarian translation I found of Széchenyi's speech cited his words completely out of context, carefully deleting all references made by him to Germans and Poles. Cf. Mihály Csery-Clauser, ed., *Széchenyi napjai* (Széchenyi's Days) (Budapest: n.d. [1942]), pp. 118f.

The bitter debate on the relation of Catholics and Protestants, on the other hand, gave him an opportunity to put his best foot forward. Despite the reluctance of the church hierarchy to make any concessions, Széchenyi supported without qualification what he considered to be the cause of freedom of conscience. This meant that in such questions as mixed marriages, the religion of illegitimate children and foundlings, the conversion of Catholics to Protestantism, and the enrollment of Catholic children in Protestant schools—to mention those in which he took the floor—Széchenyi proposed complete equality and reciprocity between followers of the two major branches of Western Christianity on the basis of true Christian love, siding thereby with the majority of the chamber of deputies. He emphatically approved the admonition of Baron Joseph Eötvös, who insisted that discriminatory practices against Protestants must be abolished for the interests of Catholics rather than Protestants.[149] It is noteworthy that, in addition to Count Louis Batthyány, spokesman of the liberals in the upper table, the leader of the conservatives, Count Aurel Dessewffy also pleaded the Protestant cause. To the charge that Protestants continually put forward new demands, he retorted that the Catholic cause would be impeccable only after all the just demands of Protestants had been met. He also added that doing justice to Protestants ended where doing wrong to Catholics began.[150]

Just as did the Catholic deputies of the previous Diet,[151] the new generation of Catholic magnates of the Diet of 1839–40 decided to bridge the gulf separating the members of the different branches of Western Christendom. The arguments used in this demonstration of the ecumenical spirit 125 years before the *aggiornamento* of the Church were sometimes couched in terms reminiscent of the language used by modern leaders of the civil rights movement in the United States; yet the driving force behind the impressive tour de force of this early 19th-century Hungarian renaissance was Magyar nationalism. It was in the name of national unity that Aurel Dessewffy, the talented young tory, managed to convince a majority of the church-dominated chamber of magnates to accept most of the provisions of the bill favoring complete Protestant equality with Catholics. However, the bill failed to become law because the Catholic high clergy sent a special emissary to the curia for advice,

---

[149] Speeches of Dec. 21, 1839; Jan. 2, 3, 4, 1840, in Zoltán Ferenczi, "Gróf Széchenyi István kiadatlan beszédei az 1839/40-liki országgyűlésről" (Count Stephen Széchenyi's Unpublished Speeches Given at the Diet of 1839–40), *Akadémiai Értesítő*, xxiv, (1913), 634–40.

[150] Antal Csengery, "Dessewffy Aurél" (Aurel Dessewffy), in Csengery ed., *Magyar szónokok*, 236–41; Horváth, *Huszonöt év*, ii, 170–78.

[151] Cf. Ch. VII, 292ff.

and the administration, anxious to avoid complications, agreed to shelve the issue until the completion of Bishop Joseph Lonovics's mission in Rome.

The mission, however, failed to bring immediate results, which further exacerbated the situation. After the Diet the majority of counties decided to bring lawsuits against priests who, following the instructions of the hierarchy, refused to bless mixed marriages in the absence of a binding promise to educate the children in the Roman Catholic faith. According to Act XXVI of 1791, mixed marriages had to be performed by a Catholic priest who was not supposed, however, to hinder them under any pretext. Refusal of the blessing, or "passive assistance" (mere presence of the priest), could be interpreted as a violation of the law of the land, because such an attitude could, and sometimes did, prevent the recognition of a marriage.[152] In counties where clerical influence prevailed, efforts of the liberal opposition to enforce the law were defeated, occasionally by violent means. Pest county, on the other hand, decided to sue the primate of Hungary, along with the local priest, in cases involving refusal of the blessing. More symbolic than practical, such actions added fuel to an already charged atmosphere. It was only at the Diet of 1843–44 that a formula was found which proved acceptable to all parties involved, by permitting the performance of mixed marriages by Protestant ministers.

The new law, which made other concessions to Protestants in the matter of conversions,[153] was confined strictly to Hungary. Its significance is shown by the circumstance that some 20 years later Pope Pius IX still refused to extend the concessions made to Hungary to the hereditary provinces of the Habsburgs.[154] Actually, Hungarian insistence on Protestant rights, supported by the palatine and less openly by the administration, challenged the Holy See at a time when it attempted, not without hope, to "restore the liberty of the Church" by doing away with the remnants of Josephinism in ecclesiastic affairs.[155] The general advancement of the cause of Catholicism in the Habsburg Monarchy as a whole thus made it psychologically difficult for the Hungarian church hierarchy

---

[152] Law XXVI of 1791 did not grant complete reciprocity to Protestants in either the performance of the marriage ceremony or the religion of children born of a mixed marriage; this is why the liberal opposition wanted to modify the law. But the Catholic clergy wanted to abolish the practices based on it since they did not correspond to canon law. Cf. Marczali, *Enchiridion*, p. 774. See also Kónyi, ed., *Deák beszédei*, I, 554–65.

[153] Horváth, *Huszonöt év*, II, 277–86, 398–406.

[154] Engel-Janosi, *Die politische Korrespondenz*, pp. 35ff., and docs. 124–26, pp. 258–66; Weinzierl-Fischer, *Die österreichischen Kondordate*, pp. 23ff.

[155] *Ibid.*, pp. 17–23; Engel-Janosi, *Die politische Korrespondenz*, pp. 16–25 and the pertinent documents. For evidence of pressure on the hierarchy, cf. Beauvale to Palmerston, June 1, 1839, *F.O. 7/281*, PRO (London).

to retreat. Yet the subtle pressure of Metternich, an advocate of the papacy at court, but who warned that the great number of non-Catholics in Hungary deserved special attention,[156] made it advisable, for the sake of the curia's goals, to help the administration get out of an embarrassing situation. Indeed, Vienna was blamed for unlawful actions of high prelates against whom it could not enforce the law unless it wished to risk a crisis much worse than the one in Prussia.

Besides the relations of the Catholic Church with the state, the debate on the rights of Protestants raised important constitutional issues. Those opposing the Protestant demands stressed the king's right to prevent people from changing their religion and to defend the royal prerogative of supervising religious and educational affairs. To them, Széchenyi replied that if he would never submit his body to arbitrary rule, how could he do it with his soul?[157] In reference to the pastoral letter of the bishop of Nagyvárad, Széchenyi, like Dessewffy, could not help pointing out that the bishop decided to refuse a blessing which had been freely given by the Hungarian clergy in the last 50 years to mixed marriages. Said the loyal Catholic:

The apostolic king of Hungary has always succeeded in defending himself and his constitutional nation against the supremacy of Rome. The high clergy has never been and could never be a state within the state. As we progress in the development of the spirit of constitutionalism in our country, such an influence of an external power upon our nation would be increasingly in conflict with, and intolerable to, this spirit. How could a nation, safeguarded by law against the despotism of his own sovereign, be submitted to foreign despotism?[158]

[156] In February 1841 Metternich asked the bishop of Csanád to urge the curia to take some decision soon, and to remind the curia of its responsibilities in view of the differences between Hungary and the overwhelmingly Catholic Austrian provinces of the Habsburg Monarchy. Metternich to Lonovics, Feb. 28, 1841, No. 187, 1841, Kabinettsarchiv, Staatskonferenzakten, Staatsarchiv (Vienna). See also Metternich to Lützow, Feb. 18, 1840, Docs. 70, 70a–b, 71, in Mass, ed., Der Josephinismus, v, 556–67. For the implications of the Lonovics mission to Rome from the point of view of the monarchy as a whole, cf. ibid., pp. 115–23.

[157] Dec. 30, 31, 1839; Jan. 2, 3, 4, 8, Apr. 10–14, 1840, Viszota, ed., Naplók, v, 344–47 and n. 2, 373.

[158] Cited in Falk, Széchenyi és kora, pp. 117f. For the title and prerogatives of the "apostolic" king, cf. Marczali, Hungary in the Eighteenth Century, pp. 309–12. Széchenyi's arguments have their legal drawbacks, for it was exactly his prerogative as "apostolic" king which gave the monarch the "right" to interfere in favor of the Protestants in Hungary. Bariska has thoroughly documented Voltaire's influence on the formulation of Széchenyi's concept of religious tolerance. Széchenyi és a francia irodalom, pp. 35f. Cf. István Sőtér, Magyar-francia kapcsolatok (Hungarian-French Relations) (Budapest: Teleki Intézet, 1946), pp. 129f. But in order to understand Voltaire's impact on the thinking of Széchenyi and other enlightened Hungarians, one must keep in mind the strength and centuries-old traditions of Hungarian Protestantism, especially its Calvinist branch, and the latter's close identification with Magyardom's fate.

The nuncio reported about the dietal debates with increasing bitterness. Shortly after its opening, he deplored the turbulence and nationalistic spirit prevalent in the Diet, identifying liberal doctrines with anti-Catholic and democratic ideas. A few months later, he complained that the administration and the palatine were too lenient toward the "revolutionaries" whose natural allies were the Protestants. The "sad truth" was, he stated, that "the spirit of religious indifference and political liberalism has invaded the majority of fairly powerful and influential Hungarian magnates and noblemen," whose yearning for popularity might destroy the Church and the monarchy as well. The papal envoy emphasized that besides acatholics, Catholics, too, played an important role in the deliberations, which he described as being very much in conflict with both the doctrine and discipline of the church and the established legal order. Indignant that following the injunction of the government, the docile Hungarian episcopate condoned the scandal of the anti-canonical prescriptions of the "famous" law of 1790–91, the nuncio was even more shocked by the "enormous scandal" of the legislative proposals aimed at granting full citizenship to Jews and Unitarians. The reports repeatedly referred to "the famous Count Stephen Széchenyi," lamenting his buffoonish (*"al buffonesco"*) and ironical treatment of those defending the rigid and dogmatic stand of the church. In his evaluation of the debates toward the end of the Diet, the nuncio extolled the primate and the bishops, who defended Rome's directives, adding that even Protestants showed themselves moderate enough (*"assai moderati"*), whereas the young Catholic magnates spoke like heretics.[159]

The papacy's sensitivity to the fight over religious affairs in the Hungarian Diet was understandable, since its outcome could well influence broader trends in the rest of the realm of the Habsburgs. Yet the latter were the foremost Catholic dynasty at a time when thrones were challenged with increasing frequency. In the 1830s the pope himself was forced to ask for Austrian troops to save his throne. But military strength alone was not enough where ideologies were bound to clash. Hence the Holy See was interested in reversing Josephinian trends in order to rely on an unadulterated Catholic power in the great competition for men's minds.

On the other hand, Metternich was also aware of the multiple domestic and international ramifications of the religious issue. In addition to stressing that Hungary and Transylvania warranted special treatment, he reminded the pope of the Prussian challenge to Austria in the German

---

[159] Altieri to Lambruschini, June 21, 1839, Feb. 28, Mar. 13, 27; Apr. 10; May 8 A-B, 11, 22, 1840, Anni 1838–1842, Rubrica 247, Busta 409, *Segreteria di Stato, Esteri, 1814–1850*, Archivio Segreto Vaticano. Széchenyi favored the complete emancipation of Unitarians. Antal Zichy, *Gróf Széchenyi István beszédei* (Count Stephen Széchenyi's Speeches), in *SzIM*, II (Budapest: Athenaeum, 1887), 169.

lands where the number of mixed marriages was increasing and could not be stemmed without strengthening Protestantism and Prussia as well. To the archbishop of Lemberg, who demanded a clearcut papal resolution affecting mixed marriages between Catholics and Uniates, he replied that this question was not raised in the present debate because he did not wish to justify the anti-Catholic measures taken by Prussia and Russia or to drive the Greek Catholics in Galicia or other parts of the monarchy into the arms of the Orthodox church.[160] In fact, the curia knew that to be successful in its work among either "heretic" Protestant or "schismatic" Orthodox populations (e.g., in Transylvania), it needed much assistance.[161] It was also cognizant of the violent aspects of the struggle between the Uniate and Orthodox clergies in the Banat of Temesvár: in their petition to the Holy Father, the people who were converted to Greek Catholicism from Orthodoxy in 1839 and whose houses were burned down by the revengeful defenders of Eastern Orthodoxy, requested the nuncio's intercession "at the most serene Austrian court" (*apud serenissimam austriacam aulam*) to prevent what happened in Russia![162]

Thus Széchenyi's assessment of the explosive nature of religious conflicts in Hungary was not wrong. He was also quite outspoken in the discussions that focused on the freedom of speech, which involved the case of Wesselényi, Kossuth, and the Dietal youth. Despite his personal reservations and his preference for petitioning the government for a political amnesty as a matter of expediency, he was indefatigable in protecting the constitutional principles inherent in the issue.[163] His speech of April 22, 1840 was most important in this respect. After the resolutions of the lower table had been rejected 22 times (taking into account the ones sent during the Diet of 1832–36) by the upper chamber, the magnates debated the 23rd message of the deputies. Széchenyi began by emphasizing that he hoped to reconcile the different parties, the two houses, and the nation and government. The main cause of all troubles, he said, lay in Hungary's "heterogeneous connections" with Austria. Whereas Hungary was a constitutional country, Austria was not. It was the duty of Hungarians to maintain their constitution in its immaculate integrity; similarly, the administration must respect and sincerely help the country's constitutional evolution. Instead, the government not only

---

[160] Docs. 68, 78, Maass, ed., *Der Josephinismus*, v, 523–53, 629ff. and the ones quoted in n. 156, *ibid.*

[161] Meszlényi, *A jozefinizmus*, pp. 283–86.

[162] Altieri to Lambruschini, Oct. 21, 1842, "Greci-Uniti della Monarchia Austriaca," Anni 1838–42, Rubrica 247, Busta 410, *Segreteria di Stato Esteri, 1814–1850*, Archivio Segreto Vaticano.

[163] Nov. 4, 1839; Jan. 11, Apr. 22, 1840, Viszota, ed., *Naplók*, v, 326, 347f., 375f.

tolerated but actually stimulated the publication of anti-Hungarian articles abroad to stir up foreign public opinion against Hungary. According to these articles, continued Széchenyi, the country's structure, based on privilege, could be overthrown—if certain locks were opened. The government's connivance in these suggestions was particularly repulsive, because it questioned the loyalty of a nation which had proved its fidelity to the dynasty during the times of Maria Theresa and Napoleon when there was no lack of temptations and promises from abroad. But Hungarians knew their duty to the sovereign and fatherland; therefore, he said, the grievances formulated by the lower table should at long last be submitted to the throne so that the general excitement could come to an end.

Széchenyi did not question the government's goodwill, but he did regret the lack of its respect for constitutional principles. This, in the opinion of the author of *Hitel,* was partly due to the fact that the nation was not yet mature enough for a more advanced constitution. But the respect commanded by Hungarians would increase in proportion to the growth in the nation's "intellectual and moral intrinsic value." Hence excesses and seeking of popularity must cease because they led directly to absolutism, and because all extremes were neighbors. Citing examples of the French Revolution, Széchenyi then turned to the government, asking it to abandon its plans for centralization, just as it had dropped its efforts at Germanization. Stating that the Hungarian nation could no longer be annihilated, he reiterated his hope in Hungary's future, referring to the conclusion of *Hitel.* In a final note, he spoke of the need for mutual trust:

> We need a complete regeneration. Can anybody doubt this if one takes into consideration the situation in our counties? the great need for communication with the outside world and for internal lines? the little weight of cities and the fact that they do not even have a voice in the Diet? But how shall we begin the regeneration so urgently needed by our nation if we do not understand the government and the government does not want to understand us? Here is the time for union, and until all our troubles are cured, let us at least submit the grievance regarding the violation of freedom of speech.[164]

Széchenyi's dignified and conciliatory plea made a deep impression on his listeners, but failed to move the majority of the chamber of

---

[164] Széchenyi's speech is quoted by Falk, *Széchenyi és kora,* pp. 112ff. Concerning the articles referred to by Széchenyi, cf. Apr. 22, 1840, Viszota, ed., *Naplók,* v, 375f. and n. 2.

magnates. His appeal went unheeded when a few months earlier he implored his peers to take a positive stand by formulating a bill of their own instead of simply rejecting the resolutions of the deputies. Unlike some, who under the influence of Western parliamentarian practices, assumed that all bills must originate in the lower house, Széchenyi contended that in Hungary, the upper table, too, had the right to initiate legislation. He intended to activate this right for the sake of a better cooperation between the two chambers of the Diet. Speaking about the Austrian and Hungarian "heterogeneous" halves of the realm—namely, the provinces where absolute rule was traditional and strong, and the lands belonging to the Crown of St. Stephen, which formed a constitutional but weak country—he said: ". . . we always had to fear the link with a powerful German intelligentsia menacing our nationality which, however, I prefer to the constitution. A nation can attain everything, even a free constitution, but it cannot regain its nationality and idiom any more once it has lost them. It is, therefore, nationality toward which we must direct our main concern."

Nationality, above or at the expense of liberty—this characteristic feature of Central European nationalisms was clearly formulated by the father of modern Magyar nationalism at this point. Its justification as fear of "a powerful German intelligentsia" was also clearly articulated despite Széchenyi's insistence that the administration had abandoned the policy of Germanization and accepted the idea that the Hungarian nation must have a Magyar administration. He suggested that the idea of constitutional government, which lies at the root of the freedom of speech, must also be accepted. Intoning for the first time publicly one of the leitmotifs of his book on "the people of the orient," in a pathetic passage he claimed that it was one of the miracles of history that an unknown, small people who "came from God knows where, settled here, loved liberty so much, stuck persistently to constitutional principles, without perhaps being aware of their scientific foundation but instinctively bearing them in its soul," was capable of sustaining itself amid the pressures of the Russian, Ottoman, and German Empires. He did not wish to risk "this greatest miracle," this precariously safeguarded constitutional freedom in a more scientific age that ought to have a clearer perception of the causes of its survival. Paraphrasing Kölcsey's previous admonition and unconsciously anticipating Kossuth's subsequent threat, he cautioned the upper table not to stand "like a wall between throne and nation."[165]

The magnates, however, who, thanks to Aurel Dessewffy, were willing to make concessions in the religious issue, refused to submit to the throne

[165] Speech of Jan. 11, 1840, in Ferenczi, "Széchenyi kiadatlan beszédei," pp. 641, 644f. Cf. Ch. VII, 300f.

the grievance regarding freedom of speech. Similarly, the liberal demands for reorganization of the educational system, establishment of a Hungarian military academy, and adequate representation of the cities in the Diet had to be postponed, primarily because of the administration's dilatory tactics or outright opposition to them. The only exception was the issue of city representation; a more flexible opposition could have found a modus vivendi between the need for the liberalization of city governments and the urgency of giving the urban populace a larger voice in national affairs. But it is true that a compromise solution would have been easier to achieve if the administration had not encouraged the cities to resist the attempts aimed at reforming their internal life.[166]

All this said, the 55 new laws enacted by the Diet of 1839–40 marked significant progress compared to the 49 of 1832–36.[167] In spite of the fact that some of the important bills failed to become laws and some had serious shortcomings, the new legislation indicated that the pace of progress had quickened in Hungary in only a few years. With all the controversies surrounding it, the new language law showed that the age of nationalism had dawned upon east Central Europe; its supporters and opponents, alike, were children of this new age, taking the first steps toward the modernization of their respective national societies, which were still very much in the process of being born. The new urbarial law, with its provision for manumission compensation, so violently opposed by both magnates and administration at the previous Diet,[168] as well as other laws affecting the economy, suggested that the country's ruling elite, perhaps slowly and reluctantly, but nevertheless consciously, began to respond to the challenges of modern times by choosing the road of reform. Circumspect and cautious, but eager to learn, the leaders of this elite tried to adapt the lessons obtainable from more advanced Western societies. Act XVII of 1840, which incorporated safeguards for the free development of industrial enterprises, also limited rather remarkably child labor to nine hours with one hour interruption in the age group 12 to 16, and forbade the hiring of children under 12 in

[166] For a summary of the demands of the cities cf. *Bittschrift der königl. Freystädte von Ungarn und der angehörigen Länder*, durch die Herrn Franz V. Vághy, Oedenburger, und Stephan V. Dienes, Eperiesser Reichs Deputierten Sr. geheiligten Majestät in tiefster Unterthänigkeit am 23. August 1835 in Schönbrunn unterbreitet. Deutsch übersetzt von Joseph V. Klápka, Temesvárer Reichs Deputierten (Eperjes, n.d.).

[167] For a comparison, with a brief summary of the most important acts of the two Diets, cf. Kerékgyártó, *Tiz év*, pp. 20–43. The full text of the laws was published in *Corpus juris hungarici—Magyar Törvénytár, Milleniumi Emlékkiadás*, VIII (Budapest: Franklin, 1896), 3–192.

[168] For a survey of the pros and cons in the debate on manumission compensation, and for examples of its de facto practice since the 18th century, see István Barta, "Korai örökváltság-szerződések" (Early Contracts for Manumission Compensation), *Agrártörténeti Szemle*, III (1961), 94–115.

factories where working conditions might impair their health.[169] Although the law was frequently violated, it is interesting to see how the "generation of reform" and a paternalistic administration could act together in this particular case to anticipate some of the social ills attendant upon the early phases of the industrial revolution. Likewise, the committee established by the Diet of 1839–40 for the preparation of the long overdue penal code, endeavored to acquire the best available sources for the study of the pertinent foreign (including American) legislation and practices. Its members—Aurel Dessewffy, Deák, Klauzál, Bezerédy, Eötvös, and Pulszky—knew that the control of crime was a complex social problem requiring human understanding and not just legal talent.[170]

Thus, even from the point of view of legislative activity, the record of the Diet of 1839–40 should not be underestimated. Moreover, the Diet that began under such ominous auspices ended on a rather promising note, due to the combined efforts of Széchenyi, Deák, Dessewffy, the palatine, and Chancellor Majláth. As a result of protracted behind-the-scenes bargaining, all political prisoners were freed and political trials were stopped by a royal amnesty a few days before the end of the Diet. This was less than Deák and the opposition had fought for, since the amnesty failed to recognize the nation's constitutional right to oppose the administration. Furthermore, as Széchenyi remarked some 20 years later, Metternich was smart enough to postpone the amnesty until the end of the Diet so that the opposition could not press for further concessions.[171] Although the legal views of the opposition failed to carry, the liberal forces had achieved an important moral victory.[172] The amnesty

[169] Mérei, *Magyar iparfejlődés*, p. 167.

[170] Ferencz Pulszky, *Jellemrajzok* (Character Sketches) (Budapest: Aigner Lajos, n.d.), pp. 96ff. In his defense of a leader of a gang of murderers and robbers, young Deák took a strong stand against capital punishment, which, as he put it, serves only the purpose of vengeance, which has no place in justice, cannot restore the life of the assassinated, prevents the rehabilitation of criminals demanded by brotherly love, and therefore ought to be resorted to only in cases where the sparing of a criminal's life would cause more damage to the public weal than the extinction of the life of a repentant sinner. Kónyi, ed., *Deák beszédei*, I, 1–7. See also the contemporary review of two works, published in 1838 and 1839 by Baron Joseph Eötvös and Bartholomew Szemere, respectively, both of which dealt with the improvement of prisons. Both studies, and the review article itself, stressed some of the pertinent reforms introduced in the United States, especially Pennsylvania. Gusztáv Szontagh, "Fogháztárgy!" (On the Subject of Prisons!) in *Figyelmező*, III (1839), 65–75. As early as 1834, Francis Toldy (Schedel) wrote a review article in Vol. IV of *Tudománytár*, pp. 105–119, on the American penal system. Cf. *ibid.*, II (1838), 692f. and note. Also Ballagi, "Az 1839/40-diki országgyűlés," pp. 91–103.

[171] Falk, *Széchenyi és kora*, pp. 109, 114–17. Cf. May 13, 1840, B. Szabó, ed., *Adatok*, I, 360.

[172] Pulszky, *Meine Zeit*, I, 212ff., 232f., 242f.; Wirkner, *Meine Erlebnisse*, 116–19; Ferenczi, *Deák élete*, I, 247–310. Concerning Deák's readiness to compromise and his

granted Wesselényi, Kossuth, and other political prisoners created an atmosphere of general reconciliation in the late spring of 1840, and this, naturally, did not hurt the administration. Actually, foreign envoys were very much interested in the détente in Hungary, as well as in the amnesty granted previously to political prisoners in Austria's Italian provinces.[173] The happy ending of the Hungarian Diet came in the right moment. The crisis in the Orient was approaching its climax, and Palmerston was anxious "to keep Austria firm . . . ." Anything that could give Metternich a pretext to waver in his far from enthusiastic support of the British determination to coerce Mehemet Ali, if necessary without French cooperation, was of great concern to the foreign secretary.[174] This is probably why he hastened to express to Vienna the pleasure with which Her Majesty's government, "in common with the rest of Europe," have learned about the extension of the Italian amnesty granted in 1838.[175]

Before and during the Diet Széchenyi was often frustrated, complaining in his diary that he was "nobody" and had lost his influence. Deák himself was rather pessimistic because of the repeated, rigid rejection of the lower table's resolutions.[176] But at the end of the Diet both Széchenyi and Deák shared the optimism characteristic of the country's mood. The amnesty and the enactment of new legislation augured a certain improvement in the relation of government and nation. Széchenyi, as well as the politically articulate public, gave much credit for this to Deák. He began to appreciate Deák's moderate but firm legalism which he had initially considered mere pettifogging. At the end of the Diet he felt reassured, suggesting that disregarding all jealousy, "Deák must be our center . . . . Let's give him precedence!"[177]

In fact, Deák played a major role in the "compromise of 1840." For 10 frustrating months almost no progress was made in the Diet, where

---

negotiations in Vienna prior to the opening of the Diet, cf. also Ballagi, *A nemzeti államalkotás, kora*, 459ff. and Trócsányi, "Wesselényi fogsága" in *Századok*, XCIV (1960) and XCV (1961), 799, 808f. and 285f., respectively. For Majláth's conciliatory attitude, reform ideas, and connections with the young conservatives, see Miskolczy, *A kamarilla*, pp. 107–115.

[173] Langsdorff to Thiers, Apr. 4, 1840, Vol. 428, *Correspondance politique, Autriche*, Archives du Ministère des Affaires Etrangères (Paris).

[174] Webster, *Foreign Policy of Palmerston*, II, 679–87.

[175] Palmerston to Beauvale, May 6, 1840 (no. 56), *F.O. 7/288*, PRO (London).

[176] E.g., Apr. 1, 1838; June 19, Sept. 25, Nov. 7, 1839; Feb. 29, Apr. 9, Apr. 27, May 4, 1840, Viszota, ed., *Naplók*, v, 175, 290, 316, 327, 362–73, 378, 381. Also, introduction, *ibid.*, p. xiv.

[177] June 22, July 3, Aug. 6, 14, 29, Sept. 13, Oct. 25, Nov. 20, Dec. 17, 18, 23, 25, 1839; Jan. 16, 28, Feb. 22, 26, Apr. 10, 13, 26, 27, 28, 30, *ibid.*, v, 292, 295, 303, 305, 309, 314, 324, 332, 341–44, 349, 352, 359f., 373, 378ff.; Ferenczi, *Deák élete*, I, 302f., 307–310; Kónyi, ed., *Deák beszédei*, I, 489f. Cf. Ch. VII, 313.

he tried to hold the line against the increasing pressure of the administration and his own less determined supporters. He was a skillful tactician, knowing precisely when to make concessions without hurting the national cause. His personal integrity, knowledge of constitutional law, modesty, and deep humanity—virtues that enabled him in the 1860s to restore Hungarian pride after a national tragedy and reconstruct the bridge of reconciliation between nation and dynasty—made him a natural leader even as a younger man. In situations where unassuming patience and reliability, rather than boldness and brilliance, were important to reach a compromise acceptable to all, Deák was supreme. His availability for carrying forward the work of reform begun by Széchenyi, and the very results of the Diet of 1839–40, to which they both contributed so much, makes one believe that Széchenyi's concept of a center party and of a moderate working majority in the Diet did not belong to the realm of impossibilities in the spring of 1840, especially since Chancellor Majláth and the palatine, too, urged reform and moderation.

Some people thought Széchenyi could give the same leadership to the administration's forces in the chamber of magnates as did Deák to the opposition in the chamber of deputies. But according to Lord Chief Justice George Majláth, such an endeavor on Széchenyi's part would have decreased his popularity and impaired his usefulness to the government.[178] For a moment, it even seemed to Széchenyi that if he were single and had no obligations to a large family he could take over the leadership of the government—"because there is none"—to serve his fatherland and the dynasty.[179]

Ignoring the personal factors, which would have made it extremely difficult for Széchenyi to undertake the task of being the head of a party or government with a chance of lasting success, it is questionable whether he would have been trusted in Vienna at the time. As late as January 1842 Metternich opposed Széchenyi's nomination to the rank of "Keeper of the Crown," a distinction proposed by the palatine at this time. (The title gave dignity but no particular political power to the person invested with it.) However, in the opinion of the chancellor, Széchenyi was not "sufficiently mature as yet" to receive such an award from the administration.[180]

But in Hungary Széchenyi's authority reached its zenith. He was admired by the adherents of reform, and one of the liberal leaders, Bezerédy, thought of him as a potential candidate for palatine after

[178] Apr. 24, 1840, Viszota, ed., *Naplók*, v, 377.

[179] Apr. 28, 1840, *ibid.*, v, 379.

[180] Cited in Viszota, ed., *Széchenyi és Kossuth*, i, p. cv. Cf. Miskolczy, *Ungarn in der Habsburger-Monachie*, p. 69.

the old archduke's death.[181] Like Deák, Széchenyi was enthusiastically hailed after the Diet was over. On June 4, 1840 the youth of Pest gave him a torchlight serenade and a tricolored flag with the inscription: "To Count Széchenyi 1840." There were two bands, one military and one gypsy. The choir of the National Theatre sang, and the speaker of the *jurati* declared: "We express our thanks to you who have roused the Hungarian nation from its sleep. Although your plans engendered envy, hatred, and misgivings among some blind people, we nonetheless hope that the darkness will disappear in due time and the nation will reach prosperity." In his answer, Széchenyi agreed that the nation had been asleep for a long time. The Hungarian people, which has not been a nation hitherto, would become one with God's help if, concluded Széchenyi, everyone will only do his best to contribute to the glory and benefit of the fatherland.[182]

For a while, Széchenyi thought that a new era had begun in Hungarian history, and even said so to Metternich.[183] He agreed with Deák, who had told him at the end of the Diet that there was no need for agitation and added that the leaders of the opposition would see to it that there be no excesses during the reports to the counties.[184] These words gave new confidence to Széchenyi. He felt that Hungarian patriots must rally around Deák as their political center. Whereas at the beginning of the Diet he worried that the general excitement could be calmed down only by some *vis major* such as the threat of an international crisis involving perhaps Spain or Turkey, he heaved a sigh of relief toward

[181] July 26, 1838, *ibid.*, v, 194. According to Heinrich Treitschke, Prussian Ambassador Maltzan reported as early as Feb. 8, 1836 that Széchenyi was a candidate for palatine after the death of Archduke Joseph. *Deutsche Geschichte im Neunzehnten Jahrhundert*, 2d. edn., 5 vols. (Leipzig: S. Hirzel, 1879–94), IV, 520.

[182] June 4, 1840. Police report on the homage to Széchenyi, B. Szabó, ed., *Adatok*, I, 36of. June 4, 1840, Viszota, ed., *Naplók*, v, 387 and n. 2. A report on the popular mood prevalent in Hungary, which was submitted to the *Staatskonferenz* by Count Sedlnitzky on June 22, 1840, noted the jubilation with which "the known reformer and agitator Count Stephen Széchenyi" was received by the students upon his arrival in Pest. The agent found it *most striking, to be sure* (his italics), that the band of the fifth artillery regiment could be "borrowed" from the military authorities for the occasion. No. 1,002/1840, *Kabinettsarchiv, Staatskonferenzakten*, Staatsarchiv (Vienna).—It was in the Age of Reforms that the red-white-green tricolor began to be regarded as the symbol of 1,002,1840, *Kabinettsarchiv, Staatskonferenzakten*, Staatsarchiv (Vienna). It was in the Age of Reforms that the red-white-green tricolor began to be regarded as the symbol of Hungarian sovereignty. It became Hungary's official national flag in 1848.

[183] May 12, 18, 1840, Viszota, ed., *Naplók*, v, 383, 385.

[184] I.e., during the reports of deputies to the county congregations on the results of the diet. It is worth mentioning that, besides deputies Balogh and Somssich, Deák was "particularly afraid" of Louis Batthyány, "because especially this last one will perhaps be agitating." Apr. 30, 1840, *ibid.*, v. 380. Cf. Sz. to Deák, Feb. 1, 1841, B. Szabó, ed., *Adatok*, I, 371f. Even police reports, which were extremely hostile to Széchenyi and Batthyány, the two leaders of "the renitent magnate opposition," conceded that the tone of Deák's report, although written "in an altogether oppositional spirit," was very moderate. No. 1,195/1840, *Kabinettsarchiv, Staatskonferenzakten*, Staatsarchiv (Vienna). For Deák's report cf. Kónyi, ed., *Deák beszédei*, I, 488–553.

the close of the Diet, and expressed hope in the nation's future.[185] In a letter to Pulszky he stressed both the feasibility and need for a nation-wide concentration of forces, relying, above all, on the intelligentsia and the propertied classes, but also including the government. Against the latter, he advised, the nation should never act, although it could go ahead without it on its own, "for the sake of the nation, the throne, and the joint empire," if the administration became hesitant about pro-ceeding with the work of reform. Returning again and again to Deák's words, he emphasized:

The necessity for agitation is over, thank heavens . . . . And if there is ever a time then it is now, when all intelligent and well-to-do people should ally themselves with the government, if the latter really wants to persist in progress and does not intend to kill the independent minded . . . . One has to work hard and toil daily, unceasingly. To attend the Diet every three years and to make flowery speeches is not enough yet . . . . There is no more agitation necessary, true; but the time for stretching our limbs at leisure has not come yet by any means.[186]

In this letter, Széchenyi invited Pulszky to attend his nameday party. One month later, on August 20, the traditional day of the founder of the Hungarian state, St. Stephen, about 70 prominent personalities came to honor Hungary's *pater patriae*. After the celebration of mass, Széchenyi was congratulated by Deák on behalf of the guests. At the gala dinner, his wife and children recited Hungarian poems.[187] And as if all this were not enough, Kossuth, too, gave credit for the ovation he received at the county congregation of Pest after he had come out of jail to Széchenyi, repeatedly calling him the "Greatest among the Magyars."[188]

[185] July 27, 1839; Apr. 30, 1840, Viszota, ed., *Naplók*, v, 300, 380.

[186] Széchenyi to Pulszky, July 20, 1840, Majláth, ed., *Levelek*, III, 63f. Also letter to Deák, referred to in n. 184 above.

[187] Aug. 19, 20, 1840, Viszota, ed., *Naplók*, v, 398; Friedreich, *Széchenyi élete*, I, 440; Zichy, *Széchenyi életrajza*, I, 449f. In his toast at the gala dinner, Széchenyi drank to the health of the king, members of the dynasty, especially the palatine, and Francis Deák, whose rare talents had been developed into a "real treasure for our nation, thanks to his unbending will and ironbound industry." For Széchenyi's toast cf. Gyula Viszota, "A kelet népe történetéhez" (To the Genesis of *A kelet népe*), *Budapesti Szemle*, CXVI (1903), 163f. Not knowing, apparently, that there was not much love lost between Batthyány and Széchenyi, the police attributed particular significance to the presence of "both notorious coryphaei of the magnate opposition" in Cenk. They regarded the celebration of Széchenyi's nameday a mere pretext for political consultations. No. 1,235/1840, *Kabinetssarchiv, Staatskonferenzakten*, Staatsarchiv (Vienna).

[188] On June 9 and then on Nov. 19, 1840. See Viszota, ed., *Széchenyi és Kossuth*, I, 788f. and n. 5. A little later, Kossuth honored Wesselényi with the same epithet. Cf. Trócsányi, *Wesselényi*, p. 552.

All this happened only 15 years after he had first taken the floor at the Diet of 1825. Now in 1840 he was a celebrity even in the eyes of foreigners. The storyteller Hans Christian Andersen saw his portrait on a steamship and in the windows of stores.[189] But Andersen never met Széchenyi in person, whereas Julia Pardoe saw him in the sessions of the Diet of 1839–40 and in his home. Her observations gave a vivid impression about Széchenyi, "who has won an European reputation which has made his name a watchword with the high-minded; and whose appearance greatly tends to deepen the feeling of admiration which his extraordinary career must naturally command. He has a dark, keen, eagle eye, softening, however, at intervals almost into sadness; heavy eyebrows, finely arched, and in perpetual motion, giving a character of extraordinary energy to his countenance; and one of those full, deep-toned, sonorous voices to which you cannot choose but listen."[190]

Miss Pardoe, admittedly favorably inclined to Hungarians, was charmed by Széchenyi, and said so in her book. Less idealistic was perhaps the representative of a manufacturer in Milan, who nevertheless expressed his enthusiasm on being introduced to "the Washington of Hungary." Remarked Széchenyi in his diary: "I wish to God it were true!"[191] Some two weeks later, after the county meeting of Pest, where Kossuth extolled him, he asked from his future opponent: "Why do you exalt me to heights where I shall be unable to maintain myself?"[192]

[189] See Ch. V, 183.
[190] Pardoe, *City of the Magyar*, I, 263f.
[191] Nov. 1, 1840, Viszota, ed., *Naplók*, v, 415.
[192] Nov. 19, 1840, *ibid.*, v, 422.

CHAPTER IX

People of the Orient

The hopes for creating a party of moderation had disappeared in less than one year. The "golden mean," of course, means different things to different people at different times. Metternich once used the term to describe Prussia's intermediary position among the powers.[1] Széchenyi, who poked fun at the vulgarization of the idea of the *juste milieu*, was nevertheless its champion in Hungary.[2] This was understood by contemporary observers.[3] But one must add that the "middling mind" cannot always cope with social change effectively because it seems "especially susceptible to either a nightmare view of the present or a kind of reverie in the present,"[4] a description that fits many aspects of Széchenyi's way of relating to his world. Beyond certain psychological factors, the explanation for this phenomenon lies in the circumstance that the middle of the road is at best very slippery political terrain. Exposed on two fronts, the center position requires a defensive posture almost by definition: consequently, it seldom succeeds in rapidly changing social conditions where it is most needed. Related originally to the rising middle classes in England and France in the 1830s, the ideology of the *juste milieu* proved too complex to succeed even in France, where the bourgeoisie were fragmented and the July monarchy overinstitutionalized.[5]

In Hungary, where Széchenyi and many younger members of the liberal generation tended to idealize the bourgeois king of the French and his experiment, there was no politically articulate middle class. There a middle-of-the-road policy could mean only one thing—a moderate

[1] Doc. 1,136, in Richard Metternich, ed., *Mémoires, documents et écrits divers laissés par le prince de Metternich*, 8 vols. (Paris: E. Plon, 1880–84), v, 538.

[2] Ferenczi, ed., *A kelet népe*, pp. 370ff., 392f.

[3] For Vörösmarty's and a police agent's opinions, cf. *ibid.*, pp. 643–49, 665. See also Ferenczi's introduction, pp. 10, 53, 56, *ibid.*

[4] Vincent E. Starzinger, *Middlingness, Juste Milieu. Political Theory in France and England, 1815–48* (Charlottesville: The University Press of Virginia, 1965), p. 152.

[5] *Ibid.*, pp. 13–19, 36f., 136–51.

course excluding methods that could lead either to a revolutionary upheaval or to the entrenchment of a reactionary regime opposed to the
evolution of a Hungarian nation with a Magyar middle class. It is important to remember that to Széchenyi and most of his Hungarian contemporaries, nation-building implied both the expansion of the restrictive
concept of the *natio Hungarica* of the privileged and the assimilation
of the foreign burghers into Magyardom.

Nation-building can never follow a clearcut model taken from an
advanced society. By the late 1830s Széchenyi had learned this the hard
way. One of his teachers, ironically, was Metternich. The relationship
between the chancellor and his erstwhile protégé was indeed peculiar.
For nearly a quarter of a century the two were constantly irritating
each other, although they both mellowed during the last five years of
their public lives, when they became increasingly lonesome amidst the
affairs of Hungary and the empire. It was in this period preceding
the revolution of 1848 that their mutual influence can be demonstrated
best.

Important as such personal factors were, they should be supplemented
with others. Allowed to interfere in domestic affairs only during the
last few years of Francis I, Metternich became, after the monarch's
death in 1835, the member of the *Staatskonferenz* most intimately connected with Hungarian developments. He continued to be preoccupied
with foreign problems, especially the Oriental crisis, and became ill from
overwork in August 1839.[6] One is tempted to attribute Vienna's failure
to strengthen adequately the favorable trend in Hungary during and
after the Diet of that year to such considerations. But neither before
his illness nor after the resumption of his duties in the autumn of 1839
was the chancellor in a compromising mood.

Indeed, Metternich's inclination to mix truisms, half-truths, and correct observations reached its height in the tirades about Hungary and
Széchenyi. Over the years his basic attitude did not change much although its expression in tangible suggestions was not always consistent.[7]
A memorandum revealing the chancellor's views on Hungary in early
1837 illustrates the point.[8]

---

[6] "Aus dem Tagebuche der Fürstin Melanie," June 27, July 7, 12, 18, 20, Aug. 2,
early Sept. and Dec. 20, 1839; Metternich to Apponyi, Docs. 1,357–63, in Metternich-
Winneburg, ed., *Nachgelassene Papiere*, VI, 307–12, 326, 342–52; also Aug. 12, 1839,
Viszota, ed., *Naplók*, V, 304, and Comte de Sainte-Aulaire, *Souvenirs, Vienne, 1832–41*
(Paris: 1926), pp. 261–65, 279.

[7] See Ch. VII, 302ff.

[8] *Kabinettsarchiv, Staatskonferenzakten*, No. 123/1837 (Jan. 19, 1837), Staatsarchiv
(Vienna). The italics in the memorandum follow the original. A very defective version
of the memorandum was transcribed in the doctoral dissertation of Pál Németh, "Die
politischen Prozesse in Ungarn in der Zeitperiode des Vormärz" (Innsbruck: 1962),
pp. 381–88. Cf. Appendix I, doc. no. 7.

Attempting to assess the roots of the "evil," Metternich pointed to the reign of Joseph II and the French revolution, stressing, rightly, the significance of the Diet of 1790–91 and the peace restored at the Congress of Vienna in 1814–15. Without analyzing the historical validity of either the periodization or the judgments suggested in the memorandum, one may note that according to the chancellor the year 1830 marked the beginning of a new period in Hungary's evolution. In this "new period," which was thus linked to the collapse of the restored old order in western Europe, "the Polish revolution has played an important role, precisely in its direct bearing on Hungary." The new trend, however, was alien to and conflicting with Hungarian laws, traditions, mores, and needs. Even before that, asserted Metternich, new oppositional forces emerged at the Diet of 1825, due to the tensions caused by forcible recruiting and the passive resistance of several counties to the collecting of taxes in specie instead of paper money. Going considerably beyond what he wrote about the substitution of a so-called new opposition for the old one in 1825,[9] he blamed the administration for allegedly having made "concessions of the highest significance at the Diet." Thereby, he added, the new opposition was encouraged to transgress the limits of Dietal activities.

Thus there came into being the casinos, an establishment for spreading modern liberalism; the Learned Association [Academy], an agency promoting the Magyar idiom which, regardless of the limited sphere of its applicability at the time, acquired the value of an institution thanks to its elevation to a *national* language; and the enterprises of Danubian navigation, designated as a purely national industrial goal! If it were not so ridiculous, one could take into account here the races with the participation of English jockeys, the numerous trips of young magnates to France and England for the purpose of imbibing foreign concepts and fashionable views, and finally even the new—so-called old—utterly fantastic costume.

These enterprises of the whizzing spirit of a Count Stephen Szécheny [*sic*], and of that of the by far more calculating Baron Wesseleny [*sic*], were backed by the former's publications. In spite of their proven shallowness, they yet had the merit of promoting the Magyar vernacular and of attacking directly *the previous track of life*. To shove a land away from this track means to expose it to subversion under the slogan of *reforms*. The distance left behind by Hungary in this respect in but a few years is shown by all the conditions of the present!

[9] Cf. Ch. IV, 132, note 136.

Despite the distortions and emotional overtones of the passages quoted and of the rest of the memorandum, the chancellor noted correctly the significance of the discussion of the *operata* by the county congregations of the early 1830s from the point of view of liberal propaganda.[10] Thus, in his opinion, the counties were given an opportunity to focus their attention on national rather than municipal affairs—which played into the hands of the liberal opposition. The latter excited the youth, intimidated men of good will (*"die Gutgesinnten"*), showed its power at the opening of the Diet of 1832, and was soon on the offensive: "as it always happens with *liberal* formations, it revealed *radical and demagogical* forms and tendencies. In their most extreme trends, *Hungary's separation* from the great imperial state is clearly spelled out today."

Mixing obvious exaggerations with sincere anxiety, Metternich admitted that the administration and its supporters were on the defensive in the Diet of 1832–36. Presenting the contest between the lesser nobility and the magnates, the lower and upper tables, the spirit of the age (*"Zeitgeist"*) and tradition as a struggle between the principles of preservation and destruction, he accused the government of being a passive spectator instead of acting. Claiming that the administration stood firmly on the ground of the Hungarian constitution, so often derided by him, he insisted that opponents of the government were also against the constitution. Posing as a defender of "Hungary's true civilization," the new convert to ancient Hungarian constitutionalism condemned, in one broadside, "the attempts of a false and conceited civilization" whose built-in speed could only be detrimental to countries traditionally slowly progressing, the influence of casinos and associations of law students threatening the property rights and "other conditions" of a citizen, the English races, steamships, railroads, "and all other extravagances of a morbid age."

Perhaps the most remarkable part of the memorandum was its concluding section. In it Metternich urged the administration to decide on the methods with which it wished to fight the disease spreading in Hungary. Before that, however, he reproached the government for having demonstrated inertia and a negative attitude vis-à-vis Hungary for many years, allowing the forces of evil to use the country as a free playground. Metternich pontificated: *"Hungary is not being governed today; she must be governed, and the field will be soon animated."*

This indictment of both the palatine's administration of Hungary and the governmental system of Francis I at the close of that monarch's life, by the latter's chief minister shows how divided the highest councils

[10] Cf. Ch. VII, 279–86.

of the empire were. The cynicism with which the most permanent and influential statesman of the era would sit in judgment over the breakdown of a regime intended to be both stable and immobile, and constructed, to a large extent, by himself, is only somewhat less amazing than the cavalier gesture with which he lumped together in one sentence the "extravagances of a morbid age," from horse races to railroads. Indeed, the document, which preceded the more restrained but essentially similar communications to Nicholas I,[11] anticipated not only the reactionary turn in the administration's policy (which Széchenyi so rightly feared) but the admission of the complete failure of that policy by the chancellor some seven and eight years later, in his much better known but far less important lamentations, which alleged that Hungary was in the abyss of revolution.[12]

It is useful to keep in mind a certain continuity and onesidedness in Metternich's thought, when one ventures to evaluate the chance of success that Széchenyi's ideas about gradual reform and a modus vivendi between Vienna and moderate Hungarian liberals might have had. During the Diet of 1825–27 the chancellor grossly underestimated the potential of Magyar nationalism; 10 years later, he seemed to be panic-stricken by it, although he tried to hide his worries behind supercilious remarks or complaints about the palatine in his conversations with foreign envoys or correspondence with the tsar. But if he took note of the strength of nationalism, he continued to ignore the explosive and irreversible power of technological progress, as shown by some of his statements in the memorandum of January 1837.

Neither did Metternich's opinion of Széchenyi's plans for reform change much. He went on ridiculing the paradoxical nature of Széchenyi's ideas and refused to recognize the more subtle aspects or tangible success of his enterprises. To him, the father of Hungarian reform remained "Stefferl," whom he could occasionally use as a thermometer for checking the temperature of the political atmosphere in Hungary, but for whom he had no use in the process of policy-making. While paying lip service to the need for change and progress the chancellor thus failed to move in that direction because he failed to see the difference between reform and revolution.

So it happened that, whereas Széchenyi tried to deemphasize the politi-

[11] Ch. VIII, 328f.
[12] Written at the end of 1843 and 1844, respectively, these letters to the palatine were published as Docs. 1,476 and 1,492 in Metternich-Winneburg, ed., *Nachgelassene Papiere*, vi, 672–77, and vii, 51–63, under the titles "Der Sprachenkampf in Ungarn" and "Über die ungarischen Zustände." The latter document was first published, separately, under the title "Aphoristische Bemerkungen über die ungarische Zustände zu Ende des Jahres 1844, mitgetheilt vom Fürsten Metternich." Cf. Ch. IV, 132, note, 136.

cal aspects of his reforms in order to demonstrate the common interest all classes of Hungarian society *and* Vienna had in their realization, Metternich and those close to the center of power were looking for a political solution to the ills of the monarchy in the first place. The memories of the French Revolution were still very much on the minds of these men: they thought in terms of breaking rather than accommodating the opposition. The circumstance that in order to revert to the "good old days" of the absolutistic reign of Francis I they would have to resort to a measure of "salutary terror," as Metternich put it, mattered but little: violence, rigged elections, and other oppressive methods have been part of the political tradition in "modern" Hungary,[13] as they have in some other countries.

If one reads the proposals for subduing the spirit of unrest in Hungary, one finds interesting parallels. Besides reshuffling the highest dignitaries of Hungary to strengthen the administration's control of the Diet in its next session, Hungarian Chancellor Pálffy suggested in the summer of 1838 the appointment of lieutenant governors or administrators to improve the conservative position at the county level. "Coordination" of the work of censors, shortening of the duration of Diets, clipping the wings of the Dietal youth, curbing the influence of the circular sessions, speeding up political trials, naming a primate to the vacant archiepiscopal see of Esztergom—all these were parts of Pálffy's program for Hungary, much of which was indeed put into practice during and after his tenure.[14] In a similar vein, *Staatsrat* Baron von Kübeck proposed in December 1839 the "disciplining" of the work of both Diet and county assemblies and the sending of able lieutenant governors into the counties, to reside there and behave like royal officials.[15] Even Aurel Dessewffy, who reported the opposition's demands and the foundation of the Academy in a rather liberal spirit to the British ambassador in 1825,[16] and who was not opposed to economic progress, social justice, and judicial reform, quite in accordance with the representatives of the liberal genera-

[13] Since the late 1820s tumultuous scenes, caused mostly by the *jurati* in the Diet and by agitators of both the conservative and liberal parties in the counties, were quite frequent. Horváth, *Huszonöt év*, I, 305, 325–28, 420–23, II, 101ff. In the elections of Heves county in 1833, according to a French report, seven persons were slain and 25 injured. Ste-Aulaire to Broglie, Nov. 12, 1833, Vol. 419, *Correspondance politique, Autriche*, Archives du Ministère des Affaires Etrangères (Paris); Pyrker, *Mein Leben*, pp. 165f., 322, n. 40 and 41. Cf. No. 267/1838, *Kabinettsarchiv, Staatskonferenzakten*, Staatsarchiv (Vienna). See also Kossuth's article in *Pesti Hirlap* (Feb. 27, 1841), Ferenczi, ed., *A kelet népe*, 145ff.

[14] Nos. 909 and 947/1838, *Kabinettsarchiv, Staatskonferenzakten*, Staatsarchiv (Vienna).

[15] Kübeck, ed., *Tagebücher*, I, Pt. 2, pp. 823f.

[16] See Ch. IV, 119, n. 104, 102f. Cf. Horváth, *Huszonöt év*, II, 100.

tion of which he himself used to be one, suggested that to overcome efficiently the "extravagances" of the "radical party" (the liberals), Diets must be short, the approach to reform through "systematic works" abandoned, and the autonomy of counties curtailed through appropriate new legislation.[17] Although many other proposals submitted by Dessewffy reflected Széchenyi's influence (e.g., his ideas to improve the country's credit system, communications, and the peasant's lot), the political part of his program, like some of the suggestions made by Pálffy or Kübeck, anticipated the energetic centralizing methods put into practice some five years later under the chancellorship of George Apponyi.[18]

Dessewffy's proposals, dated January 1, 1839, intimated that the gulf separating Széchenyi from the young tories of the Diet of 1839–40 was not unbridgeable. True, the basic constitutional principles from which he and "they" approached a number of issues, appeared to diverge. But many times, to mention only the religious issue, he and "they" fought for the same goals, using perhaps different arguments. The change in Széchenyi's personal attitude, however important, explains this phenomenon only in part: in a broader sense, the practical program of the noble and aristocratic liberal opposition diverged only in degree from that of the younger conservatives. None of the leaders of the opposition was disloyal to the dynasty, wanted the separation of Hungary from Austria, or intended to initiate radical social change before 1848. The heat generated by the opposition brought no significant institutional modifications in the Hungarian feudal establishment; the great problems of peasant emancipation, equality before the law, general taxation, abolition of the law of entail, and other noble privileges were left unsolved until the European revolution.[19]

All this, of course, implies that many of Metternich's allegations about the dangers of the new opposition were far-fetched. The details of the secret memoranda, written by the chancellor and those who had his ear, may not have been known to Széchenyi. Yet he had no illusions about the reactionary trend in the administration's policy that began with the arrest of the leaders of the Dietal youth in 1836 and provoked a wave of indignation in the country.[20] Nor could he have any doubts about Metternich's mood. Shortly before the opening of the Diet, the chancellor pointedly lectured Széchenyi that the construction of the

[17] *Aus den Papieren des Grafen Aurel Dessewffy*, pp. 74–86.

[18] For earlier efforts to break the autonomy of counties and govern by administrative fiat, see József Madarász, *Emlékirataim* (Memoirs) (Budapest: Franklin, 1883), pp. 36–46.

[19] Zoltán Horváth, *Teleki László* (Ladislas Teleki), 2 vols. (Budapest: Akadémiai kiadó, 1964), I, 121–24.

[20] Cf. Ch. VII, 310f.; VIII, 342–45. For the reaction of the county assemblies (before Kossuth's arrest in early May 1837, see Lajos Kossuth, *Törvényhatósági tudósitások* (Municipal Reports) (Budapest: Légrády, 1879.) Cf. Madarász, *Emlékirataim*, pp. 55ff.

bridge between Pest and Buda was the government's business, adding, "Nation, nation, what is it? The state is everything!" Upon his remark that during the last 10 years everything had been ruined in Hungary, Széchenyi caustically noted in his diary: "Ten years ago he said: 'My house on the *Rennweg* [in Vienna] marks the frontier of civilization.' "[21]

While the Diet was in session the prince, and Melanie, too, seem to have persisted in treating Széchenyi, whom they accused of being the leader of the opposition, with studied disdain.[22] There is no reason this time to attribute Széchenyi's indignant diary entries to an overdose of sensitivity. In the spring the chancellor was still sure that the forthcoming Diet would present no difficulties;[23] in October he pondered the "cracking" (*durchbrechen*) of the Hungarian constitution,[24] and as the Diet drew to its close he tried first to prevent and then to postpone until the very last minute the political amnesty.[25] By the autumn of 1840, with the defeat of Mehemet Ali in Egypt and the fall of Thiers in France, Metternich probably felt as sure of himself as ever.[26] It was at this juncture that, with his knowledge and approval, Kossuth, just released from jail, was allowed to become editor of *Pesti Hirlap*.[27] Having first turned him into a martyr, Vienna now made Kossuth a most influential factor in the country's public life.

Before this happened, Kossuth repeatedly attempted to curry Széchenyi's favor, both publicly and privately. But Széchenyi remained evasive and noncommittal. The reasons for this reservation are not hard to determine. Personal antipathy toward an upstart whose advances were thought to be mere flattery, Kossuth's alleged bad reputation, dislike of any initiative taken by others,[28] and, most important perhaps, subconscious awareness of the precarious nature of the improvement in the political atmosphere, may all have motivated Széchenyi's attitude.

Indeed, the very same county congregation of Pest that heard Kossuth

[21] Apr. 30, 1839, Viszota, ed., *Naplók*, v, 274. On another occasion Metternich is said to have referred to an estate of Prince Schwarzenberg, which was on the border of Austria and Hungary, as "the place where Europe ends and Asia begins." Ste-Aulaire to Thiers, May 6, 1836, Vol. 423, *Correspondance politique, Autriche*, Archives du Ministère des Affaires Etrangères (Paris): Langsdorff report, enc.

[22] Dec. 21, 1839; Feb. 2, 14, May 14, 18, 1840, Viszota, ed., *Naplók*, v, 342f., 353, 356, 383, 385.

[23] Aug. 5, 1839, *ibid.*, v, 303.

[24] Gustav Roloff, "Fürst Metternich über die slawische und ungarische Gefahr im Jahr 1839," *Mitteilungen des österreichischen Instituts für Geschichtsforschung*, LII (1938), 70.

[25] Falk, *Széchenyi és kora*, p. 109; Ferenczi, *Deák*, I, 279f.; Ballagi, *A nemzeti államalkotás*, pp. 471f., 486.

[26] For Metternich's sudden boldness even in regard to the Near East, see Webster, *Foreign Policy of Palmerston*, II, 729.

[27] Viszota, ed., introductions to *Naplók*, v, xvi f., and to *Széchenyi és Kossuth*, I, lxiii ff.; Ferenczi, ed., *A kelet népe*, pp. 11-16; Domokos Kosáry, *Kossuth Lajos a reformkorban* (Louis Kossuth in the Age of Reforms) (Budapest, 1946), pp. 191ff.

[28] Nov. 18, 21, Dec. 11, 28, 1840, Viszota, ed., *Naplók*, v, 421, 423, 429, 433f.

sing the praises of Széchenyi, also rejected a letter of the primate, which defended the Catholic position in the matter of mixed marriages. The letter was a protest against the punishment of priests who refused the benediction of the church and thereby broke the law. Széchenyi tried to tone down the assembly's harsh resolution on this sensitive and unsolved issue inherited from the preceding Diet. But he himself revealed his irritability in an article he showed to many of those attending the congregation, including Kossuth. In the article he sharply rebuked the few youthful pranksters, as he put it, upon whose insistence the orchestra consented to play the Marseillaise after a performance at the Hungarian Theater in early November.[29] Refusing to attribute any political significance to the incident, he claimed that Hungarians, always ready to safeguard their constitutional rights, might forget their grievances in times of chaos but would never be disloyal to their sovereign. "Away with you, intentional and unintentional assassins of our fatherland and national reputation!" he wrote in conclusion, exhorting those sincerely concerned with Hungary's future to join forces and uphold the name of the Magyar, "everywhere and on every occasion."[30]

This prelude to *A kelet népe* had nothing to do with Kossuth. But it showed Széchenyi's "overreaction" to challenges which, in his opinion, might undermine the tenuous political peace of the country. A month later he learned that a leading publisher in Pest had selected Kossuth as editor of his newspaper, and the administration had approved his choice.[31]

The government's "leniency," if leniency it was, was subsequently explained as a sign of the spirit of reconciliation prevailing after the Diet of 1839–40, and as an effort to keep Kossuth under control. We know that Kossuth's publisher was on excellent terms with Police Minister Sedlnitzky; the latter, in turn, was instrumental in obtaining from Metternich's chancery, without going through the regular channels, the required permission to hire Kossuth. For a while, there were rumors that the new editor himself had agreed to work with the government. Some people, including Széchenyi, first thought that Vienna wanted to split the opposition by using Kossuth's pen.[32]

Be that as it may, the publication of *Pesti Hirlap* on January 2, 1841,

---

[29] Nov. 18, 19, 23, 1840, *ibid.*, v, 421ff.

[30] Széchenyi's article, "The Marseillaise," which first appeared in the Nov. 17, 1840 issue of *Társalkodó* (no. 93), was republished by Antal Zichy, *Gróf Széchenyi István hirlapi czikkei* (Count Stephen Széchenyi's Newspaper Articles), 2 vols. (Budapest: Magyar Tud. Akadémia, 1893–94), I, 282–94, in *SzIM*.

[31] Dec. 30, 1840, Viszota, ed., *Naplók*, v, 434.

[32] For details cf. Ferenczi, ed., *A kelet népe*, pp. 11–16, 662f.; Viszota, "A kelet népe történetéhez," pp. 164f.

opened a new phase in Hungarian journalism. In the first issue, the publisher announced his intention to publish an interesting paper, adding that this was the reason for his asking Kossuth to be its editor. The new editor, in turn, set himself the task of starting a paper that would be the true mirror of the nation's life and would lend its pages, without prejudice and with moderation, to discussions focusing "on the great issues of the day." He also promised never to surrender his convictions to "foul interests."[33]

The first lead article was followed by others in each issue of the paper, which appeared twice a week. Along with other well-written articles dealing with important national and local issues, the new genre introduced by Kossuth into Hungary contributed to the popularity of the paper, which had quickly caught the public eye. Within six months the number of subscribers increased from 60 to almost 5,000, of whom only about ten percent lived in Pest. Thus *Pesti Hirlap* had more subscribers than the three other leading papers of the country put together; its readers constituted about one-fourth of the estimated 200,000 Hungarians who read newspapers at the time.[34] As the figures imply, Kossuth's paper soon became one of the most powerful opinion-shaping forces in the country, and Széchenyi grew increasingly uneasy because of the possible results of its "agitation." After seeing six or seven issues of the paper, and within a month of its first issue, the idea struck Széchenyi that he should resist Kossuth.[35] According to the same diary entry, Széchenyi was irked by the organization of the Association for Useful Knowledge by Eötvös, Kossuth, and Batthyány upon the initiative of a physician, Paul Balogh—who had failed to consult Széchenyi. Széchenyi also noted that he had spoken about Kossuth to Deák and Pulszky.[36] A few days later Széchenyi felt enthusiastic about swimming against the current, asked Pulszky to take a letter to Deák concerning the *Pesti Hirlap* and the palatine to enforce stricter censorship against the paper.[37]

This, as he himself remarked, was a "risky game." It involved all the ideals to which he committed himself in previous years—indeed his entire public career. According to the testimony of his diary, he knew perfectly well what was at stake. On February 6 he began to write "seriously" against Kossuth, calling his new book tentatively "The Death Knell." After working on it in cold fury for about a week, he

---

[33] Ferenczi, ed., *A kelet népe*, pp. 109f.

[34] *Ibid.*, p. 18.

[35] "*Es durchblitzt mich* die Idee, ich soll mich gegen Kossuth stemmen." Jan. 29, 1841, Viszota, ed., *Naplók*, v, 442 (italics Széchenyi's).

[36] Jan. 29, 30, 1841, *ibid.*, pp. 441f.

[37] Feb. 3, 5, 1841, *ibid.*, pp. 444f.

decided on the eventual title, *The People of the Orient*. In yet another week he began to express freely his dissatisfaction with *Pesti Hirlap* to people who would report it back to Kossuth; he also read parts of what he had written to friends.[38]

Because of his efforts to arouse people against *Pesti Hirlap,* several leaders of the opposition asked him to desist. Batthyány, who initially seemed to support the idea, told him on at least one occasion, in early March, not to write against Kossuth. Others, including Eötvös and Deák, gave similar advice.[39]

Eötvös, whose opinion about *Pesti Hirlap* Széchenyi solicited earlier in the year, reported back his findings after gauging the impact of the paper on a trip to two northern counties in Hungary. In Eötvös's view, based on conversations and a careful reading of all the leading articles published before the date of the letter—March 1—there was nothing in the paper that could incite people to revolt. To speak out against *Pesti Hirlap* would be most damaging and would shatter the public's trust not in Kossuth but in Széchenyi instead. Moreover, the principles advocated by Kossuth's paper clearly followed from the very principles announced by Széchenyi in his *Stádium*. Consequently, concluded Eötvös, Széchenyi's attack would only help the opponents of progress.[40]

To be more persuasive, Eötvös provided Széchenyi with the summary of a letter, written to his close friend Szalay with the understanding that its contents would be brought to Kossuth's attention. In this second letter, Eötvös indicated that Széchenyi continued to be a man of progress, progress that he had started in Hungary. Once he wrote to Szalay that *Hitel* was not only a book but something nobler, namely, a patriotic deed, and that its author was "the blessed destroyer" who had exposed prejudice and selfishness for what they were, "clearing the place for us so we can build."[41] Now he told his friend that although Széchenyi shared the principles of *Pesti Hirlap,* he found its style extremely bitter and feared that this could split the magnate opposition. Whether the opposing magnates would persist in their views when the consequences of progressive principles were increasingly clear, only time would show, and Széchenyi might turn out to be wrong. But if in Kossuth's opinion the magnate opposition was useful, it would be desirable to moderate the tone of his paper.[42]

[38] Feb. 6-28, 1841, *passim, ibid.,* pp. 446–52.
[39] Mar. 2, 7, 12, 1841, *ibid.,* pp. 453ff.
[40] Viszota, "A kelet népe történetéhez," pp. 168–71.
[41] Eötvös to Szalay, Dec. 19, 1837, Endre Nizsalovszky and Sándor Lukácsy, eds., *Eötvös József levelei Szalay Lászlóhoz* (The Letters of Joseph Eötvös to Ladislas Szalay) (Budapest: Akadémiai kiadó, 1967), p. 100.
[42] Viszota, "A kelet népe történetéhez," pp. 171–74.

Deák's reply to Széchenyi's inquiry was intended to be soothing. Giving Széchenyi full credit for having awakened the nation with *Hitel* and *Világ,* and for having ignited the torch from which they took the flame for their small wicks, he yet thought it premature to pass judgment on a brand new paper on the basis of a few issues. A lively press, Deák hoped, would improve the information of the public although the papers might occasionally cause confusion. The press was still in chains but the chains were somewhat looser. This, in itself, however, was an improvement that was far from the desired liberty. The trend of *Pesti Hirlap* was progressive; the paper's shortcomings, according to Deák, stemmed mainly from the fact that it discussed important topics in rather general terms. Given a little more time, however, he expected the articles to become more detailed and meaningful. An analytical approach to the necessary reforms would inevitably result in less emotional rhetoric and bitterness, and a more objective interpretation of events. Furthermore, Deák stressed, *Pesti Hirlap* was the property of the nation, open to anything good and beautiful. It would be detrimental, therefore, if people in agreement with the main principles of the paper launched an attack against it because of a style that might change. It was bad enough that no consistency could be expected from the Austrian administration in the realm of domestic policy; but to complain about too much liberality could provoke another relapse into the harsh and adverse course previously followed by the government. Deák assured Széchenyi that neither he nor Kossuth would be the cause of such retrogression. But this could happen, as it had in the past, as a result of another shift in the views of those in power. In such case, however, the instinct of progress, once aroused, could not be subdued by either government or any other force. Deák was convinced that the unfolding of Magyar nationality was in the interests of Austria, because a completely developed Hungarian nation would be that moral stronghold which could protect Austria against "the giant power of the north." Surmising that the recent favorable change in Vienna's attitude toward Hungary arose from the gradual realization of this circumstance, Deák thus articulated the false hopes of Magyar liberal nationalists of the *Vormärz.* Yet it took another quarter of a century, many defeats, and much disillusionment before this interpretation of Austria's mission by Magyar liberal nationalism was pondered seriously at court.

In the last part of his letter Deák set forth a respectful but firm warning. Széchenyi and Kossuth, he said, represented two moral forces which should unite rather than ruin each other. Instead of a contest of opinions between the two, Deák feared a clash of personalities focusing not on principles and issues but rather on name-calling and slogans.

Each of the contestants would be supported by a party because, in his words,

> . . . you have done much and Kossuth has suffered much for the public weal. To you, the nation owes gratitude. The aura of suffering hovers about Kossuth, and this secures for him enthusiastic sympathy. The struggle of the two parties would be bitter, because there is no more ferocious fight than the one fought with catchwords; when reasons are silenced by the slogan, personality is subordinated to the slogan, and even the subject of the discussion is forgotten because of the slogan.

Deák's sober anticipation of a bitter ideological struggle was accurate. He cautioned Széchenyi that in a country in which there were not too many talented and prominent people a personal struggle could dangerously weaken the public's trust and the national cause would suffer. In answer to Széchenyi's reminder of their previous agreement, according to which there was no more need for agitation, Deák drew a distinction between agitation in public meetings, supported by the spell of the spoken word and followed frequently by legislative action, and agitation in the press, which could be repudiated with calm arguments and was far removed from any legislative action. At any rate, Deák saw no danger in promoting public intelligence through newspaper discussions in a country where people could still believe that the recruits voted by the Diet were sold by their monarch for horses to the Russian court.[43]

Deák's long answer to Széchenyi's letter of February 1 was written on March 20. But Széchenyi learned about the essence of Deák's opinion from Pulszky's report, sent to him from the Austrian capital on February 18. According to another friend, Count Charles Andràssy, Kossuth's paper, forbidden in Austria, was widely discussed in Vienna, where people were looking forward to Széchenyi's forthcoming work. Andrássy also expressed his fear that Széchenyi's would place Kossuth on a pedestal by attributing him greater significance than he actually had. Conservatives, on the other hand, denied that Széchenyi had any grounds for resenting Kossuth, since Kossuth's conduct was a direct consequence of Széchenyi's activities.[44] This close association of his name with that of Kossuth by the opponents of liberalism and progress must have irked Széchenyi, although he appears to have been hurt even more by those leaders of the opposition who without exception endeavored to prevent him from speaking out publicly against *Pesti Hirlap*. Putting the warnings

[43] For the text of Deák's letter, cf. *ibid.*, pp. 177–87.
[44] *Ibid.*, pp. 174–77.

of Eötvös, Deák, Pulszky, and Andrássy in an envelope marked "Anti Kelet Népe,"[45] he yet decided to consult his conscience and continued to work on what might well turn out to be his swan song.[46]

His forebodings were to a large measure justified. The determination to publish *A kelet népe* was perhaps the most critical decision Széchenyi took during his public career. He wanted to save his soul in a crisis, which was brought about not so much by outward circumstances as by a crucial conflict within his inner self crying for solution. True, the historian can always relate such critical periods in an individual's or nation's life to external pressures, and an attempt has been made here to show how deeply embedded the roots of Széchenyi's clash with Kossuth were in the events of the day. One could add that on hearing of Széchenyi's intention to attack him, Kossuth also began to write to friends, sometimes the same friends to whom Széchenyi wrote, for opinion and support. On February 17 he published his famous article, "Calling," which was a direct challenge to the magnate class[47] and an indirect provocation of Széchenyi. In another article which appeared in late April Kossuth's allusions to Széchenyi were even more direct and defiant. To be sure, Kossuth subsequently softened the tone of his paper at the requests of Eötvös, Deák, and even Wesselényi, who all advised moderation, advice, however, that was unknown to Széchenyi.[48]

All this said, there may be some truth in the contention that there are men, frequently of great talent, who seem to harbor and nurture the seeds of crises in themselves. Sensitive and neurotic, they are essentially loners, anxious to stimulate change and create a new world, preferably in their own image. Apparently Széchenyi was such a man; for not much of a tangible reason and at a time of relative political calm, he picked his opponent and chose the moment of attack.

The new book appeared in late June. It created a sensation and the thousand copies of the first printing had to be supplemented after one month with a second edition.[49] Bearing the title *The People of the Orient,* the book was and still is controversial. Yet even contemporaries who disagreed with the main tenets of the book—such as the "Hungarian Franklin," Andrew Fáy, founder of the first savings bank and author of the first social novel in Hungary, or Vörösmarty, editor

[45] For additional references cf. Ferenczi, ed., *A kelet népe,* pp. 31f.

[46] Feb. 11, Mar. 7, 1841, Viszota, ed., *Naplók,* v, 447, 454.

[47] See Ch. VII, 294, 300. For the texts of Kossuth's articles cf. Ferenczi, ed., *A kelet népe,* pp. 138f., 188–92.

[48] *Ibid.,* pp. 31–37.

[49] *Ibid.,* p. 58; June 28, 1841, Viszota, ed., *Naplók,* v, 482. For the recurrence of Széchenyi's nightmarish dreams, suicidal thoughts, and fear of going insane, cf. Apr. 25 and 28, June 26, Aug. 11 and 28, Oct. 4 and 5, Nov. 2, 5, 21, 22 and 26, Dec. 21, 1841. *Ibid.,* pp. 468, 482, 491, 495, 503, 508, 516, 519, 529.

of the leading literary journal *Athenaeum*—called it epochal.[50] Vörösmarty, the most imaginative of Hungarian romantic poets, did not know any book of comparable length, which abounded in so many ideas, was so modern in their selection, so original in their exposition and presentation, so rich in substance and wit.[51] Indeed, of all Széchenyi's writings published in his lifetime, none reveals better the complexity and depth of his mature thought.

Toward the end of his 387-page-long book, Széchenyi claimed that his study was yet unfinished and fragmentary.[52] This is true in the same way Michelangelo's two slaves in the Louvre are torsos. Just as were the monumental artist's two creatures, marblebound yet painfully alive, Széchenyi's *People of the Orient* is hewn out of the "matter" with which he struggled, namely, his own soul and, what he felt was inseparably bound to it, Magyardom's fate.

The meaning of the work emerges only if one understands it as a *cri de coeur* of the author rather than a mere tirade against Kossuth. In the introductory section, which takes up more than one-fifth of the book, there is but one direct reference to *Pesti Hirlap,* and none whatsoever to its editor. Far from unimportant, this section is perhaps even more subjective than the rest of the work; it also abounds in personal reminiscences.[53] Beautifully written, but often with the rationalization inherent in human retrospection, these autobiographical reminiscences are most revealing to the historian. But they also show that it is seldom prudent to scrutinize a great man too closely, because, as Kossuth put it in his reply to Széchenyi, "closeness works like a magnifying glass indicating clods even on a smooth needle."[54]

According to the recurrent thesis of *A kelet népe,* unless Kossuth's journal changed its trend, it would promote anarchy or despotism, either of which might annihilate the Magyar. Without questioning Kossuth's good intentions or splendid talents, Széchenyi accused him of pitting the poor against the rich, the lesser nobles against the magnates, the masses against the privileged, and the have-nots against the propertied

[50] Ferenczi, ed., *A kelet népe,* p. 102. For Fáy, cf. Kornis, *A magyar politika hősei,* pp. 232–39.

[51] Ferenczi, ed., *A kelet népe,* p. 653. Vörösmarty's evaluation *A Kelet Népe 1841–ben* (The People of the Orient in 1841) was republished by Ferenczi in the *Fontes* edition of Széchenyi's book, as were some other important and pertinent writings, including the first 37 leading articles in *Pesti Hirlap,* Kossuth's reply to Széchenyi, the studies by Eötvös and Aurel Dessewffy, and notes concerning documents in the Austrian archives, which dealt with the origins of *Pesti Hirlap* and the discussion following the publication of *A kelet népe.*

[52] Ferenczi, ed., *A kelet népe,* pp. 391, 403.

[53] Cf. Chs. II, 13, IV, 119, and V, 139, 177.

[54] Ferenczi, ed., *A kelet népe,* p. 414.

classes.[55] Dissecting almost *ad absurdum* articles that dealt with abuses, destitution, and human misery, and were aimed at stirring the public's social conscience, Széchenyi attempted to prove that *Pesti Hirlap* intended to cast suspicion on everybody who owned something, to pillory every authority with hatred, to question everything already in existence, to undermine the popularity of all municipalities. The paper, he charged, indulged in muckraking without showing the way to improvements.[56] Instead of uplifting the fatherland to a higher level, Kossuth was pushing it toward the grave, Széchenyi contested. Still, he shared "with paternal feelings" the principles advocated by *Pesti Hirlap*, condemning only, as he stressed again and again, the style and tactics of its editor. In Széchenyi's view, Kossuth agitated against the landowning class and favored the confiscation of their possessions. Such agitation, however, was bound to result in revolutionary anarchy.[57]

The suggestion that one newspaper and one man, its editor, whose political principles or goodwill Széchenyi did not question, could create, with the assistance of the censors of the administration, a revolutionary situation in Hungary, was a poor argument. Széchenyi's critics, to mention only Eötvös and Vörösmarty, did not fail to point this out.[58] Even those few who sided with Széchenyi in his debate with Kossuth (the writer Louis Kuthy) found it difficult to detect signs of revolutionary agitation in *Pesti Hirlap*, let alone a threat to the established order. In his otherwise confused and clumsy book, Kuthy rightly emphasized that a successful political rebellion must emanate from a "centralized capital" to a country with a well-developed national consciousness. In a land where every municipality was independent of the movements arising in the capital, whose populace was split into different classes, languages, and interest groups, and where the intelligentsia was decentralized, no newspaper could foment a revolution even though it spoke with "two tongues of flame."[59]

Aurel Dessewffy, who agreed with the essence of Széchenyi's fears but disagreed with their spiteful presentation, warned that revolutionary ideas were never followed by immediate violence, although all revolutions were generated by ideas. What made false doctrines dangerous was that no one could predict when they would cause an outburst of violence. Among the "false doctrines" Dessewffy mentioned the heightened significance attributed by *Pesti Hirlap* to popular assemblies and municipal

---

[55] *Ibid.*, pp. 255, 260, 262, 265, 269.
[56] *Ibid.*, pp. 263, 325f.
[57] *Ibid.*, pp. 272f., 319f., 330f., 336–43, 356ff.
[58] *Ibid.*, pp. 558–83, 622ff., 652f.
[59] *Ibid.*, p. 97; Lajos Kuthy, *Polgári szózat kelet népéhez, 1841* (Civil Admonition Concerning *The People of the Orient*, 1841) (Pest: Heckenast, 1841), pp. 190f.

authorities, the paper's inclination to speak of "immature and unruly elements" as of representatives of public opinion, and the passionate tone with which it focused the attention, especially in the first five months of its existence, on every instance where human suffering was at issue. The leader of the young conservatives also cautioned that the grave charges against Kossuth, made by Széchenyi even at the risk of losing his own popularity, and of being accused of inconsistency, went far beyond the issues of style and tactics. Appreciating the weakness of Széchenyi's position, which stemmed from his declaration that he shared the principles of *Pesti Hirlap,* Dessewffy said that Széchenyi's pen was never inspired by a deeper sense of patriotic conviction than when he wrote *A kelet népe.* Thus the talented tory articulated the dilemma of all bona fide agitators, who must bring the excitement they have initiated under control before they themselves are absorbed by it. The more honest and unselfish the agitator the more bitter and difficult the decision, said Dessewffy. He reminded his readers of the sharp arguments Széchenyi had used ten years earlier in refuting the older Dessewffy's mild criticism of *Hitel.* Now Kossuth cited in great detail the author of *Világ* against the author of *A kelet népe.* Yet the time would inescapably come, Dessewffy added, when Kossuth himself must face the fate of all agitators, and might be overwhelmed by the very passions to which he had lent fuel.[60]

The first public debate between Széchenyi and Kossuth was linked in many visible and imponderable ways to the discussions that surrounded the appearance of Széchenyi's earlier works. Taking a leaf from *Világ* Széchenyi himself attempted to develop a chapter of his previous book, "Mind and Heart," into a full-fledged political theory, which drew a sharp line between the policy of cold reasoning and a policy of wishful thinking and emotionalism. Relating his theory to the national character, Széchenyi attributed the great progress made by England and the United States to a policy that, on the whole, seemed to have been based on a dispassionate evaluation of facts. The political instability in both France and the German lands, on the other hand, was rooted in the emotionalism of their leaders. Since *Pesti Hirlap,* in his opinion, appealed to the imagination and emotions rather than to the calculating mind, Széchenyi concluded that Kossuth, like many unselfish and dedicated figures of the French Revolution, was a fanatic whose emotionally dictated policies would ruin Hungary at the very moment of her awakening from a long somnolence. Despite the encouraging outcome of the Diet of 1839–40,

---

[60] X.Y.Z. [Pen name of Aurel Dessewffy], "Pesti Hirlap és Kelet Népe közti vitály" (The Dispute Between *Pesti Hirlap* and *Kelet Népe*), published originally in four articles in the paper *Világ* at the end of 1841, in Ferenczi, ed., *A kelet népe,* pp. 589–98.

which promised to inaugurate a period of fruitful cooperation between the government and the "young" Hungarian people, this "spirited oriental swarm" yet to be unfolded, Széchenyi feared Herder's prediction; only a hairbreadth of a chance, so he thought, separated his beloved nation from its fulfillment.[61] Repudiating all manias, from Anglomania to passionate love to intoxication with patriotism, he held that even a small people could become great and immortal if they followed the admonition of reason, whereas populous countries could perish if they succumbed to the fancies of their imagination.[62] But the same man who disapproved of utopias and preached soberness and detachment in the nation's affairs sounded almost like a mystic when he identified his Hungarians as a people of the Orient who had to be transformed into a people of reason. The development of such a heterogenous Oriental swarm, so separate and isolated in Europe, and its elevation to a flourishing nation for the benefit of mankind, was not an easy undertaking. Phantasmagorias, however heartwarming, could never accomplish the task, which had to be approached with circumspection and in the spirit of conciliatory and calm reformation. Saturated with revolutionary substances, as Széchenyi put it, the editor of *Pesti Hirlap* was unable to change his ways. Therefore, he begged Kossuth to step aside and stop using his popularity to confuse the mind of the Magyar.[63]

One is tempted to say that at this stage of his career Széchenyi treated Kossuth, *mutatis mutandis,* as Metternich treated him. Psychologically this is true, with important qualifications; the chancellor mistrusted and lectured Széchenyi, as the latter mistrusted and lectured Kossuth.[64] Naturally Metternich and Széchenyi were social equals and moved in the same aristocratic circles. They may have thought and even said very bad things of each other, but they both had a vested interest in the maintenance of a hierarchically structured social order. Their differences, reflected in confidential memoranda, were fought out in the privacy

---

[61] Ferenczi, ed., *A kelet népe,* pp. 230–38, 282, 285, 291–310, 315f., 339–46.

[62] *Ibid.,* p. 308. For Herder see Chs. II, IV–VII, 19, n. 36, 102, n. 40, 179, 236, 295.

[63] Ferenczi, ed., *A kelet népe,* pp. 236, 272, 315, 365, 373, 492f. The emphatic reference to Magyardom's presumed Oriental uniqueness, abused by 20th-century Magyar racists, was part of the romantic vision of Hungary and Hungarians in the early 19th century. Wrote the romantic poet Vörösmarty to Széchenyi in December 1832: "We are without companions in Europe." Gyula Viszota, "Széchenyi, Vörösmarty és az akadémia működésének első évei" (Széchenyi, Vörösmarty, and the First Years of the Activities of the Academy), *Budapesti Szemle,* cxxxviii (1909), 10. Frederick Schelling, in one of his famous "Lectures on Modern History" in Vienna in 1810, said: "No Christian people of Europe displayed so visibly, and preserved so faithfully, its Asiatic national character, yet none had participated so largely in the civilization of western Europe." Frederick Schlegel, *A Course of Lectures on Modern History,* trans. Lyndsey Purcell and R. H. Whitelock (London: H. G. Bohn, 1849), p. 138.

[64] Cf. Ch. VI, 214.

of the salons in Vienna, if we discount the gossips which were part of this "privacy." Kossuth, coming from the impoverished nobility, belonged to another sphere and another age. His very rise as a public figure represented a shift of political focus from the higher aristocracy to the lesser nobility. The latter, admittedly, was also "aristocratic" in the sense that it was part of the privileged peak of the Hungarian social pyramid. But the shift, which in the age of reform became so obvious in the changing political composition of the Diet, the changing function of the Diet's internal organization and committee work, and in the changing relationship of the Diet to the county assemblies, was not restricted to the relatively well-defined segment of the politically articulate. This was so because the gradual shift of political power and the slow widening of at least the intellectual elite's horizon coincided with and was in part even brought about by the dawn of the age of democracy in Central Europe. Due to the publicity it gave to issues and persons, *Pesti Hirlap* was certainly one of the harbingers of this new democratic age—and this is what Széchenyi felt in his bones.

Yet he was too committed and sincere to switch sides overnight, even though he carefully circumscribed his position vis-à-vis the magnate opposition, which appeared at the Diet of 1839–40. Historical literature has all but forgotten that while the main thrust of Széchenyi's attack in *A kelet népe* was directed against the "red thread" as represented, in his opinion, by Kossuth's "Jacobin" trend, he also took a stand against the "*schwarzgelb* thread," by which term he meant the black and yellow Austrian coloring of those opposing liberalism and completely subservient to the imperial administration. According to the *schwarz-gelb* view, to paraphase Széchenyi, savings associations, horse races, casinos, and newspapers were only whims of Hungarian enthusiasts, yet in reply to the intimation that he should never have given the impulse, which started the "domestic power plant," he proudly confirmed his "craving thirst," motivated by a "vigorous" sense of duty, to do whatever he could to arouse the Magyar from his sleep.[65]

The policy of the golden mean, as defined by Széchenyi in *A kelet népe,* was thus a determined struggle against the extremes of both the red and *schwarz-gelb* threads. It also implied subtle and personal involvement.[66] He derided the "atrocities of antiliberal anthropophagi," who hated liberals because all liberals, in their opinion, were of the same cloth: they were "yearning for other peoples' property, especially wife, subverting everything, trampling with their feet on every accepted principle and custom, scorning every religion, defiling every authority, and

[65] Ferenczi, ed., *A kelet népe*, pp. 361–66, 372–77.
[66] *Ibid.*, pp. 359, 366–72.

perhaps even stealing now and then a silver spoon out of carelessness or natural instinct." If this assumption were true, Széchenyi added, then indeed decent men ought to turn their backs on liberalism. He conceded that there were many hypocrits, and even more fools, wearing the philantropic mantle of liberalism. But he strongly objected to the outright condemnation of those whose philanthropy was manifest in deeds rather than lip service.

In a similarly sarcastic vein, he rejected the profanation of the *juste milieu*. Repaying 50 florins of a debt of hundred, or pulling out of the fire only one-half of a fellow man's burning body did not fit the rules of the golden mean. But to stand one's ground, fearless of government pressure or popular fads, was worthy of that *juste milieu* for which he longed to live and die.[67]

These telling parts of *A kelet népe* are relevant to an understanding of Széchenyi as a man and politician. Besides the sincere patriotism and anguish, that pervaded the entire work, they explain, why Eötvös could conclude his superb contribution to the debate[68] by reasserting what he had written earlier to Szalay that Széchenyi would never join the enemies of progress.[69] With tact, but convincingly, as Széchenyi himself noted,[70] Eötvös repeated in public what he tried to say in private: the dark picture presented by Széchenyi was overdrawn. Still, this noblest of Hungarian reformers ended his study on a conciliatory note. But Wesselényi, in a letter to Deák, condemned Széchenyi's work in strong language; Deák agreed with him that the book could be interpreted as an apologia of the administration's previous terroristic policy applied against the opposition. He would have given "much, very much, if the 'People of the Orient' had not appeared."[71]

Deák's resentment is understandable. Széchenyi did not stop at attacking Kossuth. He also sneered at efforts to establish kindergartens, improve prisons, support a society for the dissemination of useful knowledge, and to raise money for a statue of King Matthias Corvinus by the Hungarian sculptor Stephen Ferenczy. He reproached *Pesti Hirlap* for advocating such actions, because in his view they were either superfluous and beyond the country's means, or premature improvisations lacking adequate planning.[72] Again he wrote about the initiatives of other people,

[67] *Ibid.*, pp. 391 ff.
[68] József Eötvös, *Kelet Népe és Pesti Hirlap* (*People of the Orient* and *Pesti Hirlap*) (Pest: Landerer and Heckenast, 1841), republished in Ferenczi, ed., *A kelet népe*, pp. 525–86.
[69] *Ibid.*, p. 586.
[70] Sept. 2, 1841, Viszota, ed., *Naplók*, v, 496. Ferenczi, in his introduction to *A kelet népe*, misread, and consequently misinterpreted, the pertinent place in Széchenyi's diary (p. 75).
[71] Cited in Ferenczi, ed., *A kelet népe*, pp. 65–68.
[72] *Ibid.*, pp. 309–15.

however well-intentioned they might have been, as Metternich wrote about Széchenyi's endeavors. As Dessewffy said, Széchenyi too had some pet projects, such as the *Wallhalla,* the suggested burial place for great Hungarians, that were not urgently needed.[73] Scrutinizing Széchenyi's charges, Eötvös, whose essay was the first and perhaps the best piece of the mushrooming literature which dealt with the Széchenyi-Kossuth debate after the publication of *A kelet népe,* answered them in the true spirit of the earlier teachings of the greatest Hungarian. The enterprises scorned by Széchenyi, he said, could be regarded as parts of the process of educating the Hungarian nation. This being the case, he proceeded to examine the educational principles propounded by the author of *The People of the Orient.*[74]

As in his previous writings,[75] Széchenyi continued to assert the significance of public education, which ought to have precedence over everything else. He still thought of his time as of an age of enlightenment, when the banner of nationality and constitution must be carried on a road marked out by reason, science, and experience. In reality, however, he retreated from the enlightened educational ideals of his formative years,[76] when he decided to speak out against the principle of universal education. Unless the proponents of popular education intended "to drive the nation through a perfect revolution," he argued, the "national body," already aroused and growing, should not be artificially stimulated by education before securing a broader political existence for all the inhabitants of Hungary. Scoffing at the intellectual proletariat, composed of useless speechmakers, scribblers, and general planners, and produced by an anomalous and complicated educational system, he yet wanted to postpone the reform of education under the pretext that its implementation did not depend entirely on the nation. Fearful of revolutionary crisis, he advanced the liberal-sounding scheme of gradually strengthening Hungary's political foundations until he could submit a logical and safe plan for the education of the Magyar who had just been awakened from his deadly sleep.[77]

The arguments set forth by Széchenyi were partially true. But Eötvös, who became minister of education in the first responsible Hungarian government in 1848 and held the same post after the Compromise of 1867, refuted Széchenyi's arguments one by one. According to the future architect of modern Hungary's system of public education, no Hungarian had ever done more for progress than Széchenyi; consequently he could

[73] *Ibid.,* pp. 402f., 600.
[74] *Ibid.,* pp. 538–53.
[75] Cf. Ch. VI, 205, 207f.
[76] Ferenczi, ed., *A kelet népe,* p. 393. Cf. Ch. III, 88ff.
[77] Ferenczi, ed., *A kelet népe,* pp. 400f.

not be an enemy of education. To the question of whether the extension of constitutional rights should precede the establishment of a national system of public education, Eötvös replied, on the basis of many foreign examples, that political liberty usually followed the spread of civilization and no legislator had ever granted political rights to the people with the purpose of lessening the danger of their education, a procedure suggested by Széchenyi. On the contrary, education was the only reliable foundation of progress and prerequisite for increasing the number of those capable of exercising their civil rights. Public education was the more urgent because Eötvös agreed with Széchenyi that the maintenance and strengthening of Magyar nationality should be given even higher priority than the defense of constitutional liberty. But in Hungary, Eötvös argued, Magyars were barely one-half of the population, and "the beautiful Magyar word" could be one of the strong links which could "unite in one sentiment" the multilingual inhabitants of the country. Since, as Széchenyi said, the expansion of Magyardom depended on the extension of the blessings of the constitution to all—and in order to achieve this goal the nation must be governed by reason, which in turn could prevail only if the people were educated—Eötvös concluded that national and public education took precedence over any other issue.[78]

Eötvös's line of argument was far from flawless, as shown by his references to the Slavic "nationality," that "greatest of dangers," which menaced Magyar national culture.[79] But it was more logical than Széchenyi's involved argument, and more progressive, with the exception of the implications of the nationality question just mentioned. Besides Kossuth and other liberals, Aurel Dessewffy, too, agreed with Eötvös wholeheartedly on the matter of education.[80] In the spring of 1841 the administration itself began to give serious consideration to the establishment of training institutes for teachers (*Präparanden*) and schools for the education of village youth. This move was partly to anticipate the Diet's initiative, certain to be forthcoming, and partly to keep educational matters in the sphere of royal prerogative, where they had traditionally been.[81]

The discussion of the role of education in the nation's life showed that Széchenyi's fear of falling between two stools, which he expressed at the beginning of his work, was a possibility, although Eötvös denied it, saying that the esteemed count would neither lose his popularity nor could his nation be ungrateful to him.[82] It is noteworthy that on

---

[78] *Ibid.*, pp. 543–53.
[79] *Ibid.*, p. 551.
[80] *Ibid.*, p. 600.
[81] *Kabinettsarchiv, Staatskonferenzakten*, no. 388/1841, Staatsarchiv (Vienna).
[82] Ferenczi, ed., *A kelet népe*, pp. 230, 586.

one important point Eötvös came close to Széchenyi's view: he agreed that education of the people could create a dangerous situation, namely, if one part of the nation were in servitude while those exercising arbitrary rule over it intended to maintain their despotism. This single example implied that there was room for honest disagreement over whether or not the majority of the nobility was willing to give up its privileges. In answering this question in the negative, Széchenyi was probably more realistic than his opponents.[83]

Even so, the conservative turn in Széchenyi's public attitude, motivated by his growing abhorrence of the possibility of a revolutionary explosion in Hungary, is unmistakable. This can be judged also by his new emphasis on the potential damage from the irresponsible, reckless, and unrestricted application of "mankind's two greatest benefactors, freedom of speech and press."[84] It is true that Széchenyi much more than Deák recognized the potentialities of the press in arousing the masses. His sharp eye also detected the dynamic quality of the leadership given by Kossuth well before others would even think of its implications. But the charges he brought against Kossuth were frequently similar to the ones brought against him a decade before.[85] Like Cardinal Richelieu, Széchenyi too seemed to have become apprehensive lest literacy, profaned by being made available to "all kinds of persons" should lead more people to develop rather than resolve doubts. Like the founder of the French Academy some 200 years earlier, he thought a well-organized state needed "more masters in the mechanical arts than in the liberal arts to teach letters . . ."[86]

The ambivalence of his book *The People of the Orient* and some of his actions behind the scenes, such as the request for more rather than less censorship, suggests that Széchenyi could be swept to the brink of political reaction. That this did not go unnoticed is shown by the correspondence of Deák and Wesselényi. But only Kossuth publicly hinted at this possibility, and in a muffled and highly sophisticated manner. To the book-length critique of *Pesti Hirlap* he too answered with a book, which appeared in early September. By that time Széchenyi had all but lost his case in the eyes of his liberal friends and the public at large. The youth of Pest organized a torchlight serenade immediately after the publication of Széchenyi's attack on *Pesti Hirlap,* assuring the

[83] Sándor Imre, "A közoktatásügy és gróf Széchenyi István" (Public Education and Count Stephen Széchenyi), *Budapesti Szemle,* cxv (1903), 19.

[84] Ferenczi, ed., *A kelet népe,* pp. 296, 299, 301, 348–52.

[85] See Ch. VI, 213-17, 230f., 242f.

[86] "De l'instruction publique. La réforme des collèges," *Oeuvres du Cardinal de Richelieu,* avec une introduction et des notes par Roger Gaucheron; notice de Jacques Bainville (Paris: J. Taillandier, 1929), pp. 183f.

editor that the Hungarian people had outgrown the period of tutelage. Kossuth was asked to persist in defending truth and justice regardless of the rank and monopolistic claims of the "sower of the seed," who had been bypassed by time.[87] Upon reading Eötvös's defense of Kossuth shortly after its appearance at the end of August, Széchenyi remarked that it would be impossible to act more dangerously against him. Following Kossuth's reply a few days later, he acknowledged that Kossuth had skillfully extricated himself from the noose. Characteristically, he added in the same diary entry: "There are moments when I doubt if it was right to come out with *Hitel* and *A kelet népe*. Once doubt has taken possession of our soul, our happiness on earth is over."[88]

Thus wrote Hungary's reformer two weeks before his 50th birthday. Highly subjective, his feelings of futility about his lifework was not without tragic overtones. In *A kelet népe* he protested that at the time of his agitation Hungarians had to be aroused from their deadly sleep; yet when the nation was on the move, as it seemed to have been in the past 15 years, further agitation could undermine its very existence. Consequently any parallel between his and Kossuth's agitation was misleading and could have dangerous consequences. The transition to nationhood could be accomplished without human blood and revolutionary crises in an age of reason, he insisted, especially since the majority of Hungarians were willing to move ahead under proper guidance if shown the correct direction.[89] Admitting that Hungary was still very far from being a civilized country ("even today, the greatest part of our blood vegetates at the level of animals"), he nevertheless expressed the hope that gradual extension of the constitution, equality before the law, broad-base taxation, pending enactment of the abolition of the law of entail, fair conscription of all able-bodied men for service in the army, and a series of economic measures to be put into effect systematically and with the help of the administration—in sum, peaceful reform—made "Jacobin" propaganda and heartbreaking lamentation superfluous and most unfortunate.[90]

Kossuth failed to share Széchenyi's optimism about the imminence of the abolition of the law of aviticity, the improvement of the peasant's lot, or the fair administration of justice.[91] History proved him right,

---

[87] Ferenczi, ed., *A kelet népe*, pp. 63f., 75. Cf. June 28, 1841, Viszota, ed., *Naplók*, v, 482. For Klauzál's remark that Széchenyi had done much damage with his book, cf. Nov. 27, 1841, *ibid.*, p. 520. Cf. Sedlnitzky's report of July 5, 1841, No. 519/1841, *Kabinettsarchiv, Staatskonferenzakten*, Staatsarchiv (Vienna).

[88] Sept. 2, 7, 1841, Viszota, ed., *Naplók*, v, 496.

[89] Ferenczi, ed., *A kelet népe*, pp. 376–90.

[90] *Ibid.*, pp. 387, 393–97.

[91] *Ibid.*, pp. 483–94.

because for the majority of the Hungarian nobility even Széchenyi's moderate program was too radical before 1848. In the article that announced the publication of Széchenyi's book, and in his reply to it as well, Kossuth repeatedly stressed that Széchenyi *was* the greatest Magyar, who had contributed most to the maturing of Hungarians in the past 10 to 15 years.[92] Using some of Széchenyi's extreme statements—such as his contention that a single lead article in *Pesti Hirlap* could spark the fire, as a result of which the nation could be pushed into its grave,[93] and giving many citations from his opponent's writings and speeches— Kossuth denied that his agitation went any further than that of Széchenyi's.[94] He also questioned Széchenyi's attempt to build a theory of government on metaphors which intimated that there were young and aged peoples. This, said Kossuth, could imply that some peoples must reach a stage of decline and die, whereas human perfectibility had no limits and nations could die only by committing suicide.[95]

While he agreed with Széchenyi, that there was no more need for agitation against the administration, Kossuth stressed the necessity of continuously stimulating the development of national life. To apply the appropriate stimuli was the task of *Pesti Hirlap,* Kossuth contended, and to prove his point he himself resorted to a metaphor. When the Diet of 1839–40 appeared to have settled the major disputes of the previous four years, the nation showed signs of exhaustion. Shortly after the Diet, however, the issue of mixed marriages was put on the agenda; as a result of public discussion of this grievance the nation was prevented from falling asleep again.[96]

One of the most interesting aspects of Kossuth's restrained yet hard-hitting reply of Széchenyi's accusations was his assessment of Széchenyi's part in the Hungarian national awakening. In the autobiographical first section of his book, Széchenyi depicted himself as the carefully calculating but isolated hero who decided to enrich the world with a new nation. Ever since he was born, Széchenyi wrote, he had cherished the unspeakable desire to advance the Hungarian nation. After an internal struggle which lasted several days, he made up his mind in 1825 that he, "if no one else," would lay the foundation of Hungary's future glory.[97]

---

[92] *Ibid.*, pp. 60–63, 418, 482.

[93] *Ibid.*, pp. 317–46.

[94] *Ibid.*, pp. 502–24.

[95] *Ibid.*, pp. 428f.

[96] *Ibid.*, pp. 480f. See Ch. VIII, 360f. For the lasting excitement generated by this issue, and Széchenyi's efforts to cool the overheated atmosphere of the county congregation of Pest, cf. Jan. 28, 30, 31, 1842, Viszota, ed., *Naplók*, v, 545–48. Ironically, the Lutheran Kossuth's marriage to a Catholic became one of the first test cases in the dispute between secular authorities and the Catholic hierarchy.

[97] Ferenczi, ed., *A kelet népe*, pp. 222ff.

Kossuth, however, rejected the romantic image of the nation-creating demiurge. In his opinion, Széchenyi was the greatest of all Hungarians because "he had put his finger on the artery of the age and had felt its pulse." Accordingly, "Count Széchenyi was overwhelmed by the needs of the age at the right moment. He became the tongue of his age; he put the thoughts of the nation's best sons into words. This is the secret of his influence."[98] With one hand Kossuth sculptured Széchenyi in marble for eternity. With the other, he tried to remove him from the daily political struggle into the aloof sphere of timelessness. By making the greatest Magyar a statue on a pedestal, and by saying that this statute was the product of a historical moment, he strongly implied that monuments stay put while time moves on. Arguments that Hungarians were not a dying nation at the time of Széchenyi's emergence and that he did not appreciate the county assemblies, which were the workshop of national life, conveyed the same message.[99]

The two men's sincerely held views of Széchenyi's role in Hungarian political life were almost diametrically opposed. They gave different answers to a basic question of the day, namely, whether the initiator of Hungarian reform had the right (and power) to stop the reform movement at a certain point, and whether Széchenyi himself was creator or creature of the national renaissance.

Considered in their historical context of 1825, the two sides of the same question do not seem that far apart. True, during the decade preceding the Diet of 1825, Széchenyi accumulated a great deal of practical experience and theoretical knowledge which prepared him for the role that he assumed in the mid-twenties. If he had no elaborate, preconceived plan for the reform of Hungary, as he may have felt in 1841 on looking back over 16 years of tremendous activity, his basic ideas on the necessity for reform and his practical approach toward it were certainly formed by 1825. He learned these ideas about society, constitution, reform, and progress abroad and from foreign, mainly Western, authors. He was by no means a product of the atmosphere of national opposition, as were such leaders of the Hungarian liberal movement as Wesselényi, Kölcsey, Kossuth, and Deák. Thus far, Kossuth's interpretation as of 1825 seems insufficient, particularly if one remembers the personal motivation which stimulated Széchenyi to enter a public career. On the other hand, one must admit that from the early twenties on, Wesselényi and Hungarian constitutional thought presented a considerable challenge to Széchenyi. Leaving aside his personal drive, Széchenyi's success in demonstrating the practicability of many Western ideas

[98] *Ibid.*, p. 421.
[99] *Ibid.*, pp. 418–22, 433f.

in Hungary was an indication that Kossuth was not entirely wrong in explaining Széchenyi's "secret" by saying that he had felt the pulse of the nation. Otherwise the effect produced by Széchenyi's works on the younger generation would not be understandable. One could perhaps say, with the historian Michael Horváth, that Széchenyi was not only an expression of the latent desires of the Hungarian public, but also gave direction—a new direction—to it.[100]

In a different frame of reference, Széchenyi appeared on the political scene at a time when both he and the politically conscious Hungarians were trying to find themselves. Because of a historical coincidence, he and his compatriots, from different, cosmopolitan, and Magyar, cultural spheres yet sharing the common goal of building a broader and better national community, were able to feel each other's "pulse" because their pulses began to beat to the rhythm of modern Magyar nationalism. The newly found identity of those partaking in this national renaissance drew its inspiration from the idea of "saving a nation for mankind," as the poet-politician Kölcsey put it in his *Parainesis*. This will of Magyardom to assert itself as a nation among nations was the powerful force that gave greatness and impetus to the Hungarian age of reforms.

According to Horváth, the correct interpretation of the whole Hungarian reform period depends largely on an understanding of Széchenyi's activity as a reformer. Such an understanding involves three difficulties. First, the apparent lack of a consistent system in Széchenyi's reform plans, explained by Széchenyi's pragmatic approach, in which he put into practice what seemed workable and not what seemed desirable for an imaginary logical order. Second, as Horváth says, there are contradicting opinions about Széchenyi in different phases of his career. Finally, there is Széchenyi's "mysterious" mentality, which makes it difficult for the public to comprehend his behavior.

It has been said that there were two great trends in Széchenyi's career: he initiated the reform era and aroused his nation; then, frightened by the passions he himself had stirred up, he tried to prevent the younger generation led by Kossuth to accomplish the task. The two trends, which may be labeled the "liberal" and the "conservative," were not present in Széchenyi's activities in a strictly definable chronological succession, but coexisted in his outlook and actions from the very first moment of his career.[101] This is why Széchenyi can be called, with some justification, the father of both the Hungarian liberal and conservative movements, although he himself could hardly be categorized either as a

---

[100] Horváth, *Huszonöt év*, I, 199.
[101] Friedreich, *Széchenyi élete*, I, 160–67.

clearcut "liberal" or "conservative" statesman.[102] At the same time, this twofold aspect of his attitude, increasingly conspicuous from the early 1840s on, during the worsening political struggle, might have been the guarantee of lasting political success under more favorable circumstances, such as in a constitutional monarchy and a balanced society with a well-developed middle class. In Hungary, however, Széchenyi's constitutional liberalism was certain to arouse the suspicion of the Metternich regime at a time when, as Széchenyi later remarked, "nationality and constitution were covered with so many wounds, and there seemed to be so little possibility for national and constitutional progress . . . that even today I cannot understand how someone could possibly have chosen anything else but an oppositional stand in the political arena of those times."[103]

Széchenyi wrote this in the midst of his polemics with Kossuth in 1844. He also added that at the beginning of his career he was pushed into opposition by Vienna's policies of "fusion and centralization" and against his will and natural inclination because, as he said, "I was never a man of negation but always felt the desire to contribute a tiny bit, so to speak, to a little creation. . . . To create, to be creative from the point of view of nationality as well as constitution, this has been and will be the wish of my soul, and not to make difficulties, obstruct, let alone destroy."[104] At the very time he was writing these lines the conservative aspects of his thought had already brought Széchenyi into sharp controversy with the more radical wing of Hungarian liberalism which, in his opinion, threatened to wreck the results of the former decades—of *his* creative work. By that time he chose to believe that Vienna had at long last realized he had been right in 1825. Assuming that the government basically had changed its former attitude toward Hungary and intended to introduce serious reforms, he decided that the real danger lay not in the court party but in irresponsible opposition. Thinking that the administration had begun to see things through his eyes, he himself came nearer, *mutatis mutandis,* to Metternich's stand of 1825. Whether or not Széchenyi's political judgment was sound in the 1840s is a question open to debate. But it goes without saying that then, too, he candidly wanted to steer a middle course between the administration and opposition, and did his best to maintain his political

---

[102] János Asbóth, "Conservativek és szabadelvűek 1825-től Világosig" (Conservatives and Liberals from 1825 to Világos), in *Irodalmi és politikai arcképek* (Literary and Political Portraits) (Budapest: Légrády, 1876), p. 124.

[103] "Opposition. I" (Opposition), *Jelenkor*, No. 13 (Feb. 15, 1844), in Viszota, ed., *Széchenyi és Kossuth*, II, 345.

[104] *Ibid.* Cf. his letter to Gervay (Dec. 5, 1842) and 2 memoranda, *ibid.*, I, 716–43.

and moral independence between the extremes. In this respect, he was probably more sincere and consistent than any other contemporary politician. What in Metternich's judgment was the dream of a *Phantast* (in itself a sufficient "objective" cause for Széchenyi's ruin as a practicing politician), was in reality a humanitarian idealism coupled with a good deal of practical common sense.

Even after the opening of his bitter public debate with Kossuth, Széchenyi continued to think of himself as a middle-of-the road liberal. Pleased with Deák's unassuming attitude and moderation when talking to young patriots, Széchenyi still regarded him at the end of 1841, "a real extinguisher" of potential fires, telling him again that he was the appropriate leader of the political center.[105] But as he grew more impatient with the "Kossuth League" his relations with the conservative Aurel Dessewffy, whom he first suspected of writing against him, became more cordial, despite the warnings of some members of the opposition that his alliance with the young tories could "paralyze" him.[106] In early November he discussed the program they both would like to support at the next Diet; later in the month, at the county congregation of Pest, he cooperated with Dessewffy against the opposition on a number of issues, including mixed marriages, the penal code, and public trials.[107] In early December it still appeared to him that he, Deák, and Dessewffy could work together, but his sympathy was already on the side of the latter.[108] Embittered by an attack on the aristocracy in the literary journal *Athenaeum*, he sneered at "the base Hungarian," and reproached himself for not having had a bright spot in his life.[109] But despite his anger caused by the radical *sansculottes*,[110] he took offense when, on February 1, 1842 in the general assembly of Pest county, one of the liberal leaders first called him a conservative. One week later, upon the sudden death of Aurel Dessewffy, Széchenyi admitted to Batthyány, the leader of the magnate opposition, that he had been worried lest the energetic tory resort to violence if given too much power by the administration.[111]

Abhorrence of violent methods thus seems to have been one of Széchenyi's guidelines in his search for the moderate course between extreme right and left. The brief political truce after the Diet of 1839–40 marked the culmination of his public career, of what is known in Hungarian

---

[105] Nov. 28, Dec. 5, 1841, Viszota, ed., *Naplók*, v, 520f., 524.

[106] Sept. 13, 20, 1841, *ibid.*, pp. 498f.

[107] Nov. 3, 4, 11, 16, 17, 18, 19, 20, 21, 24, 25, 26, 30, 1841, *ibid.*, pp. 509, 511–22. Cf. Jan. 28, 29, 30, 31, 1842, *ibid.*, pp. 545–48.

[108] Dec. 7, 18, 21, 30, 1841, *ibid.*, pp. 524f., 528ff., 533; Viszota, ed., *Széchenyi és Kossuth*, i, lxxxv-cv.

[109] Nov. 22, 23, 26, 1841, Viszota, ed., *Naplók*, v, 517ff.

[110] Nov. 27, 1841, *ibid.*, p. 520.

[111] Feb. 8, 1842, *ibid.*, pp. 551f.

history as the "age of Széchenyi." With his vehement attack on Kossuth he himself facilitated the rise of a new star over the political horizon. Although to maintain his independence he kept aloof from the new magnate opposition in the Diet of 1839–40, he was yet regarded as one of its chief leaders by friend and foe alike. But as a result of the first phase of the acrimonious Széchenyi-Kossuth debate, which lasted until the outbreak of the revolution in 1848, Széchenyi became alienated from all leaders of the liberal opposition, including Deák. At the same time, he continued to be mistrusted in Vienna.[112]

Paralleling the debate on *Pesti Hirlap* and *A kelet népe,* and partly overlapping with it, was the nationwide discussion of the "Twelve Points of Szatmár." Accepted in the form of a resolution by the county congregation of Szatmár on February 22, 1841, the "Twelve Points" were revoked under conservative pressure in the same county in December of the same year. Symbolically, and chronologically, too, this formulation of liberal demands was about halfway between the 12 "laws" of *Stádium* and the revolutionary "Twelve Points" proclaimed by the youth of Pest on March 15, 1848. The Szatmár points proposed: (1) immediate abolition of the law of entail, (2) establishment of a land bank and (3) land register, (4) compulsory redemption of the serf with compensation to the lord by a special bank which in turn would collect the installment payments from the peasant over a period of 30 years. Moreover, the February resolution of Szatmár advocated: (5) the right of all citizens to own property and (6) hold office, (7) taxation of the nobility, (8) elimination of monopolies and guilds, (9) universal popular education, the cost of which was to be covered by the secularization of church land, (10) abolition of censorship, (11) enfranchisement of city dwellers, (12) separation of the executive and judicial branches of government, liquidation of the feudal legal system and introduction of jury trials, and popular representation. Most of the counties received the circular letter containing Szatmár's "Twelve Points" in the spring of 1841. Their majority discussed them in special committees during the remainder of the year. By the late summer and fall the discussion tended to merge with the Széchenyi-Kossuth debate: those in favor of radical reform used the Szatmár program to refute Széchenyi's contention that there was no more need for agitation. Széchenyi himself, in an article on "Hungarian Conditions," published by the *Augsburger Allgemeine Zeitung* in early February 1842, sharply attacked the "Twelve Points of Szatmár." The Twelve Points advocated the immediate transformation of the Hungarian constitution and—along with the resolution of Borsod county

---

[112] July 8, 9, Aug. 19, 1841, May 18, 1842, *ibid.*, pp. 485, 492, 596f.

which demanded the confiscation of ecclesiastic land—were to lead to a new French republic. Széchenyi also warned that such a program might endanger Hungary's connection with Austria.

Still, only one county (Fejér) besides Szatmár decided to discard the Twelve Points entirely. Others kept them on their agenda, since liberals regarded them as their first tentative platform at a time when there was no organized party of opposition on the national level. In subsequent years the acceptance of the essence of the Szatmár program was tantamount to being a liberal. But the Twelve Points went well beyond *Stádium,* and by 1841 Széchenyi had abandoned some of the ideas proposed in his most radical book.[113]

One of the contributing reasons for Széchenyi's separation from the liberal opposition was his public stand on the nationality question. Even in his earlier book, *Hunnia,* he condemned forcible Magyarization and cautioned against provoking ill will among non-Magyars. But this patriotic and yet moderate work was not published before his death,[114] and his timely warnings reached the unwilling ear of the public only as parts of his protest against *Pesti Hirlap.*

In the introductory section of *A kelet népe,* which set the pathetic and patriotic tone for the entire work, Széchenyi formulated the two main goals he thought Hungarians should pursue in the immediate future: "to make our race and constitution flourish without tears, and without human sacrifice." As a prerequisite for such "peaceful reformation," he immediately admonished his compatriots that Magyardom could be advanced only on a spiritual basis, by enhancing its "moral credit" and not by insisting that "everybody submit to, or love and imitate us."[115] While wishing to "protect and unfold Magyardom" he also observed that this was only the lesser half of the task, because paradoxically its more complex part implied that spreading Magyardom might occasionally contradict the effort to disseminate among the people material goods, the arts and sciences, and even the benefits of the constitution. Approvingly quoting Paul Nagy, who had once said that given the difficult choice between the principles of nationality and liberty he would prefer the former as a safer guaranty of the nation's survival, Széchenyi yet rebuked all efforts to establish an artificial Magyar melting pot whose aim would be to press for the Magyarization of schools, science, business and industry. To eliminate German intelligence, "this greatest possible solvent of Magyardom," from the nation's economic or intellectual life,

---

[113] István Rácz, "Az 1841. évi szatmári 12 pont" (The Twelve Points of Szatmár in 1841), *Acta Universitatis Debreceniensis de Ludovico Kossuth nominatae,* II (1955), 101–23.

[114] See Ch. VII. 296-300.

[115] Ferenczi, ed., *A kelet népe,* p. 239f

could be disastrous in the present underdeveloped stage of Hungarian society. Magyardom was unable to counterbalance the overwhelming "weight" of Germandom; yet to the Germans one must add the masses of Slovaks, other Slavs, and Romanians, many of whom had brethren and coreligionist sympathizers beyond the border. How could anyone in his right mind, Széchenyi wondered, think of forcing these peoples, to abandon their nationality in order to become Magyars at a time when Hungary's constitution extended only to some 80,000 privileged families? Instead of coining derogatory adages about Slovaks, Greeks, (i.e., the Orthodox Serbs, Romanians, Ruthenes) and Germans, which poisoned the youthful mind, Széchenyi proposed a modus vivendi between Hungary's Magyar and non-Magyar population. Part of this compromise would be the development and gradual extension of the privileges of the Hungarian constitution to the greatest possible number of the country's inhabitants. Undisturbed in their mother tongue, customs, and religious creed, the non-Magyars should in turn accept Magyar as the official language of Hungary in the kingdom's public affairs in harmony with the legislation enacted after the efforts of half a century.[116]

In making his critical remarks, the father of modern Magyar nationalism did not refer to *Pesti Hirlap* or its editor, perhaps because he knew that the evil of forcible Magyarization had deeper roots and further ramifications. He himself hoped for a slow and voluntary assimilation of free peoples to be encouraged by Magyardom's spiritual supremacy as soon as it became a realistic possibility. These liberated peoples, Széchenyi believed, would come to the aid of their Magyar fellow citizens in defense of the constitutional liberty previously shared with them. He urged his compatriots not to wait too long because a sudden turn in the Oriental question could produce an "inundation of Northern peoples," thus posing a direct threat to the very existence of Hungary.[117] But the liberals, whose Russophobia and fear of the largely imaginary Panslav danger went well beyond Széchenyi's anxieties, were blind to the disruptive forces created by the indigenous nationalisms of the non-Magyar peoples of Hungary. Relying on a narrow legalistic interpretation of Magyardom's "historical" rights, the younger generation of Magyar nationalists were prone to identify the Hungarian political nation with Magyardom, making an exception only in the case of the Croats, whose constitutional entity was recognized, albeit with growing reluctance. But Croatia at least had some representatives in the Hungarian Diet, besides having its own feudal legislative assembly. Other nationalities had neither an outlet nor spokesmen within the framework of the Hungarian consti-

[116] *Ibid.*, pp. 243–54.
[117] *Ibid.*, p. 252.

tution at the time of their national awakening, which to a large extent paralleled that of the Magyars.

Before the publication of *A kelet népe* Kossuth wrote several leading articles in *Pesti Hirlap* dealing with different aspects of the nationality question. True, he repudiated some of the more vulgar ingredients of *Magyarismus* that could debase it to the level of aristocratic *rowdyism;*[118] yet the comparison, and the epithet in particular, must have irked Széchenyi. But in other articles Kossuth supported the spreading of Magyar nationality "by all legal and equitable means, especially by the stimulation of schoolmasters," expressed the hope that "unpleasant" rumors, according to which Slovak was spoken in a general congregation of an overwhelmingly Slovak county, would turn out to be untrue, insinuated that those writing about the future glory of the Slavs were agents of a "colossal power," namely Russia, and advocated the introduction of Magyar as the language of instruction to prevent the "enemies of our nationality" from exerting an influence in the schools.[119] Kossuth favored the proposal of Count Charles Zay, superintendent of the Lutheran Church, that the Lutheran and Calvinist institutions of higher learning be merged, since this would be in the interest of Magyar national education and would strengthen the Magyar leadership of Protestantism in Hungary.[120] Two leaders of *Pesti Hirlap* were devoted to the problem of the political-administrative unification of Hungary and Transylvania, a necessary step, as Kossuth pointed out, toward the creation of one unified Magyar nation. Without Magyar unity Hungary had no chance of fulfilling its mission between the German and Slav giants. Consequently, the aristocratic aloofness of Transylvania from Hungary's vital problems should cease.[121]

There were many obstacles in the way of Transylvania's reincorporation into Hungary, a request going back to the 18th century and reiterated at every Hungarian Diet after 1825.[122] Hungary's Diet consisted of two chambers; Transylvania had a unicameral legislative body. This did not mean that the Transylvanian Diet was more "democratic" or representative than its Hungarian counterpart—many of its members attended ex officio or owed their seats to royal favor. The majority of Transylvania's people were Romanian, but Romanians were not one of the three constitutionally recognized nations (Magyars, Magyar-speaking Szeklers, and Saxon Germans), nor did the nonunited Romanian Orthodox Church represent one of the four "received" religions, which

---

[118] Jan. 16, 1841, *Pesti Hirlap*, in *ibid.*, p. 117 (emphasis in orginal).
[119] Jan. 9, Apr. 10, 1841, *Pesti Hirlap*, in *ibid.*, pp. 113f., 179–82.
[120] Mar. 17, 1841, *Pesti Hirlap*, in *ibid.*, pp. 159ff. Cf. Feb. 6, 1841, *ibid.*, pp. 130–33.
[121] Apr. 14, 17, 1841, *Pesti Hirlap*, in *ibid.*, pp. 183–88.
[122] No. 439/1848, *Kabinettsarchiv, Staatskonferenzakten,* Staatsarchiv (Vienna); Marczali, *Enchiridion,* p. 834.

since 1571 included the Calvinist and Lutheran branches of Protestanism, Roman Catholicism, and the Unitarian faith. The opposition was less well organized in Transylvania than in Hungary, especially since Wesselényi had had to withdraw from active politics. Some of its Protestant leaders hesitated to support the union movement because of the veto power of the upper table in the Hungarian Diet, which they felt was manipulated by the overrepresented Catholic hierarchy. And landowners—mostly Magyar—were in no hurry to introduce the urbarial legislation enacted by the Hungarian Diet in 1836.[123] The administration, in turn, was not anxious to strengthen the weak Transylvanian opposition by letting the "two Hungarian fatherlands" join forces under Magyar leadership.

All these difficulties were well known to Kossuth. Impressed by the strength of popular forces seeking to establish their national identity since Napoleonic times, he was convinced that the idea of national unification was the most important characteristic feature of the century. To him, the trend toward national unity was a global phenomenon: to weather the storm, inherent in a potential clash of Teuton and Slav, Magyars must unite. All separatistic and diverging interests, he argued, must yield to this superior point of view.[124]

Kossuth's pointed argument expressed a view which was an article of faith with almost all the prominent figures of 19th-century Magyar liberal nationalists before 1848, Széchenyi being the only exception. Wesselényi, who was more sensitive than his peers to the nationality question because of his Transylvanian background, nevertheless suffered from the same Russophobia.[125] Eötvös, whose goodwill toward any group of human beings was beyond question, was unable to find fault with the articles published by *Pesti Hirlap* on the question of nationalities in 1841. The author of the moderate "Nationality Act of 1868," who was the most farsighted among the remaining members of the great liberal generation after 1848, professed in his contribution to the Széchenyi-Kossuth debate that among all the newspapers which took a stand on the issue of Magyarization the leading articles of *Pesti Hirlap* revealed perhaps the greatest moderation and respect for "our non-Magyar speaking compatriots."[126]

Preoccupation with Panslavism also closed the eyes of the liberal lead-

[123] Trócsányi, *Wesselényi*, pp. 170–77, 243f.

[124] Apr. 14, 17, 1841, *Pesti Hirlap*, in Ferenczi, ed., *A kelet népe*, pp. 183–88.

[125] Wagner, "Széchenyi and the Nationality Problem," p. 306.

[126] Ferenczi, ed., *A kelet népe*, pp. 535f. This circumstance is frequently ignored in Western literature. See Johann Weber, *Eötvös und die ungarische Nationalitätenfrage* (Munich: Oldenbourg, 1966), p. 78. Like the Szekfű-school of the interwar period, this study, published as No. 64 of the *Südosteuropäische Arbeiten* (ed. Mathias Bernath), regards Széchenyi as "the most pronounced representative" (*profiliertester Vertreter*) of the Hungarian conservatives. *Ibid.*, pp. 71f.

ers to the realities of foreign policy. Although Aurel Dessewffy reminded his compatriots of the centuries-long struggle between Slavs and called their attention to the religious and historical differences between them,[127] the liberals failed to appreciate the importance of the existing Austro-Russian-Prussian alliance, overstated the political immediacy of the presumed Russian support of the Panslav and Panorthodox menace, and underestimated the autochthonous nation-forming processes unfolding among the non-Magyar peoples of Hungary and the other Habsburg lands. Their failure to do so was partly due to the illusion that the prospect of establishing an independent and strong Hungary in alliance with Austria was not only feasible but even preferred by Vienna to relying on the support of its traditional allies. The illusion was formulated by Deák in his reply to Széchenyi's inquiry in March 1841; a few days later he wrote to Wesselényi in a similar vein.[128]

As can be seen, Kossuth was not alone with his unrealistic conception of the international balance of forces, although his sharp pen contributed to its perpetuation. In his previously mentioned articles about the urgency of the union with Transylvania he insisted that it was the "inevitable mission" of the Magyars to ally themselves to those with whom they shared a common dynasty and "common ideals of civilization, justice, and liberty," against those who made independence impossible and who "threaten to swallow up our nationality, whose vanguard is barbarism, and whose tradition consists of bondage and servitude."[129]

In the early 1830s Széchenyi and other leaders of the liberal opposition formulated a program of gradual reform with the aim of harmonizing the interests of all social classes in Hungary. It included general taxation, equality before the law, compulsory redemption of the serf's obligation for the land he tilled, with due compensation to the lord, as well as the step-by-step extension of civil rights to the underprivileged. It is noteworthy that Kossuth was the first to include the non-Magyar peasants in the idea of the "unification of interests." This largely socio-economically oriented domestic program was supplemented, in the early forties by the increasingly emphatic demand for the redefinition of Hungary's position in the monarchy and in international relations. Fear of the "northern colossus" and the numerical superiority of non-Magyars in

---

[127] Ferenczi, *A kelet népe*, ed., p. 601.

[128] Cited by Miklós Asztalos, *Wesselényi Miklós, az első nemzetiségi politikus* (Nicholas Wesselényi, the First Politician [Aware] of the Nationality Question) (Pécs: Karl, 1927), pp. 46f.

[129] Apr. 14, 1841, *Pesti Hirlap*, in Ferenczi, ed., *A kelet népe*, pp. 184f. Cf. Kosáry, *Kossuth és a Védegylet*, pp. 25f., and Kossuth's report on the Diet of 1847–48, in István Barta, ed., *Kossuth Lajos az utolsó rendi országgyűlésen* (Louis Kossuth at the Last Feudal Diet) (Budapest: Akadémiai kiadó, 1951), pp. 742ff. (*KLÖM*, xi).

Hungary were among the chief motivating factors. Széchenyi more or less shared these fears. But whereas he tried to dissuade his liberal friends from pressing the issue, Wesselényi, Eötvös, and Kossuth refused to desist. Stressing the need for solidarity between the German and Magyar "element," all three also emphasized the desirability of the constitutional transformation of Austria increasing thereby both Vienna's and the non-Magyar population's resentment of Magyar liberalism.[130]

This expanded program of Magyar liberal nationalism, as Széchenyi correctly sensed it, had far-reaching international implications. Writing in *Pesti Hirlap* Kossuth spelled out the "historical right of the Magyar nation" as follows:

In Hungary, Magyar should be the language of the public administration, whether civil or ecclesiastic, of the legislative and executive branches of the government [including] the judiciary, and [all matters related to] public safety, the police, direct and indirect taxation, and the [local] administration.[131]

This incipient Magyar imperialism, to which even conservatives had to make concessions, turned into a widely held popular creed. In 1832 Francis I rejected a request submitted by Esztergom county, one of the strongholds of clerical influence, which suggested that foreign names be Magyarized all over Hungary.[132] But as the years went by, the younger liberal generation, inspired by the literary and national renaissance of the 1830s, succeeded in forcing Vienna to yield in some areas—as shown by the new language laws which step by step approached the goal of making Magyar the official language of the kingdom. Ironically, much of the bitterness of subsequent conflicts stemmed from the fact that some demands of Magyar patriots were quite justified. Trying to enlist Széchenyi's help in reforming the bylaws of the Academy at the end of 1832, Hungary's poet laureat, Vörösmarty, proposed the creation of an award for the writing of a good history textbook for elementary schools and the introduction of Magyar as the language of teaching *"at least in a few* disciplines."[133] From the point of view of the Magyar cultural revival, the main problem of Hungarian education was still the predominance of Latin in the schools,[134] and efforts to change this

[130] For references cf. George Barany, "Hungary: the Uncompromising Compromise," *Austrian History Yearbook*, III, Pt. 1 (1967), 239f.

[131] As cited in Asztalos, *Wesselényi*, p. 51.

[132] No. 993/1832, *MKA*, Staatsarchiv (Vienna).

[133] Viszota, "Széchenyi, Vörösmarty, és az akadémia," p. 10 (emphasis added).

[134] Mátyás Bajkó, "A debreceni felsőoktatás a reformkorban" (Higher Education in Debrecen in the Age of Reform), *Acta Universitatis Debreceniensis de Ludovico Kossuth*

anachronism were natural. Complications arose, however, because
Magyar nationalists failed to differentiate between schools in purely
Magyar- and non-Magyar-inhabited regions. In fact, they wished to use
the per se legitimate process of eliminating Latin as the language of
general instruction from schools above the elementary level as one of
the tools to speed up Magyarization among the intelligentsia. Other
powerful levers were the county administrations and the clergy, especially
after the legislation of the Diet of 1839–40.[135]

Discussions among liberals during and after the Diet focused mainly
on the issue of how to Magyarize, but did not question the goal itself.
They indicated that the relationship between large segments of the politically articulate Magyars and non-Magyars had deteriorated considerably
in the decade preceding the publication of *Pesti Hirlap;* but Kossuth's
paper and his articles further aggravated the situation. The liberal
nationalists rested their case on the mistaken assumption that no human
or national rights were violated if the use of the non-Magyar languages
was limited to private life. They deluded themselves into believing that
the non-Magyars in the kingdom would be forever grateful to the Hungarians if they only extended the constitutional privileges of the nobility
to them and guaranteed their individual, if not their national, rights.[136]

This belief, developed in Wesselényi's *Admonition in Regard to
Magyar and Slav Nationality,* a book published in 1843,[137] confirmed
forcefully by Kossuth on the eve of the revolution of 1848 and codified
by Deák in the nationality law under the concept of the Hungarian
"political nation" 20 years later, interpreted Hungary's integrity as meaning that the Magyar nation alone possessed exclusive national rights
in that ancient kingdom.[138]

The emphasis of Magyardom's exclusive claim to nationhood in the
lands of the Crown St. Stephen, which was the official creed of almost
all Magyar politicians until the end of World War II, was unacceptable
to non-Magyars. Indeed, spokesmen of the latter behaved in many respects as did their Magyar competitors who, on the whole, were in
a better strategic position to force Vienna's hand. Yet in the old game

---

nominatae, II (1955), 14–36. In 1844, the year Magyar officially became the language of
the state, there was no textbook for the teaching of the Magyar language in the high
schools. No. 105/1848, *Kabinettsarchiv, Staatskonferenzakten,* Staatsarchiv (Vienna).

[135] See Ch. VIII, 354f.

[136] Jászi, *The Dissolution of the Habsburg Monarchy,* pp. 307f.; Kornis, *A magyar művelődés,* II, 145f.; Asztalos, *Wesselényi,* pp. 19, 47f.

[137] Miklós Wesselényi, *Szózat a magyar és szláv nemzetiség ügyében* (Admonition in Regard to Magyar and Slav Nationality), ed. István Gál, 2 vols. (Kolozsvár: Minerva, n.d.
[1944]).

[138] Barany, "The Awakening of Magyar Nationalism," pp. 41ff.; Arató, *A nemzetiségi kérdés,* II, 34–48.

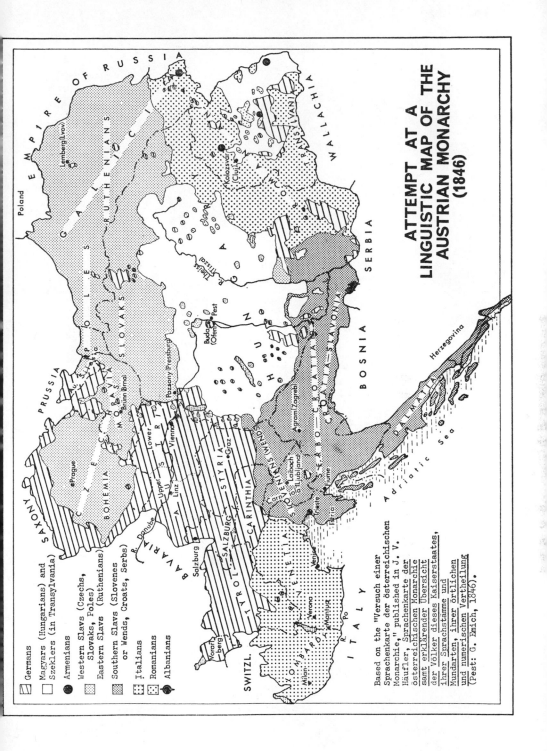

**ATTEMPT AT A
LINGUISTIC MAP OF THE
AUSTRIAN MONARCHY
(1846)**

Germans

Magyars (Hungarians) and
Szeklers (in Transylvania)

Armenians

Western Slavs (Czechs,
Slovaks, Poles)

Eastern Slavs (Ruthenians)

Southern Slavs (Slovenes
or Wends, Croats, Serbs)

Italians

Romanians

Albanians

Based on the "Versuch einer
Sprachenkarte der österreichischen
Monarchie," published in J. V.
Häufler, Sprachenkarte der
österreichischen Monarchie
samt erklärender Übersicht
der Völker dieses Kaiserstaates,
ihrer Sprachstamme und
Mundarten, ihrer örtlichen
und numerischen Vertheilung
(Pest: G. Emich, 1846).

EMPIRE OF RUSSIA

Poland

GALICIA

RUTHENIANS

Lemberg (Lvov)

POLES

PRUSSIA

SAXONY

SLOVAKS

Prague

BOHEMIA

CZECHS

MORAVIA

Brünn (Brno)

Pozsony (Pressburg)

Buda (Ofen) Pest

H U N G A R Y

Theiss (Tisza)

TRANSYLVANIA

Kolozsvár (Cluj)

WALLACHIA

SERBIA

BOSNIA

Herzegovina

DALMATIA

Adriatic Sea

CROATIA

SLAVONIA

agram (Zagreb)

Fiume

SLOVENES or WENDS

Laibach (Ljubljana)

Istria

Trieste

CARINTHIA

STYRIA

Graz

Vienna

Lower AUSTRIA

Upper AUSTRIA

Linz

R. Danube

SALZBURG

Salzburg

TYROL

Vorarlberg

SWITZL.

BAVARIA

ITALY

LOMBARDY-VENETIA

Milan

Verona

Venice

Montua

R. Po

R. Adige

of divide and rule, played cautiously but not without skill by the administration, anti-Magyar trends as represented by the Croatian Ljudevit Gaj, father of the Southern Slav ideology of Illyrism, found an influential patron in the person of Kolowrat. Potentially more menacing than the traditional autonomism advocated by the Croatian estates, the propagation of the idea of a Greater Illyria under Panslav auspices was forbidden only in 1843, when Metternich's conservative but essentially pro-Hungarian views began to prevail.[139]

Even without the reluctance of the court and the Hungarian aulic party in power, the exaggerated demands of Magyar nationalists were doomed to failure because of the socio-economic and cultural gains made by all non-Magyar nationalists of Hungary, with the possible exception of the Ruthenians.[140] Despite the relative weakness of this incipient non-Magyar bourgeoisie, if one compared it to its counterpart in more advanced Western countries and even Austria, and despite the lack of realism characteristic of the mystic dreams of the Panslav Slovak poet-pastor, Ján Kollár, Magyar nationalism alone was not strong enough to overcome the combination of forces opposed to its aggressive drive. For Magyardom, as Széchenyi correctly judged it, had yet much to learn and was only one of the peoples east of the Rhine and the Alps, all of whom "shared a common fate: they entered the age of nationalism at a time when the nation-state solution of the West was no longer applicable," although, in Hans Kohn's concise words, "The great historical dynastic states of Central and Eastern Europe were bound to undergo a thorough process of liberal and administrative reforms."[141]

Like the other liberal nationalists, Széchenyi, too, wanted to Magyarize. But he wished to rely solely on the hoped-for attraction of Magyardom's spiritual supremacy yet to be achieved. In his work, *The People of the Orient,* he openly declared that true patriotism was incompatible with forcible Magyarizing campaigns. His public stand on the nationality question thus was similar to that of Aurel Dessewffy and other conservatives, although their motives were different.[142] True, moderates such as Deák, Eötvös, and even Batthyány, were closer to Széchenyi than to Kossuth, Pulszky, and the more radical wing of the liberals in this particular question.[143] But they refrained from taking a highly unpopular

[139] *Ibid.,* II, 66–71, Kann, *The Multinational Empire,* I, 246–50.

[140] *Ibid.,* I, 160ff., 226ff., 239–50, 275ff., 285f., 309ff., 320–23; Arató, *A nemzetiségi kérdés,* II, 5–33; Harold Steinacker, *Austro-Hungarica* (Munich: Oldenbourg, 1963), pp. 348–62. In *Buchreihe der Südostdeutschen Historischen Kommission,* VIII.

[141] Hans Kohn, *Pan-Slavism,* 2d. edn., revised (New York: Vintage Russian Library, 1960), pp. 74f.

[142] See Dessewffy's article, written at the end of 1840, "Protestantismus, Magyarismus, Slavismus," in *Aus den Papieren des Grafen Aurel Dessewffy,* II, 90–97.

[143] Arató, *A nemzetiségi kérdés,* II, 52–55.

stand which might have split the ranks of the opposition. So it happened that Széchenyi's caveat, given in *A kelet népe,* which advocated decent treatment of non-Magyars, found little public echo, especially after the untimely death of Aurel Dessewffy in early 1841.

New signs of the worsening of Hungarian-Croatian relations in the spring of 1842, which led to a resolution of Pest county, favoring, upon Kossuth's suggestion, the repeal of the union between Hungary and Croatia to avoid further conflicts, and Kossuth's article on the "Slav question," taunted Széchenyi to repeat his warning in a more emphatic form. First he thought of writing another book as a sequel to *A kelet népe,* starting out with the nationality question but also taking to task, besides Kossuth, those who supported him—Pulszky, Eötvös, Batthyány, and Wesselényi. Subsequently however, he changed his mind and decided on a more dramatic course.[144]

Ever since 1832, when Count Joseph Teleki, president of the Academy, was appointed court councillor in Vienna, Széchenyi, in his capacity as vice-president, was the de facto supervisor of the Academy's affairs, although he refused the presidency offered to him.[145] In November 1842, 17 years after he had founded his "firstling," he decided to address the annual meeting of the Academy in person. Széchenyi still contended that a country should assign priority to the cultivation of the national idiom even over the sciences and applied technology, because this was the foremost guarantee of national life. But he gave no quarter to those whose patriotism was exhausted by indulging in the propagation of the outward signs of Magyardom and in the provocation of peoples of different ethnic background. Nationality is a category of quality produced by moral supremacy rather than quantity increased by administrative fiat, warned the father of Magyar nationalism, adding: "Magyar word is not Magyar feeling; to be Magyar is not necessarily identical with being virtuous; to wear the mantle of patriotism does not make you a patriot." Excesses, whipping up passions and turning the Magyar idiom into an object of hatred rather than cultivating it, Széchenyi stressed, inevitably result in retaliation, and despotism exercised over the body must not be confused with ascendancy over the soul. Deploring sermons given in Magyar upon command, and any other form of flag-waving and jingoism, the greatest Magyar summoned his compatriots to abide

[144] The fragments of Széchenyi's planned sequel to *A kelet népe,* to which he assigned the title *Garat* (Hopper), were collected and published by Gyula Viszota, who also wrote the genesis of the work beginning with Széchenyi's shock, expressed over the sudden death of Aurel Dessewffy and tracing it to the circumstances that made it sink into oblivion. Gyula Viszota, ed., *Garat,* irta 1842–ben gróf Széchenyi István (Hopper, Written by Count Stephen Széchenyi in 1842) (Budapest: Magyar Tudományos Akadémia, 1912), pp. 209–18.

[145] Viszota, "Széchenyi, Vörösmarty, és az akadémia," p. 2.

by the rules of equity and justice based on a strict observation of the letter and spirit of the law. Repeatedly in his speech, Széchenyi expressed grave doubts about Magyardom's future. The man who had once so confidently predicted the fatherland's "brighter dawn,"[146] now himself questioned his people's future, warning that unless the nation could learn to discipline itself, Hungary could soon be a country that had been.

The revocation of the winged words coined in the concluding part of *Hitel* by Széchenyi a mere dozen years later in his "Cassandra speech" stunned the public but failed to diminish Kossuth's influence. If anything, it increased his isolation, as he himself termed it in his academic address, from the overwhelming majority of Magyar patriots on one of the crucial issues Hungary must face in generations to come. Only spokesmen of different nationalities, among whom Széchenyi's economic enterprises, especially his work on the Lower Danube, had aroused much interest even before *A kelet népe* and his speech delivered at the Academy, greeted his views with enthusiasm. Leaders of the Slovak intelligentsia—Kollár, and the Croatian Gaj, the Transylvanian Saxon, Gustav Steinacker, who wrote a special poem to him, and others—referred to Széchenyi's idea of mutual tolerance and cooperation among Danubian nations as the example to be followed.[147] Admittedly, Széchenyi would probably have been reluctant to accept the formula set forth by the Czech Palacký in his famous reply to the German National Assembly of Frankfurt in 1848: ". . . with all my ardent love of my nation I always esteem more highly the good of mankind and of learning than the good of the nation . . . ."[148] But he had the moral courage of turning against the popular tide of Magyar nationalism at the acme of his career, which few statesmen are willing to do. This attitude alone makes him worthy of the respect of the "father of Czech historiography,"[149] and of posterity, too.

The outpouring of gratitude from non-Magyars, however encouraging from an ethical standpoint, did not improve Széchenyi's chances against Kossuth or more radical Magyar nationalists. He must have felt that, in Goethe's words, "Upon the creatures we have made/We are, ourselves, at last, dependent."[150] This, of course, was part of Széchenyi's personal

---

[146] Cf. Ch. VI, 212f. For complete text of Széchenyi's speech, Nov. 27, 1842, see Viszota, ed., *Széchenyi és Kossuth*, I, 149–96. For Pulszky's report on it and for Wesselényi's and Kossuth's declarations in *Pesti Hirlap*, all expressing their author's shock and dismay, cf. *ibid.*, pp. 196–207. For Viszota's analysis in the introduction, *ibid.*, pp. cv–cxxvi.

[147] For further references cf. Arató, *A nemzetiségi kérdés*, I, 166–69, 350f., II, 51f., 236f.; for possible parallelisms between Széchenyi's academic address of 1842 and Stephen Ludwig Roth's *Sprachkampf in Siebenbürgen*, published in August of the same year, see Otto Folberth, *Der Prozess Stephan Ludwig Roth* (Graz-Cologne: Böhlaus Nachf., 1959), pp. 237–46 (Vol. I of *Veröffentlichungen der Arbeitsgemeinschaft Ost.*) Roth, a Transylvanian Saxon, was the disciple of the Swiss educational reformer, Johann Heinrich Pestalozzi.

[148] Cited by Kohn, *Pan-Slavism*, p. 77.   [149] Cf. Ch. I, 8.

[150] Goethe, *Faust*, trans. Bayard Taylor (Modern Library,) Pt. II, Act II, p. 81.

tragedy. To understand why he was forced to play, to paraphrase his letter to Wesselényi, the hero in a tragedy,[151] one must look beyond the political contest with Kossuth and the continuous psychological pressure exerted on Széchenyi from Vienna, especially by Metternich, although both factors were important. In this context, the ties between the problems of the serfs and nationalities are of particular portent. The overwhelming majority of non-Magyars were serfs. Frequently they lived in the less fertile poverty-stricken regions of the country and their lords belonged to the privileged, mostly Magyar, nobility. This was not always the case, because Serbo-Croatian and German peasants cultivated some of the best land in the country; moreover, Croatian or Transylvanian Saxon landlords were not necessarily less exacting than were the Magyars or the churches that, with some exceptions, had no ethnic affiliations but owned large tracts of land.

Keeping these qualifications in mind, it is still true that the desire to extend the privileges of the constitution to the peasant masses (which implied their eventual emancipation), posed the question of how to maintain the supremacy of the Magyar "element" in Hungary. The premise from which the question arose lay at the heart of Széchenyi's reform program. Yet it could be approached by Magyar nationalists in different ways. Kossuth and the radicals who intended to speed up Hungary's overdue social transformation, urged Magyarization in order to continue the political leadership of the lesser nobility and supplement it from the ranks of a growing Magyar intelligentsia. Széchenyi, however, disliked the idea of a "changing of the guards" in the country's political life, because it meant the aristocracy would have to abandon its leading role to the common nobility, which he despised. To be sure, Magyardom's fate was foremost in his thinking. But this was precisely the reason why he wanted to avoid, almost at any cost, radical changes in Hungary's social structure. He would rather slow down social progress if it involved the risk of a social revolution. His moderate stand on the issue of nationalities was, above all, a sincere reflection of his humane feelings toward his fellow men; but it was also motivated by his apprehension that the continuous irritation of non-Magyars would result in an eruption of violence, which he abhorred. Last, but not least, a serious conflict among the various nationalities could have a disruptive effect on the monarchy, whose strengthening through gradual modernization Széchenyi thought to be in the interests of all its peoples, including the Magyar.[152]

Except for the nationality question, some of the broader implications of the Széchenyi-Kossuth debate can be traced back to a discussion between Széchenyi and Baron Langsdorff, secretary of the French embassy

[151] See Ch. VII, 272f.   [152] Arató, *A nemzetiségi kérdés*, ɪɪ, 23–33, 48ff., 55–63.

in Vienna. This hitherto unknown conversation, reported in detail by the experienced French diplomat, followed one of the stormy sessions of the general assembly of Pest county one month after the arrest of Kossuth in early May 1837.[153]

Approached by Langsdorff, who was the son-in-law of Ambassador Sainte-Aulaire, an old friend of his, Széchenyi spoke as freely as one can speak with a detached stranger, whose integrity and intellectual ability one respects. He made no secret of his dissatisfaction with Vienna's shortsighted Hungarian policy and Metternich's grandiloquent refusal to introduce meaningful reforms. Széchenyi emphasized that he was just as interested in avoiding a revolution as was the prince; furthermore, he saw no alternative to the existing government. To illustrate the administration's obsession with sinister conspiracies, he related how a vehicle carrying leeches sent by Wesselényi to a Paris doctor was searched by the secret police for an insurrectionary plan of Poles and Hungarians, allegedly destined to Lafayette who, however, had died three years earlier. Asked about the violent reaction to the arrest of the Dietal youth and the confiscation of Kossuth's *Municipal Journal,* Széchenyi replied more earnestly. He said that the opposition in the 52 counties, however strong it was in Pest and a few other places, was too disorganized to cause serious trouble to the administration. While resenting the reaction against the liberal movement (*contre le mouvement*) which seemed to have set in at the time of the palatine's illness, and the resulting uneasy atmosphere, he nevertheless thought the isolated pockets of opposition could be neglected by the government because "all the big landowners needed it, and would agree with it, unless it perpetrated some blunders or wanton provocations." Although he could not say such things in the congregation, Széchenyi continued, he was certainly not a partisan of the liberty of the press in his fatherland. In a country where, according to a feudal constitution, seignioral rights were just as legitimate as anybody else's, no meaningful public discussion could be held even on basic principles unless one wished to start a Hungarian Manifesto by declaring that "some men were born to obey, and others to command; some to possess and enjoy, others to travail and have nothing."

[153] In his diary Széchenyi noted that he spoke "a lot" with Langsdorff, gave him Hungarian newspapers, and "several" of his books. June 8, 1837, Viszota, ed., *Naplók,* v, 85. Cf. May 30, 1837, *ibid.,* p. 82. For the summary of the conversation, written in Langsdorff's hand shortly after it took place and, therefore, reflecting also some of the digressions and witty detours so characteristic of Széchenyi's style, see "Entretien avec le magnat Etienne Széchenyi sur la délibération . . . du . . . Comitat," No. 9 (Pesth, 10 juin 1837), in Vol. 51, *MDAu,* AMAE (Paris). Attached to his report on the county congregation to Ambassador Sainte-Aulaire, this document is an important source for our understanding of Széchenyi's reaction to the events of 1837. Cf. Appendix I, docs. nos. 8a–c.

Commenting on his own role, Széchenyi admitted his failure to convince Metternich of the need for a complete remodeling of Hungary, which he deemed necessary. Instead of supporting the government openly, as the chancellor wanted him to do, Széchenyi preferred "dragging the bull by the tail to taking him by the horn." To be useful, it was better for him to stay in the prompter's box because his compatriots disliked to dance to someone else's piping. Besides, he did not have the beard or shoulders of a Wesselényi, and his countrymen could not imagine great men without broad shoulders. Moreover, Széchenyi added sarcastically, in the eyes of many who were unable to determine whether he was a man of the government or belonged to the opposition, he appeared to be a double-dealer, neither fish nor fowl. Yet, Széchenyi insisted, he was simply an industrialist at the present; since Langsdorff was interested in Hungary, he would perhaps want to buy a few shares in the steamship company or visit with him on the Lower Danube to see the progress of the work. In spite of stressing his "apolitical" attitude (supra-political would perhaps be a more appropriate term), Széchenyi was far from indifferent to current affairs, as shown by his previous remarks, and by his hope that the time would yet come when his ideas would be appreciated. Occasionally, he conceded, waiting seemed to be difficult.

Without trusting that one day he would be able to sit in the shade of the trees he had planted, he would indeed be tempted to move to France or England because in Hungary, hardly the first seeds had been sown as yet. Still, he felt like staying because he wanted to keep an eye on the development of "his children."

The conversation ended on Széchenyi's repeated assurance that although a national government would be in a better position to deal with difficult Hungarian noblemen, the administration did not have to face serious and imminent dangers in Hungary. In this respect, Langsdorff's report is an interesting counterpart of the secret memorandum written by Metternich five months earlier. While the chancellor attempted to exaggerate the strength of the opposition to justify the strong-fisted policy he favored with regard to Hungary, Széchenyi appears to have played down the importance of Hungarian unrest because, as shown by a diary entry from the day following his "long talk" with the Frenchman, he was afraid of the reintroduction of dictatorial methods by the administration.[154] He might even have tried to exert indirectly a subtle

[154] Cf. Ch. VIII, 344. It is only fair to point out, however, that the reports of the secret police, although perhaps exaggerated, were not without foundation. There is evidence suggesting that the young Hungarian radicals of the 1830s had contact with the emissaries of foreign—mainly French, Polish, and German revolutionary—centers. Cf. Révész, "Das Junge Ungarn," pp. 76–83, 103f.

influence on the chancellor through the foreign diplomat knowing that Langsdorff belonged to his social circle: in March 1838 the baron was among the guests when Széchenyi's letter, which gave a graphic description of the disaster caused by the flood of the Danube at Pest, was read in the salon of Princess Melanie.[155] There is no reason to suppose that the secretary of the French embassy was unworthy of Széchenyi's friendship. To avoid the scrutiny of the police he might even have taken the report, in person, along with others which dealt with Hungary, in the diplomatic pouch to Paris. But it is noteworthy that there was hardly anything in what he heard from Széchenyi that the latter could not, and on occasions would not, tell personally to Metternich. It is also interesting that a memorandum and report on Hungary and the laws enacted by the Diet of 1832–36, which antedated both Kossuth's arrest and Langsdorff's conversations with Széchenyi, described the new legislation as the work of *un véritable parlement de réforme,* noting that the municipal reports edited by Kossuth could eventually give rise to a center of publicity and organization for the counties. The keen French observer of the Hungarian scene pointed out that he saw no signs of revolutionary ferment in Hungary; the palatine was well liked, the "radical party" was not strong enough, the government could turn the peasants against the nobility, the liberals themselves were afraid of the radicals, and there was no middle class. However, should the Austrian government

fail to recognize, or should it misjudge the instinctive taste for liberty and that nation-wide resentment of the foreigner, which are principal features of the Hungarian character, as I had already indicated—on that day it would give the radical party all it needs today—great wealth, honored and illustrious leaders, legal standing and, above all, an intimate conviction of it being in the right and of its oppressors being in the wrong.[156]

Indeed, the Frenchman had an eye for the xenophobia of Hungarians, who were *une nation fière,* a proud nation; Széchenyi expressed the same opinion a little later when he suggested that perhaps they would be more manageable under a national government. Within a lustrum Széchenyi was to remind his countrymen that other nations, too, were proud and that it was both foolish and dangerous to insult their national sentiments.

[155] Langsdorff to Molé, Mar. 21, 1838, *Correspondance politique, Autriche,* Vol. 425, Archives du Ministère des Affaires Etrangères (Paris).

[156] "Mémoir sur la hongrie [sic] et sur les lois rendues par la dernière Diète—1832–36," No. 11 (May 1837), in Vol. 51, *Mémoirs et documens [sic], Autriche, 1830 á 1847,* Archives du Ministère des Affaires Etrangères (Paris).

Langsdorff's account of his encounter with Széchenyi during the session of the general assembly of Pest county, which protested vigorously against the arrest of the Dietal youth and of Kossuth, is a valuable supplement to the Metternich memorandum analyzed at the beginning of this chapter. Taken together, the two documents provide perspective on some of the major trends that developed in the next five years and Széchenyi's role in them.

Approached from the point of view of internal Hungarian evolution, Széchenyi's conversation with the French diplomat reflected fears by the class of big landowners of any radical change in Hungary, especially if it involved the peasantry. The tone and content of his language, as reported by Langsdorff, leave no doubt that Széchenyi identified himself with the social group to which he belonged, in regard to its attitude toward experiments that might conceivably affect in a revolutionary way the power structure or social stability of his country. He was right in evaluating the weaknesses of the opposition, although he might have, perhaps intentionally, overstressed the point. But the inclination to overlook completely the middle nobility, which had produced a number of able leaders in the preceding decade, revealed what subsequently turned out to be perhaps the single most important "blind spot" limiting Széchenyi's political judgment. This handicap, never fully understood or acknowledged by him, was just as important as the unwillingness of Metternich and other influential men[157] to play their cards in accordance with Széchenyi's recommendations, as he himself, rather sadly, noted. Yet he went on trying again and again to enlist the help of whomever he needed in Vienna and Hungary to put his ideas into practice, and not only in the field of economic development. The outcome of the Diet of 1839–40 showed that there might be a chance to bring about the cooperation of the leaders of the emerging liberal and conservative parties on the basis of Magyar nationalism, since both administration and opposition were forced to modify their rigid positions in a number of instances.

Even at the Diet of 1839–40 there were signs that the platform of Magyar nationalism in itself was not an adequately strong foundation for a healthy renewal of the ancient Hungarian state. This became evident after the Austrian administration swung from one extreme, represented by the Metternich-memorandum of early 1837, to the other, symbolized by the appearance of Kossuth's paper *Pesti Hirlap*. Whether or not Széchenyi did the right thing by trying to protect the tender fruits of the Hungarian reform movement—"the children" whose father he professed to be—in his book *The People of the Orient* and in his

---

[157] Kübeck, ed., *Tagebücher*, II, 22.

academic speech of 1842, both actions were symptoms of the growing crisis not just in Hungary but in the Habsburg monarchy as a whole. This crisis was not confined to the ties between the Austrian and Hungarian halves of the realm, or to the mutual relations of its peoples, although these were involved in it. Closely, if not causally, related to this set of complex problems was a deep and worsening crisis of the imperial government, which had lingered below the surface ever since Francis I's death in 1835. The trouble was not that Hungary was not being governed, as Metternich put it, although there was an element of truth in this allegation. More important, whereas the chancellor was able to direct, cautiously but reliably, the course of the Habsburg ship of state in ruffled international waters, there was no comparable leadership in domestic affairs. The recurrent and well-known bickerings of Metternich and Kolowrat, the two most influential permanent members of the *Staatskonferenz,* were both symptoms and ingredients of what seemed to many observers as the administration's utter impotence. In a report written in the autumn of 1836, the French ambassador raised the rhetorical question: "Who is, after all, governing Austria today?" In reply, Sainte-Aulaire, who was not an ignorant or unsympathetic outsider, depicted Austria as a great empire without a sovereign, prime minister, or institutions, remarking also that the highest governing bodies of the realm suffered from chronic division and the members of the imperial family failed to see eye to eye on important issues.[158]

The governmental crisis was further aggravated by the "financial anarchy," to use Baron Kübeck's phrase, in which the state found itself. The president of the court chamber and most Austrian leaders related the unfavorable budgetary situation to the outstanding military taxes due from Hungary and Transylvania, the accumulated sum of which increased rather than decreased as the years went by. The failure to collect the disputed direct taxes had of course an adverse affect on the imperial and royal treasury. State revenues also suffered from the disproportion of the financial obligations of the different parts of the monarchy. There were endless arguments about the tariff system, the unfairness of which was one of the Hungarians' permanent grievances;

[158] Ste-Aulaire to Molé, Oct. 18, 1836, Vol. 424, *Correspondance politique, Autriche,* Archives du Ministère des Affaires Etrangères (Paris). Three years later, the same ambassador reported at the time of Metternich's illness: ". . . nobody seems to care about the government, which continues to march without anybody knowing who gives the impulse to it." Ste-Aulaire to Soult, Aug. 31, 1839, Vol. 427, *Correspondance politique, Autriche,* Archives du Ministère des Affaires Etrangères (Paris). Cf. Marquis Louis de Sainte-Aulaire to Guizot, Apr. 14, 1841, Vol. 429, *ibid.* See also Kübeck, ed. *Tagebücher,* I, Pt. 2, pp. 455f., 467-71, 520, 585, 717-22, 738-46, 752-62, 767-89, 794, 800, 805-808, 826, 842-47; Viktor Bibl, *Die Tragödie Österreichs* (Leipzig-Vienna: J. Gunther, 1937), pp. 101-21.

yet its clumsiness caused frequent complaints among the empire's foreign trade partners, too. Austrians tended to stress the tax exemption of the Hungarian nobility, which was also at the root of Hungary's domestic socio-economic difficulties. But it is fair to point out that according to Count Hartig the contribution of the Italian provinces to the burdens of the realm was out of proportion compared to that of its Slavic and German lands.[159]

The crux of the economic difficulties lay elsewhere. At the end of 1842 the unpaid military contribution of Hungary and Transylvania had over the years mounted to over 8,600,000 florins. But the deficit of the budget was 48,000,000 in the preceding two years alone, despite Kübeck's efforts to bring some order to the financial affairs of the state after his appointment as president of the treasury in 1840. According to his data, over 620,000,000 was spent on the military establishment in 1831–41. In the latter year the total state expenses was over 203,000,000. In the first two years of the decade in which Austria responded to the July Revolution by rearming feverishly, the state debt increased by 98,000,000. The public debt, which was over 554,000,000 in 1829, passed the billion mark by 1837 according to the *British and Foreign Review,* which the French thought worthy of attention.[160] Due to this crushing financial burden, the monarchy headed toward complete bankruptcy, while the overwhelming majority of the people was barely kept at the subsistence level.[161]

To eliminate the deficit and decrease the state debt Kübeck recommended three steps. First, he stressed the need for obtaining the "cooperation" of Hungary and Transylvania by changing the "menacing conditions" in those two countries. Second, he thought the army should be reduced to a peacetime footing. Finally, he suggested a few administrative reforms. As to the first recommendation, Kolowrat saw no hope for improvement in Hungary. Concerning the third, Kübeck himself complained about the immense complexity of the administrative machinery, the bewildering jungle of paperwork, and the unchecked favoritism at court; his analysis made it unlikely that the chief bureaucrats could disentangle the self-generating imbroglio of bureaucracy. Besides increas-

---

[159] No. 1,203/1836, 759/1841, 1,167 and 1,818/1842, 1,427/1843, *MKA*, Staatsarchiv (Vienna). Cf. Ch. VII, 247f., 260–65.

[160] No. 41 ("Tableau de la dette publique," Nov. 1, 1829), Vol. 49, *MDAu*, AMAE (Paris). No. 5 ("Notes historiques sur les Finances de l'Autriche," 1834) and 7, Vol. 51, *ibid.*

[161] No. 1,818/1842, 195 and 2,035/1843, *MKA*, Staatsarchiv (Vienna), Kübeck, ed., *Tagebücher,* I, Pt. 2, pp. 411ff., 505. For the significance of the military-fiscal aspects of the 19th-century history of the great empires in Eastern Europe, and for comparative data, cf. Blackwell, *Beginnings of Russian Industrialization,* pp. 177–82.

ing state revenues by stimulating taxable agricultural and industrial production and improving the tariff system, the president of the treasury left no doubt that the reduction of the inflated military establishment, supported by lobbies and pressure groups, was the most important part of his proposals. Kolowrat agreed, as did Hartig, that decreasing military expenditure was the essential thing; both stressed that the existing level of military spending in times of peace was disturbing and could impair the welfare of future generations.[162]

[162] No. 1,818/1842, 195 and 2,035/1843, *MKA*, Staatsarchiv (Vienna). For the difficulties of improving the Austrian tariff system, its relation to the Prussian-led *Zollverein*, and their relevance in the *Vormärz*, cf. Věra Vomáčková, "Österreich und der deutsche Zollverein," *Historica*, v (1963), esp. pp. 117–24.

CHAPTER X

Opening of the "Hungarian Question"

Two considerations should be mentioned concerning the governmental crisis and economic ills of the Monarchy and the cures prescribed to remedy them. One is that leaving aside the political implications of Széchenyi's economic reform program, and even Hungarian domestic resistance to it, his efforts were constantly hampered at the highest levels of government by capital shortage, mismanagement of available funds, an obtuse bureacracy, and frequently by a lack of goodwill. Awareness of the precarious economic foundations of some of his most cherished apolitical enterprises such as his work on the Lower Danube, greatly added to the nervous tensions arising from his personal life and politically motivated frustrations. In this particular sense, the conflict between him and Kossuth was a product, albeit only an indirect one, of a governmental system that one day seemed excessively cruel and another absent-mindedly impotent. Without being malicious or evil, such a government could not be relied on—hence Széchenyi's decision to try to stop Kossuth singlehandedly before it was too late.

The other aspect of this critical state of affairs, which was bound to affect the whole Monarchy and not just Hungary, should be related to the international situation. Fifteen years after the Napoleonic wars, from which Austria had not yet recuperated, it began to rearm again because of the shock of the July Revolution and the Polish uprising. After a few years, when the rash of revolutions seemed to have subsided but the financial situation looked desperate, Kolowrat and Baron Eichhoff, president of the treasury until 1840, pressed for a reduction of the army. Metternich frustrated the plan in March 1836, perhaps, as the British ambassador reported, using as a pretext the recent unrest in the Italian peninsula.[1] But a year later the chancellor again succeeded

---

[1] Kübeck, ed., *Tagebücher*, I, Pt. 2, pp. 719ff.; Lamb to Palmerston, Oct. 9, 31, 1836, *F.O. 7/258*, Public Record Office (London); Ste-Aulaire to Thiers, Apr. 13, 1836, Vol. 423, *Correspondance politique, Autriche*, Archives du Ministère des Affaires Etrangères (Paris).

in having Kolowrat overruled by declaring, if one is to believe his archrival, that even the bankruptcy of the state would be "something quite natural."[2] Besides his concern with Austrian foreign policy, Metternich might have been motivated by the growing strength of the opposition in Hungary.[3] Actually, considerations of foreign and domestic policies were closely interrelated by the mid-1830s, as intimated by Count Clam-Martinitz in early 1838. "In this union of heterogeneous provinces inclined to dissolution," said the adjutant of the emperor, the Austrian army was "the only symbol of unity and strength." It was "not a part of the nation, as in other states, but a state unto itself," which held together the various lands of the Habsburg dynasty. Characteristically, Kübeck drew the following conclusion from Clam's statement, with which he essentially agreed: "the Austrian populace does not constitute a nation, but is a compressed people, held fast by an army, dominated by an oligarchy that exploits the power of government under the label of an absolute monarchy."[4] To his own question, whether such conditions could last much longer, Kübeck answered in the affirmative. Limited and weak, occasionally even arbitrary, the government was nevertheless fair, thrifty, and took into account the basic interests of the people. Reliable in its external policy, careful and strong enough to subdue anarchic movements, the people were on the whole quite well off under its rule.[5]

Kübeck's provocative but cynical insight into the human conditions prevailing under the scepter of the "happy" house of Austria, was basically confirmed a decade later. Thanks to the army and to Russian help, the dynasty and the Habsburg state managed to muddle through in the revolutionary turbulence of 1848–49. Still, preoccupied as they were with the problems of Spain, Belgium, Italy and, above all, with the Oriental question, foreign diplomats nevertheless started to pay increasing attention to the monarchy's internal affairs. From the mid-1830s on, a "Hungarian question" began to take shape in the minds of many Austrians, as well as foreign observers. This "Hungarian question," to be sure, was formulated differently in the varied diplomatic chanceries, where it was regarded as some sort of catalyst of Austrian and Central European trends, which was tangible enough to grasp.

The worries and warnings of the Holy See about the Hungarian question stemmed from the fear that Hungary, one of the medieval shields

[2] Kübeck, ed., *Tagebücher*, i, Pt. 2, pp. 758f.

[3] Srbik, *Metternich*, ii, 8f.

[4] Kübeck, ed., *Tagebücher*, i, Pt. 2, pp. 777f. For references to the Austrian army cf. Gunther E. Rothenberg, "The Habsburg Army and the Nationality Problem in the Nineteenth Century, 1815–1914," *Austrian History Yearbook*, iii, (1967), Pt. 1, pp. 70–87.

[5] Kübeck, ed., *Tagebücher*, i, Pt. 2, p. 768.

of Western Christendom, could be subverted by Protestant heretics and Orthodox schismatics. From the standpoint of theological dogma and of the historical role played by the Church in the *Regnum Marianum,* such a trend seemed intolerable. Besides, it could dangerously weaken Austria, the only Catholic great power after 1830 on whose assistance the papacy could count, albeit with certain qualifications, in its international and Italian policies.[6]

The British, too, were concerned with the split that developed in the highest echelons of the Austrian government, where the unity of purpose derivable from a single head was wanting, to paraphrase the English ambassador. Lamb found no reason to encourage the investment of foreign capital in Hungary on the basis of the legislation of the Diet of 1832–36, although he did acknowledge that the new laws improved the serf's lot.[7] The diplomacy of Great Britain tried to combine economic and political steps to influence Austrian attitudes and promote its own vision of a Central Europe capable of resisting Russia.[8] Its interest in Hungarian affairs was revealed by the reporting and subsequent publication of the full text of the rescript with which Francis I dissolved the Transylvanian Diet. In this document, one of the last issued over his signature before he died, the monarch accused the legislature of illegal activities, unconstitutional acts, "odious licentiousness," and outright sedition. He declared null and void all its "proceedings and innovations which are obnoxious to the ancient Constitution," whose interpretation, along with the restoration of law and order, the monarch claimed as his task in view of the alleged anarchic conditions in Transylvania.[9] After the conclusion of the new treaty of trade and navigation with Austria in 1838,[10] the British intended to improve their direct commercial relations with Hungary by asking for permission to appoint a consul at Pest. Motivated in part by rumors, according to which the United States had already obtained an *exequatur* for a permanent consular representative, the request was categorically refused by Metternich, who also rejected the previous American initiative. In a letter written on May 3, 1841, two months before the appearance of *A kelet népe,* the chancellor expressed his doubts as to the prospects of English trade with an underdeveloped country like Hungary. But he seemed even more concerned with the remote possibility of the fulfillment of British expecta-

---

[6] See Chs. V, 157–62, VII, 293f., VIII, 322–26, 360–64.

[7] Lamb to Palmerston, Oct. 9, Dec. 20 (No. 33), 1836, *F.O. 7/258,* PRO (London); Lamb to Palmerston, Dec. 20 (No. 35) and 27/1836, *F.O. 7/259,* PRO (London); Beauvale to Palmerston, Mar. 10, 1840 (confidential), *F.O. 7/290,* PRO (London).

[8] Cf. Chs. VII, 256–66, VIII, 326ff.

[9] *British and Foreign State Papers,* XXIII (1834–1835), 601–608. See also Trócsányi, *Wesselényi,* pp. 284–87.

[10] Beer, *Österreichische Handelspolitik,* pp. 313–16.

tions, because such an eventuality would further increase Hungarian ambitions and demands. Six weeks later Metternich politely but firmly rejected the request of the Americans, whom he regarded as dangerous "propagandists" of the democratic disease. According to the domestic authorities, said the chancellor, "the necessity and utility of such an innovation do not appear in any manner demonstrated. It could, on the contrary, produce inconveniences of a grave nature which is the duty of every Government to avoid." In his reply to the United States chargé, the chancellor referred to the problem of establishing a precedent, implying that this was perhaps the grave inconvenience he had in mind. This, of course, was true. But the police minister was more outspoken when, in the relevant correspondence, he cautioned against admitting foreign consuls who "almost always" behaved as political agents, intriguing and trying to claim diplomatic privileges and immunities for themselves. Consequently, Sedlnitzky stressed the disadvantages of such leniency in Hungary, "where there are so many elements susceptible to agitation and temptation, and where, as in the Grandduchy of Transylvania and in the imperial-royal military frontier [district], there is no adequate police authority to control the machinations (*Antriebe*) of foreign agents, and where the necessary intervention can be exerted only through indirect means."

The foreigners of whom the Austrian officials were especially afraid, even in 1842, were French agents, in view of the "deplorable [Metternich crossed out 'political' in the draft] activity displayed by France in other countries with the direct aid of alleged commercial agents . . . ." Their admission to Hungary was "absolutely impossible . . . before things were prepared there so that their presence should not cause any noteworthy trouble. . . ."[11]

Mistrust of French intentions thus continued to linger in Metternich's mind even after the Near Eastern crisis sparked by the French-supported Mehemed Ali was solved. The rejection of the marriage alliance offered by Louis Philippe in 1836 was probably similarly motivated. This does not invalidate, however, the British ambassador's judgment, according to whom Metternich thwarted the offer not because of his "fear of or liking to [*sic*] Russia but the fear of needing her alliance . . . ," knowing that if there was a revolution in Poland, Italy, or Hungary, "France cannot assist but Russia."[12] Vienna's nervous reaction to the Hungarian question can be measured against the endeavors to nip in

---

[11] Sir Robert Gordon to Aberdeen, Apr. 10, 1842, *F.O. 7/305*, PRO (London); Metternich to Kübeck, May 3, 1841, published in Beer, *Österreichische Handelspolitik*, p. 571; Barany, "The Interest of the United States in Central Europe," pp. 283–98.

[12] Lamb to Palmerston, Aug. 5, 1836 (No. 13, confidential), *F.O. 7/257*, PRO (London). Cf. Srbik, *Metternich*, II, 53ff.

the bud any project that might conceivably lead to the palatine's founding a dynasty of his own in Hungary, thereby perhaps raising hopes for Hungary's secession from the Monarchy. Noting the popularity of the Archduke Stephen among Hungarians, the court found a pretext to transfer him to Austria and Bohemia; and subsequent efforts of Nicholas I to marry his daughter to the son of the palatine were denied for the same reason, even at the risk of alienating the Russian patron of Austria.[13]

Despite Metternich's efforts the representatives of France seem to have been the most intelligent observers of the Hungarian scene in the decade ending with 1841, although their influence on Vienna's policy was limited. Handicapped first by Austria's coolness toward the July Monarchy to the extent of being insulted by Princess Melanie,[14] Ambassador Sainte-Aulaire and his "team," which included his son-in-law Langsdorff, soon were both respected and well-informed members of the diplomatic corps. Like their English colleagues, these "conservative liberals" were more interested in bringing Austrian policy in harmony with their own government's than in undermining the Habsburg state, which France too regarded as a guarantee of the status quo against the feared encroachments of Russia in the Balkans and Near East.[15] There is little evidence to substantiate Austrian complaints about the alleged subversive activities of French agents,[16] still, in the spring of 1835 a French report called the Quai d'Orsay's special attention to Austria's relations with Hungary and Transylvania. Somewhat prematurely the same report also mentioned the possibility of the decomposition of the Austrian Empire and the establishment of an independent Hungary, whence the revolutionary ferment could spread to other countries in central, eastern, and southern Europe. Although France was in favor of the status quo, concluded the memorandum, it ought to watch closely the march of events in Hungary and Transylvania because they might have "European conse-

[13] Kübeck, ed., *Tagebucher*, I, Pt. 2, pp. 753f., 817f.; Sir Robert Gordon to Aberdeen, March 20/1844, *F.O. 7/316*, PRO (London). Cf. Ch. VIII, 325 above.

[14] Sainte-Aulaire to Broglie, Mar. 4, 1834, Vol. 420, *Correspondance politique, Autriche,* Archives du Ministère des Affaires Etrangères (Paris); Srbik, *Metternich,* I, 245.

[15] Reporting that there was calm in the interior of Austria, and that there were no disturbances in Hungary and Transylvania either, the French chargé remarked: "That's good for France." La Rochefoucauld to Broglie, July 12, 1835, Vol. 422, *Correspondance politique, Autriche,* Archives du Ministère des Affaires Etrangères (Paris). Cf. Ste-Aulaire to Broglie, Dec. 7, 1835, *ibid.;* Sainte-Aulaire to Thiers, Mar. 16, 1836, Vol. 423, *ibid.* See also Guizot's instructions to the Count Flahaut upon the latter's appointment as new ambassador to Vienna. Guizot to Flahaut, Oct. 30, 1841, Vol. 429, *ibid.*

[16] Bussière to Broglie, Mar. 28, 1833, Vol. 418, *Correspondance politique, Autriche,* Archives du Ministère des Affaires Etrangères (Paris); Broglie to Sante-Aulaire, Apr. 3, 1833, (Instructions), *ibid.*

quences" in a few years.[17] Indeed, it was one of Langsdorff's special assignments to keep in touch with Hungarian events. As shown by his numerous conscientiously prepared reports, Széchenyi was one of the informants of this excellent diplomat, although the latter did not always refer to him by name. Reporting on the political trials and the palatine's illness, Langsdorff emphasized that a revolution was not imminent, and nobody thought of separating Hungary from Austria. Yet he noted that the government of Vienna was regarded as "foreign" by most Hungarians, including aristocrats loyal to the dynasty, and that the problems inherent in the very existence of the cherished and ancient constitution of Hungary could not be solved by Metternich's skill. Besides the shortcomings of the constitution, there was the fact that the chancellor's abhorrence of constitutional government was well known and Hungarian patriots mistrusted him. In addition to reporting the antagonism between magnates and lesser noblemen, Langsdorff observed the prevalence of a certain "republican sentiment" in Upper Hungary (Bars county) and parts of Transdanubia. The "radical party," as he put it, stood for the emancipation of the peasants from the tyranny of the nobility, and for the emancipation of Hungary from the tyranny of Austria. In describing the political fermentation in Hungary, Langsdorff also mentioned that there was not much love lost between Magyars and other nationalities of the kingdom. The French diplomat expected "complications" after the death of the palatine, who was quite popular in Hungary, and seemed to agree with his British colleagues that Vienna might become more dependent on St. Petersburg, should trouble arise in Hungary.[18]

The French ambassador confirmed the opinion, repeatedly expressed in his previous correspondence, namely, that the condition of Hungary, although not menacing with an imminent revolution, "will be for a

[17] Ste-Aulaire to Broglie, Mar. 26, 1835, ("Considérations générales sur la situation actuelle de la Transylvanie") *Mémoirs et documens* [sic], *Autriche, 1814 à 1851, Archives du Ministère des Affaires Etrangères* (Paris).

[18] Ste-Aulaire to Molé, Mar. 2, 21, 30, Apr. 11-13, 24, May 2, 18, June 10, 21, July 7, 1837, Vol. 424, *Correspondance politique, Autriche*, Archives du Ministère des Affaires Etrangères (Paris). Attached to the last mentioned report was a memorandum by Langsdorff, written on June 22 in Pest. Enclosed with another report of the French ambassador was a detailed analysis and translation of the laws of the Diet of 1832-36. The introduction to this memorandum, written by Langsdorff in May 1837, paid special attention to Széchenyi's ideas and activities as a reformer, stressing, in particular, the impact of *Hitel* on the legislature and the polemics surrounding the publication of the book: at one point, the French diplomat compared *Hitel* with the *cahiers* preceding the French Revolution of 1789. "Traduction des lois rendues par la Dernière Diète 1832-36, précédée d'un [sic], Mémoire sur l'Etat de la Hongrie, #11 in Vol. 51, *Mémoires et documents, Autriche, 1830 à 1847*. Archives du Ministère des Affaires Etrangères (Paris).

long period of time a source of embarrassment to the government of Vienna, and will prevent the latter from intervening energetically in the great questions of European politics."[19] Paris, too, took notice of "the interesting reports by Langsdorff."[20] In a coded message sent to Sainte-Aulaire at the end of April 1837, one week before Kossuth's arrest, Prime Minister Molé expressed his "lively interest" in the detailed reports "on the internal situation of Hungary, and the peculiar confidences made to you on this subject by M. Metternich."[21]

There is no need to elaborate again on the chancellor's attitude toward Hungary in 1837. We are familiar with his views on the critical situation in Hungary and the interpretation he gave to it in a memorandum prepared at the beginning of the year and in his correspondence with the tsar later in the spring.[22] We also know the impact of the crisis on the country's mood and Széchenyi's thinking from Hungarian and foreign sources as well. Due to a number of international and domestic factors the administration found it advisable to relax its stand gradually, whereas the opposition, strengthened by the nationwide indignation, accepted a face-saving device although the principles advocated by it failed to obtain public recognition.

Széchenyi was one of those who worked hard at reaching a compromise between government and opposition. Using various channels behind the scenes and in public, he stressed the need for moderation on all

[19] Ste-Aulaire to Molé, June 21, 1837, Vol. 424, *Correspondance politique, Autriche*, Archives du Ministère des Affaires Etrangères (Paris).

[20] Molé to Ste-Aulaire, Aug. 10, 1837, *ibid.*

[21] Molé to Ste-Aulaire, Apr. 29, 1837, *ibid.* My findings do not support some of the interpretations of Professor Birke, who seems to have ignored the French diplomatic reports of the 1830s. Ernst Birke, *Frankreich und Ostmitteleuropa im 19. Jahrhundert* (Cologne-Graz: Vlg. Böhlau, 1960), pp. 108ff., 152. While it is true that the quality of the reports coming from Vienna deteriorated after 1841 (the year in which Sainte-Aulaire departed for London and Langsdorff became French minister in Rio de Janeiro), it is a mistake to skip the preceding decade. For examples, see, besides the references given in this chapter and elsewhere, Ste-Aulaire to Soult, June 14 and 25, 1839, Vol. 426, *Correspondance politique, Autriche*, Archives du Ministère des Affaires Etrangères (Paris); Langsdorff to Thiers, Apr. 4, May 18, 27, June 1, 1840, *ibid.*, all containing interesting information on Hungary and Transylvania, or the account of attaché Des Fayéres on Bohemian conditions, enclosed with Ste-Aulaire to Molé, Oct. 7, 1836, Vol. 423, *ibid.*

[22] See Chs. VIII, 328f., IX, 375-79. As an example of the chancellor's peculiar inconsistencies regarding Hungary, there is a letter written by him to the palatine in May 1844. In it, he suggested that Hungary had been stagnant and unchanged since 1790, and that the long reign of Francis I (1792-1835) had given nothing to Hungary. Thereby, he condemned in a cavalier fashion the entire reign of his old master. Metternich to Archduke Palatine Joseph, May 9, 1844. No. 142/1844, *Kabinettsarchiv. Separatkonferenzakten*, Staatsarchiv (Vienna). Characteristically, this admission of the total failure of the administration's policy toward Hungary by one of its chief executors and indeed architects, which constitutes an interesting supplement to Metternich's well-known opinions on the Hungarian situation written at the end of the years 1843 and 1844, has not been included in his eight-volume Memoirs, and thus has largely escaped the attention of historians.

sides. There was certainly no one happier than Széchenyi at the denouement of the crisis toward the end of the Diet of 1839–40. Francis Pulszky, who had an opportunity to observe him closely in the summer of 1840, noted: "During his twenty-year-long political career, this was the time when Széchenyi looked into the future with the greatest hope and satisfaction. I have never seen him in a jollier mood: he spoke about the immediate future with all and sundry without anxiety. . . ."[23]

Happiness, however, proved to be elusive in Széchenyi's life. Within a year after he had been feted by the leaders of the opposition, including Kossuth, he publicly raised his voice against the menace of civil strife, alienating thereby all the leaders of the opposition who disagreed with him. Yet another year, and the greatest Magyar was the most lonely and isolated of his compatriots because he had defended the basic rights of his non-Magyar countrymen. His repeated stern warning that action might beget reaction and lead to disaster, especially because of the far-reaching international implications of the nationality question, was little understood at the time.

The sharp decline in Széchenyi's popularity and his separation from prominent liberals marked the end of an era in Hungary's history. The "age of Széchenyi" was gradually transformed into an "age of Kossuth," but the many ideological and socio-economic undercurrents connecting the two periods do not warrant any simplified interpretation. The decade that witnessed the growth of Hungarian liberalism also gave birth to a "Hungarian question" in European diplomatic correspondence, and this circumstance ought not to be ignored when one deals with the diplomacy of the revolutionary years 1848 and 1849. For good or for ill, Széchenyi contributed in many ways to these intertwined historical processes. Most of the issues formulated in the period of Hungary's national awakening, and the spokesmen who debated them, were his spiritual offspring. He never disowned them publicly, although he may have wavered in private or repudiated the methods of the more radical liberal nationalists.

The opening of the public controversy between Széchenyi and Kossuth greatly helped the rise of the new star on the Hungarian political horizon. But many of Széchenyi's most significant contributions to Hungarian evolution were still ahead of him, as were the tribulations involving all the peoples of the Habsburg state in the revolution of 1848–49. This revolution was not brought about by either Kossuth or Széchenyi, al-

---

[23] Ferenc Pulszky, *Jellemrajzok* (Character Sketches) (Budapest: Aigner, 1872), p. 47. Besides frustrations and xenophobia, rising expectations and hope for a better and more meaningful life seem to be important ingredients of modern nationalism. For a sober treatment of the broader aspects of this problem, see Boyd C. Shafer, *Nationalism, Myth and Reality* (New York: Harcourt, Brace, 1955), pp. 175–81.

though their personal participation in it was significant. Viewed from a broader socio-economic perspective, however, it seems that both Széchenyi and Kossuth, in their own ways, prepared the explosion that shook Central Europe in the mid-19th century. True, the former, who divined its coming, wanted to prevent it, while the latter, when he noticed its imminence, intended to promote and thereby control it. But how restricted are the options of great leaders even in the best of historical circumstances, once the horrors of revolution, counterrevolution, and war have been unchained by the dark forces of human stupidity and irrational emotions!

The first half-century of Széchenyi's life thus coincided with the initial steps of his fatherland's modernization under the auspices of European liberalism, of which he was a most important champion in the pre-March period. He was no saint or prophet, and many of his predictions failed to come true. But he, more than any of his countrymen or even the leaders of imperial policy, thought in terms of the most significant questions of the future, although the solutions he offered were not always workable. In some instances, however, his forebodings proved to be justified: the nationality question was one of them.

All this does not mean that the trends which emerged around 1841 were bound to lead to civil war and international conflict, as in fact they did in 1848. Széchenyi, who frequently used fatalistic phrases in his diaries and published writings, never acted as though he believed in the inevitability of historical developments. Even in his moments of grave doubt he followed the advice formulated in the motto of *Stádium*—to try "again and again—incessantly."

The effort to overcome adverse circumstances and discipline destructive instincts through creative work is perhaps Széchenyi's best claim to tragic greatness. But whereas the greatness of his work was recognized by his compatriots in 1841, few could detect its tragic ingredients. Fortunately for Széchenyi, his nation, and the human race, the future is always hidden from the eyes of the children of man.

Appendices

APPENDIX I. DOCUMENTS

The transcripts of the documents in this section follow the orthography and punctuation of the originals.

DOCUMENT 1. Draft of the agreement reached by Swedish Crown Prince Bernadotte and Prussian General Blücher, at Breitenfeld, October 18, 1813. (See Chapter II, p. 51 and note 151.) *Kriget i Tyskland, 1813–1814, Nordarméns högkvater*. Handlinger från diverse personer, Vol. 31, B. I. N. 12.b Kungl. Krigsarkivet, Stockholm.

Breitenfeld 18. 8bre *1813*
8^{h} du matin

    Le Feld marechal Prince de
Shwarzenberg ayant annoncè par
Le Capitain Comte Zecheny—
que L'intention de leur majestes
L'Empereur Alexandre L'Empereur
d'Autriche et Le Roi de Prusse
etant [crossed out: "etait"] d'attaquer L'Ennemi Elles
   desirent que Les armès du Nord et
de Silesie cooperent [crossed out: "eront"] a cette grande
entreprise, et Le General Blucher s'etant
rendù au quartier General du Prince
Royal d'apres L'invitation qui lui
en avait etè faite; il a eté
convenù—
   1° que Le General Blucher—
donnerà au Prince Royal de Suede

Breitenfeld 18. 8bre 1813
5½ h. du matin

Le feld maréchal Prince de
Schwarzenberg ayant annoncé par
le capitaine comte Zechenye
que l'intention de leurs majestés
l'Empereur Alexandre l'Empereur
d'autriche et le roi de Prusse
étant d'attaquer l'ennemi elles
désirent que les armées de nord et
de Silésie coopèrent à cette grande
entreprise, le Général de Blucher s'étant
rendu au quartier Général du Prince
Royal depuis l'invitation qui lui
en avait été faite, il a été
convenu —

1° que le Général de Blucher
donnera au Prince Royal de Suède
30m. h. de son armée infanterie
cavallerie, artillerie. Qu'avec
ces troupes réunies à l'armée
de nord sous les ordres de Prince
l'armée de l'Empereur Napoléon
sera attaquée par Taucha.
que le Général Blucher avec
le reste de ses troupes gardera
ses positions devant Leipzig et
fera tous ses efforts pour —

434

s'emparer de cette ville au
moment ou l'action sera générale
de la

2. Dans le cas ou l'Empereur
Napoléon veut avec toutes ses forces
contre l'armée de Silésie et celle
du Nord alors il est convenu que
les deux armées combattront
ensemble jusqu'a tant que la
Grande armée vienne a leur
secours, ~~qu'~~ ~~les deux~~

~~qu'~~ ~~les deux~~

~~une retraite, la résolution de~~

~~pour de~~

~~ou arrêter toute le champs de~~

~~bataille;~~ dans ce dernier cas le
Prusse et Général Blücher et ~~agiront de~~

~~count~~ ensemble, les deux Généraux
en chef se concerteront pour
les opérations. —

30^m h. re Son armèe infanterie,
cavallerie, artillerie; qui'avec—
les trouppes réuniés a L'armée
du Nord Sous les ordres du Prince
L'armèe de L'Empereur Napoleon
serà attaquèe par Tauka—
   que le General Blucher avec
Le reste de ses trouppes [crossed out: one word] gardera
ses positions devant Leipzig et
fairà tous ses efforts pour—
s'emparer de cette ville au
moment ou L'action serà general
[Crossed out: "Le Gr"]
   2. Dans le cas ou l'Empereur
Napoleon vint avec toutes ses forces
contre l'armèe de Silesie et celle
du Nord, alors il est convenù que
Les deux armées combattront—
ensemble jusqu'a tant que La
Grande armèe vienne a leur
Secours, [crossed out: five lines, partly illegible]
   , dans ce dernier cas Le
Prince et General Blucher [crossed out: "et"] agiront
[crossed out: "de concert"] ensemble, et Les deux command [ants]
en chef se concerteront pour toutes
les operations.

DOCUMENT 2. Reports of Count Aurel Dessewffy on the circular sessions of the Hungarian Diet, held on Nov. 2 and 3, 1825. Enclosure of the report of Ambassador Sir Henry Wellesley to Canning, dated Jan. 1, 1826. *F.O.7/192*, Public Record Office (London). Cf. Chapter IV, p. 119 and note 104.

Le 2. de Novembre
Séance circulaire

L'ordre était à l'education de la jeunesse—on la considéra comme un des points principaux tendant à la consolidation de la constitution du pays. Pour atteindre à ce but, on crut que la voie la plus sure etoit de nationaliser l'éducation. La langue nationale est presqu'entièrement exlue de la première education et la connoissance des affaires de la patrie etant extremement limitée fait que la nation ne parvient pas à cette unité qui est la base la plus solide de la constitution, et le soutien du trône.

Le Comte Dessewffy proposa de ne recevoir dans les premières classes des écoles, que les enfans qui parlent l'Hongrois. De cette manière tous les parents seroient contreints de faire enseigner l'Hongrois à leurs enfants encore au berceau. Il fut décidé de rédiger dans cet esprit le point en question de la rémontrance. Il ne faut pas croire, que les Hongrois veuillent exclure la langue latine de l'education. Ils savent qu'elle est tres nécessaire en Hongrie, où tous les documens anciens sont dans cette langue.

Les Etats decidèrent encore de se plaindre dans cette même rémontrance, contre deux mêsures injustes du gouvernement, et qui sont propres à alimenter un esprit de dissension entre les diverses parties religieuses co-existantes, contraire à nos loix qui assurent presque les mêmes droits aux protestants qu'aux catholics.

Une de ces mesures est que les réformes sont empêchés d'envoyer leur jeunesse aux universités étrangères — chose qui est directement opposée aux loix. Les réformés ont des fonds dans ces universités placés de manière que les capitaux ne sauroient être rendus, ni les intérêts — payés a d'autres que ceux qui y viennent les consumer. Ainsi les réformés sont non seulement privés de l'avantage de voyager et de s'instruir, mais ils perdent aussi les intérêts des capitaux placés par leur ancêtres.

L'autre mêsure est qu'on a défendu aux peres Catholics de prendre des protestants pour instituteurs de leurs enfans. Cette mêsure fut considérée comme un obstacle à la liberté légale des parens, et contraire aux principes d'égalité, qui existent chez nous entre les diverses sectes.

---

3 de Novembre
Séances circulaires

La liberté de la presse étant une des plus fortes guaranties de la liberté, on se décida à la proposer à Sa Majesté. Les Etats sans entrée dans la discussion de cet objet se contentèrent de démander à Sa Majesté de faire prendre en délibération l'ouvrage du Committé de l'an 1791 sur ce sujet, rédigé par le Comte Staller, et connu comme excéllent dans tout le pays. L'ordre etoit à la langue nationale. Comme elle ne fut

Quant aux autres moyens
d'établir la Langue Hongroise
on proposa de faire rédiger
tout acte publique, plaider
tout procès, écrire toute affaire
en Hongrais — de proposer
des prix pour les écrivains
distingués, et de ne placer
que des Curés, qui parlent
l'Hongrais, et qui sont en
état de l'enseigner à leurs
paroissiens —

Animé par ces idées,
le Comte Etienne Széchenyi,
déclara sa volonté, mûrement
réfléchie

réfléchie, d'offrir un révenu d'un
année entière de ses biens
pour servir à propager la
langue nationale, et à élever
des fils dignes d'une patrie,
telle que la nôtre — L'enthousi-
=asme avec lequel la
proposition noble du fils d'un
des bienfaiteurs de la nation
fut reçue, excita l'émulation
de plusieurs autres, qui
imitèrent cet exemple dans
cette séance même. Le Comte
George Nadasdy offrit dix
mille florins, bon argent, Mr.
Bay

traitée hier que sous le rapport de l'education, qui cependant ne produit aucun effet avant une vingtaine d'années, les débats furent ouverts sur ce sujet. On cita les loix faites pour répandre la connoissance de la langue Hongroise, et les regrets de la nation de voir ce but si peu réalisé. On en chercha les causes que Mr. Nagy développa en détails. Le Comte Dessewffy exposa que la Langue Hongroise a faite dans l'espace de 25 ans des progres plus rapides, que celle d'aucune autre nation de l'Europe, et qu'un des moyen les plus sûrs pour arriver à l'établissement de la langue Hongroise, seroit de faire éléver nos Souverains futurs à l'Hongroise — à leur faire enseigner l'Hongrois à leur enpreindre dès leur enfance l'amour de notre langue, de nos coutumes, de nos institutions, afin que, étant pénétrés de'attachement pour nos lois, ils puissent être des Souverains — constitutionnelles. Quant aux autre moyens d'établir la Langue Hongroise on proposa de faire rediger tout acte publique, plaider tout procès, ecrir toute affiche en Hongrois — de proposer des prix pour les Ecrivains distingués, et de ne placer que des Curés qui parlent l'Hongrois, et qui sont en état de l'enseigner à leurs paroissiens.

Animé par ses idées, le Comte Etienne Széchenyi, declara sa volonté mûrement réfléchie, d'offrir un révénu d'une année entier de ses biens pour servir à propager la langue nationale, et à éléver des fils dignes d'une patrie, telle que la notre. L'enthusiasm avec lequel la proposition noble du fils d'un des bienfaiteurs de la nation fut reçue, excita l'émulation de plusieurs autres qui imitèrent cet example dans cette séance même. Le Comte George Nadrássy offrit dix milles florins, bon argent, M. Vay offrit huit mille, et le Comte George Karolyi en offrit mille annuellement pour un prix littéraire, et en autres la moitié de ses révénus d'une année, si l'Institut proposé venoit à se realiser. Ces offres furent encore augmentés les jours suivants. Mais pour que ces sommes ne soient pas perdue, ou employées inutilement, ces Messieurs, s'en retinrent fort sagement la surinspection, et le pouvoir de tracer eux mêmes un plan sur la manière des les employer. Les Etats exprimèrent a Messieurs la réconnoissance de la nation.

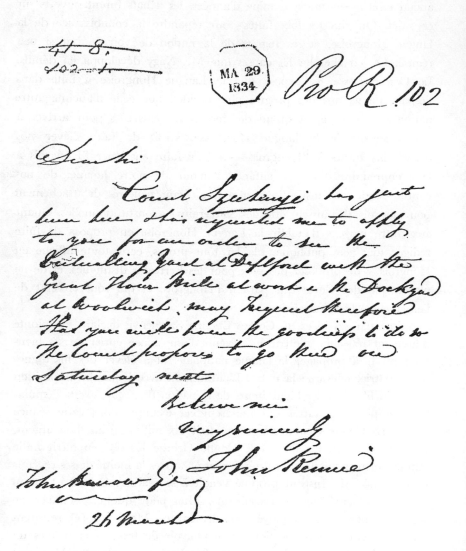

DOCUMENT 3. John Rennie's letter on Széchenyi's activities, March 26, 1834. *ADM. 1/5009. ProR 102.* Public Record Office (London). Cf. Chapter VII, pp. 273–76.

ADM 1/5009

MA 29 [Stamp]
1834

418 [crossed out]
102-1 [crossed out]   ProR 102

Dear Sir

Count *Szechenyi* has just been here & has requested me to apply to you for an order to see the Victualling Yard at Deflford with the Great Flour Mill at work & the Dockyard at Woolwich. May I request therefore that you will have the goodness to do so. The Count proposes to go there on Saturday next

> Believe me
> Very sincerely
> John Rennie

John Barrow, Esq
26 March

DOCUMENT 4. Sir Frederick Lamb to Palmerston, Aug. 5, 1836, on Hungarian conditions. *F.O.* 7/259, P.R.O. Cf. Chapter VII, pp. 300–311 and Chapter X, pp. 424f. Note the parallel between paragraph 2 in this document and paragraph 6 in Document 8c.

F.O. 7/259

Vienna, August 5th, 1836

My Lord

Count Reviczky the late Chancellor of Hungary has been removed from his high office, and a Count Palfy named in his place. Count Reviczky had the misfortune to satisfy neither the Court nor the Hungarians and both sides are equally glad to be quit of him. It is represented to me that the Diet during the latter period of its sittings was actuated by a spirit of decided hostility to the Government, a spirit which is stated to have gone far beyond the feelings of the country at large. This will be seen by the next elections but it is generally esteemed fortunate that a period of three years will elapse before the Diet shall reassemble. These three years are counted upon as a period of Tranquillity which is pretty certain to end whenever the Diet shall meet again. The measures which that Body demands are too much at variance with the

Institutions of the rest of the Empire to be granted without a general change of system, at the same time they are too much at variance with the state of society in Hungary to be put in operation without coming into conflict with the priviledges which the nobles possess and are determined to preserve.

What can be the result where an aristocratic assembly demands the freedom of the Press alongside of the most odious of the feudal institutions such as the exemption of the nobility from taxes, from arrest or any other mode of enforcing the payment of debts coupled with the existence of a Peasantry in the state of Serfs.

It is impossible to speculate upon the solution of the anomalous situation of Hungary. It is a sore place in the Austrian Empire which no man can tell how to heal. All that is counted upon for the moment is an interval of tranquillity till the reassembling of the Diet.

> I have the Honor to be
> with the greatest Truth & Respect
> My Lord
> Your Lordships
> most obedient
> humble Servant.
>
> F. Lamb

DOCUMENT 5. Draft of Palmerston's instructions to Lamb, Oct. 7, 1837, explaining British aims in southeastern and Central Europe. F. O. 7/263, P.R.O. Cf. Chapter VII, pp. 257ff.

F.O. 7/263

Foreign Office
7th October 1837

Draft, Sir. F. Lamb, No. 126
Sir,

I have received Y. E.'s dispatch no. 610 of the 22^d ult^o—reporting Prince Metternich's observations with regard to the state of Servia.

Undoubtedly, if the only choice were between the ascendancy of Russian or that of Austrian Influence in Servia, Her MY's Govt. would prefer [crossed out: the latter] the predominance of Austrian Influence [crossed out: latter,] because with Reference to the Peace and Safety of Europe it would be far better than Servia should be a Dependency of Austria than that it should [crossed out: be] become a member of the Russian System. But the ascendancy of Austrian Influence would not be unattended with Evils although of a different Nature from those which would follow the Dictation of Russia. The influence of Russia in Servia would be exerted [crossed out: with a view to] for the Purpose of rendering Servia a military advanced Post for further Territorial encroachments upon States lying beyond it; and Russia would endeavour to convert Servia into an offensive Station, from whence to threaten the Independence of other Countries. But the influence of Austria in Servia would be exerted for defensive Purposes first to render it a Bulwark against Russian attack, and next to make it a Barrier against the [crossed out: Invasion] Inroad of the principles of political Improvement. With respect to the first object, Her MY's Govt. would concur with that of Austria, with respect to the second, the views and interests of Great Britain would differ from those of the Cabinet of Vienna.

The Austrian Govt. is always so alarmed at the Progress of Political innovation, and at the appearance of Representative Institutions in any Country at all neighbouring upon Austria, that there can be no doubt that [crossed out: all] the Influence of Austria in Servia would be employed to prevent the progress of Improvement in the Govt. of that Country. But unless progressive Improvements are made in Servia, so as to render Persons and Property more secure, and to give greater Power to the Authority of the Law, it seems unlikely that the internal tranquillity of the Province can be maintained; that the Industry of the Population can be called into full activity; and that the natural resources of the Country can be properly developed.

[crossed out: But] Now the British Govt. has two objects in view with respect to Servia; First, that Servia should form a Barrier [crossed out: to] against the further encroachments of Russia; Secondly, that [crossed out: She] Servia should afford an opening for the extension of the commerce of Gt. Britain. The first object might perhaps be attained by the ascendancy of Austrian Influence, although some doubt may be felt whether if Austria were to begin to get a hold upon the Danube-bordering Provinces of Turkey, [crossed out: She] Austria and Russia might not [crossed out: insensibly] gradually [crossed out: be led to] come to an understanding [crossed out: with Russia] for a Division of those Provinces between them. —This first object, therefore, will perhaps [crossed out: be] best be attained, by keeping Servia as She is, with respect to political Dependence; but by endeavouring to give the [crossed out: People] Servians an Interest in maintainig [crossed out: that] their present political Position, and by opening to them for that Purpose such a Prospect of internal Prosperity as may render them unwilling to be [crossed out: annexed to] incorporated with the Russian Empire.

The Second of the above mentioned objects can evidently be attained by no other means than by the gradual Improvement of the Country; the advice which on this Point has been given by Colonel Hodges to Prince Milosch, seems judicious and well calculated to accomplish the desired Purpose. How far those ends are likely to be [crossed out: assisted] promoted by the Cooperation of the Austrian Consul, and how far the Austrian Govt. may be disposed to concur in [crossed out: promoting, furthering] encouraging improvement in Servia, or how far that Govt. may, on the contrary, [crossed out: prefer] wish to check such improvement, may be questions admitting of doubt; but it is certain that the experience which we have had of the action of Austrian Counsels in other Countries, would [crossed out: rather] tend to the [crossed out: conclusion, belief] apprehension that the Influence of Austria would be exerted to keep things stationary in Servia, instead of being [crossed out: employed] used to encourage Improvement in that Province.

P[almerston]

DOCUMENT 6. Excerpt from a report of the apostolic nuncio in Vienna, Ludovico Altieri, to Cardinal Secretary of State Lambruschini, May 8, 1840, on Hungarian ecclesiastic affairs and the work of the Diet. Our transcript is based on a copy of the second half of the report, which was intercepted by the Austrian secret police ("Intercepte betreffend kirchliche Angelenheiten, 1840." *StKI*, Vienna, III, HHStA). Deviations from the original have been corrected (indicating the Vienna version in brackets) on the basis of *SSE, 1814–1850*, Rubrica 247, Busta 409–410, Anni 1838–1842, No. 946 (May 8, 1840, "A"): "Affari Ecc-[lesias]tici d'Ungheria." ASV. Cf. Chapter VIII, pp. 345–48, 360–64 and Ch. X, pp. 423f.

Della Cancelleria di Stato
Il Nunzio ap[osto]lico à Lambruschini a Roma.

Vienna 8 maggio 1840

Ora sono del tutto finite le discussioni, e le deliberazioni della Dieta sulle materie *religionarie*. Nel *Renunzio* finale della Tavola de' Magnati, che avrò l'onore di sottomettere fra non molto tradotto all'E. V. si vedrà come sieno stati risoluti gli altri articoli, giacchè S. A. I. l'Arciduca Palatino ha fatto provocare gli Stati di mettere sotto gl'occhi de' Magnati alla fine della sessione tutto quanto l'articolo religionario com'essi lo vogliono, affine di evitare gli equivoci e le confusioni che potrebbero nascere dalla farragine di *Nunzi* e di *Renunzi* scambiati fra le due Camere sopra i diversi paragrafi di leggi variati, e corretti.

In seguito del suindicato *Conclusum* Dietale sullà facoltà da darsi ai Ministri delle varie religioni acattoliche di assistere, e cosí convalidare i Matrimoni Misti, il Primate e gli altri Vescovi d'Ungheria (ancora ignari di ciò che si combinò fra la S. Sede ed il Gabinetto Imp.^{le}) aveano risoluto di stare a vedere se ciò fosse o nò approvato da S. M., prima di emanare delle istruzioni ai loro Parrochi, onde vietare che benedicano i Matrimoni Misti, sforniti delle debite condizioni. Imperocchè se per legge si fosse permessa la celebrazione de' medesimi Matrimoni d'innanzi al Ministro Acattolico, sarebbe cessata l'obbligazione imposta ai Curati Cattolici di celebrarli. Che se all'incontro S. M. non avesse approvato il proposito *Conclusum,* ma si fossero lasciate le cose nello stato in cui sono, i Vescovi non avrebbero omesso di dare le analoghe istruzioni. Per ciò fare però volevano attendere la fine della Dieta, e la risoluzione che si prenderebbe in nome di S. M. intorno al *gravame* del Vescovo di Gran-Varadina, ond' evitare per quanto fosse possibile il grandissimo rumore che in essa si risveglierebbe più che mai violento contro di essi, e della Chiesa in generale, quasi che avessero imitato l'esempio del suddetto Vescovo, provocando il popolo alla ribellione, ed al disprezzo delle leggi. Appena che però fossero ritornati alle loro diocesi erano unanimemente risoluti, siccome assicurommi in voce negli scorsi giorni Mgr. Primate, di dar fuori simultaneamente le suaccennate istruzioni in forma di circolari generali, e redatte tutte negli stessi termini. Replicai in voci a Mgr. Primate le ragioni che devono persuadere della convenienza e della necessità di sottoporre preventivamente senza ulteriore indugio alla S. Sede pel mio mezzo particolare, qualora il governo continuasse a chiudere le altre vie, le prattiche che si credesse opportuno di stabilire nelle Diocesi Ungariche, onde non abbiano ad introdurvi illecitamente delle regole abrusive, e non tollerabili dal Capo della Chiesa. Persuasissimo anche il Primate della necessità di tal preventivo ricorso, dissemi essere disposto a farlo in nome di tutt'i suoi colleghi, ma che prima faceva d'uopo attendere le soraccenate risoluzioni, affine di sapere più sicuramente quali direzioni e facoltà sia necessario di richiedere al S. Padre. Tanto più si credeva obbligato di aspettare, dappoichè da una parte non poteva dirsi ancora interamente sicuro della costante ed esplicita concordia di tutt'i Vescovi del regno, e d'all'altra non sapeva operare contro le istanze che gli si faceano dall'Arciduca Palatino, non che d'a'primari membri, e Ministri del supremo governo, affinchè sospendesse co' suoi Colleghi ogni passo, fintantochè non si fosse il tutto combinato colla S. Sede, lo che gli si assicurava essere imminente. Il Palatino andava dicendo, che il Papa sarebbe stato nella necessità di dichiarare validi per tutt'i paesi, e specialmente nell'Ungheria, i Matrimoni Misti celebrati d'innanzi al Ministro non cattolico. — La prima delle suddette ragioni addotte dal Primate era purtroppo fondata sulla probabile irresoluzione et timidità, cui cederebbero alcuni de' Vescovi medesimi, allor chè si trovassero di nuovo dispersi ed isolati nelle loro Diocesi, circondati e soprasalti dalle potenti influenze del partito anticattolico, e delle stesse autorità governative, le quali non trascurarono minaccie e promesse per indebolirli e dividerli. Ciò è purtroppo vero, e ben m'avviddi, che si vuol sopratutto impaurirli, e delle rivolte, cui darebbero certamente causa, qualora non seguitassero *pro bono pacis* nella prattica finqui tranquillamente usata in riguardo ai Matrimoni Misti. E questo è il ritornello con cui si tentò spaventare anche me sulle inevitabili terribilissime conseguenze di una troppo rigida disciplina (l'unica, cioè, possibile nel senso cattolico) che si volesse imporre nell'Ungheria, con certo rischio di alienarla interamente dalla Chiesa e dal trono.

Dal canto mio non trascurai di esortare Mgr. Primate, ed alcun'altro de' Prelati com'esso ben animati, ad eseguire ciascuno senza indugio nella rispettiva loro diocesi quello che devono per obbligo, lasciando che gli altri provvedano come credono alla loro coscienza. Come anche procurai di ridurre alla giusta proporzione d'innanzi ai loro occhi le ribellioni di cui si voleano renderli ingiustamente responsabili, mentre ancor chè sieno per suscitarsi al loro ritorno nelle rispettive diocesi de' rumori sommossi dalla vendetta, e dalla rabbia de' nemici della Chiesa, non potranno certo mai attribuirsi allo loro zelo per sostenere i diritti imprescrittibili della Chiesa medesima.

Le cose sopradette potrebbero comparire inutili, ora che si sa la via concertata fra la S. Sede, e questo Imp. Governo per fare uscire d'imbarazzo i Vescovi d'Ungheria intorno alla questione di assistere ai Matrimoni Misti. Ciò non ostante ho stimato uttile di far conoscere quali sieno le disposizioni in cui si trovano attualmente i Vescovi medesimi.

Nel contemporaneo rapporto annunzierò a V. E. quello che finora si fece per rendere consapevoli i principali membri dell'Episcopato ungarico della libertà che loro è concessa di ricorrere al Sommo Pontefice sull'oggetto in questione.

Riseppi ora che il governo non permise che si pubblicasse neppure sulla gazzetta universale di Augusta la nota Dichiarazione, che il Primate fece in nome de' suoi colleghi nella seduta della Camera de' Magnati del giorno 30 Decembre passato. Si dette per ragione, che ciò avrebbe potuto dispiacere alla Prussia. E così non poterano i Vescovi rendere abbastanza manifesto un tal'atto, che mentre giustificava almeno le loro buone intenzioni per l'avvenire, avrebbe giovato eziandio a dimostrare ch'essi non volevano lasciare senza una qualche rispettosa protesta in contrario le lettere a loro dirette dall'aulica Cancelleria ungarica in nome di S.M.I.R.A. prima che si aprisse la Dieta, per renderli avvertiti a mantenere inviolabili le civile prescrizioni anticanoniche della famosa Legge del 1790/1. — La necessità di togliere lo scandalo che deriva dalla falsa opinione, che l'intero Episcopato ungarico siasi docilmente con-

qualche rispettosa protesta in contrario le lettere a loro dirette dall' Aulica Cancelleria Ungarica in nome di S. M. I. R. A. prima che si aprisse la Dieta, per renderli avvertiti a mantenere inviolabili le civili prescrizioni anticanoniche della famosa Legge Del 1790/1. — La necessità Di togliere lo scandalo che Deriva Dalla falsa opinione; che l'intero Episcopato Ungarico siasi Docilmente conformato a tali governative ingiunzioni, Diviene più urgente, Dappoichè in una Delle ultime Sedute il celebre Stefano Szechenij rinfacciò ironicamente ai laici Difensori Delle massime cattoliche del S. Matrimonio, Di voler esser più cattolici de' Vescovi; i quali si erano unanimemente guardati Dall'imitare l'esempio Di quello Di Gran-Varadino, appunto

formato a tali governative ingiunzioni, diviene più urgente, dappoichè in una delle ultime sedute il celebre Stefano Szecheny rinfacciò ironicamente ai laici difensori delle massime cattoliche sul S.º Matrimonio, di voler' esser più Cattolici de' Vescovi, i quali si erano unanimemente guardati dall'imitare l'esempio di quello di Gran-Varadino, appunto perchè irregolare. È vero che Mgr. Patriarca Pyrker si alzò a tergere li suoi Colleghi da si disonorevole imputazione, dimostrando che se finora non seguitarono l'esempio del Vescovo di Gran-Varadino, ciò fù non già perchè discordassero da' suoi lodevoli sentimenti, o perchè biasimassero il di lui operato, ma bensì perchè aspettar vollero fino a quest'estremo di essere aiutati dalla Dieta [Chiesa] e dal governo nel mantenimento de' loro diritti, che ora assolutamente erano decisi di difendere a qualunque costo.

Si querelava con ragione pur anche il Primate, perchè sulle materie di cui si tratta, di competenza intieramente ecclesiastica, neppure una volta siasi domandato dal governo alcun parere, nè a lui, nè agli altri Vescovi del Regno d'Ungheria.

Varie cose, mi soggiunse il Primate, intendono domandare i medesimi con esso lui al S. Padre, allorchè gli esporranno lo stato in cui si trovano a cagione de' Matrimoni Misti. Nel tempo stesso che per annunciarli a ricorrere alla S. Sede assicuravo in genere a Mgr. Primate, che il S. Padre avrebbe condisceso per riguardo alla odierna loro situazione in que' punti, nè quali potesse dispensare, senza offesa della essenziale ed universale disciplina, mi guardai bene dal fargli credere, che sarebbesi loro concesso tutto ciò che fossero per chiedere. E specialmente gli feci capire non esser possibile, che se non ne' singoli casi, almeno nelle facoltà quinquennali non si delegasse loro la facoltà di dispensare dall'impedimento impediente di disparità di culto, sebbene egli mi dicesse, che in ogni tempo i Vescovi d'Ungheria ne hanno dispensato per facoltà ordinaria.

In quanto al famoso Matrimonio della figlia del Consigliere Hauer con un Protestante, celebrato nella Parocchia di Kriliti nell' Archidiocesi de Strigonio di cui si menò tanto rumore mesi addietro, non fù ancor dichiarato nullo, come speravasi, pel difetto di vero domicilio, dal Concistoro Arcivescovile. Che anzi nella prima sentenza dichiarò esser valido, perchè la sposa posse[de]va una Casa in detta Parrochia. Ora si ripropose la causa per dimostrare quanto poco reale, e legale fosse cotesta illusoria possessione.

Note:
The concluding two lines of the original, acknowledging receipt of two dispatches and containing the courtesy formula, are missing from the Vienna copy.

DOCUMENT 7. Metternich's memorandum of Jan. 19, 1837, on Hungarian affairs. No. 123/1837, *CAa,* HHStA. Cf. Chapter IX, pp. 375–78, and 416ff.

Ad. Conf. Z 132.837   Conf. Z. 123.

Vide Z. 729.124.995.1700.$\overline{8}$36 $\overline{837.}$
      515.837

Ein Gegenstand, welcher wegen seiner folgereichen Wichtigkeit die höchste Aufmerksamkeit der Regierung in Anspruch nehmen muss, ist die Lage in der sich heute das Königreich Ungarn befindet.

Um diese Lage beurtheilen, — die Massregeln welche die Umstände erheischen in Erwägung zu ziehen, und mit der moralischen Beruhigung, dass sie die rechten seyen, in Anwendung bringen zu können, bedarf es vor allem *der Erkenntnis des bestehenden Übels.* Ich glaube dasselbe in grossen Zügen in das folgende Bild auffassen zu können.

Die Ursachen des dermaligen Standes der Dinge in Ungarn sind verschiedenen Ursprunges. Zwei Momente haben jedoch vorzüglich auf denselben eingewirkt.

Unter den europäischen Staaten hat Ungarn seine alten Gesetze und administrativen Formen am längsten aufrecht zu erhalten gewusst. Mit Ausnahme der Verseichtung, welche stets das Werk der Zeit ist, war dies unbedingt der Fall bis zur Epoche des Regierungs-Antrites Kaisers Joseph II. Welchen Einfluss die Regierungsprinzipien und die Massregeln dieses Monarchen in ihrer directen Anwendung auf Ungarn ausübten, hat die Thatsache bewiesen. Vor seinem Regierungsende wiederrief der Kaiser die letzteren. Dass ein ehrliches Vor- und Rückschreiten des Fürsten tief und ungedeihlich auf das Land wirken musste war unvermeidlich, und wie unheilbringend diese Einwirkung war, hat der Landtag 1790/1 handgreiflich dargethan. Das früher eingeschlummerte war erwacht; das Alte wurde neu, und dem Alten wurde Neues hinzugefügt; die früheren Beschränkungen der Königlichen Macht erhielten eine lähmende Ausdehnung, und es entstand, mit Einem Worte, ein Ungarn, welches nicht mehr das alte war, und eine unförmliche Gestaltung, ein Gewebe von Aufregung, Zweifeln, Prätensionen und Hader bildete.

Den Übeln aus dieser Veranlassung gesellte sich später ein anderes Übel zu: Es traten die Folgen der grossen socialen Umwälzung ein, welche unter der Benennung der französischen Revolution eine traurige Phase in der Geschichte unserer Zeit bildet! Die Einwirkung der

Grundsätze auf welche die französische Revolution sich stützte, und welche aus ihr hervorgegangen sind, würde in den von der Brandstätte entfernteren Theilen des europäischen Continents, zu welchen Ungarn gehört, früher bemerkbar geworden seyn, als dies wirklich der Fall war, wäre nicht die lange Krieges-Periode eingetreten. Wie verschieden von der früheren Einwirkung dieser Grundsätze jene ist, welche sich allgemein seit der Wiederkehr des politischen Friedens kundgegeben hat, liegt erwiesen vor.

Zwei Perioden sind sonach, bei der geschichtlichen Erwägung der heutigen Lage Ungarns, als Ausgangspunkte nicht aus den Augen zu verlieren: — der Landtag 1790/1, und der allgemeine Frieden in den Jahren 1814/5. Der Einfluss der ersteren dieser Perioden trift Ungarn directe; jener der zweiten ist ein allgemein vertheilter, welcher sich in Abstufungen, jedoch nicht minder deutlich in diesem Königreiche als an anderen Orten, bewährt. Als Abstufung können die Fristen zwischen den Jahren 1815 & 1830, und seit dem letzten dieser Jahre und dem heutigen Tage bezeichnet werden. In der neuen Periode nimmt, eben in ihrer directen Beziehung auf Ungarn, die polnische Revolution eine wichtige Stelle ein.

Wirft man, nach diesen Inhaltschweren Prämissen, die Blicke auf die in steter Wechselwirkung stehenden Verhältnisse Ungarns in Beziehung auf das Land selbst, und der Regierung dem Lande gegenüber: so wäre es kaum möglich diese Verhältnisse nicht in drei Zeitabschnitte zu theilen.

Den *ersten* bildet der Zeitraum zwischen dem Regierungsantritte des letztverewigten Monarchen (1792) bis zum allgemeinen Frieden (1814/15).

Als einen wegen seines eigenthümlichen Charakters, einen eigene Periode bezeichnenden *Moment,* dürfte wohl das Jahr 1811 betrachtet werden.

Die *dritte* Periode bildet der Zeitraum zwischen dem allgemeinen Frieden und dem Schlusse des letzen Landtages.

In der ersten der eben erwähnten Perioden war Ungarn, mittelst den Erwerbungen auf den Landtagen 1790/1 und 1792 befriedigt, und unter dem Lärm des Krieges zur bürgerlichen Ruhe geneigt. Die Stellung der Regierung war jedoch eine schwache, denn sie hatte grosse und unausweichliche Bedürfnisse zu decken. Ihre Rolle war auf's Ansinnen beschränkt, und die stärkere Lage — die gewährende — war jene der Stände. Wie bedeutend die Summe der Concessionen ist, welche die Regierung, auf den in diese Periode fallenden Landtagen, den Bedürfnissen ihrer oft höchst gedrängten Lage bringen zu müssen glaubte, steht in den landtäglichen Verhandlungen geschrieben.

Der Übergang aus dem Finanzdrange zu dem allerdings unhaltbaren, und nur durch eine eiserne Nothwendigkeit zu entschuldigenden Finanzsysteme im Jahre 1811, konnte für die Regierung nur dieselbe compromittirende, und ihre Stellung wäsentlich schwächende Folgen haben.

Die Ergebnisse der dritten Periode sind heute die fühlbarsten; nicht allein, weil sie die neueren sind, sondern weil sie die Dinge auf ein neues — Ungarn, dessen Gesetzen, Herkommen, Sitten und Bedürfnissen, nicht nur früher Fremdes, sondern im reinen Widerspruche mit diesen grossen Bedingungen des Staatenlebens stehendes Feld stellten. Um diese Thatsache in ein helles Licht zu ziehen, bedarf es nur der Erwägung der Verhältnisse in denen die Oppositionen sich bewegten und noch bewegen.

Bei Eröffnung des Landtages im J. 1825. befand sich die Regierung, durch die früher stattgehabte gewaltsame Recruten-Aushebung und den passiven Widerstand mehrerer Comitate gegen die Umsetzung der Contribution in Metallmünze, in einer gespannten Lage. Auf dem Landtage bewegte sich die Opposition, — so geschlossen sie auch auf demselben auftrat — dennoch in gesetzlichen Schranken. Als die Regierung sich ihrerseits fest auf das Feld der Verfassung stellte (ein Feld, welches sie seitdem, treu und unverbrüchlich, zu dem ihrigen machte) wich die alte constitutionelle Opposition, und es zeigten sich die ersten Spuren einer *neuen,* welche es sich alsbald zur Aufgabe machte, Untersuchungen über die Art und die Ausdehnung der königlichen Rechte anzustellen. Noch vor dem Schlusse des Landtages war die alte Opposition so gut als erloschen. Ihre Theilnehmer hatten sich entweder in die Königlichen Reihen gestellt, oder sie waren zu der neuen Opposition übergegangen; mehrere endlich zogen sich in Unthätigkeit zurück. — Die Regierung hatte auf dem Landtage Concessionen höchstwichtiger Art sich zu Schulden kommen lassen. Sie gereichten sämmtlich zum Gedeihen der neuen Opposition, deren Thätigkeit sich ohne Zeitverlust nicht mehr inner den Grenzen der landtäglichen Verhandlungen erhielt, sondern diese Grenzen überschritt. So entstanden die Casino's, — diese VerbreitungsAnstalt des modernen Liberalismus; — die gelehrte Gesellschaft, als die befördernde Behörde der ungarischen Sprache, welche, ohne Rücksicht auf den beschränkten Kreis ihrer damaligen Anwendbarkeit durch ihre Erhebung zur *National-* Sprache, den Werth einer Institution erhielt: —die Donauschiffarts-Unternehmungen, bezeichnet als ein rein nationaler Industrial-Zweck! — Ginge die Sache nicht in's Lächerliche, so dürften hier noch die Wettrennen mit Englischen Jokeys, die vielfachen Reisen der jungen Magnaten nach Frankreich und England, zur Einsaugung fremder Begriffe und

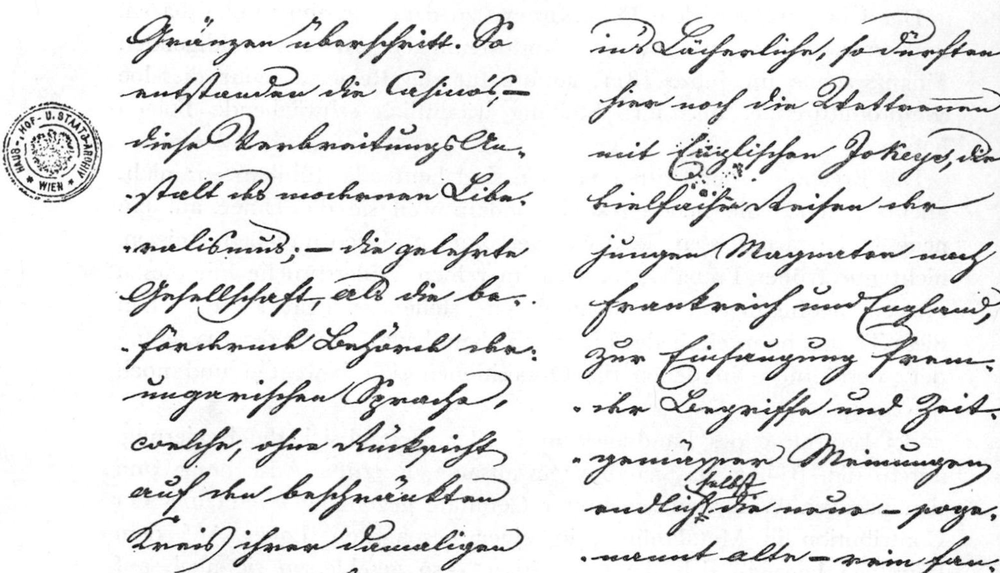

zeitgemässer Meinungen, endlich selbst die neue — sogenannte alte — rein fantastische Tracht, in Rechnung kommen.

Diese Unternehmungen des schwirrenden Geistes eines Grafen Stephan Széchény, und des weit tiefer berechnenden des Freih[n] v. Wesseleny, wurden durch die Druckschriften des Ersteren unterstützt. Ihrer erwiesenen Seichtheit ungeachtet, hatten sie dennoch den Werth der Beförderung der Sprache und eines directen Angriffs auf *das Leben im früheren Geleise*. Ein Land aus diesem Geleise schieben, heisst, es dem Umsturze unter dem Namen von *Reformen* Preis geben. Welchen Weg Ungarn in dieser Beziehung in wenigen Jahren gemacht hat, beweisen die sämmtlichen Verhältnisse des Tages!

Als einen höchst einflussreichen Entschluss, welchen die Regierung als Vorbereitung zu dem Landtage 1832. genommen hatte, muss die Abgabe der Operate, für diesen und kommende Landtage, an die Jurisdictionen bezeichnet werden. Durch diesen Schritt wurden die letzteren aus der Sphäre der Municipal-Interessen auf das höchste Feld der Gesetzgebung versetzt. Die *neue* Oppositionsparthei wirkte gleichzeitig mit allen von ihr ersonnenen und ihr täglich mehr zu Gebote stehenden Mitteln als eine liberale Propagande. Sie erhitzte die Köpfe der Jugend, schüchterte die Gutgesinnten in gleichem Masse ein, und bewies bald hierauf, bei Eröffnung des Landtages, ihre Gewalt. Von der früheren constitutionellen Opposition war gleich beim Beginnen des Landtages keine Spur mehr zu entdecken. Durch die vollkommen correcte Stellung des Königs auf dem Felde der Verfassung war ihrer Thätigkeit kein Spielraum gegönnt; aber in dieser Thatsache liegt nicht allein die Ursache ihres Nichtdaseyns: der frühere Körper war in sich selbst zerronnen. Die neue Opposition trat, ihrer Natur gemäss, nicht wie diess der Fall der früheren war, vertheidigend auf; sie ergriff alsbald die Offensive; und wie es den *liberalen* Gestaltungen stets ergeht, — sie zeigte die *radicale demagogische* Form und Tendenz. In deren äussersten Richtung steht die *Trennung Ungarns* vom grossen Kaiserstaate mit deutlichen Worten heute geschrieben.

In einer solchen Lage der Dinge, — unter dem lebendigen Einwirken einer derartigen Tendenz, — unter dem Einflusse sich bis zur Selbständigkeit erhebender Jurisdictionen, — musste das Ende des Landtages, der Thatsache ungeachtet, dass sich die Regierung keine eigentlichen Concessionen — wenigstens keine in dem constitutionellen Sinne des Wortes — zu Schulden kommen liess, ein ungedeihliches seyn, denn sie war bei dem Beginnen des Landtages bereits überflügelt, und sie konnte ihre Kraft nur auf dem Felde entfalten, welches von der Opposition verlassen war. Auch war auf dem Landtage kein Kampf zwischen den *constitutionellen Partheien* zu finden; der Kampf sprach sich — wie dies heute aller Orten mehr oder weniger offenkündig oder verkappt der Fall ist — zwischen den erhaltenden und den zerstörenden Prinzipien aus. In diesem Kampfe erhob sich der kleine gegen den grossen Adel, die untere gegen die obere Tafel, der sogenannte Zeitgeist gegen Grundsätze und Herkommen, welche als veraltet und einer finsteren Zeit angehörend verschrien wurden, und in diesem Zwiste war die Rolle der Regierung auf jene eines *Zuschauers* beschränkt!

Aus einer solchen der Wahrheit gemässen Schilderung der Lage der Dinge ergeht unbedingt die Nothwendigkeit, dass diese Lage in eine bessere umgestaltet werden müsste. Wenn hier kein Zweifel über das Bestehen dieser Nothwendigkeit obzuwalten vermag, so hat die Wahl der Mittel nicht weniger den Werth einer schweren Aufgabe!

Dort wo Sachen einmal *so* stehen wie dies der Fall in Ungarn ist, muss derjenige, welcher Hilfe zu leisten berufen ist, sich vor allem eine deutliche Ansicht *über den von ihm zu wählenden Standpunkt* verschaffen. In dem vorliegenden Falle muss die Regierung entweder sich fest *auf das Feld der Verfassung stellen,* oder sie muss ihren Standpunkt *ausser diesem Felde wählen.* Zugleich *in* und *ausser* einer Sache stehen ist nie gedeihlich.

Die Wahl zwischen den beiden Standpunkten ist um so weniger schwer, als das zur Aufstellung geeignete Feld nur das von dem Feinde nicht besetzte seyn kann. — Nun haben die Gegner das Feld der Verfassung verlassen, wäre es in dem nicht mehr auszuweichenden Kampfe nicht schon dadurch das Stärkere, weil es das gesetzliche ist, und weil in die Dauer die wilden Kräfte meist vor der Kraft des Gesetzes versiegen; so wäre es schon deshalb das zu wählende, weil es das verlassene ist, und der Regierung sonach zum freien Gebrauche offen steht.

Hiezu kömmt noch eine Betrachtung von hoher und practischer Wichtigkeit. Die *neue* Opposition steht im offenbarsten Widerspruche mit den Grundbedingungen des ungarischen Staatslebens. Das ungarische Staatsgebäude ist ein altes, in dem der Verlauf der Zeiten die verschieden-artigen Bestandtheile, aus denen Staaten bestehen, auf bestimmte Grund-bedingungen festgestellt hat, welche nicht ohne einen grossen, leicht fühlbar werdenden Schaden vernichtet werden können. Je mehr die wahre Civilisation nur ein im Vorschreiten langsames Werk zu seyn vermag, um so mehr wirken die Versuche einer falschen und eingebildeten Civilisa-tion — eben weil sie ihrer Natur gemäss stets eilig sind — unheilbringend auf die Länder. Die Ausflüsse der Casino's und der Juraten Vereine werden Ungarns alte Verfassung eben so wenig heilbringend zu ersetzen vermögen, und den Schutz, welchen die Verfassung — ihrer Mängel ungeachtet — den Eigenthums-Rechten und den sonstigen bürgerlichen Verhältnissen sichert, entbehrlich machen, als Englische Wettrennen, Dampfschiffe, Eisenbahnen, und alle sonstigen Übertreibungen in einer krankhaften Zeit die wahre Civilisation Ungarns wesentlich befördern werden. Die Zeit ist, bei solchen Verirrungen des Geistes, allerdings die beste Lehrerin; jedoch nur *der* kann ihre Früchte ernten, welcher auf einem festen Grund steht. Der festeste Grund aber ist hier unbedingt jener der Verfassung. Er muss sonach der seyn, auf dem Sich der König zu erhalten haben wird.

Hier tritt jedoch eine wesentliche Rücksicht ein. Indem wir annehmen, dass die Opposition ihr Lager ausser dem VerfassungsFelde aufgeschlagen hat, wird die Regierung — in dem sie sich auf demselben befindet — nicht die Gefahr laufen, ausser dem Kreise in welchem die Bewegung stattfindet, in Unthätigkeit zu verbleiben, und sich dazu verdammt sehen, dem Übel in träger Ruhe, ohne in dasselbe eingreifen zu können, den freien Spielraum zu überlassen? Diese Gefahr würde allerdings eintreten, verfolgte die Regierung den negativen Weg, welchen sie im Verlaufe so vieler Jahre einhielt. *Ungarn wird heute nicht regiert, es muss regiert werden, und das Feld wird sich bald beleben.*

Die Rechte des Königs sind ausser den Landtags Perioden leichter anwendbar, als in diesen Perioden. So wie die Sachen heute stehen, liegt die Königliche Gewalt in der Zwischenzeit der Landtage brach, um während dieser letzteren den ruchlosesten Angriffen ausgesetzt zu seyn. Unter solchen Bedingungen muss das Ansehen der Krone verloren gehen, wie sich dasselbe im entgegengesetzten Benehmen wieder erheben wird; denn die Regierten schliessen sich nur der Kraft an, welche sich als eine wahrhaft schützende bewährt.

Mit diesem Ausspruche hat die gegenwärtige Arbeit ihr Ziel erreicht. Ihr Zweck is kein anderer als der, in der höchsten Sphäre der Regierung Aussprüche über die folgenden Sätze herbeizuführen:

1º Ist die Lage, in welcher sich das Königreich Ungarn befindet, eine derjenigen in welcher die Regierung die Dinge ihrer eigenen Schwere überlassen kann?

2º Ist diess nicht der Fall, welche Grundlage für ihre Handlungsweise hat die Regierung zu wählen?

Ist der letztere dieser Aussprüche gefällt, so kann erst die Untersuchung der Mittel, welche dem Zwecke am besten zu entsprechen vermögen, stattfinden.

Wien, d. 19. Jäner 1837.

Metternich

DOCUMENTS 8a-c. Excerpts from Baron Langsdorff's reports to French Ambassador Sainte-Aulaire, June 6, 7, and 10, 1837, on the county assembly of Pest and on his conversation with Széchenyi. *MDAu, 1830 à 1847,* Vol. 51, #8 and 9. AMAE. Cf. Chapter IX, pp. 414ff.

8a.

Mémoirs et Documens, (sic), volume 51.

Annex à la Depeche 27, - 1837   [p.] 120
N° 2   8.

Relation de la Congrégation
du Comitat de Pesth des 6 et 7 Juin 1837
addressée à S. Ex. M^r l'ambassadeur
par le Baron de Langsdorff
Congrégation Générale   [p.] 121
du Comitat de Pesth.

. . . .

Séance du Mardi 6 Juin
[Excerpts from p. 123.]

Après cette formalité [i.e. after the new judges had been sworn in], le Comte *Szechenyi* se lève et prononce quelques paroles très accentuées: Dès les premiers mots, il est couvert d'applaudissemens.

"Ce jour est une fête pour le Comitat; mais pour qu'elle soit complète et pour répondre aux sentimens qui préoccupent l'assemblée, je demande qu'on délibère immédiatement sur le rescript impérial qui a été adressé au Comitat et que lecture en soit faite. Ce rescript impérial est celui qui depuis son arrivée excite si vivement par la dureté des expressions, la susceptibilité da la plupart des Magnats; c'est la réponse aux représentations du Comitat sur les illégalités commises dans le procès des jeunes gens du club de Presbourg. On le trouvera en entier (pièce N. 1.) . . . . . .

. . . . [pp.] 128–29

Conseils de modération donnés
par l'auteur de la motion

8b.

Le Comte *Szechenyi* demanda la parole.

". . . Ce n'est pas d'aujourd'hui que j'ai fait mes preuves, et je crois que je n'ai pas besoin d'apporter ici 'ma profession de foi' — je suis un de ceux qui ont réveillé la Patrie (bravos) pendant 20 ans on a pu la croire morte; aujourd'hui on dit qu'elle est malade, qu'elle a la fièvre — c'est un progrès. — (On rit.)

L'orateur se livre à plusieurs digressions qui captivent toujours l'attention de l'assemblée. Il excite à un très haut degré la curiosité de l'auditoire par des images vives ou des anecdotes qu'il mêle à ses raisonnemens; il intéresse et fait rire ses auditeurs, genre de succès qu'il parait ambitionner — sa parole est vive, forte, accentuée, de manière à rappeler sans cesse l'attention. D'ailleurs son discours est un peu vague et se sent de l'embarras qu'il éprouve à prêcher la modération tout en recherchant les applaudissemens que l'assemblée n'accorde qu'aux orateurs qui flattent sa passion.

456

"Je voudrais que ces jeunes gens qu'un noble amour de la liberté transporte puissent voir au fond de mon âme. — Je sais que bien des gens disent ainsi — qui souvent montrent de vilaines choses — j'ose dire que nos jeunes patriotes verraient dans mon coeur les mêmes sentimens généreux qui les animent. — Mais il faut de la modération dans notre réponse — (murmures et récriminations contre la position de l'orateur qui depuis longtemps ne paraissait plus aux congrégations.) "Il faut de la modération, parce que le droit est pour nous, et que nous voulons réussir, n'est-ce pas? — Il faut faire une petition — (oui, bravo, une pétition) — non, je me suis trompé, je voulais dire une *représentation:* c'est plus que la pétition et nous restons dans notre droit, mais il faut que notre langage soit conciliant, il ne faut pas exaspérer les vieilles têtes de la chancellerie."

L'orateur appuie d'ailleurs la proposition de Georges *Karolyi* de donner des instructions à la prochaine Diète pour une loi sur les accusations de haute trahison.

8c.

Pesth, 10 juin 1837

Entretien avec le magnat Etienne Széchényi
sur la délibération . . . du . . . Comitat.

. . . . .En sortant de la séance, j'allai chez le Comte Széchényi; eh! bien, me dit-il, maintenant que vous nous avez vus à l'oeuvre, qu'allez vous dire du nous; Est ce que vous publierez bien des méchancetés contre ce pauvre pays parce qu'on y parle un peu à tort et à travers? — Je ne publie rien ai-je répondu, vous savez bien que ce n'est pas de notre métier; mais je suis curieux, j'aime à regarder, et comme j'ai vu un peu de fumée, et que vous deviez avoir d'ailleurs, de superbes courses, je suis venu vous voir. — A la bonne heure a repris le Comte, on peut donc laisser aller sa langue avec vous; vous ne sauriez croire le tort que l'on m'a fait ici en imprimant des paroles que je disais sans crainte de cette terrible publicité; Eh bien, vous avez vu beaucoup de fumée, même un peu de feu, mais tout cela ne fera pas d'incendie."

Je vous écoute, ai-je dit, voyant qu'il m'attendait; ce que vous dites là je le crois un peu d'instinct, mais surtout parce que vous me l'assurez; Expliquez moi cependant comment tout cela pourra s'arranger? Nous autres français nous avons une certaine logique que nous portons dans le gouvernement comme ailleurs; Eh! bien voilà, par exemple, votre Comitat qui va continuer le journal de Kossuth; Si le gouvernement autrichien continue à faire arrêter les gens qui font des journaux, où cela ira-t-il? Vous avez un gouvernement qui tire à droite, et non seulement votre noblesse c.à.d. tout le pays, mais toute votre administration va à gauche:

Pesth 10 juin 1837.

Entretien avec le magnat Etienne Szécheinyi
sur la délibération . du .. Comitat. /

. . . . . . En sortant de la séance, j'allai chez le Comte
Szécheinyi ; eh! bien, me dit il, maintenant que vous nous avez
vus à l'œuvre, qu'allez vous dire de nous ; Est ce que vous
publierez bien des méchancetés contre ce pauvre pays parce qu'on
y parle un peu à tort et à travers ? — . — Je ne
publie rien ai-je répondu, vous savez bien que ce n'est pas
de notre métier ; mais je suis curieux, ; j'aime à
regarder, et comme j'ai vu un peu de fumée, et que
vous deviez avoir d'ailleurs, de superbes courses, je suis venu
vous voir . — . à la bonne heure a repris le comte,
on peut donc laisser aller sa langue avec vous ; vous ne
sauriez croire le tort que l'on m'a fait ici en
imprimant des paroles que je disais sans crainte de cette
terrible publicité ; Eh bien, vous avez vu beaucoup de fumée,
même un peu de feu, mais tout cela n . . . . . .
d'incendie . . .

Je vous écoute, ai-je dit, voyant qu'il m'attendait,
ce que vous dites là je le crois un peu d'instinct, mais
surtout parce que vous me l'assurez ; - Expliquez moi cependant
comment tout cela pourra s'arranger ? nous autres français
nous avons une certaine logique que nous portons dans le
gouvernement comme ailleurs ; Eh! bien voila, par exemple,
voici Comitat qui va . . . . . continuer le journal de
Kossuth ; - Si le gouvernement autrichien continue à faire
arrêter les gens qui font des journaux, où cela ira + il ?
vous avez un gouvernement qui tire à droite, et non seulement

votre noblesse c.-à-d. tout le pays, mais toute votre admirable
va à gauche : on vous lance vivement la Wiener, ..
vous répondez avec hauteur "— paroles, dites vous ne
les paroles amènent les actes : je vois bien voir que
vous, et les habiles, vous cherchez à renvoyer tous les
griefs à la prochaine Diète, qui tome à ce doit pas
ce sont les Calendes grecques. Mais si l'on votre dans
la légalité le tome viendra cependant ; et même
bientôt ; d'ici là vous aurez fait la boule de neige
— et même cette suspension d'armes que vous recherchez,
vous ne l'obtenez pas : — plus ou moins nettement
vous avez tous trois, vous, le Cte Dissewffy, et votre
premier vice-comte, parlé pour arriver au même but,
vous n'avez rien gagné, et sans votre éloquence, sans
l'ascendant que vous exercez toujours sur une assemblée
hongroise, vous n'auriez pas été mieux écouté que
Dissewffy. . . — — — — Il est vrai a-t-il repris que
ce pauvre garçon n'a pas été heureux ; il se perd
dans la métaphysique il faut des images et des sentiments
pour agir sur les masses : j'ai suivi assidûment
pendant deux ans le parlement anglais, j'ose dire que
leurs orateurs sont au dessous des nôtres ; ... cela se
conçoit avant 15 ans nous allons aux assemblées des
Comitats ; nous parlons comme nos hussards montent à
cheval, parce qu'ils sont en selle dès l'enfance et tout
le jour.

    Après tout si on veut y mettre de l'habileté
à Vienne on matera le pays : nous sommes gens
faciles à prendre, il faudrait nous faire quelque concession
dans la forme ; je l'ai répété vingt fois au Prince

      de Metternich ;

on vous tance vertement de Vienne, vous répondez avec hauteur "— paroles, dites vous, mais les paroles amènent les actes: je crois bien voir que vous, et les habiles, vous cherchez à renvoyer tous ces griefs à la prochaine Diète, qui terme a ne doit pas; ce sont les Calendes grecques. Mais si l'on reste dans la légalité, ce terme viendra cependant, et même bientôt; d'ici là vous aurez fait la boule de neige — et même cette suspension d'armes que vous recherchez, vous ne l'obtenez pas: — plus ou moins nettement, vous avez tous trois, vous, le Cte Désewfy, et votre premier vice-Comte, parlé pour arriver au même but; vous n'avez rien gagné, et dans votre éloquence, sans l'ascendant que vous exercerez toujours sur une assemblée hongroise, vous n'auriez pas été mieux écouté que Désewfy . . . ." Il est vrai a-t-il repris que ce pauvre garçon n'a pas été heureux; il se perd dans la métaphysique, il faut des images et des sentiments pour agir sur les masses. J'ai suivi assiduement pendant deux ans le parlement anglais, j'ose dire que leurs orateurs sont au dessous des nôtres; — cela se conçoit avant 15 ans nous allons aux assemblées des Comitats; nous parlons, comme nos hussards montent à cheval, parce qu'ils sont en selle dès l'enfance, et tout le jour.

Après tout, si on veut y mettre de l'habileté à Vienne, on *matera* ce pays: nous sommes gens faciles à prendre, il faudrait nous faire quelques concessions dans la forme; je l'ai répété vingt fois au Prince de Metternich;—"Mais pourquoi donc ne vous déclarez vous pas, nettement, hautement, pour le gouvernement me dit-il" — parce que j'aime mieux tirer le taureau par la queue, que le prendre par les cornes: le secret des forces politiques, comme celui des forces mecaniques est de n'en employer que la quantité nécessaire au but qu'on veut atteindre. — Je lui disais, distribuons nous les rôles, je serai le *traqueur,* et vous le *chasseur*; Croyez seulement que je suis aussi intéressé que vous à ce qu'il n'y ait pas de Révolution. Ce pays a besoin d'une refonte complète, et il l'aura, mais je la veux pour vous et pour nous, car nous avons besoin d'un gouvernement, et vous êtes le seul possible; je n'y mets pas de roman et de sensibilité; je ne dis pas que j'aie de l'affection, mais que vous êtes nécessaire, et que notre intérêt vous répond de notre foi. Au lieu d'entendre ce langage qui est vrai, qui est raisonnable, si l'on me fait appeler pour me consulter sur l'état du pays, on parle pendant quatre heures en me disant, "je vois toute votre affaire; il faut se retrancher dans la Constitution, bonne ou mauvaise on peut vivre avec." Je vous dire au contraire, moi que votre Constitution avec ses 2 volumes in folio est un arsenal où tout le monde va puiser: vous dites, *en vertu de, et de, je vous ordonne,* et l'on vous répond, comme aujourd'hui, *en vertu de et de, je ne vous obéirai pas;* il n'y a qu'à tourner la page.

. . . . .Non je ne crois pas qu'on veuille arrêter d'aussi gros seigneurs que ceux qui forment la commission actuelle: on nous répondra encore séchement, et nous obtiendrons, j'espère que la correspondance finisse, et que tout soit renvoyé à la prochaine Diète: il n'y a pas, croyez moi, péril en la demeure: le mal est qu'à Vienne on s'imagine qu'il y a des associations secrètes, des complots ténébreux contre la maison d'Autriche! Mon Dieu, dites moi, quand on parle, comme vous nous avez entendu parler, à quoi bon les conciliabules, imaginez qu'il y a quelque temps *Vesséliny*, qui est mal dans ses affaires, se laissa tromper par un Juif qui lui persuada de faire une expédition directe de sangsues à Paris; on achète une voiture et les sangsues partent; *Sedlnitsky* fait courir après les pauvres bêtes, la voiture contenait disait on un plan d'insurrection de la hongrie et de la Pologne, adressé à Lafayette qui était mort depuis 3 ans! on ne sait pas mieux choisir le temps pour frapper des coups; depuis la maladie du Palatin, et l'inquietude qu'elle avoit causée, il y avait une réaction marquée contre le mouvement. On choisit ce temps pour nous envoyer des paroles aigres et blessantes qui mettent de nouveau le feu aux étoupes!

. . . . .Ce n'est pas moi qui puis conduire cette conciliation; le service que je puis rendre au gouvernement c'est de me mettre dans le *trou du souffleur;* tenez ce jeune Pronay le nouvel administrateur, pourrait être utile; je tirerais les fils mais sans paraître, j'ai trop d'ennemis, trop d'envieux . . . . Je me suis brouillé avec Karolyi pour de mauvaises tracasseries; on a dit Sz . . siffle, et Ky. . danse; dès ce moment il n'a plus voulu même marcher avec moi, puis je n'ai pas le pied, je n'ai pas la barbe et les épaules de Vesséliny . . . . . — . Très sérieusement, c'est une difficulté, c'est du moins un avantage pour les autres; quand j'étais au pinacle de la faveur populaire, et qu'on voyait arriver quelque juge de village, grand, fort, aux épaules carrées, le village accourait, on criait, vivat, "voila le grand "Széchényi." Quand le vrai Sosie paraissait, on disait, quoi n'est ce que cela?

. . . . Nous avons 52 Comitatus; ils ne sont pas tous à beaucoup près aussi hostiles que celui de Pesth — c'est vrai, Sthulweissenbourg, Szalader, et en général ceux de la ligne que vous suivrez, ne sont guères meilleurs — après tout ce sont des sphères d'opposition isolées; le gouvernement autrichien peut les négliger sans péril; tous les grands propriétaires ont besoin de lui, et s'entendraient avec lui s'il ne faisait pas de maladresses ou des provocations gratuites. Par example, je ne puis pas dire ces choses là à la Congrégation, mais je ne suis pas partisan de la liberté de la presse, des journaux surtout, dans mon pays. Si vous avez aujourd'hui le journal des nobles, vous aurez demain le journal des paysans! Eh! bien sachez ce que vous voulez; votre Constitution politique et sociale, votre Constitution féodale de seigneurs et de serfs, ne peut pas supporter le discussion publique: nos droits sont aussi légitimes qu'aucun de ceux sur lesquels repose le monde, mais imaginez une discussion de journaux engagée pour les défendre, et notre manifeste commencant par établir les principes "les hommes étant nés, les uns pour obéir, les autres pour commander. . . . les uns pour posséder et jouir, les autres pour travailler et n'avoir rien." La discussion logique est impossible.

. . . . J'accepte de coeur tout ce que vous me dites d'obligeant sur ce sujet; oui, je crois aussi que mon temps ne tardera pas à revenir; En attendant je suis mal à mon aise, et si je n'avais pas l'espoir de m'abriter un jour à l'ombre des arbres que j'ai plantés, je serais quelquefois tenté d'aller vivre en France ou en Angleterre; nous n'avons guères ici que des commencements . . . . . — Je vous remercie et vous avez raison il faut rester ici pour suivre le développement de tous ces enfants dont je me reconnais le père; mais parce que je ne crie pas comme les enragés beaucoup me regardent comme un homme double; "Est-il au gouvernement ou à nous, se demandent-ils? Il n'est ni à Dieu ni à Diable; Il est à lui, il est à la raison; il n'ote pas son chapeau stupidement lorsqu'on lui dit "la Constitution." Non Széchenyi n'est plus qu'un industriel maintenant; — puisque vous vous intéressez a la hongrie, voulez vous prendre des actions pour le pont entre Pesth et Buda, voulez vous des actions de nos bateaux à vapeur, celles là sont en hausse: venez me voir à Orshowa, je vous montrerai tous nos travaux. . . .

La conversation continue longtemps sur ces matières, Nous passâmes en revue quelques uns des principaux personnages du moment, et il me les peignit toujours avec des couleurs vives, avec des apercus très rapides de ce qu'on pouvait en attendre, arrivé à l'orateur de la séance, ... vous avez bien jugé földvary me dit-il, et la scène qui vient de se passer; cet homme n'est qu'à moitié Charlatan; tel vous l'avez vu là, tel il serait devant des Commissaires Impériaux. Il a du Spartiate, . . . il veut avoir de la *popularité*, et comme tous les hommes qui n'ont qu'une seule passion, il la poursuit par tous les moyens: S'il avait vu l'assemblée froide et sans sympathie, sa démission eut été sérieusement donnée; Il l'a trouvée vive et passionnée pour lui, il reste; voilà la vérité; nous avons beaucoup de caractères de cette trempe: après tout se disent ces gens là je suis gentilhomme hongrois, membre de la couronne de hongrie, personne n'a de droit sur moi. Ce sont des hommes difficiles à manier; ce seraient des hommes précieux avec un gouvernement national, dans la situation actuelle, je conviens qu'ils sont dangereux, surtout quand ils se trouvent placés au coeur même de l'administration; ce sont des bras perpetuellement en Révolte contre la tête: mais je vous le répète je ne vois point de danger sérieux et imminent.

APPENDIX II. BIBLIOGRAPHICAL ESSAY

It has been said that each generation should try to make a new approach to any great man.[1] Due to special political and social conditions, this otherwise healthy principle has been somewhat overdone in Hungary with regard to Széchenyi. Although no high-ranking official of the administration would pay attention to his warnings in the years preceding 1848, Széchenyi was credited with almost prophetic clairvoyance during the years of the neo-absolutistic regime, after the revolution and Kossuth had failed. The classic examples of this reinterpretation of Széchenyi are Kemény's brilliant Széchenyi essays.[2]

Following this period of soul-searching, the liberal era between the Compromise of 1867 and World War I attempted to incorporate both Széchenyi and Kossuth into the national Pantheon. But the balance usually turned out to be in favor of Kossuth, for due to an unconscious attitude noticed already by Kemény in his "Memorial from 1849," ". . . the justification of one's career necessarily predetermined the other's condemnation." Despite some important exceptions, such as Angyal[3] and Gaál[4] or the literary critics Gyulai[5] and Péterfy,[6] most

[1] "Every new era asks a new question from Széchenyi." Szekfű, *A mai Széchenyi*, p. 25. Cf. Sándor Karácsonyi, *Széchenyi*, 2d. edn. (Budapest: Exodus, 1941), pp. 12–20.

[2] Kemény's "Emlékirat 1849-ből" (Memorial from 1849), "Széchenyi István" (Stephen Széchenyi), "Forradalom után" (After the Revolution) and "Még egy szó a forradalom után" (Yet Another Word after the Revolution), written in 1849–51, can be found in Pál Gyulai, ed., *Báró Kemény Zsigmond összes művei* (The Complete Works of Baron Sigismund Kemény), 12 vols. (Budapest: Franklin, 1896–1908), IX, 47–343 and XII, 7–398, respectively. (The second essay was first published in Csengery, ed., *Magyar szónokok*, pp. 332–513, in 1851.)

[3] "Les idées . . ." and *Történeti tanulmányok*, pp. 1–147.

[4] *Széchenyi nemzeti politikája.*

[5] Pál Gyulai, "Gróf Széchenyi István mint iró" (Count Stephen Széchenyi as a Writer), *SzIM²*, I, pp. v-xxiii.

[6] Jenő Péterfy, "Egy uj könyv Széchenyi Istvánról" (A New Book About Stephen Széchenyi), *BSz*, LXII (1890), 290–309. Originally published under pseudonym ("X"), this essay and Péterfy's other reviews of the volumes containing Széchenyi's letters in *SzIM* were republished in Vol. III of Dávid Angyal, ed., *Péterfy Jenő Összegyüjtött Munkái* (The Collected Works of Eugene Péterfy), 3 vols. (Budapest: Franklin, 1901–1903).

writers of this period thought of Széchenyi mainly as the great initiator of the Hungarian Age of Reforms (which he actually was) whose principles were taken over and brought to a new phase by Kossuth. Kossuth's name still had an unparalleled appeal to Hungarian hearts. Széchenyi was, at best, considered a national monument, to be respected but not studied, an aristocratic and imperfect Kossuth, who backed away from the ideas of his younger self. But more often his ability as a political leader was questioned and regarded as inferior to that of his great opponent.[7] Besides correctly pointing out the inconsistencies of Széchenyi's policy,[8] one Hungarian scholar even went so far as to refuse to see any "statesmanship" in Széchenyi's activities. In the opinion of Ákos Beöthy, Széchenyi had no political program or consistent system at all and was completely unprepared for the role of a national leader: all his works and actions were but rhapsodic improvizations of a genius.[9]

Still, the decades preceding the dissolution of Austria-Hungary witnessed a revival of interest in Széchenyi. Significant interpretations of his life work appeared, many of which have been mentioned in this study. Besides the publication of Széchenyi's main writings in numerous editions, an attempt was made to collect and publish all his works. The nine-volume edition of his letters, speeches, newspaper articles, and accounts of his foreign travels, as well as the two-volume set containing his major books (both published under the auspices of the Hungarian Academy),[10] continue to be basic tools of the researcher, despite the fact that parts of both sets have been superseded by the Széchenyi publications in the *Fontes* series and by other modern critical editions of his works. Similarly indispensable are the documentary sections and references of the biographical studies done by Falk,[11] Zichy,[12] Friedreich,[13]

---

[7] Grünwald, *Az uj Magyarország*, esp. pp. 524–28; Imre Halász, *Egy letünt nemzedék* (A Past Generation) (Budapest: Nyugat, 1911), pp. 30–53; Zichy's introduction to *Széchenyi hirlapi czikkei*, I, pp. xxi f., xxxiii.

[8] Gyula Kautz, "A 'Hitel' méltatása" (Appraisal of 'Credit'), introduction to *SzIM²*, II, pp. xviii–xxxvii.

[9] Ákos Beöthy, *A magyar államiság fejlődése, küzdelmei* (Development and Struggles of Hungarian Statehood), 3 vols. in 4 pts. (Budapest: Athenaeum, 1901–1906), II, pp. 139–91. According to the noted German historian, Gervinus, the greatness of Széchenyi was grossly overestimated. Georg Gervinus, *Geschichte des XIX. Jahrhunderts seit den Wiener Verträgen*, 8 vols. (Leipzig: Vlg. Engelmann, 1853–66), VII, pp. 114ff. Gervinus appears to have based his judgment mainly on two of Széchenyi's works read in bad German translation, *Hitel* and *Világ*, the first of which was rejected by Széchenyi himself because of the translator's distortions. (Cf. *Világ*, in *SzIM²*, I, pp. 353–56.) But in evaluating Széchenyi, one has to integrate his writings and public activities.

[10] *SzIM* and *SzIM²*.

[11] *Széchenyi és kora.*

[12] *Széchenyi életrajza.*

[13] *Széchenyi élete.*

and Bártfai Szabó.[14] Except for the third volume of Bártfai Szabó's *History of the Széchenyi Family,* all these works appeared prior to World War I, as did many of the pioneer studies of Julius Viszota, who devoted a lifetime to research on Széchenyi.[15]

No attempt will be made to enumerate collections of documents or reminiscences, written about or left by Széchenyi's Hungarian or foreign contemporaries, such as Deák, Kossuth, Eötvös, or Metternich. These monographs and memoirs have been cited whenever this seemed appropriate. Yet I should like to mention three general surveys, all classics of the older historical literature, which are most relevant to the political and socio-economic background of 19th-Hungarian history. They are Michael Horváth's history of Hungary in the years 1823–48,[16] Oscar Jászi's study on the evolution of nation-states as related to the nationality question,[17] and Maria Takács's essay on Hungarian social conditions and aspirations in 1830–47.[18] Horváth's book, written from a liberal nationalist point of view, was translated into German and served as a secondary source for sections in Knatchbull-Hugessen's *The Political Evolution of the Hungarian Nation.* Jászi's sociological approach to and radical critique of the Hungarian scene have also been incorporated into Western literature through his well-known *Dissolution of the Habsburg Monarchy.*

The last mentioned book was published in the United States 10 years after its author was forced to go into exile. Indeed, the period between the two world wars was an era of conservative reaction and rightwing nationalism in Hungary. Small wonder that Széchenyi's fear of revolution and the conservative aspects of his work received particular attention. The nationalistic side of his patriotism was overemphasized; frequently, he was presented as the forerunner of Magyar racism. This tendency, already present in Kemény's influential Széchenyi interpretation, had political overtones, too, because it could be used both for criticizing the achievements of the liberal era and for justifying Magyar claims to intellectual supremacy in the Danube basin. The most outstanding representative of this trend in Hungarian historiography was Julius Szekfű. In his opinion, Széchenyi's real claim to immortality lay in his ability to realize in time the extraordinary significance of the nationality problem within the Habsburg Empire.[19]

---

[14] *Széchényi család.*
[15] For a comprehensive list see *A Széchenyi-ábrázolás fő irányai,* pp. 355f.
[16] *Huszonöt év.*
[17] *A nemzeti államok.*
[18] *Társadalmi állapotok.*
[19] Hóman and Szekfű, *Magyar történet,* v, pp. 373f.

In the interwar period the most important contribution to Széchenyi research was the resumption of the publication of his complete works in the *Fontes* series. Besides the six volumes of Széchenyi's private diaries written before the fall of 1848, and the three volumes of his papers confiscated in Döbling in 1860, this set includes modern critical editions of *Hitel, A kelet népe* and two volumes of documents relative to the Széchenyi-Kossuth debate of the 1840's.[20] Another important source, published prior to the end of World War II, is the two-volume collection of nearly 1,500 documents for the period 1808–60.[21] The compiler of this set, Bártfai Szabó, also completed the last part of his history of the Széchenyi family, the relevant chapters and documentation of which cannot be ignored by the student of Stephen Széchenyi's life.

The new sources, unknown or not easily accessible before the first world war, but available in different Austrian and Hungarian archives in the last 50 years, made a reevaluation of many aspects of Széchenyi's activities possible. The opening of the former Secret Imperial Archives in Vienna, and the transfer of much of the material related to Hungary's history to that country on the basis of the peace treaties of 1919 and 1920, gave new opportunities to Hungarian historiography. This was reflected in the scholarly apparatus of the new source publications, biographical studies and monographs alike.[22] Many of the published documents, and considerable portions of Széchenyi's diaries and correspondence are in German, occasionally in French and English. But even if one takes into account that some of Széchenyi's writings have been translated into German, the language barrier has prevented, with minor exceptions, the incorporation of the rich Hungarian literature on Széchenyi into Western historiography, despite its European significance.[23]

The great emphasis on the anti-liberal, Christian-conservative and ethnically oriented elements of Széchenyi's nationalism, which dominated Hungarian historical writings between the two world wars, was largely attributable to the influence of Szekfű's *Three Generations* (1920) and other studies. It was an unfortunate caricature of this trend, and a sad comment on the times, when one of the infamous Nazi leaders in Hungary decided to give historical respectability to his anti-semitic

---

[20] *SzIÖM.*

[21] *Adatok.*

[22] In addition to works already cited, cf. József Östör, *A döblingi Széchenyi, 1848–1860* (Széchenyi at Döbling, 1848–1860) (Budapest: n.p., 1944).

[23] The treasures hidden in Széchenyi's diaries, from the point of view of European historiography, have been duly stressed by Fritz Valjavec, "Die neue Széchenyi-Forschung und ihre Probleme," *Jahrbücher für Geschichte Osteuropas*, IV (1939), 90–110; cf. József Östör, "Az ujabb Széchenyi-irodalom" (Recent Literature on Széchenyi), *Magyar Szemle*, XLI (1941), 233–40.

and racist concepts by choosing a phrase coined by Széchenyi—"We are alone"—as the title of his newspaper.[24] By that time, the late 1930s, Szekfű, Hungary's most influential historian in the 20th century and the initiator of the "cult of Széchenyi," began to turn against his own past. Alarmed by the growing power of the Third Reich, but still a supporter of Hungarian imperialism in the Danubian basin, he opposed Széchenyi's—and St. Stephen's—Catholic principles to Nazi neo-paganism.

The attitude of Hungarian historians toward Széchenyi in the period following World War II was also motivated by political considerations. Immediately after the Second World War, Communists claimed to be the true heirs of the revolutionary ideas of 1848 and Kossuth's program.[25] Thus the cult of Széchenyi was replaced by a cult of Kossuth in Hungarian historiography. Yet by 1954 a resolution of the Central Committee of the Party, aimed at strengthening the patriotic education of youth, suggested that the teaching of history should include, "besides revolutionary traditions, all the important progressive factors of our history (for example Széchenyi in addition to Kossuth)."[26]

Ideological considerations aside, the long overdue publication of a critical edition of *Kossuth's Complete Works*[27] and the emphasis on social and economic conditions are of immense help to the student of the Hungarian Age of Reforms. Similarly, a fresh approach to the nationality question, stimulated by the official condemnation of "bourgeois" nationalism, opened up new avenues for the understanding of conflicting Magyar and other nationalisms in East Central Europe and any research on Széchenyi is bound to benefit from this abundance of recently published materials and interpretations.[28]

New Hungarian historiography has made impressive contributions to bibliographical research. The four-volume comprehensive bibliography, begun under the direction of Zoltán I. Tóth, the last part of which

[24] Ferenc Rajniss, "Egyedül Vagyunk."

[25] József Révai in *Emlékkönyv Kossuth Lajos születésének 150. évfordulójára* (Memorial on the 150th Anniversary of the Birth of Louis Kossuth), 2 vols. (Budapest: Akadémiai kiadó, 1952), I, pp. vii f.

[26] "A Központi Vezetőség határozata a közoktatás helyzetéről és feladatairól" (Resolution of the Central Committee Concerning the State and Tasks of Public Education), *Társadalmi Szemle*, IX (1954), 99.

[27] *KLÖM.*

[28] In addition to Arató, *A nemzetiségi kérdés*, see the studies of Zoltán I. Tóth, and Gábor G. Kemény, cited in note 104 by Barany, "The Awakening of Magyar Nationalism," p. 48 and in notes 39 and 40 by Barany, "An Uncompromising Compromise," p. 248, *AHY*, II (1966) and III, Pt. 1 (1967), respectively. Cf. Robert A. Kann's review of V. Sándor and P. Hanák, eds., *Studien zur Geschichte der Österreichisch-Ungarischen Monarchie* (Budapest: Akadémiai kiadó, 1961), in *AHR*, LXVII (1962), 408f.

was edited by Gabriel G. Kemény and Ladislas Katus, covers the period 1825–67.[29] Of special interest are Zoltán Varga's one-volume study on the main trends of the Széchenyi literature in the period 1851–1918[30] and István Bakács's guide to the archives of the Széchenyi family.[31] These two works are most valuable tools in the hand of the researcher, as is the inventory of the Széchenyi Museum of the Hungarian Academy, compiled in the early years of the century by Szily and Viszota.[32]

After an initial period of hesitation, which followed the Second World War, Hungarian historians again began to pay increasing attention to Széchenyi. This is shown by numerous articles published mostly in the last decade by Barta, Kosáry, Mátyás, Sarlós, Spira and Tilkovszky, authors whose writings have been repeatedly quoted in our study. These

[29] Zoltán I. Tóth *et al*, eds., *Magyar történeti bibliográfia, 1825–1867* (Hungarian Historical Bibliography, 1825–67), 4 vols. (Budapest: Akadémiai kiadó, 1950–59), Vol. IV edited by Gábor G. Kemény and László Katus. For additional useful general information see Tibor Baráth, "L'histoire en Hongrie, 1867–1935," *RH*, CLXXVII (1936), 84–144, 596–644 and CLXXVIII (1937), 25–74; Stephen Borsody, "Modern Hungarian Historiography," *JMH*, XXIV (1952), 398–405; Peter Hanák, "Recent Hungarian Literature on the History of the Austro-Hungarian Monarchy, 1848–1918," *AHY*, I (1965), 151–63; Louis J. Lékai, "Historiography in Hungary, 1790–1848," *JCEA*, XIV (1954), 3–18; E. Lukinich, "Bibliographie historique hongroise (ouvrages publiés ou traduits dans les langues de grande circulation)," *Bulletin* of the International Committee of Historical Sciences, II (1930), 698–705; Emeric Lukinich, ed., *Les éditions des sources de l'histoire Hongroise, 1854–1930* (Budapest: Académie des Sciences Hongroise, 1931); Zoltán Sztáray, *Bibliography on Hungary* (New York: Kossuth Foundation, 1960); György Ránki, "Die Forschungsarbeit der ungarischen Historiker auf dem Gebiet der neueren Geschichte Ungarns im 19.–20. Jahrhundert," *ÖOH*, VIII (1966), 392–402; Paul Teleki, *The Evolution of Hungary and its Place in European History* (New York: Macmillan, 1923), pp. 245–312, containing a valuable bibliography compiled by Charles Feleki; Ferenc Wagner, *A magyar történetirás uj útjai, 1945–1955* (New Paths of Hungarian Historiography, 1945–55) (Washington, D. C., 1956).
[30] Z. Varga, *A Széchenyi-ábrázolás.*
[31] István Bakács, comp., *A Széchenyi család levéltára* (The Archives of the Széchenyi Family), No. 5 of *Levéltári Leltárak* (Archival Inventories) (Budapest: Levéltárak országos központja, 1958). See also Csaba Csapodi, "Széchenyi István kéziratai és egyéb Széchenyi emlékek az Akadémiai Könyvtárban" (Manuscripts of Stephen Széchenyi and Other Széchenyi Relics in the Library of the Academy), *Magyar Tudomány*, V (1960), 242–47; Antal Áldásy, "A gróf Széchenyi család levéltára" (The Archives of the Count Széchenyi Family), *Magyar Könyvszemle*, X (1902), 285–318; Miksa Storno, ed., *A Storno család Széchenyi-gyüjteményének tárgyjegyzéke. Gróf Széchenyi István kéziratainak, valamint egyéb leveleknek közlésével* (Inventory of the Széchenyi Collection of the Storno Family. With Publication of the Manuscripts of Count Stephen Széchenyi and Other Letters) (Sopron: Rottig-Romwalter, 1938). For more general information cf. Győző Ember, "Les archives et l'historiographie en Hongrie," *AH*, IV (1955), 319–43; *Kéziratos források az Országos Széchenyi Könyvtárban. 1789–1867* (Handwritten Sources in the National Széchenyi Library, 1789–1867) (Budapest: Orsz. Széchenyi Könyvtár, 1950).
[32] Kálmán Szily and Gyula Viszota, comp., *A Magy. Tud. Akadémia Széchenyi-Muzeumának tárgyjegyzéke* (Inventory of the Széchenyi Museum of the Hungarian Academy of Sciences) (Budapest: Magyar Tudományos Akadémia, 1905).

writings and the "Theses," drafted by Barta but issued under the auspices of the Hungarian Academy and its Historical Institute on the occasion of the centennial of Széchenyi's death (1960) are signs of a shift in the official attitude toward Széchenyi's public career.[33] Yet Széchenyi continues to be—as he always has been—a controversial figure. This can be seen from the mid-1961 discussion of Spira's completed manuscript, the first, and hitherto only, major monograph on Széchenyi, published in Hungary since 1945,[34] as well as from the great sensitivity with which historians in Hungary react to studies done abroad and dealing with the Hungarian Age of Reforms, Széchenyi, and Kossuth.[35]

This brief survey of Széchenyi's constant reevaluation in Hungary suggests that ever since the national rebirth of Hungary in the 19th century, the Széchenyi problem has been deeply interwoven with Hungarian social and political developments. Somehow the Széchenyi-Kossuth controversy has become and remained to this date a symbol of the clash between the ideas of peaceful evolution and revolution, of "coexistence" and "complete" national independence at all costs within the framework of one supranational state; between conservative and liberal thought. Hence its importance from the point of view of Hungarian and European history as well.

Because of the dramatic possibilities inherent in it, a description of the conflict between Széchenyi and Kossuth is both tempting and convenient to the writer. But to the historian, the crux—and challenge—of the Széchenyi drama is presented in slightly different terms. One part

---

[33] " 'Széchenyi István.' A Magyar Tudományos Akadémia Történeti Főbizottsága és Történettudományi Intézete tézisei Széchenyi halálának (1860. aprilis 8.) 100. évfordulójára" ('Stephen Széchenyi.' Theses of the General Committee on History of the Hungarian Academy of Sciences and Its Historical Institute on the Occasion of the Centennial of Széchenyi's Death, April 8, 1860), *Társadalmi Szemle*, xv (1860), 30–55.

[34] M[iklós] L[ackó], " '1848 Széchenyije.' (A Tudományos Tanács vitaülése)" ('The Széchenyi of 1848.' The Discussion Session of the Scientific Council), *TSz*, iv (1961), 524–29. The discussion of the manuscript preceded by some three years the actual publication of the book. It took about five years before a commemorative article, also written by Spira in August 1959, found its way to the printer: but the important thing is that it *was* published. György Spira, "Széchenyi tragikus utja," *TSz*, vii (1964), 583–95, published under the title "Széchenyi's Tragic Course" in *Nouvelles Etudes historiques*, publiées à l'occasion du XIIe Congrès International des Sciences Historiques par la Commission Nationale des Historiens Hongrois, 2 vols. (Budapest: Akadémiai kiadó, 1965), i, pp. 517–29.

[35] Domokos Kosáry, "Széchenyi az ujabb külföldi irodalomban," *Sz*, xcvi (1962), 275–92. Its English version under the title "Széchenyi in Recent Western Literature" in *AH*, ix (1963), 255–78. Kosáry's study on Széchenyi's Döbling period (1849–60), partly published in *ITK*, lxviii (1963), 149–70, is still in manuscript. Cf. É. Haraszti, "Széchenyi and England," *NHQ*, VIII/25 (Spring 1967), pp. 156-64.

of the dilemma was correctly formulated by Count Julius Andrássy, Jr. According to him, "*Széchenyi*'s political career was not a victorious one. He never was the political leader of the nation. First the influence of *Wesselényi*, then that of Deák, Kossuth, and later again that of Deák became decisive, and never his." And yet, continued Andrássy, Széchenyi's career, "unsuccessful from his own point of view," belonged among the most useful ones of Hungary, for Széchenyi envisaged great and significant aims for Hungary as a nation. "Széchenyi held no office, was no leader of a party and was an average speaker; still, he transformed the thinking of the nation and gave a new direction to its endeavors."[36]

This "new direction," in Széchenyi's mind, amounted to a gradual and peaceful, but complete ethical "regeneration" of his fatherland. No doubt this regeneration also implied the victory of liberalism and nationalism and the introduction of capitalism into underdeveloped feudal Hungary. Even during the years of his alliance with the Hungarian conservatives in the 1840s Széchenyi insisted that, to use a classic definition of Andrássy's, "one can conserve only through reform."[37]

Still it was Andrássy's generation, and the subsequent conservative regime of the interwar period, that eulogized Széchenyi, the *conservative reformer* ignoring, at the same time, the very essence of his reform program, namely Hungary's *progressive social and economic transformation*. Even more recently, the social function of reform began to be questioned: to children of a revolution, who view violence as the only means through which society can purge and transform itself, Széchenyi's moderate ideas have become embarrassing, if not outright meaningless.

Less directly involved in the political trends of the Hungarian domestic scene, Western historiography has been on the whole more sympathetic to Széchenyi than to Kossuth, although not many historians would agree with A.J.P. Taylor, in whose opinion Kossuth "had nothing in common with the serious, conscientious radicalism of his contemporaries; he was rather the first dictator to rise to power by prostituting idealism to the service of national passion."[38] Aside from general works dealing with

[36] Gyula Andrássy, "Széchenyi politikája" (Széchenyi's Policy), in *Széchenyi eszmevilága* (Széchenyi's World of Ideas), 3 vols. (Budapest: Franklin, 1912–14), I, pp. 120–24. Italics in original.

[37] *Ibid.*, p. 136.

[38] A.J.P. Taylor, *The Habsburg Monarchy, 1809–1918* (London: Hamish Hamilton, 1948), p. 52.

the history of Hungary,[39] the Habsburg Monarchy[40] or nationalism,[41] few modern studies done in the West have attempted to come to grips with the specific problems related to Széchenyi's (or for that matter, Kossuth's) activities.

Still, there are some important contributions published in Western languages during the last century, which are worthy of the attention of Széchenyi scholars. Perhaps the first study, done by a non-Magyar professional historian on Széchenyi, was that of Saint-René Taillandier; it appeared in the *Revue des deux mondes* in 1867.[42] Taillandier's essay, which took into account the information contained in a series of articles written by Hippolyte Desprez and the former diplomat Emile Langsdorff for the *Revue des deux mondes* in 1847 and 1848,[43] served, in turn, as basis for four articles published anonymously under the title "The Great Magyar" in the journal of Charles Dickens *All the Year Round* in 1870.[44]

Of great interest to the English reader are the special issues of two periodicals, one published in Hungary and the other in the United States. In the winter of 1941–42 *The Hungarian Quarterly* celebrated the 150th anniversary of Széchenyi's birth by publishing numerous articles on Széchenyi's life,[45] and several of them have been referred to in the present study. In October 1960 the *Journal of Central European Affairs* commemorated the centennial of Széchenyi's death by devoting three major

[39] In addition to those already mentioned, cf. C. A. Macartney, *Hungary: A Short History* (Chicago: Aldine Co., 1962); Denis Sinor, *History of Hungary* (New York: Praeger, 1959).

[40] Besides the ones cited previously, see also Hugo Hantsch, *Die Geschichte Österreichs, 1648–1918*, 2 vols., 3rd edn. (Graz-Vienna: Styria, 1959–1962); Arthur J. May, *The Age of Metternich, 1814–1848*, rev. edn. (1963) in Berkshire Studies in European History; Arnold Whitridge, *Men in Crisis. The Revolutions of 1848* (New York: Scribner's, 1949), pp. 238–82. (Ch. IV: "The Revolution in the Habsburg Monarchy. Metternich, Széchenyi and Kossuth.")

[41] Hans Kohn, *The idea of Nationalism* (New York: Macmillan, 1944).

[42] Saint-René Taillandier, "Hommes d'Etat de la Hongrie. Le comte Stephan Széchenyi," *RDM*, 2d Period, LXX and LXXI (both 1867), 628–61 and 864–903.

[43] The interest of the politically articulate French public in Hungary and Central Europe can be seen from the informative articles written by Desprez and Langsdorff. Both authors, especially Langsdorff, pay considerable attention to Széchenyi. H. Desprez, "Les paysans de l'Autriche," "La Hongrie et le mouvement magyare," "La révolution dans l'Europe orientale," Pts. I and II. *RDM*, New Series, XX (1847), 332–49, 1,068–89; XXIV (1848), 513–37 and 894–919; E. Langsdorff, "La Hongrie en 1848," Pts. I–IV, *RDM*, New series, XXII, pp. 657–73; XXIII, 395–427; XXIV, 252–79, 673–97 and 958–82 (all vols. published in 1848). Pt. III in Vol. XXIV, pp. 681–92, contains a brief survey of Széchenyi's career, and there are frequent references to him in other parts of the series as well. (For Langsdorff, cf. Ch. IX, pp. 414f.)

[44] New Series, III, pp. 450–56, 476–80, 498–504, 522–28.

[45] Vol. VII, pp. 415–512, 572–77.

articles to different aspects of Széchenyi's work;[46] these articles, too, have been cited previously. We have also quoted Szücs Nicolson's article on Széchenyi the entrepreneur[47] but have yet to mention the studies by Béla Menczer, some of which appeared in English.[48] One may add that the foreign language journals appearing in Hungary have also published a few recent articles on Széchenyi. Besides Kosáry's essay in *Acta Historica, The New Hungarian Quarterly* has published Julius Ortutay's article which analyzes three different Széchenyi portraits: the one envisioned by the poet Ady, that drawn by the historian Szekfű, and a third one preserved by the Hungarian peasant.[49] To round out the picture, one may mention an article of Francis S. Wagner in *The Hungarian Quarterly,* published in the United States, which describes the rediscovery of Széchenyi's flute in the Dayton C. Miller Collection of the Library of Congress.[50]

Due to geographical factors, and Hungary's manifold cultural and political ties with the German-speaking areas, much of the non-Magyar literature on Széchenyi is in German. As pointed out previously, some of Széchenyi's works such as *On Horses, Credit, Light, and Danubian Steam Shipping* have been translated into German, occasionally under his supervision. A considerable part of his correspondence and diaries, especially in his younger years, was written in German. Many of the reminiscences authored by Hungarians in the second half of the 19th century, are available in German, as are some of the important accounts related to Széchenyi's Döbling period.[51] Besides such general surveys

---

[46] Vol. xx, pp. 251–313.

[47] *Explorations in Entrepreneurial History,* vi (1953–54), 163–80.

[48] Béla Menczer, "Hungary's Place in European History," *Modern Age,* iii (Winter 1958–59), 66–80; "The Legacy of Metternich," *The Contemporary Review* (July 1959), pp. 36–39; "Metternich and Széchenyi," *Der Donauraum,* v (1960), 78–86; "Stephan Széchenyi/Die Romantik in der Politik," *Wort und Wahrheit,* xv (1960), 445–50; "Die geistigen Grundlagen der ungarischen Reformzeit, 1790–1848," *Der Donauraum,* ii (1957), 12–28.

[49] Gyula Ortutay, "The Living Széchenyi," *The New Hungarian Quarterly,* i (1960), 36–49. (Originally published in *Magyar Tudomány,* lxvii (1960), 179–92.)

[50] Francis S. Wagner, "The Rediscovery of Széchenyi's Flute," *The Hungarian Quarterly,* v (1965), 169–71.

[51] Max Falk, *Graf Stephan Széchenyi und seine Zeit* (Vienna: 1866, published originally in the *Österreichische Revue); Rudolph Gussmann, Graf Stephan Széchenyi im Privat-Irrenhause zu Döbling* (Pesth: Heckenast, 1860); Aurel Kecskeméthy, *Graf Stephan Széchenyis staatsmännische Laufbahn.* Seine Letzten Lebensjahre in der Döblinger Irrenanstalt und sein Tod (Pest: Hornyánszky & Hummel, 1866); K. M. Kertbeny, *Silhouetten und Reliquien,* 2 vols. (Vienna–Prague: Kober & Markgraf, 1861); Ferdinand Kürnberger, "Erinnerungen an Széchenyi," Separatdruck aus der *National-Zeitung* (Vienna: 1866); Melchior Lónyay, *Graf Stefan Széchenyi und seine hinterlassene Schriften.* Übersetzt von Adolf Dux (Budapest: Ratki, 1875); Arthur Saternus, *Der Grösste Ungar.* Gegenwartseindrücke von der Persönlichkeit und vom Werk Stefan Széchenyis. Seine Begegnung mit Friedrich List (Budapest, 1941). Reprinted from a series of articles, published

as Miskolczy's *Ungarn in der Habsburger-Monarchie,* one may note the translations of the pertinent works by Csengery and Michael Horváth.[52] From the recent literature I should like to mention in addition to Menczer's articles, the essay by Graf Georg Széchenyi, *Graf Stephan Széchenyi; ein persönliches Bekenntniss* (Cologne–Detroit–Vienna: Amerikanisch-Ungarischer Vlg., 1961), the appendix of which, compiled by Michael Ferdinándy, contains some of the *"Gedanken und Aussprüche des Grafen Stephan Széchenyi . . . ."* Finally, it is a particular pleasure to report the publication of a concise and perceptive short study, written for the general public by a scholar known from his work on late 18th-century Austro-Hungarian history: Denis Silagi's *Der grösste Ungar* (Vienna–Munich: Herold, 1967) appeared when my manuscript was about to be sent to the printer.

One additional word about the main tasks of future Széchenyi research may not be entirely out of order at this point. It would be important if the Hungarian Historical Association would resume the publication of Széchenyi's *Complete Works* in the *Fontes:* a new edition of his letters and some of his less known works is long overdue. No one but historians living in Hungary and permanently associated with the relevant archival material can accomplish this task. Others may browse around for new materials related to Széchenyi's—and Hungary's—European connections, as this writer has attempted to do. *Together,* we may come up with monographs pointing the way toward a definitive biography of the "greatest among the Magyar."

originally in the *Pester Lloyd;* Joseph Orosz, *Terra incognita. Notizen über Ungarn* (Leipzig: Wigand, 1835); Rudolph Gussmann, *Graf Stephan Széchenyi im Privat-Irrenhause zu Döbling* (Pesth: Heckenast, 1860). From the literature already cited we must mention Pulszky, *Meine Zeit, mein Leben* and Wirkner, *Meine Erlebnisse.*

[52] Anton Csengery, ed., *Ungarns Redner und Staatsmänner,* 2 vols. (Leipzig–Vienna: Manzscher Vlg., 1852); Michael Horváth, *Fünfundzwanzig Jahre aus der Geschichte Ungarns von 1823–1848,* 2 vols. (Lepzig: Brockhaus, 1867).

Index

Note: For the sake of convenience, the same entry is used for a country and its people, e.g., Austria, Austrians; Croatia, Croatians; United States, Americans.

This book has been composed
in 10 point Intertype Baskerville, leaded 2 points
with display in handset Legend, printed
by letterpress on 50 lb. Warren's
1854 Text, and bound in
Joanna Parchment
Linen